PENGUIN CLASSICS

WILLIAM WORDSWORTH: SELECTED POEMS

PENGUIN SELECTED ENGLISH POETS
GENERAL EDITOR: CHRISTOPHER RICKS

William Wordsworth was born in Cockermouth, on the coast of the Lake District, in 1770, the second of five children. His rural upbringing inspired much of his poetry, and some of his most intense visionary passages, notably in *The Prelude*, stem from childhood and adolescent experience. As a young man, Wordsworth was fired with enthusiasm for the French Revolution. After graduating from Cambridge in 1791 he spent a year in France, where he met and fell in love with Annette Vallon. On his return to England he devoted himself to literature, supporting himself by means of a legacy, and the latter course of the Revolution left him disillusioned with radical politics. He met Coleridge in 1795 and the two men became intimate friends, though they were estranged between 1810 and 1812 on account of a drawn-out quarrel.

In 1799 Wordsworth settled at Grasmere in the Lake District with his sister Dorothy, who was a close companion for most of his life and shared his deep love of nature. He married Mary Hutchinson in 1802 and they had five children. His early work was on the whole well received, and, despite some adverse reviews, his reputation grew steadily throughout his career. In 1813 he was appointed Distributor of Stamps for Westmorland, the income enabling him to continue writing. He became Poet Laureate seven years before his death in 1850.

John O. Hayden is Professor of English at the University of California. He has edited the two volumes of *William Wordsworth: The Poems*, *William Wordsworth: Selected Poems* and *Wordsworth: Selected Prose* for the Penguin Classics.

William Wordsworth

Selected Poems

EDITED BY JOHN O. HAYDEN

PENGUIN BOOKS

PENGUIN BOOKS

Published by the Penguin Group
Penguin Books Ltd, 80 Strand, London WC2R 0RL, England
Penguin Putnam Inc., 375 Hudson Street, New York, New York 10014, USA
Penguin Books Australia Ltd, 250 Camberwell Road, Camberwell, Victoria 3124, Australia
Penguin Books Canada Ltd, 10 Alcorn Avenue, Toronto, Ontario, Canada M4V 3B2
Penguin Books India (P) Ltd, 11 Community Centre, Panchsheel Park, New Delhi – 110 017, India
Penguin Books (NZ) Ltd, Cnr Rosedale and Airborne Roads, Albany, Auckland, New Zealand
Penguin Books (South Africa) (Pty) Ltd, 24 Sturdee Avenue, Rosebank 2196, South Africa

Penguin Books Ltd, Registered Offices: 80 Strand, London WC2R 0RL, England

www.penguin.com

This edition first published 1994
10

Typeset by Datix International Limited, Bungay, Suffolk
Filmset in 9.5/11.5 pt Monotype Ehrhardt
Printed in England by Clays Ltd, St Ives plc

Contents

Table of Dates

1770   *7 April*   Born at Cockermouth, Cumberland, to John Wordsworth, a lawyer.

1771   Dorothy Wordsworth, his only sister, born (three brothers: Richard b. 1768, John b. 1772, Christopher b. 1774).

1776–7   Attends nursery school in Penrith, along with Mary Hutchinson, his future wife.

1778   *c. 8 March*   Ann Wordsworth, his mother, dies.

1779   Enters Hawkshead School.

1783   *30 December*   His father dies.

1785   Earliest extant verse written (aetat. 15).

1787   Attends St John's College, Cambridge.

1789   Spends long vacation with his sister and Mary Hutchinson.

1790   Spends long vacation on a walking tour of France and Switzerland with Robert Jones, a college friend.

1791   *21 January*   Receives BA degree.
          26 November   Leaves for stay in France.

1792   Meets Michel Beaupuy and has an affair with Annette Vallon.
          December   Returns to London.
          15 December   A daughter, Anne-Caroline, by Annette Vallon, born at Orléans.

1793   *29 January*   *An Evening Walk* and *Descriptive Sketches* published.
          August–September   Walking tour over Salisbury Plain to Bristol, and thence through part of Wales.

1795   *January*   His friend Raisley Calvert dies, leaving Wordsworth a legacy.
August   Meets Samuel Taylor Coleridge.
September   Settles with Dorothy at Racedown, Dorset.

1797   *July*   Moves to Alfoxden, Somerset, to be near Coleridge at Nether Stowey.

1798   *10 July*   Visits Tintern Abbey.
September   *Lyrical Ballads* published (four poems by Coleridge included).
16 September   Embarks for Germany with Coleridge and Dorothy.

1799   *May*   Returns to England (Sockburn-on-Tees).
20 December   Settles with Dorothy at Dove Cottage at Town-End, Grasmere.

1800   *January–September*   John Wordsworth visits.

1801   *January*   *Lyrical Ballads*, second edition (dated 1800), published in two volumes with the famous Preface.

1802   *Lyrical Ballads*, third edition, published with extended Preface and Appendix.
August   Visits Annette Vallon and Caroline at Calais.
4 October   Marries Mary Hutchinson.

1803   *18 June*   A son, John, born (other children: Dora b. 1804, Thomas b. 1806, Catharine b. 1808, William b. 1810).
August–September   Tours Scotland with Coleridge and Dorothy.

1804   Coleridge sails for Malta.

1805   *6 February*   John Wordsworth, his brother, drowns.
May   *The Prelude* finished.
Lyrical Ballads, fourth edition, published.

1806   *August*   Coleridge returns from Malta.
November   Wordsworths move to Coleorton.

1807   *May*   *Poems in Two Volumes* published.

1822   *March   Ecclesiastical Sonnets* and *Memorials of a Tour on the Continent, 1820* published.
November   A Description of the Scenery of the Lakes published.

1827   *February*   Sir George Beaumont, patron, dies.
May Third collected edition of the *Poems* (5 volumes) published.

1831   *September–October*   Tours Scotland with his daughter and nephew, Charles; visits Sir Walter Scott.

1832   Fourth collected edition of the *Poems* (4 volumes) published.

1834   *25 July*   Coleridge dies.

1835   *January   Yarrow Revisited and Other Poems* published. Mental breakdown of Dorothy Wordsworth.

1836–7   Fifth collected edition of the *Poems* (in stereotype; 6 volumes) published.

1837   *March–August*   Tours France and Italy with Henry Crabb Robinson.

1838   *June*   One-volume edition of *The Sonnets* published. *21 July*   Receives DCL from the University of Durham.

1839   *12 June*   Receives DCL from Oxford University.

1842   *April   Poems, Chiefly of Early and Late Years* (with *The Borderers* and *Guilt and Sorrow*) published [volume VII of collected *Poems*].
July   Resigns Distributorship of Stamps and receives pension.

1843   *April*   Succeeds Southey as Poet Laureate. Dictates notes on his poems to Isabella Fenwick.

1845   *November*   Sixth collected edition of the *Poems* (1 volume) published.

1847   *9 July*   His daughter Dora dies.

1849–50   Seventh collected edition of the *Poems* (6 volumes) published – the last edited by Wordsworth himself.

1850   *23 April*   William Wordsworth dies.
July   *The Prelude* published.

1855   *January*   Dorothy Wordsworth dies.

1859   *January*   Mary Wordsworth dies.

Preface

To produce a selected edition of the poems of William Words-
worth is not, in the view of the Victorian critic Matthew Arnold,
like producing one for any other poet. The editor is not so much
providing a sample of the best poems as overcoming 'certain
special obstacles', chiefly the presence among Wordsworth's best
work (for Arnold, the 'shorter pieces') of large quantities of 'very
inferior' poems that 'dull and spoil' the best. Matthew Arnold
produced such a selected edition in 1879, which contained 160
poems (sixty of them sonnets) and a famous introduction arguing
the case, from which the above quotations are taken. After
claiming that Wordsworth was the greatest English poet for the
past 300 years apart from Shakespeare and Milton, Arnold argued
that his reputation was at that time low and unstable and that he
needed 'to be relieved of a great deal of the poetical baggage
which now encumbers him'.

It is, of course, no longer necessary to establish Wordsworth's
right to be included among the English poets, although he is
seldom seen as belonging, with Shakespeare and Milton, to a
triumvirate of the greatest English poets. What has been attempted
in the present edition, in any event, is a similar selection (the
great majority of Arnold's choices are contained here) with some-
what similar motives: to present the reader with the best poems
Wordsworth has to offer, in order to show him to be the very
great poet he is. With this consideration in mind, there is a
generous selection (131 complete poems, as well as a few entire
tales from *The Excursion* and well over half *The Prelude*). These
are presented in newly edited texts with complete notes that
include summaries of the important criticism devoted to each
poem. Two extra features of this edition are new versions of *The
Pedlar and the Ruined Cottage* (MS M) and the fourteen-book
Prelude (MS E), both new in the sense that neither has been
presented before in a readable text.

The texts of most of the poems are taken from the last edition (1849–50) published in Wordsworth's lifetime. Although this is standard editorial practice, there are alternatives: I might have selected the texts as first published or (as has been done) the earliest completed versions of the poems. If ordered chronologically by date of completion, either selection would have allowed for more precise study of Wordsworth's stylistic development, and some readers believe the earlier versions are preferable as poetry anyway. Yet since such versions are not the poems we know today, the textual differences can be disconcerting to a reader familiar with Wordsworth's poetry, and in the case of the earliest completed versions, it is difficult to arrive at a consistent and satisfactory policy of selection given the general difficulty of determining when a version is both earliest and complete. The editor is forced too often to make decisions only the poet should make.

Printing texts from the last edition avoids these problems, while complying with Wordsworth's strong, explicit wishes to have his final texts printed. When, however, such texts are ordered chronologically, as they are here, it is not possible to study Wordsworth's stylistic development as well as can be done using earlier versions. Yet it is a mistake, in any case, to assume that a chronological study of poems is limited to style; the poet's developing interests in themes and forms (to the extent that they can be separated from style) can also be examined.

Of those few poems not included in Wordsworth's last edition, I have used the latest printed version or, when the poem is extant only in manuscript, the latest manuscript version – all of which I have consulted at first hand. A special case is *Home at Grasmere*, taken from the latest manuscript and then reunited with its original ending, printed by Wordsworth as the Prospectus to *The Excursion*. 'The Female Vagrant', moreover, appears in the version found in *Lyrical Ballads* (1798), as part of that volume brought together as a unit in the text.

The texts, once determined, were edited in a number of ways. Spelling has been modernized when it has become archaic (except when the sound of the word has changed). Capitalization, on the other hand, has been left intact except in *The Prelude*, which contains an inordinate amount of capitalization used with no apparent rationale – possibly because it was handled by a number of amanuenses and was published posthumously (see the note to that poem). Punctuation has been respected throughout except in those very few cases when confusion was likely to result. Square brackets around titles indicate their unauthorized status – that is, as not having been provided by Wordsworth himself. Titles that are identical for two or more poems are accompanied by their opening phrases in round brackets in the Contents and Notes. A bracketed word followed by a question mark in the text of a manuscript poem signifies illegibility and conjecture, while a bracket around a letter in a manuscript poem signifies that it is missing in the manuscript.

Two exceptions to the chronological arrangement of poems by composition are the passages taken from *The Excursion* and *The Prelude*, since both poems were written over a number of years. I have placed *The Excursion* in 1814 (the year of first publication) and *The Prelude* (published posthumously) at the end. Another exception is the grouping of the 'Lucy poems', the composition of which was actually interspersed with that of a few other poems (the 'Lucy poems' also have their own introductory note). A final exception is the four poems written during the period of composition of *Lyrical Ballads* (1798) but published later, for the integrity of *Lyrical Ballads* is respected here; the poems in that publication are grouped as a unit, with the other four poems in question appearing immediately after.

The notes appear at the end of the volume except for those attached by Wordsworth directly to the beginning or end of poems. Some information is provided for every poem: the probable (sometimes certain) date of composition, the date of first publication and the category in which Wordsworth placed poems when they were collected by him. The dates of composition to 1815 inclusive are most often taken from Mark Reed's two chronologies of Wordsworth's life and works (see Further Reading) and follow his code of descending order of likelihood – probably, perhaps, possibly. The first date given for the category of a poem, moreover, is also the date of the first collected edition (if any) in which the poem appeared. If there is no indication to the contrary, poems remained in the categories to which they were first assigned.

Much of the information contained in the notes is from Words-worth himself – excerpts from letters, published notes and the manuscript notes dictated to Isabella Fenwick in 1843 ('*I. F. note*'). Such information has been limited to what concerns the composition, meaning or form of the poems. Identification of sources of other information is cited only if that information is not provided by previous editors.

A summary of important criticism of poems can be found at the end of notes. In many cases the criticism is summarized in such a way that attributions to individual critics would have been extraordinarily cumbersome and so are omitted. These summaries are in fact intended mostly to suggest ways the poem has been (and can be) approached. In any case, brief citations, when the critic's name is provided, will lead anyone interested to the original criticism.

I should like to acknowledge here the generosity of the Dove Cottage Trustees in permitting me to publish (in new versions) material under their care, especially *The Pedlar and the Ruined Cottage* (MS M) and *The Prelude* (MS E). I should also like to thank the staffs of the Dove Cottage Library (especially Jeff Cowton), the British Library and Shields Library, University of California, Davis, for making the scholarship involved in putting this edition together an easier and more enjoyable task. I should also thank Christopher Ricks, the general editor of the series, for his diligence and advice in preparing this edition. A last debt is to my typist, Susan Kancir, for her industry and patience.

Further Reading

Editions

De Selincourt, Ernest, and Helen Darbishire, eds., *The Poetical Works of William Wordsworth*, 5 volumes, Clarendon Press, 1940–49; Volumes I–III revised 1952–4 (text follows the categories of Wordsworth, with variant readings and annotations)

De Selincourt, Ernest, ed., *The Prelude, or Growth of a Poet's Mind*, Clarendon Press, 1926; second edition, revised by Helen Darbishire, 1959 (with facing texts of the 1805 and 1850 versions, variant readings, introduction and annotations)

Parrish, Stephen, Mark L. Reed and James A. Butler, gen. eds., *The Cornell Wordsworth*, Cornell University Press, in progress (each volume contains manuscript versions of the poems, often in facsimile, with variant readings and annotations)

The Salisbury Plain Poems, edited by Stephen Gill, 1975
The Prelude 1798–1799, edited by Stephen Parrish, 1977
Home at Grasmere, edited by Beth Darlington, 1977
The Ruined Cottage and *The Pedlar*, edited by James Butler, 1979
Benjamin the Waggoner, edited by Paul F. Betz, 1981
The Borderers, edited by Robert Osborn, 1982
Poems in Two Volumes, and Other Poems, 1800–1807, edited by Jared Curtis, 1983
An Evening Walk, edited by James Averill, 1984
Descriptive Sketches, edited by Eric Birdsall, with the assistance of Paul M. Zall, 1984
Peter Bell, edited by John E. Jordan, 1985
The Fourteen-Book 'Prelude', edited by W. J. B. Owen, 1985
'The Tuft of Primroses' with Other Late Poems for 'The Recluse', edited by Joseph F. Kishel, 1986
The White Doe of Rylstone, edited by Kristine Dugas, 1988
Shorter Poems, 1807–1820, edited by Carl Ketcham, 1989
The Thirteen-Book 'Prelude', 2 volumes, edited by Mark Reed, 1991

Hayden, John O., ed., *William Wordsworth: The Poems*, 2 volumes, Penguin Books, 1977 (contains all the poems except *The Prelude*, with annotations)
- *William Wordsworth: Selected Prose*, Penguin Books, 1988 (an inexpensive edition containing almost all the prose, with annotations)
Maxwell, J. C., ed., *William Wordsworth: 'The Prelude', A Parallel Text*, Penguin Books, 1971 (facing texts of the 1805 and 1850 versions, with annotations)
Wordsworth, Jonathan, M. H. Abrams and Stephen Gill, eds., *The Prelude: 1799, 1805, 1850*, W. W. Norton, 1979 (texts of the three versions and facing texts of the last two, with annotations and selected critical essays)
Owen, W. J. B., and J. W. Smyser, eds., *The Prose Works of William Wordsworth*, 3 volumes, Clarendon Press, 1974

Bibliographies and Reference Works

Bauer, N. S., *William Wordsworth: A Reference Guide to British Criticism, 1793–1899*, G. K. Hall, 1978 (an annotated bibliography of nineteenth-century criticism, with an index)
Cooper, Lane, *A Concordance to the Poems of Wordsworth*, Smith, Elder and Company, 1911
Raysor, Thomas M., ed., *The English Romantic Poets: A Review of Research*, Modern Language Association, fourth edition, revised by Frank Jordan, 1985
Reed, Mark, *Wordsworth: The Chronology of the Early Years 1770–1799*, Harvard University Press, 1967
- *Wordsworth: The Chronology of the Middle Years 1800–1815*, Harvard University Press, 1975
Thompson, T. W., *Wordsworth's Hawkshead*, edited by Robert Woof, Oxford University Press, 1970

Biographies, Letters and Journals

De Selincourt, Ernest, ed., *Journals of Dorothy Wordsworth*, 2 volumes, Macmillan, 1941
Gill, Stephen, *William Wordsworth: A Life*, Clarendon Press, 1989

Gittings, Robert, and Jo Manton, *Dorothy Wordsworth*, Clarendon Press, 1985

Hill, Alan G., ed., *The Letters of William and Dorothy Wordsworth*, arranged and edited by Ernest de Selincourt, second edition, revised, Volume II. *The Middle Years, Part I, 1806–1811*, Clarendon Press, 1969

Hill, Alan G., ed., *The Letters of William and Dorothy Wordsworth*, arranged and edited by Ernest de Selincourt, second edition, revised, Volumes IV–VII. *The Later Years, 1821–1853*, Clarendon Press, 1978–88

Moorman, Mary, ed., *Journals of Dorothy Wordsworth*, Oxford University Press, 1971 (Alfoxden and Grasmere journals)

Moorman, Mary, and Alan G. Hill, eds., *The Letters of William and Dorothy Wordsworth*, arranged and edited by Ernest de Selincourt, second edition, revised, Volume III. *The Middle Years, Part 2, 1812–1820*, Clarendon Press, 1970

Noyes, Russell, *William Wordsworth*, updated edition revised by John O. Hayden, Twayne, 1991 (a short critical biography)

Shaver, Chester L., ed., *The Letters of William and Dorothy Wordsworth*, arranged and edited by Ernest de Selincourt, second edition, revised, Volume I. *The Early Years, 1787–1805*, Clarendon Press, 1967

Woof, Pamela, ed., *Dorothy Wordsworth: The Grasmere Journals*, Clarendon Press, 1991

Selected Criticism

Arnold, Matthew, 'Wordsworth,' in *The Complete Prose Works of Matthew Arnold*, edited by R. H. Super, IV, 36–55, University of Michigan Press, 1973 (influential short study of Wordsworth originally published in 1879)

Clark, C. C., *Romantic Paradox: An Essay on the Poetry of Wordsworth*, Routledge and Kegan Paul, 1962

Coleridge, Samuel Taylor, *Biographia Literaria*, Volume VII of *The Collected Works of Samuel Taylor Coleridge*, edited by James Engel and W. J. Bate, Routledge and Kegan Paul and Princeton University Press, 1983 (Chapters 4, 14, 17–20, 22)

Danby, J. F., *The Simple Wordsworth: Studies in the Poems 1797–1807*, Routledge and Kegan Paul, 1960

Durrant, Geoffrey, *William Wordsworth*, Cambridge University Press, 1969

Hayden, John O., *William Wordsworth and the Mind of Man: The Poet as Thinker*, Bibliophile Press, 1993

Heffernan, James A. W., *Wordsworth's Theory of Poetry: The Transforming Imagination*, Cornell University Press, 1969

Jones, John, *The Egotistical Sublime: A History of Wordsworth's Imagination*, Chatto and Windus, 1954

Parrish, Stephen Maxfield, *The Art of the Lyrical Ballads*, Harvard University Press, 1973

Rader, Melvin, *Wordsworth: A Philosophical Approach*, Clarendon Press, 1967

Woodring, Carl, *Wordsworth*, Houghton Mifflin and Co., 1965

Wordsworth, Jonathan, *William Wordsworth, The Borders of Vision*, Clarendon Press, 1982

Lines Written as a School Exercise at Hawkshead, Anno Aetatis 14

'And has the Sun his flaming chariot driven
Two hundred times around the ring of heaven,
Since Science first, with all her sacred train,
Beneath yon roof began her heavenly reign?
While thus I mused, methought, before mine eyes,
The Power of Education seemed to rise;
Not she whose rigid precepts trained the boy
Dead to the sense of every finer joy;
Nor that vile wretch who bade the tender age
10 Spurn Reason's law and humour Passion's rage;
But she who trains the generous British youth
In the bright paths of fair majestic Truth:
Emerging slow from Academus' grove
In heavenly majesty she seemed to move.
Stern was her forehead, but a smile serene
"Softened the terrors of her awful mien."
Close at her side were all the powers, designed
To curb, exalt, reform the tender mind:
    With panting breast, now pale as winter snows,
20 Now flushed as Hebe, Emulation rose;
Shame followed after with reverted eye,
And hue far deeper than the Tyrian dye;
Last Industry appeared with steady pace,
A smile sat beaming on her pensive face.
I gazed upon the visionary train,
Threw back my eyes, returned, and gazed again.
When lo! the heavenly goddess thus began,
Through all my frame the pleasing accents ran.

'"When Superstition left the golden light
30 And fled indignant to the shades of night;
When pure Religion reared the peaceful breast
And lulled the warring passions into rest,
Drove far away the savage thoughts that roll
In the dark mansions of the bigot's soul,

Enlivening Hope displayed her cheerful ray,
And beamed on Britain's sons a brighter day;
So when on Ocean's face the storm subsides,
Hushed are the winds and silent are the tides;
The God of day, in all the pomp of light,
40 Moves through the vault of heaven, and dissipates the
        night;
Wide o'er the main a trembling lustre plays,
The glittering waves reflect the dazzling blaze;
Science with joy saw Superstition fly
Before the lustre of Religion's eye;
With rapture she beheld Britannia smile,
Clapped her strong wings, and sought the cheerful isle.
The shades of night no more the soul involve,
She sheds her beam, and, lo! the shades dissolve;
No jarring monks, to gloomy cell confined,
50 With mazy rules perplex the weary mind;
No shadowy forms entice the soul aside,
Secure she walks, Philosophy her guide.
Britain, who long her warriors had adored,
And deemed all merit centred in the sword;
Britain, who thought to stain the field was fame,
Now honoured Edward's less than Bacon's name.
Her sons no more in listed field advance
To ride the ring, or toss the beamy lance;
No longer steel their indurated hearts
60 To the mild influence of the finer arts;
Quick to the secret grotto they retire
To court majestic truth, or wake the golden lyre;
By generous Emulation taught to rise,
The seats of learning brave the distant skies.
    Then noble Sandys, inspired with great design,
Reared Hawkshead's happy roof, and called it mine;
There have I loved to show the tender age
The golden precepts of the classic page;
To lead the mind to those Elysian plains
70 Where, throned in gold, immortal Science reigns;
Fair to the view is sacred Truth displayed,
In all the majesty of light arrayed,

To teach, on rapid wings, the curious soul
To roam from heaven to heaven, from pole to pole,
From thence to search the mystic cause of things,
And follow Nature to her secret springs;
Nor less to guide the fluctuating youth
Firm in the sacred paths of moral truth,
To regulate the mind's disordered frame,
80 And quench the passions kindling into flame;
The glimmering fires of Virtue to enlarge,
And purge from Vice's dross my tender charge.
Oft have I said, the paths of Fame pursue,
And all that Virtue dictates, dare to do;
Go to the world, peruse the book of man,
And learn from thence thy own defects to scan;
Severely honest, break no plighted trust,
But coldly rest not here – be more than just;
Join to the rigour of the sires of Rome
90 The gentler manners of the private dome;
When Virtue weeps in agony of woe,
Teach from the heart the tender tear to flow;
If Pleasure's soothing song thy soul entice,
Or all the gaudy pomp of splendid Vice,
Arise superior to the Siren's power,
The wretch, the short-lived vision of an hour;
Soon fades her cheek, her blushing beauties fly,
As fades the chequered bow that paints the sky.
'"So shall thy sire, whilst hope his breast inspires,
100 And wakes anew life's glimmering trembling fires,
Hear Britain's sons rehearse thy praise with joy,
Look up to heaven, and bless his darling boy.
If e'er these precepts quelled the passions' strife,
If e'er they smoothed the rugged walks of life,
If e'er they pointed forth the blissful way
That guides the spirit to eternal day,
Do thou, if gratitude inspire thy breast,
Spurn the soft fetters of lethargic rest.
Awake, awake! and snatch the slumbering lyre,
110 Let this bright morn and Sandys the song inspire."
          'I looked Obedience: the celestial Fair
          Smiled like the morn, then vanished into air.'

Beauty and Moonlight

AN ODE

Fragment

High o'er the silver rocks I roved
To wander from the form I loved,
In hopes fond Fancy would be kind
And steal my Mary from my mind;
'Twas Twilight and the lunar beam
Sailed slowly o'er Winander's stream.
As down its sides the water strayed
Bright on a rock the moonbeam played.
It shone half-sheltered from the view
10 By pendent boughs of tressy yew,
True, true to love but false to rest,
So fancy whispered to my breast;
So shines her forehead smooth and fair
Gleaming through her sable hair.
    I turned to Heaven, but viewed on high
The languid lustre of her eye,
The moon's mild radiant edge I saw
Peeping a black-arched cloud below,
Nor yet its faint and paly beam
20 Could tinge its skirt with yellow gleam.
    I saw the white waves o'er and o'er
Break against a curvèd shore,
Now disappearing from the sight
Now twinkling regular and white;
Her mouth, her smiling mouth can show
As white and regular a row.
    Haste – haste, some god indulgent prove
And bear me, bear me to my Love.
Then might – for yet the sultry hour
30 Glows from the Sun's oppressive power,
Then might her bosom soft and white
Heave upon my swimming sight,

As these two Swans together ride
Upon the gently swelling tide.
Haste, haste, some god indulgent prove,
And bear me, bear me to my Love.

Extract from the Conclusion of a Poem, Composed in Anticipation of Leaving School

Dear native regions, I foretell,
From what I feel at this farewell,
That, whereso'er my steps may tend,
And whensoe'er my course shall end,
If in that hour a single tie
Survive of local sympathy,
My soul will cast the backward view,
The longing look alone on you.

Thus, while the Sun sinks down to rest
10   Far in the regions of the west,
Though to the vale no parting beam
Be given, not one memorial gleam,
A lingering light he fondly throws
On the dear hills where first he rose.

Written in Very Early Youth

Calm is all nature as a resting wheel.
The kine are couched upon the dewy grass;
The horse alone, seen dimly as I pass,
Is cropping audibly his later meal:
Dark is the ground; a slumber seems to steal
O'er vale, and mountain, and the starless sky.
Now, in this blank of things, a harmony,
Home-felt, and home-created, comes to heal

That grief for which the senses still supply
10   Fresh food; for only then, when memory
Is hushed, am I at rest. My Friends! restrain
Those busy cares that would allay my pain;
Oh! leave me to myself, nor let me feel
The officious touch that makes me droop again.

'When slow from pensive twilight's latest gleams'

When slow from pensive twilight's latest gleams
'O'er the dark mountain top descends the ray'
That stains with crimson tinge the water grey
And still, I listen while the dells and streams
And vanished woods a lulling murmur make;
As Vesper first begins to twinkle bright
And on the dark hillside the cottage light,
With long reflection streams across the lake.
The lonely grey-duck darkling on his way
10   Quacks clamorous; deep the measured strokes rebound
Of unseen oar parting with hollow sound
While the slow curfew shuts the eye of day
Soothed by the stilly scene with many a sigh,
Heaves the full heart nor knows for whom, or why.

'Sweet was the walk along the narrow lane'

Sweet was the walk along the narrow lane
At noon, the bank an[d] Hedgerows all the way
Shagged with wild pale green Tufts of fragrant Hay,
Caught by the Hawthorns from the loaded wain,
Which Age with many a slow stoop strove to gain;
And Childhood, seeming still most busy, took
His little Rake; with cunning side-long look,
Sauntering to pluck the strawberries wild, unseen.

Now too on melancholy's idle dreams
10   Musing, the lone spot with my Soul agrees,
Quiet and dark; for [through?] the thick wove Trees
Scarce peeps the curious Star till solemn gleams
The clouded Moon, and calls me forth to stray
Through tall, green, silent woods and Ruins grey.

Lines Written While Sailing in a Boat at Evening

How richly glows the water's breast
Before us, tinged with evening hues,
While, facing thus the crimson west,
The boat her silent course pursues!
And see how dark the backward stream!
A little moment past so smiling!
And still, perhaps, with faithless gleam,
Some other loiterers beguiling.

Such views the youthful Bard allure;
10   But, heedless of the following gloom,
He deems their colours shall endure
Till peace go with him to the tomb.
– And let him nurse his fond deceit,
    And what if he must die in sorrow!
Who would not cherish dreams so sweet,
    Though grief and pain may come tomorrow?

Remembrance of Collins Composed upon the Thames near Richmond

Glide gently, thus for ever glide,
O Thames! that other bards may see
As lovely visions by thy side
As now, fair river! come to me.

O glide, fair stream! for ever so,
Thy quiet soul on all bestowing,
Till all our minds for ever flow
As thy deep waters now are flowing.

Vain thought! – Yet be as now thou art,
10   That in thy waters may be seen
The image of a poet's heart,
How bright, how solemn, how serene!
Such as did once the Poet bless,
Who murmuring here a later ditty,
Could find no refuge from distress
But in the milder grief of pity.

Now let us, as we float along,
For *him* suspend the dashing oar;
And pray that never child of song
20   May know that Poet's sorrows more.
How calm! how still! the only sound,
The dripping of the oar suspended!
– The evening darkness gathers round
By virtue's holiest Powers attended.

The Female Vagrant

By Derwent's side my Father's cottage stood,
(The Woman thus her artless story told)
One field, a flock, and what the neighbouring flood
Supplied, to him were more than mines of gold.
Light was my sleep; my days in transport roll'd:
With thoughtless joy I stretch'd along the shore
My father's nets, or watched, when from the fold
High o'er the cliffs I led my fleecy store,
A dizzy depth below! his boat and twinkling oar.

10   My father was a good and pious man,
An honest man by honest parents bred,
And I believe that, soon as I began

To lisp, he made me kneel beside my bed,
And in his hearing there my prayers I said:
And afterwards, by my good father taught,
I read, and loved the books in which I read;
For books in every neighbouring house I sought,
And nothing to my mind a sweeter pleasure brought.

Can I forget what charms did once adorn
20   My garden, stored with pease, and mint, and thyme,
And rose and lily for the sabbath morn?
The sabbath bells, and their delightful chime;
The gambols and wild freaks at shèaring time;
My hens' rich nest through long grass scarce espied;
The cowslip-gathering at May's dewy prime;
The swans, that, when I sought the water-side,
From far to meet me came, spreading their snowy pride.

The staff I yet remember which upbore
The bending body of my active sire;
30   His seat beneath the honeyed sycamore
When the bees hummed, and chair by winter fire;
When market-morning came, the neat attire
With which, though bent on haste, myself I deck'd;
My watchful dog, whose starts of furious ire,
When stranger passed, so often I have check'd;
The red-breast known for years, which at my casement
       peck'd.

The suns of twenty summers danced along, –
Ah! little marked, how fast they rolled away:
Then rose a mansion proud our woods among,
40   And cottage after cottage owned its sway,
No joy to see a neighbouring house, or stray
Through pastures not his own, the master took;
My Father dared his greedy wish gainsay;
He loved his old hereditary nook,
And ill could I the thought of such sad parting brook.

But, when he had refused the proffered gold,
To cruel injuries he became a prey,

Sore-traversed in whate'er he bought and sold:
His troubles grew upon him day by day,
50 Till all his substance fell into decay.
His little range of water was denied;
All but the bed where his old body lay,
All, all was seized, and weeping, side by side,
We sought a home where we uninjured might abide.

Can I forget that miserable hour,
When from the last hill-top, my sire surveyed,
Peering above the trees, the steeple tower,
That on his marriage-day sweet music made?
Till then he hoped his bones might there be laid,
60 Close by my mother in their native bowers:
Bidding me trust in God, he stood and prayed, –
I could not pray: – through tears that fell in showers,
Glimmer'd our dear-loved home, alas! no longer ours!

There was a youth whom I had loved so long,
That when I loved him not I cannot say.
'Mid the green mountains many and many a song
We two had sung, like little birds in May.
When we began to tire of childish play
We seemed still more and more to prize each other:
70 We talked of marriage and our marriage day;
And I in truth did love him like a brother,
For never could I hope to meet with such another.

His father said, that to a distant town
He must repair, to ply the artist's trade.
What tears of bitter grief till then unknown!
What tender vows our last sad kiss delayed!
To him we turned: – we had no other aid.
Like one revived, upon his neck I wept,
And her whom he had loved in joy, he said
80 He well could love in grief: his faith he kept;
And in a quiet home once more my father slept.

Four years each day with daily bread was blest,
By constant toil and constant prayer supplied.

Three lovely infants lay upon my breast;
And often, viewing their sweet smiles, I sighed,
And knew not why. My happy father died
When sad distress reduced the children's meal:
Thrice happy! that from him the grave did hide
The empty loom, cold hearth, and silent wheel,
90   And tears that flowed for ills which patience could not
          heal.

'Twas a hard change, an evil time was come;
We had no hope, and no relief could gain.
But soon, with proud parade, the noisy drum
Beat round, to sweep the streets of want and pain.
My husband's arms now only served to strain
Me and his children hungering in his view:
In such dismay my prayers and tears were vain:
To join those miserable men he flew;
And now to the sea-coast, with numbers more, we drew.

100   There foul neglect for months and months we bore,
Nor yet the crowded fleet its anchor stirred.
Green fields before us and our native shore,
By fever, from polluted air incurred,
Ravage was made, for which no knell was heard.
Fondly we wished, and wished away, nor knew,
'Mid that long sickness, and those hopes deferr'd,
That happier days we never more must view:
The parting signal streamed, at last the land withdrew,

But from delay the summer calms were past.
110   On as we drove, the equinoctial deep
Ran mountains-high before the howling blast.
We gazed with terror on the gloomy sleep
Of them that perished in the whirlwind's sweep,
Untaught that soon such anguish must ensue,
Our hopes such harvest of affliction reap,
That we the mercy of the waves should rue.
We reached the western world, a poor, devoted crew.

Oh! dreadful price of being to resign
All that is dear *in* being! better far
120   In Want's most lonely cave till death to pine,
Unseen, unheard, unwatched by any star;
Or in the streets and walks where proud men are,
Better our dying bodies to obtrude,
Than dog-like, wading at the heels of war,
Protract a curst existence, with the brood
That lap (their very nourishment!) their brother's blood.

The pains and plagues that on our heads came down,
Disease and famine, agony and fear,
In wood or wilderness, in camp or town,
130   It would thy brain unsettle even to hear.
All perished – all, in one remorseless year,
Husband and children! one by one, by sword
And ravenous plague, all perished: every tear
Dried up, despairing, desolate, on board
A British ship I waked, as from a trance restored.

Peaceful as some immeasurable plain
By the first beams of dawning light impress'd,
In the calm sunshine slept the glittering main.
The very ocean has its hour of rest,
140   That comes not to the human mourner's breast.
Remote from man, and storms of mortal care,
A heavenly silence did the waves invest;
I looked and looked along the silent air,
Until it seemed to bring a joy to my despair.

Ah! how unlike those late terrific sleeps!
And groans, that rage of racking famine spoke,
Where looks inhuman dwelt on festering heaps!
The breathing pestilence that rose like smoke!
The shriek that from the distant battle broke!
150   The mine's dire earthquake, and the pallid host
Driven by the bomb's incessant thunder-stroke
To loathsome vaults, where heart-sick anguish toss'd,
Hope died, and fear itself in agony was lost!

Yet does that burst of woe congeal my frame,
When the dark streets appeared to heave and gape,
While like a sea the storming army came,
And Fire from Hell reared his gigantic shape,
And Murder, by the ghastly gleam, and Rape
Seized their joint prey, the mother and the child!
160 But from these crazing thoughts my brain, escape!
– For weeks the balmy air breathed soft and mild,
And on the gliding vessel Heaven and Ocean smiled.

Some mighty gulph of separation past,
I seemed transported to another world: –
A thought resigned with pain, when from the mast
The impatient mariner the sail unfurl'd,
And whistling, called the wind that hardly curled
The silent sea. From the sweet thoughts of home,
And from all hope I was forever hurled.
170 For me – farthest from earthly port to roam
Was best, could I but shun the spot where man might come.

And oft, robb'd of my perfect mind, I thought
At last my feet a resting-place had found:
Here will I weep in peace, (so fancy wrought,)
Roaming the illimitable waters round;
Here watch, of every human friend disowned,
All day, my ready tomb the ocean-flood –
To break my dream the vessel reached its bound:
And homeless near a thousand homes I stood,
180 And near a thousand tables pined, and wanted food.

By grief enfeebled was I turned adrift,
Helpless as sailor cast on desart rock;
Nor morsel to my mouth that day did lift,
Nor dared my hand at any door to knock.
I lay, where with his drowsy mates, the cock
From the cross timber of an out-house hung;
How dismal tolled, that night, the city clock!
At morn my sick heart hunger scarcely stung,
Nor to the beggar's language could I frame my tongue.

190 So passed another day, and so the third:
Then did I try, in vain, the crowd's resort,
In deep despair by frightful wishes stirr'd,
Near the sea-side I reached a ruined fort:
There, pains which nature could no more support,
With blindness linked, did on my vitals fall;
Dizzy my brain, with interruption short
Of hideous sense; I sunk, nor step could crawl,
And thence was borne away to neighbouring hospital.

Recovery came with food: but still, my brain
200 Was weak, nor of the past had memory.
I heard my neighbours, in their beds, complain
Of many things which never troubled me;
Of feet still bustling round with busy glee,
Of looks where common kindness had no part,
Of service done with careless cruelty,
Fretting the fever round the languid heart,
And groans, which, as they said, would make a dead man start.

These things just served to stir the torpid sense,
Nor pain nor pity in my bosom raised.
210 Memory, though slow, returned with strength; and thence
Dismissed, again on open day I gazed,
At houses, men, and common light, amazed.
The lanes I sought, and as the sun retired,
Came, where beneath the trees a faggot blazed;
The wild brood saw me weep, my fate enquired,
And gave me food, and rest, more welcome, more desired.

My heart is touched to think that men like these,
The rude earth's tenants, were my first relief:
How kindly did they paint their vagrant ease!
220 And their long holiday that feared not grief,
For all belonged to all, and each was chief.
No plough their sinews strained; on grating road
No wain they drove, and yet, the yellow sheaf
In every vale for their delight was stowed:
For them, in nature's meads, the milky udder flowed.

Semblance, with straw and panniered ass, they made
Of potters wandering on from door to door:
But life of happier sort to me pourtrayed,
And other joys my fancy to allure;
230 The bag-pipe dinning on the midnight moor
In barn uplighted, and companions boon
Well met from far with revelry secure,
In depth of forest glade, when jocund June
Rolled fast along the sky his warm and genial moon.

But ill it suited me, in journey dark
O'er moor and mountain, midnight theft to hatch;
To charm the surly house-dog's faithful bark,
Or hang on tiptoe at the lifted latch;
The gloomy lantern, and the dim blue match,
240 The black disguise, the warning whistle shrill,
And ear still busy on its nightly watch,
Were not for me, brought up in nothing ill;
Besides, on griefs so fresh my thoughts were brooding still.

What could I do, unaided and unblest?
Poor Father! gone was every friend of thine:
And kindred of dead husband are at best
Small help, and, after marriage such as mine,
With little kindness would to me incline.
Ill was I then for toil or service fit:
250 With tears whose course no effort could confine,
By high-way side forgetful would I sit
Whole hours, my idle arms in moping sorrow knit.

I lived upon the mercy of the fields,
And oft of cruelty the sky accused;
On hazard, or what general bounty yields,
Now coldly given, now utterly refused.
The fields I for my bed have often used:
But, what afflicts my peace with keenest ruth
Is, that I have my inner self abused,
260 Forgone the home delight of constant truth,
And clear and open soul, so prized in fearless youth.

Three years a wanderer, often have I view'd,
In tears, the sun towards that country tend
Where my poor heart lost all its fortitude:
And now across this moor my steps I bend –
Oh! tell me whither – for no earthly friend
Have I. – She ceased, and weeping turned away,
As if because her tale was at an end
She wept; – because she had no more to say
270   Of that perpetual weight which on her spirit lay.

The Convict

The glory of evening was spread through the west;
    – On the slope of a mountain I stood,
While the joy that precedes the calm season of rest
    Rang loud through the meadow and wood.

'And must we then part from a dwelling so fair?'
    In the pain of my spirit I said,
And with a deep sadness I turned, to repair
    To the cell where the convict is laid.

The thick-ribbèd walls that o'ershadow the gate
10   Resound; and the dungeons unfold:
I pause; and at length, through the glimmering grate
    That outcast of pity behold.

His black matted head on his shoulder is bent,
    And deep is the sigh of his breath,
And with steadfast dejection his eyes are intent
    On the fetters that link him to death.

'Tis sorrow enough on that visage to gaze,
    That body dismissed from his care;
Yet my fancy has pierced to his heart, and pourtrays
20   More terrible images there.

His bones are consumed, and his life-blood is dried,
    With wishes the past to undo;
And his crime, through the pains that o'erwhelm him,
        descried,
    Still blackens and grows on his view.

When from the dark synod, or blood-reeking field,
    To his chamber the monarch is led,
All soothers of sense their soft virtue shall yield,
    And quietness pillow his head.

But if grief, self-consumed, in oblivion would doze,
30   And conscience her tortures appease,
'Mid tumult and uproar this man must repose;
    In the comfortless vault of disease.

When his fetters at night have so pressed on his limbs,
    That the weight can no longer be borne,
If, while a half-slumber his memory bedims,
    The wretch on his pallet should turn,

While the jail-mastiff howls at the dull clanking chain,
    From the roots of his hair there shall start
A thousand sharp punctures of cold-sweating pain,
40   And terror shall leap at his heart.

But now he half-raises his deep-sunken eye,
    And the motion unsettles a tear;
The silence of sorrow it seems to supply,
    And asks of me why I am here.

'Poor victim! no idle intruder has stood
    With o'erweening complacence our state to compare,
But one, whose first wish is the wish to be good,
    Is come as a brother thy sorrows to share.

'At thy name though compassion her nature resign,
50   Though in virtue's proud mouth thy report be a stain,
My care, if the arm of the mighty were mine,
    Would plant thee where yet thou mightst blossom again.'

Animal Tranquillity and Decay

The little hedgerow birds,
That peck along the road, regard him not.
He travels on, and in his face, his step,
His gait, is one expression: every limb,
His look and bending figure, all bespeak
A man who does not move with pain, but moves
With thought. – He is insensibly subdued
To settled quiet: he is one by whom
All effort seems forgotten; one to whom
10 Long patience hath such mild composure given,
That patience now doth seem a thing of which
He hath no need. He is by nature led
To peace so perfect that the young behold
With envy, what the Old Man hardly feels.

Lines

Left upon a Seat in a Yew-tree, which stands near the lake of Esth-
waite, on a desolate part of the shore, commanding a beautiful prospect.

Nay, Traveller! rest. This lonely Yew-tree stands
Far from all human dwelling: what if here
No sparkling rivulet spread the verdant herb?
What if the bee love not these barren boughs?
Yet, if the wind breathe soft, the curling waves,
That break against the shore, shall lull thy mind
By one soft impulse saved from vacancy.
                                    Who he was
That piled these stones and with the mossy sod
10 First covered, and here taught this agèd Tree
With its dark arms to form a circling bower,
I well remember. – He was one who owned
No common soul. In youth by science nursed,

And led by nature into a wild scene
Of lofty hopes, he to the world went forth
A favoured Being, knowing no desire
Which genius did not hallow; 'gainst the taint
Of dissolute tongues, and jealousy, and hate,
And scorn, – against all enemies prepared,
20 All but neglect. The world, for so it thought,
Owed him no service; wherefore he at once
With indignation turned himself away,
And with the food of pride sustained his soul
In solitude. – Stranger! these gloomy boughs
Had charms for him; and here he loved to sit,
His only visitants a straggling sheep,
The stone-chat, or the glancing sand-piper:
And on these barren rocks, with fern and heath,
And juniper and thistle, sprinkled o'er,
30 Fixing his downcast eye, he many an hour
A morbid pleasure nourished, tracing here
An emblem of his own unfruitful life:
And, lifting up his head, he then would gaze
On the more distant scene, – how lovely 'tis
Thou seest, – and he would gaze till it became
Far lovelier, and his heart could not sustain
The beauty, still more beauteous! Nor, that time,
When nature had subdued him to herself,
Would he forget those Beings to whose minds
40 Warm from the labours of benevolence
The world, and human life, appeared a scene
Of kindred loveliness: then he would sigh,
Inly disturbed, to think that others felt
What he must never feel: and so, lost Man!
On visionary views would fancy feed,
Till his eye streamed with tears. In this deep vale
He died, – this seat his only monument.

If Thou be one whose heart the holy forms
Of young imagination have kept pure,

50 Stranger! henceforth be warned; and know that pride,
Howe'er disguised in its own majesty,
Is littleness; that he who feels contempt
For any living thing, hath faculties
Which he has never used; that thought with him
Is in its infancy. The man whose eye
Is ever on himself doth look on one,
The least of Nature's works, one who might move
The wise man to that scorn which wisdom holds
Unlawful, ever. O be wiser, Thou!
60 Instructed that true knowledge leads to love;
True dignity abides with him alone
Who, in the silent hour of inward thought,
Can still suspect, and still revere himself,
In lowliness of heart.

To My Sister

It is the first mild day of March:
Each minute sweeter than before,
The redbreast sings from the tall larch
That stands beside our door.

There is a blessing in the air,
Which seems a sense of joy to yield
To the bare trees, and mountains bare,
And grass in the green field.

My sister! ('tis a wish of mine)
10 Now that our morning meal is done,
Make haste, your morning task resign;
Come forth and feel the sun.

Edward will come with you; – and, pray,
Put on with speed your woodland dress;
And bring no book: for this one day
We'll give to idleness.

No joyless forms shall regulate
Our living calendar:
We from today, my Friend, will date
20   The opening of the year.

Love, now a universal birth,
From heart to heart is stealing,
From earth to man, from man to earth:
– It is the hour of feeling.

One moment now may give us more
Than years of toiling reason:
Our minds shall drink at every pore
The spirit of the season.

Some silent laws our hearts will make,
30   Which they shall long obey:
We for the year to come may take
Our temper from today.

And from the blessed power that rolls
About, below, above,
We'll frame the measure of our souls:
They shall be tuned to love.

Then come, my Sister! come, I pray,
With speed put on your woodland dress;
And bring no book: for this one day
40   We'll give to idleness.

Goody Blake and Harry Gill

A TRUE STORY

Oh! what's the matter? what's the matter?
What is't that ails young Harry Gill?
That evermore his teeth they chatter,
Chatter, chatter, chatter still!

Of waistcoats Harry has no lack,
Good duffle grey, and flannel fine;
He has a blanket on his back,
And coats enough to smother nine.

In March, December, and in July,
10   'Tis all the same with Harry Gill;
The neighbours tell, and tell you truly,
His teeth they chatter, chatter still.
At night, at morning, and at noon,
'Tis all the same with Harry Gill;
Beneath the sun, beneath the moon,
His teeth they chatter, chatter still!

Young Harry was a lusty drover,
And who so stout of limb as he?
His cheeks were red as ruddy clover;
20   His voice was like the voice of three.
Old Goody Blake was old and poor;
Ill fed she was, and thinly clad;
And any man who passed her door
Might see how poor a hut she had.

All day she spun in her poor dwelling:
And then her three hours' work at night,
Alas! 'twas hardly worth the telling,
It would not pay for candle-light.
Remote from sheltered village-green,
30   On a hill's northern side she dwelt,
Where from sea-blasts the hawthorns lean,
And hoary dews are slow to melt.

By the same fire to boil their pottage,
Two poor old Dames, as I have known,
Will often live in one small cottage;
But she, poor Woman! housed alone.
'Twas well enough, when summer came,
The long, warm, lightsome summer-day,
Then at her door the *canty* Dame
40   Would sit, as any linnet, gay.

But when the ice our streams did fetter,
Oh then how her old bones would shake!
You would have said, if you had met her,
'Twas a hard time for Goody Blake.
Her evenings then were dull and dead:
Sad case it was, as you may think,
For very cold to go to bed;
And then for cold not sleep a wink.

O joy for her! whene'er in winter
50   The winds at night had made a rout;
And scattered many a lusty splinter
And many a rotten bough about.
Yet never had she, well or sick,
As every man who knew her says,
A pile beforehand, turf or stick,
Enough to warm her for three days.

Now, when the frost was past enduring,
And made her poor old bones to ache,
Could any thing be more alluring
60   Than an old hedge to Goody Blake?
And, now and then, it must be said,
When her old bones were cold and chill,
She left her fire, or left her bed,
To seek the hedge of Harry Gill.

Now Harry he had long suspected
This trespass of old Goody Blake;
And vowed that she should be detected –
That he on her would vengeance take.
And oft from his warm fire he'd go,
70   And to the fields his road would take;
And there, at night, in frost and snow,
He watched to seize old Goody Blake.

And once, behind a rick of barley,
Thus looking out did Harry stand:
The moon was full and shining clearly,
And crisp with frost the stubble land.

– He hears a noise – he's all awake –
Again? – on tip-toe down the hill
He softly creeps – 'tis Goody Blake;
80 She's at the hedge of Harry Gill!

Right glad was he when he beheld her:
Stick after stick did Goody pull:
He stood behind a bush of elder,
Till she had filled her apron full.
When with her load she turned about,
The by-way back again to take;
He started forward, with a shout,
And sprang upon poor Goody Blake.

And fiercely by the arm he took her,
90 And by the arm he held her fast,
And fiercely by the arm he shook her,
And cried, 'I've caught you then at last!'
Then Goody, who had nothing said,
Her bundle from her lap let fall;
And, kneeling on the sticks, she prayed
To God that is the judge of all.

She prayed, her withered hand uprearing,
While Harry held her by the arm –
'God! who art never out of hearing.
100 O may he never more be warm!'
The cold, cold moon above her head,
Thus on her knees did Goody pray;
Young Harry heard what she had said:
And icy cold he turned away.

He went complaining all the morrow
That he was cold and very chill:
His face was gloom, his heart was sorrow,
Alas! that day for Harry Gill!
That day he wore a riding-coat,
110 But not a whit the warmer he:

Another was on Thursday brought,
And ere the Sabbath he had three.

'Twas all in vain, a useless matter,
And blankets were about him pinned;
Yet still his jaws and teeth they clatter,
Like a loose casement in the wind.
And Harry's flesh it fell away;
And all who see him say, 'tis plain,
That, live as long as live he may,
120   He never will be warm again.

No word to any man he utters,
A-bed or up, to young or old;
But ever to himself he mutters,
'Poor Harry Gill is very cold.'
A-bed or up, by night or day;
His teeth they chatter, chatter still.
Now think, ye farmers all, I pray,
Of Goody Blake and Harry Gill!

The Complaint of a Forsaken Indian Woman

When a Northern Indian, from sickness, is unable to continue his journey with his companions, he is left behind, covered over with deer-skins, and is supplied with water, food, and fuel, if the situation of the place will afford it. He is informed of the track which his companions intend to pursue, and if he be unable to follow, or overtake them, he perishes alone in the desert, unless he should have the good fortune to fall in with some other tribe of Indians. The females are equally, or still more, exposed to the same fate. See that very interesting work Hearne's 'Journey from Hudson's Bay to the Northern Ocean'. In the high northern latitudes, as the same writer informs us, when the northern lights vary their position in the air, they make a rustling and a crackling noise, as alluded to in the following poem.

I

Before I see another day,
Oh let my body die away!
In sleep I heard the northern gleams;
The stars, they were among my dreams;
In rustling conflict through the skies,
I heard, I saw the flashes drive,
And yet they are upon my eyes,
And yet I am alive;
Before I see another day,
10   Oh let my body die away!

II

My fire is dead: it knew no pain;
Yet is it dead, and I remain:
All stiff with ice the ashes lie;
And they are dead, and I will die.
When I was well, I wished to live,
For clothes, for warmth, for food, and fire;
But they to me no joy can give,
No pleasure now, and no desire.
Then here contented will I lie!
20   Alone, I cannot fear to die.

III

Alas! ye might have dragged me on
Another day, a single one!
Too soon I yielded to despair;
Why did ye listen to my prayer?
When ye were gone my limbs were stronger;
And oh, how grievously I rue,
That, afterwards, a little longer,
My friends, I did not follow you!
For strong and without pain I lay,
30   Dear friends, when ye were gone away.

IV

My Child! they gave thee to another,
A woman who was not thy mother.
When from my arms my Babe they took,
On me how strangely did he look!
Through his whole body something ran,
A most strange working did I see;
– As if he strove to be a man,
That he might pull the sledge for me:
And then he stretched his arms, how wild!
40　Oh mercy! like a helpless child.

V

My little joy! my little pride!
In two days more I must have died.
Then do not weep and grieve for me;
I feel I must have died with thee.
O wind, that o'er my head art flying
The way my friends their course did bend,
I should not feel the pain of dying,
Could I with thee a message send;
Too soon, my friends, ye went away;
50　For I had many things to say.

VI

I'll follow you across the snow;
Ye travel heavily and slow;
In spite of all my weary pain
I'll look upon your tents again.
– My fire is dead, and snowy white
The water which beside it stood:
The wolf has come to me tonight,
And he has stolen away my food.
For ever left alone am I;
60　Then wherefore should I fear to die?

VII

Young as I am, my course is run,
I shall not see another sun;
I cannot lift my limbs to know
If they have any life or no.
My poor forsaken Child, if I
For once could have thee close to me,
With happy heart I then would die,
And my last thought would happy be;
But thou, dear Babe, art far away,
70 Nor shall I see another day.

Her Eyes are Wild

I

Her eyes are wild, her head is bare,
The sun has burnt her coal-black hair;
Her eyebrows have a rusty stain,
And she came far from over the main.
She has a baby on her arm,
Or else she were alone:
And underneath the hay-stack warm,
And on the greenwood stone,
She talked and sung the woods among,
10 And it was in the English tongue.

II

'Sweet babe! they say that I am mad,
But nay, my heart is far too glad;
And I am happy when I sing
Full many a sad and doleful thing:
Then, lovely baby, do not fear!
I pray thee have no fear of me;
But safe as in a cradle, here
My lovely baby! thou shalt be:
To thee I know too much I owe;
20 I cannot work thee any woe.

III

'A fire was once within my brain;
And in my head a dull, dull pain;
And fiendish faces, one, two, three,
Hung at my breast, and pulled at me;
But then there came a sight of joy;
It came at once to do me good;
I waked, and saw my little boy,
My little boy of flesh and blood;
Oh joy for me that sight to see!
30   For he was here, and only he.

IV

'Suck, little babe, oh suck again!
It cools my blood; it cools my brain;
Thy lips I feel them, baby! they
Draw from my heart the pain away.
Oh! press me with thy little hand;
It loosens something at my chest;
About that tight and deadly band
I feel thy little fingers prest.
The breeze I see is in the tree:
40   It comes to cool my babe and me.

V

'Oh! love me, love me, little boy!
Thou art thy mother's only joy;
And do not dread the waves below,
When o'er the sea-rock's edge we go;
The high crag cannot work me harm,
Nor leaping torrents when they howl;
The babe I carry on my arm,
He saves for me my precious soul;
Then happy lie; for blest am I;
50   Without me my sweet babe would die.

VI
'Then do not fear, my boy! for thee
Bold as a lion will I be;
And I will always be thy guide,
Through hollow snows and rivers wide.
I'll build an Indian bower; I know
The leaves that make the softest bed:
And, if from me thou wilt not go,
But still be true till I am dead,
My pretty thing! then thou shalt sing
60 As merry as the birds in spring.

VII
'Thy father cares not for my breast,
'Tis thine, sweet baby, there to rest;
'Tis all thine own! – and, if its hue
Be changed, that was so fair to view,
'Tis fair enough for thee, my dove!
My beauty, little child, is flown,
But thou wilt live with me in love;
And what if my poor cheek be brown?
'Tis well for me, thou canst not see
70 How pale and wan it else would be.

VIII
'Dread not their taunts, my little Life;
I am thy father's wedded wife;
And underneath the spreading tree
We two will live in honesty.
If his sweet boy he could forsake,
With me he never would have stayed:
From him no harm my babe can take;
But he, poor man! is wretched made;
And every day we two will pray
80 For him that's gone and far away.

IX
'I'll teach my boy the sweetest things:
I'll teach him how the owlet sings.

My little babe! thy lips are still,
And thou hast almost sucked thy fill.
– Where art thou gone, my own dear child?
What wicked looks are those I see?
Alas! alas! that look so wild,
It never, never came from me:
If thou art mad, my pretty lad,
90   Then I must be for ever sad.

X
'Oh! smile on me, my little lamb!
For I thy own dear mother am:
My love for thee has well been tried:
I've sought thy father far and wide.
I know the poisons of the shade;
I know the earth-nuts fit for food:
Then, pretty dear, be not afraid:
We'll find thy father in the wood.
Now laugh and be gay, to the woods away!
100   And there, my babe, we'll live for aye.'

The Idiot Boy

'Tis eight o'clock, – a clear March night,
The moon is up, – the sky is blue,
The owlet, in the moonlight air,
Shouts from nobody knows where;
He lengthens out his lonely shout,
Halloo! halloo! a long halloo!

– Why bustle thus about your door,
What means this bustle, Betty Foy?
Why are you in this mighty fret?
10   And why on horseback have you set
Him whom you love, your Idiot Boy?

Scarcely a soul is out of bed;
Good Betty, put him down again;
His lips with joy they burr at you;
But, Betty! what has he to do
With stirrup, saddle, or with rein?

But Betty's bent on her intent;
For her good neighbour, Susan Gale,
Old Susan, she who dwells alone,
20   Is sick, and makes a piteous moan,
As if her very life would fail.

There's not a house within a mile,
No hand to help them in distress;
Old Susan lies a-bed in pain,
And sorely puzzled are the twain,
For what she ails they cannot guess.

And Betty's husband's at the wood,
Where by the week he doth abide,
A woodman in the distant vale;
30   There's none to help poor Susan Gale;
What must be done? what will betide?

And Betty from the lane has fetched
Her Pony, that is mild and good;
Whether he be in joy or pain,
Feeding at will along the lane,
Or bringing fagots from the wood.

And he is all in travelling trim, –
And, by the moonlight, Betty Foy
Has on the well-girt saddle set
40   (The like was never heard of yet)
Him whom she loves, her Idiot Boy.

And he must post without delay
Across the bridge and through the dale,
And by the church, and o'er the down,
To bring a Doctor from the town,
Or she will die, old Susan Gale.

There is no need of boot or spur,
There is no need of whip or wand;
For Johnny has his holly-bough,
50   And with a *hurly-burly* now
He shakes the green bough in his hand.

And Betty o'er and o'er has told
The Boy, who is her best delight,
Both what to follow, what to shun,
What do, and what to leave undone,
How turn to left, and how to right.

And Betty's most especial charge,
Was, 'Johnny! Johnny! mind that you
Come home again, nor stop at all, –
60   Come home again, whate'er befall,
My Johnny, do, I pray you, do.'

To this did Johnny answer make,
Both with his head and with his hand,
And proudly shook the bridle too;
And then! his words were not a few,
Which Betty well could understand.

And now that Johnny is just going,
Though Betty's in a mighty flurry,
She gently pats the Pony's side,
70   On which her Idiot Boy must ride,
And seems no longer in a hurry.

But when the Pony moved his legs,
Oh! then for the poor Idiot Boy!
For joy he cannot hold the bridle,
For joy his head and heels are idle,
He's idle all for very joy.

And while the Pony moves his legs,
In Johnny's left hand you may see
The green bough motionless and dead:
80   The Moon that shines above his head
Is not more still and mute than he.

His heart it was so full of glee
That, till full fifty yards were gone,
He quite forgot his holly whip,
And all his skill in horsemanship:
Oh! happy, happy, happy John.

And while the Mother, at the door,
Stands fixed, her face with joy o'erflows,
Proud of herself, and proud of him,
90   She sees him in his travelling trim,
How quietly her Johnny goes.

The silence of her Idiot Boy,
What hopes it sends to Betty's heart!
He's at the guide-post – he turns right;
She watches till he's out of sight,
And Betty will not then depart.

Burr, burr – now Johnny's lips they burr,
As loud as any mill, or near it;
Meek as a lamb the Pony moves,
100   And Johnny makes the noise he loves,
And Betty listens, glad to hear it.

Away she hies to Susan Gale:
Her Messenger's in merry tune;
The owlets hoot, the owlets curr,
And Johnny's lips they burr, burr, burr,
As on he goes beneath the moon.

His steed and he right well agree;
For of this Pony there's a rumour,
That, should he lose his eyes and ears,
110   And should he live a thousand years,
He never will be out of humour.

But then he is a horse that thinks!
And when he thinks, his pace is slack;
Now, though he knows poor Johnny well,
Yet, for his life, he cannot tell
What he has got upon his back.

So through the moonlight lanes they go,
And far into the moonlight dale,
And by the church, and o'er the down,
120   To bring a Doctor from the town,
To comfort poor old Susan Gale.

And Betty, now at Susan's side,
Is in the middle of her story,
What speedy help her Boy will bring,
With many a most diverting thing,
Of Johnny's wit, and Johnny's glory.

And Betty, still at Susan's side,
By this time is not quite so flurried:
Demure with porringer and plate
130   She sits, as if in Susan's fate
Her life and soul were buried.

But Betty, poor good woman! she,
You plainly in her face may read it,
Could lend out of that moment's store
Five years of happiness or more
To any that might need it.

But yet I guess that now and then
With Betty all was not so well;
And to the road she turns her ears,
140   And thence full many a sound she hears,
Which she to Susan will not tell.

Poor Susan moans, poor Susan groans;
'As sure as there's a moon in heaven,'
Cries Betty, 'he'll be back again;
They'll both be here – 'tis almost ten –
Both will be here before eleven.'

Poor Susan moans, poor Susan groans;
The clock gives warning for eleven;
'Tis on the stroke – 'He must be near,'
150   Quoth Betty, 'and will soon be here,
As sure as there's a moon in heaven.'

The clock is on the stroke of twelve,
And Johnny is not yet in sight:
– The Moon's in heaven, as Betty sees,
But Betty is not quite at ease;
And Susan has a dreadful night.

And Betty, half an hour ago,
On Johnny vile reflections cast:
'A little idle sauntering Thing!'
160   With other names, an endless string;
But now that time is gone and past.

And Betty's drooping at the heart,
That happy time all past and gone,
'How can it be he is so late?
The Doctor, he has made him wait;
Susan! they'll both be here anon.'

And Susan's growing worse and worse,
And Betty's in a sad *quandary*;
And then there's nobody to say
170   If she must go, or she must stay!
– She's in a sad *quandary*.

The clock is on the stroke of one;
But neither Doctor nor his Guide
Appears along the moonlight road;
There's neither horse nor man abroad,
And Betty's still at Susan's side.

And Susan now begins to fear
Of sad mischances not a few,
That Johnny may perhaps be drowned;
180   Or lost, perhaps, and never found;
Which they must both for ever rue.

She prefaced half a hint of this
With, 'God forbid it should be true!'
At the first word that Susan said
Cried Betty, rising from the bed,
'Susan, I'd gladly stay with you.

'I must be gone, I must away:
Consider, Johnny's but half-wise;
Susan, we must take care of him,
190   If he is hurt in life or limb' –
'Oh God forbid!' poor Susan cries.

'What can I do?' says Betty, going,
'What can I do to ease your pain?
Good Susan tell me, and I'll stay;
I fear you're in a dreadful way,
But I shall soon be back again.'

'Nay, Betty, go! good Betty, go!
There's nothing that can ease my pain.'
Then off she hies; but with a prayer
200   That God poor Susan's life would spare,
Till she comes back again.

So, through the moonlight lane she goes,
And far into the moonlight dale;
And how she ran, and how she walked,
And all that to herself she talked,
Would surely be a tedious tale.

In high and low, above, below,
In great and small, in round and square,
In tree and tower was Johnny seen,
210   In bush and brake, in black and green;
'Twas Johnny, Johnny, everywhere.

And while she crossed the bridge, there came
A thought with which her heart is sore –
Johnny perhaps his horse forsook,
To hunt the moon within the brook,
And never will be heard of more.

Now is she high upon the down,
Alone amid a prospect wide;
There's neither Johnny nor his Horse
220   Among the fern or in the gorse;
There's neither Doctor nor his Guide.

'Oh saints! what is become of him?
Perhaps he's climbed into an oak,
Where he will stay till he is dead;
Or sadly he has been misled,
And joined the wandering gypsy-folk.

'Or him that wicked Pony's carried
To the dark cave, the goblin's hall;
Or in the castle he's pursuing
230   Among the ghosts his own undoing;
Or playing with the waterfall.'

At poor old Susan then she railed,
While to the town she posts away;
'If Susan had not been so ill,
Alas! I should have had him still,
My Johnny, till my dying day.'

Poor Betty, in this sad distemper,
The Doctor's self could hardly spare:
Unworthy things she talked, and wild;
240   Even he, of cattle the most mild,
The Pony had his share.

But now she's fairly in the town,
And to the Doctor's door she hies;
'Tis silence all on every side;
The town so long, the town so wide,
Is silent as the skies.

And now she's at the Doctor's door,
She lifts the knocker, rap, rap, rap;
The Doctor at the casement shows
250   His glimmering eyes that peep and doze!
And one hand rubs his old night-cap.

'Oh Doctor! Doctor! where's my Johnny?'
'I'm here, what is 't you want with me?'
'Oh Sir! you know I'm Betty Foy,
And I have lost my poor dear Boy,
You know him – him you often see;

'He's not so wise as some folks be:'
'The devil take his wisdom!' said
The Doctor, looking somewhat grim,
260 'What, Woman! should I know of him?'
And, grumbling, he went back to bed!

'O woe is me! O woe is me!
Here will I die; here will I die;
I thought to find my lost one here,
But he is neither far nor near,
Oh! what a wretched Mother I!'

She stops, she stands, she looks about;
Which way to turn she cannot tell.
Poor Betty! it would ease her pain
270 If she had heart to knock again;
– The clock strikes three – a dismal knell!

Then up along the town she hies,
No wonder if her senses fail;
This piteous news so much it shocked her,
She quite forgot to send the Doctor,
To comfort poor old Susan Gale.

And now she's high upon the down,
And she can see a mile of road:
'O cruel! I'm almost threescore;
280 Such night as this was ne'er before,
There's not a single soul abroad.'

She listens, but she cannot hear
The foot of horse, the voice of man;
The streams with softest sound are flowing,
The grass you almost hear it growing,
You hear it now, if e'er you can.

The owlets through the long blue night
Are shouting to each other still:
Fond lovers! yet not quite hob nob,
290 They lengthen out the tremulous sob,
That echoes far from hill to hill.

Poor Betty now has lost all hope,
Her thoughts are bent on deadly sin,
A green-grown pond she just has past,
And from the brink she hurries fast,
Lest she should drown herself therein.

And now she sits her down and weeps;
Such tears she never shed before;
'Oh dear, dear Pony! my sweet joy!
300   Oh carry back my Idiot Boy!
And we will ne'er o'erload thee more.'

A thought is come into her head:
The Pony he is mild and good,
And we have always used him well;
Perhaps he's gone along the dell,
And carried Johnny to the wood.

Then up she springs as if on wings;
She thinks no more of deadly sin;
If Betty fifty ponds should see,
310   The last of all her thoughts would be
To drown herself therein.

Oh Reader! now that I might tell
What Johnny and his Horse are doing!
What they've been doing all this time,
Oh could I put it into rhyme,
A most delightful tale pursuing!

Perhaps, and no unlikely thought!
He with his Pony now doth roam
The cliffs and peaks so high that are,
320   To lay his hands upon a star,
And in his pocket bring it home.

Perhaps he's turned himself about,
His face unto his horse's tail,
And, still and mute, in wonder lost,
All silent as a horseman-ghost,
He travels slowly down the vale.

And now, perhaps, is hunting sheep,
A fierce and dreadful hunter he;
Yon valley, now so trim and green,
330   In five months' time, should he be seen,
A desert wilderness will be!

Perhaps, with head and heels on fire,
And like the very soul of evil,
He's galloping away, away,
And so will gallop on for aye,
The bane of all that dread the devil!

I to the Muses have been bound
These fourteen years, by strong indentures:
O gentle Muses! let me tell
340   But half of what to him befell;
He surely met with strange adventures.

O gentle Muses! is this kind?
Why will ye thus my suit repel?
Why of your further aid bereave me?
And can ye thus unfriended leave me;
Ye Muses! whom I love so well?

Who's yon, that, near the waterfall,
Which thunders down with headlong force,
Beneath the moon, yet shining fair,
350   As careless as if nothing were,
Sits upright on a feeding horse?

Unto his horse – there feeding free,
He seems, I think, the rein to give;
Of moon or stars he takes no heed;
Of such we in romances read:
– 'Tis Johnny! Johnny! as I live.

And that's the very Pony, too!
Where is she, where is Betty Foy?
She hardly can sustain her fears;
360   The roaring waterfall she hears,
And cannot find her Idiot Boy.

Your Pony's worth his weight in gold:
Then calm your terrors, Betty Foy!
She's coming from among the trees,
And now all full in view she sees
Him whom she loves, her Idiot Boy.

And Betty sees the Pony too:
Why stand you thus, good Betty Foy?
It is no goblin, 'tis no ghost,
370   'Tis he whom you so long have lost,
He whom you love, your Idiot Boy.

She looks again – her arms are up –
She screams – she cannot move for joy;
She darts, as with a torrent's force,
She almost has o'erturned the Horse,
And fast she holds her Idiot Boy.

And Johnny burrs, and laughs aloud;
Whether in cunning or in joy
I cannot tell; but while he laughs,
380   Betty a drunken pleasure quaffs
To hear again her Idiot Boy.

And now she's at the Pony's tail,
And now is at the Pony's head, –
On that side now, and now on this;
And, almost stifled with her bliss,
A few sad tears does Betty shed.

She kisses o'er and o'er again
Him whom she loves, her Idiot Boy;
She's happy here, is happy there,
390   She is uneasy everywhere;
Her limbs are all alive with joy.

She pats the Pony, where or when
She knows not, happy Betty Foy!
The little Pony glad may be,
But he is milder far than she,
You hardly can perceive his joy.

'Oh! Johnny, never mind the Doctor;
You've done your best, and that is all:'
She took the reins, when this was said,
400 And gently turned the Pony's head
From the loud waterfall.

By this the stars were almost gone,
The moon was setting on the hill,
So pale you scarcely looked at her:
The little birds began to stir,
Though yet their tongues were still.

The Pony, Betty, and her Boy,
Wind slowly through the woody dale;
And who is she, betimes abroad,
410 That hobbles up the steep rough road?
Who is it, but old Susan Gale?

Long time lay Susan lost in thought;
And many dreadful fears beset her,
Both for her Messenger and Nurse;
And, as her mind grew worse and worse,
Her body – it grew better.

She turned, she tossed herself in bed,
On all sides doubts and terrors met her;
Point after point did she discuss;
420 And, while her mind was fighting thus,
Her body still grew better.

'Alas! what is become of them?
These fears can never be endured;
I'll to the wood.' – The word scarce said,
Did Susan rise up from her bed,
As if by magic cured.

Away she goes up hill and down,
And to the wood at length is come;
She spies her Friends, she shouts a greeting;
430 Oh me! it is a merry meeting
As ever was in Christendom.

The owls have hardly sung their last,
While our four travellers homeward wend;
The owls have hooted all night long,
And with the owls began my song,
And with the owls must end.

For while they all were travelling home,
Cried Betty, 'Tell us, Johnny, do,
Where all this long night you have been,
440   What you have heard, what you have seen:
And, Johnny, mind you tell us true.'

Now Johnny all night long had heard
The owls in tuneful concert strive;
No doubt too he the moon had seen;
For in the moonlight he had been
From eight o'clock till five.

And thus, to Betty's question, he
Made answer, like a traveller bold,
(His very words I give to you,)
450   'The cocks did crow to-whoo, to-whoo,
And the sun did shine so cold!'
– Thus answered Johnny in his glory,
And that was all his travel's story.

The Last of the Flock

I

In distant countries have I been,
And yet I have not often seen
A healthy man, a man full grown,
Weep in the public roads, alone.
But such a one, on English ground,
And in the broad highway, I met;
Along the broad highway he came,
His cheeks with tears were wet:
Sturdy he seemed, though he was sad;
10   And in his arms a Lamb he had.

II

He saw me, and he turned aside,
As if he wished himself to hide:
And with his coat did then essay
To wipe those briny tears away.
I followed him, and said, 'My friend,
What ails you? wherefore weep you so?'
– 'Shame on me, Sir! this lusty Lamb,
He makes my tears to flow.
Today I fetched him from the rock;
20   He is the last of all my flock.

III

'When I was young, a single man,
And after youthful follies ran,
Though little given to care and thought,
Yet, so it was, an ewe I bought;
And other sheep from her I raised,
As healthy sheep as you might see;
And then I married, and was rich
As I could wish to be;
Of sheep I numbered a full score,
30   And every year increased my store.

IV
'Year after year my stock it grew;
And from this one, this single ewe,
Full fifty comely sheep I raised,
As fine a flock as ever grazed!
Upon the Quantock hills they fed;
They throve, and we at home did thrive:
– This lusty Lamb of all my store
Is all that is alive;
And now I care not if we die,
40   And perish all of poverty.

V
'Six Children, Sir! had I to feed;
Hard labour in a time of need!
My pride was tamed, and in our grief
I of the Parish asked relief.
They said, I was a wealthy man;
My sheep upon the uplands fed,
And it was fit that thence I took
Whereof to buy us bread.
"Do this: how can we give to you,"
50   They cried, "what to the poor is due?"

VI
'I sold a sheep, as they had said,
And bought my little children bread,
And they were healthy with their food;
For me – it never did me good.
A woeful time it was for me,
To see the end of all my gains,
The pretty flock which I had reared
With all my care and pains,
To see it melt like snow away –
60   For me it was a woeful day.

VII

'Another still! and still another!
A little lamb, and then its mother!
It was a vein that never stopped –
Like blood-drops from my heart they dropped.
Till thirty were not left alive
They dwindled, dwindled, one by one;
And I may say, that many a time
I wished they all were gone –
Reckless of what might come at last
70 Were but the bitter struggle past.

VIII

'To wicked deeds I was inclined,
And wicked fancies crossed my mind;
And every man I chanced to see,
I thought he knew some ill of me:
No peace, no comfort could I find,
No ease, within doors or without;
And, crazily and wearily
I went my work about;
And oft was moved to flee from home,
80 And hide my head where wild beasts roam.

IX

'Sir! 'twas a precious flock to me,
As dear as my own children be;
For daily with my growing store
I loved my children more and more.
Alas! it was an evil time;
God cursed me in my sore distress;
I prayed, yet every day I thought
I loved my children less;
And every week, and every day,
90 My flock it seemed to melt away.

X

'They dwindled, Sir, sad sight to see!
From ten to five, from five to three,
A lamb, a wether, and a ewe; –
And then at last from three to two;
And, of my fifty, yesterday
I had but only one:
And here it lies upon my arm,
Alas! and I have none; –
Today I fetched it from the rock;
100   It is the last of all my flock.'

We are Seven

– A simple Child,
That lightly draws its breath,
And feels its life in every limb,
What should it know of death?

I met a little cottage Girl:
She was eight years old, she said;
Her hair was thick with many a curl
That clustered round her head.

She had a rustic, woodland air,
10   And she was wildly clad:
Her eyes were fair, and very fair;
– Her beauty made me glad.

'Sisters and brothers, little Maid,
How many may you be?'
'How many? Seven in all,' she said,
And wondering looked at me.

'And where are they? I pray you tell.'
She answered, 'Seven are we;
And two of us at Conway dwell,
20   And two are gone to sea.

'Two of us in the church-yard lie,
My sister and my brother;
And, in the church-yard cottage, I
Dwell near them with my mother.'

'You say that two at Conway dwell,
And two are gone to sea,
Yet ye are seven! I pray you tell,
Sweet Maid, how this may be.'

Then did the little Maid reply,
30 'Seven boys and girls are we;
Two of us in the church-yard lie,
Beneath the church-yard tree.'

'You run about, my little Maid,
Your limbs they are alive;
If two are in the church-yard laid,
Then ye are only five.'

'Their graves are green, they may be seen,'
The little Maid replied,
'Twelve steps or more from my mother's door,
40 And they are side by side.

'My stockings there I often knit,
My kerchief there I hem;
And there upon the ground I sit,
And sing a song to them.

'And often after sun-set, Sir,
When it is light and fair,
I take my little porringer,
And eat my supper there.

'The first that died was sister Jane;
50 In bed she moaning lay,
Till God released her of her pain;
And then she went away.

'So in the church-yard she was laid;
And, when the grass was dry,
Together round her grave we played,
My brother John and I.

'And when the ground was white with snow,
And I could run and slide,
My brother John was forced to go,
60 And he lies by her side.'

'How many are you, then,' said I,
'If they two are in heaven?'
Quick was the little Maid's reply,
'O Master! we are seven.'

'But they are dead; those two are dead!
Their spirits are in heaven!'
'Twas throwing words away; for still
The little Maid would have her will,
And said, 'Nay, we are seven!'

Simon Lee, the Old Huntsman

With an incident in which he was concerned.

In the sweet shire of Cardigan,
Not far from pleasant Ivor-hall,
An old Man dwells, a little man, –
'Tis said he once was tall.
Full five-and-thirty years he lived
A running huntsman merry;
And still the centre of his cheek
Is red as a ripe cherry.

No man like him the horn could sound,
10 And hill and valley rang with glee
When Echo bandied, round and round,
The halloo of Simon Lee.

In those proud days, he little cared
For husbandry or tillage;
To blither tasks did Simon rouse
The sleepers of the village.

He all the country could outrun,
Could leave both man and horse behind;
And often, ere the chase was done,
20   He reeled, and was stone-blind.
And still there's something in the world
At which his heart rejoices;
For when the chiming hounds are out,
He dearly loves their voices!

But, oh the heavy change! – bereft
Of health, strength, friends, and kindred, see!
Old Simon to the world is left
In liveried poverty.
His Master's dead, – and no one now
30   Dwells in the Hall of Ivor;
Men, dogs, and horses, all are dead;
He is the sole survivor.

And he is lean and he is sick;
His body, dwindled and awry,
Rests upon ankles swoln and thick;
His legs are thin and dry.
One prop he has, and only one,
His wife, an aged woman,
Lives with him, near the waterfall,
40   Upon the village Common.

Beside their moss-grown hut of clay,
Not twenty paces from the door,
A scrap of land they have, but they
Are poorest of the poor.
This scrap of land he from the heath
Enclosed when he was stronger;
But what to them avails the land
Which he can till no longer?

Oft, working by her Husband's side,
50 Ruth does what Simon cannot do;
For she, with scanty cause for pride,
Is stouter of the two.
And, though you with your utmost skill
From labour could not wean them,
'Tis little, very little – all
That they can do between them.

Few months of life has he in store
As he to you will tell,
For still, the more he works, the more
60 Do his weak ankles swell.
My gentle Reader, I perceive
How patiently you've waited,
And now I fear that you expect
Some tale will be related.

O Reader! had you in your mind
Such stores as silent thought can bring,
O gentle Reader! you would find
A tale in everything.
What more I have to say is short,
70 And you must kindly take it:
It is no tale; but, should you think,
Perhaps a tale you'll make it.

One summer-day I chanced to see
This old Man doing all he could
To unearth the root of an old tree,
A stump of rotten wood.
The mattock tottered in his hand;
So vain was his endeavour,
That at the root of the old tree
80 He might have worked for ever.

'You're overtasked, good Simon Lee,
Give me your tool,' to him I said;
And at the word right gladly he
Received my proffered aid.
I struck, and with a single blow
The tangled root I severed,
At which the poor old Man so long
And vainly had endeavoured.

The tears into his eyes were brought,
90 And thanks and praises seemed to run
So fast out of his heart, I thought
They never would have done.
– I've heard of hearts unkind, kind deeds
With coldness still returning;
Alas! the gratitude of men
Hath oftener left me mourning.

The Thorn

I
'There is a Thorn – it looks so old,
In truth, you'd find it hard to say
How it could ever have been young,
It looks so old and grey.
Not higher than a two years' child
It stands erect, this aged Thorn;
No leaves it has, no prickly points;
It is a mass of knotted joints,
A wretched thing forlorn.
10 It stands erect, and like a stone
With lichens is it overgrown.

II

'Like rock or stone, it is o'ergrown,
With lichens to the very top,
And hung with heavy tufts of moss,
A melancholy crop:
Up from the earth these mosses creep,
And this poor Thorn they clasp it round
So close, you'd say that they are bent
With plain and manifest intent
20   To drag it to the ground;
And all have joined in one endeavour
To bury this poor Thorn for ever.

III

'High on a mountain's highest ridge,
Where oft the stormy winter gale
Cuts like a scythe, while through the clouds
It sweeps from vale to vale;
Not five yards from the mountain path,
This Thorn you on your left espy;
And to the left, three yards beyond,
30   You see a little muddy pond
Of water – never dry
Though but of compass small, and bare
To thirsty suns and parching air.

IV

'And, close beside this aged Thorn,
There is a fresh and lovely sight,
A beauteous heap, a hill of moss,
Just half a foot in height.
All lovely colours there you see,
All colours that were ever seen;
40   And mossy network too is there,
As if by hand of lady fair
The work had woven been;
And cups, the darlings of the eye,
So deep is their vermilion dye.

V

'Ah me! what lovely tints are there
Of olive green and scarlet bright,
In spikes, in branches, and in stars,
Green, red, and pearly white!
This heap of earth o'ergrown with moss,
50   Which close beside the Thorn you see,
So fresh in all its beauteous dyes,
Is like an infant's grave in size,
As like as like can be:
But never, never anywhere,
An infant's grave was half so fair.

VI

'Now would you see this aged Thorn,
This pond, and beauteous hill of moss,
You must take care and choose your time
The mountain when to cross.
60   For oft there sits between the heap,
So like an infant's grave in size,
And that same pond of which I spoke,
A Woman in a scarlet cloak,
And to herself she cries,
"Oh misery! oh misery!
Oh woe is me! oh misery!"

VII

'At all times of the day and night
This wretched Woman thither goes;
And she is known to every star,
70   And every wind that blows;
And there, beside the Thorn, she sits
When the blue daylight's in the skies,
And when the whirlwind's on the hill,
Or frosty air is keen and still,
And to herself she cries,
"Oh misery! oh misery!
Oh woe is me! oh misery!"'

VIII
'Now wherefore, thus, by day and night,
In rain, in tempest, and in snow,
80   Thus to the dreary mountain-top
Does this poor Woman go?
And why sits she beside the Thorn
When the blue daylight's in the sky
Or when the whirlwind's on the hill,
Or frosty air is keen and still,
And wherefore does she cry? –
O wherefore? wherefore? tell me why
Does she repeat that doleful cry?'

IX
'I cannot tell; I wish I could;
90   For the true reason no one knows:
But would you gladly view the spot,
The spot to which she goes;
The hillock like an infant's grave,
The pond – and Thorn, so old and grey;
Pass by her door –' tis seldom shut –
And, if you see her in her hut –
Then to the spot away!
I never heard of such as dare
Approach the spot when she is there.'

X
100   'But wherefore to the mountain-top
Can this unhappy Woman go,
Whatever star is in the skies,
Whatever wind may blow?'
'Full twenty years are past and gone
Since she (her name is Martha Ray)
Gave with a maiden's true good-will
Her company to Stephen Hill;
And she was blithe and gay,
While friends and kindred all approved
110   Of him whom tenderly she loved.

XI

'And they had fixed the wedding day,
The morning that must wed them both;
But Stephen to another Maid
Had sworn another oath;
And, with this other Maid, to church
Unthinking Stephen went –
Poor Martha! on that woeful day
A pang of pitiless dismay
Into her soul was sent;
120   A fire was kindled in her breast,
Which might not burn itself to rest.

XII

'They say, full six months after this,
While yet the summer leaves were green,
She to the mountain-top would go,
And there was often seen.
What could she seek? – or wish to hide?
Her state to any eye was plain;
She was with child, and she was mad;
Yet often was she sober sad
130   From her exceeding pain.
O guilty Father – would that death
Had saved him from that breach of faith!

XIII

'Sad case for such a brain to hold
Communion with a stirring child!
Sad case, as you may think, for one
Who had a brain so wild!
Last Christmas-eve we talked of this,
And grey-haired Wilfred of the glen
Held that the unborn infant wrought
140   About its mother's heart, and brought
Her senses back again:
And, when at last her time drew near,
Her looks were calm, her senses clear.

XIV

'More know I not, I wish I did,
And it should all be told to you;
For what became of this poor child
No mortal ever knew;
Nay – if a child to her was born
No earthly tongue could ever tell;
150   And if 'twas born alive or dead,
Far less could this with proof be said;
But some remember well,
That Martha Ray about this time
Would up the mountain often climb.

XV

'And all that winter, when at night
The wind blew from the mountain-peak,
'Twas worth your while, though in the dark,
The churchyard path to seek:
For many a time and oft were heard
160   Cries coming from the mountain head:
Some plainly living voices were;
And others, I've heard many swear,
Were voices of the dead:
I cannot think, whate'er they say,
They had to do with Martha Ray.

XVI

'But that she goes to this old Thorn,
The Thorn which I described to you,
And there sits in a scarlet cloak,
I will be sworn is true.
170   For one day with my telescope,
To view the ocean wide and bright,
When to this country first I came,
Ere I had heard of Martha's name,
I climbed the mountain's height: –
A storm came on, and I could see
No object higher than my knee.

XVII
"Twas mist and rain, and storm and rain:
No screen, no fence could I discover;
And then the wind! in sooth, it was
180 A wind full ten times over.
I looked around, I thought I saw
A jutting crag, – and off I ran,
Head-foremost, through the driving rain,
The shelter of the crag to gain;
And, as I am a man,
Instead of jutting crag, I found
A Woman seated on the ground.

XVIII
'I did not speak – I saw her face;
Her face! – it was enough for me;
190 I turned about and heard her cry,
"Oh misery! oh misery!"
And there she sits, until the moon
Through half the clear blue sky will go;
And when the little breezes make
The waters of the pond to shake,
As all the country know,
She shudders, and you hear her cry,
"Oh misery! oh misery!"'

XIX
'But what's the Thorn? and what the pond?
200 And what the hill of moss to her?
And what the creeping breeze that comes
The little pond to stir?'
'I cannot tell; but some will say
She hanged her baby on the tree;
Some say she drowned it in the pond,
Which is a little step beyond:
But all and each agree,
The little Babe was buried there,
Beneath that hill of moss so fair.

XX

210 'I've heard, the moss is spotted red
      With drops of that poor infant's blood;
      But kill a new-born infant thus,
      I do not think she could!
      Some say, if to the pond you go,
      And fix on it a steady view,
      The shadow of a babe you trace,
      A baby and a baby's face,
      And that it looks at you;
      Whene'er you look on it, 'tis plain
220 The baby looks at you again.

XXI

      'And some had sworn an oath that she
      Should be to public justice brought;
      And for the little infant's bones
      With spades they would have sought.
      But instantly the hill of moss
      Before their eyes began to stir!
      And, for full fifty yards around,
      The grass — it shook upon the ground!
      Yet all do still aver
230 The little Babe lies buried there,
      Beneath that hill of moss so fair.

XXII

      'I cannot tell how this may be,
      But plain it is the Thorn is bound
      With heavy tufts of moss that strive
      To drag it to the ground;
      And this I know, full many a time,
      When she was on the mountain high,
      By day, and in the silent night,
      When all the stars shone clear and bright,
240 That I have heard her cry,
      "Oh misery! oh misery!
      Oh woe is me! oh misery!"'

Lines Written in Early Spring

I heard a thousand blended notes,
While in a grove I sate reclined,
In that sweet mood when pleasant thoughts
Bring sad thoughts to the mind.

To her fair works did Nature link
The human soul that through me ran;
And much it grieved my heart to think
What man has made of man.

Through primrose tufts, in that green bower,
10   The periwinkle trailed its wreaths;
And 'tis my faith that every flower
Enjoys the air it breathes.

The birds around me hopped and played,
Their thoughts I cannot measure: —
But the least motion which they made,
It seemed a thrill of pleasure.

The budding twigs spread out their fan,
To catch the breezy air;
And I must think, do all I can,
20   That there was pleasure there.

If this belief from heaven be sent,
If such be Nature's holy plan,
Have I not reason to lament
What man has made of man?

Anecdote for Fathers

'Retine vim istam, falsa enim dicam, si coges.'
EUSEBIUS

I have a boy of five years old;
His face is fair and fresh to see;
His limbs are cast in beauty's mould,
And dearly he loves me.

One morn we strolled on our dry walk,
Our quiet home all full in view,
And held such intermitted talk
As we are wont to do.

My thoughts on former pleasures ran;
10   I thought of Kilve's delightful shore,
Our pleasant home when spring began,
A long, long year before.

A day it was when I could bear
Some fond regrets to entertain;
With so much happiness to spare,
I could not feel a pain.

The green earth echoed to the feet
Of lambs that bounded through the glade,
From shade to sunshine, and as fleet
20   From sunshine back to shade.

Birds warbled round me – and each trace
Of inward sadness had its charm;
Kilve, thought I, was a favoured place,
And so is Liswyn farm.

My boy beside me tripped, so slim
And graceful in his rustic dress!
And, as we talked, I questioned him,
In very idleness.

'Now tell me, had you rather be,'
30 I said, and took him by the arm,
'On Kilve's smooth shore, by the green sea,
Or here at Liswyn farm?'

In careless mood he looked at me,
While still I held him by the arm,
And said, 'At Kilve I'd rather be
Than here at Liswyn farm.'

'Now, little Edward, say why so:
My little Edward, tell me why.' –
'I cannot tell, I do not know.' –
40 'Why, this is strange,' said I;

'For, here are woods, hills smooth and warm:
There surely must some reason be
Why you would change sweet Liswyn farm
For Kilve by the green sea.'

At this, my boy hung down his head,
He blushed with shame, nor made reply;
And three times to the child I said,
'Why, Edward, tell me why?'

His head he raised – there was in sight,
50 It caught his eye, he saw it plain –
Upon the house-top, glittering bright,
A broad and gilded vane.

Then did the boy his tongue unlock,
And eased his mind with this reply:
'At Kilve there was no weather-cock;
And that's the reason why.'

O dearest, dearest boy! my heart
For better lore would seldom yearn,
Could I but teach the hundredth part
60 Of what from thee I learn.

Expostulation and Reply

'Why, William, on that old grey stone,
Thus for the length of half a day,
Why, William, sit you thus alone,
And dream your time away?

'Where are your books? – that light bequeathed
To Beings else forlorn and blind!
Up! up! and drink the spirit breathed
From dead men to their kind.

'You look round on your Mother Earth,
10 As if she for no purpose bore you;
As if you were her first-born birth,
And none had lived before you!'

One morning thus, by Esthwaite lake,
When life was sweet, I knew not why,
To me my good friend Matthew spake,
And thus I made reply:

'The eye – it cannot choose but see;
We cannot bid the ear be still;
Our bodies feel, where'er they be,
20 Against or with our will.

'Nor less I deem that there are Powers
Which of themselves our minds impress;
That we can feed this mind of ours
In a wise passiveness.

'Think you, 'mid all this mighty sum
Of things for ever speaking,
That nothing of itself will come,
But we must still be seeking?

'– Then ask not wherefore, here, alone,
30 Conversing as I may,
I sit upon this old grey stone,
And dream my time away.'

The Tables Turned

AN EVENING SCENE ON THE SAME SUBJECT

Up! up! my Friend, and quit your books;
Or surely you'll grow double:
Up! up! my Friend, and clear your looks;
Why all this toil and trouble?

The sun, above the mountain's head,
A freshening lustre mellow
Through all the long green fields has spread,
His first sweet evening yellow.

Books! 'tis a dull and endless strife:
10   Come, hear the woodland linnet,
How sweet his music! on my life,
There's more of wisdom in it.

And hark! how blithe the throstle sings!
He, too, is no mean preacher:
Come forth into the light of things,
Let Nature be your Teacher.

She has a world of ready wealth,
Our minds and hearts to bless –
Spontaneous wisdom breathed by health,
20   Truth breathed by cheerfulness.

One impulse from a vernal wood
May teach you more of man,
Of moral evil and of good,
Than all the sages can.

Sweet is the lore which Nature brings;
Our meddling intellect
Mis-shapes the beauteous forms of things: –
We murder to dissect.

Enough of Science and of Art;
30   Close up those barren leaves;
Come forth, and bring with you a heart
That watches and receives.

Lines Composed a Few Miles above Tintern Abbey,
on Revisiting the Banks of the Wye during a Tour.
July 13, 1798

Five years have past; five summers, with the length
Of five long winters! and again I hear
These waters, rolling from their mountain-springs
With a soft inland murmur. – Once again
Do I behold these steep and lofty cliffs,
That on a wild secluded scene impress
Thoughts of more deep seclusion; and connect
The landscape with the quiet of the sky.
The day is come when I again repose
10 Here, under this dark sycamore, and view
These plots of cottage-ground, these orchard-tufts,
Which at this season, with their unripe fruits,
Are clad in one green hue, and lose themselves
'Mid groves and copses. Once again I see
These hedgerows, hardly hedgerows, little lines
Of sportive wood run wild: these pastoral farms,
Green to the very door; and wreaths of smoke
Sent up, in silence, from among the trees!
With some uncertain notice, as might seem
20 Of vagrant dwellers in the houseless woods,
Or of some Hermit's cave, where by his fire
The Hermit sits alone.
                                    These beauteous forms,
Through a long absence, have not been to me
As is a landscape to a blind man's eye:
But oft, in lonely rooms, and 'mid the din
Of towns and cities, I have owed to them
In hours of weariness, sensations sweet,
Felt in the blood, and felt along the heart;
And passing even into my purer mind,
30 With tranquil restoration: – feelings too
Of unremembered pleasure: such, perhaps,
As have no slight or trivial influence
On that best portion of a good man's life,

His little, nameless, unremembered, acts
Of kindness and of love. Nor less, I trust,
To them I may have owed another gift,
Of aspect more sublime; that blessed mood,
In which the burden of the mystery,
In which the heavy and the weary weight
40 Of all this unintelligible world,
Is lightened: – that serene and blessed mood,
In which the affections gently lead us on, –
Until, the breath of this corporeal frame
And even the motion of our human blood
Almost suspended, we are laid asleep
In body, and become a living soul:
While with an eye made quiet by the power
Of harmony, and the deep power of joy,
We see into the life of things.
                          If this
50 Be but a vain belief, yet, oh! how oft –
In darkness and amid the many shapes
Of joyless daylight; when the fretful stir
Unprofitable, and the fever of the world,
Have hung upon the beatings of my heart –
How oft, in spirit, have I turned to thee,
O sylvan Wye! thou wanderer through the woods,
How often has my spirit turned to thee!

    And now, with gleams of half-extinguished thought,
With many recognitions dim and faint,
60 And somewhat of a sad perplexity,
The picture of the mind revives again:
While here I stand, not only with the sense
Of present pleasure, but with pleasing thoughts
That in this moment there is life and food
For future years. And so I dare to hope,
Though changed, no doubt, from what I was when first
I came among these hills; when like a roe
I bounded o'er the mountains, by the sides
Of the deep rivers, and the lonely streams,
70 Wherever nature led: more like a man

Flying from something that he dreads, than one
Who sought the thing he loved. For nature then
(The coarser pleasures of my boyish days,
And their glad animal movements all gone by)
To me was all in all. – I cannot paint
What then I was. The sounding cataract
Haunted me like a passion: the tall rock,
The mountain, and the deep and gloomy wood,
Their colours and their forms, were then to me
80 An appetite; a feeling and a love,
That had no need of a remoter charm,
By thought supplied, nor any interest
Unborrowed from the eye. – That time is past,
And all its aching joys are now no more,
And all its dizzy raptures. Not for this
Faint I, nor mourn nor murmur; other gifts
Have followed; for such loss, I would believe,
Abundant recompense. For I have learned
To look on nature, not as in the hour
90 Of thoughtless youth; but hearing oftentimes
The still, sad music of humanity,
Nor harsh nor grating, though of ample power
To chasten and subdue. And I have felt
A presence that disturbs me with the joy
Of elevated thoughts; a sense sublime
Of something far more deeply interfused,
Whose dwelling is the light of setting suns,
And the round ocean and the living air,
And the blue sky, and in the mind of man:
100 A motion and a spirit, that impels
All thinking things, all objects of all thought,
And rolls through all things. Therefore am I still
A lover of the meadows and the woods,
And mountains; and of all that we behold
From this green earth; of all the mighty world
Of eye, and ear, – both what they half create,
And what perceive; well pleased to recognize
In nature and the language of the sense,
The anchor of my purest thoughts, the nurse,

110   The guide, the guardian of my heart, and soul
        Of all my moral being.
                                    Nor perchance,
        If I were not thus taught, should I the more
        Suffer my genial spirits to decay:
        For thou art with me here upon the banks
        Of this fair river; thou my dearest Friend,
        My dear, dear Friend; and in thy voice I catch
        The language of my former heart, and read
        My former pleasures in the shooting lights
        Of thy wild eyes. Oh! yet a little while
120   May I behold in thee what I was once,
        My dear, dear Sister! and this prayer I make,
        Knowing that Nature never did betray
        The heart that loved her; 'tis her privilege,
        Through all the years of this our life, to lead
        From joy to joy: for she can so inform
        The mind that is within us, so impress
        With quietness and beauty, and so feed
        With lofty thoughts, that neither evil tongues,
        Rash judgements, nor the sneers of selfish men,
130   Nor greetings where no kindness is, nor all
        The dreary intercourse of daily life,
        Shall e'er prevail against us, or disturb
        Our cheerful faith, that all which we behold
        Is full of blessings. Therefore let the moon
        Shine on thee in thy solitary walk;
        And let the misty mountain-winds be free
        To blow against thee: and, in after years,
        When these wild ecstasies shall be matured
        Into a sober pleasure; when thy mind
140   Shall be a mansion for all lovely forms,
        Thy memory be as a dwelling-place
        For all sweet sounds and harmonies; oh! then,
        If solitude, or fear, or pain, or grief,
        Should be thy portion, with what healing thoughts
        Of tender joy wilt thou remember me,
        And these my exhortations! Nor, perchance –
        If I should be where I no more can hear

Thy voice, nor catch from thy wild eyes these gleams
Of past existence – wilt thou then forget
150 That on the banks of this delightful stream
We stood together; and that I, so long
A worshipper of Nature, hither came
Unwearied in that service: rather say
With warmer love – oh! with far deeper zeal
Of holier love. Nor wilt thou then forget,
That after many wanderings, many years
Of absence, these steep woods and lofty cliffs,
And this green pastoral landscape, were to me
More dear, both for themselves and for thy sake!

The Reverie of Poor Susan

At the corner of Wood Street, when daylight appears,
Hangs a Thrush that sings loud, it has sung for three years:
Poor Susan has passed by the spot, and has heard
In the silence of morning the song of the Bird.

'Tis a note of enchantment; what ails her? She sees
A mountain ascending, a vision of trees;
Bright volumes of vapour through Lothbury glide,
And a river flows on through the vale of Cheapside.

Green pastures she views in the midst of the dale,
10 Down which she so often has tripped with her pail;
And a single small cottage, a nest like a dove's,
The one only dwelling on earth that she loves.

She looks, and her heart is in heaven: but they fade,
The mist and the river, the hill and the shade:
The stream will not flow, and the hill will not rise,
And the colours have all passed away from her eyes!

A Night-Piece

         – The sky is overcast
With a continuous cloud of texture close,
Heavy and wan, all whitened by the Moon,
Which through that veil is indistinctly seen,
A dull, contracted circle, yielding light
So feebly spread, that not a shadow falls,
Chequering the ground – from rock, plant, tree, or tower.
At length a pleasant instantaneous gleam
Startles the pensive traveller while he treads
His lonesome path, with unobserving eye
Bent earthwards; he looks up – the clouds are split
Asunder, – and above his head he sees
The clear Moon, and the glory of the heavens.
There, in a black-blue vault she sails along,
Followed by multitudes of stars, that, small
And sharp, and bright, along the dark abyss
Drive as she drives: how fast they wheel away,
Yet vanish not! – the wind is in the tree,
But they are silent; – still they roll along
Immeasurably distant; and the vault,
Built round by those white clouds, enormous clouds,
Still deepens its unfathomable depth.
At length the Vision closes; and the mind,
Not undisturbed by the delight it feels,
Which slowly settles into peaceful calm,
Is left to muse upon the solemn scene.

The Old Cumberland Beggar

The class of Beggars, to which the Old Man here described belongs,
will probably soon be extinct. It consisted of poor, and, mostly, old
and infirm persons, who confined themselves to a stated round in
their neighbourhood, and had certain fixed days, on which, at different
houses, they regularly received alms, sometimes in money, but mostly
in provisions.

I saw an aged Beggar in my walk;
And he was seated, by the highway side,
On a low structure of rude masonry
Built at the foot of a huge hill, that they
Who lead their horses down the steep rough road
May thence remount at ease. The aged Man
Had placed his staff across the broad smooth stone
That overlays the pile; and, from a bag
All white with flour, the dole of village dames,
10   He drew his scraps and fragments, one by one;
And scanned them with a fixed and serious look
Of idle computation. In the sun,
Upon the second step of that small pile,
Surrounded by those wild unpeopled hills,
He sat, and ate his food in solitude:
And ever, scattered from his palsied hand,
That, still attempting to prevent the waste,
Was baffled still, the crumbs in little showers
Fell on the ground; and the small mountain birds,
20   Not venturing yet to peck their destined meal,
Approached within the length of half his staff.

Him from my childhood have I known; and then
He was so old, he seems not older now;
He travels on, a solitary Man,
So helpless in appearance, that for him
The sauntering Horseman throws not with a slack
And careless hand his alms upon the ground,
But stops, – that he may safely lodge the coin
Within the old Man's hat; nor quits him so,
30   But still, when he has given his horse the rein,

Watches the aged Beggar with a look
Sidelong, and half-reverted. She who tends
The toll-gate, when in summer at her door
She turns her wheel, if on the road she sees
The aged Beggar coming, quits her work,
And lifts the latch for him that he may pass.
The post-boy, when his rattling wheels o'ertake
The aged Beggar in the woody lane,
Shouts to him from behind; and, if thus warned
40 The old Man does not change his course, the boy
Turns with less noisy wheels to the roadside,
And passes gently by, without a curse
Upon his lips, or anger at his heart.

He travels on, a solitary Man;
His age has no companion. On the ground
His eyes are turned, and, as he moves along,
They move along the ground; and, evermore,
Instead of common and habitual sight
Of fields with rural works, of hill and dale,
50 And the blue sky, one little span of earth
Is all his prospect. Thus, from day to day,
Bow-bent, his eyes for ever on the ground,
He plies his weary journey; seeing still,
And seldom knowing that he sees, some straw,
Some scattered leaf, or marks which, in one track,
The nails of cart or chariot-wheel have left
Impressed on the white road, – in the same line,
At distance still the same. Poor Traveller!
His staff trails with him; scarcely do his feet
60 Disturb the summer dust; he is so still
In look and motion, that the cottage curs,
Ere he has passed the door, will turn away,
Weary of barking at him. Boys and girls,
The vacant and the busy, maids and youths,
And urchins newly breeched – all pass him by:
Him even the slow-paced waggon leaves behind.

But deem not this Man useless – Statesmen! ye
Who are so restless in your wisdom, ye

Who have a broom still ready in your hands
70   To rid the world of nuisances; ye proud,
Heart-swoln, while in your pride ye contemplate
Your talents, power, or wisdom, deem him not
A burden of the earth! 'Tis Nature's law
That none, the meanest of created things,
Of forms created the most vile and brute,
The dullest or most noxious, should exist
Divorced from good – a spirit and pulse of good,
A life and soul, to every mode of being
Inseparably linked. Then be assured
80   That least of all can aught – that ever owned
The heaven-regarding eye and front sublime
Which man is born to – sink, howe'er depressed,
So low as to be scorned without a sin;
Without offence to God cast out of view;
Like the dry remnant of a garden-flower
Whose seeds are shed, or as an implement
Worn out and worthless. While from door to door,
This old Man creeps, the villagers in him
Behold a record which together binds
90   Past deeds and offices of charity,
Else unremembered, and so keeps alive
The kindly mood in hearts which lapse of years,
And that half-wisdom half-experience gives,
Make slow to feel, and by sure steps resign
To selfishness and cold oblivious cares.
Among the farms and solitary huts,
Hamlets and thinly-scattered villages,
Where'er the aged Beggar takes his rounds,
The mild necessity of use compels
100 To acts of love; and habit does the work
Of reason; yet prepares that after-joy
Which reason cherishes. And thus the soul,
By that sweet taste of pleasure unpursued,
Doth find herself insensibly disposed
To virtue and true goodness. Some there are,
By their good works exalted, lofty minds
And meditative, authors of delight

And happiness, which to the end of time
Will live, and spread, and kindle: even such minds
110   In childhood, from this solitary Being,
Or from like wanderer, haply have received
(A thing more precious far than all that books
Or the solicitudes of love can do!)
That first mild touch of sympathy and thought,
In which they found their kindred with a world
Where want and sorrow were. The easy man
Who sits at his own door, – and, like the pear
That overhangs his head from the green wall,
Feeds in the sunshine; the robust and young,
120   The prosperous and unthinking, they who live
Sheltered, and flourish in a little grove
Of their own kindred; – all behold in him
A silent monitor, which on their minds
Must needs impress a transitory thought
Of self-congratulation, to the heart
Of each recalling his peculiar boons,
His charters and exemptions; and, perchance,
Though he to no one give the fortitude
And circumspection needful to preserve
130   His present blessings, and to husband up
The respite of the season, he, at least,
And 'tis no vulgar service, makes them felt.

Yet further. – Many, I believe, there are
Who live a life of virtuous decency,
Men who can hear the Decalogue and feel
No self-reproach; who of the moral law
Established in the land where they abide
Are strict observers; and not negligent
In acts of love to those with whom they dwell,
140   Their kindred, and the children of their blood.
Praise be to such, and to their slumbers peace!
– But of the poor man ask, the abject poor;
Go, and demand of him, if there be here
In this cold abstinence from evil deeds,
And these inevitable charities,

Wherewith to satisfy the human soul?
No – man is dear to man; the poorest poor
Long for some moments in a weary life
When they can know and feel that they have been,
150 Themselves, the fathers and the dealers-out
Of some small blessings; have been kind to such
As needed kindness, for this single cause,
That we have all of us one human heart.
– Such pleasure is to one kind Being known,
My neighbour, when with punctual care, each week,
Duly as Friday comes, though pressed herself
By her own wants, she from her store of meal
Takes one unsparing handful for the scrip
Of this old Mendicant, and, from her door
160 Returning with exhilarated heart,
Sits by her fire, and builds her hope in heaven.

Then let him pass, a blessing on his head!
And while in that vast solitude to which
The tide of things has borne him, he appears
To breathe and live but for himself alone,
Unblamed, uninjured, let him bear about
The good which the benignant law of Heaven
Has hung around him: and, while life is his,
Still let him prompt the unlettered villagers
170 To tender offices and pensive thoughts.
– Then let him pass, a blessing on his head!
And, long as he can wander, let him breathe
The freshness of the valleys; let his blood
Struggle with frosty air and winter snows;
And let the chartered wind that sweeps the heath
Beat his grey locks against his withered face.
Reverence the hope whose vital anxiousness
Gives the last human interest to his heart.
May never HOUSE, misnamed of INDUSTRY,
180 Make him a captive! – for that pent-up din,
Those life-consuming sounds that clog the air,
Be his the natural silence of old age!
Let him be free of mountain solitudes;

And have around him, whether heard or not,
The pleasant melody of woodland birds.
Few are his pleasures: if his eyes have now
Been doomed so long to settle upon earth
That not without some effort they behold
The countenance of the horizontal sun,
190 Rising or setting, let the light at least
Find a free entrance to their languid orbs.
And let him, *where* and *when* he will, sit down
Beneath the trees, or on a grassy bank
Of highway side, and with the little birds
Share his chance-gathered meal; and, finally,
As in the eye of Nature he has lived,
So in the eye of Nature let him die!

'A whirl-blast from behind the hill'

A whirl-blast from behind the hill
Rushed o'er the wood with startling sound;
Then – all at once the air was still,
And showers of hailstones pattered round.
Where leafless oaks towered high above,
I sat within an undergrove
Of tallest hollies, tall and green;
A fairer bower was never seen.
From year to year the spacious floor
10 With withered leaves is covered o'er,
And all the year the bower is green.
But see! where'er the hailstones drop
The withered leaves all skip and hop;
There's not a breeze – no breath of air –
Yet here, and there, and everywhere
Along the floor, beneath the shade
By those embowering hollies made,
The leaves in myriads jump and spring,
As if with pipes and music rare
20 Some Robin Good-fellow were there,
And all those leaves, in festive glee,
Were dancing to the minstrelsy.

'A slumber did my spirit seal'

A slumber did my spirit seal;
   I had no human fears:
She seemed a thing that could not feel
   The touch of earthly years.

No motion has she now, no force;
   She neither hears nor sees;
Rolled round in earth's diurnal course,
   With rocks, and stones, and trees.

'She dwelt among the untrodden ways'

She dwelt among the untrodden ways
   Beside the springs of Dove,
A Maid whom there were none to praise
   And very few to love:

A violet by a mossy stone
   Half hidden from the eye!
– Fair as a star, when only one
   Is shining in the sky.

She lived unknown, and few could know
10   When Lucy ceased to be;
But she is in her grave, and, oh,
   The difference to me!

'Strange fits of passion have I known'

Strange fits of passion have I known:
And I will dare to tell,
But in the Lover's ear alone,
What once to me befell.

When she I loved looked every day
Fresh as a rose in June,
I to her cottage bent my way,
Beneath an evening moon.

Upon the moon I fixed my eye,
10 All over the wide lea;
With quickening pace my horse drew nigh
Those paths so dear to me.

And now we reached the orchard-plot;
And, as we climbed the hill,
The sinking moon to Lucy's cot
Came near, and nearer still.

In one of those sweet dreams I slept,
Kind Nature's gentlest boon!
And all the while my eyes I kept
20 On the descending moon.

My horse moved on; hoof after hoof
He raised, and never stopped:
When down behind the cottage roof,
At once, the bright moon dropped.

What fond and wayward thoughts will slide
Into a Lover's head!
'O mercy!' to myself I cried,
'If Lucy should be dead!'

'Three years she grew in sun and shower'

Three years she grew in sun and shower,
Then Nature said, 'A lovelier flower
On earth was never sown;
This Child I to myself will take;
She shall be mine, and I will make
A Lady of my own.

'Myself will to my darling be
Both law and impulse: and with me
The Girl, in rock and plain,
10   In earth and heaven, in glade and bower,
Shall feel an overseeing power
To kindle or restrain.

'She shall be sportive as the fawn
That wild with glee across the lawn
Or up the mountain springs;
And hers shall be the breathing balm,
And hers the silence and the calm
Of mute insensate things.

'The floating clouds their state shall lend
20   To her; for her the willow bend;
Nor shall she fail to see
Even in the motions of the Storm
Grace that shall mould the Maiden's form
By silent sympathy.

'The stars of midnight shall be dear
To her; and she shall lean her ear
In many a secret place
Where rivulets dance their wayward round,
And beauty born of murmuring sound
30   Shall pass into her face.

'And vital feelings of delight
Shall rear her form to stately height,
Her virgin bosom swell;
Such thoughts to Lucy I will give
While she and I together live
Here in this happy dell.'

Thus Nature spake – The work was done –
How soon my Lucy's race was run!
She died, and left to me
40   This heath, this calm, and quiet scene;
The memory of what has been,
And never more will be.

'*I travelled among unknown men*'

I travelled among unknown men,
    In lands beyond the sea;
Nor, England! did I know till then
    What love I bore to thee.

'Tis past, that melancholy dream!
    Nor will I quit thy shore
A second time; for still I seem
    To love thee more and more.

Among thy mountains did I feel
10   The joy of my desire;
And she I cherished turned her wheel
    Beside an English fire.

Thy mornings showed, thy nights concealed,
    The bowers where Lucy played;
And thine too is the last green field
    That Lucy's eyes surveyed.

Nutting

——————————It seems a day
(I speak of one from many singled out)
One of those heavenly days that cannot die;
When, in the eagerness of boyish hope,
I left our cottage-threshold, sallying forth
With a huge wallet o'er my shoulders slung,
A nutting-crook in hand; and turned my steps
Toward some far-distant wood, a Figure quaint,
Tricked out in proud disguise of cast-off weeds
10 Which for that service had been husbanded,
By exhortation of my frugal Dame –
Motley accoutrement, of power to smile
At thorns, and brakes, and brambles, – and, in truth,

More ragged than need was! O'er pathless rocks,
Through beds of matted fern, and tangled thickets,
Forcing my way, I came to one dear nook
Unvisited, where not a broken bough
Drooped with its withered leaves, ungracious sign
Of devastation; but the hazels rose
20   Tall and erect, with tempting clusters hung,
A virgin scene! – A little while I stood,
Breathing with such suppression of the heart
As joy delights in; and, with wise restraint
Voluptuous, fearless of a rival, eyed
The banquet; – or beneath the trees I sate
Among the flowers, and with the flowers I played;
A temper known to those who, after long
And weary expectation, have been blest
With sudden happiness beyond all hope.
30   Perhaps it was a bower beneath whose leaves
The violets of five seasons re-appear
And fade, unseen by any human eye;
Where fairy water-breaks do murmur on
For ever; and I saw the sparkling foam,
And – with my cheek on one of those green stones
That, fleeced with moss, under the shady trees,
Lay round me, scattered like a flock of sheep –
I heard the murmur and the murmuring sound,
In that sweet mood when pleasure loves to pay
40   Tribute to ease; and, of its joy secure,
The heart luxuriates with indifferent things,
Wasting its kindliness on stocks and stones,
And on the vacant air. Then up I rose,
And dragged to earth both branch and bough, with crash
And merciless ravage: and the shady nook
Of hazels, and the green and mossy bower,
Deformed and sullied, patiently gave up
Their quiet being: and, unless I now
Confound my present feelings with the past,
50   Ere from the mutilated bower I turned
Exulting, rich beyond the wealth of kings,
I felt a sense of pain when I beheld

The silent trees, and saw the intruding sky. –
Then, dearest Maiden, move along these shades
In gentleness of heart; with gentle hand
Touch – for there is a spirit in the woods.

Matthew

In the School of — is a tablet, on which are inscribed, in gilt letters,
the Names of the several persons who have been Schoolmasters there
since the foundation of the School, with the time at which they
entered upon and quitted their office. Opposite to one of those Names
the Author wrote the following lines.

If Nature, for a favourite child,
In thee hath tempered so her clay,
That every hour thy heart runs wild,
Yet never once doth go astray,

Read o'er these lines; and then review
This tablet, that thus humbly rears
In such diversity of hue
Its history of two hundred years.

– When through this little wreck of fame,
10 Cipher and syllable! thine eye
Has travelled down to Matthew's name,
Pause with no common sympathy.

And, if a sleeping tear should wake,
Then be it neither checked nor stayed:
For Matthew a request I make
Which for himself he had not made.

Poor Matthew, all his frolics o'er,
Is silent as a standing pool;
Far from the chimney's merry roar,
20 And murmur of the village school.

The sighs which Matthew heaved were sighs
Of one tired out with fun and madness;
The tears which came to Matthew's eyes
Were tears of light, the dew of gladness.

Yet, sometimes, when the secret cup
Of still and serious thought went round,
It seemed as if he drank it up –
He felt with spirit so profound.

– Thou soul of God's best earthly mould!
30 Thou happy Soul! and can it be
That these two words of glittering gold
Are all that must remain of thee?

The Two April Mornings

We walked along, while bright and red
Uprose the morning sun;
And Matthew stopped, he looked, and said,
'The will of God be done!'

A village schoolmaster was he,
With hair of glittering grey;
As blithe a man as you could see
On a spring holiday.

And on that morning, through the grass,
10 And by the steaming rills,
We travelled merrily, to pass
A day among the hills.

'Our work,' said I, 'was well begun,
Then, from thy breast what thought,
Beneath so beautiful a sun,
So sad a sigh has brought?'

A second time did Matthew stop;
And fixing still his eye
Upon the eastern mountain-top,
20   To me he made reply:

'Yon cloud with that long purple cleft
Brings fresh into my mind
A day like this which I have left
Full thirty years behind.

'And just above yon slope of corn
Such colours, and no other,
Were in the sky, that April morn,
Of this the very brother.

'With rod and line I sued the sport
30   Which that sweet season gave,
And, to the churchyard come, stopped short
Beside my daughter's grave.

'Nine summers had she scarcely seen,
The pride of all the vale;
And then she sang; – she would have been
A very nightingale.

'Six feet in earth my Emma lay;
And yet I loved her more,
For so it seemed, than till that day
40   I e'er had loved before.

'And, turning from her grave, I met,
Beside the churchyard yew,
A blooming Girl, whose hair was wet
With points of morning dew.

'A basket on her head she bare;
Her brow was smooth and white:
To see a child so very fair,
It was a pure delight!

'No fountain from its rocky cave
50 E'er tripped with foot so free;
She seemed as happy as a wave
That dances on the sea.

'There came from me a sigh of pain
Which I could ill confine;
I looked at her, and looked again:
And did not wish her mine!'

Matthew is in his grave, yet now,
Methinks, I see him stand,
As at that moment, with a bough
60 Of wilding in his hand.

The Fountain

A CONVERSATION

We talked with open heart, and tongue
Affectionate and true,
A pair of friends, though I was young,
And Matthew seventy-two.

We lay beneath a spreading oak,
Beside a mossy seat;
And from the turf a fountain broke,
And gurgled at our feet.

'Now, Matthew!' said I, 'let us match
10 This water's pleasant tune
With some old border-song, or catch
That suits a summer's noon;

'Or of the church-clock and the chimes
Sing here beneath the shade,
That half-mad thing of witty rhymes
Which you last April made!'

In silence Matthew lay, and eyed
The spring beneath the tree;
And thus the dear old Man replied,
20   The grey-haired man of glee:

'No check, no stay, this Streamlet fears;
How merrily it goes!
'Twill murmur on a thousand years,
And flow as now it flows.

'And here, on this delightful day,
I cannot choose but think
How oft, a vigorous man, I lay
Beside this fountain's brink.

'My eyes are dim with childish tears,
30   My heart is idly stirred,
For the same sound is in my ears
Which in those days I heard.

'Thus fares it still in our decay:
And yet the wiser mind
Mourns less for what age takes away
Than what it leaves behind.

'The blackbird amid leafy trees,
The lark above the hill,
Let loose their carols when they please,
40   Are quiet when they will.

'With Nature never do *they* wage
A foolish strife; they see
A happy youth, and their old age
Is beautiful and free:

'But we are pressed by heavy laws;
And often, glad no more,
We wear a face of joy, because
We have been glad of yore.

'If there be one who need bemoan
50 His kindred laid in earth,
The household hearts that were his own;
It is the man of mirth.

'My days, my Friend, are almost gone,
My life has been approved,
And many love me; but by none
Am I enough beloved.'

'Now both himself and me he wrongs,
The man who thus complains!
I live and sing my idle songs
60 Upon these happy plains;

'And, Matthew, for thy children dead
I'll be a son to thee!'
At this he grasped my hand, and said,
'Alas! that cannot be.'

We rose up from the fountain-side;
And down the smooth descent
Of the green sheep-track did we glide;
And through the wood we went;

And, ere we came to Leonard's rock,
70 He sang those witty rhymes
About the crazy old church-clock,
And the bewildered chimes.

Lucy Gray; or, Solitude

Oft I had heard of Lucy Gray:
And, when I crossed the wild,
I chanced to see at break of day
The solitary child.

No mate, no comrade Lucy knew;
She dwelt on a wide moor,
– The sweetest thing that ever grew
Beside a human door!

You yet may spy the fawn at play,
10 The hare upon the green;
But the sweet face of Lucy Gray
Will never more be seen.

'Tonight will be a stormy night –
You to the town must go;
And take a lantern, Child, to light
Your mother through the snow.'

'That, Father! will I gladly do:
'Tis scarcely afternoon –
The minster-clock has just struck two,
20 And yonder is the moon!'

At this the Father raised his hook,
And snapped a faggot-band;
He plied his work; – and Lucy took
The lantern in her hand.

Not blither is the mountain roe:
With many a wanton stroke
Her feet disperse the powdery snow,
That rises up like smoke.

The storm came on before its time:
30 She wandered up and down;
And many a hill did Lucy climb:
But never reached the town.

The wretched parents all that night
Went shouting far and wide;
But there was neither sound nor sight
To serve them for a guide.

At day-break on a hill they stood
That overlooked the moor;
And thence they saw the bridge of wood,
40 A furlong from their door.

They wept – and, turning homeward, cried,
'In heaven we all shall meet;'
– When in the snow the mother spied
The print of Lucy's feet.

Then downwards from the steep hill's edge
They tracked the footmarks small;
And through the broken hawthorn hedge,
And by the long stone-wall;

And then an open field they crossed:
50 The marks were still the same;
They tracked them on, nor ever lost;
And to the bridge they came.

They followed from the snowy bank
Those footmarks, one by one,
Into the middle of the plank;
And further there were none!

– Yet some maintain that to this day
She is a living child;
That you may see sweet Lucy Gray
60 Upon the lonesome wild.

O'er rough and smooth she trips along,
And never looks behind;
And sings a solitary song
That whistles in the wind.

A Poet's Epitaph

Art thou a Statist in the van
Of public conflicts trained and bred?
– First learn to love one living man;
Then mayst thou think upon the dead.

A Lawyer art thou? – draw not nigh!
Go, carry to some fitter place
The keenness of that practised eye,
The hardness of that sallow face.

Art thou a Man of purple cheer?
10 A rosy Man, right plump to see?
Approach; yet, Doctor, not too near,
This grave no cushion is for thee.

Or art thou one of gallant pride,
A Soldier and no man of chaff?
Welcome! – but lay thy sword aside,
And lean upon a peasant's staff.

Physician art thou? – one, all eyes,
Philosopher! – a fingering slave,
One that would peep and botanize
20 Upon his mother's grave?

Wrapt closely in thy sensual fleece,
O turn aside, – and take, I pray,
That he below may rest in peace,
Thy ever-dwindling soul, away!

A Moralist perchance appears;
Led, Heaven knows how! to this poor sod:
And he has neither eyes nor ears;
Himself his world, and his own God;

One to whose smooth-rubbed soul can cling
30 Nor form, nor feeling, great or small;
A reasoning, self-sufficing thing,
An intellectual All-in-all!

Shut close the door; press down the latch;
Sleep in thy intellectual crust;
Nor lose ten tickings of thy watch
Near this unprofitable dust.

But who is He, with modest looks,
And clad in homely russet brown?
He murmurs near the running brooks
40   A music sweeter than their own.

He is retired as noontide dew,
Or fountain in a noon-day grove;
And you must love him, ere to you
He will seem worthy of your love.

The outward shows of sky and earth,
Of hill and valley, he has viewed;
And impulses of deeper birth
Have come to him in solitude.

In common things that round us lie
50   Some random truths he can impart, –
The harvest of a quiet eye
That broods and sleeps on his own heart.

But he is weak; both Man and Boy,
Hath been an idler in the land;
Contented if he might enjoy
The things which others understand.

– Come hither in thy hour of strength;
Come, weak as is a breaking wave!
Here stretch thy body at full length;
60   Or build thy house upon this grave.

The Brothers

'These Tourists, heaven preserve us! needs must live
A profitable life: some glance along,
Rapid and gay, as if the earth were air,
And they were butterflies to wheel about
Long as the summer lasted: some, as wise,
Perched on the forehead of a jutting crag,
Pencil in hand and book upon the knee,
Will look and scribble, scribble on and look,
Until a man might travel twelve stout miles,
10   Or reap an acre of his neighbour's corn.
But, for that moping Son of Idleness,
Why can he tarry *yonder*? – In our church-yard
Is neither epitaph nor monument,
Tombstone nor name – only the turf we tread
And a few natural graves.'
                                    To Jane, his wife,
Thus spake the homely Priest of Ennerdale.
It was a July evening; and he sate
Upon the long stone-seat beneath the eaves
Of his old cottage, – as it chanced, that day,
20   Employed in winter's work. Upon the stone
His wife sate near him, teasing matted wool,
While, from the twin cards toothed with glittering wire,
He fed the spindle of his youngest child,
Who, in the open air, with due accord
Of busy hands and back-and-forward steps,
Her large round wheel was turning. Towards the field
In which the Parish Chapel stood alone,
Girt round with a bare ring of mossy wall,
While half an hour went by, the Priest had sent
30   Many a long look of wonder: and at last,
Risen from his seat, beside the snow-white ridge
Of carded wool which the old man had piled
He laid his implements with gentle care,
Each in the other locked; and, down the path,
That from his cottage to the church-yard led,

He took his way, impatient to accost
The Stranger, whom he saw still lingering there.

'Twas one well known to him in former days,
A Shepherd-lad; who ere his sixteenth year
40 Had left that calling, tempted to entrust
His expectations to the fickle winds
And perilous waters; with the mariners
A fellow-mariner; – and so had fared
Through twenty seasons; but he had been reared
Among the mountains, and he in his heart
Was half a shepherd on the stormy seas.
Oft in the piping shrouds had Leonard heard
The tones of waterfalls, and inland sounds
Of caves and trees: – and, when the regular wind
50 Between the tropics filled the steady sail,
And blew with the same breath through days and weeks,
Lengthening invisibly its weary line
Along the cloudless Main, he, in those hours
Of tiresome indolence, would often hang
Over the vessel's side, and gaze and gaze;
And, while the broad blue wave and sparkling foam
Flashed round him images and hues that wrought
In union with the employment of his heart,
He, thus by feverish passion overcome,
60 Even with the organs of his bodily eye,
Below him, in the bosom of the deep,
Saw mountains; saw the forms of sheep that grazed
On verdant hills – with dwellings among trees,
And shepherds clad in the same country grey
Which he himself had worn.
                              And now, at last,
From perils manifold, with some small wealth
Acquired by traffic 'mid the Indian Isles,
To his paternal home he is returned,
With a determined purpose to resume
70 The life he had lived there; both for the sake
Of many darling pleasures, and the love
Which to an only brother he has borne

In all his hardships, since that happy time
When, whether it blew foul or fair, they two
Were brother-shepherds on their native hills.
– They were the last of all their race: and now,
When Leonard had approached his home, his heart
Failed in him; and, not venturing to inquire
Tidings of one so long and dearly loved,
80 He to the solitary church-yard turned;
That, as he knew in what particular spot
His family were laid, he thence might learn
If still his Brother lived, or to the file
Another grave was added. – He had found
Another grave, – near which a full half-hour
He had remained; but, as he gazed, there grew
Such a confusion in his memory,
That he began to doubt; and even to hope
That he had seen this heap of turf before, –
90 That it was not another grave; but one
He had forgotten. He had lost his path,
As up the vale, that afternoon, he walked
Through fields which once had been well known to him:
And oh what joy this recollection now
Sent to his heart! he lifted up his eyes,
And, looking round, imagined that he saw
Strange alteration wrought on every side
Among the woods and fields, and that the rocks,
And everlasting hills themselves were changed.

100   By this the Priest, who down the field had come,
Unseen by Leonard, at the church-yard gate
Stopped short, – and thence, at leisure, limb by limb
Perused him with a gay complacency.
Ay, thought the Vicar, smiling to himself,
'Tis one of those who needs must leave the path
Of the world's business to go wild alone:
His arms have a perpetual holiday;
The happy man will creep about the fields,
Following his fancies by the hour, to bring
110 Tears down his cheek, or solitary smiles

Into his face, until the setting sun
Write fool upon his forehead. – Planted thus
Beneath a shed that over-arched the gate
Of this rude church-yard, till the stars appeared
The good Man might have communed with himself,
But that the Stranger, who had left the grave,
Approached; he recognized the Priest at once,
And, after greetings interchanged, and given
By Leonard to the Vicar as to one
120   Unknown to him, this dialogue ensued.
    LEONARD. You live, Sir, in these dales, a quiet life:
Your years make up one peaceful family;
And who would grieve and fret, if, welcome come
And welcome gone, they are so like each other,
They cannot be remembered? Scarce a funeral
Comes to this church-yard once in eighteen months;
And yet, some changes must take place among you:
And you, who dwell here, even among these rocks,
Can trace the finger of mortality,
130   And see, that with our threescore years and ten
We are not all that perish. – I remember,
(For many years ago I passed this road)
There was a foot-way all along the fields
By the brook-side – 'tis gone – and that dark cleft!
To me it does not seem to wear the face
Which then it had!
    PRIEST.   Nay, Sir, for aught I know,
That chasm is much the same –
    LEONARD.   But, surely, yonder –
    PRIEST. Ay, there, indeed, your memory is a friend
That does not play you false. – On that tall pike
140   (It is the loneliest place of all these hills)
There were two springs which bubbled side by side,
As if they had been made that they might be
Companions for each other: the huge crag
Was rent with lightning – one hath disappeared;
The other, left behind, is flowing still.
For accidents and changes such as these,
We want not store of them; – a waterspout

Will bring down half a mountain; what a feast
For folks that wander up and down like you,
150   To see an acre's breadth of that wide cliff
One roaring cataract! a sharp May-storm
Will come with loads of January snow,
And in one night send twenty score of sheep
To feed the ravens; or a shepherd dies
By some untoward death among the rocks:
The ice breaks up and sweeps away a bridge;
A wood is felled: – and then for our own homes!
A child is born or christened, a field ploughed,
A daughter sent to service, a web spun,
160   The old house-clock is decked with a new face;
And hence, so far from wanting facts or dates
To chronicle the time, we all have here
A pair of diaries, – one serving, Sir,
For the whole dale, and one for each fire-side –
Yours was a stranger's judgement: for historians,
Commend me to these valleys!
    LEONARD.   Yet your Church-yard
Seems, if such freedom may be used with you,
To say that you are heedless of the past:
An orphan could not find his mother's grave:
170   Here's neither head nor foot-stone, plate of brass,
Cross-bones nor skull, – type of our earthly state
Nor emblem of our hopes: the dead man's home
Is but a fellow to that pasture-field.
    PRIEST. Why, there, Sir, is a thought that's new to me!
The stone-cutters, 'tis true, might beg their bread
If every English church-yard were like ours;
Yet your conclusion wanders from the truth:
We have no need of names and epitaphs;
We talk about the dead by our fire-sides.
180   And then, for our immortal part! *we* want
No symbols, Sir, to tell us that plain tale:
The thought of death sits easy on the man
Who has been born and dies among the mountains.
    LEONARD. Your Dalesmen, then, do in each other's
        thoughts

Possess a kind of second life: no doubt
You, Sir, could help me to the history
Of half these graves?

    PRIEST.   For eight-score winters past,
With what I've witnessed, and with what I've heard,
Perhaps I might; and, on a winter-evening,
190 If you were seated at my chimney's nook,
By turning o'er these hillocks one by one,
We two could travel, Sir, through a strange round;
Yet all in the broad highway of the world.
Now there's a grave – your foot is half upon it, –
It looks just like the rest; and yet that man
Died broken-hearted.

    LEONARD.   'Tis a common case.
We'll take another: who is he that lies
Beneath yon ridge, the last of those three graves?
It touches on that piece of native rock
Left in the church-yard wall.
200 PRIEST.   That's Walter Ewbank.
He had as white a head and fresh a cheek
As ever were produced by youth and age
Engendering in the blood of hale four-score.
Through five long generations had the heart
Of Walter's forefathers o'erflowed the bounds
Of their inheritance, that single cottage –
You see it yonder! and those few green fields.
They toiled and wrought, and still, from sire to son,
Each struggled, and each yielded as before
210 A little – yet a little, – and old Walter,
They left to him the family heart, and land
With other burdens than the crop it bore.
Year after year the old man still kept up
A cheerful mind, – and buffeted with bond,
Interest, and mortgages; at last he sank,
And went into his grave before his time.
Poor Walter! whether it was care that spurred him
God only knows, but to the very last
He had the lightest foot in Ennerdale:
220 His pace was never that of an old man:

I almost see him tripping down the path
With his two grandsons after him: — but you,
Unless our Landlord be your host tonight,
Have far to travel, — and on these rough paths
Even in the longest day of midsummer —
   LEONARD. But those two Orphans!
   PRIEST.   Orphans! — Such they were —
Yet not while Walter lived: — for, though their parents
Lay buried side by side as now they lie,
The old man was a father to the boys,
230 Two fathers in one father: and if tears,
Shed when he talked of them where they were not,
And hauntings from the infirmity of love,
Are aught of what makes up a mother's heart,
This old Man, in the day of his old age,
Was half a mother to them. — If you weep, Sir,
To hear a stranger talking about strangers,
Heaven bless you when you are among your kindred!
Ay — you may turn that way — it is a grave
Which will bear looking at.
   LEONARD.   These boys — I hope
They loved this good old Man? —
240   PRIEST.   They did — and truly:
But that was what we almost overlooked,
They were such darlings of each other. Yes,
Though from the cradle they had lived with Walter,
The only kinsman near them, and though he
Inclined to both by reason of his age,
With a more fond, familiar, tenderness;
They, notwithstanding, had much love to spare,
And it all went into each other's hearts.
Leonard, the elder by just eighteen months,
250 Was two years taller: 'twas a joy to see,
To hear, to meet them! — From their house the school
Is distant three short miles, and in the time
Of storm and thaw, when every water-course
And unbridged stream, such as you may have noticed
Crossing our roads at every hundred steps,
Was swoln into a noisy rivulet,

Would Leonard then, when elder boys remained
At home, go staggering through the slippery fords,
Bearing his brother on his back. I have seen him,
260   On windy days, in one of those stray brooks,
Ay, more than once I have seen him, mid-leg deep,
Their two books lying both on a dry stone,
Upon the hither side: and once I said,
As I remember, looking round these rocks
And hills on which we all of us were born,
That God who made the great book of the world
Would bless such piety –
    LEONARD.   It may be then –
    PRIEST. Never did worthier lads break English bread;
The very brightest Sunday Autumn saw,
270   With all its mealy clusters of ripe nuts,
Could never keep those boys away from church,
Or tempt them to an hour of sabbath breach.
Leonard and James! I warrant, every corner
Among these rocks, and every hollow place
That venturous foot could reach, to one or both
Was known as well as to the flowers that grow there.
Like roe-bucks they went bounding o'er the hills;
They played like two young ravens on the crags:
Then they could write, ay, and speak too, as well
280   As many of their betters – and for Leonard!
The very night before he went away,
In my own house I put into his hand
A Bible, and I'd wager house and field
That, if he be alive, he has it yet.
    LEONARD. It seems, these Brothers have not lived to be
A comfort to each other –
    PRIEST.   That they might
Live to such end is what both old and young
In this our valley all of us have wished,
And what, for my part, I have often prayed:
But Leonard –
290   LEONARD. Then James still is left among you!
    PRIEST. 'Tis of the elder brother I am speaking:
They had an uncle; – he was at that time

A thriving man, and trafficked on the seas:
And, but for that same uncle, to this hour
Leonard had never handled rope or shroud:
For the boy loved the life which we lead here;
And though of unripe years, a stripling only,
His soul was knit to this his native soil.
But, as I said, old Walter was too weak
300 To strive with such a torrent; when he died,
The estate and house were sold; and all their sheep,
A pretty flock, and which, for aught I know,
Had clothed the Ewbanks for a thousand years: –
Well – all was gone, and they were destitute,
And Leonard, chiefly for his Brother's sake,
Resolved to try his fortune on the seas.
Twelve years are past since we had tidings from him.
If there were one among us who had heard
That Leonard Ewbank was come home again,
310 From the Great Gavel, down by Leeza's banks,
And down the Enna, far as Egremont,
The day would be a joyous festival;
And those two bells of ours, which there you see –
Hanging in the open air – but, O good Sir!
This is sad talk – they'll never sound for him –
Living or dead. – When last we heard of him,
He was in slavery among the Moors
Upon the Barbary coast. – 'Twas not a little
That would bring down his spirit; and no doubt,
320 Before it ended in his death, the Youth
Was sadly crossed. – Poor Leonard! when we parted,
He took me by the hand, and said to me,
If e'er he should grow rich, he would return,
To live in peace upon his father's land,
And lay his bones among us.
    LEONARD.   If that day
Should come, 'twould needs be a glad day for him;
He would himself, no doubt, be happy then
As any that should meet him –
    PRIEST.   Happy! Sir –
    LEONARD. You said his kindred all were in their graves,

And that he had one Brother –

330   PRIEST.   That is but
A fellow-tale of sorrow. From his youth
James, though not sickly, yet was delicate;
And Leonard being always by his side
Had done so many offices about him,
That, though he was not of a timid nature,
Yet still the spirit of a mountain-boy
In him was somewhat checked; and, when his Brother
Was gone to sea, and he was left alone,
The little colour that he had was soon

340   Stolen from his cheek; he drooped, and pined, and pined –
    LEONARD. But these are all the graves of full-grown men!
    PRIEST. Ay, Sir, that passed away: we took him to us;
He was the child of all the dale – he lived
Three months with one, and six months with another;
And wanted neither food, nor clothes, nor love:
And many, many happy days were his.
But, whether blithe or sad, 'tis my belief
His absent Brother still was at his heart.
And, when he dwelt beneath our roof, we found

350   (A practice till this time unknown to him)
That often, rising from his bed at night,
He in his sleep would walk about, and sleeping
He sought his brother Leonard. – You are moved!
Forgive me, Sir: before I spoke to you,
I judged you most unkindly.
    LEONARD.   But this Youth,
How did he die at last?
    PRIEST.   One sweet May-morning,
(It will be twelve years since when Spring returns)
He had gone forth among the new-dropped lambs,
With two or three companions, whom their course

360   Of occupation led from height to height
Under a cloudless sun – till he, at length,
Through weariness, or, haply, to indulge
The humour of the moment, lagged behind.
You see yon precipice; – it wears the shape

Of a vast building made of many crags;
And in the midst is one particular rock
That rises like a column from the vale,
Whence by our shepherds it is called, THE PILLAR.
Upon its aëry summit crowned with heath,
370   The loiterer, not unnoticed by his comrades,
Lay stretched at ease; but, passing by the place
On their return, they found that he was gone.
No ill was feared; till one of them by chance
Entering, when evening was far spent, the house
Which at that time was James's home, there learned
That nobody had seen him all that day:
The morning came, and still he was unheard of:
The neighbours were alarmed, and to the brook
Some hastened; some ran to the lake: ere noon
380   They found him at the foot of that same rock
Dead, and with mangled limbs. The third day after
I buried him, poor Youth, and there he lies!
　　LEONARD. And that then *is* his grave! – Before his death
You say that he saw many happy years?
　　PRIEST. Ay, that he did –
　　LEONARD.　　　　　　And all went well with him? –
　　PRIEST. If he had one, the Youth had twenty homes.
　　LEONARD. And you believe, then, that his mind was
　　　easy? –
　　PRIEST. Yes, long before he died, he found that time
Is a true friend to sorrow; and unless
390   His thoughts were turned on Leonard's luckless fortune,
He talked about him with a cheerful love.
　　LEONARD. He could not come to an unhallowed end!
　　PRIEST. Nay, God forbid! – You recollect I mentioned
A habit which disquietude and grief
Had brought upon him; and we all conjectured
That, as the day was warm, he had lain down
On the soft heath, – and, waiting for his comrades,
He there had fallen asleep; that in his sleep
He to the margin of the precipice
400   Had walked, and from the summit had fallen headlong:
And so no doubt he perished. When the Youth

Fell, in his hand he must have grasped, we think,
His shepherd's staff; for on that Pillar of rock
It had been caught mid-way; and there for years
It hung; – and mouldered there.
                              The Priest here ended –
The Stranger would have thanked him, but he felt
A gushing from his heart, that took away
The power of speech. Both left the spot in silence;
And Leonard, when they reached the church-yard gate,
410   As the Priest lifted up the latch, turned round, –
And, looking at the grave, he said, 'My Brother!'
The Vicar did not hear the words: and now,
He pointed towards his dwelling-place, entreating
That Leonard would partake his homely fare:
The other thanked him with an earnest voice;
But added, that, the evening being calm,
He would pursue his journey. So they parted.
    It was not long ere Leonard reached a grove
That overhung the road: he there stopped short,
420   And, sitting down beneath the trees, reviewed
All that the Priest had said: his early years
Were with him: – his long absence, cherished hopes,
And thoughts which had been his an hour before,
All pressed on him with such a weight, that now,
This vale, where he had been so happy, seemed
A place in which he could not bear to live:
So he relinquished all his purposes.
He travelled back to Egremont: and thence,
That night, he wrote a letter to the Priest,
430   Reminding him of what had passed between them;
And adding, with a hope to be forgiven,
That it was from the weakness of his heart
He had not dared to tell him who he was.
This done, he went on shipboard, and is now
A Seaman, a grey-headed Mariner.

To M. H.

Our walk was far among the ancient trees:
There was no road, nor any woodman's path;
But a thick umbrage – checking the wild growth
Of weed and sapling, along soft green turf
Beneath the branches – of itself had made
A track, that brought us to a slip of lawn,
And a small bed of water in the woods.
All round this pool both flocks and herds might drink
On its firm margin, even as from a well,
10   Or some stone-basin which the herdsman's hand
Had shaped for their refreshment; nor did sun,
Or wind from any quarter, ever come,
But as a blessing to this calm recess,
This glade of water and this one green field.
The spot was made by Nature for herself;
The travellers know it not, and 'twill remain
Unknown to them; but it is beautiful;
And if a man should plant his cottage near,
Should sleep beneath the shelter of its trees,
20   And blend its waters with his daily meal,
He would so love it, that in his death-hour
Its image would survive among his thoughts:
And therefore, my sweet MARY, this still Nook,
With all its beeches, we have named from You!

Hart-Leap Well

Hart-Leap Well is a small spring of water, about five miles from
Richmond in Yorkshire, and near the side of the road that leads from
Richmond to Askrigg. Its name is derived from a remarkable Chase,
the memory of which is preserved by the monuments spoken of in the
second Part of the following Poem, which monuments do now exist as
I have there described them.

The Knight had ridden down from Wensley Moor
With the slow motion of a summer's cloud,
And now, as he approached a vassal's door,
'Bring forth another horse!' he cried aloud.

'Another horse!' – That shout the vassal heard
And saddled his best Steed, a comely grey;
Sir Walter mounted him; he was the third
Which he had mounted on that glorious day.

Joy sparkled in the prancing courser's eyes;
10　The horse and horseman are a happy pair;
But, though Sir Walter like a falcon flies,
There is a doleful silence in the air.

A rout this morning left Sir Walter's Hall,
That as they galloped made the echoes roar;
But horse and man are vanished, one and all;
Such race, I think, was never seen before.

Sir Walter, restless as a veering wind,
Calls to the few tired dogs that yet remain:
Blanch, Swift, and Music, noblest of their kind,
20　Follow, and up the weary mountain strain.

The Knight hallooed, he cheered and chid them on
With suppliant gestures and upbraidings stern;
But breath and eyesight fail; and, one by one,
The dogs are stretched among the mountain fern.

Where is the throng, the tumult of the race?
The bugles that so joyfully were blown?
– This chase it looks not like an earthly chase;
Sir Walter and the Hart are left alone.

The poor Hart toils along the mountain-side;
30　I will not stop to tell how far he fled,
Nor will I mention by what death he died;
But now the Knight beholds him lying dead.

Dismounting, then, he leaned against a thorn;
He had no follower, dog, nor man, nor boy:
He neither cracked his whip, nor blew his horn,
But gazed upon the spoil with silent joy.

Close to the thorn on which Sir Walter leaned
Stood his dumb partner in this glorious feat;
Weak as a lamb the hour that it is yeaned;
40   And white with foam as if with cleaving sleet.

Upon his side the Hart was lying stretched:
His nostril touched a spring beneath a hill,
And with the last deep groan his breath had fetched
The waters of the spring were trembling still.

And now, too happy for repose or rest,
(Never had living man such joyful lot!)
Sir Walter walked all round, north, south, and west,
And gazed and gazed upon that darling spot.

And climbing up the hill – (it was at least
50   Four roods of sheer ascent) Sir Walter found
Three several hoof-marks which the hunted Beast
Had left imprinted on the grassy ground.

Sir Walter wiped his face, and cried, 'Till now
Such sight was never seen by human eyes:
Three leaps have borne him from this lofty brow,
Down to the very fountain where he lies.

'I'll build a pleasure-house upon this spot,
And a small arbour, made for rural joy;
'Twill be the traveller's shed, the pilgrim's cot,
60   A place of love for damsels that are coy.

'A cunning artist will I have to frame
A basin for that fountain in the dell!
And they who do make mention of the same,
From this day forth, shall call it HART-LEAP WELL.

'And, gallant Stag! to make thy praises known,
Another monument shall here be raised;
Three several pillars, each a rough-hewn stone,
And planted where thy hoofs the turf have grazed.

'And, in the summer-time when days are long,
70 I will come hither with my Paramour;
And with the dancers and the minstrel's song
We will make merry in that pleasant bower.

'Till the foundations of the mountains fail
My mansion with its arbour shall endure; –
The joy of them who till the fields of Swale,
And them who dwell among the woods of Ure!'

Then home he went, and left the Hart, stone-dead,
With breathless nostrils stretched above the spring.
– Soon did the Knight perform what he had said;
80 And far and wide the fame thereof did ring.

Ere thrice the Moon into her port had steered,
A cup of stone received the living well;
Three pillars of rude stone Sir Walter reared,
And built a house of pleasure in the dell.

And near the fountain, flowers of stature tall
With trailing plants and trees were intertwined, –
Which soon composed a little sylvan hall,
A leafy shelter from the sun and wind.

And thither, when the summer days were long,
90 Sir Walter led his wondering Paramour;
And with the dancers and the minstrel's song
Made merriment within that pleasant bower.

The Knight, Sir Walter, died in course of time,
And his bones lie in his paternal vale. –
But there is matter for a second rhyme,
And I to this would add another tale.

PART SECOND

The moving accident is not my trade;
To freeze the blood I have no ready arts:
'Tis my delight, alone in summer shade,
100 To pipe a simple song for thinking hearts.

As I from Hawes to Richmond did repair,
It chanced that I saw standing in a dell
Three aspens at three corners of a square;
And one, not four yards distant, near a well.

What this imported I could ill divine:
And, pulling now the rein my horse to stop,
I saw three pillars standing in a line, –
The last stone-pillar on a dark hill-top.

The trees were grey, with neither arms nor head;
110 Half wasted the square mound of tawny green;
So that you just might say, as then I said,
'Here in old time the hand of man hath been.'

I looked upon the hill both far and near,
More doleful place did never eye survey;
It seemed as if the spring-time came not here,
And Nature here were willing to decay.

I stood in various thoughts and fancies lost,
When one, who was in shepherd's garb attired,
Came up the hollow: – him did I accost,
120 And what this place might be I then inquired.

The Shepherd stopped, and that same story told
Which in my former rhyme I have rehearsed.
'A jolly place,' said he, 'in times of old!
But something ails it now: the spot is curst.

'You see these lifeless stumps of aspen wood –
Some say that they are beeches, others elms –
These were the bower; and here a mansion stood,
The finest palace of a hundred realms!

'The arbour does its own condition tell;
130   You see the stones, the fountain, and the stream;
But as to the great Lodge! you might as well
Hunt half a day for a forgotten dream.

'There's neither dog nor heifer, horse nor sheep,
Will wet his lips within that cup of stone;
And oftentimes, when all are fast alseep,
This water doth send forth a dolorous groan.

'Some say that here a murder has been done,
And blood cries out for blood: but, for my part,
I've guessed, when I've been sitting in the sun,
140   That it was all for that unhappy Hart.

'What thoughts must through the creature's brain have past!
Even from the topmost stone, upon the steep,
Are but three bounds – and look, Sir, at this last –
O Master! it has been a cruel leap.

'For thirteen hours he ran a desperate race;
And in my simple mind we cannot tell
What cause the Hart might have to love this place,
And come and make his death-bed near the well.

'Here on the grass perhaps asleep he sank,
150   Lulled by the fountain in the summer-tide;
This water was perhaps the first he drank
When he had wandered from his mother's side.

'In April here beneath the flowering thorn
He heard the birds their morning carols sing;
And he, perhaps, for aught we know, was born
Not half a furlong from that self-same spring.

'Now, here is neither grass nor pleasant shade;
The sun on drearier hollow never shone;
So will it be, as I have often said,
160   Till trees, and stones, and fountain, all are gone.'

'Grey-headed Shepherd, thou hast spoken well;
Small difference lies between thy creed and mine:
This Beast not unobserved by Nature fell;
His death was mourned by sympathy divine.

'The Being, that is in the clouds and air,
That is in the green leaves among the groves,
Maintains a deep and reverential care
For the unoffending creatures whom he loves.

'The pleasure-house is dust: – behind, before,
170   This is no common waste, no common gloom;
But Nature, in due course of time, once more
Shall here put on her beauty and her bloom.

'She leaves these objects to a slow decay,
That what we are, and have been, may be known;
But at the coming of the milder day,
These monuments shall all be overgrown.

'One lesson, Shepherd, let us two divide,
Taught both by what she shows, and what conceals;
Never to blend our pleasure or our pride
180   With sorrow of the meanest thing that feels.'

'It was an April morning: fresh and clear'

It was an April morning: fresh and clear
The Rivulet, delighting in its strength,
Ran with a young man's speed; and yet the voice
Of waters which the winter had supplied
Was softened down into a vernal tone.
The spirit of enjoyment and desire,
And hopes and wishes, from all living things
Went circling, like a multitude of sounds.

The budding groves seemed eager to urge on
10 The steps of June; as if their various hues
Were only hindrances that stood between
Them and their object: but, meanwhile, prevailed
Such an entire contentment in the air
That every naked ash, and tardy tree
Yet leafless, showed as if the countenance
With which it looked on this delightful day
Were native to the summer. – Up the brook
I roamed in the confusion of my heart,
Alive to all things and forgetting all.
20 At length I to a sudden turning came
In this continuous glen, where down a rock
The Stream, so ardent in its course before,
Sent forth such sallies of glad sound, that all
Which I till then had heard, appeared the voice
Of common pleasure: beast and bird, the lamb,
The shepherd's dog, the linnet and the thrush
Vied with this waterfall, and made a song,
Which, while I listened, seemed like the wild growth
Or like some natural produce of the air,
30 That could not cease to be. Green leaves were here;
But 'twas the foliage of the rocks – the birch,
The yew, the holly, and the bright green thorn,
With hanging islands of resplendent furze:
And, on a summit, distant a short space,
By any who should look beyond the dell,
A single mountain-cottage might be seen.
I gazed and gazed, and to myself I said,
'Our thoughts at least are ours; and this wild nook,
MY EMMA, I will dedicate to thee.'
40 – Soon did the spot become my other home,
My dwelling, and my out-of-doors abode.
And, of the Shepherds who have seen me there,
To whom I sometimes in our idle talk
Have told this fancy, two or three, perhaps,
Years after we are gone and in our graves,
When they have cause to speak of this wild place,
May call it by the name of EMMA'S DELL.

To Joanna

Amid the smoke of cities did you pass
The time of early youth; and there you learned,
From years of quiet industry, to love
The living Beings by your own fire-side,
With such a strong devotion, that your heart
Is slow to meet the sympathies of them
Who look upon the hills with tenderness,
And make dear friendships with the streams and groves.
Yet we, who are transgressors in this kind,
Dwelling retired in our simplicity
Among the woods and fields, we love you well,
Joanna! and I guess, since you have been
So distant from us now for two long years,
That you will gladly listen to discourse,
However trivial, if you thence be taught
That they, with whom you once were happy, talk
Familiarly of you and of old times.

  While I was seated, now some ten days past,
Beneath those lofty firs, that overtop
Their ancient neighbour, the old steeple-tower,
The Vicar from his gloomy house hard by
Came forth to greet me; and when he had asked,
'How fares Joanna, that wild-hearted Maid!
And when will she return to us?' he paused;
And, after short exchange of village news,
He with grave looks demanded, for what cause,
Reviving obsolete idolatry,
I, like a Runic Priest, in characters
Of formidable size had chiselled out
Some uncouth name upon the native rock,
Above the Rotha, by the forest-side.
– Now, by those dear immunities of heart
Engendered between malice and true love,
I was not loth to be so catechised,
And this was my reply: – 'As it befell,

One summer morning we had walked abroad
At break of day, Joanna and myself.
– 'Twas that delightful season when the broom,
Full-flowered, and visible on every steep,
40   Along the copses runs in veins of gold.
Our pathway led us on to Rotha's banks;
And when we came in front of that tall rock
That eastward looks, I there stopped short – and stood
Tracing the lofty barrier with my eye
From base to summit; such delight I found
To note in shrub and tree, in stone and flower,
That intermixture of delicious hues,
Along so vast a surface, all at once,
In one impression, by connecting force
50   Of their own beauty, imaged in the heart.
– When I had gazed perhaps two minutes' space,
Joanna, looking in my eyes, beheld
That ravishment of mine, and laughed aloud.
The Rock, like something starting from a sleep,
Took up the Lady's voice, and laughed again;
That ancient Woman seated on Helm-crag
Was ready with her cavern; Hammar-scar,
And the tall Steep of Silver-how, sent forth
A noise of laughter; southern Loughrigg heard,
60   And Fairfield answered with a mountain tone;
Helvellyn far into the clear blue sky
Carried the Lady's voice, – old Skiddaw blew
His speaking-trumpet; – back out of the clouds
Of Glaramara southward came the voice;
And Kirkstone tossed it from his misty head.
– Now whether (said I to our cordial Friend,
Who in the hey-day of astonishment
Smiled in my face) this were in simple truth
A work accomplished by the brotherhood
70   Of ancient mountains, or my ear was touched
With dreams and visionary impulses
To me alone imparted, sure I am
That there was a loud uproar in the hills.
And, while we both were listening, to my side

The fair Joanna drew, as if she wished
To shelter from some object of her fear.
– And hence, long afterwards, when eighteen moons
Were wasted, as I chanced to walk alone
Beneath this rock, at sunrise, on a calm
80   And silent morning, I sat down, and there,
In memory of affections old and true,
I chiselled out in those rude characters
Joanna's name deep in the living stone: –
And I, and all who dwell by my fireside,
Have called the lovely rock, JOANNA'S ROCK.'

NOTE. – In Cumberland and Westmoreland are several Inscriptions, upon the native rock, which, from the wasting of time, and the rudeness of the workmanship, have been mistaken for Runic. They are, without doubt, Roman.

The Rotha, mentioned in this poem, is the River which, flowing through the lakes of Grasmere and Rydal, falls into Wynandermere. On Helm-crag, that impressive single mountain at the head of the Vale of Grasmere, is a rock which from most points of view bears a striking resemblance to an old Woman cowering. Close by this rock is one of those fissures or caverns, which in the language of the country are called dungeons. Most of the mountains here mentioned immediately surround the Vale of Grasmere; of the others, some are at a considerable distance, but they belong to the same cluster.

'When, to the attractions of the busy world'

When, to the attractions of the busy world,
Preferring studious leisure, I had chosen
A habitation in this peaceful Vale,
Sharp season followed of continual storm
In deepest winter; and, from week to week,
Pathway, and lane, and public road, were clogged
With frequent showers of snow. Upon a hill
At a short distance from my cottage, stands
A stately Fir-grove, whither I was wont
10   To hasten, for I found, beneath the roof

Of that perennial shade, a cloistral place
Of refuge, with an unencumbered floor.
Here, in safe covert, on the shallow snow,
And, sometimes, on a speck of visible earth,
The redbreast near me hopped; nor was I loth
To sympathize with vulgar coppice birds
That, for protection from the nipping blast,
Hither repaired. – A single beech-tree grew
Within this grove of firs! and, on the fork
20 Of that one beech, appeared a thrush's nest;
A last year's nest, conspicuously built
At such small elevation from the ground
As gave sure sign that they, who in that house
Of nature and of love had made their home
Amid the fir-trees, all the summer long
Dwelt in a tranquil spot. And oftentimes
A few sheep, stragglers from some mountain-flock,
Would watch my motions with suspicious stare,
From the remotest outskirts of the grove, –
30 Some nook where they had made their final stand,
Huddling together from two fears – the fear
Of me and of the storm. Full many an hour
Here did I lose. But in this grove the trees
Had been so thickly planted, and had thriven
In such perplexed and intricate array,
That vainly did I seek, beneath their stems
A length of open space, where to and fro
My feet might move without concern or care;
And, baffled thus, though earth from day to day
40 Was fettered, and the air by storm disturbed,
I ceased the shelter to frequent, – and prized,
Less than I wished to prize, that calm recess.

The snows dissolved, and genial Spring returned
To clothe the fields with verdure. Other haunts
Meanwhile were mine; till, one bright April day,
By chance retiring from the glare of noon
To this forsaken covert, there I found
A hoary pathway traced between the trees,

And winding on with such an easy line
50   Along a natural opening, that I stood
Much wondering how I could have sought in vain
For what was now so obvious. To abide,
For an allotted interval of ease,
Under my cottage-roof, had gladly come
From the wild sea a cherished Visitant;
And with the sight of this same path – begun,
Begun and ended, in the shady grove,
Pleasant conviction flashed upon my mind
That, to this opportune recess allured,
60   He had surveyed it with a finer eye,
A heart more wakeful; and had worn the track
By pacing here, unwearied and alone,
In that habitual restlessness of foot
That haunts the Sailor measuring o'er and o'er
His short domain upon the vessel's deck,
While she pursues her course through the dreary sea.

When thou hadst quitted Esthwaite's pleasant shore,
And taken thy first leave of those green hills
And rocks that were the play-ground of thy youth,
70   Year followed year, my Brother! and we two,
Conversing not, knew little in what mould
Each other's mind was fashioned; and at length,
When once again we met in Grasmere Vale,
Between us there was little other bond
Than common feelings of fraternal love.
But thou, a School-boy, to the sea hadst carried
Undying recollections; Nature there
Was with thee; she, who loved us both, she still
Was with thee; and even so didst thou become
80   A *silent* Poet; from the solitude
Of the vast sea didst bring a watchful heart
Still couchant, an inevitable ear,
And an eye practised like a blind man's touch.
– Back to the joyless Ocean thou art gone;
Nor from this vestige of thy musing hours
Could I withhold thy honoured name, – and now
I love the fir-grove with a perfect love.

Thither do I withdraw when cloudless suns
Shine hot, or wind blows troublesome and strong;
90 And there I sit at evening, when the steep
Of Silver-how, and Grasmere's peaceful lake,
And one green island, gleam between the stems
Of the dark firs, a visionary scene!
And, while I gaze upon the spectacle
Of clouded splendour, on this dream-like sight
Of solemn loveliness, I think on thee,
My Brother, and on all which thou hast lost.
Nor seldom, if I rightly guess, while Thou,
Muttering the verses which I muttered first
100 Among the mountains, through the midnight watch
Art pacing thoughtfully the vessel's deck
In some far region, here, while o'er my head,
At every impulse of the moving breeze,
The fir-grove murmurs with a sea-like sound,
Alone I tread this path; – for aught I know,
Timing my steps to thine; and, with a store
Of undistinguishable sympathies,
Mingling most earnest wishes for the day
When we, and others whom we love, shall meet
110 A second time, in Grasmere's happy Vale.

NOTE. – This wish was not granted; the lamented Person not long after
perished by shipwreck, in discharge of his duty as Commander of the
Honourable East India Company's Vessel, the Earl of Abergavenny.

Michael

A PASTORAL POEM

If from the public way you turn your steps
Up the tumultuous brook of Green-head Ghyll,
You will suppose that with an upright path
Your feet must struggle; in such bold ascent
The pastoral mountains front you, face to face.
But, courage! for around that boisterous brook
The mountains have all opened out themselves,

And made a hidden valley of their own.
No habitation can be seen; but they
10   Who journey thither find themselves alone
With a few sheep, with rocks and stones, and kites
That overhead are sailing in the sky.
It is in truth an utter solitude;
Nor should I have made mention of this Dell
But for one object which you might pass by,
Might see and notice not. Beside the brook
Appears a straggling heap of unhewn stones!
And to that simple object appertains
A story – unenriched with strange events,
20   Yet not unfit, I deem, for the fireside,
Or for the summer shade. It was the first
Of those domestic tales that spake to me
Of Shepherds, dwellers in the valleys, men
Whom I already loved; – not verily
For their own sakes, but for the fields and hills
Where was their occupation and abode.
And hence this Tale, while I was yet a Boy
Careless of books, yet having felt the power
Of Nature, by the gentle agency
30   Of natural objects, led me on to feel
For passions that were not my own, and think
(At random and imperfectly indeed)
On man, the heart of man, and human life.
Therefore, although it be a history
Homely and rude, I will relate the same
For the delight of a few natural hearts;
And, with yet fonder feeling, for the sake
Of youthful Poets, who among these hills
Will be my second self when I am gone.

40   Upon the forest-side in Grasmere Vale
There dwelt a Shepherd, Michael was his name;
An old man, stout of heart, and strong of limb.
His bodily frame had been from youth to age
Of an unusual strength: his mind was keen,
Intense, and frugal, apt for all affairs,
And in his shepherd's calling he was prompt
And watchful more than ordinary men.

Hence had he learned the meaning of all winds,
Of blasts of every tone; and, oftentimes,
50 When others heeded not, he heard the South
Make subterraneous music, like the noise
Of bagpipers on distant Highland hills.
The Shepherd, at such warning, of his flock
Bethought him, and he to himself would say,
'The winds are now devising work for me!'
And, truly, at all times, the storm, that drives
The traveller to a shelter, summoned him
Up to the mountains: he had been alone
Amid the heart of many thousand mists,
60 That came to him, and left him, on the heights.
So lived he till his eightieth year was past.
And grossly that man errs, who should suppose
That the green valleys, and the streams and rocks,
Were things indifferent to the Shepherd's thoughts.
Fields, where with cheerful spirits he had breathed
The common air; hills, which with vigorous step
He had so often climbed; which had impressed
So many incidents upon his mind
Of hardship, skill or courage, joy or fear;
70 Which, like a book, preserved the memory
Of the dumb animals, whom he had saved,
Had fed or sheltered, linking to such acts
The certainty of honourable gain;
Those fields, those hills – what could they less? had laid
Strong hold on his affections, were to him
A pleasurable feeling of blind love,
The pleasure which there is in life itself.

His days had not been passed in singleness.
His Helpmate was a comely matron, old –
80 Though younger than himself full twenty years.
She was a woman of a stirring life,
Whose heart was in her house: two wheels she had
Of antique form; this large, for spinning wool;
That small, for flax; and if one wheel had rest,
It was because the other was at work.
The Pair had but one inmate in their house,
An only Child, who had been born to them

When Michael, telling o'er his years, began
To deem that he was old, – in shepherd's phrase,
90   With one foot in the grave. This only Son,
With two brave sheep-dogs tried in many a storm,
The one of an inestimable worth,
Made all their household. I may truly say,
That they were as a proverb in the vale
For endless industry. When day was gone,
And from their occupations out of doors
The Son and Father were come home, even then,
Their labour did not cease; unless when all
Turned to the cleanly supper-board, and there,
100   Each with a mess of pottage and skimmed milk,
Sat round the basket piled with oaten cakes,
And their plain home-made cheese. Yet when the meal
Was ended, Luke (for so the Son was named)
And his old Father both betook themselves
To such convenient work as might employ
Their hands by the fire-side; perhaps to card
Wool for the Housewife's spindle, or repair
Some injury done to sickle, flail, or scythe,
Or other implement of house or field.

110   Down from the ceiling, by the chimney's edge,
That in our ancient uncouth country style
With huge and black projection overbrowed
Large space beneath, as duly as the light
Of day grew dim the Housewife hung a lamp;
An aged utensil, which had performed
Service beyond all others of its kind.
Early at evening did it burn – and late,
Surviving comrade of uncounted hours,
Which, going by from year to year, had found,
120   And left the couple neither gay perhaps
Nor cheerful, yet with objects and with hopes,
Living a life of eager industry.
And now, when Luke had reached his eighteenth year,
There by the light of this old lamp they sate,
Father and Son, while far into the night
The Housewife plied her own peculiar work,

Making the cottage through the silent hours
Murmur as with the sound of summer flies.
This light was famous in its neighbourhood,
130   And was a public symbol of the life
That thrifty Pair had lived. For, as it chanced,
Their cottage on a plot of rising ground
Stood single, with large prospect, north and south,
High into Easedale, up to Dunmail-Raise,
And westward to the village near the lake;
And from this constant light, so regular
And so far seen, the House itself, by all
Who dwelt within the limits of the vale,
Both old and young, was named THE EVENING STAR.

140   Thus living on through such a length of years,
The Shepherd, if he loved himself, must needs
Have loved his Helpmate; but to Michael's heart
This son of his old age was yet more dear –
Less from instinctive tenderness, the same
Fond spirit that blindly works in the blood of all –
Than that a child, more than all other gifts
That earth can offer to declining man,
Brings hope with it, and forward-looking thoughts,
And stirrings of inquietude, when they
150   By tendency of nature needs must fail.
Exceeding was the love he bare to him,
His heart and his heart's joy! For often-times
Old Michael, while he was a babe in arms,
Had done him female service, not alone
For pastime and delight, as is the use
Of fathers, but with patient mind enforced
To acts of tenderness; and he had rocked
His cradle, as with a woman's gentle hand.

And, in a later time, ere yet the Boy
160   Had put on boy's attire, did Michael love,
Albeit of a stern unbending mind,
To have the Young-one in his sight, when he
Wrought in the field, or on his shepherd's stool
Sate with a fettered sheep before him stretched
Under the large old oak, that near his door

Stood single, and, from matchless depth of shade,
Chosen for the Shearer's covert from the sun,
Thence in our rustic dialect was called
The CLIPPING TREE, a name which yet it bears.
170 There, while they two were sitting in the shade,
With others round them, earnest all and blithe,
Would Michael exercise his heart with looks
Of fond correction and reproof bestowed
Upon the Child, if he disturbed the sheep
By catching at their legs, or with his shouts
Scared them, while they lay still beneath the shears.

And when by Heaven's good grace the boy grew up
A healthy Lad, and carried in his cheek
Two steady roses that were five years old;
180 Then Michael from a winter coppice cut
With his own hand a sapling, which he hooped
With iron, making it throughout in all
Due requisites a perfect shepherd's staff,
And gave it to the Boy; wherewith equipt
He as a watchman oftentimes was placed
At gate or gap, to stem or turn the flock;
And, to his office prematurely called,
There stood the urchin, as you will divine,
Something between a hindrance and a help;
190 And for this cause not always, I believe,
Receiving from his Father hire of praise;
Though naught was left undone which staff, or voice,
Or looks, or threatening gestures, could perform.

But soon as Luke, full ten years old, could stand
Against the mountain blasts; and to the heights,
Not fearing toil, nor length of weary ways,
He with his Father daily went, and they
Were as companions, why should I relate
That objects which the Shepherd loved before
200 Were dearer now? that from the Boy there came
Feelings and emanations – things which were
Light to the sun and music to the wind;
And that the old Man's heart seemed born again?

Thus in his Father's sight the Boy grew up:
And now, when he had reached his eighteenth year,
He was his comfort and his daily hope.

While in this sort the simple household lived
From day to day, to Michael's ear there came
Distressful tidings. Long before the time
210 Of which I speak, the Shepherd had been bound
In surety for his brother's son, a man
Of an industrious life, and ample means;
But unforeseen misfortunes suddenly
Had prest upon him; and old Michael now
Was summoned to discharge the forfeiture,
A grievous penalty, but little less
Than half his substance. This unlooked-for claim,
At the first hearing, for a moment took
More hope out of his life than he supposed
220 That any old man ever could have lost.
As soon as he had armed himself with strength
To look his trouble in the face, it seemed
The Shepherd's sole resource to sell at once
A portion of his patrimonial fields.
Such was his first resolve; he thought again,
And his heart failed him. 'Isabel,' said he,
Two evenings after he had heard the news,
'I have been toiling more than seventy years,
And in the open sunshine of God's love
230 Have we all lived; yet if these fields of ours
Should pass into a stranger's hand, I think
That I could not lie quiet in my grave.
Our lot is a hard lot; the sun himself
Has scarcely been more diligent than I;
And I have lived to be a fool at last
To my own family. An evil man
That was, and made an evil choice, if he
Were false to us; and if he were not false,
There are ten thousand to whom loss like this
240 Had been no sorrow. I forgive him; – but
'Twere better to be dumb than to talk thus.

'When I began, my purpose was to speak
Of remedies and of a cheerful hope.
Our Luke shall leave us, Isabel; the land
Shall not go from us, and it shall be free;
He shall possess it, free as is the wind
That passes over it. We have, thou know'st,
Another kinsman – he will be our friend
In this distress. He is a prosperous man,
250 Thriving in trade – and Luke to him shall go,
And with his kinsman's help and his own thrift
He quickly will repair this loss, and then
He may return to us. If here he stay,
What can be done? Where every one is poor,
What can be gained?'
                    At this the old Man paused,
And Isabel sat silent, for her mind
Was busy, looking back into past times.
There's Richard Bateman, thought she to herself,
He was a parish-boy – at the church-door
260 They made a gathering for him, shillings, pence,
And halfpennies, wherewith the neighbours bought
A basket, which they filled with pedlar's wares;
And, with this basket on his arm, the lad
Went up to London, found a master there,
Who, out of many, chose the trusty boy
To go and overlook his merchandise
Beyond the seas; where he grew wondrous rich,
And left estates and monies to the poor,
And, at his birth-place, built a chapel floored
270 With marble, which he sent from foreign lands.
These thoughts, and many others of like sort,
Passed quickly through the mind of Isabel,
And her face brightened. The old Man was glad,
And thus resumed: – 'Well, Isabel! this scheme
These two days, has been meat and drink to me.
Far more than we have lost is left us yet.
– We have enough – I wish indeed that I
Were younger; – but this hope is a good hope.

Make ready Luke's best garments, of the best
280 Buy for him more, and let us send him forth
Tomorrow, or the next day, or tonight:
– If he *could* go, the Boy should go tonight.'

Here Michael ceased, and to the fields went forth
With a light heart. The Housewife for five days
Was restless morn and night and all day long
Wrought on with her best fingers to prepare
Things needful for the journey of her son.
But Isabel was glad when Sunday came
To stop her in her work: for, when she lay
290 By Michael's side, she through the last two nights
Heard him, how he was troubled in his sleep:
And when they rose at morning she could see
That all his hopes were gone. That day at noon
She said to Luke, while they two by themselves
Were sitting at the door, 'Thou must not go:
We have no other Child but thee to lose,
None to remember – do not go away,
For if thou leave thy Father he will die.'
The Youth made answer with a jocund voice;
300 And Isabel, when she had told her fears,
Recovered heart. That evening her best fare
Did she bring forth, and all together sat
Like happy people round a Christmas fire.

With daylight Isabel resumed her work;
And all the ensuing week the house appeared
As cheerful as a grove in Spring: at length
The expected letter from their kinsman came,
With kind assurances that he would do
His utmost for the welfare of the Boy;
310 To which, requests were added, that forthwith
He might be sent to him. Ten times or more
The letter was read over; Isabel
Went forth to show it to the neighbours round;
Nor was there at that time on English land
A prouder heart than Luke's. When Isabel
Had to her house returned, the old Man said,
'He shall depart tomorrow.' To this word

The Housewife answered, talking much of things
Which, if at such short notice he should go,
320　Would surely be forgotten. But at length
She gave consent, and Michael was at ease.

　　Near the tumultuous brook of Green-head Ghyll,
In that deep valley, Michael had designed
To build a Sheep-fold; and, before he heard
The tidings of his melancholy loss,
For this same purpose he had gathered up
A heap of stones, which by the streamlet's edge
Lay thrown together, ready for the work.
With Luke that evening thitherward he walked:
330　And soon as they had reached the place he stopped,
And thus the old Man spake to him: – 'My Son,
Tomorrow thou wilt leave me: with full heart
I look upon thee, for thou art the same
That wert a promise to me ere thy birth,
And all thy life hast been my daily joy.
I will relate to thee some little part
Of our two histories; 'twill do thee good
When thou art from me, even if I should touch
On things thou canst not know of. – After thou
340　First cam'st into the world – as oft befalls
To new-born infants – thou didst sleep away
Two days, and blessings from thy Father's tongue
Then fell upon thee. Day by day passed on,
And still I loved thee with increasing love.
Never to living ear came sweeter sounds
Than when I heard thee by our own fire-side
First uttering, without words, a natural tune;
While thou, a feeding babe, didst in thy joy
Sing at thy Mother's breast. Month followed month,
350　And in the open fields my life was passed
And on the mountains; else I think that thou
Hadst been brought up upon thy Father's knees.
But we were playmates, Luke: among these hills,
As well thou knowest, in us the old and young
Have played together, nor with me didst thou
Lack any pleasure which a boy can know.'

Luke had a manly heart; but at these words
He sobbed aloud. The old Man grasped his hand,
And said, 'Nay, do not take it so – I see
360 That these are things of which I need not speak.
– Even to the utmost I have been to thee
A kind and a good Father: and herein
I but repay a gift which I myself
Received at others' hands; for, though now old
Beyond the common life of man, I still
Remember them who loved me in my youth.
Both of them sleep together: here they lived,
As all their Forefathers had done; and when
At length their time was come, they were not loth
370 To give their bodies to the family mould.
I wished that thou should'st live the life they lived:
But 'tis a long time to look back, my Son,
And see so little gain from threescore years.
These fields were burdened when they came to me;
Till I was forty years of age, not more
Than half of my inheritance was mine.
I toiled and toiled; God blessed me in my work,
And till these three weeks past the land was free.
– It looks as if it never could endure
380 Another Master. Heaven forgive me, Luke,
If I judge ill for thee, but it seems good
That thou shouldst go.'
                            At this the old Man paused;
Then, pointing to the stones near which they stood,
Thus, after a short silence, he resumed:
'This was a work for us; and now, my Son,
It is a work for me. But, lay one stone –
Here, lay it for me, Luke, with thine own hands.
Nay, Boy, be of good hope; – we both may live
To see a better day. At eighty-four
390 I still am strong and hale; – do thou thy part;
I will do mine. – I will begin again
With many tasks that were resigned to thee:
Up to the heights, and in among the storms,

Will I without thee go again, and do
All works which I was wont to do alone,
Before I knew thy face. – Heaven bless thee, Boy!
Thy heart these two weeks has been beating fast
With many hopes; it should be so – yes – yes –
I knew that thou couldst never have a wish
400 To leave me, Luke: thou hast been bound to me
Only by links of love: when thou art gone,
What will be left to us! – But, I forget
My purposes. Lay now the corner-stone,
As I requested; and hereafter, Luke,
When thou art gone away, should evil men
Be thy companions, think of me, my Son,
And of this moment; hither turn thy thoughts,
And God will strengthen thee: amid all fear
And all temptation, Luke, I pray that thou
410 May'st bear in mind the life thy Fathers lived,
Who, being innocent, did for that cause
Bestir them in good deeds. Now, fare thee well –
When thou return'st, thou in this place wilt see
A work which is not here: a covenant
'Twill be between us; but, whatever fate
Befall thee, I shall love thee to the last,
And bear thy memory with me to the grave.'

     'The Shepherd ended here; and Luke stooped down,
And, as his Father had requested, laid
420 The first stone of the Sheep-fold. At the sight
The old Man's grief broke from him; to his heart
He pressed his Son, he kissèd him and wept;
And to the house together they returned.
– Hushed was that House in peace, or seeming peace,
Ere the night fell: – with morrow's dawn the Boy
Began his journey, and when he had reached
The public way, he put on a bold face;
And all the neighbours, as he passed their doors,
Came forth with wishes and with farewell prayers,
430 That followed him till he was out of sight.

A good report did from their Kinsman come,
Of Luke and his well-doing: and the Boy
Wrote loving letters, full of wondrous news,
Which, as the Housewife phrased it, were throughout
'The prettiest letters that were ever seen.'
Both parents read them with rejoicing hearts.
So, many months passed on: and once again
The Shepherd went about his daily work
With confident and cheerful thoughts; and now
440 Sometimes when he could find a leisure hour
He to that valley took his way, and there
Wrought at the Sheep-fold. Meantime Luke began
To slacken in his duty; and, at length,
He in the dissolute city gave himself
To evil courses: ignominy and shame
Fell on him, so that he was driven at last
To seek a hiding-place beyond the seas.

There is a comfort in the strength of love;
'Twill make a thing endurable, which else
450 Would overset the brain, or break the heart:
I have conversed with more than one who well
Remember the old Man, and what he was
Years after he had heard this heavy news.
His bodily frame had been from youth to age
Of an unusual strength. Among the rocks
He went, and still looked up to sun and cloud,
And listened to the wind; and, as before,
Performed all kinds of labour for his sheep,
And for the land, his small inheritance.
460 And to that hollow dell from time to time
Did he repair, to build the Fold of which
His flock had need. 'Tis not forgotten yet
The pity which was then in every heart
For the old Man – and 'tis believed by all
That many and many a day he thither went,
And never lifted up a single stone.

There, by the Sheep-fold, sometimes was he seen
Sitting alone, or with his faithful Dog,

Then old, beside him, lying at his feet.
470 The length of full seven years, from time to time,
He at the building of this Sheep-fold wrought,
And left the work unfinished when he died.
Three years, or little more, did Isabel
Survive her Husband: at her death the estate
Was sold, and went into a stranger's hand.
The Cottage which was named the EVENING STAR
Is gone – the ploughshare has been through the ground
On which it stood; great changes have been wrought
In all the neighbourhood: – yet the oak is left
480 That grew beside their door; and the remains
Of the unfinished Sheep-fold may be seen
Beside the boisterous brook of Green-head Ghyll.

To a Young Lady Who Had Been Reproached for Taking Long Walks in the Country

Dear Child of Nature, let them rail!
– There is a nest in a green dale,
A harbour and a hold;
Where thou, a Wife and Friend, shalt see
Thy own heart-stirring days, and be
A light to young and old.

There, healthy as a shepherd boy,
And treading among flowers of joy
Which at no season fade,
10 Thou, while thy babes around thee cling,
Shalt show us how divine a thing
A Woman may be made.

Thy thoughts and feelings shall not die,
Nor leave thee, when grey hairs are nigh,
A melancholy slave;
But an old age serene and bright,
And lovely as a Lapland night,
Shall lead thee to thy grave.

The Sailor's Mother

One morning (raw it was and wet –
A foggy day in winter time)
A Woman on the road I met,
Not old, though something past her prime:
Majestic in her person, tall and straight;
And like a Roman matron's was her mien and gait.

The ancient spirit is not dead;
Old times, thought I, are breathing there;
Proud was I that my country bred
10   Such strength, a dignity so fair:
She begged an alms, like one in poor estate;
I looked at her again, nor did my pride abate.

When from these lofty thoughts I woke,
'What is it,' said I, 'that you bear,
Beneath the covert of your Cloak,
Protected from this cold damp air?'
She answered, soon as she the question heard,
'A simple burden, Sir, a little Singing-bird.'

And, thus continuing, she said,
20   'I had a Son, who many a day
Sailed on the seas, but he is dead;
In Denmark he was cast away:
And I have travelled weary miles to see
If aught which he had owned might still remain for me.

'The bird and cage they both were his:
'Twas my Son's bird; and neat and trim
He kept it: many voyages
The singing-bird had gone with him;
When last he sailed, he left the bird behind;
30   From bodings, as might be, that hung upon his mind.

'He to a fellow-lodger's care
Had left it, to be watched and fed,
And pipe its song in safety; – there
I found it when my Son was dead;
And now, God help me for my little wit!
I bear it with me, Sir; – he took so much delight in it.'

Alice Fell; or, Poverty

The post-boy drove with fierce career,
For threatening clouds the moon had drowned;
When, as we hurried on, my ear
Was smitten with a startling sound.

As if the wind blew many ways,
I heard the sound, – and more and more;
It seemed to follow with the chaise,
And still I heard it as before.

At length I to the boy called out;
10   He stopped his horses at the word,
But neither cry, nor voice, nor shout,
Nor aught else like it, could be heard.

The boy then smacked his whip, and fast
The horses scampered through the rain;
But, hearing soon upon the blast
The cry, I bade him halt again.

Forthwith alighting on the ground,
'Whence comes,' said I, 'this piteous moan?'
And there a little Girl I found
20   Sitting behind the chaise, alone.

'My cloak!' no other word she spake,
But loud and bitterly she wept,
As if her innocent heart would break;
And down from off her seat she leapt.

'What ails you, child?' – she sobbed, 'Look here!'
I saw it in the wheel entangled,
A weather-beaten rag as e'er
From any garden scare–crow dangled.

There, twisted between nave and spoke,
30   It hung, nor could at once be freed;
But our joint pains unloosed the cloak,
A miserable rag indeed!

'And whither are you going, child,
Tonight along these lonesome ways?'
'To Durham,' answered she, half wild –
'Then come with me into the chaise.'

Insensible to all relief
Sat the poor girl, and forth did send
Sob after sob, as if her grief
40   Could never, never have an end.

'My child, in Durham do you dwell?'
She checked herself in her distress,
And said, 'My name is Alice Fell;
I'm fatherless and motherless.

'And I to Durham, Sir, belong.'
Again, as if the thought would choke
Her very heart, her grief grew strong;
And all was for her tattered cloak!

The chaise drove on; our journey's end
50   Was nigh; and, sitting by my side,
As if she had lost her only friend
She wept, nor would be pacified.

Up to the tavern-door we post;
Of Alice and her grief I told;
And I gave money to the host,
To buy a new cloak for the old.

'And let it be of duffle grey,
As warm a cloak as man can sell!'
Proud creature was she the next day,
60   The little orphan, Alice Fell!

Beggars

She had a tall man's height or more;
Her face from summer's noontide heat
No bonnet shaded, but she wore
A mantle, to her very feet
Descending with a graceful flow,
And on her head a cap as white as new-fallen snow.

Her skin was of Egyptian brown:
Haughty, as if her eye had seen
Its own light to a distance thrown,
10 She towered, fit person for a Queen
To lead those ancient Amazonian files;
Or ruling Bandit's wife among the Grecian isles.

Advancing, forth she stretched her hand
And begged an alms with doleful plea
That ceased not; on our English land
Such woes, I knew, could never be;
And yet a boon I gave her, for the creature
Was beautiful to see – a weed of glorious feature.

I left her, and pursued my way;
20 And soon before me did espy
A pair of little Boys at play,
Chasing a crimson butterfly;
The taller followed with his hat in hand,
Wreathed round with yellow flowers the gayest of the land.

The other wore a rimless crown
With leaves of laurel stuck about;
And, while both followed up and down,
Each whooping with a merry shout,
In their fraternal features I could trace
30 Unquestionable lines of that wild Suppliant's face.

Yet *they*, so blithe of heart, seemed fit
For finest tasks of earth or air:
Wings let them have, and they might flit
Precursors to Aurora's car,
Scattering fresh flowers; though happier far, I ween,
To hunt their fluttering game o'er rock and level green.

They dart across my path – but lo,
Each ready with a plaintive whine!
Said I, 'not half an hour ago
40   Your Mother has had alms of mine.'
'That cannot be,' one answered – 'she is dead:' –
I looked reproof – they saw – but neither hung his head.

'She has been dead, Sir, many a day.' –
'Hush, boys! you're telling me a lie;
It was your Mother, as I say!'
And, in the twinkling of an eye,
'Come! come!' cried one, and without more ado,
Off to some other play the joyous Vagrants flew!

To a Butterfly

Stay near me – do not take thy flight!
A little longer stay in sight!
Much converse do I find in thee,
Historian of my infancy!
Float near me; do not yet depart!
Dead times revive in thee:
Thou bring'st, gay creature as thou art!
A solemn image to my heart,
My father's family!

10 Oh! pleasant, pleasant were the days,
The time, when, in our childish plays,
My sister Emmeline and I
Together chased the butterfly!
A very hunter did I rush
Upon the prey: – with leaps and springs
I followed on from brake to bush;
But she, God love her! feared to brush
The dust from off its wings.

To the Cuckoo

O blithe New-comer! I have heard,
I hear thee and rejoice.
O Cuckoo! shall I call thee Bird,
Or but a wandering Voice?

While I am lying on the grass
Thy twofold shout I hear,
From hill to hill it seems to pass,
At once far off, and near.

Though babbling only to the Vale,
10 Of sunshine and of flowers,
Thou bringest unto me a tale
Of visionary hours.

Thrice welcome, darling of the Spring!
Even yet thou art to me
No bird, but an invisible thing,
A voice, a mystery;

The same whom in my schoolboy days
I listened to; that Cry
Which made me look a thousand ways
20 In bush, and tree, and sky.

To seek thee did I often rove
Through woods and on the green;
And thou wert still a hope, a love;
Still longed for, never seen.

And I can listen to thee yet;
Can lie upon the plain
And listen, till I do beget
That golden time again.

O blessèd Bird! the earth we pace
30 Again appears to be
An unsubstantial, faery place;
That is fit home for Thee!

'My heart leaps up when I behold'

My heart leaps up when I behold
   A rainbow in the sky:
So was it when my life began;
So is it now I am a man;
So be it when I shall grow old,
   Or let me die!
The Child is father of the Man;
And I could wish my days to be
Bound each to each by natural piety.

To H. C., Six Years Old

O thou! whose fancies from afar are brought;
Who of thy words dost make a mock apparel,
And fittest to unutterable thought
The breeze-like motion and the self-born carol;
Thou faery voyager! that dost float
In such clear water, that thy boat

May rather seem
To brood on air than on an earthly stream;
Suspended in a stream as clear as sky,
10 Where earth and heaven do make one imagery;
O blessèd vision! happy child!
Thou art so exquisitely wild,
I think of thee with many fears
For what may be thy lot in future years.

I thought of times when Pain might be thy guest,
Lord of thy house and hospitality;
And Grief, uneasy lover! never rest
But when she sate within the touch of thee.
O too industrious folly!
20 O vain and causeless melancholy!
Nature will either end thee quite;
Or, lengthening out thy season of delight,
Preserve for thee, by individual right,
A young lamb's heart among the full-grown flocks.
What hast thou to do with sorrow,
Or the injuries of tomorrow?
Thou art a dew-drop, which the morn brings forth,
Ill fitted to sustain unkindly shocks,
Or to be trailed along the soiling earth;
30 A gem that glitters while it lives,
And no forewarning gives;
But, at the touch of wrong, without a strife
Slips in a moment out of life.

Ode: Intimations of Immortality from Recollections of Early Childhood

The Child is Father of the Man;
And I could wish my days to be
Bound each to each by natural piety.

I

There was a time when meadow, grove, and stream,
The earth, and every common sight,
    To me did seem
    Apparelled in celestial light,
The glory and the freshness of a dream.
It is not now as it hath been of yore;-
    Turn wheresoe'er I may,
      By night or day,
The things which I have seen I now can see no more.

II

10   The Rainbow comes and goes,
      And lovely is the Rose;
      The Moon doth with delight
Look round her when the heavens are bare;
      Waters on a starry night
      Are beautiful and fair;
    The sunshine is a glorious birth;
    But yet I know, where'er I go,
That there hath past away a glory from the earth.

III

Now, while the birds thus sing a joyous song,
20   And while the young lambs bound
      As to the tabor's sound,
To me alone there came a thought of grief:
A timely utterance gave that thought relief,
      And I again am strong:
The cataracts blow their trumpets from the steep;
No more shall grief of mine the season wrong;
I hear the Echoes through the mountains throng,
The Winds come to me from the fields of sleep,
      And all the earth is gay;
30   Land and sea
      Give themselves up to jollity,
      And with the heart of May
    Doth every Beast keep holiday;-
      Thou Child of Joy,
Shout round me, let me hear thy shouts, thou happy
    Shepherd-boy!

IV

Ye blessèd Creatures, I have heard the call
   Ye to each other make; I see
The heavens laugh with you in your jubilee;
   My heart is at your festival,
40   My head hath its coronal,
The fulness of your bliss, I feel – I feel it all.
     Oh evil day! if I were sullen
     While Earth herself is adorning,
       This sweet May-morning,
     And the Children are culling
       On every side,
     In a thousand valleys far and wide,
     Fresh flowers; while the sun shines warm,
And the Babe leaps up on his Mother's arm: –
50   I hear, I hear, with joy I hear!
     – But there's a Tree, of many, one,
A single Field which I have looked upon,
Both of them speak of something that is gone:
     The Pansy at my feet
     Doth the same tale repeat:
Whither is fled the visionary gleam?
Where is it now, the glory and the dream?

V

Our birth is but a sleep and a forgetting:
The Soul that rises with us, our life's Star,
60   Hath had elsewhere its setting,
      And cometh from afar:
     Not in entire forgetfulness,
     And not in utter nakedness,
But trailing clouds of glory do we come
     From God, who is our home:
Heaven lies about us in our infancy!
Shades of the prison-house begin to close
     Upon the growing Boy,
       But He
70 Beholds the light, and whence it flows,
     He sees it in his joy;

The Youth, who daily farther from the east
    Must travel, still is Nature's Priest,
    And by the vision splendid
    Is on his way attended;
At length the Man perceives it die away,
And fade into the light of common day.

VI

Earth fills her lap with pleasures of her own;
Yearnings she hath in her own natural kind,
80   And, even with something of a Mother's mind,
    And no unworthy aim,
    The homely Nurse doth all she can
To make her Foster-child, her Inmate Man,
    Forget the glories he hath known,
And that imperial palace whence he came.

VII

Behold the Child among his new-born blisses,
A six years' Darling of a pigmy size!
See, where 'mid work of his own hand he lies,
Fretted by sallies of his mother's kisses,
90   With light upon him from his father's eyes!
See, at his feet, some little plan or chart,
Some fragment from his dream of human life,
Shaped by himself with newly-learnèd art;
    A wedding or a festival,
    A mourning or a funeral;
      And this hath now his heart,
    And unto this he frames his song:
      Then will he fit his tongue
To dialogues of business, love, or strife;
100   But it will not be long
    Ere this be thrown aside,
    And with new joy and pride
The little Actor cons another part;
Filling from time to time his 'humorous stage'
With all the Persons, down to palsied Age,
That Life brings with her in her equipage;
    As if his whole vocation
    Were endless imitation.

VIII
Thou, whose exterior semblance doth belie
110   Thy Soul's immensity;
Thou best Philosopher, who yet dost keep
Thy heritage, thou Eye among the blind,
That, deaf and silent, read'st the eternal deep,
Haunted for ever by the eternal mind, –
         Mighty Prophet! Seer blest!
         On whom those truths do rest,
Which we are toiling all our lives to find,
In darkness lost, the darkness of the grave;
Thou, over whom thy Immortality
120 Broods like the Day, a Master o'er a Slave,
A Presence which is not to be put by;
Thou little Child, yet glorious in the might
Of heaven-born freedom on thy being's height,
Why with such earnest pains dost thou provoke
The years to bring the inevitable yoke,
Thus blindly with thy blessedness at strife?
Full soon thy Soul shall have her earthly freight,
And custom lie upon thee with a weight,
Heavy as frost, and deep almost as life!

IX
130   O joy! that in our embers
         Is something that doth live,
         That nature yet remembers
         What was so fugitive!
The thought of our past years in me doth breed
Perpetual benediction: not indeed
For that which is most worthy to be blest;
Delight and liberty, the simple creed
Of Childhood, whether busy or at rest,
With new-fledged hope still fluttering in his breast: –
140   Not for these I raise
         The song of thanks and praise;
      But for those obstinate questionings
      Of sense and outward things,
      Fallings from us, vanishings;

Blank misgivings of a Creature
Moving about in worlds not realized,
High instincts before which our mortal Nature
Did tremble like a guilty Thing surprised:
    But for those first affections,
150   Those shadowy recollections,
    Which, be they what they may,
Are yet the fountain light of all our day,
Are yet a master light of all our seeing;
    Uphold us, cherish, and have power to make
Our noisy years seem moments in the being
Of the eternal Silence: truths that wake,
    To perish never;
Which neither listlessness, nor mad endeavour,
    Nor Man nor Boy,
160 Nor all that is at enmity with joy,
Can utterly abolish or destroy!
    Hence in a season of calm weather
    Though inland far we be,
Our Souls have sight of that immortal sea
    Which brought us hither,
    Can in a moment travel thither,
And see the Children sport upon the shore,
And hear the mighty waters rolling evermore.

X
Then sing, ye Birds, sing, sing a joyous song!
170   And let the young Lambs bound
    As to the tabor's sound!
We in thought will join your throng,
    Ye that pipe and ye that play,
    Ye that through your hearts today
    Feel the gladness of the May!
What though the radiance which was once so bright
Be now for ever taken from my sight,
    Though nothing can bring back the hour
Of splendour in the grass, of glory in the flower;
180   We will grieve not, rather find
    Strength in what remains behind;

In the primal sympathy
Which having been must ever be;
In the soothing thoughts that spring
Out of human suffering;
In the faith that looks through death,
In years that bring the philosophic mind.

XI

And O, ye Fountains, Meadows, Hills, and Groves,
Forebode not any severing of our loves!
190 Yet in my heart of hearts I feel your might;
I only have relinquished one delight
To live beneath your more habitual sway.
I love the Brooks which down their channels fret,
Even more than when I tripped lightly as they;
The innocent brightness of a new-born Day
      Is lovely yet;
The Clouds that gather round the setting sun
Do take a sober colouring from an eye
That hath kept watch o'er man's mortality;
200 Another race hath been, and other palms are won.
Thanks to the human heart by which we live,
Thanks to its tenderness, its joys, and fears,
To me the meanest flower that blows can give
Thoughts that do often lie too deep for tears.

The Sparrow's Nest

Behold, within the leafy shade,
Those bright blue eggs together laid!
On me the chance-discovered sight
Gleamed like a vision of delight.
I started – seeming to espy
The home and sheltered bed,
The Sparrow's dwelling, which, hard by
My Father's house, in wet or dry
My sister Emmeline and I
10   Together visited.

She looked at it and seemed to fear it;
Dreading, though wishing, to be near it:
Such heart was in her, being then
A little Prattler among men.
The Blessing of my later years
Was with me when a boy:
She gave me eyes, she gave me ears;
And humble cares, and delicate fears;
A heart, the fountain of sweet tears;
20   And love, and thought, and joy.

Written in March While Resting on the Bridge at the Foot of Brother's Water

The Cock is crowing,
The stream is flowing,
The small birds twitter,
The lake doth glitter,
The green field sleeps in the sun;
The oldest and youngest
Are at work with the strongest;
The cattle are grazing,
Their heads never raising;
10 There are forty feeding like one!

Like an army defeated
The snow hath retreated,
And now doth fare ill
On the top of the bare hill;
The Ploughboy is whooping – anon – anon:
There's joy in the mountains;
There's life in the fountains;
Small clouds are sailing,
Blue sky prevailing;
20 The rain is over and gone!

The Green Linnet

Beneath these fruit-tree boughs that shed
Their snow-white blossoms on my head,
With brightest sunshine round me spread
    Of spring's unclouded weather,
In this sequestered nook how sweet
To sit upon my orchard-seat!
And birds and flowers once more to greet,
    My last year's friends together.

One have I marked, the happiest guest
10 In all this covert of the blest:
Hail to Thee, far above the rest
    In joy of voice and pinion!
Thou, Linnet! in thy green array,
Presiding Spirit here today,
Dost lead the revels of the May;
    And this is thy dominion.

While birds, and butterflies, and flowers,
Make all one band of paramours,
Thou, ranging up and down the bowers,
20   Art sole in thy employment:
A Life, a Presence like the Air,
Scattering thy gladness without care,
Too blest with anyone to pair;
    Thyself thy own enjoyment.

Amid yon tuft of hazel trees,
That twinkle to the gusty breeze,
Behold him perched in ecstasies,
    Yet seeming still to hover;
There! where the flutter of his wings
30 Upon his back and body flings
Shadows and sunny glimmerings,
    That cover him all over.

My dazzled sight he oft deceives,
A Brother of the dancing leaves;
Then flits, and from the cottage-eaves
   Pours forth his song in gushes;
As if by that exulting strain
He mocked and treated with disdain
The voiceless Form he chose to feign,
40   While fluttering in the bushes.

To the Daisy

Bright Flower! whose home is everywhere,
Bold in maternal Nature's care,
And all the long year through the heir
   Of joy and sorrow;
Methinks that there abides in thee
Some concord with humanity,
Given to no other flower I see
   The forest thorough!

Is it that Man is soon deprest?
10 A thoughtless Thing! who, once unblest,
Does little on his memory rest,
   Or on his reason,
And Thou wouldst teach him how to find
A shelter under every wind,
A hope for times that are unkind
   And every season?

Thou wander'st the wide world about,
Unchecked by pride or scrupulous doubt,
With friends to greet thee, or without,
20   Yet pleased and willing;
Meek, yielding to the occasion's call,
And all things suffering from all,
Thy function apostolical
   In peace fulfilling.

To a Butterfly

I've watched you now a full half-hour,
Self-poised upon that yellow flower;
And, little Butterfly! indeed
I know not if you sleep or feed.
How motionless! – not frozen seas
More motionless! and then
What joy awaits you, when the breeze
Hath found you out among the trees,
And calls you forth again!

10   This plot of orchard-ground is ours;
My trees they are, my Sister's flowers;
Here rest your wings when they are weary;
Here lodge as in a sanctuary!
Come often to us, fear no wrong;
Sit near us on the bough!
We'll talk of sunshine and of song,
And summer days, when we were young;
Sweet childish days, that were as long
As twenty days are now.

To the Small Celandine

Pansies, lilies, kingcups, daisies,
Let them live upon their praises;
Long as there's a sun that sets,
Primroses will have their glory;
Long as there are violets,
They will have a place in story:
There's a flower that shall be mine,
'Tis the little Celandine.

Eyes of some men travel far
10 For the finding of a star;
Up and down the heavens they go,
Men that keep a mighty rout!
I'm as great as they, I trow,
Since the day I found thee out,
Little Flower! – I'll make a stir,
Like a sage astronomer.

Modest, yet withal an Elf
Bold, and lavish of thyself;
Since we needs must first have met
20 I have seen thee, high and low,
Thirty years or more, and yet
'Twas a face I did not know;
Thou hast now, go where I may,
Fifty greetings in a day.

Ere a leaf is on a bush,
In the time before the thrush
Has a thought about her nest,
Thou wilt come with half a call,
Spreading out thy glossy breast
30 Like a careless Prodigal;
Telling tales about the sun,
When we've little warmth, or none.

Poets, vain men in their mood!
Travel with the multitude:
Never heed them; I aver
That they all are wanton wooers;
But the thrifty cottager,
Who stirs little out of doors,
Joys to spy thee near her home;
40 Spring is coming, Thou art come!

Comfort have thou of thy merit,
Kindly, unassuming Spirit!
Careless of thy neighbourhood,
Thou dost show thy pleasant face
On the moor, and in the wood,
In the lane; – there's not a place,
Howsoever mean it be,
But 'tis good enough for thee.

Ill befall the yellow flowers,
50   Children of the flaring hours!
Buttercups, that will be seen,
Whether we will see or no;
Others, too, of lofty mien;
They have done as worldlings do,
Taken praise that should be thine,
Little, humble Celandine.

Prophet of delight and mirth,
Ill-requited upon earth;
Herald of a mighty band,
60   Of a joyous train ensuing,
Serving at my heart's command,
Tasks that are no tasks renewing,
I will sing, as doth behove,
Hymns in praise of what I love!

To the Same Flower

Pleasures newly found are sweet
When they lie about our feet:
February last, my heart
First at sight of thee was glad;
All unheard of as thou art,
Thou must needs, I think, have had,
Celandine! and long ago,
Praise of which I nothing know.

I have not a doubt but he,
10   Whosoe'er the man might be,
Who the first with pointed rays
(Workman worthy to be sainted)
Set the sign-board in a blaze,
When the rising sun he painted,
Took the fancy from a glance
At thy glittering countenance.

Soon as gentle breezes bring
News of winter's vanishing,
And the children build their bowers,
20   Sticking 'kerchief-plots of mould
All about with full-blown flowers,
Thick as sheep in shepherd's fold!
With the proudest thou art there,
Mantling in the tiny square.

Often have I sighed to measure
By myself a lonely pleasure,
Sighed to think, I read a book
Only read, perhaps, by me;
Yet I long could overlook
30   Thy bright coronet and Thee,
And thy arch and wily ways,
And thy store of other praise.

Blithe of heart, from week to week
Thou dost play at hide-and-seek;
While the patient primrose sits
Like a beggar in the cold,
Thou, a flower of wiser wits,
Slip'st into thy sheltering hold;
Liveliest of the vernal train
40   When ye all are out again.

Drawn by what peculiar spell,
By what charm of sight or smell,
Does the dim-eyed curious Bee,
Labouring for her waxen cells,
Fondly settle upon Thee
Prized above all buds and bells
Opening daily at thy side,
By the season multiplied?

Thou art not beyond the moon,
50   But a thing 'beneath our shoon':
Let the bold Discoverer thrid
In his bark the polar sea;
Rear who will a pyramid;
Praise it is enough for me,
If there be but three or four
Who will love my little Flower.

Resolution and Independence

I

There was a roaring in the wind all night;
The rain came heavily and fell in floods;
But now the sun is rising calm and bright;
The birds are singing in the distant woods;
Over his own sweet voice the Stock-dove broods;
The Jay makes answer as the Magpie chatters;
And all the air is filled with pleasant noise of waters.

II

All things that love the sun are out of doors;
The sky rejoices in the morning's birth;
10   The grass is bright with rain-drops; – on the moors
The hare is running races in her mirth;
And with her feet she from the plashy earth
Raises a mist; that, glittering in the sun,
Runs with her all the way, wherever she doth run.

III
I was a Traveller then upon the moor;
I saw the hare that raced about with joy;
I heard the woods and distant waters roar;
Or heard them not, as happy as a boy:
The pleasant season did my heart employ:
20   My old remembrances went from me wholly;
And all the ways of men, so vain and melancholy.

IV
But, as it sometimes chanceth, from the might
Of joy in minds that can no further go,
As high as we have mounted in delight
In our dejection do we sink as low;
To me that morning did it happen so;
And fears and fancies thick upon me came;
Dim sadness – and blind thoughts, I knew not, nor could
        name.

V
I heard the sky-lark warbling in the sky;
30   And I bethought me of the playful hare:
Even such a happy Child of earth am I;
Even as these blissful creatures do I fare;
Far from the world I walk, and from all care;
But there may come another day to me –
Solitude, pain of heart, distress, and poverty.

VI
My whole life I have lived in pleasant thought,
As if life's business were a summer mood;
As if all needful things would come unsought
To genial faith, still rich in genial good;
40   But how can He expect that others should
Build for him, sow for him, and at his call
Love him, who for himself will take no heed at all?

VII

I thought of Chatterton, the marvellous Boy,
The sleepless Soul that perished in his pride;
Of Him who walked in glory and in joy
Following his plough, along the mountain-side:
By our own spirits are we deified:
We Poets in our youth begin in gladness;
But thereof come in the end despondency and madness.

VIII

50 Now, whether it were by peculiar grace,
A leading from above, a something given,
Yet it befell, that, in this lonely place,
When I with these untoward thoughts had striven,
Beside a pool bare to the eye of heaven
I saw a Man before me unawares:
The oldest man he seemed that ever wore grey hairs.

IX

As a huge stone is sometimes seen to lie
Couched on the bald top of an eminence;
Wonder to all who do the same espy,
60 By what means it could thither come, and whence;
So that it seems a thing endued with sense:
Like a sea-beast crawled forth, that on a shelf
Of rock or sand reposeth, there to sun itself;

X

Such seemed this Man, not all alive nor dead,
Nor all asleep – in his extreme old age:
His body was bent double, feet and head
Coming together in life's pilgrimage;
As if some dire constraint of pain, or rage
Of sickness felt by him in times long past,
70 A more than human weight upon his frame had cast.

XI

Himself he propped, limbs, body, and pale face,
Upon a long grey staff of shaven wood:
And, still as I drew near with gentle pace,
Upon the margin of that moorish flood
Motionless as a cloud the old Man stood,
That heareth not the loud winds when they call;
And moveth all together, if it move at all.

XII

At length, himself unsettling, he the pond
Stirred with his staff, and fixedly did look
80 Upon the muddy water, which he conned,
As if he had been reading in a book:
And now a stranger's privilege I took;
And, drawing to his side, to him did say,
'This morning gives us promise of a glorious day.'

XIII

A gentle answer did the old Man make,
In courteous speech which forth he slowly drew:
And him with further words I thus bespake,
'What occupation do you there pursue?
This is a lonesome place for one like you.'
90 Ere he replied, a flash of mild surprise
Broke from the sable orbs of his yet-vivid eyes.

XIV

His words came feebly, from a feeble chest,
But each in solemn order followed each,
With something of a lofty utterance drest –
Choice word and measured phrase, above the reach
Of ordinary men; a stately speech;
Such as grave Livers do in Scotland use,
Religious men, who give to God and man their dues.

XV

He told, that to these waters he had come
100 To gather leeches, being old and poor:
Employment hazardous and wearisome!
And he had many hardships to endure:
From pond to pond he roamed, from moor to moor;
Housing, with God's good help, by choice or chance;
And in this way he gained an honest maintenance.

XVI

The old Man still stood talking by my side;
But now his voice to me was like a stream
Scarce heard; nor word from word could I divide;
And the whole body of the Man did seem
110 Like one whom I had met with in a dream;
Or like a man from some far region sent,
To give me human strength, by apt admonishment.

XVII

My former thoughts returned: the fear that kills;
And hope that is unwilling to be fed;
Cold, pain, and labour, and all fleshly ills;
And mighty Poets in their misery dead.
– Perplexed, and longing to be comforted,
My question eagerly did I renew,
'How is it that you live, and what is it you do?'

XVIII

120 He with a smile did then his words repeat;
And said that, gathering leeches, far and wide
He travelled; stirring thus about his feet
The waters of the pools where they abide.
'Once I could meet with them on every side;
But they have dwindled long by slow decay;
Yet still I persevere, and find them where I may.'

XIX

While he was talking thus, the lonely place,
The old Man's shape, and speech – all troubled me:
In my mind's eye I seemed to see him pace
130   About the weary moors continually,
Wandering about alone and silently.
While I these thoughts within myself pursued,
He, having made a pause, the same discourse renewed.

XX

And soon with this he other matter blended,
Cheerfully uttered, with demeanour kind,
But stately in the main; and when he ended,
I could have laughed myself to scorn to find
In that decrepit Man so firm a mind.
'God,' said I, 'be my help and stay secure;
140   I'll think of the Leech-gatherer on the lonely moor!'

Travelling

This is the spot: – how mildly does the sun
Shine in between the fading leaves! the air
In the habitual silence of this wood
Is more than silent; and this bed of heath –
Where shall we find so sweet a resting-place?
Come, let me see thee sink into a dream
Of quiet thoughts, protracted till thine eye
Be calm as water when the winds are gone
And no one can tell whither. My sweet Friend,
10   We two have had such happy hours together
That my heart melts in me to think of it.

Stanzas Written in my Pocket-Copy of Thomson's 'Castle of Indolence'

Within our happy Castle there dwelt One
Whom without blame I may not overlook;
For never sun on living creature shone
Who more devout enjoyment with us took:
Here on his hours he hung as on a book,
On his own time here would he float away,
As doth a fly upon a summer brook;
But go tomorrow, or belike today,
Seek for him, – he is fled; and whither none can say.

10 Thus often would he leave our peaceful home,
And find elsewhere his business or delight;
Out of our Valley's limits did he roam:
Full many a time, upon a stormy night,
His voice came to us from the neighbouring height:
Oft could we see him driving full in view
At mid-day when the sun was shining bright;
What ill was on him, what he had to do,
A mighty wonder bred among our quiet crew.

Ah! piteous sight it was to see this Man
20 When he came back to us, a withered flower, –
Or like a sinful creature, pale and wan.
Down would he sit; and without strength or power
Look at the common grass from hour to hour:
And oftentimes, how long I fear to say,
Where apple-trees in blossom made a bower,
Retired in that sunshiny shade he lay;
And, like a naked Indian, slept himself away.

Great wonder to our gentle tribe it was
Whenever from our Valley he withdrew;
30 For happier soul no living creature has
Than he had, being here the long day through.

Some thought he was a lover, and did woo:
Some thought far worse of him, and judged him wrong;
But verse was what he had been wedded to;
And his own mind did like a tempest strong
Come to him thus, and drove the weary Wight along.

With him there often walked in friendly guise,
Or lay upon the moss by brook or tree,
A noticeable Man with large grey eyes,
40 And a pale face that seemed undoubtedly
As if a blooming face it ought to be;
Heavy his low-hung lip did oft appear,
Deprest by weight of musing Phantasy;
Profound his forehead was, though not severe;
Yet some did think that he had little business here:

Sweet heaven forefend! his was a lawful right;
Noisy he was, and gamesome as a boy;
His limbs would toss about him with delight,
Like branches when strong winds the trees annoy.
50 Nor lacked his calmer hours device or toy
To banish listlessness and irksome care;
He would have taught you how you might employ
Yourself; and many did to him repair, –
And certes not in vain; he had inventions rare.

Expedients, too, of simplest sort he tried:
Long blades of grass, plucked round him as he lay,
Made, to his ear attentively applied,
A pipe on which the wind would deftly play;
Glasses he had, that little things display,
60 The beetle panoplied in gems and gold,
A mailèd angel on a battle-day;
The mysteries that cups of flowers enfold,
And all the gorgeous sights which fairies do behold.

He would entice that other Man to hear
His music, and to view his imagery:
And, sooth, these two were each to the other dear:
No livelier love in such a place could be:
There did they dwell – from earthly labour free,
As happy spirits as were ever seen;

70 If but a bird, to keep them company,
Or butterfly sate down, they were, I ween,
As pleased as if the same had been a Maiden-queen.

1801

I grieved for Buonaparté, with a vain
And an unthinking grief! The tenderest mood
Of that Man's mind – what can it be? what food
Fed his first hopes? what knowledge could *he* gain?
'Tis not in battles that from youth we train
The Governor who must be wise and good,
And temper with the sternness of the brain
Thoughts motherly, and meek as womanhood.
Wisdom doth live with children round her knees:
10 Books, leisure, perfect freedom, and the talk
Man holds with week-day man in the hourly walk
Of the mind's business: these are the degrees
By which true Sway doth mount; this is the stalk
True Power doth grow on; and her rights are these.

'Methought I saw the footsteps of a throne'

Methought I saw the footsteps of a throne
Which mists and vapours from mine eyes did shroud –
Nor view of who might sit thereon allowed;
But all the steps and ground about were strown
With sights the ruefullest that flesh and bone
Ever put on; a miserable crowd,
Sick, hale, old, young, who cried before that cloud,
'Thou art our king, O Death! to thee we groan.'
Those steps I clomb; the mists before me gave
10 Smooth way; and I beheld the face of one
Sleeping alone within a mossy cave,
With her face up to heaven; that seemed to have
Pleasing remembrance of a thought foregone;
A lovely Beauty in a summer grave!

'England! the time is come when thou shouldst wean'

England! the time is come when thou shouldst wean
Thy heart from its emasculating food;
The truth should now be better understood;
Old things have been unsettled; we have seen
Fair seed-time, better harvest might have been
But for thy trespasses; and, at this day,
If for Greece, Egypt, India, Africa,
Aught good were destined, thou wouldst step between.
England! all nations in this charge agree:
10 But worse, more ignorant in love and hate,
Far – far more abject, is thine Enemy:
Therefore the wise pray for thee, though the freight
Of thy offences be a heavy weight:
Oh grief that Earth's best hopes rest all with Thee!

'It is not to be thought of that the Flood'

It is not to be thought of that the Flood
Of British freedom, which, to the open sea
Of the world's praise, from dark antiquity
Hath flowed, 'with pomp of waters, unwithstood,'
Roused though it be full often to a mood
Which spurns the check of salutary bands,
That this most famous Stream in bogs and sands
Should perish; and to evil and to good
Be lost for ever. In our halls is hung
10 Armoury of the invincible Knights of old:
We must be free or die, who speak the tongue
That Shakespeare spake; the faith and morals hold
Which Milton held. – In everything we are sprung
Of Earth's first blood, have titles manifold.

'When I have borne in memory what has tamed'

When I have borne in memory what has tamed
Great Nations, how ennobling thoughts depart
When men change swords for ledgers, and desert
The student's bower for gold, some fears unnamed
I had, my Country! – am I to be blamed?
Now, when I think of thee, and what thou art,
Verily, in the bottom of my heart,
Of those unfilial fears I am ashamed.
For dearly must we prize thee; we who find
10 In thee a bulwark for the cause of men;
And I by my affection was beguiled:
What wonder if a Poet now and then,
Among the many movements of his mind,
Felt for thee as a lover or a child!

'"Beloved Vale!" I said, "when I shall con"'

'Beloved Vale!' I said, 'when I shall con
Those many records of my childish years,
Remembrance of myself and of my peers
Will press me down: to think of what is gone
Will be an awful thought, if life have one.'
But, when into the Vale I came, no fears
Distressed me; from mine eyes escaped no tears;
Deep thought, or dread remembrance, had I none.
By doubts and thousand petty fancies crost
10 I stood, of simple shame the blushing Thrall;
So narrow seemed the brooks, the fields so small!
A Juggler's balls old Time about him tossed;
I looked, I stared, I smiled, I laughed; and all
The weight of sadness was in wonder lost.

Personal Talk

I

I am not One who much or oft delight
To season my fireside with personal talk, –
Of friends, who live within an easy walk,
Or neighbours, daily, weekly, in my sight:
And, for my chance-acquaintance, ladies bright,
Sons, mothers, maidens withering on the stalk,
These all wear out of me, like Forms, with chalk
Painted on rich men's floors, for one feast-night.
Better than such discourse doth silence long,
10 Long, barren silence, square with my desire;
To sit without emotion, hope, or aim,
In the loved presence of my cottage-fire,
And listen to the flapping of the flame,
Or kettle whispering its faint undersong.

II

'Yet life,' you say, 'is life; we have seen and see,
And with a living pleasure we describe;
And fits of sprightly malice do but bribe
The languid mind into activity.
Sound sense, and love itself, and mirth and glee
20 Are fostered by the comment and the gibe.'
Even be it so: yet still among your tribe,
Our daily world's true Worldlings, rank not me!
Children are blest, and powerful; their world lies
More justly balanced; partly at their feet,
And part far from them: – sweetest melodies
Are those that are by distance made more sweet;
Whose mind is but the mind of his own eyes,
He is a Slave; the meanest we can meet!

III

Wings have we, – and as far as we can go
30 We may find pleasure: wilderness and wood,
Blank ocean and mere sky, support that mood
Which with the lofty sanctifies the low.
Dreams, books, are each a world; and books, we know,
Are a substantial world, both pure and good:
Round these, with tendrils strong as flesh and blood,
Our pastime and our happiness will grow.
There find I personal themes, a plenteous store,
Matter wherein right voluble I am,
To which I listen with a ready ear;
40 Two shall be named, pre-eminently dear, –
The gentle Lady married to the Moor;
And heavenly Una with her milk-white Lamb.

IV

Nor can I not believe but that hereby
Great gains are mine; for thus I live remote
From evil-speaking; rancour, never sought,
Comes to me not; malignant truth, or lie.
Hence have I genial seasons, hence have I
Smooth passions, smooth discourse, and joyous thought:
And thus from day to day my little boat
50 Rocks in its harbour, lodging peaceably.
Blessings be with them – and eternal praise,
Who gave us nobler loves, and nobler cares –
The Poets, who on earth have made us heirs
Of truth and pure delight by heavenly lays!
Oh! might my name be numbered among theirs,
Then gladly would I end my mortal days.

'The world is too much with us; late and soon'

The world is too much with us; late and soon,
Getting and spending, we lay waste our powers:
Little we see in Nature that is ours;
We have given our hearts away, a sordid boon!
This Sea that bares her bosom to the moon;
The winds that will be howling at all hours,
And are up-gathered now like sleeping flowers;
For this, for everything, we are out of tune;
It moves us not. – Great God! I'd rather be
10   A Pagan suckled in a creed outworn;
So might I, standing on this pleasant lea,
Have glimpses that would make me less forlorn;
Have sight of Proteus rising from the sea;
Or hear old Triton blow his wreathèd horn.

To the Memory of Raisley Calvert

Calvert! it must not be unheard by them
Who may respect my name, that I to thee
Owed many years of early liberty.
This care was thine when sickness did condemn
Thy youth to hopeless wasting, root and stem –
That I, if frugal and severe, might stray
Where'er I liked; and finally array
My temples with the Muse's diadem.
Hence, if in freedom I have loved the truth;
10   If there be aught of pure, or good, or great,
In my past verse; or shall be, in the lays
Of higher mood, which now I meditate; –
It gladdens me, O worthy, short-lived, Youth!
To think how much of this will be thy praise.

'Where lies the Land to which yon Ship must go?'

Where lies the Land to which yon Ship must go?
Fresh as a lark mounting at break of day,
Festively she puts forth in trim array;
Is she for tropic suns, or polar snow?
What boots the inquiry? – Neither friend nor foe
She cares for; let her travel where she may,
She finds familiar names, a beaten way
Ever before her, and a wind to blow.
Yet still I ask, what haven is her mark?
10   And, almost as it was when ships were rare,
(From time to time, like Pilgrims, here and there
Crossing the waters) doubt, and something dark,
Of the old Sea some reverential fear,
Is with me at thy farewell, joyous Bark!

'With Ships the sea was sprinkled far and nigh'

With Ships the sea was sprinkled far and nigh,
Like stars in heaven, and joyously it showed;
Some lying fast at anchor in the road,
Some veering up and down, one knew not why.
A goodly Vessel did I then espy
Come like a giant from a haven broad;
And lustily along the bay she strode,
Her tackling rich, and of apparel high.
This Ship was naught to me, nor I to her,
10   Yet I pursued her with a Lover's look;
This Ship to all the rest did I prefer:
When will she turn, and whither? She will brook
No tarrying; where She comes the winds must stir:
On went She, and due north her journey took.

On the Extinction of the Venetian Republic

Once did She hold the gorgeous east in fee;
And was the safeguard of the west: the worth
Of Venice did not fall below her birth,
Venice, the eldest Child of Liberty.
She was a maiden City, bright and free;
No guile seduced, no force could violate;
And, when she took unto herself a Mate,
She must espouse the everlasting Sea.
And what if she had seen those glories fade,
10 Those titles vanish, and that strength decay;
Yet shall some tribute of regret be paid
When her long life hath reached its final day:
Men are we, and must grieve when even the Shade
Of that which once was great, is passed away.

A Farewell

Farewell, thou little Nook of mountain-ground,
Thou rocky corner in the lowest stair
Of that magnificent temple which doth bound
One side of our whole vale with grandeur rare;
Sweet garden-orchard, eminently fair,
The loveliest spot that man hath ever found,
Farewell! – we leave thee to Heaven's peaceful care,
Thee, and the Cottage which thou dost surround.

Our boat is safely anchored by the shore,
10 And there will safely ride when we are gone;
The flowering shrubs that deck our humble door
Will prosper, though untended and alone:
Fields, goods, and far-off chattels we have none:
These narrow bounds contain our private store
Of things earth makes, and sun doth shine upon;
Here are they in our sight – we have no more.

Sunshine and shower be with you, bud and bell!
For two months now in vain we shall be sought;
We leave you here in solitude to dwell
20   With these our latest gifts of tender thought;
Thou, like the morning, in thy saffron coat,
Bright gowan, and marsh-marigold, farewell!
Whom from the borders of the Lake we brought,
And placed together near our rocky Well.

We go for One to whom ye will be dear;
And she will prize this Bower, this Indian shed,
Our own contrivance, Building without peer!
– A gentle Maid, whose heart is lowly bred,
Whose pleasures are in wild fields gatherèd,
30   With joyousness, and with a thoughtful cheer,
Will come to you; to you herself will wed;
And love the blessed life that we lead here.

Dear Spot! which we have watched with tender heed,
Bringing thee chosen plants and blossoms blown
Among the distant mountains, flower and weed,
Which thou hast taken to thee as thy own,
Making all kindness registered and known;
Thou for our sakes, though Nature's child indeed,
Fair in thyself and beautiful alone,
40   Hast taken gifts which thou dost little need.

And O most constant, yet most fickle Place,
That hast thy wayward moods, as thou dost show
To them who look not daily on thy face;
Who, being loved, in love no bounds dost know,
And say'st, when we forsake thee, 'Let them go!'
Thou easy-hearted Thing, with thy wild race
Of weeds and flowers, till we return be slow,
And travel with the year at a soft pace.

Help us to tell Her tales of years gone by,
50   And this sweet spring, the best beloved and best;
Joy will be flown in its mortality;
Something must stay to tell us of the rest.

50   Here, thronged with primroses, the steep rock's breast
      Glittered at evening like a starry sky;
      And in this bush our sparrow built her nest,
      Of which I sang one song that will not die.

      O happy Garden! whose seclusion deep
      Hath been so friendly to industrious hours;
      And to soft slumbers, that did gently steep
60   Our spirits, carrying with them dreams of flowers.
      And wild notes warbled among leafy bowers;
      Two burning months let summer overleap,
      And, coming back with Her who will be ours,
      Into thy bosom we again shall creep.

Composed Upon Westminster Bridge, September 3,
1802

      Earth has not anything to show more fair:
      Dull would he be of soul who could pass by
      A sight so touching in its majesty:
      This City now doth, like a garment, wear
      The beauty of the morning; silent, bare,
      Ships, towers, domes, theatres, and temples lie
      Open unto the fields, and to the sky;
      All bright and glittering in the smokeless air.
      Never did sun more beautifully steep
10   In his first splendour, valley, rock, or hill;
      Ne'er saw I, never felt, a calm so deep!
      The river glideth at his own sweet will:
      Dear God! the very houses seem asleep;
      And all that mighty heart is lying still!

Calais, August, 1802

Is it a reed that's shaken by the wind,
Or what is it that ye go forth to see?
Lords, lawyers, statesmen, squires of low degree,
Men known, and men unknown, sick, lame, and blind,
Post forward all, like creatures of one kind,
With first-fruit offerings crowd to bend the knee
In France, before the new-born Majesty.
'Tis ever thus. Ye men of prostrate mind,
A seemly reverence may be paid to power;
10   But that's a loyal virtue, never sown
In haste, nor springing with a transient shower:
When truth, when sense, when liberty were flown,
What hardship had it been to wait an hour?
Shame on you, feeble Heads, to slavery prone!

Composed by the Sea-Side, near Calais, August, 1802

Fair Star of evening, Splendour of the west,
Star of my Country! – on the horizon's brink
Thou hangest, stooping, as might seem, to sink
On England's bosom; yet well pleased to rest,
Meanwhile, and be to her a glorious crest
Conspicuous to the Nations. Thou, I think,
Shouldst be my Country's emblem; and shouldst wink,
Bright Star! with laughter on her banners, drest
In thy fresh beauty. There! that dusky spot
10   Beneath thee, that is England; there she lies.
Blessings be on you both! one hope, one lot,
One life, one glory! – I, with many a fear
For my dear Country, many heartfelt sighs,
Among men who do not love her, linger here.

'It is a beauteous evening, calm and free'

It is a beauteous evening, calm and free,
The holy time is quiet as a Nun
Breathless with adoration; the broad sun
Is sinking down in its tranquillity;
The gentleness of heaven broods o'er the Sea:
Listen! the mighty Being is awake,
And doth with his eternal motion make
A sound like thunder – everlastingly.
Dear Child! dear Girl! that walkest with me here,
10 If thou appear untouched by solemn thought,
Thy nature is not therefore less divine:
Thou liest in Abraham's bosom all the year;
And worshipp'st at the Temple's inner shrine,
God being with thee when we know it not.

To Toussaint l'Ouverture

Toussaint, the most unhappy man of men!
Whether the whistling Rustic tend his plough
Within thy hearing, or thy head be now
Pillowed in some deep dungeon's earless den; –
O miserable Chieftain! where and when
Wilt thou find patience! Yet die not; do thou
Wear rather in thy bonds a cheerful brow:
Though fallen thyself, never to rise again,
Live, and take comfort. Thou hast left behind
10 Powers that will work for thee; air, earth, and skies;
There's not a breathing of the common wind
That will forget thee; thou hast great allies;
Thy friends are exultations, agonies,
And love, and man's unconquerable mind.

September, 1802. Near Dover

Inland, within a hollow vale, I stood;
And saw, while sea was calm and air was clear,
The coast of France – the coast of France how near!
Drawn almost into frightful neighbourhood.
I shrunk; for verily the barrier flood
Was like a lake, or river bright and fair,
A span of waters; yet what power is there!
What mightiness for evil and for good!
Even so doth God protect us if we be
10 Virtuous and wise. Winds blow, and waters roll,
Strength to the brave, and Power, and Deity;
Yet in themselves are nothing! One decree
Spake laws to *them*, and said that by the soul
Only, the Nations shall be great and free.

London, 1802

Milton! thou shouldst be living at this hour:
England hath need of thee: she is a fen
Of stagnant waters: altar, sword, and pen,
Fireside, the heroic wealth of hall and bower,
Have forfeited their ancient English dower
Of inward happiness. We are selfish men;
Oh! raise us up, return to us again;
And give us manners, virtue, freedom, power.
Thy soul was like a Star, and dwelt apart:
10 Thou hadst a voice whose sound was like the sea:
Pure as the naked heavens, majestic, free,
So didst thou travel on life's common way,
In cheerful godliness; and yet thy heart
The lowliest duties on herself did lay.

Written in London, September, 1802

O Friend! I know not which way I must look
For comfort, being, as I am, opprest,
To think that now our life is only drest
For show; mean handy-work of craftsman, cook,
Or groom! – We must run glittering like a brook
In the open sunshine, or we are unblest:
The wealthiest man among us is the best:
No grandeur now in nature or in book
Delights us. Rapine, avarice, expense,
10   This is idolatry; and these we adore:
Plain living and high thinking are no more:
The homely beauty of the good old cause
Is gone; our peace, our fearful innocence,
And pure religion breathing household laws.

'Nuns fret not at their convent's narrow room'

Nuns fret not at their convent's narrow room;
And hermits are contented with their cells;
And students with their pensive citadels;
Maids at the wheel, the weaver at his loom,
Sit blithe and happy; bees that soar for bloom,
High as the highest Peak of Furness-fells,
Will murmur by the hour in foxglove bells:
In truth the prison, unto which we doom
Ourselves, no prison is: and hence for me,
10   In sundry moods, 'twas pastime to be bound
Within the Sonnet's scanty plot of ground;
Pleased if some Souls (for such there needs must be)
Who have felt the weight of too much liberty,
Should find brief solace there, as I have found.

To the Men of Kent. October, 1803

Vanguard of Liberty, ye men of Kent,
Ye children of a Soil that doth advance
Her haughty brow against the coast of France,
Now is the time to prove your hardiment!
To France be words of invitation sent!
They from their fields can see the countenance
Of your fierce war, may ken the glittering lance
And hear you shouting forth your brave intent.
Left single, in bold parley, ye, of yore,
10 Did from the Norman win a gallant wreath;
Confirmed the charters that were yours before; –
No parleying now! In Britain is one breath;
We all are with you now from shore to shore: –
Ye men of Kent, 'tis victory or death!

Sonnet in the Pass of Killicranky

An invasion being expected, October, 1803.

Six thousand veterans practised in war's game,
Tried men, at Killicranky were arrayed
Against an equal host that wore the plaid,
Shepherds and herdsmen. – Like a whirlwind came
The Highlanders, the slaughter spread like flame;
And Garry, thundering down his mountain-road,
Was stopped, and could not breathe beneath the load
Of the dead bodies. – 'Twas a day of shame
For them whom precept and the pedantry
10 Of cold mechanic battle do enslave.
O for a single hour of that Dundee,
Who on that day the word of onset gave!
Like conquest would the Men of England see;
And her Foes find a like inglorious grave.

October, 1803

These times strike monied worldlings with dismay:
Even rich men, brave by nature, taint the air
With words of apprehension and despair:
While tens of thousands, thinking on the affray,
Men unto whom sufficient for the day
And minds not stinted or untilled are given,
Sound, healthy, children of the God of heaven,
Are cheerful as the rising sun in May.
What do we gather hence but firmer faith
10   That every gift of noble origin
Is breathed upon by Hope's perpetual breath;
That virtue and the faculties within
Are vital, – and that riches are akin
To fear, to change, to cowardice, and death?

Yarrow Unvisited

See the various Poems the scene of which is laid upon the banks of the
Yarrow; in particular, the exquisite Ballad of Hamilton beginning
'Busk ye, busk ye, my bonny, bonny Bride,
Busk ye, busk ye, my winsome Marrow!' –

From Stirling castle we had seen
The mazy Forth unravelled;
Had trod the banks of Clyde, and Tay,
And with the Tweed had travelled;
And when we came to Clovenford,
Then said my '*winsome Marrow*,'
'Whate'er betide, we'll turn aside,
And see the Braes of Yarrow.'

'Let Yarrow folk, *frae* Selkirk town,
10   Who have been buying, selling,
Go back to Yarrow, 'tis their own;
Each maiden to her dwelling!
On Yarrow's banks let herons feed,
Hares couch, and rabbits burrow!
But we will downward with the Tweed,
Nor turn aside to Yarrow.

'There's Galla Water, Leader Haughs,
Both lying right before us;
And Dryborough, where with chiming Tweed
20   The lintwhites sing in chorus;
There's pleasant Tiviot-dale, a land
Made blithe with plough and harrow:
Why throw away a needful day
To go in search of Yarrow?

'What's Yarrow but a river bare,
That glides the dark hills under?
There are a thousand such elsewhere
As worthy of your wonder.'
– Strange words they seemed of slight and scorn;
30   My True-love sighed for sorrow;
And looked me in the face, to think
I thus could speak of Yarrow!

'Oh! green,' said I, 'are Yarrow's holms,
And sweet is Yarrow flowing!
Fair hangs the apple frae the rock,
But we will leave it growing.
O'er hilly path, and open Strath,
We'll wander Scotland thorough;
But, though so near, we will not turn
40   Into the dale of Yarrow.

'Let beeves and home-bred kine partake
The sweets of Burn-mill meadow;
The swan on still St Mary's Lake
Float double, swan and shadow!
We will not see them; will not go,
Today, nor yet tomorrow;
Enough if in our hearts we know
There's such a place as Yarrow.

'Be Yarrow stream unseen, unknown!
50   It must, or we shall rue it:
We have a vision of our own;
Ah! why should we undo it?
The treasured dreams of times long past,
We'll keep them, winsome Marrow!
For when we're there, although 'tis fair,
'Twill be another Yarrow!

'If Care with freezing years should come,
And wandering seem but folly, –
Should we be loth to stir from home,
60   And yet be melancholy;
Should life be dull, and spirits low,
'Twill soothe us in our sorrow,
That earth hath something yet to show,
The bonny holms of Yarrow!'

The Pedlar and the Ruined Cottage (MS M)

'Twas summer and the sun was mounted high.
Travelling on foot, and distant from my home
Several days' journey, over the flat Plain
Of a bare Common I had toiled along
With languid steps; and when I stretched myself
On the brown earth my limbs from very heat
Could find no rest; nor my weak arm disperse
The host of insects gathering round my face.

The time was hot, the place was shelterless;
10   And, rising, right across the open Plain
On to the spot I hastened whither I
Was bound that morning, a small Group of Trees
Which midway on the Common stood alone.
I made no second stop, and soon had gained
The Port that lay before me full in view.
It was a knot of clustering Elms that sprang
As if from the same root, beneath whose shade
I found a Ruined House, four naked walls
That stared upon each other. Glad I was
20   And cast immediately my eyes about
In search of the Old Man whom I that morning
Had come to meet; this was the appointed place
And here he was upon the Cottage Bench
Lying within the shade, as if asleep;
An Iron-pointed Staff lay at his side.

   Him had I seen the day before – alone
And in the middle of the public way
Standing to rest himself. His eyes were turned
Towards the setting sun; while with that Staff
30   Behind him fixed he propped a long white Pack
Which crossed his shoulders, wares for them who live
In lonely villages or straggling huts.
At sight of one thus standing in the road,
With slackened footsteps I advanced, but soon
As I came up to him, great joy was ours
At such unthought-of meeting. For the night
We parted, nothing willingly, and now
He by appointment waited for me here
Beneath the shelter of these clustering elms.
40   We were dear Friends: I from my Childhood up
Had known him. In a little town obscure,
Or market village hidden in a tract
Of mountains where my school-boy days were passed
One Room he owned, the fifth part of a house,
A place to which he drew from time to time
And found a kind of home or harbour there.

- He loved me, from a swarm of rosy Boys
Singled out me, as he in sport would say,
For my grave looks, too thoughtful for my years.
50 Glad was I when he from his rounds returned:
As I grew up it was my best delight
To be his chosen comrade. Many a time
He made a holiday and left his Pack
Behind, and we two wandered through the Hills,
A Pair of random Travellers – we sate,
We walked; he pleased me with his sweet discourse
Of things which he had seen, and oft-times touched
Abstrusest matter, reasonings of the mind
Turned inwards, or, in other mood, he sang
60 Old songs, and sometimes, too, at my request
More solemn music, which he in his youth
Had learned, religious anthems, sounds sedate
And soft, and most refreshing to the heart.
    In that same Town of Hawkshead where we dwelt
There was a little Girl (and though, in truth,
This incident be something like a nook
Or pleasant corner which from my right path
Diverts me, yet I cannot pass it by),
There was a little Girl, ten years of age,
70 But tiny for her years, a pretty Dwarf,
Fair-haired, fair-faced, and, though of stature small,
In heart as forward as a lusty child.
This Girl, when from his travels he returned,
To his abiding-place would daily come
To play with the good Man, and he was wont
To tell her stories of his early life.
Nay, would she answer him, unsaying thus
All he had said to her, 'You never could
Be a poor ragged little Boy, and hired
80 By the poor Man you talk of to tend cattle
On a hill side, for forty pence a year.'
All which did to the Child appear so strange
She could not give it faith; and when she used
To doubt his words, as I remember well,

Spite of himself, the good Man smiled, and held
His hand up to his face to hide his smiles,
Because he knew that if the little Girl
Once spied them, she would then be sure, past doubt
That it was but a story framed in sport.
90   His History which he would thus in part
Tell to this Child I from himself have heard
Minutely, after I grew up, and he
Found in my heart, as he would kindly say,
A kindred heart to his. I was a Boy
When first he noticed me, and I began
To love him, and to seek him, and rejoice
In the plain presence of his dignity.
Oh! many are the Poets that are sown
By nature, men endued with highest gifts,
100   The vision and the faculty divine,
Yet wanting the accomplishment of verse
And never being led by accident
Or circumstance to take unto the height
By estimate comparative, at least,
The measure of themselves, live out their time
Husbanding that which they possess within
And go to the grave unthought of. Strongest minds
Are often those of which the noisy world
Hears least, else, surely, this Man had not left,
110   And sundry others, too, whom I have known,
His graces unrevealed and unproclaimed.
Though born in low estate, and earning bread
By a low calling, yet this very Man
Was as the prime and choice of sterling minds:
I honored him, respected, nay, revered.
And some small portion of his eloquent words,
The feeling pleasures of his loneliness,
And something that may serve to set in view
The doings, observations, which his life
120   Had dealt with, I will here record in verse.
     Among the Hills of Perthshire he was born:
His Father, he being yet an Infant, died
In poverty, and left three Sons behind.

The Mother married for a second Mate
A Schoolmaster, who taught the Boys to read
And brought them up, and gave them, as he could,
Needful instruction, shewing them the ways
Of honesty and holiness severe.
A virtuous household, though exceeding poor,
130 Pure livers were they all, austere and grave,
And fearing God, the very children taught
Stern self-respect, a reverence for God's word,
And piety scarce known on English Land.
    From his sixth year, the Boy of whom I speak
In summer tended cattle on the Hills,
But in the winter time he duly went
To his Step-father's School, that stood alone,
Sole Building on a Mountain's dreary edge,
Far from the sight of City Spire, or Sound
140 Of Minster Clock. From that bleak Tenement
He, many an evening, to his distant home
In solitude returning, saw the hills
Grow larger in the darkness, all alone
Beheld the stars come out above his head
And travelled through the wood with no one near
To whom he might confess the things he saw.
So the foundations of his mind were laid.
In such communion, not from terror free,
While yet a Child, and long before his time,
150 He had perceived the presence and the power
Of greatness, and deep feelings had impressed
Great objects on his mind, with portraiture
And colours so distinct that on his mind they lay
Like substances, and almost seemed
To haunt the bodily sense. He had received
(Vigorous in mind by nature, as he was)
A precious gift; for, as he grew in years,
With these impressions would he still compare
All his Remembrances, thoughts, shapes, and forms.

160   And being still unsatisfied with aught
       Of dimmer character, he thence attained
       An active power to fasten images
       Upon his brain, and on their pictured lines
       Intensely brooded, even till they acquired
       The liveliness of dreams. Nor did he fail,
       While yet a child, with a child's eagerness
       Incessantly to turn his ear and eye
       On all things which the moving seasons brought
       To feed such appetite: nor this alone
170   Appeased his yearning. In the after day
       Of boyhood, many an hour in caves forlorn,
       And in the hollow depths of naked crags
       He sate, and even in their fixed lineaments
       Or from the power of a peculiar eye,
       Or by creative feeling overborne,
       Or by predominance of thought oppressed,
       Even in their fixed and steady lineaments,
       He traced an ebbing and a flowing mind,
       Expression ever varying.
                          Thus informed
180   He had small need of books; for many a Tale
       Traditionary round the mountains hung:
       And many a legend peopling the dark woods
       Nourished Imagination in her growth
       And gave the mind that apprehensive power
       By which she is made quick to recognise
       The moral properties and scope of things.
       But greedily he read and read again
       Whate'er the Minister's old Shelf supplied,
       The life and death of Martyrs who sustained
190   Intolerable pangs, the Records left
       Of Persecution and the Covenant, times
       Whose echo rings through Scotland to this hour;
       Nor haply was there wanting here and there
       A straggling volume torn and incomplete
       That left half-told the preternatural Tale,

Romance of Giants, Chronicle of Fiends,
Profuse in garniture of wooden cuts,
Strange and uncouth, dire faces, figures dire,
Sharp-kneed, sharp-elbowed, and lean-ankled too,
200 With long and ghostly shanks, forms which once seen
Could never be forgotten.
                              In his heart
Where fear sate thus a cherished Visitant
A milder Spirit yet had found no place.
Love yet was wanting, the pure joy of love
By sound diffused, or by the breathing air,
Or by the silent looks of happy things,
Or flowing from the universal face
Of earth and sky. But he had felt the power
Of nature, and already was prepared
210 By his intense conceptions to receive
Deeply, the lesson deep of love, which he
Whom Nature, by whatever means, has taught
To feel intensely cannot but receive.
     From early childhood, even, as I have said,
From his sixth year, he had been sent abroad
In summer, to tend herds: such was his task
Henceforward till the later day of youth.
Oh! then what soul was his when on the tops
Of the high mountains he beheld the sun
220 Rise up, and bathe the world in light. He looked;
The ocean and the earth beneath him lay
In gladness and deep joy. The clouds were touched
And in their silent faces did he read
Unutterable love. Sound needed none,
Nor any voice of joy: his spirit drank
The spectacle; sensation, soul, and form
All melted into him; they swallowed up
His animal being: in them did he live,
And by them did he live: they were his life.
230 In such access of mind, in such high hour
Of visitation from the living God,
Thought was not. In enjoyment it expired.

No thanks he breathed, he proffered no request;
Rapt into still communion that transcends
The imperfect offices of prayer and praise,
His mind was a thanksgiving to the Power
That made him: it was blessedness and love.
A Herdsman on the lonely mountain tops,
Such intercourse was his, and in this sort
240   Was his existence oftentimes *possessed*.
Oh! then how beautiful, how bright appeared
The written Promise! He had early learned
To reverence the Volume which displays
The mystery, the life which cannot die:
But in the mountains did he *feel* his faith.
There did he see the writing. All things there
Breathed immortality, revolving life,
And greatness still revolving: infinite.
There littleness was not; the least of things
250   Seemed infinite, and there his spirit shaped
Her prospects, nor did he *believe* – he saw.
What wonder if his being thus became
Sublime and comprehensive! Low desires,
Low thoughts had there no place, yet was his mind
Lowly; for he was meek in gratitude
Oft as he called to mind those ecstasies
And whence they flowed, and from them he acquired
Wisdom which works through patience; thence he learned
In many a calmer hour of sober thought
260   To look on nature with an humble heart,
Self-questioned where it did not understand,
And with a superstitious eye of love.
    Thus passed the time; yet to the neighbouring Town
He often went with what small overplus
His earnings might supply, and brought away
The book which most had tempted his desires
While at the Stall he read. Among the hills
He gazed upon that mighty Orb of Song,
The divine Milton. Lore of different kind,
270   The annual savings of a toilsome life,
His Step-father supplied, books that explain

The purer elements of truth involved
In lines and numbers, and by charm severe
(Especially perceived where nature droops
And feeling is suppressed) preserve the mind
Busy in solitude and poverty.
And, thus employed, he many a time o'erlooked
The listless hours when in the hollow vale,
Hollow and green, he lay on the green turf
280 In pensive idleness. What could he do,
With blind endeavours, in that lonesome life
Thus thirsting daily? Yet, still uppermost,
Nature was at his heart, as if he felt,
Though yet he knew not how, a wasting power
In all things which from her sweet influence
Might tend to wean him. Therefore with her hues,
Her forms, and with the spirit of her forms,
He clothed the nakedness of austere truth.
While yet he lingered in the elements
290 Of science, and among her simplest laws,
His triangles they were the stars of Heaven,
The silent stars: oft did he take delight
To measure th'altitude of some tall crag
Which is the eagle's birth-place, or some peak
Familiar with forgotten years, which shews
Inscribed, as with the silence of the thought,
Upon its bleak and visionary sides
The history of many a winter storm,
Or obscure records of the path of fire.
300 And thus before his eighteenth year was gone
Accumulated feelings pressed his heart
With an encreasing weight: he was o'erpowered
By his own nature, by the turbulence
Of his own heart, by mystery, and hope,
And the first virgin passion of a mind
Communing with the glorious universe.
Full often wished he that the winds might rage
When they were silent; far more fondly now
Than in his earlier season did he love
310 Tempestuous nights, the uproar and the sounds
That live in darkness: from his intellect,

And from the stillness of abstracted thought,
He sought repose in vain. I have heard him say
That at this time he scanned the laws of light
Amid the roar of torrents, where they send
From hollow clefts up to the clearer air
A cloud of mist which in the shining sun
Varies its rainbow hues. But vainly thus,
And vainly by all other means he strove
320 To mitigate the fever of his heart.
  In dreams, in study, and in ardent thought,
Thus, even from childhood upward, was he reared,
Doubtless in want of much, yet gaining more,
Breathing a piercing air of poverty,
And drinking from the Well of homely life.
And now, brought near to manhood, he began
To think upon life's future course, and how
He best might earn his worldly maintenance.
His Mother strove to make her Son perceive
330 With what advantage he might teach a School
In the adjoining Village; but the Youth,
Who of this service made a short essay,
Found that the wanderings of his thought were then
A misery to him, that he must resign
A task he was unable to perform.
  He had a Brother elder than himself
Six years, who, long before, had left his home
To journey far and wide with Pedlar's Wares
In England, where he trafficked at that time,
340 Healthy and prosperous. 'What should hinder now,'
Said he within himself, 'but that I go
And toil in the same calling?' And, in truth,
This plan long time had been his favorite thought.
He asked his Mother's blessing, did with tears
Thank the good Man, his second Father, asked
From him paternal blessings, and set forth
A Traveller bound to England. The good Pair
Offered up prayers, and blessed him; but with hearts
Foreboding evil. From his native Hills
350 He wandered far: much did he see of men,

Their manners, their enjoyments and pursuits,
Their passions and their feelings, chiefly those
Essential and eternal in the heart,
Which, mid the simpler forms of rural life,
Exist more simple in their elements,
And speak a plainer language. In the woods,
A lone enthusiast, and among the fields,
Itinerant in this labour, he had passed
The better portion of his time; and there
360 From day to day had his affections breathed
The wholesome air of nature; there he kept,
In solitude and solitary thought,
His mind in a just equipoise of love.
Serene it was, unclouded by the cares
Of ordinary life, unvexed, unwarped
By partial bondage. In his steady course
No piteous revolutions had he felt,
No wild varieties of joy or grief;
Unoccupied by sorrow of its own
370 His heart lay open; and, by Nature tuned
And constant disposition of his thoughts
To sympathy with man, he was alive
To all that was enjoyed where'er he went
And all that was endured; and in himself
Happy, and quiet in his cheerfulness,
He had no painful pressure from without
Which made him turn aside from wretchedness
With coward fears. He could afford to suffer
With them whom he saw suffer. Hence it was
380 That in our best experience he was rich
And in the wisdom of our daily life:
For hence minutely in his various rounds
He had observed the progress and decay
Of many minds, of minds and bodies too,
The history of many families,
And how they prospered; how they were o'erthrown
By passion or mischance, or such misrule
Among the unthinking Masters of the earth

As makes the Nations groan. Untouched by taint
390   Of worldly mindedness or anxious care,
Observant, studious, thoughtful, and refreshed
By knowledge gathered up from day to day –
Thus had he lived a long and innocent life.
    The Scottish Church both on himself, and those
With whom from childhood he grew up, had held
The strong hand of her purity; and still
Had watched him with an unrelenting eye.
This he remembered in his riper years
With gratitude and reverential thoughts.
400   But by the native vigour of his mind,
By his habitual wanderings out of doors,
By loneliness, and goodness, and kind works,
Whatever in his childhood or in youth
He had imbibed of fear or darker thought
Was melted all away: so true was this
That sometimes his religion seemed to me
Self-taught, as of a dreamer of the woods.
– And surely never did there live on earth
A man of sweeter temper. Birds and beasts,
410   He loved them all, chickens and household dogs,
And to the kitten of a neighbour's house
Would carry crumbs and feed it. Poor and plain
Was his appearance, yet he was a man
Whom no one could have passed without remark.
Active and nervous was his gait; his limbs
And his whole figure breathed intelligence.
Age had compressed the freshness of his cheek
Into a narrower circle of deep red
But had not tamed his eye, which under brows,
420   Shaggy and grey, had meanings which it brought
From years of youth, which, like a being made
Of many beings he had wondrous skill
To blend with knowledge of the years to come,
Human, or such as lie beyond the grave.

Such was, in brief, the history of my Friend:
So was he framed. Now on the Bench he lay
And of his Pack of Merchandise had made
A pillow for his head: his eyes were shut;
The shadows of the breezy elms above
430   Dappled his face. He had not heard my steps
As I approached; and near him did I sit
Unnoticed in the shade some minute's space;
At length I hailed him, seeing that his hat
Was moist with water-drops, as if the brim
Had newly scooped a running stream. He rose,
And ere the pleasant greeting that ensued
Was ended, ''Tis a burning day,' said I,
'My lips are parched with thirst; but you, I guess
Have somewhere found relief.' He, at the word,
440   Pointing towards a sweet-briar, bade me climb
The fence hard by, where that tall, slender shrub
Looked out upon the road. It was a plot
Of garden-ground run wild, its matted weeds
Marked with the steps of those whom, as they passed,
The gooseberry trees that shot in long, lank slips
Or currants hanging from their leafless stems
In scanty strings, had tempted to o'erleap
The broken wall. I looked about, and there,
Where two tall hedge-rows of thick alder boughs
450   Joined in a damp cold nook, I found a Well,
Half covered up with willow flowers and grass;
My thirst I slaked, and from the cheerless spot
Withdrew, and while beside the shady Bench
I yet was standing with uncovered head,
Intent to catch the motion of the air,
The Old Man spake, 'I see around me here
Things which you cannot see: we die, my Friend,
Nor we alone, but that which each man loved
And prized in his peculiar nook of earth
460   Dies with him, or is changed; and very soon
Even of the good is no memorial left.
The Poets in their elegies and songs,
Lamenting the departed, call the groves,

They call upon the hills and streams to mourn
And senseless rocks; nor idly; for they speak
In these their invocations, with a voice
Obedient to the strong creative power
Of human passion. Sympathies there are
More tranquil, yet perhaps of kindred birth
470   That steal upon the meditative mind
And grow with thought. Beside yon Spring I stood,
And eyed its waters till we seemed to feel
One sadness, they and I. For them a bond
Of brotherhood is broken: time has been
When every day the touch of human hand
Dislodged the natural sleep that binds them up
In mortal stillness, and they ministered
To human comfort. When I stooped to drink,
Upon the slimy foot-stone I espied
480   The useless fragment of a wooden bowl;
Green with the moss of years, a sight it was;
It moved my heart, recalling former times
When I could never pass this road but she
Who lived within these walls, when I appeared,
A daughter's welcome gave me, and I loved her
As my own child. O Sir! the good die first,
And they whose hearts are dry as summer dust
Burn to the socket. Many a passenger
Hath blessed poor Margaret for her gentle looks
490   When she upheld the cool refreshment, drawn
From that forsaken Spring; and no one came
But he was welcome; no one went away
But that it seemed she loved him. She is dead,
Forgotten in the quiet of the grave.
    I speak of a poor Woman who dwelt here:
This Cottage was her home, and she the best
Of many thousands who are good and poor.
She was a Woman of a steady mind,
Tender and deep in her excess of love,
500   Not speaking much, pleased rather with the joy
Of her own thoughts: by some especial care
Her temper had been framed as if to make

A being, who by adding love to peace,
Might live on earth a life of happiness.
Her wedded Partner lacked not on his side
The humble worth that satisfied her heart:
Frugal, affectionate, sober, and therewith
Keenly industrious. I have heard her say
That he was up, and busy at his loom
510   In summer ere the mower was abroad
Among the grass, and oft in early spring
Ere the last star had vanished. – They who passed
At evening, from behind the garden fence
Might hear his busy spade, which he would ply
After his daily work, till the day-light
Was gone, and every leaf and flower were lost
In the dark hedges. So their days were spent
In peace and comfort, and a pretty Boy
Was their best hope, next to the God in Heaven.
520   Some twenty years ago, but you, I think,
Can scarcely bear it now in mind, there came
Two blighting seasons when the fields were left
With half a harvest. It pleased Heaven to add
A worse affliction in the plague of war:
A happy Land was stricken to the heart;
'Twas a sad time of sorrow and distress:
A wanderer among the cottages,
I, with my Pack of winter raiment, saw
The hardships of that season: many rich
530   Sank down, as in a dream, among the poor,
And of the poor did many cease to be
And their place knew them not. Meanwhile, abridged
Of daily comforts, gladly reconciled
To numerous self-denials, Margaret
Went struggling on through those calamitous years
With cheerful hope: but ere the second autumn
Her husband to a sick bed was confined
Labouring with perilous fever. In disease
He lingered long; and when his strength returned
540   He found the little he had stored to meet
The hour of accident or crippling age

Was all consumed. Two children had they now,
One newly born. As I have said, it was
A time of trouble; shoals of artisans
Were from their daily labour turned adrift
To seek their bread from public charity,
They and their wives and children, happier far
Could they have lived as do the little birds
That peck along the hedges, or the kite
550   That makes his dwelling on the mountain rocks.
    Ill fared it now with Robert, he who dwelt
Here in this Cottage. At his door he stood
And whistled many a snatch of merry tunes
That had no mirth in them; or with his knife
Carved uncouth figures on the heads of sticks,
Then idly sought about through every nook
In house or garden any casual work
Of use or ornament, and with a strange,
Amusing, but uneasy novelty
560   He blended, where he might, the various tasks
Of summer, autumn, winter, and of spring.
But this endured not; his good-humour soon
Became a weight in which no pleasure was
And poverty brought on a petted mood
And a sore temper: day by day he drooped,
And he would leave his home, and to the Town
Without an errand would direct his steps
Or wander here and there among the fields.
One while he would speak lightly of his Babes
570   And with a cruel tongue: at other times
He tossed them with a false unnatural joy
And 'twas a rueful thing to see the looks
Of the poor innocent Children. "Every smile,"
Said Margaret to me, here, beneath these trees,
"Made my heart bleed."'
                      At this the Old Man paused
And, looking up to those enormous Elms,
He said, "'Tis now the hour of deepest noon.
At this still season of repose and peace
This hour when all things which are not at rest

580 Are cheerful; while this multitude of flies
Is filling all the air with melody;
Why should a tear be in an old Man's eye?
Why should we thus with an untoward mind
And in the weakness of humanity,
From natural wisdom turn our hearts away,
To natural comfort shut our eyes and ears
And, feeding on disquiet, thus disturb
The calm of nature with our restless thoughts?'

He spake with somewhat of a solemn tone
590 But when he ended there was in his face
Such easy cheerfulness, a look so mild,
That for a little time it stole away
All recollection, and that simple Tale
Passed from my mind like a forgotten sound.
A while on trivial things we held discourse,
To me soon tasteless. In my own despite
I thought of that poor Woman as of one
Whom I had known and loved. He had rehearsed
Her homely Tale with such familiar power,
600 With such an active countenance, an eye
So busy, that the things of which he spake
Seemed present, and, attention now relaxed,
There was a heartfelt chillness in my veins.
I rose, and, turning from that breezy shade,
Went forth into the open air, and stood
To drink the comfort of the warmer sun.
Long time I had not stayed, ere, looking round
Upon that tranquil Ruin, I returned
And begged of the Old Man that for my sake
610 He would resume his story. He replied,
'It were a wantonness and would demand
Severe reproof if we were men whose hearts
Could hold vain dalliance with the misery
Even of the dead; contented thence to draw
A momentary pleasure, never marked
By reason, barren of all future good.

But we have known that there is often found
In mournful thoughts, and always might be found,
A power to virtue friendly; were't not so
620   I am a dreamer among men, indeed
An idle dreamer. 'Tis a common Tale,
An ordinary sorrow of man's life,
A tale of silent suffering, hardly clothed
In bodily form. But without further bidding
I will proceed.
　　　　　　　While thus it fared with them
To whom this Cottage till those hapless years
Had been a blessed home, it was my chance
To travel in a country far remote
And glad I was, when, halting by yon gate
630   That leads from the green lane, again I saw
These lofty Elm-trees. Long I did not rest:
With many pleasant thoughts I cheered my way
Over the flat Common. At the door arrived,
I knocked, and when I entered with the hope
Of usual greeting, Margaret looked at me
A little while, then turned her head away
Speechless, and sitting down upon a chair,
Wept bitterly. I wist not what to do
Or how to speak to her. Poor Wretch! at last
640   She rose from off her seat, and then, O Sir!
I cannot tell how she pronounced my name:
With fervent love, and with a face of grief
Unutterably helpless and a look
That seemed to cling upon me she inquired
If I had seen her Husband. As she spake
A strange surprise and fear came to my heart
Nor had I power to answer, ere she told
That he had disappeared just two months gone.
He left his house; two wretched days had passed
650   And on the third, by the first break of light
Within her casement full in view she saw
A letter, such it seemed, which she forthwith
Opened and found no writing, but therein
Pieces of money carefully wrapped up,

Silver and gold. "I trembled at the sight,"
Said Margaret, "for I knew it was his hand
Which placed it there; and on that very day,
By one who from my Husband had been sent,
The tidings came that he had joined a Troop
660   Of Soldiers going to a distant Land.
He left me thus – Poor Man! he had not heart
To take a farewell of me; and he feared
That I should follow with my Babes, and sink
Beneath the misery of that wandering life."
      This Tale did Margaret tell with many tears
And when she ended I had little power
To give her comfort, and was glad to take
Such words of hope from her own mouth as served
To cheer us both: but long she had not talked
670   Ere we built up a pile of better thoughts,
And with a brighter eye she looked around
As if she had been shedding tears of joy.
We parted. It was then the early spring;
I left her busy with her garden tools;
And well remember, o'er that fence she looked
And, while I paced along the foot-way path,
Called out; and sent a blessing after me
With tender cheerfulness, and with a voice
That seemed the very sound of happy thoughts.
680   I roved o'er many a hill, and many a dale
With this my weary load, in heat and cold,
Through many a wood, and many an open ground,
In sunshine, or in shade, in wet or fair,
Drooping, or blithe of heart, as might befall,
My best companions now the driving winds
And now the 'trotting brooks,' and whispering trees,
And now the music of my own sad steps,
With many a short-lived thought that passed between
And disappeared. I came this way again
690   Towards the wane of summer, when the wheat
Was yellow and the soft and bladed grass
Sprang up afresh, and o'er the hay-field spread
Its tender green. When I had reached the door

I found that she was absent. In the shade
Where now we sit, I waited her return.
Her Cottage wore its customary look,
As cheerful as before; but that I thought
The honeysuckle crowded round the door
And from the wall hung down in heavier tufts,
700   And knots of worthless stonecrop started out
Along the window's edge and grew like weeds
Against the lower panes. I turned aside
And strolled into her garden. It appeared
To lag behind the season, and had lost
Its pride of neatness. From the border lines
Composed of daisy and resplendent thrift,
Flowers straggling forth had on those paths encroached
Which they were used to deck: Carnations, once
Prized for surpassing beauty, and no less
710   For that peculiar pain they had required,
Hung down their languished heads without support.
The cumbrous bindweed with its wreaths and bells
Had twined about her two small rows of peas
And dragged them to the earth. Ere this an hour
Was wasted. Back I turned my restless steps
And, as I walked before the door it chanced
A Stranger passed, and guessing whom I sought
He said that she was used to ramble far.
The sun was sinking in the west; and now
720   I sate with sad impatience. From within
Her solitary Infant cried aloud.
The spot, though fair, seemed very desolate.
The longer I remained more desolate.
And, looking round, I saw the corner stones,
Till then unnoticed, on either side the door
With dull red stains discoloured, and stuck o'er
With tufts and hairs of wool, as if the sheep
That fed upon the Common thither came
Familiarly, and found a couching-place
730   Even at her threshold. The house-clock struck eight;
I turned, and saw her distant a few steps.
Her face was pale and thin, her figure too

Was changed. As she unlocked the door, she said,
"It grieves me you have waited here so long
But, in good truth, I've wandered much of late
And sometimes, to my shame I speak, have need
Of my best prayers to bring me back again."
While on the board she spread our evening meal
She told me, she had lost her elder Child,
740   That he, for months, had been a Serving-boy
Apprenticed by the Parish. "I perceive
You look at me, and you have cause. Today
I have been travelling far, and many days
About the fields I wander, knowing this
Only, that what I seek I cannot find.
And so I waste my time: for I am changed
And to myself," said she, "have done much wrong,
And to this helpless Infant. I have slept
Weeping, and weeping I have waked; my tears
750   Have flowed as if my body were not such
As others are, and I could never die.
But I am now in mind and in my heart
More easy, and I hope," said she, "that Heaven
Will give me patience to endure the things
Which I behold at home." It would have grieved
Your very soul to see her. Sir, I feel
The story linger in my heart; I fear
'Tis long and tedious, but my spirit clings
To that poor Woman: so familiarly
760   Do I perceive her manner and her look
And presence, and so deeply do I feel
Her goodness, that, not seldom, in my walks
A momentary trance comes over me
And to myself I seem to muse on one
By sorrow laid asleep, or borne away,
A human being destined to awake
To human life, or something very near
To human life, when he shall come again
For whom she suffered. Sir, it would have grieved
770   Your very soul to see her: evermore
Her eyelids drooped, her eyes were downward cast;

And when she at her table gave me food
She did not look at me. Her voice was low,
Her body was subdued. In every act
Pertaining to her house affairs appeared
The careless stillness of a thinking mind,
Self-occupied, to which all outward things
Are like an idle matter. Still she sighed,
But yet no motion of the breast was seen,
780   No heaving of the heart. While by the fire
We sate together sighs came on my ear,
I knew not how, and hardly whence they came.
I gave her for her Son, the Parish Boy,
A kerchief and a book wherewith she seemed
Pleased; and I counselled her to have her trust
In God's good love, and seek his help by prayer.
I took my Staff and when I kissed her Babe,
The tears stood in her eyes. I left her then
With the best hope and comfort I could give;
790   She thanked me for my will, but for my hope
It seemed she did not thank me.
                                    I returned
And took my rounds along this road again
Ere on its sunny bank the primrose flower
Peeped forth to give an earnest of the spring.
I found her sad and drooping; she had learned
No tidings of her Husband: if he lived
She knew not that he lived; if he were dead
She knew not he was dead. She seemed the same
In person and appearance; but her house
800   Bespake a sleepy hand of negligence;
The floor was neither dry nor neat, the hearth
Was comfortless, and her small lot of books,
Which, one upon the other, heretofore
Had been piled up against the corner panes
In seemly order, now, with straggling leaves
Lay scattered here and there, open or shut
As they had chanced to fall. Her Infant Babe
Had from its Mother caught the trick of grief
And sighed among its playthings. Once again

810   I turned towards the garden gate, and saw
       More plainly still that poverty and grief
       Were now come nearer to her; the earth was hard,
       With weeds defaced and knots of withered grass;
       No ridges there appeared of clear black mould,
       No winter greenness; of her herbs and flowers
       It seemed the better part were gnawed away
       Or trampled on the earth; a chain of straw,
       Which had been twisted round the slender stem
       Of a young apple-tree, lay at its root;
820   The bark was nibbled round by truant sheep.
       Margaret stood near, her Infant in her arms,
       And, seeing that my eye was on the tree,
       She said, "I fear it will be dead and gone
       Ere Robert come again." Towards the House
       Together we returned, and she inquired
       If I had any hope. But for her Babe,
       And for her little friendless Boy, she said
       She had no wish to live, that she must die
       Of sorrow. Yet I saw the idle loom
830   Still in its place. His Sunday garments hung
       Upon the self-same nail; his very Staff
       Stood undisturbed behind the door. And when
       This way the ensuing winter I returned,
       She told me that her little Babe was dead
       And she was left alone. She now, I learned,
       After her Infant's death had taken up
       The employment common through these parts, and gained,
       By spinning hemp, a pittance for herself
       And, for that end, had hired a neighbour's boy
840   To help her in her work. That very time
       Most willingly she put her work aside,
       And walked with me a mile, and, in such sort
       That any heart had ached to hear her, begged
       That, wheresoe'er I went, I still would ask
       For him whom she had lost. We parted then,
       Our final parting; for, from that time forth,
       Did many seasons pass ere I returned
       Into this tract again.

                            Nine tedious years,
            From their first separation, nine long years,
850   She lingered in unquiet widowhood,
            A Wife and Widow. Needs must it have been
            A sore heart-wasting. I have heard, my Friend,
            That in yon broken arbour she would sit
            The idle length of half a sabbath day
            And, when a dog passed by she still would quit
            The shade, and look abroad. On this old Bench
            For hours she sate; and evermore her eye
            Was busy in the distance, shaping things
            That made her heart beat quick. You see that Path,
860   Now faint? The grass has crept o'er its grey line;
            There to and fro she paced through many a day
            Of the warm summer; from a belt of hemp
            That girt her waist spinning the long-drawn thread
            With backward steps. Yet, ever as there passed
            A Man whose garments shewed the Soldier's red,
            Or crippled Mendicant in Sailor's garb
            The little Child who sate to turn the wheel
            Ceased from his task, and she with faltering voice
            Expecting still to hear her Husband's fate,
870   Made many a fond inquiry; and when they
            Whose presence gave no comfort were gone by,
            Her heart was still more sad. And by yon Gate
            That bars the Traveller's road she often stood,
            And, when a Stranger Horseman came, the latch
            Would lift, and in his face look wistfully,
            Most happy if from aught discovered there
            Of tender feeling she might dare repeat
            The same sad question. Meanwhile her poor Hut
            Sank to decay: for he was gone whose hand,
880   At the first nippings of October frost,
            Closed up each chink, and with fresh bands of straw
            Chequered the green-grown thatch. And so she lived
            Through the long winter, reckless and alone,
            Until her House by frost, and thaw and rain
            Was sapped; and when she slept, the nightly damps
            Did chill her breast; and, in the stormy day,

Her tattered clothes were ruffled by the wind
Even at the side of her own fire. Yet still
She loved this wretched spot nor would for worlds
890   Have parted hence; and still that length of road,
And this rude Bench one torturing hope endeared
Fast rooted at her heart; and here, my Friend,
In sickness she remained, and here she died,
Last human tenant of these ruined Walls.'
     The Old Man ceased: he saw that I was moved;
From that low Bench rising instinctively,
I turned aside in weakness, nor had power
To thank him for the Tale which he had told.
I stood, and leaning o'er the Garden wall
900   Reviewed that Woman's sufferings, and it seemed
To comfort me while with a Brother's love
I blessed her in the impotence of grief.
At length towards the Cottage I returned
Fondly, and traced with interest more mild
That secret spirit of humanity,
Which, mid the calm oblivious tendencies
Of Nature, mid her plants, and weeds, and flowers
And silent overgrowings still survived.
The Old Man noting this, resumed, and said,
910   'My Friend, enough to sorrow have you given,
The purposes of wisdom ask no more;
Be wise and cheerful, and no longer read
The forms of things with an unworthy eye.
She sleeps in the calm earth, and peace is here,
I well remember that those very plumes,
Those weeds, and the high spear grass on that wall,
By mist and silent rain-drops silvered o'er,
As once I passed did to my heart convey
So still an image of tranquillity,
920   So calm and still, and looked so beautiful
Amid the uneasy thoughts which filled my mind
That what we feel of sorrow and despair
From ruin and from change, and all the grief
The passing shows of being leave behind
Appeared an idle dream that could not live

Where meditation was: I turned away
And walked along my road in happiness.'
   He ceased. Ere long, the sun, declining, shot
A slant and mellow radiance which began
930 To fall upon us where beneath the trees
We sate on that low Bench: and now we felt,
Admonished thus, the sweet hour coming on.
A linnet warbled from those lofty Elms,
A thrush sang loud, and other melodies,
At distance heard, peopled the milder air.
The Old Man rose, and lifted up his load;
Together, casting then a farewell look
Upon those silent Walls, we left the shade
And, ere the stars were visible, had reached
940 A Village Inn – our Evening resting-place.

'She was a Phantom of delight'

She was a Phantom of delight
When first she gleamed upon my sight;
A lovely Apparition, sent
To be a moment's ornament;
Her eyes as stars of Twilight fair;
Like Twilight's, too, her dusky hair;
But all things else about her drawn
From May-time and the cheerful Dawn;
A dancing Shape, an Image gay,
10 To haunt, to startle, and way-lay.

I saw her upon nearer view,
A Spirit, yet a Woman too!
Her household motions light and free,
And steps of virgin-liberty;
A countenance in which did meet
Sweet records, promises as sweet;
A Creature not too bright or good
For human nature's daily food;
For transient sorrows, simple wiles,
20 Praise, blame, love, kisses, tears, and smiles.

And now I see with eye serene
The very pulse of the machine;
A Being breathing thoughtful breath,
A Traveller between life and death;
The reason firm, the temperate will,
Endurance, foresight, strength, and skill;
A perfect Woman, nobly planned,
To warn, to comfort, and command;
And yet a Spirit still, and bright
30   With something of angelic light.

The Small Celandine

There is a Flower, the lesser Celandine,
That shrinks, like many more, from cold and rain;
And, the first moment that the sun may shine,
Bright as the sun himself, 'tis out again!

When hailstones have been falling, swarm on swarm,
Or blasts the green field and the trees distrest,
Oft have I seen it muffled up from harm,
In close self-shelter, like a Thing at rest.

But lately, one rough day, this Flower I passed
10   And recognized it, though an altered form,
Now standing forth an offering to the blast,
And buffeted at will by rain and storm.

I stopped, and said with inly-muttered voice,
'It doth not love the shower, nor seek the cold:
This neither is its courage nor its choice,
But its necessity in being old.

'The sunshine may not cheer it, nor the dew;
It cannot help itself in its decay;
Stiff in its members, withered, changed of hue.'
20   And, in my spleen, I smiled that it was grey.

To be a Prodigal's Favourite – then, worse truth,
A Miser's Pensioner – behold our lot!
O Man, that from thy fair and shining youth
Age might but take the things Youth needed not!

Ode to Duty

'Jam non consilio bonus, sed more eò perductus, ut non tantum
rectè facere possim, sed nisi rectè facere non possim.'

Stern Daughter of the Voice of God!
O Duty! if that name thou love
Who art a light to guide, a rod
To check the erring, and reprove;
Thou, who art victory and law
When empty terrors overawe;
From vain temptations dost set free;
And calm'st the weary strife of frail humanity!

There are who ask not if thine eye
10 Be on them; who, in love and truth,
Where no misgiving is, rely
Upon the genial sense of youth:
Glad Hearts! without reproach or blot;
Who do thy work, and know it not:
Oh! if through confidence misplaced
They fail, thy saving arms, dread Power! around them cast.

Serene will be our days and bright,
And happy will our nature be,
When love is an unerring light,
20 And joy its own security.
And they a blissful course may hold
Even now, who, not unwisely bold,
Live in the spirit of this creed;
Yet seek thy firm support, according to their need.

I, loving freedom, and untried;
No sport of every random gust,
Yet being to myself a guide,
Too blindly have reposed my trust:
And oft, when in my heart was heard
30   Thy timely mandate, I deferred
The task, in smoother walks to stray;
But thee I now would serve more strictly, if I may.

Through no disturbance of my soul,
Or strong compunction in me wrought,
I supplicate for thy control;
But in the quietness of thought:
Me this unchartered freedom tires;
I feel the weight of chance-desires:
My hopes no more must change their name,
40   I long for a repose that ever is the same.

[Yet not the less would I throughout
Still act according to the voice
Of my own wish; and feel past doubt
That my submissiveness was choice:
Not seeking in the school of pride
For 'precepts over dignified',
Denial and restraint I prize
No farther than they breed a second Will more wise.]

Stern Lawgiver! yet thou dost wear
50   The Godhead's most benignant grace;
Nor know we anything so fair
As is the smile upon thy face:
Flowers laugh before thee on their beds
And fragrance in thy footing treads;
Thou dost preserve the stars from wrong;
And the most ancient heavens, through Thee, are fresh and
        strong.

To humbler functions, awful Power!
I call thee: I myself commend
Unto thy guidance from this hour;
60   Oh, let my weakness have an end!
Give unto me, made lowly wise,
The spirit of self-sacrifice;
The confidence of reason give;
And in the light of truth thy Bondman let me live!

'I wandered lonely as a cloud'

I wandered lonely as a cloud
That floats on high o'er vales and hills,
When all at once I saw a crowd,
A host, of golden daffodils;
Beside the lake, beneath the trees,
Fluttering and dancing in the breeze.

Continuous as the stars that shine
And twinkle on the milky way,
They stretched in never-ending line
10   Along the margin of a bay:
Ten thousand saw I at a glance,
Tossing their heads in sprightly dance.

The waves beside them danced; but they
Out-did the sparkling waves in glee:
A poet could not but be gay,
In such a jocund company:
I gazed – and gazed – but little thought
What wealth the show to me had brought:

For oft, when on my couch I lie
20   In vacant or in pensive mood,
They flash upon that inward eye
Which is the bliss of solitude;
And then my heart with pleasure fills,
And dances with the daffodils.

Yew-Trees

There is a Yew-tree, pride of Lorton Vale,
Which to this day stands single, in the midst
Of its own darkness, as it stood of yore:
Not loth to furnish weapons for the bands
Of Umfraville or Percy ere they marched
To Scotland's heaths; or those that crossed the sea
And drew their sounding bows at Azincour,
Perhaps at earlier Crecy, or Poictiers.
Of vast circumference and gloom profound
10   This solitary Tree! a living thing
Produced too slowly ever to decay;
Of form and aspect too magnificent
To be destroyed. But worthier still of note
Are those fraternal Four of Borrowdale,
Joined in one solemn and capacious grove;
Huge trunks! and each particular trunk a growth
Of intertwisted fibres serpentine
Up-coiling, and inveterately convolved;
Nor uninformed with Phantasy, and looks
20   That threaten the profane; – a pillared shade,
Upon whose grassless floor of red-brown hue,
By sheddings from the pining umbrage tinged
Perennially – beneath whose sable roof
Of boughs, as if for festal purpose, decked
With unrejoicing berries – ghostly Shapes
May meet at noontide; Fear and trembling Hope,
Silence and Foresight; Death the Skeleton
And Time the Shadow; – there to celebrate,
As in a natural temple scattered o'er
30   With altars undisturbed of mossy stone,
United worship; or in mute repose
To lie, and listen to the mountain flood
Murmuring from Glaramara's inmost caves.

Elegiac Stanzas Suggested by a Picture
Castle, in a Storm, Painted by Sir George Beaumont

I was thy neighbour once, thou rugged Pile!
Four summer weeks I dwelt in sight of thee:
I saw thee every day; and all the while
Thy Form was sleeping on a glassy sea.

So pure the sky, so quiet was the air!
So like, so very like, was day to day!
Whene'er I looked, thy Image still was there;
It trembled, but it never passed away.

How perfect was the calm! it seemed no sleep;
10 No mood, which season takes away, or brings:
I could have fancied that the mighty Deep
Was even the gentlest of all gentle Things.

Ah! THEN, if mine had been the Painter's hand,
To express what then I saw; and add the gleam,
The light that never was, on sea or land,
The consecration, and the Poet's dream;

I would have planted thee, thou hoary Pile
Amid a world how different from this!
Beside a sea that could not cease to smile;
20 On tranquil land, beneath a sky of bliss.

Thou shouldst have seemed a treasure-house divine
Of peaceful years; a chronicle of heaven; –
Of all the sunbeams that did ever shine
The very sweetest had to thee been given.

A Picture had it been of lasting ease,
Elysian quiet, without toil or strife;
No motion but the moving tide, a breeze,
Or merely silent Nature's breathing life.

Such, in the fond illusion of my heart,
30 Such Picture would I at that time have made:
And seen the soul of truth in every part,
A steadfast peace that might not be betrayed.

So once it would have been, – 'tis so no more;
I have submitted to a new control:
A power is gone, which nothing can restore;
A deep distress hath humanized my Soul.

Not for a moment could I now behold
A smiling sea, and be what I have been:
The feeling of my loss will ne'er be old;
40   This, which I know, I speak with mind serene.

Then, Beaumont, Friend! who would have been the
            Friend,
If he had lived, of Him whom I deplore,
This work of thine I blame not, but commend;
This sea in anger, and that dismal shore.

O 'tis a passionate Work! – yet wise and well,
Well chosen is the spirit that is here;
That Hulk which labours in the deadly swell,
This rueful sky, this pageantry of fear!

And this huge Castle, standing here sublime,
50   I love to see the look with which it braves,
Cased in the unfeeling armour of old time,
The lightning, the fierce wind, and trampling waves.

Farewell, farewell the heart that lives alone,
Housed in a dream, at distance from the Kind!
Such happiness, wherever it be known,
Is to be pitied; for 'tis surely blind.

But welcome fortitude, and patient cheer,
And frequent sights of what is to be borne!
Such sights, or worse, as are before me here. –
60   Not without hope we suffer and we mourn.

Stepping Westward

While my Fellow-traveller and I were walking by the side of Loch
Ketterine, one fine evening after sunset, in our road to a hut where, in
the course of our Tour, we had been hospitably entertained some
weeks before, we met, in one of the loneliest parts of that solitary
region, two well-dressed Women, one of whom said to us, by way of
greeting, 'What, you are stepping westward?'

'*What, you are stepping westward?*' – '*Yea.*'
– 'Twould be a *wildish* destiny,
If we, who thus together roam
In a strange Land, and far from home,
Were in this place the guests of Chance:
Yet who would stop, or fear to advance,
Though home or shelter he had none,
With such a sky to lead him on?

The dewy ground was dark and cold;
10 Behind, all gloomy to behold;
And stepping westward seemed to be
A kind of *heavenly* destiny:
I liked the greeting; 'twas a sound
Of something without place or bound;
And seemed to give me spiritual right
To travel through that region bright.

The voice was soft, and she who spake
Was walking by her native lake:
The salutation had to me
20 The very sound of courtesy:
Its power was felt; and while my eye
Was fixed upon the glowing Sky,
The echo of the voice enwrought
A human sweetness with the thought
Of travelling through the world that lay
Before me in my endless way.

The Solitary Reaper

Behold her, single in the field,
Yon solitary Highland Lass!
Reaping and singing by herself;
Stop here, or gently pass!
Alone she cuts and binds the grain,
And sings a melancholy strain;
O listen! for the Vale profound
Is overflowing with the sound.

No Nightingale did ever chaunt
10   More welcome notes to weary bands
Of travellers in some shady haunt,
Among Arabian sands:
A voice so thrilling ne'er was heard
In spring-time from the Cuckoo-bird,
Breaking the silence of the seas
Among the farthest Hebrides.

Will no one tell me what she sings? –
Perhaps the plaintive numbers flow
For old, unhappy, far-off things,
20   And battles long ago:
Or is it some more humble lay,
Familiar matter of today?
Some natural sorrow, loss, or pain,
That has been, and may be again?

Whate'er the theme, the Maiden sang
As if her song could have no ending;
I saw her singing at her work,
And o'er the sickle bending; –
I listened, motionless and still;
30   And, as I mounted up the hill,
The music in my heart I bore,
Long after it was heard no more.

Character of the Happy Warrior

Who is the happy Warrior? Who is he
That every man in arms should wish to be?
– It is the generous Spirit, who, when brought
Among the tasks of real life, hath wrought
Upon the plan that pleased his boyish thought:
Whose high endeavours are an inward light
That makes the path before him always bright:
Who, with a natural instinct to discern
What knowledge can perform, is diligent to learn;
10 Abides by this resolve, and stops not there,
But makes his moral being his prime care;
Who, doomed to go in company with Pain,
And Fear, and Bloodshed, miserable train!
Turns his necessity to glorious gain;
In face of these doth exercise a power
Which is our human nature's highest dower;
Controls them and subdues, transmutes, bereaves
Of their bad influence, and their good receives:
By objects, which might force the soul to abate
20 Her feeling, rendered more compassionate;
Is placable – because occasions rise
So often that demand such sacrifice;
More skilful in self-knowledge, even more pure,
As tempted more; more able to endure,
As more exposed to suffering and distress;
Thence, also, more alive to tenderness.
– 'Tis he whose law is reason; who depends
Upon that law as on the best of friends;
Whence, in a state where men are tempted still
30 To evil for a guard against worse ill,
And what in quality or act is best
Doth seldom on a right foundation rest,
He labours good on good to fix, and owes
To virtue every triumph that he knows:
– Who, if he rise to station of command,
Rises by open means; and there will stand

On honourable terms, or else retire,
And in himself possess his own desire;
Who comprehends his trust, and to the same
40   Keeps faithful with a singleness of aim;
And therefore does not stoop, nor lie in wait
For wealth, or honours, or for worldly state;
Whom they must follow; on whose head must fall,
Like showers of manna, if they come at all:
Whose powers shed round him in the common strife,
Or mild concerns of ordinary life,
A constant influence, a peculiar grace;
But who, if he be called upon to face
Some awful moment to which Heaven has joined
50   Great issues, good or bad for human kind,
Is happy as a Lover; and attired
With sudden brightness, like a Man inspired;
And, through the heat of conflict, keeps the law
In calmness made, and sees what he foresaw;
Or if an unexpected call succeed,
Come when it will, is equal to the need:
– He who, though thus endued as with a sense
And faculty for storm and turbulence,
Is yet a Soul whose master-bias leans
60   To homefelt pleasures and to gentle scenes;
Sweet images! which, whereso'er he be,
Are at his heart; and such fidelity
It is his darling passion to approve;
More brave for this, that he hath much to love: –
'Tis, finally, the Man, who, lifted high,
Conspicuous object in a Nation's eye,
Or left unthought-of in obscurity, –
Who, with a toward or untoward lot,
Prosperous or adverse, to his wish or not –
70   Plays, in the many games of life, that one
Where what he most doth value must be won:
Whom neither shape of danger can dismay,
Nor thought of tender happiness betray;

Who, not content that former worth stand fast,
Looks forward, persevering to the last,
From well to better, daily self-surpast:
Who, whether praise of him must walk the earth
For ever, and to noble deeds give birth,
Or he must fall, to sleep without his fame,
80 And leave a dead unprofitable name –
Finds comfort in himself and in his cause;
And, while the mortal mist is gathering, draws
His breath in confidence of Heaven's applause:
This is the happy Warrior; this is He
That every Man in arms should wish to be.

The Waggoner

'In Cairo's crowded streets
The impatient Merchant, wondering, waits in vain,
And Mecca saddens at the long delay.'   THOMSON.

TO CHARLES LAMB, ESQ.
MY DEAR FRIEND,
    When I sent you, a few weeks ago, the Tale of Peter Bell, you asked 'why THE WAGGONER was not added?' – To say the truth, – from the higher tone of imagination, and the deeper touches of passion aimed at in the former, I apprehended this little Piece could not accompany it without disadvantage. In the year 1806, if I am not mistaken, THE WAGGONER was read to you in manuscript, and, as you have remembered it for so long a time, I am the more encouraged to hope that, since the localities on which the Poem partly depends did not prevent its being interesting to you, it may prove acceptable to others. Being therefore in some measure the cause of its present appearance, you must allow me the gratification of inscribing it to you; in acknowledgement of the pleasure I have derived from your Writings, and of the high esteem with which

                                        I am very truly yours,
                                        WILLIAM WORDSWORTH.

RYDAL MOUNT, *May 20, 1819*

CANTO FIRST

'Tis spent – this burning day of June!
Soft darkness o'er its latest gleams is stealing;
The buzzing dor-hawk, round and round, is wheeling, –
That solitary bird
Is all that can be heard
In silence deeper far than that of deepest noon!

   Confiding Glow-worms, 'tis a night
Propitious to your earth-born light!
But, where the scattered stars are seen
In hazy straits the clouds between,
Each, in his station twinkling not,
Seems changed into a pallid spot.
The mountains against heaven's grave weight
Rise up, and grow to wondrous height.
The air, as in a lion's den,
Is close and hot; – and now and then
Comes a tired and sultry breeze
With a haunting and a panting,
Like the stifling of disease;
But the dews allay the heat,
And the silence makes it sweet.

   Hush, there is someone on the stir!
'Tis Benjamin the Waggoner;
Who long hath trod this toilsome way,
Companion of the night and day.
That far-off tinkling's drowsy cheer,
Mixed with a faint yet grating sound
In a moment lost and found,
The Wain announces – by whose side
Along the banks of Rydal Mere
He paces on, a trusty Guide, –
Listen! you can scarcely hear!
Hither he his course is bending; –
Now he leaves the lower ground,
And up the craggy hill ascending

Many a stop and stay he makes,
Many a breathing-fit he takes; –
Steep the way and wearisome,
Yet all the while his whip is dumb!

40   The Horses have worked with right good-will,
And so have gained the top of the hill;
He was patient, they were strong,
And now they smoothly glide along,
Recovering breath, and pleased to win
The praises of mild Benjamin.
Heaven shield him from mishap and snare!
But why so early with this prayer?
Is it for threatenings in the sky?
Or for some other danger nigh?
50 No; none is near him yet, though he
Be one of much infirmity;
For at the bottom of the brow,
Where once the DOVE and OLIVE-BOUGH
Offered a greeting of good ale
To all who entered Grasmere Vale;
And called on him who must depart
To leave it with a jovial heart;
There, where the DOVE and OLIVE-BOUGH
Once hung, a Poet harbours now,
60 A simple water-drinking Bard;
Why need our Hero then (though frail
His best resolves) be on his guard?
He marches by, secure and bold;
Yet while he thinks on times of old,
It seems that all looks wondrous cold;
He shrugs his shoulders, shakes his head,
And, for the honest folk within,
It is a doubt with Benjamin
Whether they be alive or dead!

70   *Here* is no danger, – none at all!
Beyond his wish he walks secure;
But pass a mile – and *then* for trial, –
Then for the pride of self-denial;

If he resist that tempting door,
Which with such friendly voice will call;
If he resist those casement panes,
And that bright gleam which thence will fall
Upon his Leaders' bells and manes,
Inviting him with cheerful lure:
80   For still, though all be dark elsewhere,
Some shining notice will be *there*,
Of open house and ready fare.

   The place to Benjamin right well
Is known, and by as strong a spell
As used to be that sign of love
And hope – the OLIVE-BOUGH and DOVE;
He knows it to his cost, good Man!
Who does not know the famous SWAN?
Object uncouth! and yet our boast,
90   For it was painted by the Host;
His own conceit the figure planned,
'Twas coloured all by his own hand;
And that frail Child of thirsty clay,
Of whom I sing this rustic lay,
Could tell with self-dissatisfaction
Quaint stories of the bird's attraction!

   Well! that is past – and in despite
Of open door and shining light.
And now the conqueror essays
100   The long ascent of Dunmail-raise;
And with his team is gentle here
As when he clomb from Rydal Mere;
His whip they do not dread – his voice
They only hear it to rejoice.
To stand or go is at *their* pleasure;
Their efforts and their time they measure
By generous pride within the breast;
And, while they strain, and while they rest,
He thus pursues his thoughts at leisure.

110   Now am I fairly safe tonight –
        And with proud cause my heart is light:
        I trespassed lately worse than ever –
        But Heaven has blest a good endeavour;
        And, to my soul's content, I find
        The evil One is left behind.
        Yes, let my master fume and fret,
        Here am I – with my horses yet!
        My jolly team, he finds that ye
        Will work for nobody but me!
120   Full proof of this the Country gained;
        It knows how ye were vexed and strained,
        And forced unworthy stripes to bear,
        When trusted to another's care.
        Here was it – on this rugged slope,
        Which now ye climb with heart and hope,
        I saw you, between rage and fear,
        Plunge, and fling back a spiteful ear,
        And ever more and more confused,
        As ye were more and more abused:
130   As chance would have it, passing by
        I saw you in that jeopardy:
        A word from me was like a charm;
        Ye pulled together with one mind;
        And your huge burden, safe from harm,
        Moved like a vessel in the wind!
        – Yes, without me, up hills so high
        'Tis vain to strive for mastery.
        Then grieve not, jolly team! though tough
        The road we travel, steep, and rough;
140   Though Rydal-heights and Dunmail-raise,
        And all their fellow banks and braes,
        Full often make you stretch and strain,
        And halt for breath and halt again,
        Yet to their sturdiness 'tis owing
        That side by side we still are going!

While Benjamin in earnest mood
His meditations thus pursued,
A storm, which had been smothered long,
Was growing inwardly more strong;
150   And, in its struggles to get free,
Was busily employed as he.
The thunder had begun to growl –
He heard not, too intent of soul;
The air was now without a breath –
He marked not that 'twas still as death.
But soon large rain-drops on his head
Fell with the weight of drops of lead; –
He starts – and takes, at the admonition,
A sage survey of his condition.
160   The road is black before his eyes,
Glimmering faintly where it lies;
Black is the sky – and every hill,
Up to the sky, is blacker still –
Sky, hill, and dale, one dismal room,
Hung round and overhung with gloom;
Save that above a single height
Is to be seen a lurid light,
Above Helm-crag – a streak half dead,
A burning of portentous red;
170   And near that lurid light, full well
The ASTROLOGER, sage Sidrophel,
Where at his desk and book he sits,
Puzzling aloft his curious wits;
He whose domain is held in common
With no one but the ANCIENT WOMAN,
Cowering beside her rifted cell,
As if intent on magic spell; –
Dread pair that, spite of wind and weather,
Still sit upon Helm-crag together!

180   The ASTROLOGER was not unseen
        By solitary Benjamin;
        But total darkness came anon,
        And he and everything was gone:
        And suddenly a ruffling breeze,
        (That would have rocked the sounding trees
        Had aught of sylvan growth been there)
        Swept through the Hollow long and bare:
        The rain rushed down – the road was battered,
        As with the force of billows shattered;
190   The horses are dismayed, nor know
        Whether they should stand or go;
        And Benjamin is groping near them,
        Sees nothing, and can scarcely hear them.
        He is astounded, – wonder not, –
        With such a charge in such a spot;
        Astounded in the mountain gap
        With thunder-peals, clap after clap,
        Close-treading on the silent flashes –
        And somewhere, as he thinks, by crashes
200   Among the rocks; with weight of rain,
        And sullen motions long and slow,
        That to a dreary distance go –
        Till, breaking in upon the dying strain,
        A rending o'er his head begins the fray again.

            Meanwhile, uncertain what to do,
        And oftentimes compelled to halt,
        The horses cautiously pursue
        Their way, without mishap or fault;
        And now have reached that pile of stones,
210   Heaped over brave King Dunmail's bones,
        He who had once supreme command,
        Last king of rocky Cumberland;
        His bones, and those of all his Power,
        Slain here in a disastrous hour!

When, passing through this narrow strait,
Stony, and dark, and desolate,
Benjamin can faintly hear
A voice that comes from someone near,
A female voice: – 'Whoe'er you be,
220   Stop,' it exclaimed, 'and pity me!'
And, less in pity than in wonder,
Amid the darkness and the thunder,
The Waggoner, with prompt command,
Summons his horses to a stand.

While, with increasing agitation,
The Woman urged her supplication,
In rueful words, with sobs between –
The voice of tears that fell unseen;
There came a flash – a startling glare,
230   And all Seat-Sandal was laid bare!
'Tis not a time for nice suggestion,
And Benjamin, without a question,
Taking her for some way-worn rover,
Said, 'Mount, and get you under cover!'

Another voice, in tone as hoarse
As a swoln brook with rugged course,
Cried out, 'Good brother, why so fast?
I've had a glimpse of you – *avast*!
Or, since it suits you to be civil,
240   Take her at once – for good and evil!'

'It is my Husband,' softly said
The Woman, as if half afraid:
By this time she was snug within,
Through help of honest Benjamin;
She and her Babe, which to her breast
With thankfulness the Mother pressed;
And now the same strong voice more near
Said cordially, 'My Friend, what cheer?
Rough doings these! as God's my judge,
250   The sky owes somebody a grudge!
We've had in half an hour or less
A twelvemonth's terror and distress!'

Then Benjamin entreats the Man
Would mount, too, quickly as he can:
The Sailor – Sailor now no more
But such he had been heretofore –
To courteous Benjamin replied,
'Go you your way, and mind not me;
For I must have, whate'er betide,
260   My Ass and fifty things beside, –
Go, and I'll follow speedily!'

The Waggon moves – and with its load
Descends along the sloping road;
And the rough Sailor instantly
Turns to a little tent hard by:
For when, at closing-in of day,
The family had come that way,
Green pasture and the soft warm air
Tempted them to settle there. –
270   Green is the grass for beast to graze,
Around the stones of Dunmail-raise!

The Sailor gathers up his bed,
Takes down the canvas overhead;
And, after farewell to the place,
A parting word – though not of grace,
Pursues, with Ass and all his store,
The way the Waggon went before.

CANTO SECOND

If Wythburn's modest House of prayer,
As lowly as the lowliest dwelling,
Had, with its belfry's humble stock,
A little pair that hang in air,
Been mistress also of a clock,
(And one, too, not in crazy plight)
Twelve strokes that clock would have been telling
Under the brow of old Helvellyn –
Its bead-roll of midnight,

10 Then, when the Hero of my tale
     Was passing by, and, down the vale
     (The vale now silent, hushed, I ween,
     As if a storm had never been)
     Proceeding with a mind at ease;
     While the old Familiar of the seas,
     Intent to use his utmost haste,
     Gained ground upon the Waggon fast,
     And gives another lusty cheer;
     For, spite of rumbling of the wheels,
20 A welcome greeting he can hear; –
     It is a fiddle in its glee
     Dinning from the CHERRY TREE!

     Thence the sound – the light is there –
     As Benjamin is now aware,
     Who, to his inward thoughts confined,
     Had almost reached the festive door,
     When, startled by the Sailor's roar,
     He hears a sound and sees the light,
     And in a moment calls to mind
30 That 'tis the village MERRY-NIGHT!

     Although before in no dejection,
     At this insidious recollection
     His heart with sudden joy is filled, –
     His ears are by the music thrilled,
     His eyes take pleasure in the road
     Glittering before him bright and broad;
     And Benjamin is wet and cold,
     And there are reasons manifold
     That make the good, towards which he's yearning,
40 Look fairly like a lawful earning.

     Nor has thought time to come and go,
     To vibrate between yes and no;
     For, cries the Sailor, 'Glorious chance
     That blew us hither! – let him dance,

Who can or will! – my honest soul,
Our treat shall be a friendly bowl!'
He draws him to the door – 'Come in,
Come, come,' cries he to Benjamin!
And Benjamin – ah, woe is me!
50 Gave the word – the horses heard
And halted, though reluctantly.

'Blithe souls and lightsome hearts have we,
Feasting at the CHERRY TREE!'
This was the outside proclamation,
This was the inside salutation;
What bustling – jostling – high and low!
A universal overflow!
What tankards foaming from the tap!
What store of cakes in every lap!
60 What thumping – stumping – overhead!
The thunder had not been more busy:
With such a stir you would have said,
This little place may well be dizzy!
'Tis who can dance with greatest vigour –
'Tis what can be most prompt and eager;
As if it heard the fiddle's call,
The pewter clatters on the wall;
The very bacon shows its feeling,
Swinging from the smoky ceiling!

70 A steaming bowl, a blazing fire,
What greater good can heart desire?
'Twere worth a wise man's while to try
The utmost anger of the sky:
To *seek* for thoughts of a gloomy cast,
If such the bright amends at last.
Now should you say I judge amiss,
The CHERRY TREE shows proof of this;
For soon, of all the happy there,
Our Travellers are the happiest pair:

80　All care with Benjamin is gone –
　　A Caesar past the Rubicon!
　　He thinks not of his long, long, strife; –
　　The Sailor, Man by nature gay,
　　Hath no resolves to throw away;
　　And he hath now forgot his Wife,
　　Hath quite forgotten her – or may be
　　Thinks her the luckiest soul on earth,
　　Within that warm and peaceful berth,
　　　Under cover,
90　　Terror over,
　　Sleeping by her sleeping Baby.

　　With bowl that sped from hand to hand,
　　The gladdest of the gladsome band,
　　Amid their own delight and fun,
　　They hear – when every dance is done,
　　When every whirling bout is o'er –
　　The fiddle's *squeak* – that call to bliss,
　　Ever followed by a kiss;
　　They envy not the happy lot,
100　But enjoy their own the more!

　　While thus our jocund Travellers fare,
　　Up springs the Sailor from his chair –
　　Limps (for I might have told before
　　That he was lame) across the floor –
　　Is gone – returns – and with a prize;
　　With what? – a Ship of lusty size;
　　A gallant stately Man-of-war,
　　Fixed on a smoothly-sliding car.
　　Surprise to all, but most surprise
110　To Benjamin, who rubs his eyes,
　　Not knowing that he had befriended
　　A Man so gloriously attended!

　　'This,' cries the Sailor, 'a Third-rate is –
　　Stand back, and you shall see her gratis!

This was the Flag-ship at the Nile,
The VANGUARD – you may smirk and smile,
But, pretty Maid, if you look near,
You'll find you've much in little here!
A nobler ship did never swim,
120   And you shall see her in full trim:
I'll set, my friends, to do you honour,
Set every inch of sail upon her.'
So said, so done; and masts, sails, yards,
He names them all; and interlards
His speech with uncouth terms of art,
Accomplished in the showman's part;
And then, as from a sudden check,
Cries out – ''Tis there, the quarter-deck
On which brave Admiral Nelson stood –
130   A sight that would have roused your blood! –
One eye he had, which, bright as ten,
Burned like a fire among his men;
Let this be land, and that be sea,
Here lay the French – and *thus* came we!'

     Hushed was by this the fiddle's sound,
The dancers all were gathered round,
And, such the stillness of the house,
You might have heard a nibbling mouse;
While, borrowing helps where'er he may,
140   The Sailor through the story runs
Of ships to ships and guns to guns;
And does his utmost to display
The dismal conflict, and the might
And terror of that marvellous night!
'A bowl, a bowl of double measure,'
Cries Benjamin, 'a draught of length,
To Nelson, England's pride and treasure,
Her bulwark and her tower of strength!'
When Benjamin had seized the bowl,
150   The mastiff, from beneath the waggon,
Where he lay, watchful as a dragon,

Rattled his chain; – 'twas all in vain,
For Benjamin, triumphant soul!
He heard the monitory growl;
Heard – and in opposition quaffed
A deep, determined, desperate draught!
Nor did the battered Tar forget,
Or flinch from what he deemed his debt:
Then, like a hero crowned with laurel,
160 Back to her place the ship he led;
Wheeled her back in full apparel;
And so, flag flying at mast head,
Re-yoked her to the Ass: – anon,
Cries Benjamin, 'We must be gone.'
Thus, after two hours' hearty stay,
Again behold them on their way!

CANTO THIRD

Right gladly had the horses stirred,
When they the wished-for greeting heard,
The whip's loud notice from the door,
That they were free to move once more.
You think, those doings must have bred
In them disheartening doubts and dread;
No, not a horse of all the eight,
Although it be a moonless night,
Fears either for himself or freight;
10 For this they know (and let it hide,
In part, the offences of their guide)
That Benjamin, with clouded brains,
Is worth the best with all their pains;
And, if they had a prayer to make,
The prayer would be that they may take
With him whatever comes in course,
The better fortune or the worse;
That no one else may have business near them,
And, drunk or sober, he may steer them.

20   So forth in dauntless mood they fare,
And with them goes the guardian pair.

Now, heroes, for the true commotion,
The triumph of your late devotion!
Can aught on earth impede delight,
Still mounting to a higher height;
And higher still – a greedy flight!
Can any low-born care pursue her,
Can any mortal clog come to her?
No notion have they – not a thought,
30   That is from joyless regions brought!
And, while they coast the silent lake,
Their inspiration I partake;
Share their empyrcal spirits – yea,
With their enraptured vision, see –
O fancy – what a jubilee!
What shifting pictures – clad in gleams
Of colour bright as feverish dreams!
Earth, spangled sky, and lake serene,
Involved and restless all – a scene
40   Pregnant with mutual exaltation,
Rich change, and multiplied creation!
This sight to me the Muse imparts; –
And then, what kindness in their hearts!
What tears of rapture, what vow-making,
Profound entreaties, and hand-shaking!
What solemn, vacant, interlacing,
As if they'd fall asleep embracing!
Then, in the turbulence of glee,
And in the excess of amity,
50   Says Benjamin, 'That Ass of thine,
He spoils thy sport, and hinders mine:
If he were tethered to the waggon,
He'd drag as well what he is dragging;
And we, as brother should with brother,
Might trudge it alongside each other!'

Forthwith, obedient to command,
The horses made a quiet stand;
And to the waggon's skirts was tied
The Creature, by the Mastiff's side,
60 The Mastiff wondering, and perplext
With dread of what will happen next;
And thinking it but sorry cheer,
To have such company so near!

This new arrangement made, the Wain
Through the still night proceeds again;
No Moon hath risen her light to lend;
But indistinctly may be kenned
The VANGUARD, following close behind,
Sails spread, as if to catch the wind!

70 'Thy wife and child are snug and warm,
Thy ship will travel without harm;
I like,' said Benjamin, 'her shape and stature:
And this of mine – this bulky creature
Of which I have the steering – this,
Seen fairly, is not much amiss!
We want your streamers, friend, you know;
But, altogether as we go,
We make a kind of handsome show!
Among these hills, from first to last,
80 We've weathered many a furious blast;
Hard passage forcing on, with head
Against the storm, and canvas spread.
I hate a boaster; but to thee
Will say't, who know'st both land and sea,
The unluckiest hulk that stems the brine
Is hardly worse beset than mine,
When cross-winds on her quarter beat;
And, fairly lifted from my feet,
I stagger onward – heaven knows how;
90 But not so pleasantly as now:
Poor pilot I, by snows confounded,
And many a foundrous pit surrounded!

Yet here we are, by night and day
Grinding through rough and smooth our way;
Through foul and fair our task fulfilling;
And long shall be so yet – God willing!'

    'Ay,' said the Tar, 'through fair and foul –
But save us from yon screeching owl!'
That instant was begun a fray
100 Which called their thoughts another way:
The Mastiff, ill-conditioned carl!
What must he do but growl and snarl,
Still more and more dissatisfied
With the meek comrade at his side!
Till, not incensed though put to proof,
The Ass, uplifting a hind hoof,
Salutes the Mastiff on the head;
And so were better manners bred,
And all was calmed and quieted.

110   'Yon screech-owl,' says the Sailor, turning
Back to his former cause of mourning,
'Yon owl! – pray God that all be well!
'Tis worse than any funeral bell;
As sure as I've the gift of sight,
We shall be meeting ghosts tonight!'
– Said Benjamin, 'This whip shall lay
A thousand, if they cross our way.
I know that Wanton's noisy station,
I know him and his occupation;
120 The jolly bird hath learned his cheer
Upon the banks of Windermere;
Where a tribe of them make merry,
Mocking the Man that keeps the ferry;
Hallooing from an open throat,
Like travellers shouting for a boat.
– The tricks he learned at Windermere
This vagrant owl is playing here –
That is the worst of his employment:
He's at the top of his enjoyment!'

130   This explanation stilled the alarm,
          Cured the foreboder like a charm;
          This, and the manner, and the voice,
          Summoned the Sailor to rejoice;
          His heart is up – he fears no evil
          From life or death, from man or devil;
          He wheels – and, making many stops,
          Brandished his crutch against the mountain tops;
          And, while he talked of blows and scars,
          Benjamin, among the stars,
140   Beheld a dancing – and a glancing;
          Such retreating and advancing
          As, I ween, was never seen
          In bloodiest battle since the days of Mars!

CANTO FOURTH

          Thus they, with freaks of proud delight,
          Beguile the remnant of the night;
          And many a snatch of jovial song
          Regales them as they wind along;
          While to the music, from on high,
          The echoes make a glad reply. –
          But the sage Muse the revel heeds
          No farther than her story needs;
          Nor will she servilely attend
10   The loitering journey to its end.
          – Blithe spirits of her own impel
          The Muse, who scents the morning air,
          To take of this transported pair
          A brief and unreproved farewell;
          To quit the slow-paced waggon's side,
          And wander down yon hawthorn dell,
          With murmuring Greta for her guide.
          – There doth she ken the awful form
          Of Raven-crag – black as a storm –
20   Glimmering through the twilight pale;

And Ghimmer-crag, his tall twin brother,
Each peering forth to meet the other: –
And, while she roves through St John's Vale,
Along the smooth unpathwayed plain,
By sheep-track or through cottage lane,
Where no disturbance comes to intrude
Upon the pensive solitude,
Her unsuspecting eye, perchance,
With the rude shepherd's favourcd glance,
30   Beholds the faeries in array,
Whose party-coloured garments gay
The silent company betray:
Red, green, and blue; a moment's sight!
For Skiddaw-top with rosy light
Is touched – and all the band take flight.
– Fly also, Muse! and from the dell
Mount to the ridge of Nathdale Fell;
Thence, look thou forth o'er wood and lawn
Hoar with the frost-like dews of dawn;
40   Across yon meadowy bottom look,
Where close fogs hide their parent brook;
And see, beyond that hamlet small,
The ruined towers of Threlkeld-hall,
Lurking in a double shade,
By trees and lingering twilight made!
There, at Blencathara's rugged feet,
Sir Lancelot gave a safe retreat
To noble Clifford; from annoy
Concealed the persecuted boy,
50   Well pleased in rustic garb to feed
His flock, and pipe on shepherd's reed
Among this multitude of hills,
Crags, woodlands, waterfalls, and rills;
Which soon the morning shall enfold,
From east to west, in ample vest
Of massy gloom and radiance bold.

The mists, that o'er the streamlet's bed
Hung low, begin to rise and spread;
Even while I speak, their skirts of grey
60 Are smitten by a silver ray;
And lo! – up Castrigg's naked steep
(Where, smoothly urged, the vapours sweep
Along – and scatter and divide,
Like fleecy clouds self-multiplied)
The stately waggon is ascending,
With faithful Benjamin attending,
Apparent now beside his team –
Now lost amid a glittering stream:
And with him goes his Sailor-friend,
70 By this time near their journey's end;
And, after their high-minded riot,
Sickening into thoughtful quiet;
As if the morning's pleasant hour
Had for their joys a killing power.
And, sooth, for Benjamin a vein
Is opened of still deeper pain,
As if his heart by notes were stung
From out the lowly hedge-rows flung;
As if the warbler lost in light
80 Reproved his soarings of the night,
In strains of rapture pure and holy
Upbraided his distempered folly.

Drooping is he, his step is dull;
But the horses stretch and pull;
With increasing vigour climb,
Eager to repair lost time;
Whether, by their own desert,
Knowing what cause there is for shame,
They are labouring to avert
90 As much as may be of the blame,
Which, they foresee, must soon alight
Upon *his* head, whom, in despite
Of all his failings, they love best;
Whether for him they are distrest;

Or, by length of fasting roused,
Are impatient to be housed:
Up against the hill they strain
Tugging at the iron chain,
Tugging all with might and main,
100 Last and foremost, every horse
To the utmost of his force!
And the smoke and respiration,
Rising like an exhalation,
Blend with the mist – a moving shroud
To form, an undissolving cloud;
Which, with slant ray, the merry sun
Takes delight to play upon.
Never golden-haired Apollo,
Pleased some favourite chief to follow
110 Through accidents of peace or war,
In a perilous moment threw
Around the object of his care
Veil of such celestial hue;
Interposed so bright a screen –
Him and his enemies between!

Alas! what boots it? – who can hide,
When the malicious Fates are bent
On working out an ill intent?
Can destiny be turned aside?
120 No – sad progress of my story!
Benjamin, this outward glory
Cannot shield thee from thy Master,
Who from Keswick has pricked forth,
Sour and surly as the north;
And, in fear of some disaster,
Comes to give what help he may,
And to hear what thou canst say;
If, as needs he must forbode,
Thou hast been loitering on the road!
130 His fears, his doubts, may now take flight –
The wished-for object is in sight;

Yet, trust the Muse, it rather hath
Stirred him up to livelier wrath;
Which he stifles, moody man!
With all the patience that he can;
To the end that, at your meeting,
He may give thee decent greeting.

There he is – resolved to stop,
Till the waggon gains the top;
140 But stop he cannot – must advance:
Him Benjamin, with lucky glance,
Espies – and instantly is ready,
Self-collected, poised, and steady:
And, to be the better seen,
Issues from his radiant shroud,
From his close-attending cloud,
With careless air and open mien.
Erect his port, and firm his going;
So struts yon cock that now is crowing;
150 And the morning light in grace
Strikes upon his lifted face,
Hurrying the pallid hue away
That might his trespasses betray.
But what can all avail to clear him,
Or what need of explanation,
Parley or interrogation?
For the Master sees, alas!
That unhappy Figure near him,
Limping o'er the dewy grass,
160 Where the road it fringes, sweet,
Soft and cool to way-worn feet;
And, O indignity! an Ass,
By his noble Mastiff's side,
Tethered to the waggon's tail:
And the ship, in all her pride,
Following after in full sail!
Not to speak of babe and mother;
Who, contented with each other,
And snug as birds in leafy arbour,
170 Find, within, a blessed harbour!

With eager eyes the Master pries;
Looks in and out, and through and through;
Says nothing – till at last he spies
A wound upon the Mastiff's head,
A wound, where plainly might be read
What feats an Ass's hoof can do!
But drop the rest: – this aggravation,
This complicated provocation,
A hoard of grievances unsealed;
180 All past forgiveness it repealed;
And thus, and through distempered blood
On both sides, Benjamin the good,
The patient, and the tender-hearted,
Was from his team and waggon parted;
When duty of that day was o'er,
Laid down his whip – and served no more. –
Nor could the waggon long survive,
When Benjamin had ceased to drive:
It lingered on; – guide after guide
190 Ambitiously the office tried;
But each unmanageable hill
Called for *his* patience and *his* skill; –
And sure it is, that through this night,
And what the morning brought to light,
Two losses had we to sustain,
We lost both WAGGONER and WAIN!

Accept, O Friend, for praise or blame,
The gift of this adventurous song;
A record which I dared to frame,
200 Though timid scruples checked me long;
They checked me – and I left the theme
Untouched; – in spite of many a gleam
Of fancy which thereon was shed,
Like pleasant sunbeams shifting still
Upon the side of a distant hill:
But Nature might not be gainsaid;
For what I have and what I miss
I sing of these; – it makes my bliss!

Nor is it I who play the part,
210   But a shy spirit in my heart,
That comes and goes – will sometimes leap
From hiding-places ten years deep;
Or haunts me with familiar face,
Returning, like a ghost unlaid,
Until the debt I owe be paid.
Forgive me, then; for I had been
On friendly terms with this Machine:
In him, while he was wont to trace
Our roads, through many a long year's space,
220   A living almanack had we;
We had a speaking diary,
That in this uneventful place,
Gave to the days a mark and name
By which we knew them when they came.
– Yes, I, and all about me here,
Through all the changes of the year,
Had seen him through the mountains go,
In pomp of mist or pomp of snow,
Majestically huge and slow:
230   Or, with a milder grace adorning
The landscape of a summer's morning;
While Grasmere smoothed her liquid plain
The moving image to detain;
And mighty Fairfield, with a chime
Of echoes, to his march kept time;
When little other business stirred,
And little other sound was heard;
In that delicious hour of balm,
Stillness, solitude, and calm,
240   While yet the valley is arrayed,
On this side with a sober shade;
On that is prodigally bright –
Crag, lawn, and wood – with rosy light.
– But most of all, thou lordly Wain!
I wish to have thee here again,
When windows flap and chimney roars,
And all is dismal out of doors;

And, sitting by my fire, I see
Eight sorry carts, no less a train!
250 Unworthy successors of thee,
Come straggling through the wind and rain:
And oft, as they pass slowly on,
Beneath my windows, one by one,
See, perched upon the naked height
The summit of a cumbrous freight,
A single traveller – and there
Another; then perhaps a pair –
The lame, the sickly, and the old;
Men, women, heartless with the cold;
260 And babes in wet and starveling plight;
Which once, be weather as it might,
Had still a nest within a nest,
Thy shelter – and their mother's breast!
Then most of all, then far the most,
Do I regret what we have lost;
Am grieved for that unhappy sin
Which robbed us of good Benjamin; –
And of his stately Charge, which none
Could keep alive when He was gone!

Star-Gazers

What crowd is this? what have we here! we must not pass
    it by;
A Telescope upon its frame, and pointed to the sky:
Long is it as a barber's pole, or mast of little boat,
Some little pleasure-skiff, that doth on Thames's waters
    float.

The Show-man chooses well his place, 'tis Leicester's busy
    Square;
And is as happy in his night, for the heavens are blue and
    fair;

Calm, though impatient, is the crowd; each stands ready
    with the fee,
And envies him that's looking; – what an insight must it
    be!

Yet, Show-man, where can lie the cause? Shall thy
    Implement have blame,
10 A boaster that, when he is tried, fails, and is put to shame?
Or is it good as others are, and be their eyes in fault?
Their eyes, or minds? or, finally, is yon resplendent vault?

Is nothing of that radiant pomp so good as we have here?
Or gives a thing but small delight that never can be dear?
The silver moon with all her vales, and hills of mightiest
    fame,
Doth she betray us when they're seen? or are they but a
    name?

Or is it rather that Conceit rapacious is and strong,
And bounty never yields so much but it seems to do her
    wrong?
Or is it that, when human Souls a journey long have had
20 And are returned into themselves, they cannot but be sad?

Or must we be constrained to think that these Spectators
    rude,
Poor in estate, of manners base, men of the multitude,
Have souls which never yet have risen, and therefore
    prostrate lie?
No, no, this cannot be; – men thirst for power and majesty!

Does, then, a deep and earnest thought the blissful mind
    employ
Of him who gazes, or has gazed? a grave and steady joy,
That doth reject all show of pride, admits no outward sign,
Because not of this noisy world, but silent and divine!

Whatever be the cause, 'tis sure that they who pry and
    pore
30 Seem to meet with little gain, seem less happy than before:
One after One they take their turn, nor have I one espied
That doth not slackly go away, as if dissatisfied.

'Yes, it was the mountain Echo'

Yes, it was the mountain Echo,
Solitary, clear, profound,
Answering to the shouting Cuckoo,
Giving to her sound for sound!

Unsolicited reply
To a babbling wanderer sent;
Like her ordinary cry,
Like – but oh, how different!

Hears not also mortal Life?
10   Hear not we, unthinking Creatures!
Slaves of folly, love, or strife –
Voices of two different natures?

Have not *we* too? – yes, we have
Answers, and we know not whence;
Echoes from beyond the grave,
Recognized intelligence!

Such rebounds our inward ear
Catches sometimes from afar –
Listen, ponder, hold them dear;
20   For of God, – of God they are.

The Recluse. Part First. Book First. Home at Grasmere

Once to the verge of yon steep barrier came
A roving School-boy – what the Adventurer's age
Hath now escaped his memory – but the hour,
One of a golden summer holiday,
He well remembers, though the year be gone.
Alone and devious from afar he came;
And, with a sudden influx overpowered
At sight of this seclusion, he forgot

His haste, for hasty had his footsteps been
10   As boyish his pursuits; and, sighing said,
'What happy fortune were it here to live!
And, if a thought of dying, if a thought
Of mortal separation, could intrude
With paradise before him, here to die!'
No Prophet was he, had not even a hope,
Scarcely a wish, but one bright pleasing thought,
A fancy in the heart of what might be
The lot of Others, never could be his.

      The Station whence he looked was soft and green,
20   Not giddy yet aërial, with a depth
Of Vale below, a height of hills above.
For rest of body, perfect was the Spot,
All that luxurious nature could desire,
But stirring to the Spirit; who could gaze
And not feel motions there? He thought of clouds
That sail on winds; of Breezes that delight
To play on water, or in endless chase
Pursue each other through the yielding plain
Of grass or corn, over and through and through,
30   In billow after billow, evermore
Disporting. Nor unmindful was the Boy
Of sunbeams, shadows, butterflies and birds;
Of fluttering Sylphs, and softly-gliding Fays,
Genii, and winged Angels that are Lords
Without restraint, of all which they behold.
The illusion strengthening as he gazed, he felt
That such unfettered liberty was his,
Such power and joy; but only for this end,
To flit from field to rock, from rock to field,
40   From shore to island, and from isle to shore,
From open ground to covert, from a bed
Of meadow-flowers into a tuft of wood;
From high to low, from low to high, yet still
Within the bound of this huge Concave; here
Must be his Home, this Valley be his World.

Since that day forth the place to him – *to me*
(For I who live to register the truth
Was that same young and happy Being) became
As beautiful to thought, as it had been,
50   When present, to the bodily sense; a haunt
Of pure affections, shedding upon joy
A brighter joy; and through such damp and gloom
Of the gay mind, as ofttimes splenetic Youth
Mistakes for sorrow darting beams of light
That no self-cherished sadness could withstand:
And now 'tis mine, perchance for life, dear Vale,
Beloved Grasmere (let the Wandering Streams
Take up, the cloud-capt hills repeat, the name),
One of thy lowly Dwellings is my Home.

60   And was the cost so great? and could it seem
An act of courage, and the thing itself
A conquest? who must bear the blame? sage Man
Thy prudence, thy experience – thy desires,
Thy apprehensions – blush thou for them all.

Yes, the realities of life so cold,
So cowardly, so ready to betray,
So stinted in the measure of their grace
As we pronounce them doing them much wrong
Have been to me more bountiful than hope,
70   Less timid than desire – but that is passed.

On Nature's invitation do I come
By Reason sanctioned. Can the choice mislead
That made the calmest, fairest spot of earth,
With all its unappropriated good,
My own; and not mine only, for with me
Entrenched, say rather peacefully embowered,
Under yon Orchard, in yon humble Cot,
A younger Orphan of a Home extinct,
The only Daughter of my Parents, dwells.

80   Aye, think on that, my Heart, and cease to stir,
        Pause upon that and let the breathing frame
        No longer breathe, but all be satisfied.
        – Oh if such silence be not thanks to God
        For what hath been bestowed, then where, where then
        Shall gratitude find rest? Mine eyes did ne'er
        Fix on a lovely object nor my mind
        Take pleasure in the midst of happy thoughts,
        But either She whom now I have, who now
        Divides with me this loved Abode, was there,

90   Or not far off. Where'er my footsteps turned,
        Her Voice was like a hidden Bird that sang,
        The thought of her was like a flash of light,
        Or an *unseen* companionship, a breath
        Or fragrance independent of the wind.
        In all my goings, in the new and old
        Of all my meditations, and in this
        Favourite of all, in this the most of all.
        – What Being, therefore, since the birth of Man
        Had ever more abundant cause to speak

100   Thanks, and if favours of the heavenly Muse
        Make him more thankful, then to call on verse
        To aid him, and in Song resound his joy.
        The boon is absolute; surpassing grace
        To me hath been vouchsafed; among the bowers
        Of blissful Eden this was neither given
        Nor could be given, possession of the good
        Which had been sighed for, ancient thought fulfilled
        And dear Imaginations realized,
        Up to their highest measure, yea, and more.

110   Embrace me then, ye Hills, and close me in;
        Now in the clear and open day I feel
        Your guardianship; I take it to my heart;
        'Tis like the solemn shelter of the night.
        But I would call thee beautiful, for mild,
        And soft, and gay, and beautiful thou art,
        Dear Valley, having in thy face a smile
        Though peaceful, full of gladness. Thou art pleased,

Pleased with thy crags, and woody steeps, thy Lake,
Its one green Island and its winding shores;
120   The multitude of little rocky hills,
Thy Church and Cottages of mountain stone –
Clustered like stars some few, but single most,
And lurking dimly in their shy retreats,
Or glancing at each other cheerful looks
Like separated stars with clouds between.
What want we? have we not perpetual streams,
Warm woods, and sunny hills, and fresh green fields,
And mountains not less green, and flocks and herds,
And thickets full of songsters, and the voice
130   Of lordly birds, an unexpected sound
Heard now and then from morn to latest eve,
Admonishing the man who walks below
Of solitude and silence in the sky?
These have we, and a thousand nooks of earth
Have also these, but *no* where else is found,
Nowhere (or is it fancy?) *can* be found
The one sensation that is here; 'tis here,
Here as it found its way into my heart
In childhood, here as it abides by day,
140   By night, here only; or in chosen minds
That take it with them hence, where'er they go.
'Tis, but I cannot name it, 'tis the sense
Of majesty, and beauty, and repose,
A blended holiness of earth and sky,
Something that makes this individual Spot,
This small Abiding-place of many Men,
A termination, and a last retreat,
A Centre, come from wheresoe'er you will,
A Whole without dependence or defect,
150   Made for itself, and happy in itself,
Perfect Contentment, Unity entire.

Bleak season was it, turbulent and bleak,
When hitherward we journeyed, side by side
Through burst of sunshine and through flying showers;
Paced the long Vales, how long they were, and yet

How fast that length of way was left behind,
Wensley's rich Vale and Sedbergh's naked heights.
The frosty wind, as if to make amends
For its keen breath, was aiding to our steps
160 And drove us onward like two Ships at sea,
Or like two Birds, companions in mid-air,
Parted and re-united by the blast.
Stern was the face of Nature; we rejoiced
In that stern countenance, for our Souls thence drew
A feeling of their strength. The naked Trees,
The icy brooks, as on we passed, appeared
To question us. 'Whence come ye? to what end?'
They seemed to say; 'What would ye,' said the shower,
'Wild Wanderers, whither through my dark domain?'
170 The sunbeam said, 'Be happy.' When this Vale
We entered, bright and solemn was the sky
That faced us with a passionate welcoming,
And led us to our threshold. Daylight failed
Insensibly, and round us gently fell
Composing darkness, with a quiet load
Of full contentment, in a little Shed
Disturbed, uneasy in itself as seemed,
And wondering at its new inhabitants.
It loves us now, this Vale so beautiful
180 Begins to love us! By a sullen storm,
Two months unwearied of severest storm,
It put the temper of our minds to proof
And found us faithful through the gloom, and heard
The Poet mutter his prelusive songs
With cheerful heart, an unknown voice of joy
Among the silence of the woods and hills;
Silent to any gladsomeness of sound
With all their Shepherds.
                              But the gates of Spring
Are opened; churlish Winter hath given leave
190 That she should entertain for this one day,
Perhaps for many genial days to come,
His guests, and make them jocund. They are pleased,

But most of all the Birds that haunt the flood
With the mild summons; inmates though they be
Of Winter's household, they keep festival
This day, who drooped, or seemed to droop, so long;
They show their pleasure, and shall I do less?
Happier of happy though I be, like them
I cannot take possession of the sky,
200 Mount with a thoughtless impulse, and wheel there,
One of a mighty multitude, whose way
Is a perpetual harmony and dance
Magnificent. Behold, how with a grace
Of ceaseless motion, that might scarcely seem
Inferior to angelical, they prolong
Their curious pastime, shaping in mid-air,
And sometimes with ambitious wing that soars
High as the level of the mountain tops,
A circuit ampler than the lake beneath,
210 Their own domain; – but ever, while intent
On tracing and retracing that large round,
Their jubilant activity evolves
Hundreds of curves and circlets, to and fro,
Upwards and downwards, progress intricate
Yet unperplexed, as if one spirit swayed
Their indefatigable flight. 'Tis done;
Ten times and more I fancied it had ceased,
But lo! the vanished company again
Ascending, they approach – I hear their wings
220 Faint, faint at first; and then an eager sound
Passed in a moment – and as faint again!
They tempt the sun to sport among their plumes;
Tempt the smooth water, or the gleaming ice,
To show them a fair image, – 'tis themselves,
Their own fair forms, upon the glimmering plain,
Painted more soft and fair as they descend,
Almost to touch, – then up again aloft,
Up with a sally and a flash of speed,
As if they scorned both resting-place and rest!

230   This day is a thanksgiving, 'tis a day
         Of glad emotion and deep quietness;
         Not upon me alone hath been bestowed,
         Me rich in many onward-looking thoughts,
         The penetrating bliss; oh surely these
         Have felt it, not the happy Choirs of Spring,
         Her own peculiar family of love
         That sport among green leaves, a blither train.

             But two are missing – two, a lonely pair
         Of milk-white Swans, wherefore are they not seen
240   Partaking this day's pleasure? From afar
         They came, to sojourn here in solitude,
         Choosing this Valley, they who had the choice
         Of the whole world. We saw them day by day,
         Through those two months of unrelenting storm,
         Conspicuous at the centre of the Lake
         Their safe retreat; we knew them well, I guess
         That the whole Valley knew them; but to us
         They were more dear than may be well believed,
         Not only for their beauty, and their still
250   And placid way of life and constant love
         Inseparable, not for these alone,
         But that their state so much resembled ours,
         They having also chosen this abode;
         They strangers, and we strangers; they a pair,
         And we a solitary pair like them.
         They should not have departed; many days
         Did I look forth in vain, nor on the wing
         Could see them, nor in that small open space
         Of blue unfrozen water, where they lodged,
260   And lived so long in quiet, side by side.
         Shall we behold them, consecrated friends,
         Faithful Companions, yet another year
         Surviving, they for us, and we for them,
         And neither pair be broken? Nay perchance
         It is too late already for such hope,
         The Dalesmen may have aimed the deadly tube,
         And parted them; or haply both are gone
         One death, and that were mercy given to both.

Recall my song the ungenerous thought; forgive,
270 Thrice favoured Region, the conjecture harsh
Of such inhospitable penalty
Inflicted upon confidence so pure.
Ah, if I wished to follow where the sight
Of all that is before my eyes, the voice
Which speaks from a presiding Spirit here,
Would lead me – I should whisper to myself;
They who are dwellers in this holy place
Must needs themselves be hallowed, they require
No benediction from the Stranger's lips,
280 For they are blest already; none would give
The greeting 'peace be with you' unto them
For peace they have, it cannot but be theirs,
And mercy, and forbearance nay – not these,
Their healing offices a pure good-will
Precludes, and charity beyond the bounds
Of charity – an overflowing love,
Not for the Creature only, but for all
That is around them, love for everything
Which in this happy Region they behold!

290   Thus do we soothe ourselves, and when the thought
Is passed we blame it not for having come.
– What if I floated down a pleasant Stream
And now am landed, and the motion gone,
Shall I reprove myself? Ah no, the Stream
Is flowing, and will never cease to flow,
And I shall float upon that Stream again.
By such forgetfulness the Soul becomes,
Words cannot say, how beautiful: then hail,
Hail to the visible Presence, hail to thee,
300 Delightful Valley, habitation fair!
And to whatever else of outward form
Can give us inward help, can purify,
And elevate, and harmonize, and soothe,
And steal away, and for a while deceive
And lap in pleasing rest, and bear us on
Without desire in full complacency,
Contemplating perfection absolute
And entertained as in a placid sleep.

But not betrayed by tenderness of mind
310 That feared, or wholly overlooked, the truth,
Did we come hither, with romantic hope
To find in midst of so much loveliness,
Love, perfect love; of so much majesty
A like majestic frame of mind, in those
Who here abide, the persons like the place.
Not from such hope, or aught of such belief
Hath issued any portion of the joy
Which I have felt this day. An awful voice,
'Tis true, hath in my walks been often heard
320 Sent from the mountains or the sheltered fields,
Shout after shout – reiterated whoop
In manner of a bird that takes delight
In answering to itself; or like a hound
Single at chase among the lonely woods,
His yell repeating; yet it was in truth
A human voice – a Spirit of coming night;
How solemn when the sky is dark, and earth
Not dark, nor yet enlightened, but by snow
Made visible, amid a noise of winds
330 And bleatings manifold of mountain sheep,
Which in that iteration recognize
Their summons, and are gathering round for food,
Devoured with keenness ere to grove or bank
Or rocky *bield* with patience they retire.

That very voice, which, in some timid mood
Of superstitious fancy, might have seemed
Awful as ever stray Demoniac uttered,
His steps to govern in the Wilderness;
Or, as the Norman Curfew's regular beat,
340 To hearths when first they darkened at the knell:
That Shepherd's voice, it may have reached mine ear
Debased and under profanation, made
The ready Organ of articulate sounds
From ribaldry, impiety, or wrath
Issuing when shame hath ceased to check the brawls
Of some abused Festivity – so be it.

I came not dreaming of unruffled life,
Untainted manners; born among the hills,
Bred also there, I wanted not a scale
350 To regulate my hopes; pleased with the good,
I shrink not from the evil with disgust,
Or with immoderate pain. I look for Man,
The common Creature of the brotherhood,
Differing but little from the Man elsewhere,
For selfishness, and envy, and revenge,
Ill neighbourhood, pity that this should be,
Flattery and double-dealing, strife and wrong.

 Yet is it something gained, it is in truth
A mighty gain, that Labour here preserves
360 His rosy face, a Servant only here
Of the fire-side or of the open field,
A Freeman, therefore sound and unimpaired;
That extreme penury is here unknown
And cold and hunger's abject wretchedness,
Mortal to body and the heaven-born mind;
That they who want, are not too great a weight
For those who can relieve; here may the heart
Breathe in the air of fellow-suffering
Dreadless, as in a kind of fresher breeze
370 Of her own native element, the hand
Be ready and unwearied without plea
From tasks too frequent, or beyond its power
For languor or indifference or despair.
And as these lofty barriers break the force
Of winds, this deep Vale, as it doth in part
Conceal us from the Storm, so here abides
A Power and a protection for the mind
Dispensed indeed to other Solitudes
Favoured by noble privilege like this,
380 Where kindred independence of estate
Is prevalent, where he who tills the field,
He, happy Man! is Master of the field,
And treads the mountains which his Fathers trod.

  Not less than half-way up *yon* mountain's side
Behold a dusky spot, a grove of Firs
That seems still smaller than it is; this grove
Is haunted – by what ghost? – a gentle Spirit
Of memory faithful to the call of love,
For, as reports the Dame, whose fire sends up
390 Yon curling smoke from the grey cot below,
The trees (her first-born Child being then a babe)
Were planted by her husband and herself
That ranging o'er the high and houseless ground
Their sheep might neither want (from perilous storm
Of winter, nor from summer's sultry heat)
A friendly Covert. 'And they knew it well,'
Said she, 'for thither as the trees grew up,
We to the patient creatures carried food
In times of heavy snow.' She then began
400 In fond obedience to her private thoughts
To speak of her dead Husband: is there not
An art, a music, and a strain of words
That shall be life, the acknowledged voice of life,
Shall speak of what is done among the fields,
Done truly there, or felt, of solid good
And real evil, yet be sweet withal,
More grateful, more harmonious than the breath,
The idle breath of softest pipe attuned
To pastoral fancies? Is there such a stream
410 Pure and unsullied flowing from the heart
With motions of true dignity and grace?
Or must we seek that stream where Man is not?
Methinks I could repeat in tuneful verse
Delicious as the gentlest breeze that sounds
Through that aërial fir-grove, could preserve
Some portion of its human history
As gathered from the Matron's lips, and tell
Of tears that have been shed at sight of it
And moving dialogues between this Pair,
420 Who in their prime of wedlock, with joint hands
Did plant the grove, now flourishing, while they

No longer flourish, he entirely gone,
She withering in her loneliness. Be this
A task above my skill: the silent mind
Has her own treasures, and I think of these,
Love what I see, and honour humankind.

No, we are not alone, we do not stand,
My Sister, here misplaced and desolate,
Loving what no one cares for but ourselves;
430 We shall not scatter through the plains and rocks
Of this fair Vale, and o'er its spacious heights
Unprofitable kindliness, bestowed
On objects unaccustomed to the gifts
Of feeling, which were cheerless and forlorn
But few weeks past, and would be so again
Were we not here; we do not tend a lamp
Whose lustre we alone participate,
Which shines dependent upon us alone,
Mortal though bright, a dying, dying flame.
440 Look where we will, some human hand has been
Before us with its offering; not a tree
Sprinkles these little pastures but the same
Hath furnished matter for a thought; perchance
For someone serves as a familiar friend.
Joy spreads and sorrow spreads; and this whole Vale,
Home of untutored Shepherds as it is,
Swarms with sensation, as with gleams of sunshine,
Shadows or breezes, scents or sounds. Nor deem
These feelings, though subservient more than ours
450 To every day's demand for daily bread
And borrowing more their spirit, and their shape
From self-respecting interests, deem them not
Unworthy therefore, and unhallowed – no,
They lift the animal being, do themselves
By nature's kind and ever-present aid
Refine the selfishness from which they spring,
Redeem by love the individual sense
Of anxiousness with which they are combined.

And thus it is that fitly they become
460   Associates in the joy of purest minds
They blend therewith congenially: meanwhile
Calmly they breathe their own undying life
Through this their mountain sanctuary; – long,
Oh long may it remain inviolate,
Diffusing health and sober cheerfulness
And giving to the moments as they pass
Their little boons of animating thought
That sweeten labour, make it seen and felt
To be no arbitrary weight imposed,
470   But a glad function natural to Man.

Fair proof of this, Newcomer though I be,
Already have I gained; the inward frame
Though slowly opening, opens every day
With process not unlike to that which cheers
A pensive Stranger journeying at his leisure
Through some Helvetian Dell, when low-hung mists
Break up, and are beginning to recede;
How pleased he is where thin and thinner grows
The veil, or where it parts at once, to spy
480   The dark pines thrusting forth their spiky heads;
To watch the spreading lawns with cattle grazed,
Then to be greeted by the scattered huts
As they shine out; and *see* the streams whose murmur
Had soothed his ear while they were hidden: how pleased
To have about him, which way e'er he goes,
Something on every side concealed from view,
In every quarter something visible,
Half-seen or wholly, lost and found again,
Alternate progress and impediment
490   And yet a growing prospect in the main.

Such pleasure now is mine, albeit forced,
Herein less happy than the Traveller
To cast from time to time a painful look
Upon unwelcome things which unawares
Reveal themselves; not therefore is my heart

Depressed nor does it fear what is to come,
But confident, enriched at every glance.
The more I see the more delight my mind
Receives, or by reflexion can create.
500   Truth justifies herself, and as she dwells
With Hope, who would not follow where she leads?

    Nor let me pass unheeded other loves
Where no fear is, and humbler sympathies.
Already hath sprung up within my heart
A liking for the small grey horse that bears
The paralytic Man, and for the brute
In Scripture sanctified – the patient brute
On which the Cripple, in the Quarry maimed,
Rides to and fro: I know them and their ways.
510   The famous Sheep-dog, first in all the Vale
Though yet to me a Stranger, will not be
A Stranger long; nor will the blind man's guide,
Meek and neglected thing, of no renown!
Soon will peep forth the primrose; ere it fades
Friends shall I have at dawn, blackbird and thrush
To rouse me, and a hundred Warblers more;
And if those Eagles to their ancient Hold
Return, Helvellyn's Eagles! with the Pair
From my own door I shall be free to claim
520   Acquaintance as they sweep from cloud to cloud.
The Owl that gives the name to Owlet-Crag
Have I heard whooping, and he soon will be
A chosen one of my regards. See there.
The Heifer in yon little Croft belongs
To one who holds it dear; with duteous care
She reared it, and in speaking of her Charge
I heard her scatter some endearing words
Domestic, and in spirit motherly,
She being herself a Mother, happy Beast
530   If the caresses of a human voice
Can make it so, and care of human hands.

And ye as happy under Nature's care,
Strangers to me and all men, or at least
Strangers to all particular amity,
All intercourse of knowledge or of love
That parts the individual from his kind,
Whether in large communities ye keep
From year to year, not shunning Man's abode,
A settled residence, or be from far,
540   Wild creatures, and of many homes, that come
The gift of winds, and whom the winds again
Take from us at your pleasure; yet shall ye
Not want, for this, your own subordinate place
In my affections. Witness the delight
With which erewhile I saw that multitude
Wheel through the sky, and see them now at rest,
Yet not at rest, upon the glassy lake.
They *cannot* rest – they gambol like young whelps;
Active as lambs, and overcome with joy,
550   They try all frolic motions; flutter, plunge
And beat the passive water with their wings.
Too distant are they for plain view, but lo!
Those little fountains, sparkling in the sun,
Betray their occupation, rising up,
First one and then another silver spout,
As one or other takes the fit of glee,
Fountains and spouts, yet somewhat in the guise
Of plaything fire-works, that on festal nights
Sparkle about the feet of wanton boys.
560   – How vast the compass of this theatre,
Yet nothing to be seen but lovely pomp
And silent majesty; the birch-tree woods
Are hung with thousand thousand diamond drops
Of melted hoar-frost, every tiny knot
In the bare twigs, each little budding-place
Cased with its several bead, what myriads there
Upon one tree, while all the distant grove
That rises to the summit of the steep
Shows like a mountain built of silver light:

570 See yonder the same pageant, and again
    Behold the universal imagery
    Inverted, all its sun-bright features touched
    As with the varnish, and the gloss of dreams;
    Dreamlike the blending also of the whole
    Harmonious Landscape; all along the shore
    The boundary lost, the line invisible
    That parts the image from reality;
    And the clear hills, as high as they ascend
    Heavenward, so deep piercing the lake below.
580 Admonished of the days of love to come
    The raven croaks, and fills the upper air
    With a strange sound of genial harmony;
    And in and all about that playful band,
    Incapable although they be of rest
    And in their fashion very rioters,
    There is a stillness; and they seem to make
    Calm revelry in that their calm abode.
    Them leaving to their joyous hours I pass,
    Pass with a thought the life of the whole year
590 That is to come: the throng of woodland flowers,
    And lilies that will dance upon the waves.

    Say boldly then that solitude is not
    Where these things are: he truly is alone,
    He of the multitude whose eyes are doomed
    To hold a vacant commerce day by day
    With objects wanting life – repelling love;
    He by the vast Metropolis immured,
    Where pity shrinks from unremitting calls,
    Where numbers overwhelm humanity,
600 And neighbourhood serves rather to divide
    Than to unite. What sighs more deep than his,
    Whose nobler will hath long been sacrificed;
    Who must inhabit, under a black sky,
    A city where, if indifference to disgust
    Yield not, to scorn, or sorrow, living Men
    Are ofttimes to their fellow-men no more
    Than to the Forest Hermit are the leaves

That hang aloft in myriads, nay, far less,
For they protect his walk from sun and shower,
610   Swell his devotion with their voice in storms
And whisper while the stars twinkle among them
His lullaby. From crowded streets remote
Far from the living and dead wilderness
Of the thronged World, Society is here
A true Community – a genuine frame
Of many into one incorporate.
That must be looked for here; paternal sway,
One household, under God, for high and low,
One family and one mansion; to themselves
620   Appropriate, and divided from the world
As if it were a cave, a multitude
Human and brute, possessors undisturbed
Of this Recess, their legislative Hall,
Their Temple and their glorious Dwelling-place.

　　Dismissing therefore all Arcadian dreams,
All golden fancies of the golden Age,
The bright array of shadowy thoughts from times
That were before all time, or are to be
Ere time expire, the pageantry that stirs
630   And will be stirring when our eyes are fixed
On lovely objects and we wish to part
With all remembrance of a jarring world,
– Take we at once this one sufficient hope,
What need of more? that we shall neither droop
Nor pine for want of pleasure in the life
Scattered about us, nor through dearth of aught
That keeps in health the insatiable mind;
– That we shall have for knowledge and for love
Abundance, and that, feeling as we do
640   How goodly, how exceeding fair, how pure
From all reproach is yon ethereal vault
And this deep Vale, its earthly counterpart,
By which, and under which, we are enclosed
To breathe in peace; we shall moreover find
(If sound, and what we ought to be ourselves

If rightly we observe and justly weigh)
The Inmates not unworthy of their home,
The Dwellers of their Dwelling.
                     And if this
Were otherwise, we have within ourselves
650   Enough to fill the present day with joy
And overspread the future years with hope,
Our beautiful and quiet home, enriched
Already with a Stranger whom we love
Deeply, a Stranger of our Father's House,
A never-resting Pilgrim of the Sea,
Who finds at last an hour to his content
Beneath our roof. And others whom we love
Will seek us also, Sisters of our hearts
And One, like them, a Brother of our hearts,
660   Philosopher and Poet in whose sight
These Mountains will rejoice with open joy
– Such is our wealth; O Vale of Peace, we are
And must be, with God's will, a happy Band.

   Yet 'tis not to enjoy that we exist,
For that end only; something must be done.
I must not walk in unreproved delight
These narrow bounds, and think of nothing more,
No duty that looks further, and no care.
Each Being has *his* office, lowly some
670   And common, yet all worthy if fulfilled
With zeal, acknowledgement that with the gift
Keeps pace, a harvest answering to the seed.
Of ill-advised Ambition, and of Pride
I would stand clear, but yet to me I feel
That an internal brightness is vouchsafed
That must not die, that must not pass away.
Why does this inward lustre fondly seek
And gladly blend with outward fellowship?
Why do *they* shine around me whom I love?
680   Why do they teach me whom I thus revere?
Strange question yet it answers not itself.

That humble Roof embowered among the trees,
That calm fire-side, it is not even in them,
Blest as they are, to furnish a reply
That satisfies and ends in perfect rest.
Possessions have I that are solely mine,
Something within which yet is shared by none,
Not even the nearest to me and most dear,
Something which power and effort may impart,
690 I would impart it, I would spread it wide,
Immortal in the world which is to come.
Forgive me if I add another claim
And would not wholly perish even in this,
Lie down and be forgotten in the dust,
I and the modest Partners of my days
Making a silent company in death.
Love, Knowledge, all my manifold delights
All buried with me without monument
Or profit unto any but ourselves.
700 It must not be, if I, divinely taught,
Be privileged to speak as I have felt
Of what in man is human or divine.

   While yet an innocent Little-one, with a heart
That doubtless wanted not its tender moods,
I breathed (for this I better recollect)
Among wild appetites and blind desires,
Motions of savage instinct my delight
And exaltation. Nothing at that time
So welcome, no temptation half so dear
710 As that which urged me to a daring feat.
Deep pools, tall trees, black chasms and dizzy crags,
And tottering towers, I loved to stand and read
Their looks forbidding, read and disobey,
Sometimes in act, and evermore in thought.
With impulses that scarcely were by these
Surpassed in strength, I heard of danger, met
Or sought with courage; enterprise forlorn
By one, sole keeper of his own intent,
Or by a resolute few who for the sake
720 Of glory fronted multitudes in arms.

Yea to this hour I cannot read a Tale
Of two brave Vessels matched in deadly fight
And fighting to the death, but I am pleased
More than a wise man ought to be. I wish,
Fret, burn, and struggle, and in soul am there;
But me hath Nature tamed and bade to seek
For other agitations or be calm;
Hath dealt with me as with a turbulent stream,
Some nursling of the mountains, which she leads
730 Through quiet meadows after he has learnt
His strength and had his triumph and his joy,
His desperate course of tumult and of glee.
That which in stealth by Nature was performed
Hath Reason sanctioned: her deliberate Voice
Hath said, 'Be mild and cleave to gentle things,
Thy glory and thy happiness be there.
Nor fear, though thou confide in me, a want
Of aspirations that *have* been – of foes
To wrestle with, and victory to complete,
740 Bounds to be leapt, darkness to be explored,
All that inflamed thy infant heart, the love,
The longing, the contempt, the undaunted quest,
All shall survive though changed their office, all
Shall live – it is not in their power to die.'

Then farewell to the Warrior's schemes, farewell
The forwardness of Soul which looks that way
Upon a less incitement than the cause
Of Liberty endangered, and farewell
That other hope, long mine, the hope to fill
750 The heroic trumpet with the Muse's breath!
Yet in this peaceful Vale we will not spend
Unheard-of days, though loving peaceful thoughts.
A Voice shall speak, and what will be the Theme?
On Man, on Nature, and on Human Life
Musing in solitude, I oft perceive
Fair trains of imagery before me rise,
Accompanied by feelings of delight
Pure, or with no unpleasing sadness mixed;

And I am conscious of affecting thoughts
760   And dear remembrances, whose presence soothes
Or elevates the Mind, intent to weigh
The good and evil of our mortal state.
– To these emotions, whencesoe'er they come,
Whether from breath of outward circumstance,
Or from the Soul – an impulse to herself –
I would give utterance in numerous verse.
Of Truth, of Grandeur, Beauty, Love, and Hope,
And melancholy Fear subdued by Faith;
Of blessèd consolations in distress;
770   Of moral strength, and intellectual Power;
Of joy in widest commonalty spread;
Of the individual Mind that keeps her own
Inviolate retirement, subject there
To Conscience only, and the law supreme
Of that Intelligence which governs all –
I sing: – 'fit audience let me find though few!'

'So prayed, more gaining than he asked, the Bard –
In holiest mood. Urania, I shall need
Thy guidance, or a greater Muse, if such
780   Descend to earth or dwell in highest heaven!
For I must tread on shadowy ground, must sink
Deep – and, aloft ascending, breathe in worlds
To which the heaven of heavens is but a veil.
All strength – all terror, single or in bands,
That ever was put forth in personal form –
Jehovah – with his thunder, and the choir
Of shouting Angels, and the empyreal thrones –
I pass them unalarmed. Not Chaos, not
The darkest pit of lowest Erebus,
790   Nor aught of blinder vacancy, scooped out
By help of dreams – can breed such fear and awe
As fall upon us often when we look
Into our Minds, into the Mind of Man –
My haunt, and the main region of my song.
– Beauty – a living Presence of the earth,
Surpassing the most fair ideal Forms

Which craft of delicate Spirits hath composed
From earth's materials – waits upon my steps;
Pitches her tents before me as I move,
800　An hourly neighbour. Paradise, and groves
Elysian, Fortunate Fields – like those of old
Sought in the Atlantic Main – why should they be
A history only of departed things,
Or a mere fiction of what never was?
For the discerning intellect of Man,
When wedded to this goodly universe
In love and holy passion, shall find these
A simple produce of the common day.
　– I, long before the blissful hour arrives,
810　Would chant, in lonely peace, the spousal verse
Of this great consummation: – and, by words
Which speak of nothing more than what we are,
Would I arouse the sensual from their sleep
Of Death, and win the vacant and the vain
To noble raptures; while my voice proclaims
How exquisitely the individual Mind
(And the progressive powers perhaps no less
Of the whole species) to the external World
Is fitted: – and how exquisitely, too –
820　Theme this but little heard of among men –
The external World is fitted to the Mind;
And the creation (by no lower name
Can it be called) which they with blended might
Accomplish: – this is our high argument.
　– Such grateful haunts foregoing, if I oft
Must turn elsewhere – to travel near the tribes
And fellowships of men, and see ill sights
Of madding passions mutually inflamed;
Must hear Humanity in fields and groves
830　Pipe solitary anguish; or must hang
Brooding above the fierce confederate storm
Of sorrow, barricadoed evermore
Within the walls of cities – may these sounds
Have their authentic comment; that even these
Hearing, I be not downcast or forlorn! –

Descend, prophetic Spirit! that inspir'st
The human Soul of universal earth,
Dreaming on things to come; and dost possess
A metropolitan temple in the hearts
840   Of mighty Poets: upon me bestow
A gift of genuine insight; that my Song
With star-like virtue in its place may shine,
Shedding benignant influence, and secure,
Itself, from all malevolent effect
Of those mutations that extend their sway
Throughout the nether sphere! – and if with this
I mix more lowly matter; with the thing
Contemplated, describe the Mind and Man
Contemplating; and who, and what he was –
850   The transitory Being that beheld
This Vision; when and where, and how he lived; –
Be not this labour useless. If such theme
May sort with highest objects, then – dread Power!
Whose gracious favour is the primal source
Of all illumination – may my Life
Express the image of a better time,
More wise desires, and simpler manners; – nurse
My Heart in genuine freedom: – all pure thoughts
Be with me; – so shall thy unfailing love
860   Guide, and support, and cheer me to the end!'

Lines

Composed at Grasmere, during a walk one Evening, after a stormy
day, the Author having just read in a Newspaper that the dissolution
of Mr Fox was hourly expected.

Loud is the Vale! the Voice is up
With which she speaks when storms are gone,
A mighty unison of streams!
Of all her Voices, One!

Loud is the Vale; – this inland Depth
In peace is roaring like the Sea;
Yon star upon the mountain-top
Is listening quietly.

Sad was I, even to pain deprest,
10   Importunate and heavy load!
The Comforter hath found me here,
Upon this lonely road;

And many thousands now are sad –
Wait the fulfilment of their fear;
For he must die who is their stay,
Their glory disappear.

A Power is passing from the earth
To breathless Nature's dark abyss;
But when the great and good depart
20   What is it more than this –

That Man, who is from God sent forth,
Doth yet again to God return? –
Such ebb and flow must ever be,
Then wherefore should we mourn?

Thought of a Briton on the Subjugation of Switzerland

Two Voices are there; one is of the sea,
One of the mountains; each a mighty Voice:
In both from age to age thou didst rejoice,
They were thy chosen music, Liberty!
There came a Tyrant, and with holy glee
Thou fought'st against him; but hast vainly striven:
Thou from thy Alpine holds at length art driven,
Where not a torrent murmurs heard by thee.
Of one deep bliss thine ear hath been bereft:
10   Then cleave, O cleave to that which still is left;
For, high-souled Maid, what sorrow would it be
That Mountain floods should thunder as before,
And Ocean bellow from his rocky shore,
And neither awful Voice be heard by thee!

November, 1806

Another year! – another deadly blow!
Another mighty Empire overthrown!
And We are left, or shall be left, alone;
The last that dare to struggle with the Foe.
'Tis well! from this day forward we shall know
That in ourselves our safety must be sought;
That by our own right hands it must be wrought;
That we must stand unpropped, or be laid low.
O dastard whom such foretaste doth not cheer!
10   We shall exult, if they who rule the land
Be men who hold its many blessings dear,
Wise, upright, valiant; not a servile band,
Who are to judge of danger which they fear,
And honour which they do not understand.

Song at the Feast of Brougham Castle upon the Restoration of Lord Clifford, the Shepherd, to the Estates and Honours of His Ancestors

High in the breathless Hall the Minstrel sate,
And Emont's murmur mingled with the Song. –
The words of ancient time I thus translate,
A festal strain that hath been silent long: –

  'From town to town, from tower to tower,
  The red rose is a gladsome flower.
  Her thirty years of winter past,
  The red rose is revived at last;
  She lifts her head for endless spring,
10   For everlasting blossoming:
  Both roses flourish, red and white:
  In love and sisterly delight
  The two that were at strife are blended,
  And all old troubles now are ended. –
  Joy! joy to both! but most to her

Who is the flower of Lancaster!
Behold her how She smiles today
On this great throng, this bright array!
Fair greeting doth she send to all
20 From every corner of the hall;
But chiefly from above the board
Where sits in state our rightful Lord,
A Clifford to his own restored!

'They came with banner, spear, and shield;
And it was proved in Bosworth-field.
Not long the Avenger was withstood –
Earth helped him with the cry of blood:
St George was for us, and the might
Of blessed Angels crowned the right.
30 Loud voice the Land has uttered forth,
We loudest in the faithful north:
Our fields rejoice, our mountains ring,
Our streams proclaim a welcoming;
Our strong-abodes and castles see
The glory of their loyalty.

'How glad is Skipton at this hour –
Though lonely, a deserted Tower;
Knight, squire, and yeoman, page and groom:
We have them at the feast of Brough'm.
40 How glad Pendragon – though the sleep
Of years be on her! – She shall reap
A taste of this great pleasure, viewing
As in a dream her own renewing.
Rejoiced is Brough, right glad, I deem,
Beside her little humble stream;
And she that keepeth watch and ward
Her statelier Eden's course to guard;
They both are happy at this hour,
Though each is but a lonely Tower: –
50 But here is perfect joy and pride
For one fair House by Emont's side,
This day, distinguished without peer,
To see her Master and to cheer –
Him, and his Lady-mother dear!

'Oh! it was a time forlorn
When the fatherless was born –
Give her wings that she may fly,
Or she sees her infant die!
Swords that are with slaughter wild
60 Hunt the Mother and the Child.
Who will take them from the light?
– Yonder is a man in sight –
Yonder is a house – but where?
No, they must not enter there.
To the caves, and to the brooks,
To the clouds of heaven she looks;
She is speechless, but her eyes
Pray in ghostly agonies.
Blissful Mary, Mother mild,
70 Maid and Mother undefiled,
Save a Mother and her Child!

'Now Who is he that bounds with joy
On Carrock's side, a Shepherd-boy?
No thoughts hath he but thoughts that pass
Light as the wind along the grass.
Can this be He who hither came
In secret, like a smothered flame?
O'er whom such thankful tears were shed
For shelter, and a poor man's bread!
80 God loves the Child; and God hath willed
That those dear words should be fulfilled,
The Lady's words, when forced away,
The last she to her Babe did say:
"My own, my own, thy Fellow-guest
I may not be; but rest thee, rest,
For lowly shepherd's life is best!"

'Alas! when evil men are strong
No life is good, no pleasure long.
The Boy must part from Mosedale's groves,
90 And leave Blencathara's rugged coves,
And quit the flowers that summer brings
To Glenderamakin's lofty springs;

Must vanish, and his careless cheer
Be turned to heaviness and fear.
– Give Sir Lancelot Threlkeld praise!
Hear it, good man, old in days!
Thou tree of covert and of rest
For this young Bird that is distrest;
Among thy branches safe he lay,
And he was free to sport and play,
When falcons were abroad for prey.

    'A recreant harp, that sings of fear
And heaviness in Clifford's ear!
I said, when evil men are strong,
No life is good, no pleasure long,
A weak and cowardly untruth!
Our Clifford was a happy Youth,
And thankful through a weary time,
That brought him up to manhood's prime.
– Again he wanders forth at will,
And tends a flock from hill to hill:
His garb is humble; ne'er was seen
Such garb with such a noble mien;
Among the shepherd-grooms no mate
Hath he, a Child of strength and state!
Yet lacks not friends for simple glee,
Nor yet for higher sympathy.
To his side the fallow-deer
Came, and rested without fear;
The eagle, lord of land and sea,
Stooped down to pay him fealty;
And both the undying fish that swim
Through Bowscale-tarn did wait on him;
The pair were servants of his eye
In their immortality;
And glancing, gleaming, dark or bright,
Moved to and fro, for his delight.
He knew the rocks which Angels haunt
Upon the mountains visitant;
He hath kenned them taking wing:

And into caves where Faeries sing
He hath entered; and been told
By Voices how men lived of old.
Among the heavens his eye can see
The face of thing that is to be;
And, if that men report him right,
His tongue could whisper words of might.
— Now another day is come,
Fitter hope, and nobler doom;
He hath thrown aside his crook,
And hath buried deep his book;
Armour rusting in his halls
On the blood of Clifford calls; —
"Quell the Scot," exclaims the Lance —
Bear me to the heart of France,
Is the longing of the Shield —
Tell thy name, thou trembling Field;
Field of death, where'er thou be,
Groan thou with our victory!
Happy day, and mighty hour,
When our Shepherd, in his power,
Mailed and horsed, with lance and sword,
To his ancestors restored
Like a re-appearing Star,
Like a glory from afar,
First shall head the flock of war!'

Alas! the impassioned minstrel did not know
How, by Heaven's grace, this Clifford's heart was framed:
How he, long forced in humble walks to go,
Was softened into feeling, soothed, and tamed.

Love had he found in huts where poor men lie;
His daily teachers had been woods and rills,
The silence that is in the starry sky,
The sleep that is among the lonely hills.

In him the savage virtue of the Race,
Revenge, and all ferocious thoughts were dead:
Nor did he change; but kept in lofty place
The wisdom which adversity had bred.

Glad were the vales, and every cottage-hearth;
170 The Shepherd-lord was honoured more and more;
And, ages after he was laid in earth,
'The good Lord Clifford' was the name he bore.

Gypsies

Yet are they here the same unbroken knot
Of human Beings, in the self-same spot!
    Men, women, children, yea the frame
    Of the whole spectacle the same!
Only their fire seems bolder, yielding light,
Now deep and red, the colouring of night;
    That on their Gypsy-faces falls,
    Their bed of straw and blanket-walls.
– Twelve hours, twelve bounteous hours are gone, while I
10 Have been a traveller under open sky,
    Much witnessing of change and cheer,
    Yet as I left I find them here!
The weary Sun betook himself to rest; –
Then issued Vesper from the fulgent west,
    Outshining like a visible God
    The glorious path in which he trod.
And now, ascending, after one dark hour
And one night's diminution of her power,
    Behold the mighty Moon! this way
20   She looks as if at them – but they
Regard not her: – oh better wrong and strife
(By nature transient) than this torpid life;
    Life which the very stars reprove
    As on their silent tasks they move!
Yet, witness all that stirs in heaven or earth!
In scorn I speak not; – they are what their birth
    And breeding suffer them to be;
    Wild outcasts of society!

[St Paul's]

Pressed with conflicting thoughts of love and fear
I parted from thee, Friend, and took my way
Through the great City, pacing with an eye
Downcast, ear sleeping, and feet masterless
That were sufficient guide unto themselves,
And step by step went pensively. Now, mark!
Not how my trouble was entirely hushed,
(That might not be) but how, by sudden gift,
Gift of Imagination's holy power,
10 My Soul in her uneasiness received
An anchor of stability. – It chanced
That while I thus was pacing, I raised up
My heavy eyes and instantly beheld,
Saw at a glance in that familiar spot
A visionary scene – a length of street
Laid open in its morning quietness,
Deep, hollow, unobstructed, vacant, smooth,
And white with winter's purest white, as fair,
As fresh and spotless as he ever sheds
20 On field or mountain. Moving Form was none
Save here and there a shadowy Passenger
Slow, shadowy, silent, dusky, and beyond
And high above this winding length of street,
This moveless and unpeopled avenue,
Pure, silent, solemn, beautiful, was seen
The huge majestic Temple of St Paul
In awful sequestration, through a veil,
Through its own sacred veil of falling snow.

Epitaph

Six months to six years added he remained
Upon this sinful earth, by sin unstained:
O blessèd Lord! whose mercy then removed
A Child whom every eye that looked on loved;
Support us, teach us calmly to resign
What we possessed, and now is wholly thine!

Characteristics of a Child Three Years Old

Loving she is, and tractable, though wild;
And Innocence hath privilege in her
To dignify arch looks and laughing eyes;
And feats of cunning; and the pretty round
Of trespasses, affected to provoke
Mock-chastisement and partnership in play.
And, as a faggot sparkles on the hearth,
Not less if unattended and alone
Than when both young and old sit gathered round
10 And take delight in its activity;
Even so this happy Creature of herself
Is all-sufficient; solitude to her
Is blithe society, who fills the air
With gladness and involuntary songs.
Light are her sallies as the tripping fawn's
Forth-startled from the fern where she lay couched;
Unthought-of, unexpected, as the stir
Of the soft breeze ruffling the meadow-flowers,
Or from before it chasing wantonly
20 The many-coloured images imprest
Upon the bosom of a placid lake.

'Surprised by joy – impatient as the Wind'

Surprised by joy – impatient as the Wind
I turned to share the transport – Oh! with whom
But Thee, deep buried in the silent tomb,
That spot which no vicissitude can find?
Love, faithful love, recalled thee to my mind –
But how could I forget thee? Through what power,
Even for the least division of an hour,
Have I been so beguiled as to be blind
To my most grievous loss! – That thought's return
10 Was the worst pang that sorrow ever bore,
Save one, one only, when I stood forlorn,

Knowing my heart's best treasure was no more;
That neither present time, nor years unborn
Could to my sight that heavenly face restore.

The Excursion

from BOOK IV

[Greek Nature Myths]

'Once more to distant ages of the world
Let us revert, and place before our thoughts
The face which rural solitude might wear
850 To the unenlightened swains of pagan Greece.
– In that fair clime, the lonely herdsman, stretched
On the soft grass through half a summer's day,
With music lulled his indolent repose:
And, in some fit of weariness, if he,
When his own breath was silent, chanced to hear
A distant strain, far sweeter than the sounds
Which his poor skill could make, his fancy fetched,
Even from the blazing chariot of the sun,
A beardless Youth, who touched a golden lute,
860 And filled the illumined groves with ravishment.
The nightly hunter, lifting a bright eye
Up towards the crescent moon, with grateful heart
Called on the lovely wanderer who bestowed
That timely light, to share his joyous sport:
And hence, a beaming Goddess with her Nymphs,
Across the lawn and through the darksome grove,
Not unaccompanied with tuneful notes
By echo multiplied from rock or cave,
Swept in the storm of chase; as moon and stars
870 Glance rapidly along the clouded heaven,
When winds are blowing strong. The traveller slaked
His thirst from rill or gushing fount, and thanked
The Naiad. Sunbeams, upon distant hills

Gliding apace, with shadows in their train,
Might, with small help from fancy, be transformed
Into fleet Oreads sporting visibly.
The Zephyrs fanning, as they passed, their wings,
Lacked not, for love, fair objects whom they wooed
With gentle whisper. Withered boughs grotesque,
880   Stripped of their leaves and twigs by hoary age,
From depth of shaggy covert peeping forth
In the low vale, or on steep mountain-side;
And, sometimes, intermixed with stirring horns
Of the live deer, or goat's depending beard, –
These were the lurking Satyrs, a wild brood
Of gamesome Deities; or Pan himself,
The simple shepherd's awe-inspiring god!'

from BOOK VI

[*The Tale of the Whig and the Jacobite*]

    'Yes,' said the Priest, 'the Genius of our hills –
Who seems, by these stupendous barriers cast
Round his domain, desirous not alone
To keep his own, but also to exclude
All other progeny – doth sometimes lure,
Even by his studied depth of privacy,
The unhappy alien hoping to obtain
Concealment, or seduced by wish to find,
400   In place from outward molestation free,
Helps to internal ease. Of many such
Could I discourse; but as their stay was brief,
So their departure only left behind
Fancies, and loose conjectures. Other trace
Survives, for worthy mention, of a pair
Who, from the pressure of their several fates,
Meeting as strangers, in a petty town
Whose blue roofs ornament a distant reach
Of this far-winding vale, remained as friends
410   True to their choice; and gave their bones in trust

To this loved cemetery, here to lodge
With unescutcheoned privacy interred
Far from the family vault. – A Chieftain one
By right of birth; within whose spotless breast
The fire of ancient Caledonia burned:
He, with the foremost whose impatience hailed
The Stuart, landing to resume, by force
Of arms, the crown which bigotry had lost,
Aroused his clan; and, fighting at their head,
420   With his brave sword endeavoured to prevent
Culloden's fatal overthrow. Escaped
From that disastrous rout, to foreign shores
He fled; and when the lenient hand of time
Those troubles had appeased, he sought and gained,
For his obscured condition, an obscure
Retreat, within this nook of English ground.

'The other, born in Britain's southern tract,
Had fixed his milder loyalty, and placed
His gentler sentiments of love and hate,
430   There, where *they* placed them who in conscience prized
The new succession, as a line of kings
Whose oath had virtue to protect the land
Against the dire assaults of papacy
And arbitrary rule. But launch thy bark
On the distempered flood of public life,
And cause for most rare triumph will be thine
If, spite of keenest eye and steadiest hand,
The stream, that bears thee forward, prove not, soon
Or late, a perilous master. He – who oft,
440   Beneath the battlements and stately trees
That round his mansion cast a sober gloom,
Had moralized on this, and other truths
Of kindred import, pleased and satisfied –
Was forced to vent his wisdom with a sigh
Heaved from the heart in fortune's bitterness,
When he had crushed a plentiful estate
By ruinous contest, to obtain a seat
In Britain's senate. Fruitless was the attempt:

And while the uproar of that desperate strife
450   Continued yet to vibrate on his ear,
The vanquished Whig, under a borrowed name,
(For the mere sound and echo of his own
Haunted him with sensations of disgust
That he was glad to lose) slunk from the world
To the deep shade of those untravelled Wilds;
In which the Scottish Laird had long possessed
An undisturbed abode. Here, then, they met,
Two doughty champions; flaming Jacobite
And sullen Hanoverian! You might think
460   That losses and vexations, less severe
Than those which they had severally sustained,
Would have inclined each to abate his zeal
For his ungrateful cause; no, – I have heard
My reverend Father tell that, 'mid the calm
Of that small town encountering thus, they filled,
Daily, its bowling-green with harmless strife;
Plagued with uncharitable thoughts the church;
And vexed the market-place. But in the breasts
Of these opponents gradually was wrought,
470   With little change of general sentiment,
Such leaning towards each other, that their days
By choice were spent in constant fellowship;
And if, at times, they fretted with the yoke,
Those very bickerings made them love it more.

'A favourite boundary to their lengthened walks
This Churchyard was. And, whether they had come
Treading their path in sympathy and linked
In social converse, or by some short space
Discreetly parted to preserve the peace,
480   One spirit seldom failed to extend its sway
Over both minds, when they awhile had marked
The visible quiet of this holy ground,
And breathed its soothing air; – the spirit of hope
And saintly magnanimity; that – spurning
The field of selfish difference and dispute,
And every care which transitory things,

Earth and the kingdoms of the earth, create –
Doth, by a rapture of forgetfulness,
Preclude forgiveness, from the praise debarred,
490   Which else the Christian virtue might have claimed.

'There live who yet remember here to have seen
Their courtly figures, seated on the stump
Of an old yew, their favourite resting-place.
But as the remnant of the long-lived tree
Was disappearing by a swift decay,
They, with joint care, determined to erect,
Upon its site, a dial, that might stand
For public use preserved, and thus survive
As their own private monument: for this
500   Was the particular spot, in which they wished
(And Heaven was pleased to accomplish the desire)
That, undivided, their remains should lie.
So, where the mouldered tree had stood, was raised
Yon structure, framing, with the ascent of steps
That to the decorated pillar lead,
A work of art more sumptuous than might seem
To suit this place; yet built in no proud scorn
Of rustic homeliness; they only aimed
To ensure for it respectful guardianship.
510   Around the margin of the plate, whereon
The shadow falls to note the stealthy hours,
Winds an inscriptive legend.' – At these words
Thither we turned; and gathered, as we read,
The appropriate sense, in Latin numbers couched:
'*Time flies; it is his melancholy task*
To bring, and bear away, delusive hopes,
And re-produce the troubles he destroys.
But, while his blindness thus is occupied,
Discerning Mortal! do thou serve the will
520   *Of Time's eternal Master, and that peace,*
Which the world wants, shall be for thee confirmed!'

from BOOK VI

[*The Story of Ellen*]

'As on a sunny bank, a tender lamb
Lurks in safe shelter from the winds of March,
Screened by its parent, so that little mound
790 Lies guarded by its neighbour; the small heap
Speaks for itself; an Infant there doth rest;
The sheltering hillock is the Mother's grave.
If mild discourse, and manners that conferred
A natural dignity on humblest rank;
If gladsome spirits, and benignant looks,
That for a face not beautiful did more
Than beauty for the fairest face can do;
And if religious tenderness of heart,
Grieving for sin, and penitential tears
800 Shed when the clouds had gathered and distained
The spotless ether of a maiden life;
If these may make a hallowed spot of earth
More holy in the sight of God or Man;
Then, o'er that mould, a sanctity shall brood
Till the stars sicken at the day of doom.

'Ah! what a warning for a thoughtless man,
Could field or grove, could any spot of earth,
Show to his eye an image of the pangs
Which it hath witnessed; render back an echo
810 Of the sad steps by which it hath been trod!
There, by her innocent Baby's precious grave,
And on the very turf that roofs her own,
The Mother oft was seen to stand, or kneel
In the broad day, a weeping Magdalene.
Now she is not; the swelling turf reports
Of the fresh shower, but of poor Ellen's tears
Is silent; nor is any vestige left
Of the path worn by mournful tread of her
Who, at her heart's light bidding, once had moved
820 In virgin fearlessness, with step that seemed
Caught from the pressure of elastic turf
Upon the mountains gemmed with morning dew,

In the prime hour of sweetest scents and airs.
– Serious and thoughtful was her mind; and yet,
By reconcilement exquisite and rare,
The form, port, motions, of this Cottage-girl
Were such as might have quickened and inspired
A Titian's hand, addrest to picture forth
Oread or Dryad glancing through the shade
830 What time the hunter's earliest horn is heard
Startling the golden hills.
                                A wide-spread elm
Stands in our valley, named THE JOYFUL TREE;
From dateless usage which our peasants hold
Of giving welcome to the first of May
By dances round its trunk. – And if the sky
Permit, like honours, dance and song, are paid
To the Twelfth Night, beneath the frosty stars
Or the clear moon. The queen of these gay sports,
If not in beauty yet in sprightly air,
840 Was hapless Ellen. – No one touched the ground
So deftly, and the nicest maiden's locks
Less gracefully were braided; – but this praise,
Methinks, would better suit another place.

   'She loved, and fondly deemed herself beloved.
– The road is dim, the current unperceived,
The weakness painful and most pitiful,
By which a virtuous woman, in pure youth,
May be delivered to distress and shame.
Such fate was hers. – The last time Ellen danced,
850 Among her equals, round THE JOYFUL TREE,
She bore a secret burden; and full soon
Was left to tremble for a breaking vow, –
Then, to bewail a sternly-broken vow,
Alone, within her widowed Mother's house.
It was the season of unfolding leaves,
Of days advancing toward their utmost length,
And small birds singing happily to mates
Happy as they. With spirit-saddening power
Winds pipe through fading woods; but those blithe notes

860 Strike the deserted to the heart; I speak
Of what I know, and what we feel within.
– Beside the cottage in which Ellen dwelt
Stands a tall ash-tree; to whose topmost twig
A thrush resorts and annually chants,
At morn and evening from that naked perch,
While all the undergrove is thick with leaves,
A time-beguiling ditty, for delight
Of his fond partner, silent in the nest.
– "Ah why," said Ellen, sighing to herself,
870 "Why do not words, and kiss, and solemn pledge,
And nature that is kind in woman's breast,
And reason that in man is wise and good,
And fear of Him who is a righteous judge;
Why do not these prevail for human life,
To keep two hearts together, that began
Their spring-time with one love, and that have need
Of mutual pity and forgiveness, sweet
To grant, or be received; while that poor bird –
O come and hear him! Thou who hast to me
880 Been faithless, hear him, though a lowly creature,
One of God's simple children that yet know not
The universal Parent, how he sings
As if he wished the firmament of heaven
Should listen, and give back to him the voice
Of his triumphant constancy and love;
The proclamation that he makes, how far
His darkness doth transcend our fickle light!"

     'Such was the tender passage, not by me
Repeated without loss of simple phrase,
890 Which I perused, even as the words had been
Committed by forsaken Ellen's hand
To the blank margin of a Valentine,
Bedropped with tears. 'Twill please you to be told
That, studiously withdrawing from the eye
Of all companionship, the Sufferer yet
In lonely reading found a meek resource:
How thankful for the warmth of summer days,

When she could slip into the cottage-barn,
And find a secret oratory there;
900 Or, in the garden, under friendly veil
Of their long twilight, pore upon her book
By the last lingering help of the open sky
Until dark night dismissed her to her bed!
Thus did a waking fancy sometimes lose
The unconquerable pang of despised love.

'A kindlier passion opened on her soul
When that poor Child was born. Upon its face
She gazed as on a pure and spotless gift
Of unexpected promise, where a grief
910 Or dread was all that had been thought of, – joy
Far livelier than bewildered traveller feels,
Amid a perilous waste that all night long
Hath harassed him toiling through fearful storm,
When he beholds the first pale speck serene
Of day-spring, in the gloomy east, revealed,
And greets it with thanksgiving. "Till this hour,"
Thus, in her Mother's hearing Ellen spake,
"There was a stony region in my heart;
But He, at whose command the parchèd rock
920 Was smitten, and poured forth a quenching stream,
Hath softened that obduracy, and made
Unlooked-for gladness in the desert place,
To save the perishing; and, henceforth, I breathe
The air with cheerful spirit, for thy sake,
My Infant! and for that good Mother dear,
Who bore me; and hath prayed for me in vain; –
Yet not in vain; it shall not be in vain."
She spake, nor was the assurance unfulfilled;
And if heart-rending thoughts would oft return,
930 They stayed not long. – The blameless Infant grew;
The Child whom Ellen and her Mother loved
They soon were proud of; tended it and nursed;
A soothing comforter, although forlorn;
Like a poor singing-bird from distant lands;
Or a choice shrub, which he, who passes by

With vacant mind, not seldom may observe
Fair-flowering in a thinly-peopled house,
Whose window, somewhat sadly, it adorns.

'Through four months' space the Infant drew its food
940   From the maternal breast; then scruples rose;
Thoughts, which the rich are free from, came and crossed
The fond affection. She no more could bear
By her offence to lay a twofold weight
On a kind parent willing to forget
Their slender means: so, to that parent's care
Trusting her child, she left their common home,
And undertook with dutiful content
A Foster-mother's office.
                              'Tis, perchance,
Unknown to you that in these simple vales
950   The natural feeling of equality
Is by domestic service unimpaired;
Yet, though such service be, with us, removed
From sense of degradation, not the less
The ungentle mind can easily find means
To impose severe restraints and laws unjust,
Which hapless Ellen now was doomed to feel:
For (blinded by an over-anxious dread
Of such excitement and divided thought
As with her office would but ill accord)
960   The pair, whose infant she was bound to nurse,
Forbad her all communion with her own:
Week after week, the mandate they enforced.
– So near! yet not allowed, upon that sight
To fix her eyes – alas! 'twas hard to bear!
But worse affliction must be borne – far worse;
For 'tis Heaven's will – that, after a disease
Begun and ended within three days' space,
Her child should die; as Ellen now exclaimed,
Her own – deserted child! – Once, only once,
970   She saw it in that mortal malady;
And, on the burial-day, could scarcely gain
Permission to attend its obsequies.

She reached the house, last of the funeral train;
And someone, as she entered, having chanced
To urge unthinkingly their prompt departure,
"Nay," said she, with commanding look, a spirit
Of anger never seen in her before,
"Nay, ye must wait my time!" and down she sate,
And by the unclosed coffin kept her seat
980 Weeping and looking, looking on and weeping,
Upon the last sweet slumber of her Child,
Until at length her soul was satisfied.

'You see the Infant's Grave; and to this spot,
The Mother, oft as she was sent abroad,
On whatsoever errand, urged her steps:
Hither she came; here stood, and sometimes knelt
In the broad day, a rueful Magdalene!
So call her; for not only she bewailed
A mother's loss, but mourned in bitterness
990 Her own transgression; penitent sincere
As ever raised to heaven a streaming eye!
– At length the parents of the foster-child,
Noting that in despite of their commands
She still renewed and could not but renew
Those visitations, ceased to send her forth;
Or, to the garden's narrow bounds, confined.
I failed not to remind them that they erred;
For holy Nature might not thus be crossed,
Thus wronged in woman's breast: in vain I pleaded –
1000 But the green stalk of Ellen's life was snapped,
And the flower drooped; as every eye could see,
It hung its head in mortal languishment.
– Aided by this appearance, I at length
Prevailed; and, from those bonds released, she went
Home to her mother's house.
                                    The Youth was fled;
The rash betrayer could not face the shame
Or sorrow which his senseless guilt had caused;
And little would his presence, or proof given
Of a relenting soul, have now availed;

1010   For, like a shadow, he was passed away
        From Ellen's thoughts; had perished to her mind
        For all concerns of fear, or hope, or love,
        Save only those which to their common shame,
        And to his moral being appertained:
        Hope from that quarter would, I know, have brought
        A heavenly comfort; there she recognized
        An unrelaxing bond, a mutual need;
        There, and, as seemed, there only.
                                She had built,
        Her fond maternal heart had built, a nest
1020   In blindness all too near the river's edge;
        That work a summer flood with hasty swell
        Had swept away; and now her Spirit longed
        For its last flight to heaven's security.
        – The bodily frame wasted from day to day;
        Meanwhile, relinquishing all other cares,
        Her mind she strictly tutored to find peace
        And pleasure in endurance. Much she thought,
        And much she read; and brooded feelingly
        Upon her own unworthiness. To me,
1030   As to a spiritual comforter and friend,
        Her heart she opened; and no pains were spared
        To mitigate, as gently as I could,
        The sting of self-reproach, with healing words.
        Meek Saint! through patience glorified on earth!
        In whom, as by her lonely hearth she sate,
        The ghastly face of cold decay put on
        A sun-like beauty, and appeared divine!
        May I not mention – that, within those walls,
        In due observance of her pious wish,
1040   The congregation joined with me in prayer
        For her soul's good? Nor was that office vain.
        – Much did she suffer: but, if any friend,
        Beholding her condition, at the sight
        Gave way to words of pity or complaint,
        She stilled them with a prompt reproof, and said,
        "He who afflicts me knows what I can bear;

And, when I fail, and can endure no more,
Will mercifully take me to Himself."
So, through the cloud of death, her Spirit passed
1050 Into that pure and unknown world of love
Where injury cannot come: – and here is laid
The mortal Body by her Infant's side.'

from BOOK VIII

[*The Pastor's Children*]

He gazed, with admiration unsuppressed,
Upon the landscape of the sun-bright vale,
Seen, from the shady room in which we sate,
In softened pérspective; and more than once
Praised the consummate harmony serene
Of gravity and elegance, diffused
540 Around the mansion and its whole domain;
Not, doubtless, without help of female taste
And female care. – 'A blessed lot is yours!'
The words escaped his lip, with a tender sigh
Breathed over them: but suddenly the door
Flew open, and a pair of lusty Boys
Appeared, confusion checking their delight.
– Not brothers they in feature or attire,
But fond companions, so I guessed, in field,
And by the river's margin – whence they come,
550 Keen anglers with unusual spoil elated.
One bears a willow-pannier on his back,
The boy of plainer garb, whose blush survives
More deeply tinged. Twin might the other be
To that fair girl who from the garden-mount
Bounded: – triumphant entry this for him!
Between his hands he holds a smooth blue stone,
On whose capacious surface see outspread
Large store of gleaming crimson-spotted trouts;
Ranged side by side, and lessening by degrees
560 Up to the dwarf that tops the pinnacle.

Upon the board he lays the sky-blue stone
With its rich freight; their number he proclaims;
Tells from what pool the noblest had been dragged;
And where the very monarch of the brook,
After long struggle, had escaped at last –
Stealing alternately at them and us
(As doth his comrade too) a look of pride:
And, verily, the silent creatures made
A splendid sight, together thus exposed;
570   Dead – but not sullied or deformed by death,
That seemed to pity what he could not spare.

But O, the animation in the mien
Of those two boys! yea in the very words
With which the young narrator was inspired,
When, as our questions led, he told at large
Of that day's prowess! Him might I compare,
His looks, tones, gestures, eager eloquence,
To a bold brook that splits for better speed,
And at the self-same moment, works its way
580   Through many channels, ever and anon
Parted and re-united: his compeer
To the still lake, whose stillness is to sight
As beautiful – as grateful to the mind.
– But to what object shall the lovely Girl
Be likened? She whose countenance and air
Unite the graceful qualities of both,
Even as she shares the pride and joy of both.

Yarrow Visited

September, 1814

And is this – Yarrow? – *This* the Stream
Of which my fancy cherished,
So faithfully, a waking dream?
An image that hath perished!
O that some Minstrel's harp were near,
To utter notes of gladness,
And chase this silence from the air,
That fills my heart with sadness!

Yet why? – a silvery current flows
10   With uncontrolled meanderings;
Nor have these eyes by greener hills
Been soothed, in all my wanderings.
And, through her depths, Saint Mary's Lake
Is visibly delighted;
For not a feature of those hills
Is in the mirror slighted.

A blue sky bends o'er Yarrow vale,
Save where that pearly whiteness
Is round the rising sun diffused,
20   A tender hazy brightness;
Mild dawn of promise! that excludes
All profitless dejection;
Though not unwilling here to admit
A pensive recollection.

Where was it that the famous Flower
Of Yarrow Vale lay bleeding?
His bed perchance was yon smooth mound
On which the herd is feeding:
And haply from this crystal pool,
30   Now peaceful as the morning,
The Water-wraith ascended thrice –
And gave his doleful warning.

Delicious is the Lay that sings
The haunts of happy Lovers,
The path that leads them to the grove,
The leafy grove that covers:
And Pity sanctifies the Verse
That paints, by strength of sorrow,
The unconquerable strength of love;
40   Bear witness, rueful Yarrow!

But thou, that didst appear so fair
To fond imagination,
Dost rival in the light of day
Her delicate creation:
Meek loveliness is round thee spread,
A softness still and holy;
The grace of forest charms decayed,
And pastoral melancholy.

That region left, the vale unfolds
50   Rich groves of lofty stature,
With Yarrow winding through the pomp
Of cultivated nature;
And, rising from those lofty groves,
Behold a Ruin hoary!
The shattered front of Newark's Towers,
Renowned in Border story.

Fair scenes for childhood's opening bloom,
For sportive youth to stray in;
For manhood to enjoy his strength;
60   And age to wear away in!
Yon cottage seems a bower of bliss,
A covert for protection
Of tender thoughts, that nestle there –
The brood of chaste affection.

How sweet, on this autumnal day,
The wild-wood fruits to gather,
And on my True-love's forehead plant
A crest of blooming heather!
And what if I enwreathed my own!
70   'Twere no offence to reason;
The sober Hills thus deck their brows
To meet the wintry season.

I see – but not by sight alone,
Loved Yarrow, have I won thee;
A ray of fancy still survives –
Her sunshine plays upon thee!
Thy ever-youthful waters keep
A course of lively pleasure;
And gladsome notes my lips can breathe,
80   Accordant to the measure.

The vapours linger round the Heights,
They melt, and soon must vanish;
One hour is theirs, nor more is mine –
Sad thought, which I would banish,
But that I know, where'er I go,
Thy genuine image, Yarrow!
Will dwell with me – to heighten joy,
And cheer my mind in sorrow.

Laodamia

'With sacrifice before the rising morn
Vows have I made by fruitless hope inspired;
And from the infernal Gods, mid shades forlorn
Of night, my slaughtered Lord have I required;
Celestial pity I again implore; –
Restore him to my sight – great Jove, restore!'

So speaking, and by fervent love endowed
With faith, the Suppliant heavenward lifts her hands;
While, like the sun emerging from a cloud,
10   Her countenance brightens – and her eye expands;
Her bosom heaves and spreads, her stature grows;
And she expects the issue in repose.

O terror! what hath she perceived? – O joy!
What doth she look on? – whom doth she behold?
Her Hero slain upon the beach of Troy?
His vital presence? his corporeal mould?
It is – if sense deceive her not – 'tis He!
And a God leads him, wingèd Mercury!

Mild Hermes spake – and touched her with his wand
20   That calms all fear; 'Such grace hath crowned thy prayer,
Laodamía! that at Jove's command
Thy Husband walks the paths of upper air:
He comes to tarry with thee three hours' space;
Accept the gift, behold him face to face!'

Forth sprang the impassioned Queen her Lord to clasp;
Again that consummation she essayed;
But unsubstantial Form eludes her grasp
As often as that eager grasp was made.
The Phantom parts – but parts to re-unite,
30   And re-assume his place before her sight.

'Protesiláus, lo! thy guide is gone!
Confirm, I pray, the vision with thy voice:
This is our palace, – yonder is thy throne;
Speak, and the floor thou tread'st on will rejoice.
Not to appal me have the gods bestowed
This precious boon; and blest a sad abode.'

'Great Jove, Laodamía! doth not leave
His gifts imperfect: – Spectre though I be,
I am not sent to scare thee or deceive;
40 But in reward of thy fidelity.
And something also did my worth obtain;
For fearless virtue bringeth boundless gain.

'Thou knowest, the Delphic oracle foretold
That the first Greek who touched the Trojan strand
Should die; but me the threat could not withhold:
A generous cause a victim did demand;
And forth I leapt upon the sandy plain;
A self-devoted chief – by Hector slain.'

'Supreme of Heroes – bravest, noblest, best!
50 Thy matchless courage I bewail no more,
Which then, when tens of thousands were deprest
By doubt, propelled thee to the fatal shore;
Thou found'st – and I forgive thee – here thou art –
A nobler counsellor than my poor heart.

'But thou, though capable of sternest deed,
Wert kind as resolute, and good as brave;
And he, whose power restores thee, hath decreed
Thou should'st elude the malice of the grave:
Redundant are thy locks, thy lips as fair
60 As when their breath enriched Thessalian air.

'No Spectre greets me, – no vain Shadow this;
Come, blooming Hero, place thee by my side!
Give, on this well-known couch, one nuptial kiss
To me, this day, a second time thy bride!'
Jove frowned in heaven: the conscious Parcae threw
Upon those roseate lips a Stygian hue.

'This visage tells thee that my doom is past:
Nor should the change be mourned, even if the joys
Of sense were able to return as fast
70 And surely as they vanish. Earth destroys
Those raptures duly – Erebus disdains:
Calm pleasures there abide – majestic pains.

'Be taught, O faithful Consort, to control
Rebellious passion: for the Gods approve
The depth, and not the tumult, of the soul;
A fervent, not ungovernable, love.
Thy transports moderate; and meekly mourn
When I depart, for brief is my sojourn –'

'Ah, wherefore? – Did not Hercules by force
80 Wrest from the guardian Monster of the tomb
Alcestis, a reanimated corse,
Given back to dwell on earth in vernal bloom?
Medea's spells dispersed the weight of years,
And Aeson stood a youth mid youthful peers.

'The Gods to us are merciful – and they
Yet further may relent: for mightier far
Than strength of nerve and sinew, or the sway
Of magic potent over sun and star,
Is love, though oft to agony distrest,
90 And though his favourite seat be feeble woman's breast.

'But if thou goest, I follow –' 'Peace!' he said, –
She looked upon him and was calmed and cheered;
The ghastly colour from his lips had fled;
In his deportment, shape, and mien, appeared
Elysian beauty, melancholy grace,
Brought from a pensive though a happy place.

He spake of love, such love as Spirits feel
In worlds whose course is equable and pure;
No fears to beat away – no strife to heal –
100 The past unsighed for, and the future sure;
Spake of heroic arts in graver mood
Revived, with finer harmony pursued;

Of all that is most beauteous – imaged there
In happier beauty; more pellucid streams,
An ampler ether, a diviner air,
And fields invested with purpureal gleams;
Climes which the sun, who sheds the brightest day
Earth knows, is all unworthy to survey.

Yet there the Soul shall enter which hath earned
110   That privilege by virtue. – 'Ill,' said he,
'The end of man's existence I discerned,
Who from ignoble games and revelry
Could draw, when we had parted, vain delight,
While tears were thy best pastime, day and night;

'And while my youthful peers before my eyes
(Each hero following his peculiar bent)
Prepared themselves for glorious enterprise
By martial sports, – or, seated in the tent,
Chieftains and kings in council were detained;
120   What time the fleet at Aulis lay enchained,

'The wished-for wind was given: – I then revolved
The oracle, upon the silent sea;
And, if no worthier led the way, resolved
That, of a thousand vessels, mine should be
The foremost prow in pressing to the strand, –
Mine the first blood that tinged the Trojan sand.

'Yet bitter, oft-times bitter, was the pang
When of thy loss I thought, belovèd Wife!
On thee too fondly did my memory hang,
130   And on the joys we shared in mortal life, –
The paths which we had trod – these fountains, flowers;
My new-planned cities, and unfinished towers.

'But should suspense permit the Foe to cry,
"Behold they tremble! – haughty their array,
Yet of their number no one dares to die?"
In soul I swept the indignity away:
Old frailties then recurred: – but lofty thought,
In act embodied, my deliverance wrought.

'And Thou, though strong in love, art all too weak
140   In reason, in self-government too slow;
I counsel thee by fortitude to seek
Our blest re-union in the shades below.
The invisible world with thee hath sympathized;
Be thy affections raised and solemnized.

'Learn, by a mortal yearning, to ascend –
Seeking a higher object. Love was given,
Encouraged, sanctioned, chiefly for that end;
For this the passion to excess was driven –
That self might be annulled: her bondage prove
150 The fetters of a dream, opposed to love.' –

Aloud she shrieked! for Hermes reappears!
Round the dear Shade she would have clung – 'tis vain:
The hours are past – too brief had they been years;
And him no mortal effort can detain:
Swift, toward the realms that know not earthly day,
He through the portal takes his silent way,
And on the palace-floor a lifeless corse She lay.

Thus, all in vain exhorted and reproved,
She perished; and, as for a wilful crime,
160 By the just Gods whom no weak pity moved,
Was doomed to wear out her appointed time,
Apart from happy Ghosts, that gather flowers
Of blissful quiet 'mid unfading bowers.

– Yet tears to human suffering are due;
And mortal hopes defeated and o'erthrown
Are mourned by man, and not by man alone,
As fondly he believes. – Upon the side
Of Hellespont (such faith was entertained)
A knot of spiry trees for ages grew
170 From out the tomb of him for whom she died;
And ever, when such stature they had gained
That Ilium's walls were subject to their view,
The trees' tall summits withered at the sight;
A constant interchange of growth and blight!

Composed upon an Evening of Extraordinary Splendour and Beauty

I

Had this effulgence disappeared
With flying haste, I might have sent,
Among the speechless clouds, a look
Of blank astonishment;
But 'tis endued with power to stay,
And sanctify one closing day,
That frail Mortality may see –
What is? – ah no, but what *can* be!
Time was when field and watery cove
10   With modulated echoes rang,
While choirs of fervent Angels sang
Their vespers in the grove;
Or, crowning, star-like, each some sovereign height,
Warbled, for heaven above and earth below,
Strains suitable to both. – Such holy rite,
Methinks, if audibly repeated now
From hill or valley, could not move
Sublimer transport, purer love,
Than doth this silent spectacle – the gleam –
20   The shadow – and the peace supreme!

II

No sound is uttered, – but a deep
And solemn harmony pervades
The hollow vale from steep to steep,
And penetrates the glades.
Far-distant images draw nigh,
Called forth by wondrous potency
Of beamy radiance, that imbues
Whate'er it strikes with gem-like hues!
In vision exquisitely clear,
30   Herds range along the mountain side;
And glistening antlers are descried;
And gilded flocks appear.
Thine is the tranquil hour, purpureal Eve!

But long as god-like wish, or hope divine,
Informs my spirit, ne'er can I believe
That this magnificence is wholly thine!
– From worlds not quickened by the sun
A portion of the gift is won;
An intermingling of Heaven's pomp is spread
40   On ground which British shepherds tread!

III
And, if there be whom broken ties
Afflict, or injuries assail,
Yon hazy ridges to their eyes
Present a glorious scale,
Climbing suffused with sunny air,
To stop – no record hath told where!
And tempting Fancy to ascend,
And with immortal Spirits blend!
– Wings at my shoulders seem to play;
50   But, rooted here, I stand and gaze
On those bright steps that heavenward raise
Their practicable way.
Come forth, ye drooping old men, look abroad,
And see to what fair countries ye are bound!
And if some traveller, weary of his road,
Hath slept since noon-tide on the grassy ground,
Ye Genii! to his covert speed;
And wake him with such gentle heed
As may attune his soul to meet the dower
60   Bestowed on this transcendent hour!

IV
Such hues from their celestial Urn
Were wont to stream before mine eye,
Where'er it wandered in the morn
Of blissful infancy.
This glimpse of glory, why renewed?
Nay, rather speak with gratitude;
For, if a vestige of those gleams
Survived, 'twas only in my dreams.

Dread Power! whom peace and calmness serve
70 No less than Nature's threatening voice,
If aught unworthy be my choice,
From THEE if I would swerve;
Oh, let Thy grace remind me of the light
Full early lost, and fruitlessly deplored;
Which, at this moment, on my waking sight
Appears to shine, by miracle restored;
My soul, though yet confined to earth,
Rejoices in a second birth!
– 'Tis past, the visionary splendour fades;
80 And night approaches with her shades.

NOTE – The multiplication of mountain-ridges, described at the
commencement of the third Stanza of this Ode as a kind of Jacob's
Ladder, leading to Heaven, is produced either by watery vapours, or
sunny haze; – in the present instance by the latter cause. Allusions to
the Ode entitled 'Intimations of Immortality' pervade the last Stanza
of the foregoing Poem.

'Sole listener, Duddon! to the breeze that played'

Sole listener, Duddon! to the breeze that played
With thy clear voice, I caught the fitful sound
Wafted o'er sullen moss and craggy mound –
Unfruitful solitudes, that seemed to upbraid
The sun in heaven! – but now, to form a shade
For Thee, green alders have together wound
Their foliage; ashes flung their arms around;
And birch-trees risen in silver colonnade.
And thou hast also tempted here to rise,
10 Mid sheltering pines, this Cottage rude and grey
Whose ruddy children, by the mother's eyes
Carelessly watched, sport through the summer day,
Thy pleased associates: – light as endless May
On infant bosoms lonely Nature lies.

'Return, Content! for fondly I pursued'

Return, Content! for fondly I pursued,
Even when a child, the Streams – unheard, unseen;
Through tangled woods, impending rocks between;
Or, free as air, with flying inquest viewed
The sullen reservoirs whence their bold brood –
Pure as the morning, fretful, boisterous, keen,
Green as the salt-sea billows, white and green –
Poured down the hills, a choral multitude!
Nor have I tracked their course for scanty gains;
They taught me random cares and truant joys,
That shield from mischief and preserve from stains
Vague minds, while men are growing out of boys;
Maturer Fancy owes to their rough noise
Impetuous thoughts that brook not servile reins.

After-thought

I THOUGHT of Thee, my partner and my guide,
As being past away. – Vain sympathies!
For, backward, Duddon! as I cast my eyes,
I see what was, and is, and will abide;
Still glides the Stream, and shall for ever glide;
The Form remains, the Function never dies;
While we, the brave, the mighty, and the wise,
We Men, who in our morn of youth defied
The elements, must vanish; – be it so!
Enough, if something from our hands have power
To live, and act, and serve the future hour;
And if, as toward the silent tomb we go,
Through love, through hope, and faith's transcendent
       dower,
We feel that we are greater than we know.

Yarrow Revisited

The following Stanzas are a memorial of a day passed with Sir Walter Scott and other Friends visiting the Banks of the Yarrow under his guidance, immediately before his departure from Abbotsford, for Naples.

The title 'Yarrow Revisited' will stand in no need of explanation for Readers acquainted with the Author's previous poems suggested by that celebrated Stream.

The gallant Youth, who may have gained,
 Or seeks, a 'winsome Marrow,'
Was but an Infant in the lap
 When first I looked on Yarrow;
Once more, by Newark's Castle-gate
 Long left without a warder,
I stood, looked, listened, and with Thee,
 Great Minstrel of the Border!

Grave thoughts ruled wide on that sweet day,
10   Their dignity installing
In gentle bosoms, while sere leaves
 Were on the bough, or falling;
But breezes played, and sunshine gleamed –
 The forest to embolden;
Reddened the fiery hues, and shot
 Transparence through the golden.

For busy thoughts the Stream flowed on
 In foamy agitation;
And slept in many a crystal pool
20   For quiet contemplation:
No public and no private care
 The freeborn mind enthralling,
We made a day of happy hours,
 Our happy days recalling.

Brisk Youth appeared, the Morn of youth,
　　With freaks of graceful folly, –
Life's temperate Noon, her sober Eve,
　　Her Night not melancholy;
Past, present, future, all appeared
30　　In harmony united,
Like guests that meet, and some from far,
　　By cordial love invited.

And if, as Yarrow, through the woods
　　And down the meadow ranging,
Did meet us with unaltered face,
　　Though we were changed and changing;
If, *then*, some natural shadows spread
　　Our inward prospect over,
The soul's deep valley was not slow
40　　Its brightness to recover.

Eternal blessings on the Muse,
　　And her divine employment!
The blameless Muse, who trains her Sons
　　For hope and calm enjoyment;
Albeit sickness, lingering yet,
　　Has o'er their pillow brooded;
And Care waylays their steps – a Sprite
　　Not easily eluded.

For thee, O SCOTT! compelled to change
50　　Green Eildon-hill and Cheviot
For warm Vesuvio's vine-clad slopes;
　　And leave thy Tweed and Tiviot
For mild Sorento's breezy waves;
　　May classic Fancy, linking
With native Fancy her fresh aid,
　　Preserve thy heart from sinking!

Oh! while they minister to thee,
　　Each vying with the other,
May Health return to mellow Age,
60　　With Strength, her venturous brother;
And Tiber, and each brook and rill
　　Renowned in song and story,
With unimagined beauty shine,
　　Nor lose one ray of glory!

For Thou, upon a hundred streams,
  By tales of love and sorrow,
Of faithful love, undaunted truth,
  Hast shed the power of Yarrow;
And streams unknown, hills yet unseen,
70 Wherever they invite Thee,
At parent Nature's grateful call,
  With gladness must requite Thee.

A gracious welcome shall be thine,
  Such looks of love and honour
As thy own Yarrow gave to me
  When first I gazed upon her;
Beheld what I had feared to see,
  Unwilling to surrender
Dreams treasured up from early days,
80 The holy and the tender.

And what, for this frail world, were all
  That mortals do or suffer,
Did no responsive harp, no pen,
  Memorial tribute offer?
Yea, what were mighty Nature's self?
  Her features, could they win us,
Unhelped by the poetic voice
  That hourly speaks within us?

Nor deem that localized Romance
90 Plays false with our affections;
Unsanctifies our tears – made sport
  For fanciful dejections:
Ah, no! the visions of the past
  Sustain the heart in feeling
Life as she is – our changeful Life,
  With friends and kindred dealing.

Bear witness, Ye, whose thoughts that day
  In Yarrow's groves were centred;
Who through the silent portal arch
100 Of mouldering Newark entered;
And clomb the winding stair that once
  Too timidly was mounted
By the 'last Minstrel,' (not the last!)
  Ere he his Tale recounted.

Flow on for ever, Yarrow Stream!
  Fulfil thy pensive duty,
Well pleased that future Bards should chant
  For simple hearts thy beauty;
To dream-light dear while yet unseen,
110 Dear to the common sunshine,
And dearer still, as now I feel,
  To memory's shadowy moonshine!

On the Departure of Sir Walter Scott from Abbotsford, for Naples

A trouble, not of clouds, or weeping rain,
Nor of the setting sun's pathetic light
Engendered, hangs o'er Eildon's triple height:
Spirits of Power, assembled there, complain
For kindred Power departing from their sight;
While Tweed, best pleased in chanting a blithe strain,
Saddens his voice again, and yet again.
Lift up your hearts, ye Mourners! for the might
Of the whole world's good wishes with him goes;
10 Blessings and prayers in nobler retinue
Than sceptred king or laurelled conqueror knows,
Follow this wondrous Potentate. Be true,
Ye winds of ocean, and the midland sea,
Wafting your Charge to soft Parthenope!

'Calm is the fragrant air, and loth to lose'

Calm is the fragrant air, and loth to lose
Day's grateful warmth, though moist with falling dews.
Look for the stars, you'll say that there are none;
Look up a second time, and, one by one,
You mark them twinkling out with silvery light,
And wonder how they could elude the sight!

The birds, of late so noisy in their bowers,
Warbled a while with faint and fainter powers,
But now are silent as the dim-seen flowers:
10 Nor does the village Church-clock's iron tone
The time's and season's influence disown;
Nine beats distinctly to each other bound
In drowsy sequence – how unlike the sound
That, in rough winter, oft inflicts a fear
On fireside listeners, doubting what they hear!
The shepherd, bent on rising with the sun,
Had closed his door before the day was done,
And now with thankful heart to bed doth creep,
And joins his little children in their sleep.
20 The bat, lured forth where trees the lane o'ershade,
Flits and reflits along the close arcade;
The busy dor-hawk chases the white moth
With burring note, which Industry and Sloth
Might both be pleased with, for it suits them both.
A stream is heard – I see it not, but know
By its soft music whence the waters flow:
Wheels and the tread of hoofs are heard no more;
One boat there was, but it will touch the shore
With the next dipping of its slackened oar;
30 Faint sound, that, for the gayest of the gay,
Might give to serious thought a moment's sway,
As a last token of man's toilsome day!

'Most sweet it is with unuplifted eyes'

Most sweet it is with unuplifted eyes
To pace the ground, if path be there or none,
While a fair region round the traveller lies
Which he forbears again to look upon;
Pleased rather with some soft ideal scene,
The work of Fancy, or some happy tone
Of meditation, slipping in between
The beauty coming and the beauty gone.

If Thought and Love desert us, from that day
10   Let us break off all commerce with the Muse:
With Thought and Love companions of our way,
Whate'er the senses take or may refuse,
The Mind's internal heaven shall shed her dews
Of inspiration on the humblest lay.

Extempore Effusion upon the Death of James Hogg

When first, descending from the moorlands,
I saw the Stream of Yarrow glide
Along a bare and open valley,
The Ettrick Shepherd was my guide.

When last along its banks I wandered,
Through groves that had begun to shed
Their golden leaves upon the pathways,
My steps the Border-minstrel led.

The mighty Minstrel breathes no longer,
10   'Mid mouldering ruins low he lies;
And death upon the braes of Yarrow,
Has closed the Shepherd-poet's eyes:

Nor has the rolling year twice measured,
From sign to sign, its steadfast course,
Since every mortal power of Coleridge
Was frozen at its marvellous source;

The rapt One, of the godlike forehead,
The heaven-eyed creature sleeps in earth:
And Lamb, the frolic and the gentle,
20   Has vanished from his lonely hearth.

Like clouds that rake the mountain-summits,
Or waves that own no curbing hand,
How fast has brother followed brother,
From sunshine to the sunless land!

Yet I, whose lids from infant slumber
Were earlier raised, remain to hear
A timid voice, that asks in whispers,
'Who next will drop and disappear?'

Our haughty life is crowned with darkness,
30   Like London with its own black wreath,
On which with thee, O Crabbe! forth-looking,
I gazed from Hampstead's breezy heath.

As if but yesterday departed,
Thou too art gone before; but why,
O'er ripe fruit, seasonably gathered,
Should frail survivors heave a sigh?

Mourn rather for that holy Spirit,
Sweet as the spring, as ocean deep;
For Her who, ere her summer faded,
40   Has sunk into a breathless sleep.

No more of old romantic sorrows,
For slaughtered Youth or love-lorn Maid!
With sharper grief is Yarrow smitten,
And Ettrick mourns with her their Poet dead.

The Prelude
[Final, Fourteen-Book Version; MS E]

BOOK FIRST

Introduction, Childhood, & School-time

O there is blessing in this gentle breeze,
A visitant that while he fans my cheek
Doth seem half-conscious of the joy he brings
From the green fields, and from yon azure sky.
Whate'er his mission, the soft breeze can come
To none more grateful than to me; escaped
From the vast city, where I long had pined
A discontented sojourner – Now free,

Free as a bird to settle where I will.
10   What dwelling shall receive me? in what vale
Shall be my harbour? underneath what grove
Shall I take up my home? and what clear stream
Shall with its murmur lull me into rest?
The earth is all before me: with a heart
Joyous, nor scared at its own liberty,
I look about; and should the chosen guide
Be nothing better than a wandering cloud
I cannot miss my way. I breathe again;
Trances of thought and mountings of the mind
20   Come fast upon me: it is shaken off,
That burthen of my own unnatural self,
The heavy weight of many a weary day
Not mine, and such as were not made for me.
Long months of peace (if such bold word accord
With any promises of human life),
Long months of ease and undisturbed delight
Are mine in prospect; whither shall I turn
By road or pathway, or through trackless field,
Up hill or down, or shall some floating thing
30   Upon the river point me out my course?
Dear Liberty! Yet what would it avail
But for a gift that consecrates the joy?
For I, methought, while the sweet breath of heaven
Was blowing on my body, felt within
A correspondent breeze, that gently moved
With quickening virtue, but is now become
A tempest, a redundant energy,
Vexing its own creation. Thanks to both
And their congenial powers that while they join
40   In breaking up a long continued frost,
Bring with them vernal promises, the hope
Of active days urged on by flying hours,
Days of sweet leisure taxed with patient thought
Abstruse, nor wanting punctual service high,
Matins and vespers of harmonious verse!

Thus far, O Friend! did I, not used to make
A present joy the matter of a song,
Pour forth, that day, my soul in measured strains
That would not be forgotten, and are here
50 Recorded: to the open fields I told
A prophecy: – poetic numbers came
Spontaneously to clothe in priestly robe
A renovated spirit singled out,
Such hope was mine, for holy services:
My own voice cheered me, and far more, the mind's
Internal echo of the imperfect sound;
To both I listened, drawing from them both
A cheerful confidence in things to come.

Content and not unwilling now to give
60 A respite to this passion, I paced on
With brisk and eager steps; and came at length
To a green shady place where down I sate
Beneath a tree, slackening my thoughts by choice,
And settling into gentler happiness.
'Twas autumn and a clear and placid day,
With warmth as much as needed from a sun
Two hours declined towards the west, a day
With silver clouds, and sunshine on the grass
And in the sheltered and the sheltering grove,
70 A perfect stillness. Many were the thoughts
Encouraged and dismissed, till choice was made
Of a known Vale whither my feet should turn
Nor rest till they had reached the very door
Of the one cottage which methought I saw.
No picture of mere memory ever looked
So fair, and while upon the fancied scene
I gazed with growing love, a higher power
Than Fancy gave assurance of some work
Of glory there forthwith to be begun,
80 Perhaps too there performed. Thus long I mused,
Nor e'er lost sight of what I mused upon,
Save where, amid the stately grove of oaks,
Now here, now there, an acorn, from its cup

Dislodged, through sere leaves rustled, or at once
To the bare earth dropped with a startling sound.
From that soft couch I rose not, till the sun
Had almost touched the horizon, casting then
A backward glance upon the curling cloud
Of city smoke, by distance ruralised,
90 Keen as a Truant or a Fugitive
But as a Pilgrim resolute, I took,
Even with the chance equipment of that hour,
The road that pointed tow'rd the chosen Vale.
It was a splendid evening and my soul
Once more made trial of her strength nor lacked
Æolian visitations, but the harp
Was soon defrauded, and the banded host
Of harmony dispersed in straggling sounds;
And lastly utter silence! 'Be it so;
100 Why think of anything but present good?'
So, like a home-bound labourer I pursued
My way beneath the mellowing sun, that shed
Mild influence; nor left in me one wish
Again to bend the Sabbath of that time
To a servile yoke. What need of many words?
A pleasant loitering journey, through three days
Continued, brought me to my hermitage.
I spare to tell of what ensued, the life
In common things – the endless store of things,
110 Rare, or at least so seeming, every day
Found all about me in one neighbourhood –
The self-congratulation, and from morn
To night unbroken cheerfulness serene.
But speedily an earnest longing rose
To brace myself to some determined aim,
Reading or thinking; either to lay up
New stores, or rescue from decay the old
By timely interference: and therewith
Came hopes still higher, that with outward life
120 I might endue some airy phantasies
That had been floating loose about for years,
And to such beings temperately deal forth
The many feelings that oppressed my heart.

That hope hath been discouraged; welcome light
Dawns from the east but dawns to disappear
And mock me with a sky that ripens not
Into a steady morning: if my mind,
Remembering the bold promise of the past,
Would gladly grapple with some noble theme,
130 Vain is her wish; where'er she turns, she finds
Impediments, from day to day, renewed.

    And now it would content me to yield up
Those lofty hopes awhile, for present gifts
Of humbler industry. But, O, dear Friend!
The Poet, gentle creature as he is,
Hath like the Lover his unruly times,
His fits when he is neither sick nor well,
Though no distress be near him but his own
Unmanageable thoughts: his mind, best pleased
140 While she as duteous as the mother dove
Sits brooding, lives not always to that end
But like the innocent bird, hath goadings on
That drive her as in trouble through the groves;
With me is now such passion, to be blamed
No otherwise than as it lasts too long.
    When as becomes a man who would prepare
For such an arduous work, I through myself
Make rigorous inquisition, the report
Is often cheering; for I neither seem
150 To lack that first great gift, the vital soul,
Nor general Truths which are themselves a sort
Of Elements and Agents, Under-powers,
Subordinate helpers of the living mind:
Nor am I naked of external things,
Forms, images, nor numerous other aids
Of less regard, though won perhaps with toil
And needful to build up a Poet's praise.
Time, place and manners do I seek, and these
Are found in plenteous store, but nowhere such
160 As may be singled out with steady choice;
No little band of yet remembered names
Whom I, in perfect confidence, might hope

To summon back from lonesome banishment
And make them dwellers in the hearts of men
Now living, or to live in future years.
Sometimes the ambitious Power of choice, mistaking
Proud spring-tide swellings for a regular sea,
Will settle on some British theme, some old
Romantic tale by Milton left unsung:
170   More often turning to some gentle place
Within the groves of Chivalry, I pipe
To shepherd swains, or seated harp in hand
Amid reposing knights by a river side
Or fountain, listen to the grave reports
Of dire enchantments faced, and overcome
By the strong mind, and tales of warlike feats
Where spear encountered spear and sword with sword
Fought, as if conscious of the blazonry
That the shield bore, so glorious was the strife;
180   Whence inspiration for a song that winds
Through ever changing scenes of votive quest
Wrongs to redress, harmonious tribute paid
To patient courage and unblemished truth,
To firm devotion, zeal unquenchable,
And Christian meekness hallowing faithful loves.
Sometimes more sternly moved I would relate
How vanquished Mithridates northward passed
And, hidden in the cloud of years, became
Odin, the Father of a race by whom
190   Perished the Roman Empire; how the friends
And followers of Sertorius, out of Spain
Flying, found shelter in the Fortunate Isles
And left their usages, their arts and laws
To disappear by a slow gradual death;
To dwindle and to perish one by one,
Starved in those narrow bounds: but not the soul
Of Liberty, which fifteen hundred years
Survived, and when the European came
With skill and power that might not be withstood,
200   Did, like a pestilence, maintain its hold
And wasted down by glorious death that race

Of natural heroes: – or I would record
How, in tyrannic times, some high-souled man,
Unnamed among the chronicles of kings,
Suffered in silence for Truth's sake: or tell
How that one Frenchman, through continued force
Of meditation on the inhuman deeds
Of those who conquered first the Indian Isles,
Went single in his ministry across
210   The Ocean; not to comfort the oppressed,
But like a thirsty wind to roam about
Withering the Oppressor: how Gustavus sought
Help at his need in Dalecarlia's mines:
How Wallace fought for Scotland, left the name
Of Wallace to be found, like a wild flower,
All over his dear Country, left the deeds
Of Wallace, like a family of Ghosts,
To people the steep rocks and river banks,
Her natural sanctuaries, with a local soul
220   Of independence and stern liberty.
Sometimes it suits me better to invent
A tale from my own heart, more near akin
To my own passions and habitual thoughts;
Some variegated story, in the main
Lofty, but the unsubstantial structure melts
Before the very sun that brightens it,
Mist into air dissolving! Then a wish,
My best and favourite aspiration, mounts
With yearning, tow'rd some philosophic song
230   Of Truth that cherishes our daily life;
With meditations passionate, from deep
Recesses in man's heart, immortal verse
Thoughtfully fitted to the Orphean lyre;
But from this awful burthen I full soon
Take refuge and beguile myself with trust
That mellower years will bring a riper mind
And clearer insight. Thus my days are past
In contradiction; with no skill to part
Vague longing, haply bred by want of power,
240   From paramount impulse – not to be withstood;

A timorous capacity from prudence;
From circumspection infinite delay.
Humility and modest awe themselves
Betray me, serving often for a cloak
To a more subtle selfishness; that now
Locks every function up in blank reserve,
Now dupes me, trusting to an anxious eye
That with intrusive restlessness beats off
Simplicity and self-presented truth.
250 Ah! better far than this to stray about
Voluptuously through fields and rural walks
And ask no record of the hours, resigned
To vacant musing, unreproved neglect
Of all things and deliberate holiday.
Far better never to have heard the name
Of zeal and just ambition, than to live
Baffled and plagued by a mind that every hour
Turns recreant to her task, takes heart again,
Then feels immediately some hollow thought
260 Hang like an interdict upon her hopes.
This is my lot; for either still I find
Some imperfection in the chosen theme,
Or see of absolute accomplishment
Much wanting, so much wanting, in myself
That I recoil and droop, and seek repose
In listlessness from vain perplexity,
Unprofitably travelling toward the grave
Like a false steward who hath much received
And renders nothing back.
                              Was it for this
270 That one, the fairest of all rivers, loved
To blend his murmurs with my nurse's song
And, from his alder shades and rocky falls,
And from his fords and shallows, sent a voice
That flowed along my dreams? For this, didst thou,
O Derwent! winding among grassy holms
Where I was looking on, a babe in arms,
Make ceaseless music that composed my thoughts
To more than infant softness, giving me

      Amid the fretful dwellings of mankind
280   A foretaste, a dim earnest, of the calm
      That Nature breathes among the hills and groves?
      When he had left the mountains and received
      On his smooth breast the shadow of those towers
      That yet survive, a shattered monument
      Of feudal sway, the bright blue river passed
      Along the margin of our terrace walk;
      A tempting playmate whom we dearly loved.
      O, many a time have I, a five years' child
      In a small mill-race severed from his stream
290   Made one long bathing of a summer's day;
      Basked in the sun and plunged and basked again
      Alternate, all a summer's day, or scoured
      The sandy fields, leaping through flowery groves
      Of yellow ragwort; or when rock and hill,
      The woods and distant Skiddaw's lofty height
      Were bronzed with deepest radiance, stood alone
      Beneath the sky, as if I had been born
      On Indian plains, and from my mother's hut
      Had run abroad in wantonness, to sport
300   A naked savage, in the thunder shower.

        Fair seed-time had my soul and I grew up
      Fostered alike by beauty, and by fear:
      Much favoured in my birth-place, and no less
      In that beloved Vale to which erelong
      We were transplanted – there were we let loose
      For sports of wider range. Ere I had told
      Ten birth-days, when among the mountain slopes
      Frost, and the breath of frosty wind, had snapped
      The last autumnal crocus, 'twas my joy
310   With store of springes o'er my shoulder hung
      To range the open heights where woodcocks ran
      Along the smooth green turf. Through half the night
      Scudding away from snare to snare, I plied
      That anxious visitation; – moon and stars
      Were shining o'er my head. I was alone
      And seemed to be a trouble to the peace

That dwelt among them. Sometimes it befell
In these night wanderings, that a strong desire
O'erpowered my better reason, and the bird
320   Which was the captive of another's toil
Became my prey; and when the deed was done
I heard among the solitary hills
Low breathings coming after me and sounds
Of undistinguishable motion, steps
Almost as silent as the turf they trod.

Nor less when spring had warmed the cultured Vale,
Moved we as plunderers where the mother-bird
Had in high places built her lodge; though mean
Our object and inglorious, yet the end
330   Was not ignoble. Oh! when I have hung
Above the raven's nest, by knots of grass
And half-inch fissures in the slippery rock
But ill-sustained, and almost (so it seemed)
Suspended by the blast that blew amain,
Shouldering the naked crag, oh, at that time
While on the perilous ridge I hung alone,
With what strange utterance did the loud dry wind
Blow through my ear! the sky seemed not a sky
Of earth and with what motion moved the clouds!

340   Dust as we are, the immortal spirit grows
Like harmony in music; there is a dark
Inscrutable workmanship that reconciles
Discordant elements, makes them cling together
In one society – How strange that all
The terrors, pains, and early miseries,
Regrets, vexations, lassitudes interfused
Within my mind, should e'er have borne a part,
And that a needful part, in making up
The calm existence that is mine when I
350   Am worthy of myself. Praise to the end!
Thanks to the means which Nature deigned to employ
Whether her fearless visitings or those
That came with soft alarm like hurtless lightning
Opening the peaceful clouds, or she may use

Severer interventions, ministry
More palpable, as best might suit her aim.

One summer evening (led by her) I found
A little boat tied to a willow tree
Within a rocky cave, its usual home.
360 Straight I unloosed her chain, and stepping in
Pushed from the shore. It was an act of stealth
And troubled pleasure, nor without the voice
Of mountain-echoes did my boat move on,
Leaving behind her still on either side,
Small circles glittering idly in the moon,
Until they melted all into one track
Of sparkling light. But now, like one who rows
(Proud of his skill) to reach a chosen point
With an unswerving line, I fixed my view
370 Upon the summit of a craggy ridge,
The horizon's utmost boundary; far above
Was nothing but the stars and the grey sky.
She was an elfin pinnace; lustily
I dipped my oars into the silent lake
And, as I rose upon the stroke, my boat
Went heaving through the water like a swan;
When, from behind that craggy steep till then
The horizon's bound, a huge peak, black and huge,
As if with voluntary power instinct
380 Upreared its head. I struck and struck again
And growing still in stature the grim shape
Towered up between me and the stars, and still,
For so it seemed, with purpose of its own
And measured motion like a living thing
Strode after me. With trembling oars I turned
And through the silent water stole my way
Back to the covert of the willow tree;
There in her mooring-place I left my bark, –
And through the meadows homeward went in grave
390 And serious mood, but after I had seen
That spectacle, for many days, my brain
Worked with a dim and undetermined sense

Of unknown modes of being; o'er my thoughts
There hung a darkness, call it solitude
Or blank desertion. No familiar shapes
Remained, no pleasant images of trees,
Of sea or sky, no colours of green fields;
But huge and mighty forms, that do not live
Like living men, moved slowly through the mind
400   By day, and were a trouble to my dreams.

Wisdom and Spirit of the universe!
Thou Soul that art the eternity of thought,
That giv'st to forms and images a breath
And everlasting motion, not in vain
By day or star-light thus from my first dawn
Of childhood didst thou intertwine for me
The passions that build up our human soul;
Not with the mean and vulgar works of man,
But with high objects, with enduring things –
410   With life and nature, purifying thus
The elements of feeling and of thought
And sanctifying, by such discipline,
Both pain and fear until we recognise
A grandeur in the beatings of the heart.
Nor was this fellowship vouchsafed to me
With stinted kindness. In November days,
When vapours rolling down the valley made
A lonely scene more lonesome, among woods
At noon and mid the calm of summer nights,
420   When, by the margin of the trembling lake,
Beneath the gloomy hills homeward I went
In solitude, such intercourse was mine;
Mine was it in the fields both day and night
And by the waters, all the summer long.

And in the frosty season, when the sun
Was set, and visible for many a mile
The cottage windows blazed through twilight gloom,
I heeded not their summons – happy time
It was indeed for all of us, for me
430   It was a time of rapture! Clear and loud

The village clock tolled six – I wheeled about,
Proud and exulting like an untired horse
That cares not for his home. All shod with steel
We hissed along the polished ice in games
Confederate, imitative of the chase
And woodland pleasures, – the resounding horn,
The pack loud chiming, and the hunted hare.
So through the darkness and the cold we flew,
And not a voice was idle; with the din
440   Smitten, the precipices rang aloud;
The leafless trees and every icy crag
Tinkled like iron; while far distant hills
Into the tumult sent an alien sound
Of melancholy, not unnoticed, while the stars
Eastward were sparkling clear, and in the west
The orange sky of evening died away.
Not seldom from the uproar I retired
Into a silent bay, or sportively
Glanced sideway, leaving the tumultuous throng
450   To cut across the reflex of a star
That fled and flying still before me gleamed
Upon the glassy plain; and oftentimes
When we had given our bodies to the wind
And all the shadowy banks on either side
Came sweeping through the darkness, spinning still
The rapid line of motion, then at once
Have I, reclining back upon my heels,
Stopped short, yet still the solitary cliffs
Wheeled by me – even as if the earth had rolled
460   With visible motion her diurnal round!
Behind me did they stretch in solemn train,
Feebler and feebler, and I stood and watched
Till all was tranquil as a dreamless sleep.

Ye Presences of Nature in the sky
And on the earth! Ye Visions of the hills!
And Souls of lonely places! can I think
A vulgar hope was yours when ye employed
Such ministry, when ye through many a year
Haunting me thus among my boyish sports,

470 On caves and trees, upon the woods and hills,
Impressed upon all forms the characters
Of danger or desire; and thus did make
The surface of the universal earth
With triumph and delight, with hope and fear,
Work like a sea?
                    Not uselessly employed,
Might I pursue this theme through every change
Of exercise and play, to which the year
Did summon us in his delightful round.

We were a noisy crew, the sun in heaven
480 Beheld not vales more beautiful than ours;
Nor saw a band in happiness and joy
Richer, or worthier of the ground they trod.
I could record with no reluctant voice
The woods of autumn, and their hazel bowers
With milk-white clusters hung; the rod and line,
True symbol of hope's foolishness, whose strong
And unreproved enchantment led us on,
By rocks and pools shut out from every star
All the green summer, to forlorn cascades
490 Among the windings hid of mountain brooks.
– Unfading recollections! at this hour
The heart is almost mine with which I felt
From some hill-top on sunny afternoons
The paper kite high among fleecy clouds
Pull at her rein like an impetuous courser
Or, from the meadows sent on gusty days,
Beheld her breast the wind, then suddenly
Dashed headlong, and rejected by the storm.

Ye lowly cottages wherein we dwelt,
500 A ministration of your own was yours;
Can I forget you, being as ye were
So beautiful among the pleasant fields
In which ye stood? or can I here forget
The plain and seemly countenance with which
Ye dealt out your plain comforts? Yet had ye
Delights and exultations of your own.

Eager and never weary we pursued
Our home-amusements by the warm peat-fire
At evening, when with pencil and smooth slate
510   In square divisions parcelled out, and all
With crosses and with cyphers scribbled o'er,
We schemed and puzzled, head opposed to head
In strife too humble to be named in verse:
Or round the naked table, snow-white deal,
Cherry or maple, sate in close array,
And to the combat, Loo or Whist, led on
A thick-ribbed army, not, as in the world
Neglected and ungratefully thrown by
Even for the very service they had wrought,
520   But husbanded through many a long campaign.
Uncouth assemblage was it where no few
Had changed their functions; some, plebeian cards
Which Fate, beyond the promise of their birth,
Had dignified, and called to represent
The persons of departed potentates.
Oh, with what echoes on the board they fell!
Ironic diamonds, clubs, hearts, diamonds, spades,
A congregation piteously akin!
Cheap matter offered they to boyish wit,
530   Those sooty knaves, precipitated down
With scoffs and taunts like Vulcan out of heaven:
The paramount ace, a moon in her eclipse,
Queens gleaming through their splendour's last decay,
And monarchs surly at the wrongs sustained
By royal visages. Meanwhile abroad
Incessant rain was falling, or the frost
Raged bitterly, with keen and silent tooth;
And, interrupting oft that eager game,
From under Esthwaite's splitting fields of ice
540   The pent-up air, struggling to free itself,
Gave out to meadow grounds and hills a loud
Protracted yelling, like the noise of wolves
Howling in troops along the Bothnic Main.

Nor, sedulous as I have been to trace
How Nature by extrinsic passion first

Peopled the mind with forms sublime or fair
And made me love them, may I here omit
How other pleasures have been mine and joys
Of subtler origin; how I have felt,
550 Not seldom even in that tempestuous time,
Those hallowed and pure motions of the sense
Which seem, in their simplicity, to own
An intellectual charm; that calm delight
Which, if I err not, surely must belong
To those first-born affinities that fit
Our new existence to existing things
And, in our dawn of being, constitute
The bond of union between life and joy.

Yes, I remember when the changeful earth
560 And twice five summers on my mind had stamped
The faces of the moving year, even then
I held unconscious intercourse with beauty
Old as creation, drinking in a pure
Organic pleasure from the silver wreaths
Of curling mist, or from the level plain
Of waters coloured by impending clouds.

The sands of Westmoreland, the creeks and bays
Of Cumbria's rocky limits, they can tell
How, when the Sea threw off his evening shade,
570 And to the shepherd's hut on distant hills
Sent welcome notice of the rising moon,
How I have stood, to fancies such as these
A stranger, linking with the spectacle
No conscious memory of a kindred sight
And bringing with me no peculiar sense
Of quietness or peace, yet have I stood,
Even while mine eye hath moved o'er many a league
Of shining water, gathering as it seemed
Through every hair-breadth in that field of light
580 New pleasure like a bee among the flowers.

Thus oft amid those fits of vulgar joy
Which, through all seasons, on a child's pursuits

Are prompt attendants, mid that giddy bliss
Which like a tempest works along the blood
And is forgotten; even then I felt
Gleams like the flashing of a shield; – the earth
And common face of Nature spake to me
Rememberable things; sometimes, 'tis true,
By chance collisions and quaint accidents
590   (Like those ill-sorted unions, work supposed
Of evil-minded fairies), yet not vain
Nor profitless, if haply they impressed
Collateral objects and appearances,
Albeit lifeless then, and doomed to sleep
Until maturer seasons called them forth
To impregnate and to elevate the mind.
– And if the vulgar joy by its own weight
Wearied itself out of the memory,
The scenes which were a witness of that joy
600   Remained in their substantial lineaments
Depicted on the brain and to the eye
Were visible, a daily sight; and thus
By the impressive discipline of fear,
By pleasure and repeated happiness,
So frequently repeated, and by force
Of obscure feelings representative
Of things forgotten, these same scenes so bright,
So beautiful, so majestic in themselves,
Though yet the day was distant, did become
610   Habitually dear, and all their forms
And changeful colours by invisible links
Were tied and bound to the affections.

My story early I began, not misled, I trust,
By an infirmity of love for days
Disowned by memory, fancying flowers where none,
Not even the sweetest, do or can survive
For him at least whose dawning day they cheered.
Nor will it seem to thee, O Friend! so prompt
In sympathy, that I have lengthened out
620   With fond and feeble tongue a tedious tale.

Meanwhile, my hope has been, that I might fetch
Invigorating thoughts from former years;
Might fix the wavering balance of my mind
And haply meet reproaches too, whose power
May spur me on, in manhood now mature,
To honourable toil. Yet should these hopes
Prove vain, and thus should neither I be taught
To understand myself, nor thou to know
With better knowledge how the heart was framed
630 Of him thou lovest, need I dread from thee
Harsh judgements, if the song be loth to quit
Those recollected hours that have the charm
Of visionary things, those lovely forms
And sweet sensations that throw back our life
And almost make remotest infancy
A visible scene, on which the sun is shining?

One end at least hath been attained; my mind
Hath been revived, and if this genial mood
Desert me not, forthwith shall be brought down
640 Through later years the story of my life.
The road lies plain before me; – 'tis a theme
Single and of determined bounds; and hence
I choose it rather at this time, than work
Of ampler or more varied argument,
Where I might be discomfited and lost:
And certain hopes are with me, that to thee
This labour will be welcome, honoured Friend!

BOOK SECOND

School-time continued

Thus far, O Friend! have we, though leaving much
Unvisited, endeavoured to retrace
The simple ways in which my childhood walked;
Those chiefly that first led me to the love
Of rivers, woods, and fields. The passion yet
Was in its birth, sustained, as might befall,
By nourishment that came unsought; for still

From week to week, from month to month, we lived
A round of tumult. Duly were our games
10 Prolonged in summer till the day-light failed:
No chair remained before the doors; the bench
And threshold steps were empty; fast asleep
The labourer and the old man who had sate
A later lingerer; yet the revelry
Continued and the loud uproar: at last,
When all the ground was dark, and twinkling stars
Edged the black clouds, home, and to bed we went,
Feverish with weary joints and beating minds.
Ah! is there one who ever has been young,
20 Nor needs a warning voice to tame the pride
Of intellect and virtue's self-esteem?
One is there, though the wisest and the best
Of all mankind, who covets not at times
Union that cannot be; – who would not give,
If so he might, to duty and to truth
The eagerness of infantine desire?
A tranquillising spirit presses now
On my corporeal frame, so wide appears
The vacancy between me and those days
30 Which yet have such self-presence in my mind,
That musing on them, often do I seem
Two consciousnesses, conscious of myself
And of some other Being. A rude mass
Of native rock, left midway in the square
Of our small market village, was the goal
Or centre of these sports; and when, returned
After long absence, thither I repaired,
Gone was the old grey stone, and in its place
A smart Assembly-room usurped the ground
40 That had been ours. There let the fiddle scream
And be ye happy! Yet, my Friends! I know
That more than one of you will think with me
Of those soft starry nights, and that old Dame
From whom the stone was named, who there had sate
And watched her table with its huckster's wares
Assiduous, through the length of sixty years.

– We ran a boisterous course; the year span round
With giddy motion. But the time approached
That brought with it a regular desire
50 For calmer pleasures, when the winning forms
Of Nature were collaterally attached
To every scheme of holiday delight
And every boyish sport, less grateful else
And languidly pursued.
                  When summer came,
Our pastime was on bright half-holidays
To sweep along the plain of Windermere
With rival oars, and the selected bourne
Was now an Island musical with birds
That sang and ceased not; now a Sister Isle
60 Beneath the oaks' umbrageous covert, sown
With lilies of the valley like a field;
And now a third small Island, where survived
In solitude the ruins of a shrine
Once to Our Lady dedicate, and served
Daily with chaunted rites. In such a race
So ended, disappointment could be none,
Uneasiness, or pain, or jealousy:
We rested in the shade, all pleased alike,
Conquered and conqueror. Thus the pride of strength,
70 And the vain-glory of superior skill,
Were tempered; thus was gradually produced
A quiet independence of the heart;
And to my Friend who knows me I may add,
Fearless of blame, that hence for future days
Ensued a diffidence and modesty
And I was taught to feel, perhaps too much,
The self-sufficing power of Solitude.

Our daily meals were frugal, Sabine fare!
More than we wished we knew the blessing then
80 Of vigorous hunger – hence corporeal strength
Unsapped by delicate viands; for, exclude
A little weekly stipend, and we lived
Through three divisions of the quartered year
In penniless poverty. But now to school

From the half-yearly holidays returned,
We came with weightier purses, that sufficed
To furnish treats more costly than the Dame
Of th' old grey stone, from her scant board, supplied.
Hence rustic dinners on the cool green ground,
90 Or in the woods, or by a river side
Or shady fountains, while among the leaves
Soft airs were stirring, and the mid-day sun
Unfelt shone brightly round us in our joy.
Nor is my aim neglected if I tell
How sometimes in the length of those half-years,
We from our funds drew largely – proud to curb
And eager to spur on, the galloping steed;
And with the courteous inn-keeper, whose stud
Supplied our want, we haply might employ
100 Sly subterfuges, if the adventure's bound
Were distant: some framed temple where of yore
The Druids worshipped, or the antique walls
Of that large abbey, which within the Vale
Of Nightshade, to St Mary's honour built,
Stands yet, a mouldering pile, with fractured arch,
Belfry, and images, and living trees,
A holy scene! Along the smooth green turf
Our horses grazed; to more than inland peace
Left by the west wind sweeping overhead
110 From a tumultuous ocean, trees and towers
In that sequestered valley may be seen,
Both silent and both motionless alike;
Such the deep shelter that is there, and such
The safeguard for repose and quietness.

Our steeds remounted and the summons given,
With whip and spur we through the chauntry flew
In uncouth race, and left the cross-legged knight
And the stone-abbot and that single wren
Which one day sang so sweetly in the nave
120 Of the old church, that – though from recent showers
The earth was comfortless, and, touched by faint
Internal breezes, sobbings of the place
And respirations, from the roofless walls

The shuddering ivy dripped large drops, yet still
So sweetly mid the gloom the invisible bird
Sang to herself, that there I could have made
My dwelling-place and lived for ever there
To hear such music. Through the walls we flew
And down the valley, and, a circuit made
130 In wantonness of heart, through rough and smooth
We scampered homewards. Oh, ye rocks and streams
And that still spirit shed from evening air!
Even in this joyous time I sometimes felt
Your presence, when with slackened step we breathed
Along the sides of the steep hills, or when
Lighted by gleams of moonlight from the sea
We beat with thundering hoofs the level sand.

　　Midway on long Winander's eastern shore,
Within the crescent of a pleasant bay,
140 A tavern stood; no homely-featured house,
Primeval like its neighbouring cottages,
But 'twas a splendid place, the door beset
With chaises, grooms, and liveries, and within
Decanters, glasses, and the blood-red wine.
In ancient times and ere the Hall was built
On the large island, had this dwelling been
More worthy of a poet's love, a hut
Proud of its own bright fire and sycamore shade.
But, though the rhymes were gone that once inscribed
150 The threshold and large golden characters
Spread o'er the spangled sign-board had dislodged
The old Lion and usurped his place in slight
And mockery of the rustic painter's hand,
Yet to this hour the spot to me is dear
With all its foolish pomp. The garden lay
Upon a slope surmounted by a plain
Of a small bowling-green; beneath us stood
A grove, with gleams of water through the trees
And over the tree-tops; nor did we want
160 Refreshment, strawberries and mellow cream.
There, while through half an afternoon we played

On the smooth platform, whether skill prevailed
Or happy blunder triumphed, bursts of glee
Made all the mountains ring. But ere night-fall,
When in our pinnace we returned at leisure
Over the shadowy lake, and to the beach
Of some small island steered our course with one,
The Minstrel of the Troop, and left him there
And rowed off gently, while he blew his flute
170 Alone upon the rock – oh then the calm
And dead still water lay upon my mind
Even with a weight of pleasure, and the sky,
Never before so beautiful, sank down
Into my heart, and held me like a dream!
Thus were my sympathies enlarged and thus
Daily the common range of visible things
Grew dear to me: already I began
To love the sun; a boy I loved the sun,
Not as I since have loved him, as a pledge
180 And surety of our earthly life, a light
Which we behold and feel we are alive;
Nor for his bounty to so many worlds –
But for this cause, that I had seen him lay
His beauty on the morning hills, had seen
The western mountain touch his setting orb
In many a thoughtless hour, when, from excess
Of happiness, my blood appeared to flow
For its own pleasure, and I breathed with joy.
And from like feelings, humble though intense,
190 To patriotic and domestic love
Analogous, the moon to me was dear;
For I could dream away my purposes,
Standing to gaze upon her while she hung
Midway between the hills, as if she knew
No other region, but belonged to thee,
Yea, appertained by a peculiar right
To thee and thy grey huts, thou one dear Vale!

      Those incidental charms which first attached
My heart to rural objects, day by day

200 Grew weaker, and I hasten on to tell
How Nature, intervenient till this time
And secondary, now at length was sought
For her own sake. But who shall parcel out
His intellect by geometric rules,
Split like a province into round and square?
Who knows the individual hour in which
His habits were first sown, even as a seed?
Who that shall point as with a wand and say,
'This portion of the river of my mind
210 Came from yon fountain?' Thou, my Friend! art one
More deeply read in thy own thoughts; to thee,
Science appears but what in truth she is,
Not as our glory and our absolute boast,
But as a succedaneum, and a prop
To our infirmity. No officious slave
Art thou of that false secondary power
By which we multiply distinctions, then
Deem that our puny boundaries are things
That we perceive, and not that we have made.
220 To thee, unblinded by these formal arts,
The unity of all hath been revealed,
And thou wilt doubt with me, less aptly skilled
Than many are to range the faculties
In scale and order, class the cabinet
Of their sensations, and in voluble phrase
Run through the history and birth of each
As of a single independent thing.
Hard task, vain hope, to analyse the mind
If each most obvious and particular thought,
230 Not in a mystical and idle sense
But in the words of Reason deeply weighed,
Hath no beginning.
                              Blest the infant Babe
(For with my best conjecture I would trace
Our Being's earthly progress), blest the Babe,
Nursed in his Mother's arms, who sinks to sleep
Rocked on his Mother's breast; who with his soul
Drinks in the feelings of his Mother's eye!

For him, in one dear Presence, there exists
A virtue which irradiates and exalts
240   Objects through widest intercourse of sense.
No outcast he, bewildered and depressed:
Along his infant veins are interfused
The gravitation and the filial bond
Of nature that connect him with the world.
Is there a flower, to which he points with hand
Too weak to gather it, already love
Drawn from love's purest earthly fount for him
Hath beautified that flower; already shades
Of pity cast from inward tenderness
250   Do fall around him upon aught that bears
Unsightly marks of violence or harm.
Emphatically such a Being lives,
Frail creature as he is, helpless as frail,
An inmate of this active universe.
For feeling has to him imparted power
That through the growing faculties of sense
Doth like an agent of the one great Mind
Create, creator and receiver both,
Working but in alliance with the works
260   Which it beholds. – Such, verily, is the first
Poetic spirit of our human life,
By uniform control of after years
In most abated or suppressed; in some,
Through every change of growth and of decay,
Pre-eminent till death.
                              From early days,
Beginning not long after that first time
In which, a Babe, by intercourse of touch
I held mute dialogues with my Mother's heart,
I have endeavoured to display the means
270   Whereby this infant sensibility,
Great birthright of our being, was in me
Augmented and sustained. Yet is a path
More difficult before me; and I fear
That in its broken windings we shall need
The chamois' sinews, and the eagle's wing:

For now a trouble came into my mind
From unknown causes. I was left alone
Seeking the visible world, nor knowing why.
The props of my affections were removed
280   And yet the building stood, as if sustained
By its own spirit! All that I beheld
Was dear, and hence to finer influxes
The mind lay open, to a more exact
And close communion. Many are our joys
In youth, but oh! what happiness to live
When every hour brings palpable access
Of knowledge, when all knowledge is delight
And sorrow is not there! The seasons came,
And every season wheresoe'er I moved
290   Unfolded transitory qualities
Which, but for this most watchful power of love,
Had been neglected, left a register
Of permanent relations, else unknown.
Hence life and change and beauty, solitude
More active even than 'best society' –
Society made sweet as solitude
By inward concords, silent, inobtrusive
And gentle agitations of the mind
From manifold distinctions, difference
300   Perceived in things where to the unwatchful eye
No difference is, and hence from the same source
Sublimer joy; for I would walk alone
Under the quiet stars and at that time
Have felt whate'er there is of power in sound
To breathe an elevated mood, by form
Or image unprofaned; and I would stand,
If the night blackened with a coming storm,
Beneath some rock, listening to notes that are
The ghostly language of the ancient earth
310   Or make their dim abode in distant winds.
Thence did I drink the visionary power;
And deem not profitless those fleeting moods
Of shadowy exultation: not for this,
That they are kindred to our purer mind

And intellectual life; but that the soul,
Remembering how she felt, but what she felt
Remembering not, retains an obscure sense
Of possible sublimity, whereto
With growing faculties she doth aspire,
320 With faculties still growing, feeling still
That whatsoever point they gain, they yet
Have something to pursue.
                    And not alone
Mid gloom and tumult, but no less mid fair
And tranquil scenes, that universal power
And fitness in the latent qualities
And essences of things, by which the mind
Is moved with feelings of delight, to me
Came strengthened with a superadded soul,
A virtue not its own. My morning walks
330 Were early; – oft before the hours of school
I travelled round our little lake, five miles
Of pleasant wandering. Happy time! more dear
For this, that one was by my side, a Friend,
Then passionately loved; with heart how full
Would he peruse these lines! For many years
Have since flowed in between us, and, our minds
Both silent to each other, at this time
We live as if those hours had never been.
Nor seldom did I lift our cottage latch
340 Far earlier, and ere one smoke-wreath had risen
From human dwelling, or the thrush, high perched,
Piped to the woods his shrill *reveillè*, sate
Alone upon some jutting eminence
At the first gleam of dawn-light, when the Vale,
Yet slumbering, lay in utter solitude.
How shall I seek the origin, where find
Faith in the marvellous things which then I felt?
Oft in these moments such a holy calm
Would overspread my soul, that bodily eyes
350 Were utterly forgotten, and what I saw
Appeared like something in myself, a dream,
A prospect in the mind.

                    'Twere long to tell
What spring and autumn, what the winter snows
And what the summer shade, what day and night,
Evening and morning, sleep and waking thought,
From sources inexhaustible, poured forth
To feed the spirit of religious love
In which I walked with Nature. But let this
Be not forgotten, that I still retained
360 My first creative sensibility,
That by the regular action of the world
My soul was unsubdued. A plastic power
Abode with me, a forming hand, at times
Rebellious, acting in a devious mood,
A local spirit of his own, at war
With general tendency, but for the most
Subservient strictly to external things
With which it communed. An auxiliar light
Came from my mind, which on the setting sun
370 Bestowed new splendour; the melodious birds,
The fluttering breezes, fountains that ran on
Murmuring so sweetly in themselves, obeyed
A like dominion and the midnight storm
Grew darker in the presence of my eye:
Hence my obeisance, my devotion hence,
And hence my transport.
                    Nor should this, perchance,
Pass unrecorded, that I still had loved
The exercise and produce of a toil
Than analytic industry to me
380 More pleasing, and whose character I deem
Is more poetic as resembling more
Creative agency. The song would speak
Of that interminable building reared
By observation of affinities
In objects where no brotherhood exists
To passive minds. My seventeenth year was come
And whether from this habit rooted now
So deeply in my mind, or from excess
In the great social principle of life

390 Coercing all things into sympathy,
    To unorganic natures were transferred
    My own enjoyments, or the power of truth
    Coming in revelation, did converse
    With things that really are, I, at this time,
    Saw blessings spread around me like a sea.
    Thus while the days flew by and years passed on,
    From Nature overflowing on my soul,
    I had received so much, that every thought
    Was steeped in feeling; I was only then
400 Contented when with bliss ineffable
    I felt the sentiment of Being spread
    O'er all that moves and all that seemeth still;
    O'er all that, lost beyond the reach of thought
    And human knowledge, to the human eye
    Invisible, yet liveth to the heart;
    O'er all that leaps and runs and shouts and sings,
    Or beats the gladsome air; o'er all that glides
    Beneath the wave, yea, in the wave itself
    And mighty depth of waters. Wonder not
410 If high the transport, great the joy I felt,
    Communing in this sort through earth and heaven
    With every form of creature as it looked
    Towards the Uncreated with a countenance
    Of adoration, with an eye of love.
    One song they sang and it was audible,
    Most audible, then, when the fleshly ear,
    O'ercome by humblest prelude of that strain,
    Forgot her functions and slept undisturbed.

    If this be error, and another faith
420 Find easier access to the pious mind,
    Yet were I grossly destitute of all
    Those human sentiments that make this earth
    So dear, if I should fail with grateful voice
    To speak of you, ye mountains, and ye lakes
    And sounding cataracts, ye mists and winds
    That dwell among the hills where I was born;
    If in my youth I have been pure in heart,

If, mingling with the world, I am content
With my own modest pleasures and have lived
430 With God and Nature communing, removed
From little enmities and low desires,
The gift is yours; if in these times of fear,
This melancholy waste of hopes o'erthrown,
If, mid indifference and apathy
And wicked exultation when good men
On every side fall off, we know not how,
To selfishness disguised in gentle names
Of peace and quiet and domestic love
Yet mingled not unwillingly with sneers
440 On visionary minds; if, in this time
Of dereliction and dismay, I yet
Despair not of our nature but retain
A more than Roman confidence, a faith
That fails not, in all sorrow my support,
The blessing of my life, the gift is yours,
Ye winds and sounding cataracts 'tis yours,
Ye mountains! thine, O Nature! Thou hast fed
My lofty speculations; and in thee,
For this uneasy heart of ours, I find
450 A never-failing principle of joy
And purest passion.
                            Thou, my Friend! wert reared
In the great city, mid far other scenes;
But we, by different roads, at length have gained
The self-same bourne. And for this cause to thee
I speak, unapprehensive of contempt,
The insinuated scoff of coward tongues,
And all that silent language which so oft
In conversation between man and man
Blots from the human countenance all trace
460 Of beauty and of love. For thou hast sought
The truth in solitude and since the days
That gave thee liberty full long desired
To serve in Nature's temple, thou hast been
The most assiduous of her ministers,
In many things my brother, chiefly here

In this our deep devotion.
                              Fare thee well!
Health and the quiet of a healthful mind
Attend thee! seeking oft the haunts of men
And yet more often living with thyself
470   And for thyself, so haply shall thy days
Be many and a blessing to mankind.

from BOOK THIRD

Residence at Cambridge

It was a dreary morning when the wheels
Rolled over a wide plain o'erhung with clouds,
And nothing cheered our way till first we saw
The long-roofed chapel of King's College lift
Turrets and pinnacles in answering files
Extended high above a dusky grove.

      Advancing, we espied upon the road
A student clothed in gown and tasselled cap
Striding along as if o'ertasked by Time
10   Or covetous of exercise and air;
He passed – nor was I master of my eyes
Till he was left an arrow's flight behind.
As near and nearer to the spot we drew,
It seemed to suck us in with an eddy's force;
Onward we drove beneath the Castle, caught,
While crossing Magdalene Bridge, a glimpse of Cam,
And at the *Hoop* alighted, famous Inn.

      My spirit was up, my thoughts were full of hope;
Some friends I had, acquaintances who there
20   Seemed friends, poor simple school-boys, now hung round
With honour and importance: in a world
Of welcome faces up and down I roved;
Questions, directions, warnings and advice
Flowed in upon me, from all sides; fresh day
Of pride and pleasure! to myself I seemed
A man of business and expense, and went
From shop to shop about my own affairs,

To Tutor or to Tailor, as befell,
From street to street with loose and careless mind.

30   I was the Dreamer, they the Dream; I roamed
Delighted through the motley spectacle;
Gowns grave, or gaudy, doctors, students, streets,
Courts, cloisters, flocks of churches, gateways, towers:
Migration strange for a stripling of the hills,
A northern villager. As if the change
Had waited on some Fairy's wand, at once
Behold me rich in monies, and attired
In splendid garb, with hose of silk, and hair
Powdered like rimy trees, when frost is keen.
40   My lordly dressing-gown, I pass it by,
With other signs of manhood that supplied
The lack of beard. – The weeks went roundly on
With invitations, suppers, wine and fruit.
Smooth housekeeping within and all without
Liberal, and suiting gentleman's array.

The Evangelist St. John my patron was;
Three Gothic courts are his, and in the first
Was my abiding-place, a nook obscure;
Right underneath, the College kitchens made
50   A humming sound, less tuneable than bees
But hardly less industrious; with shrill notes
Of sharp command and scolding intermixed.
Near me hung Trinity's loquacious clock,
Who never let the quarters, night or day,
Slip by him unproclaimed, and told the hours
Twice over with a male and female voice.
Her pealing organ was my neighbour too,
And from my pillow, looking forth by light
Of moon or favouring stars, I could behold
60   The antechapel where the statue stood
Of Newton with his prism and silent face,
The marble index of a mind for ever
Voyaging through strange seas of Thought, alone.

Of College labours, of the Lecturer's room
All studded round, as thick as chairs could stand,

With loyal students faithful to their books,
Half-and-half idlers, hardy recusants
And honest dunces – of important days,
Examinations when the man was weighed
70 As in a balance! of excessive hopes,
Tremblings withal and commendable fears;
Small jealousies, and triumphs good or bad,
Let others that know more speak as they know.
Such glory was but little sought by me,
And little won. Yet from the first crude days
Of settling time in this untried abode
I was disturbed at times by prudent thoughts,
Wishing to hope without a hope, some fears
About my future worldly maintenance,
80 And, more than all, a strangeness in the mind,
A feeling that I was not for that hour
Nor for that place. But wherefore be cast down?
For (not to speak of Reason and her pure
Reflective acts to fix the moral law
Deep in the conscience, nor of Christian Hope
Bowing her head before her sister Faith
As one far mightier) hither I had come,
Bear witness, Truth, endowed with holy powers
And faculties, whether to work or feel.
90 Oft when the dazzling show no longer new
Had ceased to dazzle, ofttimes did I quit
My comrades, leave the crowd, buildings and groves,
And as I paced alone the level fields
Far from those lovely sights and sounds sublime
With which I had been conversant, the mind
Drooped not but there into herself returning
With prompt rebound seemed fresh as heretofore.
At least I more distinctly recognized
Her native instincts; let me dare to speak
100 A higher language, say that now I felt
What independent solaces were mine
To mitigate the injurious sway of place
Or circumstance, how far soever changed
In youth, or *to* be changed in manhood's prime;

Or for the few who shall be called to look
On the long shadows, in our evening years,
Ordained precursors to the night of death.
As if awakened, summoned, roused, constrained,
I looked for universal things, perused
110 The common countenance of earth and sky:
Earth nowhere unembellished by some trace
Of that first Paradise whence man was driven;
And sky whose beauty and bounty are expressed
By the proud name she bears – the name of Heaven.
I called on both to teach me what they might,
Or turning the mind in upon herself
Pored, watched, expected, listened, spread my thoughts
And spread them with a wider creeping; felt
Incumbencies more awful, visitings
120 Of the Upholder of the tranquil soul
That tolerates the indignities of Time
And, from the centre of Eternity
All finite motions overruling, lives
In glory immutable. But peace! enough
Here to record I had ascended now
To such community with highest truth
– A track pursuing, not untrod before,
From strict analogies by thought supplied
Or consciousnesses not to be subdued.
130 To every natural form, rock, fruit or flower,
Even the loose stones that cover the high-way,
I gave a moral life; I saw them feel
Or linked them to some feeling: the great mass
Lay bedded in a quickening soul, and all
That I beheld respired with inward meaning.
Add that whate'er of Terror or of Love
Or Beauty, Nature's daily face put on
From transitory passion, unto this
I was as sensitive as waters are
140 To the sky's influence, in a kindred mood
Of passion, was obedient as a lute
That waits upon the touches of the wind.
Unknown, unthought of, yet I was most rich;

I had a world about me; 'twas my own;
I made it, for it only lived to me
And to the God who sees into the heart.
Such sympathies, though rarely, were betrayed
By outward gestures and by visible looks:
Some called it madness – so indeed it was,
150   If child-like fruitfulness in passing joy,
If steady moods of thoughtfulness matured
To inspiration, sort with such a name;
If prophecy be madness, if things viewed
By poets in old time, and higher up
By the first men, earth's first inhabitants,
May in these tutored days no more be seen
With undisordered sight. But leaving this,
It was no madness, for the bodily eye
Amid my strongest workings evermore
160   Was searching out the lines of difference
As they lie hid in all external forms
Near or remote, minute or vast, an eye
Which from a tree, a stone, a withered leaf,
To the broad ocean and the azure heavens
Spangled with kindred multitudes of stars,
Could find no surface where its power might sleep;
Which spake perpetual logic to my soul,
And by an unrelenting agency
Did bind my feelings even as in a chain.

170   And here, O Friend! have I retraced my life
Up to an eminence, and told a tale
Of matters which not falsely may be called
The glory of my youth. Of genius, power,
Creation and divinity itself
I have been speaking, for my theme has been
What passed within me. Not of outward things
Done visibly for other minds, words, signs,
Symbols or actions, but of my own heart
Have I been speaking, and my youthful mind.
180   O Heavens! how awful is the might of souls
And what they do within themselves while yet

The yoke of earth is new to them, the world
Nothing but a wild field where they were sown.
This is, in truth, heroic argument,
This genuine prowess, which I wished to touch
With hand however weak, but in the main
It lies far hidden from the reach of words.
Points have we all of us within our souls
Where all stand single; this I feel, and make
190 Breathings for incommunicable powers;
But is not each a memory to himself?
And therefore now that we must quit this theme
I am not heartless, for there's not a man
That lives who hath not known his godlike hours
And feels not what an empire we inherit
As natural beings in the strength of Nature.

No more, for now into a populous plain
We must descend. A Traveller I am
Whose tale is only of himself; even so,
200 So be it, if the pure of heart be prompt
To follow, and if thou, O honoured Friend!
Who in these thoughts art ever at my side,
Support, as heretofore, my fainting steps.

It hath been told that when the first delight
That flashed upon me from this novel show
Had failed, the mind returned into herself;
Yet true it is, that I had made a change
In climate, and my nature's outward coat
Changed also slowly and insensibly.
210 Full oft the quiet and exalted thoughts
Of loneliness gave way to empty noise
And superficial pastimes. Now and then
Forced labour and more frequently forced hopes
And, worst of all, a treasonable growth
Of indecisive judgments, that impaired
And shook the mind's simplicity. – And yet
This was a gladsome time. Could I behold –
Who, less insensible than sodden clay
In a sea-river's bed at ebb of tide,

220   Could have beheld – with undelighted heart,
So many happy youths, so wide and fair
A congregation in its budding-time
Of health and hope and beauty, all at once
So many divers samples from the growth
Of life's sweet season – could have seen unmoved
That miscellaneous garland of wild flowers
Decking the matron temples of a place
So famous through the world? To me at least
It was a goodly prospect: for, in sooth,
230   Though I had learnt betimes to stand unpropped
And independent musings pleased me so
That spells seemed on me when I was alone,
Yet could I only cleave to solitude
In lonely places; if a throng was near
That way I leaned by nature; for my heart
Was social and loved idleness and joy.

    Not seeking those who might participate
My deeper pleasures (nay, I had not once,
Though not unused to mutter lonesome songs,
240   Even with myself divided such delight
Or looked that way for aught that might be clothed
In human language), easily I passed
From the remembrance of better things
And slipped into the ordinary works
Of careless youth, unburthened, unalarmed.
Caverns there were within my mind which sun
Could never penetrate, yet did there not
Want store of leafy *arbours* where the light
Might enter in at will. Companionships,
250   Friendships, acquaintances, were welcome all.
We sauntered, played, or rioted; we talked
Unprofitable talk at morning hours,
Drifted about along the streets and walks,
Read lazily in trivial books, went forth
To gallop through the country in blind zeal
Of senseless horsemanship, or on the breast
Of Cam sailed boisterously, and let the stars
Come forth, perhaps without one quiet thought.

Such was the tenor of the second act
260 In this new life. Imagination slept
And yet not utterly. I could not print
Ground where the grass had yielded to your steps
Ye generations of illustrious men,
Unmoved. I could not always lightly pass
Through the same gateways, sleep where ye had slept,
Wake where ye waked, range that inclosure old,
That garden of great intellects, undisturbed.
Place also by the side of this dark sense
Of noble feeling, that those spiritual men,
270 Even the great Newton's own ethereal self,
Seemed humbled in these precincts, thence to be
The more endeared. Their several memories here
(Even like their persons in their portraits clothed
With the accustomed garb of daily life)
Put on a lowly and a touching grace
Of more distinct humanity, that left
All genuine admiration unimpaired.
– Beside the pleasant Mill of Trompington
I laughed with Chaucer in the hawthorn shade,
280 Heard him, while birds were warbling, tell his tales
Of amorous passion. And that gentle Bard,
Chosen by the Muses for their Page of State –
Sweet Spenser, moving through his clouded heaven
With the moon's beauty and the moon's soft pace,
I called him Brother, Englishman, and Friend!
Yea, our blind Poet, who, in his later day,
Stood almost single, uttering odious truth
– Darkness before and danger's voice behind,
Soul awful – if the earth hath ever lodged
290 An awful soul – I seemed to see him here
Familiarly, and in his scholar's dress
Bounding before me, yet a stripling youth –
A boy, no better, with his rosy cheeks
Angelical, keen eye, courageous look
And conscious step of purity and pride.
Among the band of my compeers was one
Whom chance had stationed in the very room

Honoured by Milton's name. O temperate Bard!
Be it confest that, for the first time, seated
300   Within thy innocent lodge and oratory,
One of a festive circle, I poured out
Libations, to thy memory drank, till pride
And gratitude grew dizzy in a brain
Never excited by the fumes of wine
Before that hour or since. Then, forth I ran
From the assembly; through a length of streets
Ran, ostrich-like, to reach our chapel door
In not a desperate or opprobrious time,
Albeit long after the importunate bell
310   Had stopped, with wearisome Cassandra voice
No longer haunting the dark winter night. –
Call back, O Friend! a moment to thy mind
The place itself and fashion of the rites.
With careless ostentation shouldering up
My surplice, through the inferior throng I clove
Of the plain Burghers, who in audience stood
On the last skirts of their permitted ground
Under the pealing organ. Empty thoughts!
I am ashamed of them: and that great Bard
320   And thou, O Friend! who in thy ample mind
Hast placed me high above my best deserts,
Ye will forgive the weakness of that hour,
In some of its unworthy vanities,
Brother to many more.
                              In this mixed sort
The months passed on, remissly, not given up
To wilful alienation from the right,
Or walks of open scandal, but in vague
And loose indifference, easy likings, aims
Of a low pitch – duty and zeal dismissed,
330   Yet Nature, or a happy course of things,
Not doing in their stead the needful work.
The memory languidly revolved, the heart
Reposed in noontide rest, the inner pulse
Of contemplation almost failed to beat.
Such life might not inaptly be compared

To a floating island, an amphibious spot
Unsound, of spongy texture, yet withal
Not wanting a fair face of water weeds
And pleasant flowers. The thirst of living praise,
340   Fit reverence for the glorious Dead, the sight
Of those long vistas, sacred catacombs
Where mighty *minds* lie visibly entombed,
Have often stirred the heart of youth and bred
A fervent love of vigorous discipline.
Alas! such high emotion touched not me.
Look was there none within these walls to shame
My easy spirits, and discountenance
Their light composure, far less to instil
A calm resolve of mind, firmly addressed
350   To puissant efforts. Nor was this the blame
Of others but my own; I should, in truth,
As far as doth concern my single self,
Misdeem most widely, lodging it elsewhere:
For I, bred up mid Nature's luxuries,
Was a spoiled child, and rambling like the wind
As I had done in daily intercourse
With those crystalline rivers, solemn heights
And mountains, ranging like a fowl of the air,
I was ill-tutored for captivity,
360   To quit my pleasure and from month to month
Take up a station calmly on the perch
Of sedentary peace. Those lovely forms
Had also left less space within my mind,
Which, wrought upon instinctively, had found
A freshness in those objects of her love,
A winning power, beyond all other power.
Not that I slighted books – that were to lack
All sense – but other passions in me ruled,
Passions more fervent, making me less prompt
370   To indoor study than was wise or well
Or suited to those years. Yet I, though used
In magisterial liberty to rove,
Culling such flowers of learning as might tempt
A random choice, could shadow forth a place

(If now I yield not to a flattering dream)
Whose studious aspect should have bent me down
To instantaneous service, should at once
Have made me pay to science and to arts
And written lore, acknowledged my liege lord,
380 A homage frankly offered up, like that
Which I had paid to Nature. Toil and pains
In this recess by thoughtful Fancy built
Should spread from heart to heart and stately groves,
Majestic edifices, should not want
A corresponding dignity within.
The congregating temper that pervades
Our unripe years, not wasted, should be taught
To minister to works of high attempt –
Works which the enthusiast would perform with love.
390 Youth should be awed, religiously possessed
With a conviction of the power that waits
On knowledge, when sincerely sought and prized
For its own sake, on glory and on praise
If but by labour won and fit to endure.
The passing day should learn to put aside
Her trappings here, should strip them off abashed
Before antiquity and steadfast truth
And strong book-mindedness, and over all
A healthy sound simplicity should reign,
400 A seemly plainness, name it what you will,
Republican or pious.

*   *   *   *   *

    Thus in submissive idleness, my Friend,
The labouring time of autumn, winter, spring,
Eight months! rolled pleasingly away; the ninth
Came and returned me to my native hills.

from BOOK FOURTH

Summer Vacation

Bright was the summer's noon when quickening steps
Followed each other till a dreary moor
Was crossed, and a bare ridge clomb, upon whose top

Standing alone, as from a rampart's edge
I overlooked the bed of Windermere
Like a vast river stretching in the sun.
With exultation, at my feet I saw
Lake, islands, promontories, gleaming bays,
A universe of Nature's fairest forms
10   Proudly revealed with instantaneous burst,
Magnificent and beautiful and gay.
I bounded down the hill shouting amain
For the old Ferryman; to the shout the rocks
Replied, and when the Charon of the flood
Had staid his oars and touched the jutting pier
I did not step into the well-known boat
Without a cordial greeting. Thence with speed
Up the familiar hill I took my way
Towards that sweet Valley where I had been reared;
20   'Twas but a short hour's walk ere veering round
I saw the snow-white church upon her hill
Sit like a thronèd Lady sending out
A gracious look all over her domain.
Yon azure smoke betrays the lurking town;
With eager footsteps I advance and reach
The cottage threshold where my journey closed –
Glad welcome had I, with some tears, perhaps,
From my old Dame, so kind and motherly
While she perused me with a parent's pride.
30   The thoughts of gratitude shall fall like dew
Upon thy grave, good creature! While my heart
Can beat never will I forget thy name.
Heaven's blessing be upon thee where thou liest
After thy innocent and busy stir
In narrow cares, thy little daily growth
Of calm enjoyments; after eighty years
And more than eighty of untroubled life,
Childless, yet by the strangers to thy blood
Honoured with little less than filial love.
40   What joy was mine to see thee once again,
Thee and thy dwelling, and a crowd of things
About its narrow precincts all beloved,

And many of them seeming yet my own.
Why should I speak of what a thousand hearts
Have felt, and every man alive can guess?
The rooms, the court, the garden were not left
Long unsaluted nor the sunny seat
Round the stone table under the dark pine,
Friendly to studious or to festive hours,
50 Nor that unruly child of mountain birth,
The famous brook, who, soon as he was boxed
Within our garden, found himself at once,
As if by trick insidious and unkind
Stripped of his voice and left to dimple down
(Without an effort and without a will)
A channel paved by man's officious care.
I looked at him and smiled, and smiled again,
And in the press of twenty thousand thoughts,
'Ha', quoth I, 'pretty prisoner, are you there!'
60 Well might sarcastic Fancy then have whispered,
'An emblem here behold of thy own life
In its late course of even days with all
Their smooth enthralment'; but the heart was full,
Too full for that reproach. My aged Dame
Walked proudly at my side: she guided me,
I willing, nay – nay, wishing to be led.
– The face of every neighbour whom I met
Was like a volume to me; some were hailed
Upon the road, some busy at their work,
70 Unceremonious greetings interchanged
With half the length of a long field between.
Among my schoolfellows I scattered round
Like recognitions, but with some constraint
Attended, doubtless, with a little pride
But with more shame for my habiliments,
The transformation wrought by gay attire.
Not less delighted did I take my place
At our domestic table, and, dear Friend,
In this endeavour simply to relate
80 A Poet's history, may I leave untold
The thankfulness with which I laid me down

In my accustomed bed, more welcome now
Perhaps than if it had been more desired
Or been more often thought of with regret;
That lowly bed whence I had heard the wind
Roar and the rain beat hard, where I so oft
Had lain awake on summer nights to watch
The moon in splendour couched among the leaves
Of a tall ash, that near our cottage stood;
90 Had watched her with fixed eyes while to and fro
In the dark summit of the waving tree
She rocked with every impulse of the breeze.

Among the favourites whom it pleased me well
To see again, was one, by ancient right
Our inmate, a rough terrier of the hills;
By birth and call of nature pre-ordained
To hunt the badger and unearth the fox
Among the impervious crags, but having been
From youth our own adopted, he had passed
100 Into a gentler service. And when first
The boyish spirit flagged and day by day
Along my veins I kindled with the stir,
The fermentation, and the vernal heat
Of poesy, affecting private shades
Like a sick Lover, then this dog was used
To watch me, an attendant and a friend
Obsequious to my steps early and late,
Though often of such dilatory walk
Tired, and uneasy at the halts I made.
110 A hundred times when, roving high and low,
I have been harassed with the toil of verse,
Much pains and little progress, and at once
Some lovely Image in the song rose up
Full-formed, like Venus rising from the sea;
Then have I darted forwards to let loose
My hand upon his back with stormy joy,
Caressing him again and yet again.
And when at evening on the public way
I sauntered, like a river murmuring

120 And talking to itself when all things else
Are still, the creature trotted on before.
Such was his custom but whene'er he met
A passenger approaching he would turn
To give me timely notice, and straightway,
Grateful for that admonishment, I hushed
My voice, composed my gait, and with the air
And mien of one whose thoughts are free, advanced
To give and take a greeting that might save
My name from piteous rumours, such as wait
130 On men suspected to be crazed in brain.

Those walks well worthy to be prized and loved,
Regretted! that word too was on my tongue,
But they were richly laden with all good
And cannot be remembered but with thanks
And gratitude and perfect joy of heart;
Those walks in all their freshness now came back
Like a returning Spring. When first I made
Once more the circuit of our little lake,
If ever happiness hath lodged with man,
140 That day consummate happiness was mine,
Wide-spreading, steady, calm, contemplative.
The sun was set, or setting, when I left
Our cottage door, and evening soon brought on
A sober hour, not winning or serene,
For cold and raw the air was and untuned
But as a face we love is sweetest then
When sorrow damps it or, whatever look
It chance to wear, is sweetest if the heart
Have fulness in herself, even so with me
150 It fared that evening. Gently did my soul
Put off her veil, and, self-transmuted, stood
Naked, as in the presence of her God.
While on I walked a comfort seemed to touch
A heart that had not been disconsolate.
Strength came where weakness was not known to be,
At least not felt; and restoration came
Like an intruder knocking at the door

Of unacknowledged weariness. I took
The balance and with firm hand weighed myself.
160   – Of that external scene which round me lay,
Little, in this abstraction, did I see,
Remembered less, but I had inward hopes
And swellings of the spirit, was rapt and soothed,
Conversed with promises, had glimmering views
How life pervades the undecaying mind,
How the immortal soul with God-like power
Informs, creates, and thaws the deepest sleep
That time can lay upon her; how on earth
Man, if he do but live within the light
170   Of high endeavours, daily spreads abroad
His being armed with strength that cannot fail.
Nor was there want of milder thoughts, of love,
Of innocence, and holiday repose;
And more than pastoral quiet, mid the stir
Of boldest projects and a peaceful end
At last, or glorious, by endurance won.
Thus musing, in a wood I sate me down
Alone, continuing there to muse: the slopes
And heights meanwhile were slowly overspread
180   With darkness and before a rippling breeze
The long lake lengthened out its hoary line
And in the sheltered coppice where I sate,
Around me from among the hazel leaves,
Now here, now there, moved by the straggling wind,
Came ever and anon a breath-like sound,
Quick as the pantings of the faithful dog,
The off and on companion of my walk;
And such, at times, believing them to be,
I turned my head to look if he were there;
190   Then into solemn thought I passed once more.

*   *   *   *   *

Nor less do I remember to have felt
Distinctly manifested at this time
A human-heartedness about my love
For objects hitherto the absolute wealth

Of my own private being and no more:
Which I had loved, even as a blessed spirit
Or Angel, if he were to dwell on earth,
Might love in individual happiness.
But now there opened on me other thoughts
240   Of change, congratulation or regret,
A pensive feeling! It spread far and wide;
The trees, the mountains shared it, and the brooks,
The stars of Heaven, now seen in their old haunts –
White Sirius glittering o'er the southern crags,
Orion with his belt, and those fair Seven,
Acquaintances of every little child,
And Jupiter, my own beloved star!
Whatever shadings of mortality,
Whatever imports from the world of death
250   Had come among these objects heretofore,
Were, in the main, of mood less tender: strong,
Deep, gloomy were they, and severe; the scatterings
Of awe or tremulous dread, that had given way
In later youth to yearnings of a love
Enthusiastic, to delight and hope.
– As one who hangs down-bending from the side
Of a slow-moving boat, upon the breast
Of a still water, solacing himself
With such discoveries as his eye can make
260   Beneath him in the bottom of the deep,
Sees many beauteous sights, weeds, fishes, flowers,
Grots, pebbles, roots of trees, and fancies more
Yet often is perplexed and cannot part
The shadow from the substance, rocks and sky,
Mountains and clouds reflected in the depth
Of the clear flood, from things which there abide
In their true dwelling: now is crossed by gleam
Of his own image, by a sun-beam now,
And wavering motions sent he knows not whence,
270   Impediments that make his task more sweet,
Such pleasant office have we long pursued
Incumbent o'er the surface of past time
With like success nor often have appeared

Shapes fairer or less doubtfully discerned
Than these to which the Tale, indulgent Friend,
Would now direct thy notice: yet in spite
Of pleasure won and knowledge not withheld,
There was an inner falling off – I loved,
Loved deeply all that had been loved before,
280   More deeply even than ever: but a swarm
Of heady schemes jostling each other, gawds
And feast and dance, and public revelry
And sports, and games (too grateful in themselves
Yet in themselves less grateful, I believe,
Than as they were a badge glossy and fresh
Of manliness and freedom) all conspired
To lure my mind from firm habitual quest
Of feeding pleasures, to depress the zeal
And damp those daily yearnings which had once been
         mine –
290   A wild unworldly minded youth given up
To his own eager thoughts. It would demand
Some skill, and longer time than may be spared,
To paint these vanities and how they wrought
In haunts where they, till now, had been unknown.
It seemed the very garments that I wore
Preyed on my strength and stopped the quiet stream
Of self-forgetfulness.
                        Yes, that heartless chase
Of trivial pleasures was a poor exchange
For books and nature at that early age.
300   'Tis true some casual knowledge might be gained
Of character or life; but at that time,
Of manners put to school I took small note
And all my deeper passions lay elsewhere.
Far better had it been to exalt the mind
By solitary study, to uphold
Intense desire through meditative peace
And yet for chastisement of these regrets
The memory of one particular hour
Doth here rise up against me. Mid a throng
310   Of maids and youths, old men and matrons staid,

A medley of all tempers, I had passed
The night in dancing, gaiety and mirth,
With din of instruments and shuffling feet
And glancing forms and tapers glittering
And unaimed prattle flying up and down –
Spirits upon the stretch and here and there
Slight shocks of young love-liking interspersed,
Whose transient pleasure mounted to the head
And tingled through the veins. Ere we retired
320 The cock had crowed and now the eastern sky
Was kindling, not unseen, from humble copse
And open field, through which the pathway wound
And homeward led my steps. Magnificent
The morning rose, in memorable pomp,
Glorious as e'er I had beheld – in front
The sea lay laughing at a distance; near
The solid mountains shone, bright as the clouds,
Grain-tinctured, drenched in empyrean light
And in the meadows and the lower grounds
330 Was all the sweetness of a common dawn;
Dews, vapours, and the melody of birds,
And labourers going forth to till the fields.

Ah! need I say, dear Friend! that to the brim
My heart was full; I made no vows, but vows
Were then made for me; bond unknown to me
Was given that I should be, else sinning greatly,
A dedicated Spirit. On I walked
In thankful blessedness, which yet survives.

Strange rendezvous my mind was at that time,
340 A parti-coloured show of grave and gay,
Solid and light, short-sighted and profound;
Of inconsiderate habits and sedate,
Consorting in one mansion unreproved.
The worth I knew of powers that I possessed,
Though slighted and too oft misused. Besides,
That summer, swarming as it did with thoughts
Transient and idle, lacked not intervals
When Folly from the frown of fleeting Time

Shrunk, and the mind experienced in herself
350 Conformity as just as that of old
To the end and written spirit of God's works,
Whether held forth in Nature or in Man,
In pregnant vision, separate or conjoined.

When from our better selves we have too long
Been parted by the hurrying world and droop,
Sick of its business, of its pleasures tired,
How gracious, how benign, is Solitude;
How potent a mere image of her sway;
Most potent when impressed upon the mind
360 With an appropriate human centre – hermit
Deep in the bosom of the wilderness;
Votary (in vast cathedral, where no foot
Is treading and no other face is seen)
Kneeling at prayers or watchman on the top
Of lighthouse beaten by Atlantic waves;
Or as the soul of that great Power is met
Sometimes embodied on a public road
When for the night deserted it assumes
A character of quiet more profound
Than pathless wastes.
370   Once, when those summer months
Were flown and autumn brought its annual show
Of oars with oars contending, sails with sails,
Upon Winander's spacious breast, it chanced
That after I had left a flower-decked room
(Whose in-door pastime, lighted up, survived
To a late hour) and spirits overwrought
Were making night do penance for a day
Spent in a round of strenuous idleness,
My homeward course led up a long ascent
380 Where the road's watery surface to the top
Of that sharp rising glittered to the moon
And bore the semblance of another stream
Stealing with silent lapse to join the brook
That murmured in the vale. All else was still;
No living thing appeared in earth or air
And save the flowing water's peaceful voice

Sound there was none – but lo! an uncouth shape
Shown by a sudden turning of the road,
So near that, slipping back into the shade
390 Of a thick hawthorn, I could mark him well,
Myself unseen. He was of stature tall,
A span above man's common measure tall,
Stiff, lank, and upright; a more meagre man
Was never seen before by night or day.
Long were his arms, pallid his hands; his mouth
Looked ghastly in the moonlight: from behind
A mile-stone propped him; I could also ken
That he was clothed in military garb,
Though faded yet entire. Companionless,
400 No dog attending, by no staff sustained,
He stood and in his very dress appeared
A desolation, a simplicity
To which the trappings of a gaudy world
Make a strange background. From his lips ere long
Issued low muttered sounds, as if of pain
Or some uneasy thought; yet still his form
Kept the same awful steadiness – at his feet
His shadow lay and moved not. From self-blame
Not wholly free I watched him thus; at length
410 Subduing my heart's specious cowardice
I left the shady nook where I had stood
And hailed him. Slowly from his resting-place
He rose and with a lean and wasted arm
In measured gesture lifted to his head
Returned my salutation; then resumed
His station as before and when I asked
His history, the veteran in reply
Was neither slow nor eager; but unmoved
And with a quiet uncomplaining voice,
420 A stately air of mild indifference,
He told in few plain words a soldier's tale –
That in the Tropic Islands he had served
Whence he had landed scarcely three weeks past,
That on his landing he had been dismissed
And now was travelling towards his native home.

This heard, I said in pity, 'Come with me.'
He stooped and straightway from the ground took up
An oaken staff by me yet unobserved,
A staff which must have dropt from his slack hand
430   And lay till now neglected in the grass.
Though weak his step and cautious, he appeared
To travel without pain, and I beheld
With an astonishment but ill suppressed
His ghostly figure moving at my side;
Nor could I, while we journeyed thus, forbear
To turn from present hardships to the past
And speak of war, battle, and pestilence,
Sprinkling this talk with questions better spared
On what he might himself have seen or felt.
440   He all the while was in demeanour calm,
Concise in answer; solemn and sublime
He might have seemed but that in all he said
There was a strange half-absence, as of one
Knowing too well the importance of his theme
But feeling it no longer. Our discourse
Soon ended and together on we passed
In silence through a wood gloomy and still.
Up-turning then along an open field
We reached a cottage. At the door I knocked
450   And earnestly to charitable care
Commended him as a poor friendless man,
Belated and by sickness overcome.
Assured that now the traveller would repose
In comfort, I entreated that henceforth
He would not linger in the public ways
But ask for timely furtherance and help
Such as his state required. At this reproof,
With the same ghastly mildness in his look,
He said, 'My trust is in the God of Heaven
460   And in the eye of him who passes me.'

The cottage door was speedily unbarred
And now the soldier touched his hat once more
With his lean hand and in a faltering voice
Whose tone bespake reviving interests

Till then unfelt, he thanked me; I returned
The farewell blessing of the patient man
And so we parted. Back I cast a look
And lingered near the door a little space,
Then sought with quiet heart my distant home.

470   This passed and he who deigns to mark with care
By what rules governed, with what end in view
This Work proceeds, *he* will not wish for more.

from BOOK FIFTH

Books

. . . Once in the stillness of a summer's noon
While I was seated in a rocky cave
By the sea-side, perusing, so it chanced,
60   The famous history of the errant knight
Recorded by Cervantes, these same thoughts
Beset me and to height unusual rose,
While listlessly I sate, and, having closed
The book, had turned my eyes toward the wide sea.
On poetry and geometric truth,
And their high privilege of lasting life,
From all internal injury exempt,
I mused: upon these chiefly and at length,
My senses yielding to the sultry air,
70   Sleep seized me and I passed into a dream.
I saw before me stretched a boundless plain
Of sandy wilderness, all black and void,
And as I looked around, distress and fear
Came creeping over me, when at my side,
Close at my side, an uncouth shape appeared
Upon a dromedary, mounted high.
He seemed an Arab of the Bedouin tribes;
A lance he bore, and underneath one arm
A stone, and, in the opposite hand a shell
80   Of a surpassing brightness. At the sight
Much I rejoiced, not doubting but a guide
Was present, one who with unerring skill
Would through the desert lead me; and while yet

I looked, and looked, self-questioned what this freight
Which the new-comer carried through the waste
Could mean, the Arab told me that the stone
(To give it in the language of the dream)
'Was Euclid's Elements' and 'This', said he,
'Is something of more worth'; and at the word
90   Stretched forth the shell, so beautiful in shape,
In colour so resplendent, with command
That I should hold it to my ear. I did so,
And heard, that instant in an unknown tongue
Which yet I understood, articulate sounds,
A loud prophetic blast of harmony;
An Ode, in passion uttered, which foretold
Destruction to the children of the earth
By deluge now at hand. No sooner ceased
The song than the Arab with calm look declared
100   That all would come to pass of which the voice
Had given forewarning, and that he himself
Was going then to bury those two books:
The one that held acquaintance with the stars,
And wedded soul to soul in purest bond
Of reason, undisturbed by space or time;
The other that was a god, yea many gods,
Had voices more than all the winds, with power
To exhilarate the spirit, and to soothe,
Through every clime, the heart of human kind.
110   While this was uttering, strange as it may seem,
I wondered not, although I plainly saw
The one to be a stone, the other a shell,
Nor doubted once but that they both were books,
Having a perfect faith in all that passed.
Far stronger now grew the desire I felt
To cleave unto this man, but when I prayed
To share his enterprise he hurried on
Reckless of me: I followed, not unseen,
For oftentimes he cast a backward look,
120   Grasping his twofold treasure. Lance in rest,
He rode, I keeping pace with him; and now
He to my fancy had become the knight

Whose tale Cervantes tells; yet not the knight,
But was an Arab of the desert, too;
Of these was neither, and was both at once.
His countenance, meanwhile, grew more disturbed
And looking backwards when he looked, mine eyes
Saw, over half the wilderness diffused,
A bed of glittering light: I asked the cause:
130 'It is', said he, 'the waters of the deep
Gathering upon us'; quickening then the pace
Of the unwieldly creature he bestrode,
He left me; I called after him aloud;
He heeded not; but with his twofold charge
Still in his grasp, before me full in view
Went hurrying o'er the illimitable waste,
With the fleet waters of a drowning world
In chase of him; whereat I waked in terror
And saw the sea before me, and the book
140 In which I had been reading, at my side.

Full often, taking from the world of sleep
This Arab phantom, which I thus beheld,
This semi-Quixote, I to him have given
A substance, fancied him a living man,
A gentle dweller in the desert, crazed
By love and feeling, and internal thought
Protracted among endless solitudes;
Have shaped him wandering upon this quest!
Nor have I pitied him; but rather felt
150 Reverence was due to a being thus employed;
And thought that, in the blind and awful lair
Of such a madness, reason did lie couched.
Enow there are on earth to take in charge
Their wives, their children, and their virgin loves
Or whatsoever else the heart holds dear:
Enow to stir for these; yea, will I say,
Contemplating in soberness the approach
Of an event so dire, by signs, in earth
Or heaven made manifest, that I could share
160 That maniac's fond anxiety and go

Upon like errand. Oftentimes at least
Me hath such strong entrancement overcome
When I have held a volume in my hand,
Poor earthly casket of immortal verse,
Shakespeare, or Milton, labourers divine!

Great and benign, indeed, must be the power
Of living nature, which could thus so long
Detain me from the best of other guides
And dearest helpers, left unthanked, unpraised.
170 Even in the time of lisping infancy
And later down, in prattling childhood even,
While I was travelling back among those days,
How could I ever play an ingrate's part?
Once more should I have made those bowers resound
By intermingling strains of thankfulness
With their own thoughtless melodies; at least
It might have well beseemed me to repeat
Some simply fashioned tale, to tell again,
In slender accents of sweet verse, some tale
180 That did bewitch me then, and soothes me now.
O Friend! O Poet! brother of my soul,
Think not that I could pass along untouched
By these remembrances. Yet wherefore speak?
Why call upon a few weak words to say
What is already written in the hearts
Of all that breathe? what in the path of all
Drops daily from the tongue of every child
Wherever man is found? The trickling tear
Upon the cheek of listening Infancy
Proclaims it, and the insuperable look
190 That drinks as if it never could be full.

That portion of my story I shall leave
There registered; whatever else of power
Or pleasure sown or fostered thus may be
Peculiar to myself, let that remain
Where still it works, though hidden from all search
Among the depths of time. Yet is it just
That here in memory of all books which lay

Their sure foundations in the heart of man,
200 Whether by native prose, or numerous verse,
That in the name of all inspirèd souls,
From Homer the great Thunderer, from the voice
That roars along the bed of Jewish song,
And that more varied and elaborate –
Those trumpet-tones of harmony that shake
Our shores in England, from those loftiest notes
Down to the low and wren-like warblings, made
For cottagers and spinners at the wheel
And sun-burnt travellers resting their tired limbs,
210 Stretched under wayside hedge-rows, ballad tunes,
Food for the hungry ears of little ones,
And of old men who have survived their joys;
'Tis just that in behalf of these, the works,
And of the men that framed them, whether known
Or sleeping nameless in their scattered graves,
That I should here assert their rights, attest
Their honours, and should, once for all, pronounce
Their benediction: speak of them as Powers
For ever to be hallowed; only less,
220 For what we are and what we may become,
Than Nature's self, which is the breath of God,
Or His pure Word by miracle revealed.

*   *   *   *   *

There was a Boy: ye knew him well, ye cliffs
And islands of Winander! – many a time
At evening, when the earliest stars began
To move along the edges of the hills,
Rising or setting, would he stand alone
Beneath the trees or by the glimmering lake
370 And there with fingers interwoven, both hands
Pressed closely palm to palm and to his mouth
Uplifted, he, as through an instrument,
Blew mimic hootings to the silent owls
That they might answer him. And they would shout
Across the watery vale and shout again,
Responsive to his call, with quivering peals

And long halloos and screams, and echoes loud
Redoubled and redoubled, concourse wild
Of jocund din – and, when a lengthened pause
380 Of silence came and baffled his best skill,
Then sometimes, in that silence while he hung
Listening, a gentle shock of mild surprise
Has carried far into his heart the voice
Of mountain torrents; or the visible scene
Would enter unawares into his mind
With all its solemn imagery, its rocks,
Its woods, and that uncertain heaven, received
Into the bosom of the steady lake.

This Boy was taken from his mates and died
390 In childhood ere he was full twelve years old:
Fair is the spot, most beautiful the vale,
Where he was born; the grassy churchyard hangs
Upon a slope above the village school;
And through that churchyard when my way has led
On summer evenings I believe that there
A long half hour together I have stood
Mute-looking at the grave in which he lies!
– Even now appears before the mind's clear eye
That self-same village church; I see her sit
400 (The thronèd Lady whom erewhile we hailed)
On her green hill, forgetful of this Boy
Who slumbers at her feet, forgetful, too,
Of all her silent neighbourhood of graves,
And listening only to the gladsome sounds
That, from the rural school ascending, play
Beneath her, and about her. May she long
Behold a race of young ones like to those
With whom I herded! – (easily, indeed,
We might have fed upon a fatter soil
410 Of arts and letters – but be that forgiven)
A race of real children; not too wise,
Too learned or too good; but wanton, fresh,
And bandied up and down by love and hate;
Not unresentful, where self-justified;
Fierce, moody, patient, venturous, modest, shy,

Mad at their sports like withered leaves in winds:
Though doing wrong and suffering, and full oft
Bending beneath our life's mysterious weight
Of pain, and doubt, and fear; yet yielding not
420   In happiness to the happiest upon earth.
Simplicity in habit, truth in speech,
Be these the daily strengtheners of their minds;
May books and Nature be their early joy!
And knowledge, rightly honoured with that name –
Knowledge not purchased by the loss of power!

Well do I call to mind the very week
When I was first intrusted to the care
Of that sweet Valley; when its paths, its shores,
And brooks were like a dream of novelty
430   To my half-infant thoughts; that very week
While I was roving up and down alone,
Seeking I knew not what, I chanced to cross
One of those open fields, which, shaped like ears,
Make green peninsulas on Esthwaite's Lake.
Twilight was coming on, yet through the gloom
Appeared distinctly on the opposite shore
A heap of garments, as if left by one
Who might have there been bathing – long I watched
But no one owned them; meanwhile the calm lake
440   Grew dark with all the shadows on its breast
And, now and then, a fish up-leaping snapped
The breathless stillness. The succeeding day
Those unclaimed garments telling a plain tale
Drew to the spot an anxious crowd; some looked
In passive expectation from the shore,
While from a boat others hung o'er the deep,
Sounding with grappling irons and long poles.
At last, the dead man, mid that beauteous scene
Of trees and hills and water, bolt upright
450   Rose with his ghastly face, a spectre shape
Of terror; yet no soul-debasing fear,
Young as I was, a child not nine years old,
Possessed me, for my inner eye had seen

Such sights before among the shining streams
Of fairy land, the forests of romance.
Their spirit hallowed the sad spectacle
With decoration and ideal grace;
A dignity, a smoothness, like the works
Of Grecian art and purest poesy.

*   *   *   *   *

Thus far a scanty record is deduced
Of what I owed to books in early life;
Their later influence yet remains untold;
But as this work was taking in my mind
610   Proportions that seemed larger than had first
Been meditated, I was indisposed
To any further progress at a time
When these acknowledgements were left unpaid.

From BOOK SIXTH

Cambridge and the Alps

The leaves were fading when to Esthwaite's banks
And the simplicities of cottage life
I bade farewell; and one among the youth
Who, summoned by that season, reunite
As scattered birds troop to the fowler's lure,
Went back to Granta's cloisters, not so prompt
Or eager, though as gay and undepressed
In mind as when I thence had taken flight
A few short months before. I turned my face
10   Without repining from the coves and heights
Clothed in the sunshine of the withering fern;
Quitted, not loth, the mild magnificence
Of calmer lakes and louder streams; and you,
Frank-hearted maids of rocky Cumberland,
You and your not unwelcome days of mirth
Relinquished, and your nights of revelry,
And in my own unlovely cell sate down
In lightsome mood – such privilege has youth
That cannot take long leave of pleasant thoughts.

20   The bonds of indolent society
Relaxing in their hold, henceforth I lived
More to myself. Two winters may be passed
Without a separate notice: many books
Were skimmed, devoured, or studiously perused,
But with no settled plan. I was detached
Internally from academic cares;
Yet independent study seemed a course
Of hardy disobedience toward friends
And kindred, proud rebellion and unkind.
30   This spurious virtue, rather let it bear
A name it more deserves, this cowardice,
Gave treacherous sanction to that over-love
Of freedom which encouraged me to turn
From regulations even of my own
As from restraints and bonds. Yet who can tell –
Who knows what thus may have been gained, both then
And at a later season, or preserved;
What love of nature, what original strength
Of contemplation, what intuitive truths
40   The deepest and the best, what keen research
Unbiassed, unbewildered, and unawed!

                *   *   *   *   *

190   In summer, making quest for works of art
Or scenes renowned for beauty, I explored
That streamlet whose blue current works its way
Between romantic Dovedale's spiry rocks;
Pried into Yorkshire dales, or hidden tracts
Of my own native region and was blest
Between these sundry wanderings with a joy
Above all joys, that seemed another morn
Risen on mid noon, blest with the presence, Friend,
Of that sole Sister, she who hath been long
200   Dear to thee also, thy true friend and mine,
Now, after separation desolate,
Restored to me, such absences that she seemed
A gift then first bestowed. The varied banks
Of Emont, hitherto unnamed in song,

And that monastic castle mid tall trees
Low-standing by the margin of the stream,
A mansion visited (as fame reports)
By Sidney, where, in sight of our Helvellyn
Or stormy Cross-fell, snatches he might pen
210 Of his Arcadia by fraternal love
Inspired; – that river and those mouldering towers
Have seen us side by side when having clomb
The darksome windings of a broken stair
And crept along a ridge of fractured wall,
Not without trembling, we in safety looked
Forth through some Gothic window's open space
And gathered with one mind a rich reward
From the far-stretching landscape by the light
Of morning beautified, or purple eve,
220 Or, not less pleased, lay on some turret's head,
Catching from tufts of grass and hare-bell flowers
Their faintest whisper, to the passing breeze
Given out while mid-day heat oppressed the plains.

Another maid there was who also shed
A gladness o'er that season, then to me,
By her exulting outside look of youth
And placid under-countenance, first endeared;
That other spirit, Coleridge! who is now
So near to us, that meek confiding heart
230 So reverenced by us both. O'er paths and fields
In all that neighbourhood, through narrow lanes
Of eglantine and through the shady woods
And o'er the Border Beacon, and the waste
Of naked pools, and common crags that lay
Exposed on the bare fell, were scattered love,
The spirit of pleasure and youth's golden gleam.
O Friend! we had not seen thee at that time
And yet a power is on me and a strong
Confusion and I seem to plant thee there.
240 Far art thou wandered now in search of health
And milder breezes, melancholy lot!
But thou art with us, with us in the past,

The present, with us in the times to come:
There is no grief, no sorrow, no despair,
No languor, no dejection, no dismay,
No absence scarcely can there be, for those
Who love as we do. Speed thee well! divide
With us thy pleasure; thy returning strength,
Receive it daily as a joy of ours;
250 Share with us thy fresh spirits, whether gift
Of gales Etesian or of tender thoughts.

*   *   *   *   *

When the third summer freed us from restraint,
A youthful friend, he too a mountaineer,
Not slow to share my wishes, took his staff
And sallying forth, we journeyed, side by side,
Bound to the distant Alps – A hardy slight
Did this unprecedented course imply
Of college studies and their set rewards
Nor had in truth the scheme been formed by me
330 Without uneasy forethought of the pain,
The censures and ill-omening of those
To whom my worldly interests were dear.
But Nature then was sovereign in my mind,
And mighty Forms, seizing a youthful fancy,
Had given a charter to irregular hopes.
In any age of uneventful calm
Among the nations, surely would my heart
Have been possessed by similar desire;
But Europe at that time was thrilled with joy,
340 France standing on the top of golden hours
And human nature seeming born again.

Lightly equipped and but a few brief looks
Cast on the white cliffs of our native shore
From the receding vessel's deck, we chanced
To land at Calais on the very eve
Of that great federal day; and there we saw
In a mean city and among a few,
How bright a face is worn when joy of one
Is joy for tens of millions. Southward thence

350   We held our way direct through hamlets, towns,
       Gaudy with reliques of that festival,
       Flowers left to wither on triumphal arcs,
       And window-garlands. On the public roads
       And, once, three days successively through paths
       By which our toilsome journey was abridged,
       Among sequestered villages we walked
       And found benevolence and blessedness
       Spread like a fragrance everywhere, when spring
       Hath left no corner of the land untouched.
360   Where elms for many and many a league in files
       With their thin umbrage, on the stately roads
       Of that great kingdom, rustled o'er our heads
       For ever near us as we paced along;
       How sweet at such a time, with such delight
       On every side, in prime of youthful strength,
       To feed a Poet's tender melancholy
       And fond conceit of sadness, with the sound
       Of undulations varying as might please
       The wind that swayed them; once and more than once
370   Unhoused beneath the evening star we saw
       Dances of liberty, and in late hours
       Of darkness, dances in the open air
       Deftly prolonged, though grey-haired lookers-on
       Might waste their breath in chiding.

                *   *   *   *   *

       . . . From a bare ridge we also first beheld
       Unveiled the summit of Mont Blanc and grieved
       To have a soulless image on the eye
       That had usurped upon a living thought
       That never more could be. The wondrous Vale
       Of Chamouny stretched far below, and soon
530   With its dumb cataracts and streams of ice,
       A motionless array of mighty waves,
       Five rivers broad and vast, made rich amends
       And reconciled us to realities;
       There small birds warble from the leafy trees,
       The eagle soars high in the element,

There doth the reaper bind the yellow sheaf,
The maiden spread the haycock in the sun,
While Winter like a well-tamed lion walks,
Descending from the mountain to make sport
540 Among the cottages by beds of flowers.

    Whate'er in this wide circuit we beheld
Or heard was fitted to our unripe state
Of intellect and heart. With such a book
Before our eyes we could not choose but read
Lessons of genuine brotherhood, the plain
And universal reason of mankind,
The truths of young and old. Nor, side by side
Pacing, two social pilgrims, or alone
Each with his humour, could we fail to abound
550 In dreams and fictions pensively composed,
Dejection taken up for pleasure's sake,
And gilded sympathies, the willow wreath,
And sober posies of funereal flowers
Gathered among those solitudes sublime
From formal gardens of the Lady Sorrow,
Did sweeten many a meditative hour.

    Yet still in me, with those soft luxuries
Mixed something of stern mood, an under-thirst
Of vigour seldom utterly allayed.
560 And from that source how different a sadness
Would issue, let one incident make known.
When from the Vallais we had turned, and clomb
Along the Simplon's steep and rugged road,
Following a band of muleteers, we reached
A halting-place where all together took
Their noon-tide meal. Hastily rose our guide,
Leaving *us* at the board; awhile we lingered,
Then paced the beaten downward way that led
Right to a rough stream's edge and there broke off.
570 The only track now visible was one
That from the torrent's further brink held forth
Conspicuous invitation to ascend
A lofty mountain. After brief delay

Crossing the unbridged stream, that road we took
And clomb with eagerness, till anxious fears
Intruded, for we failed to overtake
Our comrades gone before. By fortunate chance,
While every moment added doubt to doubt,
A peasant met us from whose mouth we learned
580   That to the spot which had perplexed us first
We must descend and there should find the road,
Which in the stony channel of the stream
Lay a few steps, and then along its banks,
And that our future course, all plain to sight,
Was downwards, with the current of that stream.
Loth to believe what we so grieved to hear,
For still we had hopes that pointed to the clouds,
We questioned him again, and yet again;
But every word that from the peasant's lips
590   Came in reply, translated by our feelings,
Ended in this, *that we had crossed the Alps.*

Imagination – here the Power so called
Through sad incompetence of human speech,
That awful Power rose from the mind's abyss
Like an unfathered vapour that enwraps,
At once, some lonely traveller. I was lost,
Halted without an effort to break through;
But to my conscious soul I now can say –
'I recognise thy glory'; in such strength
600   Of usurpation, when the light of sense
Goes out, but with a flash that has revealed
The invisible world, doth greatness make abode,
There harbours, whether we be young or old;
Our destiny, our being's heart and home,
Is with infinitude, and only there;
With hope it is, hope that can never die,
Effort, and expectation, and desire,
And something evermore about to be.
Under such banners militant the soul
610   Seeks for no trophies, struggles for no spoils
That may attest her prowess, blest in thoughts

That are their own perfection and reward,
Strong in herself and in beatitude
That hides her like the mighty flood of Nile
Poured from his fount of Abyssinian clouds
To fertilise the whole Egyptian plain.

    The melancholy slackening that ensued
Upon those tidings by the peasant given
Was soon dislodged. Downwards we hurried fast
620 And, with the half-shaped road which we had missed,
Entered a narrow chasm. The brook and road
Were fellow-travellers in this gloomy strait
And with them did we journey several hours
At a slow pace. The immeasurable height
Of woods decaying, never to be decayed,
The stationary blasts of waterfalls,
And in the narrow rent at every turn
Winds thwarting winds, bewildered and forlorn,
The torrents shooting from the clear blue sky,
630 The rocks that muttered close upon our ears,
Black drizzling crags that spake by the way-side
As if a voice were in them, the sick sight
And giddy prospect of the raving stream,
The unfettered clouds and region of the Heavens,
Tumult and peace, the darkness and the light
Were all like workings of one mind, the features
Of the same face, blossoms upon one tree,
Characters of the great Apocalypse,
The types and symbols of Eternity,
640 Of first, and last, and midst, and without end.

    That night our lodging was a house that stood
Alone within the valley, at a point
Where tumbling from aloft a torrent swelled
The rapid stream whose margin we had trod;
A dreary mansion large beyond all need,
With high and spacious rooms, deafened and stunned
By noise of waters, making innocent sleep
Lie melancholy among weary bones.

       *   *   *   *   *

But here I must break off and bid farewell
To days each offering some new sight, or fraught
With some untried adventure in a course
730 Prolonged till sprinklings of autumnal snow
Checked our unwearied steps. Let this alone
Be mentioned as a parting word, that not
In hollow exultation, dealing out
Hyperboles of praise comparative,
Not rich one moment to be poor for ever,
Not prostrate, overborne, as if the mind
Herself were nothing, a mere pensioner
On outward forms, did we in presence stand
Of that magnificent region. On the front
740 Of this whole Song is written that my heart
Must in such Temple needs have offered up
A different worship. Finally, whate'er
I saw, or heard, or felt, was but a stream
That flowed into a kindred stream; a gale
Confederate with the current of the soul,
To speed my voyage; every sound or sight
In its degree of power, administered
To grandeur or to tenderness, to the one
Directly, but to tender thoughts by means
750 Less often instantaneous in effect:
Led me to these by paths that in the main
Were more circuitous, but not less sure
Duly to reach the point marked out by Heaven.

from BOOK SEVENTH

Residence in London

Returned from that excursion, soon I bade
Farewell for ever to the sheltered seats
Of gownèd students, quitted hall and bower
And every comfort of that privileged ground,
Well pleased to pitch a vagrant tent among
The unfenced regions of society.

Yet undetermined to what course of life
I should adhere, and seeming to possess
60   A little space of intermediate time
At full command, to London first I turned,
In no disturbance of excessive hope,
By personal ambition unenslaved,
Frugal as there was need, and though self-willed
From dangerous passions free. Three years had flown
Since I had felt in heart and soul the shock
Of the huge town's first presence, and had paced
Her endless streets, a transient visitant.
Now fixed amid that concourse of mankind
70   Where Pleasure whirls about incessantly
Or life and labour seem but one, I filled
An idler's place – an idler well content
To have a house (what matter for a home?)
That owned him; living cheerfully abroad
With unchecked fancy ever on the stir
And all my young affections out of doors.

*   *   *   *   *

Those simple days
Are now my theme, and foremost of the scenes
Which yet survive in memory appears
One at whose centre sate a lovely Boy,
A sportive infant who for six months' space,
Not more, had been of age to deal about
Articulate prattle; Child as beautiful
340   As ever clung around a mother's neck
Or father fondly gazed upon with pride.
There, too, conspicuous for stature tall
And large dark eyes, beside her infant stood
The mother but upon her cheeks diffused
False tints too well accorded with the glare
From play-house lustres thrown without reserve
On every object near. The Boy had been
The pride and pleasure of all lookers-on
In whatsoever place; but seemed in this
350   A sort of alien scattered from the clouds.

Of lusty vigour more than infantine
He was in limb, in cheek a summer rose,
Just three parts blown – a cottage child if e'er
By cottage-door on breezy mountain side
Or in some sheltering vale was seen a babe
By Nature's gifts so favoured. Upon a board
Decked with refreshments had this child been placed,
His little stage in the vast theatre,
And there he sate surrounded with a throng
360 Of chance spectators, chiefly dissolute men
And shameless women; treated and caressed,
Ate, drank, and with the fruit and glasses played,
While oaths and laughter and indecent speech
Were rife about him as the songs of birds
Contending after showers. The mother now
Is fading out of memory but I see
The lovely Boy as I beheld him then
Among the wretched and the falsely gay,
Like one of those who walked with hair unsinged
370 Amid the fiery furnace. Charms and spells
Muttered on black and spiteful instigation
Have stopped, as some believe, the kindliest growths.
Ah – with how different spirit might a prayer
Have been preferred that this fair creature, checked
By special privilege of Nature's love,
Should in his childhood be detained for ever.

*   *   *   *   *

Pass we from entertainments that are such
Professedly to others titled higher,
Yet, in the estimate of youth at least,
More near akin to those than names imply;
490 I mean the brawls of lawyers in their courts
Before the ermined judge, or that great stage
Where senators, tongue-favoured men, perform,
Admired and envied. Oh! the beating heart
When one among the prime of these rose up,
One of whose name from childhood we had heard
Familiarly, a household term, like those,

The Bedfords, Glosters, Salisburys, of old
Whom the fifth Harry talks of. Silence! hush!
This is no trifler, no short-flighted wit,
500 No stammerer of a minute, painfully
Delivered, No! the Orator hath yoked
The Hours, like young Aurora, to his car:
Thrice welcome Presence! how can patience e'er
Grow weary of attending on a track
That kindles with such glory. All are charmed,
Astonished; like a hero in romance
He winds away his never-ending horn;
Words follow words, sense seems to follow sense;
What memory and what logic! till the strain
510 Transcendent, superhuman, as it seemed,
Grows tedious even in a young man's ears.

      Genius of Burke! forgive the pen seduced
By specious wonders, and too slow to tell
Of what the ingenuous, what bewildered men,
Beginning to mistrust their boastful guides,
And wise men, willing to grow wiser, caught,
Rapt auditors! from thy most eloquent tongue –
Now mute, for ever mute in the cold grave.
I see him, – old, but vigorous in age, –
520 Stand like an oak whose stag-horn branches start
Out of its leafy brow, the more to awe
The younger brethren of the grove. But some –
While he forewarns, denounces, launches forth,
Against all systems built on abstract rights,
Keen ridicule; the majesty proclaims
Of Institutes and Laws, hallowed by time;
Declares the vital power of social ties
Endeared by Custom; and with high disdain,
Exploding upstart Theory, insists
530 Upon the allegiance to which men are born –
Some – say at once a froward multitude –
Murmur (for truth is hated, where not loved)
As the winds fret within the Æolian cave,
Galled by their monarch's chain. The times were big

With ominous change, which, night by night, provoked
Keen struggles, and black clouds of passion raised;
But memorable moments intervened,
When Wisdom, like the Goddess from Jove's brain,
Broke forth in armour of resplendent words,
540   Startling the Synod. Could a youth, and one
In ancient story versed, whose breast had heaved
Under the weight of classic eloquence,
Sit, see, and hear, unthankful, uninspired?

*   *   *   *   *

    But foolishness and madness in parade
Though most at home in this their dear domain
Are scattered everywhere, no rarities
Even to the rudest novice of the Schools.
Me, rather, it employed to note and keep
In memory those individual sights
600   Of courage, or integrity, or truth,
Or tenderness, which there, set off by foil,
Appeared more touching. One will I select,
A Father – for he bore that sacred name!
Him saw I sitting in an open square
Upon a corner-stone of that low wall
Wherein were fixed the iron pales that fenced
A spacious grass-plot; there in silence sate
This one Man, with a sickly babe outstretched
Upon his knee, whom he had thither brought
610   For sunshine, and to breathe the fresher air.
Of those who passed, and me who looked at him,
He took no heed; but in his brawny arms
(The Artificer was to the elbow bare
And from his work this moment had been stolen)
He held the child, and, bending over it,
As if he were afraid both of the sun
And of the air which he had come to seek,
Eyed the poor babe with love unutterable.
As the black storm upon the mountain top
620   Sets off the sunbeam in the valley, so
That huge fermenting mass of human-kind
Serves as a solemn back-ground or relief

To single forms and objects, whence they draw,
For feeling and contemplative regard
More than inherent liveliness and power.
How oft amid those overflowing streets
Have I gone forward with the crowd and said
Unto myself, 'The face of every one
That passes by me is a mystery!'
630   Thus have I looked, nor ceased to look, oppressed
By thoughts of what and whither, when and how,
Until the shapes before my eyes became
A second-sight procession such as glides
Over still mountains or appears in dreams.
And once, far-travelled in such mood, beyond
The reach of common indication, lost
Amid the moving pageant, I was smitten
Abruptly with the view (a sight not rare)
Of a blind Beggar who, with upright face,
640   Stood propped against a wall; upon his chest
Wearing a written paper to explain
His story, whence he came and who he was.
Caught by the spectacle my mind turned round
As with the might of waters; an apt type
This label seemed, of the utmost we can know
Both of ourselves and of the universe;
And on the shape of that unmoving man,
His steadfast face and sightless eyes, I gazed
As if admonished from another world.

650   Though reared upon the base of outward things,
Structures like these the excited spirit mainly
Builds for herself. Scenes different there are,
Full-formed, that take with small internal help
Possession of the faculties – the peace
That comes with night, the deep solemnity
Of nature's intermediate hours of rest,
When the great tide of human life stands still,
The business of the day to come – unborn,
Of that gone by – locked up as in the grave;
660   The blended calmness of the heavens and earth,

Moonlight and stars and empty streets and sounds
Unfrequent as in deserts; at late hours
Of winter evenings when unwholesome rains
Are falling hard, with people yet astir,
The feeble salutation from the voice
Of some unhappy woman, now and then
Heard as we pass; when no one looks about,
Nothing is listened to. But these, I fear,
Are falsely catalogued; things that are, are not,
670   As the mind answers to them, or the heart
Is prompt, or slow, to feel. What say you, then,
To times when half the city shall break out
Full of one passion, vengeance, rage, or fear?
To executions, to a street on fire,
Mobs, riots or rejoicings? From these sights
Take one, that ancient festival, the Fair
Holden where martyrs suffered in past time
And named of St. Bartholomew; there see
A work completed to our hands, that lays,
680   If any spectacle on earth can do,
The whole creative powers of man asleep!
For once the Muse's help will we implore
And she shall lodge us, wafted on her wings
Above the press and danger of the crowd,
Upon some showman's platform. What a shock
For eyes and ears! what anarchy and din
Barbarian and infernal – a phantasma
Monstrous in colour, motion, shape, sight, sound!
Below, the open space, through every nook
690   Of the wide area, twinkles, is alive
With heads; the midway region and above
Is thronged with staring pictures and huge scrolls,
Dumb proclamations of the Prodigies.
With chattering monkeys dangling from their poles
And children whirling in their roundabouts;
With those that stretch the neck and strain the eyes
And crack the voice in rivalship, the crowd
Inviting; with buffoons against buffoons
Grimacing, writhing, screaming, him who grinds

700 The hurdy-gurdy, at the fiddle weaves,
Rattles the salt-box, thumps the kettle-drum;
And him who at the trumpet puffs his cheeks;
The silver-collared Negro with his timbrel;
Equestrians, tumblers, women, girls and boys,
Blue-breeched, pink-vested, with high-towering plumes.
– All moveables of wonder from all parts
Are here, Albinos, painted Indians, Dwarfs,
The Horse of knowledge and the learned Pig,
The Stone-eater, the man that swallows fire –
710 Giants, Ventriloquists, the Invisible Girl,
The Bust that speaks and moves its goggling eyes,
The Wax-work, Clock-work, all the marvellous craft
Of modern Merlins, Wild Beasts, Puppet shows,
All out-o'-the-way, far-fetched, perverted things,
All freaks of nature, all Promethean thoughts
Of man, his dullness, madness, and their feats
All jumbled up together to compose
A Parliament of Monsters. Tents and Booths
Meanwhile, as if the whole were one vast mill,
720 Are vomiting, receiving on all sides
Men, Women, three-years' Children, Babes in arms.

    Oh blank confusion! true epitome
Of what the mighty City is herself
To thousands upon thousands of her sons
Living amid the same perpetual whirl
Of trivial objects, melted and reduced
To one identity, by differences
That have no law, no meaning and no end;
Oppression under which even highest minds
730 Must labour, whence the strongest are not free!
But though the picture weary out the eye,
By nature an unmanageable sight,
It is not wholly so to him who looks
In steadiness, who hath among least things
An under-sense of greatest; sees the parts
As parts, but with a feeling of the whole.

       *   *   *   *   *

... This did I feel in London's vast domain;
The Spirit of Nature was upon me there;
The soul of Beauty and enduring Life
740   Vouchsafed her inspiration and diffused,
Through meagre lines and colours, and the press
Of self-destroying transitory things,
Composure, and ennobling Harmony.

from BOOK EIGHTH

Retrospect, – Love of Nature leading to Love of Man

What sounds are those, Helvellyn, that are heard
Up to thy summit, through the depth of air
Ascending, as if distance had the power
To make the sounds more audible? What crowd
Covers, or sprinkles o'er yon village green?
Crowd seems it, solitary hill! to thee,
Though but a little family of men,
Shepherds and tillers of the ground – betimes
Assembled with their children and their wives,
10   And here and there a stranger interspersed.
They hold a rustic fair – a festival,
Such as, on this side now, and now on that,
Repeated through his tributary vales,
Helvellyn, in the silence of his rest,
Sees annually, if clouds towards either ocean
Blown from their favourite resting place, or mists
Dissolved have left him an unshrouded head.
Delightful day it is for all who dwell
In this secluded glen, and eagerly
20   They give it welcome. Long ere heat of noon
From byre or field the kine were brought; the sheep
Are penned in cotes: the chaffering is begun.
The heifer lows uneasy at the voice
Of a new master; bleat the flocks aloud;
Booths are there none; a stall or two is here;
A lame man or a blind, the one to beg,
The other to make music; hither, too,

From far, with basket slung upon her arm
Of hawker's wares, books, pictures, combs, and pins,
30 Some aged woman finds her way again
Year after year, a punctual visitant!
There also stands a speech-maker by rote,
Pulling the strings of his boxed raree-show;
And in the lapse of many years may come
Prouder itinerant, mountebank or he
Whose wonders in a covered wain lie hid.
But one there is, the loveliest of them all,
Some sweet lass of the valley, looking out
For gains, and who that sees her would not buy?
40 Fruits of her father's orchard are *her* wares
And with the ruddy produce she walks round
Among the crowd, half-pleased with, half-ashamed
Of her new office, blushing restlessly.
The children now are rich for the old to-day
Are generous as the young, and if content
With looking on, some ancient wedded pair
Sit in the shade together, while they gaze,
'A cheerful smile unbends the wrinkled brow,
The days departed start again to life,
50 And all the scenes of childhood reappear,
Faint but more tranquil, like the changing sun
To him who slept at noon and wakes at eve.'
Thus gaiety and cheerfulness prevail,
Spreading from young to old, from old to young,
And no one seems to want his part. – Immense
Is the recess, the circumambient world
Magnificent by which they are embraced:
They move about upon the soft green turf:
How little they, they and their doings seem,
60 And all that they can further or obstruct!
Through utter weakness pitiably dear,
As tender infants are: and yet how great!
For all things serve them: them the morning light
Loves as it glistens on the silent rocks;
And them the silent rocks which now from high
Look down upon them: the reposing clouds,

The wild brooks prattling from invisible haunts,
And old Helvellyn, conscious of the stir
Which animates this day their calm abode.

70 With deep devotion, Nature, did I feel
In that enormous City's turbulent world
Of men and things, what benefit I owed
To thee and those domains of rural peace
Where to the sense of beauty first my heart
Was opened . . .

* * * * *

      Yet hail to you
Moors, mountains, headlands, and ye hollow vales,
Ye long deep channels for the Atlantic's voice,
Powers of my native region. – Ye that seize
The heart with firmer grasp! Your snows and streams
220 Ungovernable, and your terrifying winds
That howl so dismally for him who treads
Companionless your awful solitudes!
There 'tis the shepherd's task the winter long,
To wait upon the storms: of their approach
Sagacious, into sheltering coves he drives
His flock and thither from the homestead bears
A toilsome burden up the craggy ways,
And deals it out, their regular nourishment
Strewn on the frozen snow. And when the spring
230 Looks out and all the pastures dance with lambs
And when the flock, with warmer weather, climbs
Higher and higher, him his office leads
To watch their goings, whatsoever track
The wanderers choose. For this he quits his home
At day-spring, and no sooner doth the sun
Begin to strike him with a fire-like heat
Than he lies down upon some shining rock
And breakfasts with his dog. When they have stolen,
As is their wont, a pittance from strict time,
240 For rest, not needed, or exchange of love,
Then from his couch he starts; and now his feet
Crush out a livelier fragrance from the flowers

Of lowly thyme, by Nature's skill enwrought
In the wild turf: the lingering dews of morn
Smoke round him, as from hill to hill he hies,
His staff portending like a hunter's spear,
Or by its aid leaping from crag to crag
And o'er the brawling beds of unbridged streams.
Philosophy, methinks, at Fancy's call
250 Might deign to follow him through what he does
Or sees in his day's march: himself he feels,
In those vast regions where his service lies,
A freeman, wedded to his life of hope
And hazard, and hard labour interchanged
With that majestic indolence so dear
To native man. A rambling school-boy, thus
I felt his presence in his own domain
As of a lord and master or a power
Or genius, under Nature, under God
260 Presiding; and severest solitude
Had more commanding looks when he was there.
When up the lonely brooks on rainy days
Angling I went, or trod the trackless hills
By mists bewildered, suddenly mine eyes
Have glanced upon him distant a few steps,
In size a giant, stalking through thick fog,
His sheep like Greenland bears; or as he stepped
Beyond the boundary line of some hill-shadow,
His form hath flashed upon me, glorified
270 By the deep radiance of the setting sun:
Or him have I descried in distant sky,
A solitary object and sublime,
Above all height! like an aerial cross
Stationed alone upon a spiry rock
Of the Chartreuse, for worship. Thus was man
Ennobled outwardly before my sight
And thus my heart was early introduced
To an unconscious love and reverence
Of human nature; hence the human form
280 To me became an index of delight,
Of grace and honour, power and worthiness.

Meanwhile this creature, spiritual almost
As those of books, but more exalted far;
Far more of an imaginative form
Than the gay Corin of the groves, who lives
For his own fancies, or to dance by the hour
In coronal, with Phyllis in the midst –
Was, for the purposes of kind, a man
With the most common; husband, father; learned,
290   Could teach, admonish, suffered with the rest
From vice and folly, wretchedness and fear;
Of this I little saw, cared less for it,
But something must have felt.
                                        Call ye these appearances
Which I beheld of shepherds in my youth,
This sanctity of Nature given to man –
A shadow, a delusion, ye who pore
On the dead letter, miss the spirit of things;
Whose truth is not a motion or a shape
Instinct with vital functions, but a block
300   Or waxen image which yourselves have made,
And ye adore. But blessed be the God
Of Nature and of Man that this was so,
That men before my inexperienced eyes
Did first present themselves thus purified,
Removed and to a distance that was fit.
And so we all of us in some degree
Are led to knowledge, whencesoever led,
And howsoever; were it otherwise
And we found evil fast as we find good
310   In our first years, or think that it is found,
How could the innocent heart bear up and live!
But doubly fortunate my lot; not here
Alone, that something of a better life
Perhaps was round me than it is the privilege
Of most to move in, but that first I looked
At Man through objects that were great or fair;
First communed with him by their help. And thus
Was founded a sure safeguard and defence
Against the weight of meanness, selfish cares,

320 Coarse manners, vulgar passions, that beat in
On all sides from the ordinary world
In which we traffic. Starting from this point
I had my face turned toward the truth, began
With an advantage furnished by that kind
Of prepossession without which the soul
Receives no knowledge that can bring forth good,
No genuine insight ever comes to her.
From the restraint of over-watchful eyes
Preserved, I moved about, year after year
330 Happy, and now most thankful, that my walk
Was guarded from too early intercourse
With the deformities of crowded life,
And those ensuing laughters and contempts,
Self-pleasing, which, if we would wish to think
With a due reverence on earth's rightful lord,
Here placed to be the inheritor of heaven,
Will not permit us; but pursue the mind,
That to devotion willingly would rise,
Into the temple and the temple's heart.

340   Yet deem not, Friend, that human kind with me
Thus early took a place pre-eminent;
Nature herself was at this unripe time
But secondary to my own pursuits
And animal activities, and all
Their trivial pleasures; and when these had drooped
And gradually expired, and Nature, prized
For her own sake, became my joy, even then
And upwards through late youth, until not less
Than two-and-twenty summers had been told
350 Was Man in my affections and regards
Subordinate to her; her visible forms
And viewless agencies: a passion she,
A rapture often, and immediate love
Ever at hand; *he* only a delight
Occasional, an accidental grace,
His hour being not yet come.

*   *   *   *   *

Thus from a very early age, O Friend!
My thoughts by slow gradations had been drawn
To human-kind and to the good and ill
Of human life: Nature had led me on
680 And oft amid the 'busy hum' I seemed
To travel independent of her help,
As if I had forgotten her; but no,
The world of human-kind outweighed not hers
In my habitual thoughts; the scale of love
Though filling daily still was light compared
With that in which *her* mighty objects lay.

from BOOK NINTH

Residence in France

Even as a river – partly (it might seem)
Yielding to old remembrances, and swayed
In part by fear to shape a way direct
That would engulph him soon in the ravenous sea –
Turns and will measure back his course, far back
Seeking the very regions which he crossed
In his first outset; so have we, my Friend!
Turned and returned with intricate delay.
Or as a traveller, who has gained the brow
10 Of some aerial Down, while there he halts
For breathing-time, is tempted to review
The region left behind him; and if aught
Deserving notice have escaped regard
Or been regarded with too careless eye,
Strives, from that height, with one, and yet one more
Last look, to make the best amends he may,
So have we lingered. Now we start afresh
With courage, and new hope risen on our toil.
Fair greetings to this shapeless eagerness
20 Whene'er it comes! needful in work so long,
Thrice needful to the argument which now
Awaits us! Oh, how much unlike the past!

Free as a colt, at pasture on the hill,
I ranged at large through London's wide domain
Month after month. Obscurely did I live,
Not seeking frequent intercourse with men
By literature, or elegance, or rank
Distinguished. Scarcely was a year thus spent
Ere I forsook the crowded solitude
30 With less regret for its luxurious pomp
And all the nicely-guarded shows of art,
Than for the humble bookstalls in the streets,
Exposed to eye and hand where'er I turned.
– France lured me forth, the realm that I had crossed
So lately, journeying toward the snow-clad Alps.
But now relinquishing the scrip and staff
And all enjoyment which the summer sun
Sheds round the steps of those who meet the day
With motion constant as his own, I went
40 Prepared to sojourn in a pleasant town
Washed by the current of the stately Loire.

Through Paris lay my readiest course and there
Sojourning a few days, I visited
In haste each spot of old or recent fame,
The latter chiefly; from the field of Mars
Down to the suburbs of St. Anthony
And from Mont Martyr southward to the Dome
Of Genevieve. In both her clamorous Halls,
The National Synod and the Jacobins,
50 I saw the Revolutionary Power
Toss like a ship at anchor, rocked by storms;
The Arcades I traversed, in the Palace huge
Of Orleans, coasted round and round the line
Of Tavern, Brothel, Gaming-house and Shop,
Great rendezvous of worst and best, the walk
Of all who had a purpose, or had not;
I stared and listened with a stranger's ears
To Hawkers and Haranguers, hubbub wild!
And hissing Factionists with ardent eyes,
60 In knots or pairs or single. Not a look

Hope takes, or Doubt or Fear are forced to wear
But seemed there present, and I scanned them all,
Watched every gesture uncontrollable
Of anger and vexation and despite,
All side by side and struggling face to face
With gaiety and dissolute idleness.
– Where silent zephyrs sported with the dust
Of the Bastille, I sate in the open sun
And from the rubbish gathered up a stone
70   And pocketed the relic in the guise
Of an enthusiast, yet in honest truth
I looked for something that I could not find,
Affecting more emotion than I felt;
For 'tis most certain that these various sights,
However potent their first shock, with me
Appeared to recompense the traveller's pains
Less than the painted Magdalene of Le Brun,
A beauty exquisitely wrought, with hair
Dishevelled, gleaming eyes, and rueful cheek
80   Pale and bedropped with everflowing tears.

But hence to my more permanent abode
I hasten; there by novelties in speech,
Domestic manners, customs, gestures, looks
And all the attire of ordinary life,
Attention was engrossed; and thus amused
I stood mid those concussions unconcerned,
Tranquil almost, and careless as a flower
Glassed in a green-house, or a parlour shrub
That spreads its leaves in unmolested peace
90   While every bush and tree, the country through,
Is shaking to the roots; indifference this
Which may seem strange; but I was unprepared
With needful knowledge, had abruptly passed
Into a theatre whose stage was filled
And busy with an action far advanced.
Like others I had skimmed and sometimes read
With care the master pamphlets of the day;
Nor wanted such half-insight as grew wild

Upon that meagre soil, helped out by talk
100 And public news; but having never seen
A chronicle that might suffice to show
Whence the main organs of the public power
Had sprung, their transmigrations, when and how
Accomplished, giving thus unto events
A form and body; all things were to me
Loose and disjointed, and the affections left
Without a vital interest. At that time,
Moreover, the first storm was overblown
And the strong hand of outward violence
110 Locked up in quiet. For myself I fear
Now in connection with so great a theme
To speak (as I must be compelled to do)
Of one so unimportant; night by night
Did I frequent the formal haunts of men
Whom, in the city, privilege of birth
Sequestered from the rest; societies
Polished in arts, and in punctilio versed;
Whence, and from deeper causes, all discourse
Of good and evil of the time was shunned
120 With scrupulous care; but these restrictions soon
Proved tedious, and I gradually withdrew
Into a noisier world, and thus ere long
Became a patriot; and my heart was all
Given to the people, and my love was theirs.

    A band of military Officers
Then stationed in the city were the chief
Of my associates: some of these wore swords
That had been seasoned in the wars, and all
Were men well born; the chivalry of France.
130 In age and temper differing, they had yet
One spirit ruling in each heart, alike
(Save only one, hereafter to be named)
Were bent upon undoing what was done . . .

        *   *   *   *   *

                          An Englishman,
            Born in a land whose very name appeared
190   To license some unruliness of mind,
            A stranger, with youth's further privilege,
            And the indulgence that a half-learnt speech
            Wins from the courteous, I, who had been else
            Shunned and not tolerated, freely lived
            With these defenders of the Crown and talked
            And heard their notions, nor did they disdain
            The wish to bring me over to their cause.

                    *   *   *   *   *

                For, born in a poor district, and which yet
            Retaineth more of ancient homeliness,
            Than any other nook of English ground,
            It was my fortune scarcely to have seen
            Through the whole tenor of my school-day time
220   The face of one, who, whether boy or man,
            Was vested with attention or respect
            Through claims of wealth or blood; nor was it least
            Of many benefits, in later years
            Derived from academic institutes
            And rules, that they held something up to view
            Of a Republic, where all stood thus far
            Upon equal ground, that we were brothers all
            In honour, as in one community,
            Scholars, and gentlemen, where, furthermore,
230   Distinction lay open to all that came
            And wealth and titles were in less esteem
            Than talents, worth, and prosperous industry.
            Add unto this, subservience from the first
            To presences of God's mysterious power
            Made manifest in Nature's sovereignty,
            And fellowship with venerable books
            To sanction the proud workings of the soul
            And mountain liberty. It could not be
            But that one tutored thus, should look with awe
240   Upon the faculties of man, receive
            Gladly the highest promises, and hail,

As best, the government of equal rights
And individual worth. And hence, O Friend,
If at the first great outbreak I rejoiced
Less than might well befit my youth, the cause
In part lay here, that unto me the events
Seemed nothing out of Nature's certain course,
A gift that was rather come late than soon.
No wonder then if advocates like these,
250   Inflamed by passion, blind with prejudice,
And stung with injury, at this riper day,
Were impotent to make my hopes put on
The shape of theirs, my understanding bend
In honour to their honour – zeal, which yet
Had slumbered, now in opposition burst
Forth like a Polar summer: every word
They uttered was a dart, by counter-winds
Blown back upon themselves; their reason seemed
Confusion-stricken by a higher power
260   Than human understanding, their discourse
Maimed, spiritless; and, in their weakness strong,
I triumphed.

*   *   *   *   *

Among that band of Officers was one,
Already hinted at, of other mould,
290   A patriot, thence rejected by the rest
And with an oriental loathing spurned
As of a different caste. A meeker man
Than this, lived never, nor a more benign,
Meek though enthusiastic. Injuries
Made *him* more gracious, and his nature then
Did breathe its sweetness out most sensibly
As aromatic flowers on Alpine turf
When foot hath crushed them. He through the events
Of that great change wandered in perfect faith,
300   As through a book, an old romance or tale
Of Fairy, or some dream of actions wrought
Behind the summer clouds. By birth he ranked
With the most noble, but unto the poor

Among mankind he was in service bound
As by some tie invisible, oaths professed
To a religious order. Man he loved
As man; and to the mean and the obscure
And all the homely in their homely works
Transferred a courtesy which had no air
310 Of condescension; but did rather seem
A passion and a gallantry, like that
Which he, a soldier, in his idler day
Had paid to woman: somewhat vain he was
Or seemed so, yet it was not vanity
But fondness, and a kind of radiant joy
Diffused around him while he was intent
On works of love or freedom, or revolved
Complacently the progress of a cause
Whereof he was a part: yet this was meek
320 And placid, and took nothing from the man
That was delightful: oft in solitude
With him did I discourse about the end
Of civil government, and its wisest forms,
Of ancient loyalty, and chartered rights,
Custom and habit, novelty and change,
Of self-respect, and virtue in the few
For patrimonial honour set apart
And ignorance in the labouring multitude.
For he, to all intolerance indisposed,
330 Balanced these contemplations in his mind
And I, who at that time was scarcely dipped
Into the turmoil, bore a sounder judgment
Than later days allowed, carried about me
With less alloy to its integrity
The experience of past ages, as through help
Of books and common life it makes sure way
To youthful minds, by objects over near
Not pressed upon, nor dazzled or misled
By struggling with the crowd for present ends.

*   *   *   *   *

And when we chanced
510 One day to meet a hunger-bitten girl
Who crept along fitting her languid gait
Unto a heifer's motion, by a cord
Tied to her arm, and picking thus from the lane
Its sustenance, while the girl with pallid hands
Was busy knitting in a heartless mood
Of solitude, and at the sight my friend
In agitation said, ''Tis against *that*
That we are fighting', I with him believed
That a benignant spirit was abroad
520 Which might not be withstood, that poverty
Abject as this would in a little time
Be found no more, that we should see the earth
Unthwarted in her wish to recompense
The meek, the lowly, patient child of toil,
All institutes for ever blotted out
That legalised exclusion, empty pomp
Abolished, sensual state and cruel power,
Whether by edict of the one or few.
And finally, as sum and crown of all,
530 Should see the people having a strong hand
In framing their own laws, whence better days
To all mankind.

from BOOK TENTH

France continued

. . . To Paris I returned;
And ranged with ardour heretofore unfelt
50 The spacious city, and in progress passed
The prison where the unhappy Monarch lay,
Associate with his children and his wife
In bondage; and the palace lately stormed
With roar of cannon by a furious host.
I crossed the square (an empty area then!)
Of the Carrousel, where so late had lain
The dead, upon the dying heaped; and gazed

On this and other spots as doth a man
Upon a volume whose contents he knows
60 Are memorable, but from him locked up,
Being written in a tongue he cannot read;
So that he questions the mute leaves with pain
And half upbraids their silence. But that night
I felt most deeply in what world I was,
What ground I trod on, and what air I breathed.
High was my room and lonely, near the roof
Of a large mansion or hotel, a lodge
That would have pleased me in more quiet times,
Nor was it wholly without pleasure then.
70 With unextinguished taper I kept watch,
Reading at intervals; the fear gone by
Pressed on me almost like a fear to come.
I thought of those September massacres,
Divided from me by one little month,
Saw them and touched; the rest was conjured up
From tragic fictions, or true history,
Remembrances and dim admonishments.
The horse is taught his manage, and no star
Of wildest course but treads back his own steps;
80 For the spent hurricane the air provides
As fierce a successor. The tide retreats
But to return out of its hiding-place
In the great deep; all things have second birth;
The earthquake is not satisfied at once;
And in this way I wrought upon myself
Until I seemed to hear a voice that cried
To the whole city, 'Sleep no more'. The trance
Fled with the voice to which it had given birth,
But vainly comments of a calmer mind
90 Promised soft peace and sweet forgetfulness.
The place, all hushed and silent as it was,
Appeared unfit for the repose of night,
Defenceless as a wood where tigers roam.

*   *   *   *   *

Yet did I grieve, nor only grieved, but thought
Of opposition and of remedies:
An insignificant stranger and obscure,
And one, moreover, little graced with power
150 Of eloquence even in my native speech,
And all unfit for tumult or intrigue,
Yet would I at this time with willing heart
Have undertaken for a cause so great
Service however dangerous.

*   *   *   *   *

In this frame of mind,
Dragged by a chain of harsh necessity,
So seemed it, – now I thankfully acknowledge,
Forced by the gracious providence of Heaven –
To England I returned, else (though assured
That I both was and must be of small weight,
No better than a landsman on the deck
Of a ship struggling with a hideous storm),
Doubtless I should have then made common cause
230 With some who perished, haply, perished too,
A poor mistaken and bewildered offering,
Should to the breast of Nature have gone back
With all my resolutions, all my hopes,
A Poet only to myself, to men
Useless, and even, beloved Friend! a soul
To thee unknown!

*   *   *   *   *

What then were my emotions when in arms
Britain put forth her free-born strength in league,
O pity and shame! with those confederate Powers!
Not in my single self alone I found,
But in the minds of all ingenuous youth,
Change and subversion from that hour. No shock
Given to my moral nature had I known
270 Down to that very moment; neither lapse
Nor turn of sentiment that might be named
A revolution, save at this one time;
All else was progress on the self-same path

On which with a diversity of pace
I had been travelling: this a stride at once
Into another region. – As a light
And pliant harebell swinging in the breeze
On some grey rock, its birth-place, so had I
Wantoned, fast rooted on the ancient tower
280 Of my beloved country, wishing not
A happier fortune than to wither there.
Now was I from that pleasant station torn
And tossed about in whirlwind. I rejoiced,
Yea, afterwards, truth most painful to record!
Exulted in the triumph of my soul,
When Englishmen by thousands were o'erthrown,
Left without glory on the field, or driven,
Brave hearts, to shameful flight. It was a grief,
Grief call it not, 'twas anything but that,
290 A conflict of sensations without name,
Of which *he* only who may love the sight
Of a village steeple as I do can judge,
When in the congregation bending all
To their great Father, prayers were offered up
Or praises for our country's victories;
And mid the simple worshippers, perchance
I only, like an uninvited guest
Whom no one owned, sate silent, shall I add,
Fed on the day of vengeance yet to come.

*   *   *   *   *

Domestic carnage now filled the whole year
With feast days; old men from the chimney-nook,
The maiden from the bosom of her love,
The mother from the cradle of her babe,
360 The warrior from the field, all perished, all,
Friends, enemies, of all parties, ages, ranks,
Head after head, and never heads enough
For those that bade them fall. They found their joy,
They made it proudly eager as a child,
(If like desires of innocent little ones
May with such heinous appetites be compared),

Pleased in some open field to exercise
A toy that mimics with revolving wings
The motion of a wind-mill; though the air
370   Do of itself blow fresh and make the vanes
Spin in his eyesight, *that* contents him not,
But, with the plaything at arm's length, he sets
His front against the blast, and runs amain
That it may whirl the faster.
                                 Mid the depth
Of those enormities, even thinking minds
Forgot at seasons whence they had their being,
Forgot that such a sound was ever heard
As Liberty upon earth; yet all beneath
Her innocent authority was wrought,
380   Nor could have been without her blessed name.
The illustrious wife of Roland, in the hour
Of her composure, felt that agony
And gave it vent in her last words. O Friend!
It was a lamentable time for man,
Whether a hope had e'er been his or not,
A woful time for them whose hopes survived
The shock – most woful for those few who still
Were flattered, and had trust in human kind:
They had the deepest feeling of the grief.
390   Meanwhile the Invaders fared as they deserved:
The Herculean Commonwealth had put forth her arms,
And throttled with an infant godhead's might
The snakes about her cradle; that was well
And as it should be, yet no cure for them
Whose souls were sick with pain of what would be
Hereafter brought in charge against mankind:
Most melancholy at that time, O Friend!
Were my day-thoughts, my nights were miserable;
Through months, through years, long after the last beat
400   Of those atrocities, the hour of sleep
To me came rarely charged with natural gifts,
Such ghastly visions had I of despair
And tyranny, and implements of death,
And innocent victims sinking under fear,

And momentary hope and worn-out prayer,
Each in his separate cell, or penned in crowds
For sacrifice, and struggling with forced mirth
And levity in dungeons where the dust
Was laid with tears. Then suddenly the scene
410 Changed, and the unbroken dream entangled me
In long orations which I strove to plead
Before unjust tribunals – with a voice
Labouring, a brain confounded, and a sense,
Death-like of treacherous desertion, felt
In the last place of refuge, my own soul.

*   *   *   *   *

Not far from that still ruin all the plain
Lay spotted with a variegated crowd
Of vehicles and travellers, horse and foot,
Wading beneath the conduct of their guide
In loose procession through the shallow stream
Of inland waters; the great sea meanwhile
Heaved at safe distance, far retired. I paused,
Longing for skill to paint a scene so bright
570 And cheerful, but the foremost of the band
As he approached, no salutation given
In the familiar language of the day,
Cried, 'Robespierre is dead!' nor was a doubt,
After strict question, left within my mind
That he and his supporters all were fallen.

Great was my transport, deep my gratitude
To everlasting Justice, by this fiat
Made manifest. 'Come now, ye golden times',
Said I forth pouring on those open sands
580 A hymn of triumph, 'as the morning comes
From out the bosom of the night come ye:
Thus far our trust is verified; behold!
They who with clumsy desperation brought
A river of blood, and preached that nothing else
Could cleanse the Augean stable, by the might
Of their own helper have been swept away;
Their madness stands declared and visible;

Elsewhere will safety now be sought and earth
March firmly towards righteousness and peace.'
590   – Then schemes I framed more calmly, when and how
The madding factions might be tranquillised,
And how through hardships manifold and long
The glorious renovation would proceed.
Thus interrupted by uneasy bursts
Of exultation, I pursued my way
Along that very shore which I had skimmed
In former days when, spurring from the Vale
Of Nightshade, and St. Mary's mouldering fane
And the stone abbot, after circuit made
600   In wantonness of heart, a joyous band
Of schoolboys hastening to their distant home
Along the margin of the moonlight sea,
We beat with thundering hoofs the level sand.

from BOOK ELEVENTH

France concluded

O pleasant exercise of hope and joy!
For mighty were the auxiliars which then stood
Upon our side, we who were strong in love!
Bliss was it in that dawn to be alive,
But to be young was very Heaven! O times
110   In which the meagre, stale, forbidding ways
Of custom, law, and statute, took at once
The attraction of a country in romance!
When Reason seemed the most to assert her rights
When most intent on making of herself
A prime enchantress – to assist the work,
Which then was going forward in her name!
Not favoured spots alone, but the whole Earth
The beauty wore of promise – that which sets
(As at some moments might not be unfelt
120   Among the bowers of Paradise itself)
The budding rose above the rose full blown.

What temper at the prospect did not wake
To happiness unthought of? The inert
Were roused, and lively natures rapt away!
They who had fed their childhood upon dreams,
The play-fellows of fancy, who had made
All powers of swiftness, subtilty, and strength
Their ministers, – who in lordly wise had stirred
Among the grandest objects of the sense,
130   And dealt with whatsoever they found there
As if they had within some lurking right
To wield it; – they, too, who of gentle mood
Had watched all gentle motions, and to these
Had fitted their own thoughts, schemers more mild,
And in the region of their peaceful selves; –
Now was it that *both* found, the meek and lofty
Did both find helpers to their hearts' desire,
And stuff at hand, plastic as they could wish, –
Were called upon to exercise their skill,
140   Not in Utopia, – subterranean fields, –
Or some secreted island, Heaven knows where!
But in the very world, which is the world
Of all of us, – the place where in the end
We find our happiness, or not at all!

Why should I not confess that Earth was then
To me what an inheritance new-fallen
Seems, when the first time visited, to one
Who thither comes to find in it his home?
He walks about and looks upon the spot
150   With cordial transport, moulds it and remoulds,
And is half-pleased with things that are amiss,
'Twill be such joy to see them disappear.

An active partisan, I thus convoked
From every object pleasant circumstance
To suit my ends; I moved among mankind
With genial feelings still predominant;
When erring, erring on the better part,
And in the kinder spirit; placable,
Indulgent, as not uninformed that men

160 See as they have been taught – and that Antiquity
Gives rights to error; and aware no less
That throwing off oppression must be work
As well of License as of Liberty;
And above all, for this was more than all,
Not caring if the wind did now and then
Blow keen upon an eminence that gave
Prospect so large into futurity;
In brief, a child of Nature, as at first,
Diffusing only those affections wider
170 That from the cradle had grown up with me,
And losing, in no other way than light
Is lost in light, the weak in the more strong.

    In the main outline, such it might be said
Was my condition, till with open war
Britain opposed the liberties of France.
This threw me first out of the pale of love,
Soured and corrupted, upwards to the source,
My sentiments; was not as hitherto
A swallowing up of lesser things in great,
180 But change of them into their contraries:
And thus a way was opened for mistakes
And false conclusions, in degree as gross,
In kind more dangerous. What had been a pride
Was now a shame: my likings and my loves
Ran in new channels, leaving old ones dry,
And hence a blow that in maturer age
Would but have touched the judgment, struck more deep
Into sensations near the heart: meantime,
As from the first, wild theories were afloat
190 To whose pretensions sedulously urged
I had but lent a careless ear, assured
That time was ready to set all things right,
And that the multitude so long oppressed
Would be oppressed no more.
                    But when events
Brought less encouragement, and unto these
The immediate proof of principles no more

Could be entrusted, while the events themselves,
Worn out in greatness, stripped of novelty,
Less occupied the mind, and sentiments
200 Could through my understanding's natural growth
No longer keep their ground, by faith maintained
Of inward consciousness, and hope that laid
Her hand upon her object; evidence
Safer, of universal application, such
As could not be impeached, was sought elsewhere.

But now, become oppressors in their turn,
Frenchmen had changed a war of self-defence
For one of conquest, losing sight of all
Which they had struggled for: and mounted up,
210 Openly in the eye of earth and heaven,
The scale of Liberty. I read her doom
With anger vexed, with disappointment sore,
But not dismayed, nor taking to the shame
Of a false prophet. While resentment rose
Striving to hide, what nought could heal, the wounds
Of mortified presumption, I adhered
More firmly to old tenets, and, to prove
Their temper, strained them more, and thus in heat
Of contest did opinions every day
220 Grow into consequence, till round my mind
They clung, as if they were its life, nay more,
The very being of the immortal soul.

This was the time when all things tending fast
To depravation, speculative schemes
That promised to abstract the hopes of Man
Out of his feelings, to be fixed thenceforth
For ever in a purer element
Found ready welcome. Tempting region *that*
For Zeal to enter and refresh herself,
230 Where passions had the privilege to work,
And never hear the sound of their own names.
But speaking more in charity, the dream
Flattered the young, pleased with extremes, nor least
With that which makes our Reason's naked self

The object of its fervour: What delight!
How glorious! in self-knowledge and self-rule
To look through all the frailties of the world,
And with a resolute mastery shaking off
Infirmities of nature, time and place,
240   Build social upon personal Liberty,
Which, to the blind restraints of general laws
Superior, magisterially adopts
One guide, the light of circumstances, flashed
Upon an independent intellect.

*　　*　　*　　*　　*

270   A strong shock
Was given to old opinions; all men's minds
Had felt its power, and mine was both let loose,
Let loose and goaded. After what hath been
Already said of patriotic love,
Suffice it here to add, that somewhat stern
In temperament, withal a happy man,
And therefore bold to look on painful things,
Free likewise of the world, and thence more bold,
I summoned my best skill, and toiled, intent
280   To anatomise the frame of social life,
Yea, the whole body of society
Searched to its heart. Share with me, Friend! the wish
That some dramatic tale endued with shapes
Livelier, and flinging out less guarded words
Than suit the work we fashion, might set forth
What then I learned or think I learned of truth,
And the errors into which I fell, betrayed
By present objects, and by reasonings false
From their beginnings, inasmuch as drawn
290   Out of a heart that had been turned aside
From Nature's way by outward accidents,
And which was thus confounded, more and more
Misguided and misguiding. So I fared,
Dragging all precepts, judgments, maxims, creeds,
Like culprits to the bar; calling the mind,
Suspiciously, to establish in plain day

Her titles and her honours, now believing,
Now disbelieving, endlessly perplexed
With impulse, motive, right and wrong, the ground
300   Of obligation, what the rule and whence
The sanction; till, demanding formal *proof*
And seeking it in every thing, I lost
All feeling of conviction, and in fine
Sick, wearied out with contrarieties,
Yielded up moral question in despair.

    This was the crisis of that strong disease,
This the soul's last and lowest ebb; I drooped,
Deeming our blessed reason of least use
Where wanted most . . .

      *   *   *   *   *

                          Then it was,
Thanks to the bounteous Giver of all good!
That the beloved woman in whose sight
Those days were passed, now speaking in a voice
Of sudden admonition like a brook
That does but *cross* a lonely road, and now
Seen, heard, and felt, and caught at every turn,
340   Companion never lost through many a wind,
Maintained for me a saving intercourse
With my true self; for, though bedimmed and changed
Both as a clouded and a waning moon
She whispered still that brightness would return,
She in despite of all preserved me still
A Poet, made me seek beneath that name,
And that alone, my office upon earth.
And lastly, as hereafter will be shown
If willing audience fail not, Nature's self,
350   By all varieties of human love
Assisted, led me back through opening day
To those sweet counsels between head and heart
Whence grew that genuine knowledge fraught with peace,
Which through the later sinkings of this cause
Hath still upheld me and upholds me now
In the catastrophe (for so they dream

And nothing less) when finally to close
And rivet down the gains of France, a Pope
Is summoned in, to crown an Emperor:
360   This last opprobrium, when we see a people,
That once looked up in faith as if to Heaven
For manna take a lesson from the dog
Returning to his vomit . . .

from BOOK TWELFTH

Imagination and Taste, how impaired and restored

Long time have human ignorance and guilt
Detained us, on what spectacles of woe
Compelled to look, and inwardly oppressed
With sorrow, disappointment, vexing thoughts,
Confusion of the judgment, zeal decayed,
And lastly utter loss of hope itself
And things to hope for. Not with these began
Our song, and not with these our song must end.
Ye motions of delight that haunt the sides
10   Of the green hills. Ye breezes and soft airs
Whose subtle intercourse with breathing flowers
Feelingly watched, might teach Man's haughty race
How without injury to take, to give
Without offence; ye who, as if to show
The wondrous influence of power gently used,
Bend the complying heads of lordly pines,
And with a touch shift the stupendous clouds
Through the whole compass of the sky; ye brooks,
Muttering along the stones, a busy noise
20   By day, a quiet sound in silent night;
Ye waves that out of the great deep steal forth
In a calm hour to kiss the pebbly shore,
Not mute, and then retire, fearing no storm;
And you, ye groves, whose ministry it is
To interpose the covert of your shades,
Even as a sleep, between the heart of man
And outward troubles, between man himself,

Not seldom, and his own uneasy heart!
Oh! that I had a music and a voice
30   Harmonious as your own, that I might tell
What ye have done for me. The morning shines
Nor heedeth Man's perverseness; Spring returns,
I saw the Spring return and could rejoice,
In common with the children of her love,
Piping on boughs or sporting on fresh fields
Or boldly seeking pleasure nearer heaven
On wings that navigate cerulean skies.
So neither were complacency nor peace
Nor tender yearnings, wanting for my good
40   Through those distracted times; in Nature still
Glorying, I found a counterpoise in her,
Which when the spirit of evil reached its height
Maintained for me a secret happiness.

*   *   *   *   *

What wonder then, if to a mind so far
Perverted, even the visible Universe
90   Fell under the dominion of a taste
Less spiritual, with microscopic view
Was scanned, as I had scanned the moral world?

O Soul of Nature! excellent and fair!
That didst rejoice with me, with whom I too
Rejoiced, through early youth before the winds
And roaring waters, and in lights and shades
That marched and countermarched about the hills
In glorious apparition, Powers on whom
I daily waited, now all eye and now
100   All ear; but never long without the heart
Employed and man's unfolding intellect.
O Soul of Nature! that, by laws divine
Sustained and governed, still dost overflow
With an impassioned life, what feeble ones
Walk on this earth! how feeble have I been
When thou wert in thy strength! Nor this through stroke
Of human suffering, such as justifies
Remissness and inaptitude of mind,

But through presumption; even in pleasure pleased
110 Unworthily, disliking here, and there
Liking, by rules of mimic art transferred
To things above all art; but more, – for this,
Although a strong infection of the age,
Was never much my habit, giving way
To a comparison of scene with scene,
Bent overmuch on superficial things,
Pampering myself with meagre novelties
Of colour and proportion, to the moods
Of time and season, to the moral power,
120 The affections and the spirit of the place
Insensible. Nor only did the love
Of sitting thus in judgment interrupt
My deeper feelings, but another cause,
More subtle and less easily explained,
That almost seems inherent in the creature,
A twofold frame of body and of mind.
I speak in recollection of a time
When the bodily eye, in every stage of life
The most despotic of our senses, gained
130 Such strength in *me* as often held my mind
In absolute dominion. Gladly here,
Entering upon abstruser argument
Could I endeavour to unfold the means
Which Nature studiously employs to thwart
This tyranny, summons all the senses each
To counteract the other, and themselves,
And makes them all, and the objects with which all
Are conversant, subservient in their turn
To the great ends of Liberty and Power.
140 But leave we this: enough that my delights
(Such as they were) were sought insatiably.
Vivid the transport, vivid though not profound;
I roamed from hill to hill, from rock to rock,
Still craving combinations of new forms,
New pleasure, wider empire for the sight,
Proud of her own endowments, and rejoiced
To lay the inner faculties asleep.
Amid the turns and counterturns, the strife

And various trials of our complex being,
150 As we grow up such thraldom of that sense
Seems hard to shun. And yet I knew a maid,
A young enthusiast, who escaped these bonds;
Her eye was not the mistress of her heart.
Far less did rules prescribed by passive taste
Or barren intermeddling subtleties
Perplex her mind; but wise as women are
When genial circumstance hath favoured them,
She welcomed what was given and craved no more;
Whate'er the scene presented to her view,
160 That was the best, to that she was attuned
By her benign simplicity of life
And through a perfect happiness of soul
Whose variegated feelings were in this
Sisters, that they were each some new delight.
Birds in the bower, and lambs in the green field,
Could they have known her, would have loved; methought
Her very presence such a sweetness breathed
That flowers, and trees, and even the silent hills
And every thing she looked on should have had
170 An intimation how she bore herself
Towards them and to all creatures. God delights
In such a being; for her common thoughts
Are piety, her life is gratitude.

Even like this maid, before I was called forth
From the retirement of my native hills,
I loved whate'er I saw: nor lightly loved,
But most intensely, never dreamt of aught
More grand, more fair, more exquisitely framed
Than those few nooks to which my happy feet
180 Were limited. I had not at that time
Lived long enough, nor in the least survived
The first diviner influence of this world
As it appears to unaccustomed eyes.
Worshipping then among the depth of things
As piety ordained, could I submit
To measured admiration or to aught

That should preclude humility and love?
I felt, observed, and pondered; did not judge,
Yea, never thought of judging; with the gift
190 Of all this glory filled and satisfied.
And afterwards, when through the gorgeous Alps
Roaming, I carried with me the same heart:
In truth, the degradation howsoe'er
Induced, effect in whatsoe'er degree
Of custom that prepares a partial scale
In which the little oft outweighs the great,
Or any other cause that hath been named;
Or lastly, aggravated by the times
And their impassioned sounds, which well might make
200 The milder minstrelsies of rural scenes
Inaudible, was transient; I had known
Too forcibly, too early in my life,
Visitings of imaginative power
For this to last: I shook the habit off
Entirely and for ever, and again
In Nature's presence stood, as now I stand,
A sensitive being, a *creative* soul.

There are in our existence spots of time
That with distinct pre-eminence retain
210 A renovating virtue, whence, depressed
By false opinion and contentious thought,
Or aught of heavier or more deadly weight,
In trivial occupations, and the round
Of ordinary intercourse, our minds
Are nourished and invisibly repaired;
A virtue by which pleasure is enhanced,
That penetrates, enables us to mount
When high, more high, and lifts us up when fallen.
This efficacious spirit chiefly lurks
220 Among those passages of life that give
Profoundest knowledge, to what point, and how
The mind is lord and master – outward sense
The obedient servant of her will. Such moments
Are scattered everywhere, taking their date

From our first childhood. I remember well
That once, while yet my inexperienced hand
Could scarcely hold a bridle, with proud hopes
I mounted, and we journeyed towards the hills:
An ancient servant of my father's house
230   Was with me, my encourager and guide.
We had not travelled long ere some mischance
Disjoined me from my comrade, and through fear
Dismounting, down the rough and stony moor
I led my horse, and stumbling on, at length
Came to a bottom, where in former times
A murderer had been hung in iron chains.
The gibbet-mast had mouldered down, the bones
And iron case were gone, but on the turf
Hard by, soon after that fell deed was wrought,
240   Some unknown hand had carved the murderer's name.
The monumental letters were inscribed
In times long past, but still from year to year,
By superstition of the neighbourhood
The grass is cleared away and to that hour
The characters were fresh and visible.
A casual glance had shown them, and I fled,
Faltering and faint and ignorant of the road:
Then, reascending the bare common, saw
A naked pool that lay beneath the hills,
250   The beacon on its summit, and more near
A girl who bore a pitcher on her head
And seemed with difficult steps to force her way
Against the blowing wind. It was in truth
An ordinary sight; but I should need
Colours and words that are unknown to man,
To paint the visionary dreariness
Which while I looked all round for my lost guide
Invested moorland waste, and naked pool,
The beacon crowning the lone eminence,
260   The female and her garments vexed and tossed
By the strong wind. – When in the blessed hours
Of early love, the loved one at my side,
I roamed, in daily presence of this scene,

Upon the naked pool and dreary crags,
And on the melancholy beacon fell
A spirit of pleasure and youth's golden gleam;
And think ye not with radiance more sublime
For these remembrances, and for the power
They had left behind? So feeling comes in aid
270 Of feeling, and diversity of strength
Attends us, if but once we have been strong.
Oh! mystery of Man, from what a depth
Proceed thy honours. I am lost, but see
In simple childhood something of the base
On which thy greatness stands; but this I feel,
That from thy self it comes, that thou must give,
Else never canst receive. The days gone by
Return upon me almost from the dawn
Of life: the hiding-places of man's power
280 Open; I would approach them, but they close.
I see by glimpses now; when age comes on
May scarcely see at all, and I would give
While yet we may, as far as words can give,
Substance and life to what I feel, enshrining,
Such is my hope, the spirit of the Past
For future restoration. – Yet another
Of these memorials.
                One Christmas-time
On the glad eve of its dear holidays,
Feverish, and tired, and restless, I went forth
290 Into the fields, impatient for the sight
Of those led palfreys that should bear us home;
My brothers and myself. There rose a crag
That, from the meeting-point of two highways
Ascending, overlooked them both, far stretched;
Thither, uncertain on which road to fix
My expectation, thither I repaired,
Scout-like, and gained the summit; 'twas a day
Tempestuous, dark, and wild, and on the grass
I sate half-sheltered by a naked wall;
300 Upon my right hand couched a single sheep,
Upon my left a blasted hawthorn stood;

With those companions at my side, I sate
Straining my eyes intensely, as the mist
Gave intermitting prospect of the copse
And plain beneath. Ere wc to school returned,
That dreary time, ere we had been ten days
Sojourners in my father's house, he died
And I and my three brothers, orphans then,
Followed his body to the grave. The event,
310   With all the sorrow that it brought, appeared
A chastisement, and when I called to mind
That day so lately past, when from the crag
I looked in such anxiety of hope,
With trite reflections of morality,
Yet in the deepest passion, I bowed low
To God, Who thus corrected my desires;
And afterwards, the wind and sleety rain
And all the business of the elements,
The single sheep, and the one blasted tree,
320   And the bleak music of that old stone wall,
The noise of wood and water, and the mist
That on the line of each of those two roads
Advanced in such indisputable shapes:
All these were kindred spectacles and sounds
To which I oft repaired, and thence would drink
As at a fountain; and on winter nights
Down to this *very* time, when storm and rain
Beat on my roof, or haply at noon-day
While in a grove I walk, whose lofty trees
330   Laden with summer's thickest foliage rock
In a strong wind, some working of the spirit,
Some inward agitations thence are brought,
Whate'er their office, whether to beguile
Thoughts over busy in the course they took
Or animate an hour of vacant ease.

from BOOK THIRTEENTH

Subject concluded

From Nature doth emotion come, and moods
Of calmness equally are Nature's gift;
This is her glory; these two attributes
Are sister horns that constitute her strength.
Hence Genius, born to thrive by interchange
Of peace and excitation, finds in her
His best and purest friend, from her receives
That energy by which he seeks the truth,
From her that happy stillness of the mind
10   Which fits him to receive it when unsought.

Such benefit the humblest intellects
Partake of, each in their degree; 'tis mine
To speak of what myself have known and felt.
Smooth task! for words find easy way, inspired
By gratitude and confidence in truth.
Long time in search of knowledge did I range
The field of human life, in heart and mind
Benighted, but, the dawn beginning now
To re-appear, 'twas proved that not in vain
20   I had been taught to reverence a Power
That is the visible quality and shape
And image of right reason, that matures
Her processes by steadfast laws, gives birth
To no impatient or fallacious hopes,
No heat of passion or excessive zeal,
No vain conceits, – provokes to no quick turns
Of self-applauding intellect – but trains
To meekness and exalts by humble faith,
Holds up before the mind intoxicate
30   With present objects, and the busy dance
Of things that pass away, a temperate show
Of objects that endure; and by this course
Disposes her, when over-fondly set
On throwing off incumbrances, to seek
In man, and in the frame of social life,
Whate'er there is desirable and good

Of kindred permanence, unchanged in form
And function, or through strict vicissitude
Of life and death revolving. Above all
40   Were re-established now those watchful thoughts
Which, seeing little worthy or sublime
In what the Historian's pen so much delights
To blazon, power and energy detached
From moral purpose, early tutored me
To look with feelings of fraternal love
Upon the unassuming things that hold
A silent station in this beauteous world.

Thus moderated, thus composed, I found
Once more in Man an object of delight,
50   Of pure imagination, and of love;
And, as the horizon of my mind enlarged,
Again I took the intellectual eye
For my instructor, studious more to see
Great truths, than touch and handle little ones.
Knowledge was given accordingly; my trust
Became more firm in feelings that had stood
The test of such a trial; clearer far
My sense of excellence – of right and wrong:
The promise of the present time retired
60   Into its true proportion: sanguine schemes,
Ambitious projects, pleased me less; I sought
For present good in life's familiar face,
And built thereon my hopes of good to come.

*   *   *   *   *

There are who think that strong affections, love,
Known by whatever name, is falsely deemed
A gift, to use a term which they would use,
Of vulgar nature, that its growth requires
Retirement, leisure, language purified
190   By manners studied and elaborate;
That whoso feels such passion in its strength
Must live within the very light and air
Of courteous usages refined by art.
True is it where oppression worse than death

Salutes the being at his birth, where grace
Of culture hath been utterly unknown,
And poverty and labour in excess
From day to day pre-occupy the ground
Of the affections, and to Nature's self
200 Oppose a deeper nature; there indeed
Love cannot be, nor does it thrive with ease
Among the close and overcrowded haunts
Of cities, where the human heart is sick,
And the eye feeds it not and cannot feed.
– Yes, in those wanderings deeply did I feel
How we mislead each other; above all,
How books mislead us, seeking their reward
From judgments of the wealthy Few, who see
By artificial lights; how they debase
210 The Many for the pleasure of those Few,
Effeminately level down the truth
To certain general notions for the sake
Of being understood at once, or else
Through want of better knowledge in the heads
That framed them; flattering self-conceit with words,
That, while they most ambitiously set forth
Extrinsic differences, the outward marks
Whereby society has parted man
From man, neglect the universal heart.

220   Here, calling up to mind what then I saw,
A youthful traveller, and see daily now
In the familiar circuit of my home,
Here might I pause, and bend in reverence
To Nature, and the power of human minds,
To men as they are men within themselves.
How oft high service is performed within,
When all the external man is rude in show,
Not like a temple rich with pomp and gold,
But a mere mountain chapel that protects
230 Its simple worshippers from sun and shower.
Of these, said I, shall be my song; of these,
If future years mature me for the task,

Will I record the praises, making verse
Deal boldly with substantial things; in truth
And sanctity of passion speak of these,
That justice may be done, obeisance paid
Where it is due: thus haply shall I teach,
Inspire, through unadulterated ears
Pour rapture, tenderness, and hope, my theme
240   No other than the very heart of man
As found among the best of those who live
Not unexalted by religious faith,
Nor uninformed by books, good books, though few,
In Nature's presence: thence may I select
Sorrow, that is not sorrow, but delight;
And miserable love, that is not pain
To hear of, for the glory that redounds
Therefrom to human kind and what we are.
Be mine to follow with no timid step
250   Where knowledge leads me; it shall be my pride
That I have dared to tread this holy ground,
Speaking no dream, but things oracular,
Matter not lightly to be heard by those
Who to the letter of the outward promise
Do read the invisible soul, by men adroit
In speech, and for communion with the world
Accomplished, minds whose faculties are then
Most active when they are most eloquent,
And elevated most when most admired.
260   Men may be found of other mould than these,
Who are their own upholders, to themselves
Encouragement and energy and will,
Expressing liveliest thoughts in lively words
As native passion dictates. Others, too,
There are among the walks of homely life
Still higher, men for contemplation framed,
Shy, and unpractised in the strife of phrase;
Meek men, whose very souls perhaps would sink
Beneath them, summoned to such intercourse:
270   Theirs is the language of the heavens, the power,
The thought, the image, and the silent joy:

Words are but under-agents in their souls;
When they are grasping with their greatest strength
They do not breathe among them; this I speak
In gratitude to God, Who feeds our hearts
For His own service; knoweth, loveth us,
When we are unregarded by the world.

    Also, about this time did I receive
Convictions still more strong than heretofore
280 Not only that the inner frame is good,
And graciously composed, but that, no less,
Nature for all conditions wants not power
To consecrate, if we have eyes to see,
The outside of her creatures, and to breathe
Grandeur upon the very humblest face
Of human life. I felt that the array
Of act and circumstance, and visible form,
Is mainly to the pleasure of the mind
What passion makes them; that meanwhile the forms
290 Of Nature have a passion in themselves,
That intermingles with those works of man
To which she summons him; although the works
Be mean, have nothing lofty of their own;
And that the Genius of the Poet hence
May boldly take his way among mankind
Wherever Nature leads, that he hath stood
By Nature's side among the men of old,
And so shall stand for ever. Dearest Friend!
If thou partake the animating faith
300 That Poets, even as Prophets, each with each
Connected in a mighty scheme of truth,
Have each his own peculiar faculty,
Heaven's gift, a sense that fits him to perceive
Objects unseen before, thou wilt not blame
The humblest of this band who dares to hope
That unto him hath also been vouchsafed
An insight that in some sort he possesses
A privilege whereby a work of his,
Proceeding from a source of untaught things

310   Creative and enduring, may become
      A power like one of Nature's. To a hope
      Not less ambitious once among the wilds
      Of Sarum's Plain my youthful spirit was raised:
      There, as I ranged at will the pastoral downs
      Trackless and smooth, or paced the bare white roads
      Lengthening in solitude their dreary line,
      Time with his retinue of ages fled
      Backwards, nor checked his flight until I saw
      Our dim ancestral Past in Vision clear;
320   Saw multitudes of men, and, here and there,
      A single Briton clothed in wolf-skin vest,
      With shield and stone-axe, stride across the wold;
      The voice of spears was heard, the rattling spear
      Shaken by arms of mighty bone, in strength
      Long mouldered of barbaric majesty.
      I called on Darkness – but before the word
      Was uttered, midnight darkness seemed to take
      All objects from my sight; and lo! again
      The Desert visible by dismal flames;
330   It is the sacrificial altar fed
      With living men – how deep the groans! the voice
      Of those that crowd the giant wicker thrills
      The monumental hillocks, and the pomp
      Is for both worlds, the living and the dead.

                *   *   *   *   *

      Moreover, each man's Mind is to herself
      Witness and judge; and I remember well
      That in life's every-day appearances
      I seemed about this time to gain clear sight
      Of a new world, a world, too, that was fit
370   To be transmitted and to other eyes
      Made visible; as ruled by those fixed laws
      Whence spiritual dignity originates,
      Which do both give it being and maintain
      A balance, an ennobling interchange
      Of action from without, and from within;
      The excellence, pure function and best power
      Both of the object seen, and eye that sees.

from BOOK FOURTEENTH

Conclusion

In one of those excursions (may they ne'er
Fade from remembrance) through the Northern tracts
Of Cambria ranging with a youthful friend,
I left Bethgelert's huts at couching-time,
And westward took my way, to see the sun
Rise from the top of Snowdon. To the door
Of a rude cottage at the mountain's base
We came, and roused the shepherd who attends
The adventurous stranger's steps, a trusty guide;
10   Then, cheered by short refreshment, sallied forth.
– It was a close, warm, breezeless summer night,
Wan, dull, and glaring, with a dripping fog
Low-hung and thick, that covered all the sky:
But, undiscouraged, we began to climb
The mountain-side. The mist soon girt us round,
And after ordinary travellers' talk
With our conductor, pensively we sank
Each into commerce with his private thoughts:
Thus did we breast the ascent, and by myself
20   Was nothing either seen or heard that checked
Those musings or diverted, save that once
The shepherd's lurcher, who, among the crags,
Had to his joy unearthed a hedgehog, teased
His coiled-up prey with barkings turbulent.
This small adventure, for even such it seemed
In that wild place, and at the dead of night,
Being over and forgotten, on we wound
In silence as before. With forehead bent
Earthward, as if in opposition set
30   Against an enemy, I panted up
With eager pace, and no less eager thoughts.
Thus might we wear a midnight hour away,
Ascending at loose distance each from each,
And I, as chanced, the foremost of the band;
When at my feet the ground appeared to brighten,

And with a step or two seemed brighter still,
Nor was time given to ask or learn the cause;
For instantly a light upon the turf
Fell like a flash, and lo! as I looked up,
40   The Moon hung naked in a firmament
Of azure without cloud, and at my feet
Rested a silent sea of hoary mist.
A hundred hills their dusky backs upheaved
All over this still ocean; and beyond,
Far, far beyond, the solid vapours stretched,
In headlands, tongues, and promontory shapes,
Into the main Atlantic, that appeared
To dwindle, and give up his majesty,
Usurped upon far as the sight could reach.
50   Not so the ethereal vault; encroachment none
Was there, nor loss; only the inferior stars
Had disappeared, or shed a fainter light
In the clear presence of the full-orbed Moon;
Who, from her sovereign elevation, gazed
Upon the billowy ocean, as it lay
All meek and silent, save that through a rift
Not distant from the shore whereon we stood,
A fixed, abysmal, gloomy breathing-place,
Mounted the roar of waters – torrents – streams
60   Innumerable, roaring with one voice!
Heard over earth and sea, and in that hour,
For so it seemed, felt by the starry heavens.

When into air had partially dissolved
That vision given to spirits of the night
And three chance human wanderers, in calm thought
Reflected, it appeared to me, the type
Of a majestic intellect, its acts
And its possessions, what it has and craves,
What in itself it is, and would become.
70   There I beheld the emblem of a mind
That feeds upon infinity, that broods
Over the dark abyss, intent to hear
Its voices issuing forth to silent light

In one continuous stream, a mind sustained
By recognitions of transcendent power,
In sense conducting to ideal form,
In soul of more than mortal privilege.
One function, above all, of such a mind
Had Nature shadowed there, by putting forth,
80   Mid circumstances awful and sublime,
That mutual domination which she loves
To exert upon the face of outward things,
So moulded, joined, abstracted; so endowed
With interchangeable supremacy,
That men, least sensitive, see, hear, perceive,
And cannot choose but feel. The power which all
Acknowledge when thus moved, which Nature thus
To bodily sense exhibits, is the express
Resemblance of that glorious faculty
90   That higher minds bear with them as their own.
This is the very spirit in which they deal
With the whole compass of the universe:
They from their native selves can send abroad
Kindred mutations, for themselves create
A like existence, and whene'er it dawns
Created for them, catch it or are caught
By its inevitable mastery,
Like angels stopped upon the wing by sound
Of harmony from Heaven's remotest spheres.
100 Them the enduring and the transient both
Serve to exalt; they build up greatest things
From least suggestions; ever on the watch,
Willing to work and to be wrought upon,
They need not extraordinary calls
To rouse them; in a world of life they live;
By sensible impressions not enthralled,
But by their quickening impulse made more prompt
To hold fit converse with the spiritual world,
And with the generations of mankind
110 Spread over time, past, present, and to come,
Age after age till Time shall be no more.
Such minds are truly from the Deity,

Age after age till Time shall be no more.
Such minds are truly from the Deity,
For they are powers; and hence the highest bliss
That flesh can know is theirs – the consciousness
Of Whom they are, habitually infused
Through every image and through every thought,
And all affections, by communion raised
From earth to heaven, from human to divine.
Hence endless occupation for the Soul,
120   Whether discursive or intuitive;
Hence cheerfulness for acts of daily life,
Emotions which best foresight need not fear,
Most worthy then of trust when most intense.
Hence, amid ills that vex and wrongs that crush
Our hearts, if here the words of Holy Writ
May with fit reverence be applied, that peace
Which passeth understanding – that repose
In moral judgments which from this pure source
Must come, or will by man be sought in vain.

130   Oh! who is he that hath his whole life long
Preserved, enlarged, this freedom in himself,
For this alone is genuine liberty?
Where is the favoured being who hath held
That course unchecked, unerring, and untired,
In one perpetual progress smooth and bright?
– A humbler destiny have we retraced,
And told of lapse and hesitating choice,
And backward wanderings along thorny ways:
Yet compassed round by mountain solitudes,
140   Within whose solemn temple I received
My earliest visitations, careless then
Of what was given me; and which now I range
A meditative, oft a suffering man,
Do I declare, in accents which, from truth
Deriving cheerful confidence, shall blend
Their modulation with these vocal streams,
That, whatsoever falls my better mind
Revolving with the accidents of life

May have sustained, that howsoe'er misled,
150   Never did I, in quest of right and wrong,
Tamper with conscience from a private aim;
Nor was in any public hope the dupe
Of selfish passions; nor did ever yield
Wilfully to mean cares or low pursuits,
But shrunk with apprehensive jealousy
From every combination which might aid
The tendency, too potent in itself,
Of use and custom to bow down the soul
Under a growing weight of vulgar sense,
160 And substitute a universe of death
For that which moves with light and life informed,
Actual, divine, and true – To fear and love,
To love as prime and chief, for there fear ends,
Be this ascribed; to early intercourse,
In presence of sublime or beautiful forms,
With the adverse principles of pain and joy,
Evil as one is rashly named by men
Who know not what they speak. By love subsists
All lasting grandeur, by pervading love;
170 That gone, we are as dust. – Behold the fields
In balmy spring-time full of rising flowers
And joyous creatures; see that pair, the lamb
And the lamb's mother, and their tender ways
Shall touch thee to the heart; thou callest this love,
And not inaptly so, for love it is,
Far as it carries thee. In some green bower
Rest, and be not alone, but have thou there
The One who is thy choice of all the world:
There linger, listening, gazing with delight
180 Impassioned, but delight how pitiable
Unless this love by a still higher love
Be hallowed, love that breathes not without awe,
Love that adores, but on the knees of prayer
By heaven inspired; that frees from chains the soul,
Bearing, in union with the purest, best
Of earth-born passions, on the wings of praise,
A mutual tribute to the Almighty's Throne.

  This spiritual Love acts not, nor can exist
Without Imagination, which, in truth,
190 Is but another name for absolute power
And clearest insight, amplitude of mind,
And reason in her most exalted mood.
This faculty hath been the feeding source
Of our long labour: we have traced the stream
From the blind cavern whence is faintly heard
Its natal murmur; followed it to light
And open day; accompanied its course
Among the ways of Nature, for a time
Lost sight of it, bewildered and engulfed;
200 Then given it greeting as it rose once more
In strength, reflecting from its placid breast
The works of man, and face of human life;
And lastly, from its progress have we drawn
Faith in life endless, the sustaining thought
Of human being, Eternity and God.

  Imagination having been our theme,
So also hath that intellectual love,
For they are each in each, and cannot stand
Dividually. – Here must thou be, O Man!
210 Power to thyself; no Helper hast thou here;
Here keepest thou in singleness thy state.
No other can divide with thee this work:
No secondary hand can intervene
To fashion this ability; 'tis thine,
The prime and vital principle is thine
In the recesses of thy nature, far
From any reach of outward fellowship,
Else is not thine at all. But joy to him,
Oh, joy to him who here hath sown, hath laid
220 Here the foundation of his future years!
For all that friendship, all that love can do,
All that a darling countenance can look
Or dear voice utter to complete the man,
Perfect him, made imperfect in himself,
All shall be his: and he whose soul hath risen

Up to the height of feeling intellect
Shall want no humbler tenderness, his heart
Be tender as a nursing mother's heart;
Of female softness shall his life be full,
230 Of humble cares and delicate desires,
Mild interests and gentlest sympathies.

Child of my parents! Sister of my soul!
Thanks in sincerest verse have been elsewhere
Poured out for all the early tenderness
Which I from thee imbibed: and 'tis most true
That later seasons owed to thee no less;
For spite of thy sweet influence and the touch
Of kindred hands that opened out the springs
Of genial thought in childhood, and in spite
240 Of all that, unassisted, I had marked
In life or nature of those charms minute
That win their way into the heart by stealth
(Still to the very going out of youth),
I too exclusively esteemed *that* love,
And sought that beauty, which, as Milton sings,
Hath terror in it. Thou didst soften down
This over-sternness; but for thee, dear Friend!
My soul, too reckless of mild grace, had stood
In her original self too confident,
250 Retained too long a countenance severe;
A rock with torrents roaring, with the clouds
Familiar, and a favourite of the stars:
But thou didst plant its crevices with flowers,
Hang it with shrubs that twinkle in the breeze,
And teach the little birds to build their nests
And warble in its chambers. At a time
When Nature, destined to remain so long
Foremost in my affections, had fallen back
Into a second place, pleased to become
260 A handmaid to a nobler than herself,
When every day brought with it some new sense
Of exquisite regard for common things,
And all the earth was budding with these gifts

Of more refined humanity, thy breath,
Dear Sister, was a kind of gentler spring
That went before my steps. Thereafter came
One whom with thee friendship had early paired;
She came, no more a phantom to adorn
A moment, but an inmate of the heart,
270 And yet a spirit, there for me enshrined
To penetrate the lofty and the low;
Even as one essence of pervading light
Shines in the brightest of ten thousand stars,
And the meek worm that feeds her lonely lamp
Couched in the dewy grass.
                                    With such a theme,
Coleridge! with this my argument, of thee
Shall I be silent? O capacious Soul!
Placed on this earth to love and understand,
And from thy presence shed the light of love,
280 Shall I be mute ere thou be spoken of?
Thy kindred influence to my heart of hearts
Did also find its way. Thus fear relaxed
Her overweening grasp; thus thoughts and things
In the self-haunting spirit learned to take
More rational proportions; mystery,
The incumbent mystery of sense and soul,
Of life and death, time and eternity,
Admitted more habitually a mild
Interposition – a serene delight
290 In closelier gathering cares, such as become
A human creature, howsoe'er endowed,
Poet, or destined for a humbler name;
And so the deep enthusiastic joy,
The rapture of the hallelujah sent
From all that breathes and is, was chastened, stemmed
And balanced by pathetic truth, by trust,
In hopeful reason, leaning on the stay
Of Providence; – and in reverence for duty,
Here, if need be, struggling with storms, and there
300 Strewing in peace life's humblest ground with herbs
At every season green, sweet at all hours.

And now, O Friend! this history is brought
To its appointed close: the discipline
And consummation of a Poet's mind,
In everything that stood most prominent,
Have faithfully been pictured; we have reached
The time (our guiding object from the first)
When we may, not presumptuously, I hope,
Suppose my powers so far confirmed, and such
310   My knowledge, as to make me capable
Of building up a Work that shall endure.

*   *   *   *   *

Oh! yet a few short years of useful life,
And all will be complete, thy race be run,
Thy monument of glory will be raised;
Then, though (too weak to tread the ways of truth)
This age fall back to old idolatry,
Though men return to servitude as fast
As the tide ebbs, to ignominy and shame
By nations sink together, we shall still
440   Find solace – knowing what we have learnt to know,
Rich in true happiness if allowed to be
Faithful alike in forwarding a day
Of firmer trust, joint labourers in the work
(Should Providence such grace to us vouchsafe)
Of their deliverance, surely yet to come.
Prophets of Nature, we to them will speak
A lasting inspiration, sanctified
By reason, blest by faith: what we have loved
Others will love, and we will teach them how,
450   Instruct them how the mind of man becomes
A thousand times more beautiful than the earth
On which he dwells, above this frame of things
(Which mid all revolutions in the hopes
And fears of men doth still remain unchanged)
In beauty exalted, as it is itself
Of quality and fabric more divine.

Appendix I   Preface to Lyrical Ballads, with Pastoral and Other Poems (*1802*)

[Wordsworth's notes have been incorporated into the text in square brackets.]

The first Volume of these Poems has already been submitted to general perusal. It was published, as an experiment, which, I hoped, might be of some use to ascertain, how far, by fitting to metrical arrangement a selection of the real language of men in a state of vivid sensation, that sort of pleasure and that quantity of pleasure may be imparted, which a Poet may rationally endeavour to impart.

I had formed no very inaccurate estimate of the probable effect of those Poems: I flattered myself that they who should be pleased with them would read them with more than common pleasure: and, on the other hand, I was well aware, that by those who should dislike them they would be read with more than common dislike. The result has differed from my expectation in this only, that I have pleased a greater number, than I ventured to hope I should please.

For the sake of variety, and from a consciousness of my own weakness, I was induced to request the assistance of a Friend, who furnished me with the Poems of the ANCIENT MARINER, the FOSTER-MOTHER'S TALE, the NIGHTINGALE, and the Poem entitled LOVE. I should not, however, have requested this assistance, had I not believed that the Poems of my Friend would in a great measure have the same tendency as my own, and that, though there would be found a difference, there would be found no discordance in the colours of our style; as our opinions on the subject of poetry do almost entirely coincide.

Several of my Friends are anxious for the success of these Poems from a belief, that, if the views with which they were composed were indeed realized, a class of Poetry would be produced, well adapted to interest mankind permanently, and not unimportant in the multiplicity, and in the quality of its moral relations: and on this account they have advised me to prefix a systematic defence of the theory upon which the poems were written. But I was unwilling to undertake the task, because I knew that on this occasion the Reader would look coldly upon my arguments, since I might be suspected of having been principally influenced by the selfish and foolish hope of *reasoning* him into an approbation of these particular Poems: and I was still more unwilling to undertake the task, because, adequately to display my opinions, and fully to enforce my arguments, would require a space wholly disproportionate to the nature of a preface. For to treat the subject with the clearness and coherence, of which I believe it susceptible, it would be necessary to give a full account of the present state of the public taste in this country, and to determine how far this taste is healthy or depraved; which, again, could not be determined, without pointing out, in what manner language and the human mind act and re-act on each other, and without retracing the revolutions, not of literature alone, but likewise of society itself. I have therefore altogether declined to enter regularly upon this defence; yet I am sensible, that there would be some impropriety in abruptly obtruding upon the Public, without a few words of introduction, Poems so materially different from those upon which general approbation is at present bestowed.

It is supposed, that by the act of writing in verse an Author makes a formal engagement that he will gratify certain known habits of association; that he not only thus apprises the Reader that certain classes of ideas and expressions will be found in his book, but that others will be carefully excluded. This exponent or symbol held forth by metrical language must in different eras of literature have excited very different expectations: for example, in the age of Catullus, Terence, and Lucretius, and that of Statius or Claudian; and in our own country, in the age of Shakespeare and Beaumont and Fletcher, and that of Donne and Cowley, or Dryden, or Pope. I will not take upon me to determine the exact import of the promise which by the act of writing in verse an Author, in the present day, makes to his Reader; but I am certain, it will appear to many persons that I have not fulfilled the terms of an engagement thus voluntarily contracted. They who have been accustomed to the gaudiness and inane phraseology of many modern writers, if they persist in reading this book to its conclusion, will, no doubt, frequently have to struggle with feelings of strangeness and awkwardness: they will look round for poetry, and will be induced to inquire by what species of courtesy these attempts can be permitted to assume that title. I hope therefore the Reader will not censure me, if I attempt to state what I have proposed to myself to perform; and also (as far as the limits of a preface will permit) to explain some of the chief reasons which have determined me in the choice of my purpose: that at least he may be spared any unpleasant feeling of disappointment, and that I myself may be protected from the most dishonourable accusation which can be brought against an Author, namely, that of an indolence which prevents him from endeavouring to ascertain what is his duty, or, when his duty is ascertained, prevents him from performing it.

The principal object, then, which I proposed to myself in these Poems was to choose incidents and situations from common life, and to relate or describe them, throughout, as far as was possible, in a selection of language really used by men; and, at the same time, to throw over them a certain colouring of imagination, whereby ordinary things should be presented to the mind in an unusual way; and, further, and above all, to make these incidents and situations interesting by tracing in them, truly though not ostentatiously, the primary laws of our nature: chiefly, as far as regards the manner in which we associate ideas in a state of excitement. Low and rustic life was generally chosen, because in that condition, the essential passions of the heart find a better soil in which they can attain their maturity, are less under restraint, and speak a plainer and more emphatic language; because in that condition of life our elementary feelings co-exist in a state of greater simplicity, and, consequently, may be more accurately contemplated, and more forcibly communicated; because the manners of rural life germinate from those elementary feelings; and, from the necessary character of rural occupations, are more easily comprehended; and are more durable; and lastly, because in that condition the passions of men are incorporated with the beautiful and permanent forms of nature. The language, too, of these men is adopted (purified indeed from what appear to be its real defects, from all lasting and rational causes of dislike or disgust) because such men hourly communicate with the best objects from which the best part of language is originally derived; and because, from their rank in society and the sameness and narrow circle of their intercourse, being less under the influence of social vanity, they convey their feelings and notions in simple and unelaborated expressions. Accordingly, such a language, arising out of repeated experience and regular feelings, is a more permanent, and a far more philosophical language, than that which is frequently substituted for it by Poets, who think that they are conferring honour upon themselves and their art, in proportion as they separate themselves from the sympathies of men, and indulge in arbitrary and capricious habits of expression, in order to furnish food for fickle tastes, and fickle appetites, of their own creation. [It is worthwhile here to observe that the affecting parts of Chaucer are almost always expressed in language pure and universally intelligible even to this day. – W.]

I cannot, however, be insensible of the present outcry against the triviality and meanness both of thought and language, which some of my contemporaries have occasionally introduced into their metrical compositions; and I acknowledge that this defect, where it exists, is more dishonourable to the Writer's own character than false refinement or arbitrary innovation, though I should contend at the same time that it is far less pernicious in the sum of its consequences. From such verses the Poems in these volumes will be found distinguished at least by one mark of difference, that each of them has a worthy *purpose*. Not that I mean to say, that I always began to write with a distinct purpose formally conceived; but I believe that my habits of meditation have so formed my feelings, as that my descriptions of such objects as strongly excite those feelings, will be found to carry along with them a *purpose*. If in this opinion I am mistaken, I can have little right to the name of a Poet. For all good poetry is the spontaneous overflow of powerful feelings: but though this be true, Poems to which any value can be attached, were never produced on any variety of subjects but by a man, who being possessed of more than usual organic sensibility, had also thought long and deeply. For our continued influxes of feeling are modified and directed by our thoughts, which are indeed the representatives of all our past feelings; and, as by contemplating the relation of these general representatives to each other we discover what is really important to men, so, by the repetition and continuance of this act, our feelings will be connected with important subjects, till at length, if we be originally possessed of much sensibility, such habits of mind will be produced, that, by obeying blindly and mechanically the impulses of those habits, we shall describe objects, and utter sentiments, of such a nature and in such connexion with each other, that the understanding of the being to whom we address ourselves, if he be in a healthful state of association, must necessarily be in some degree enlightened, and his affections ameliorated.

I have said that each of these poems has a purpose. I have also informed my Reader what this purpose will be found principally to be: namely, to illustrate the manner in which our feelings and ideas are associated in a state of excitement. But, speaking in language somewhat more appropriate, it is to follow the fluxes and refluxes of the mind when agitated by the great and simple affections of our nature. This object I have endeavoured in these short essays to attain by various means; by tracing the maternal passion through many of its more subtle windings, as in the poems of the IDIOT BOY and the MAD MOTHER; by accompanying the last struggles of a human being, at the approach of death, cleaving in solitude to life and society, as in the Poem of the FORSAKEN INDIAN; by showing, as in the Stanzas entitled WE ARE SEVEN, the perplexity and obscurity which in childhood attend our notion of death, or rather our utter inability to admit that notion; or by displaying the strength of fraternal, or to speak more philosophically, of moral attachment when early associated with the great and beautiful objects of nature, as in THE BROTHERS; or, as in the Incident of SIMON LEE, by placing my Reader in the way of receiving from ordinary moral sensations another and more salutary impression than we are accustomed to receive from them. It has also been part of my general purpose to attempt to sketch characters under the influence of less impassioned feelings, as in the TWO APRIL MORNINGS, THE FOUNTAIN, THE OLD MAN TRAVELLING, THE TWO THIEVES, &c. characters of which the elements are simple, belonging rather to nature than to manners, such as exist now, and will probably always exist, and which from their constitution may be distinctly and profitably contemplated. I will not abuse the indulgence of my Reader by dwelling longer upon this subject; but it is proper that I should mention one other circumstance which distinguishes these Poems from the popular Poetry of the day; it is this, that the feeling therein developed gives importance to the action and situation, and not the action and situation to the feeling. My meaning will be rendered perfectly intelligible by referring my Reader to the Poems entitled POOR SUSAN and the CHILDLESS FATHER, particularly to the last Stanza of the latter Poem.

I will not suffer a sense of false modesty to prevent me from asserting, that I point my Reader's attention to this mark of distinction, far less for the sake of these particular Poems than from the general importance of the subject. The subject is indeed important! For the human mind is capable of being excited without the application of gross and violent stimulants; and he must have a very faint perception of its beauty and dignity who does not know this, and who does not further know, that one being is elevated above another, in proportion as he possesses this capability. It has therefore appeared to me, that to endeavour to produce or enlarge this capability is one of the best services in which, at any period, a Writer can be engaged; but this service, excellent at all times, is especially so at the present day. For a multitude of causes, unknown to former times, are now acting with a combined force to blunt the discriminating powers of the mind, and unfitting it for all voluntary exertion to reduce it to a state of almost savage torpor. The most effective of these causes are the great national events which are daily taking place, and the increasing accumulation of men in cities, where the uniformity of their occupations produces a craving for extraordinary incident, which the rapid communication of intelligence hourly gratifies. To this tendency of life and manners the literature and theatrical exhibitions of the country have conformed themselves. The invaluable works of our elder writers, I had almost said the works of Shakespeare and Milton, are driven into neglect by frantic novels, sickly and stupid German Tragedies, and deluges of idle and extravagant stories in verse. — When I think upon this degrading thirst after outrageous stimulation, I am almost ashamed to have spoken of the feeble effort with which I have endeavoured to counteract it; and, reflecting upon the magnitude of the general evil, I should be oppressed with no dishonourable melancholy, had I not a deep impression of certain inherent and indestructible qualities of the human mind, and likewise of certain powers in the great and permanent objects that act upon it, which are equally inherent and indestructible; and did I not further add to this impression a belief, that the time is approaching when the evil will be systematically opposed, by men of greater powers, and with far more distinguished success.

Having dwelt thus long on the subjects and aim of these Poems, I shall request the Reader's permission to apprise him of a few circumstances relating to their *style*, in order, among other reasons, that I may not be censured for not having performed what I never attempted. The Reader will find that personifications of abstract ideas rarely occur in these volumes; and, I hope, are utterly rejected as an ordinary device to elevate the style, and raise it above prose. I have proposed to myself to imitate, and, as far as is possible, to adopt the very language of men; and assuredly such personifications do not make any natural or regular part of that language. They are, indeed, a figure of speech occasionally prompted by passion, and I have made use of them as such; but I have endeavoured utterly to reject them as a mechanical device of style, or as a family language which Writers in metre seem to lay claim to by prescription. I have wished to keep my Reader in the company of flesh and blood, persuaded that by so doing I shall interest him. I am, however, well aware that others who pursue a different track may interest him likewise; I do not interfere with their claim, I only wish to prefer a different claim of my own. There will also be found in these volumes little of what is usually called poetic diction; I have taken as much pains to avoid it as others ordinarily take to produce it; this I have done for the reason already alleged, to bring my language near to the language of men, and further, because the pleasure which I have proposed to myself to impart is of a kind very different from that which is supposed by many persons to be the proper object of poetry. I do not know how without being culpably particular I can give my Reader a more exact notion of the style in which I wished these poems to be written than by informing him that I have at all times endeavoured to look steadily at my subject; consequently, I hope that there is in these Poems little falsehood of description, and that my ideas are expressed in language fitted to their respective importance. Something I must have gained by this practise, as it is friendly to one property of all good poetry, namely good sense; but it has necessarily cut me off from a large portion of phrases and figures of speech which from father to son have long been regarded as the common inheritance of Poets. I have also thought it expedient to restrict myself still further, having abstained from the use of many expressions, in themselves proper and beautiful, but which have been foolishly repeated by bad Poets, till such feelings of disgust are connected with them as it is scarcely possible by any art of association to overpower.

If in a poem there should be found a series of lines, or even a single line, in which the language, though naturally arranged, and according to the strict laws of metre, does not differ from that of prose, there is a numerous class of critics, who, when they stumble upon these prosaisms, as they call them, imagine that they have made a notable discovery, and exult over the Poet as over a man ignorant of his own profession. Now these men would establish a canon of criticism which the Reader will conclude he must utterly reject, if he wishes to be pleased with these volumes. And it would be a most easy task to prove to him, that not only the language of a large portion of every good poem, even of the most elevated character, must necessarily, except with reference to the metre, in no respect differ from that of good prose, but likewise that some of the most interesting parts of the best poems will be found to be strictly the language of prose, when prose is well written. The truth of this assertion might be demonstrated by innumerable passages from almost all the poetical writings, even of Milton himself. I have not space for much quotation; but, to illustrate the subject in a general manner, I will here adduce a short composition of Gray, who was at the head of those who by their reasonings have attempted to widen the space of separation betwixt Prose and Metrical composition, and was more than any other man curiously elaborate in the structure of his own poetic diction.

In vain to me the smiling mornings shine,
And reddening Phoebus lifts his golden fire:
The birds in vain their amorous descant join,
Or cheerful fields resume their green attire:
These ears, alas! for other notes repine;
A different object do these eyes require;
My lonely anguish melts no heart but mine;
And in my breast the imperfect joys expire;
Yet morning smiles the busy race to cheer,
And new-born pleasure brings to happier men;
The fields do all their wonted tribute bear;
To warm their little loves the birds complain.
I fruitless mourn to him that cannot hear
And weep the more because I weep in vain.

It will easily be perceived that the only part of this Sonnet which is of any value is the lines printed in Italics: it is equally obvious, that, except in the rhyme, and in the use of the single word 'fruitless' for fruitlessly, which is so far a defect, the language of these lines does in no respect differ from that of prose.

By the foregoing quotation I have shown that the language of Prose may yet be well adapted to Poetry; and I have previously asserted that a large portion of the language of every good poem can in no respect differ from that of good Prose. I will go further. I do not doubt that it may be safely affirmed, that there neither is, nor can be, any essential difference between the language of prose and metrical composition. We are fond of tracing the resemblance between Poetry and Painting, and, accordingly, we call them Sisters: but where shall we find bonds of connexion sufficiently strict to typify the affinity betwixt metrical and prose composition? They both speak by and to the same organs; the bodies in which both of them are clothed may be said to be of the same substance, their affections are kindred and almost identical, not necessarily differing even in degree; Poetry [I here use the word 'Poetry' (though against my own judgement) as opposed to the word Prose, and synonymous with metrical composition. But much confusion has been introduced into criticism by this contra-distinction of Poetry and Prose, instead of the more philosophical one of Poetry and Matter of Fact, or Science. The only strict antithesis to Prose is Metre; nor is this, in truth, a *strict* antithesis; because lines and passages of metre so naturally occur in writing prose, that it would be scarcely possible to avoid them, even were it desirable. – W.] sheds no tears 'such as Angels weep,' but natural and human tears; she can boast of no celestial Ichor that distinguishes her vital juices from those of prose; the same human blood circulates through the veins of them both.

If it be affirmed that rhyme and metrical arrangement of themselves constitute a distinction which overturns what I have been saying on the strict affinity of metrical language with that of prose, and paves the way for other artificial distinctions which the mind voluntarily admits, I answer that [*added 1802*: the language of such Poetry as I am recommending is, as far as is possible, a selection of the language really spoken by men; that this selection, wherever it is made with true taste and feeling, will of itself form a distinction far greater than would at first be imagined, and will entirely separate the composition from the vulgarity and meanness of ordinary life; and, if metre be superadded thereto, I believe that a dissimilitude will be produced altogether sufficient for the gratification of a rational mind. What other distinction would we have? Whence is it to come? And where is it to exist? Not, surely, where the Poet speaks through the mouths of his characters: it cannot be necessary here, either for elevation of style, or any of its supposed ornaments; for, if the Poet's subject be judiciously chosen, it will naturally, and upon fit occasion, lead him to passions the language of which, if selected truly and judiciously, must necessarily be dignified and variegated, and alive with metaphors and figures. I forbear to speak of an incongruity which would shock the intelligent Reader, should the Poet interweave any foreign splendour of his own with that which the passion naturally suggests: it is sufficient to say that such addition is unnecessary. And, surely, it is more probable that those passages, which with propriety abound with metaphors and figures, will have their due effect, if, upon other occasions where the passions are of a milder character, the style also be subdued and temperate.

But, as the pleasure which I hope to give by the Poems I now present to the Reader must depend entirely on just notions upon this subject, and, as it is in itself of the highest importance to our taste and moral feelings, I cannot content myself with these detached remarks. And if, in what I am about to say, it shall appear to some that my labour is unnecessary, and that I am like a man fighting a battle without enemies, I would remind such persons that, whatever may be the language outwardly holden by men, a practical faith in the opinions which I am wishing to establish is almost unknown. If my conclusions are admitted, and carried as far as they must be carried if admitted at all, our judgements concerning the works of the greatest Poets both ancient and modern will be far different from what they are at present, both when we praise, and when we censure: and our moral feelings influencing, and influenced by these judgements will, I believe, be corrected and purified.

Taking up the subject, then, upon general grounds, I ask what is meant by the word Poet? What is a Poet? To whom does he address himself? And what language is to be expected from him? He is a man speaking to men: a man, it is true, endued with more lively sensibility, more enthusiasm and tenderness, who has a greater knowledge of human nature, and a more comprehensive soul, than are supposed to be common among mankind; a man pleased with his own passions and volitions, and who rejoices more than other men in the spirit of life that is in him; delighting to contemplate similar volitions and passions as manifested in the goings-on of the Universe, and habitually impelled to create them where he does not find them. To these qualities he has added a disposition to be affected more than other men by absent things as if they were present; an ability of conjuring up in himself passions, which are indeed far from being the same as those produced by real events, yet (especially in those parts of the general sympathy which are pleasing and delightful) do more nearly resemble the passions produced by real events, than anything which, from the motions of their own minds merely, other men are accustomed to feel in themselves; whence, and from practise, he has acquired a greater readiness and power in expressing what he thinks and feels, and especially those thoughts and feelings which, by his own choice, or from the structure of his own mind, arise in him without immediate external excitement.

But, whatever portion of this faculty we may suppose even the greatest Poet to possess, there cannot be a doubt but that the language which it will suggest to him, must, in liveliness and truth, fall far short of that which is uttered by men in real life, under the actual pressure of those passions, certain shadows of which the Poet thus produces, or feels to be produced, in himself. However exalted a notion we would wish to cherish of the character of a Poet, it is obvious that, while he describes and imitates passions, his situation is altogether slavish and mechanical, compared with the freedom and power of real and substantial action and suffering. So that it will be the wish of the Poet to bring his feelings near to those of the persons whose feelings he describes, nay, for short spaces of time perhaps, to let himself slip into an entire delusion, and even confound and identify his own feelings with theirs; modifying only the language which is thus suggested to him, by a consideration that he describes for a particular purpose, that of giving pleasure. Here, then, he will apply the principle on which I have so much insisted, namely, that of selection; on this he will depend for removing what would otherwise be painful or disgusting in the passion; he will feel that there is no necessity to trick out or to elevate nature: and, the more industriously he applies this principle, the deeper will be his faith that no words, which his fancy or imagination can suggest, will be to be compared with those which are the emanations of reality and truth.

But it may be said by those who do not object to the general spirit of these remarks, that, as it is impossible for the Poet to produce upon all occasions language as exquisitely fitted for the passion as that which the real passion itself suggests, it is proper that he should consider himself as in the situation of a translator, who deems himself justified when he substitutes excellences of another kind for those which are unattainable by him; and endeavours occasionally to surpass his original, in order to make some amends for the general inferiority to which he feels that he must submit. But this would be to encourage idleness and unmanly despair. Further, it is the language of men who speak of what they do not understand; who talk of Poetry as of a matter of amusement and idle pleasure; who will converse with us as gravely about a *taste* for Poetry, as they express it, as if it were a thing as indifferent as a taste for Rope-dancing, or Frontiniac or Sherry. Aristotle, I have been told, hath said, that Poetry is the most philosophic of all writing: it is so: its object is truth, not individual and local, but general, and operative; not standing upon external testimony, but carried alive into the heart by passion; truth which is its own testimony, which gives strength and divinity to the tribunal to which it appeals, and receives them from the same tribunal. Poetry is the image of man and nature. The obstacles which stand in the way of the fidelity of the Biographer and Historian, and of their consequent utility, are incalculably greater than those which are to be encountered by the Poet who has an adequate notion of the dignity of his art. The Poet writes under one restriction only, namely, that of the necessity of giving immediate pleasure to a human Being possessed of that information which may be expected from him, not as a lawyer, a physician, a mariner, an astronomer or a natural philosopher, but as a Man. Except this one restriction, there is no object standing between the Poet and the image of things; between this, and the Biographer and Historian there are a thousand.

Nor let this necessity of producing immediate pleasure be considered as a degradation of the Poet's art. It is far otherwise. It is an acknowledgement of the beauty of the universe, an acknowledgement the more sincere, because it is not formal, but indirect; it is a task light and easy to him who looks at the world in the spirit of love: further, it is a homage paid to the native and naked dignity of man, to the grand elementary principle of pleasure, by which he knows, and feels, and lives, and moves. We have no sympathy but what is propagated by pleasure: I would not be misunderstood; but wherever we sympathize with pain it will be found that the sympathy is produced and carried on by subtle combinations with pleasure. We have no knowledge, that is, no general principles drawn from the contemplation of particular facts, but what has been built up by pleasure, and exists in us by pleasure alone. The Man of Science, the Chemist and Mathematician, whatever difficulties and disgusts they may have had to struggle with, know and feel this. However painful may be the objects with which the Anatomist's knowledge is connected, he feels that his knowledge is pleasure; and where he has no pleasure he has no knowledge. What then does the Poet? He considers man and the objects that surround him as acting and re-acting upon each other, so as to produce an infinite complexity of pain and pleasure; he considers man in his own nature and in his ordinary life as contemplating this with a certain quantity of immediate knowledge, with certain convictions, intuitions, and deductions which by habit become of the nature of intuitions; he considers him as looking upon this complex scene of ideas and sensations, and finding everywhere objects that immediately excite in him sympathies which, from the necessities of his nature, are accompanied by an over-balance of enjoyment.

To this knowledge which all men carry about with them, and to these sympathies in which without any other discipline than that of our daily life we are fitted to take delight, the Poet principally directs his attention. He considers man and nature as essentially adapted to each other, and the mind of man as naturally the mirror of the fairest and most interesting qualities of nature. And thus the Poet, prompted by this feeling of pleasure which accompanies him through the whole course of his studies, converses with general nature with affections akin to those, which, through labour and length of time, the Man of Science has raised up in himself, by conversing with those particular parts of nature which are the objects of his studies. The knowledge both of the Poet and the Man of Science is pleasure; but the knowledge of the one cleaves to us as a necessary part of our existence, our natural and unalienable inheritance; the other is a personal and individual acquisition, slow to come to us, and by no habitual and direct sympathy connecting us with our fellow-beings. The Man of Science seeks truth as a remote and unknown benefactor; he cherishes and loves it in his solitude: the Poet, singing a song in which all human beings join with him, rejoices in the presence of truth as our visible friend and hourly companion. Poetry is the breath and finer spirit of all knowledge; it is the impassioned expression which is in the countenance of all Science. Emphatically may it be said of the Poet, as Shakespeare hath said of man, 'that he looks before and after.' He is the rock of defence of human nature; an upholder and preserver, carrying everywhere with him relationship and love. In spite of difference of soil and climate, of language and manners, of laws and customs, in spite of things silently gone out of mind and things violently destroyed, the Poet binds together by passion and knowledge the vast empire of human society, as it is spread over the whole earth, and over all time. The objects of the Poet's thoughts are everywhere; though the eyes and senses of man are, it is true, his favourite guides, yet he will follow wheresoever he can find an atmosphere of sensation in which to move his wings. Poetry is the first and last of all knowledge – it is as immortal as the heart of man. If the labours of Men of Science should ever create any material revolution, direct or indirect, in our condition, and in the impressions which we habitually receive, the Poet will sleep then no more than at present, but he will be ready to follow the steps of the Man of Science, not only in those general indirect effects, but he will be at his side, carrying sensation into the midst of the objects of the Science itself. The remotest discoveries of the Chemist, the Botanist, or Mineralogist, will be as proper objects of the Poet's art as any upon which it can be employed, if the time should ever come when these things shall be familiar to us, and the relations under which they are contemplated by the followers of these respective Sciences shall be manifestly and palpably material to us as enjoying and suffering beings. If the time should ever come when what is now called Science, thus familiarized to men, shall be ready to put on, as it were, a form of flesh and blood, the Poet will lend his divine spirit to aid the transfiguration, and will welcome the Being thus produced, as a dear and genuine inmate of the household of man. – It is not, then, to be supposed that anyone, who holds that sublime notion of Poetry which I have attempted to convey, will break in upon the sanctity and truth of his pictures by transitory and accidental ornaments, and endeavour to excite admiration of himself by arts, the necessity of which must manifestly depend upon the assumed meanness of his subject.

What I have thus far said applies to Poetry in general; but especially to those parts of composition where the Poet speaks through the mouths of his characters; and upon this point it appears to have such weight that I will conclude, there are few persons of good sense, who would not allow that the dramatic parts of composition are defective, in proportion as they deviate from the real language of nature, and are coloured by a diction of the Poet's own, either peculiar to him as an individual Poet, or belonging simply to Poets in general, to a body of men who, from the circumstance of their compositions being in metre, it is expected will employ a particular language.

It is not, then, in the dramatic parts of composition that we look for this distinction of language; but still it may be proper and necessary where the Poet speaks to us in his own person and character. To this I answer by referring my Reader to the description which I have before given of a Poet. Among the qualities which I have enumerated as principally conducing to form a Poet, is implied nothing differing in kind from other men, but only in degree. The sum of what I have there said is, that the Poet is chiefly distinguished from other men by a greater promptness to think and feel without immediate external excitement, and a greater power in expressing such thoughts and feelings as are produced in him in that manner. But these passions and thoughts and feelings are the general passions and thoughts and feelings of men. And with what are they connected? Undoubtedly with our moral sentiments and animal sensations, and with the causes which excite these; with the operations of the elements and the appearances of the visible universe; with storm and sunshine, with the revolutions of the seasons, with cold and heat, with loss of friends and kindred, with injuries and resentments, gratitude and hope, with fear and sorrow. These, and the like, are the sensations and objects which the Poet describes, as they are the sensations of other men, and the objects which interest them. The Poet thinks and feels in the spirit of the passions of men. How, then, can his language differ in any material degree from that of all other men who feel vividly and see clearly? It might be *proved* that it is impossible. But supposing that this were not the case, the Poet might then be allowed to use a peculiar language, when expressing his feelings for his own gratification, or that of men like himself. But Poets do not write for Poets alone, but for men. Unless therefore we are advocates for that admiration which depends upon ignorance, and that pleasure which arises from hearing what we do not understand, the Poet must descend from this supposed height, and, in order to excite rational sympathy, he must express himself as other men express themselves. To this it may be added, that while he is only selecting from the real language of men, or, which amounts to the same thing, composing accurately in the spirit of such selection, he is treading upon safe ground, and we know what we are to expect from him. Our feelings are the same with respect to metre; for, as it may be proper to remind the Reader the, *end of 1802 addition*] distinction of metre is regular and uniform, and not like that which is produced by what is usually called poetic diction, arbitrary, and subject to infinite caprices upon which no calculation whatever can be made. In the one case, the Reader is utterly at the mercy of the Poet respecting what imagery or diction he may choose to connect with the passion, whereas, in the other, the metre obeys certain laws, to which the Poet and Reader both willingly submit because they are certain, and because no interference is made by them with the passion but such as the concurring testimony of ages has shown to heighten and improve the pleasure which co-exists with it.

It will now be proper to answer an obvious question, namely, why, professing these opinions, have I written in verse? To this, in addition to such answer as is included in what I have already said, I reply in the first place, because, however I may have restricted myself, there is still left open to me what confessedly constitutes the most valuable object of all writing whether in prose or verse, the great and universal passions of men, the most general and interesting of their occupations, and the entire world of nature, from which I am at liberty to supply myself with endless combinations of forms and imagery. Now, supposing for a moment that whatever is interesting in these objects may be as vividly described in prose, why am I to be condemned, if to such description I have endeavoured to superadd the charm which, by the consent of all nations, is acknowledged to exist in metrical language? To this, by such as are unconvinced by what I have already said, it may be answered, that a very small part of the pleasure given by Poetry depends upon the metre, and that it is injudicious to write in metre, unless it be accompanied with the other artificial distinctions of style with which metre is usually accompanied, and that by such deviation more will be lost from the shock which will be thereby given to the Reader's associations, than will be counterbalanced by any pleasure which he can derive from the general power of numbers. In answer to those who still contend for the necessity of accompanying metre with certain appropriate colours of style in order to the accomplishment of its appropriate end, and who also, in my opinion, greatly underrate the power of metre in itself, it might perhaps, as far as relates to these Poems, have been almost sufficient to observe, that poems are extant, written upon more humble subjects, and in a more naked and simple style than I have aimed at, which poems have continued to give pleasure from generation to generation. Now, if nakedness and simplicity be a defect, the fact here mentioned affords a strong presumption that poems somewhat less naked and simple are capable of affording pleasure at the present day; and, what I wished *chiefly* to attempt, at present, was to justify myself for having written under the impression of this belief.

But I might point out various causes why, when the style is manly, and the subject of some importance, words metrically arranged will long continue to impart such a pleasure to mankind as he who is sensible of the extent of that pleasure will be desirous to impart. The end of Poetry is to produce excitement in co-existence with an over-balance of pleasure. Now, by the supposition, excitement is an unusual and irregular state of the mind; ideas and feelings do not in that state succeed each other in accustomed order. But, if the words by which this excitement is produced are in themselves powerful, or the images and feelings have an undue proportion of pain connected with them, there is some danger that the excitement may be carried beyond its proper bounds. Now the co-presence of something regular, something to which the mind has been accustomed in various moods and in a less excited state, cannot but have great efficacy in tempering and restraining the passion by an intertexture of ordinary feeling, and of feeling not strictly and necessarily connected with the passion. This is unquestionably true, and hence, though the opinion will at first appear paradoxical, from the tendency of metre to divest language in a certain degree of its reality, and thus to throw a sort of half consciousness of unsubstantial existence over the whole composition, there can be little doubt but that more pathetic situations and sentiments, that is, those which have a greater proportion of pain connected with them, may be endured in metrical composition, especially in rhyme, than in prose. The metre of the old ballads is very artless; yet they contain many passages which would illustrate this opinion, and, I hope, if the following Poems be attentively perused, similar instances will be found in them. This opinion may be further illustrated by appealing to the Reader's own experience of the reluctance with which he comes to the reperusal of the distressful parts of Clarissa Harlowe, or the Gamester. While Shakespeare's writings, in the most pathetic scenes, never act upon us as pathetic beyond the bounds of pleasure – an effect which, in a much greater degree than might at first be imagined, is to be ascribed to small, but continual and regular impulses of pleasurable surprise from the metrical arrangement. – On the other hand (what it must be allowed will much more frequently happen) if the Poet's words should be incommensurate with the passion, and inadequate to raise the Reader to a height of desirable excitement, then (unless the Poet's choice of his metre has been grossly injudicious) in the feelings of pleasure which the Reader has been accustomed to connect with metre in general, and in the feeling, whether cheerful or melancholy, which he has been accustomed to connect with that particular movement of metre, there will be found something which will greatly contribute to impart passion to the words, and to effect the complex end which the Poet proposes to himself.

If I had undertaken a systematic defence of the theory upon which these poems are written, it would have been my duty to develop the various causes upon which the pleasure received from metrical language depends. Among the chief of these causes is to be reckoned a principle which must be well known to those who have made any of the Arts the object of accurate reflection; I mean the pleasure which the mind derives from the perception of similitude in dissimilitude. This principle is the great spring of the activity of our minds, and their chief feeder. From this principle the direction of the sexual appetite, and all the passions connected with it, take their origin: it is the life of our ordinary conversation; and upon the accuracy with which similitude in dissimilitude, and dissimilitude in similitude are perceived, depend our taste and our moral feelings. It would not have been a useless employment to have applied this principle to the consideration of metre, and to have shown that metre is hence enabled to afford much pleasure, and to have pointed out in what manner that pleasure is produced. But my limits will not permit me to enter upon this subject, and I must content myself with a general summary.

I have said that Poetry is the spontaneous overflow of powerful feelings: it takes its origin from emotion recollected in tranquillity:

the emotion is contemplated till by a species of reaction the tranquillity gradually disappears, and an emotion, kindred to that which was before the subject of contemplation, is gradually produced, and does itself actually exist in the mind. In this mood successful composition generally begins, and in a mood similar to this it is carried on; but the emotion, of whatever kind and in whatever degree, from various causes is qualified by various pleasures, so that in describing any passions whatsoever, which are voluntarily described, the mind will upon the whole be in a state of enjoyment. Now, if Nature be thus cautious in preserving in a state of enjoyment a being thus employed, the Poet ought to profit by the lesson thus held forth to him, and ought especially to take care, that whatever passions he communicates to his Reader, those passions, if his Reader's mind be sound and vigorous, should always be accompanied with an over-balance of pleasure. Now the music of harmonious metrical language, the sense of difficulty overcome, and the blind association of pleasure which has been previously received from works of rhyme or metre of the same or similar construction, an indistinct perception perpetually renewed of language closely resembling that of real life, and yet, in the circumstance of metre, differing from it so widely — all these imperceptibly make up a complex feeling of delight, which is of the most important use in tempering the painful feeling which will always be found intermingled with powerful descriptions of the deeper passions. This effect is always produced in pathetic and impassioned poetry; while, in lighter compositions, the ease and gracefulness with which the Poet manages his numbers are themselves confessedly a principal source of the gratification of the Reader. I might perhaps include all which it is *necessary* to say upon this subject by affirming, what few persons will deny, that, of two descriptions, either of passions, manners, or characters, each of them equally well executed, the one in prose and the other in verse, the verse will be read a hundred times where the prose is read once. We see that Pope, by the power of verse alone, has contrived to render the plainest common sense interesting, and even frequently to invest it with the appearance of passion. In consequence of these convictions I related in metre the Tale of GOODY BLAKE AND HARRY GILL, which is one of the rudest of this collection. I wished to draw attention to the truth, that the power of the human imagination is sufficient to produce such changes even in our physical nature as might almost appear miraculous. The truth is an important one; the fact (for it is a *fact*) is a valuable illustration of it. And I have the satisfaction of knowing that it has been communicated to many hundreds of people who would never have heard of it, had it not been narrated as a Ballad, and in a more impressive metre than is usual in Ballads.

Having thus explained a few of the reasons why I have written in verse, and why I have chosen subjects from common life, and endeavoured to bring my language near to the real language of men, if I have been too minute in pleading my own cause, I have at the same time been treating a subject of general interest; and it is for this reason that I request the Reader's permission to add a few words with reference solely to these particular poems, and to some defects which will probably be found in them. I am sensible that my associations must have sometimes been particular instead of general, and that, consequently, giving to things a false importance, sometimes from diseased impulses I may have written upon unworthy subjects; but I am less apprehensive on this account, than that my language may frequently have suffered from those arbitrary connexions of feelings and ideas with particular words and phrases, from which no man can altogether protect himself. Hence I have no doubt, that, in some instances, feelings even of the ludicrous may be given to my Readers by expressions which appeared to me tender and pathetic. Such faulty expressions, were I convinced they were faulty at present, and that they must necessarily continue to be so, I would willingly take all reasonable pains to correct. But it is dangerous to make these alterations on the simple authority of a few individuals, or even of certain classes of men; for where the understanding of an Author is not convinced, or his feelings altered, this cannot be done without great injury to himself: for his own feelings are his stay and support, and, if he sets them aside in one instance, he may be induced to repeat this act till his mind loses all confidence in itself, and becomes utterly debilitated. To this it may be added, that the Reader ought never to forget that he is himself exposed to the same errors as the Poet, and perhaps in a much greater degree: for there can be no presumption in saying, that it is not probable he will be so well acquainted with the various stages of meaning through which words have passed, or with the fickleness or stability of the relations of particular ideas to each other; and above all, since he is so much less interested in the subject, he may decide lightly and carelessly.

Long as I have detained my Reader, I hope he will permit me to caution him against a mode of false criticism which has been applied to Poetry in which the language closely resembles that of life and nature. Such verses have been triumphed over in parodies of which Dr Johnson's Stanza is a fair specimen.

> 'I put my hat upon my head,
> And walked into the Strand.
> And there I met another man
> Whose hat was in his hand.'

Immediately under these lines I will place one of the most justly admired stanzas of the '*Babes in the Wood*.'

> 'These pretty Babes with hand in hand
> Went wandering up and down;
> But never more they saw the Man
> Approaching from the Town.'

In both these stanzas the words, and the order of the words, in no respect differ from the most unimpassioned conversation. There are words in both, for example, 'the Strand,' and 'the Town,' connected with none but the most familiar ideas; yet the one stanza we admit as admirable, and the other as a fair example of the superlatively contemptible. Whence arises this difference? Not from the metre, not from the language, not from the order of the words; but the *matter* expressed in Dr Johnson's stanza is contemptible. The proper method of treating trivial and simple verses, to which Dr Johnson's stanza would be a fair parallelism, is not to say, this is a bad kind of poetry, or this is not poetry; but this wants sense; it is neither interesting in itself, nor can *lead* to anything interesting; the images neither originate in that sane state of feeling which arises out of thought, nor can excite thought or feeling in the Reader. This is the only sensible manner of dealing with such verses: Why trouble yourself about the species till you have previously decided upon the genus? Why take pains to prove that an ape is not a Newton, when it is self-evident that he is not a man?

I have one request to make of my Reader, which is, that in judging these Poems he would decide by his own feelings genuinely, and not by reflection upon what will probably be the judgement of others. How common is it to hear a person say, 'I myself do not object to this style of composition, or this or that expression, but to such and such classes of people it will appear mean or ludicrous.' This mode of criticism, so destructive of all sound unadulterated judgement, is almost universal: I have therefore to request, that the Reader would abide independently by his own feelings, and that if he finds himself affected he would not suffer such conjectures to interfere with his pleasure.

If an Author by any single composition has impressed us with respect for his talents, it is useful to consider this as affording a presumption, that, on other occasions where we have been displeased, he nevertheless may not have written ill or absurdly; and, further, to give him so much credit for this one composition as may induce us to review what has displeased us with more care than we should otherwise have bestowed upon it. This is not only an act of justice, but, in our decisions upon poetry especially, may conduce in a high degree to the improvement of our own taste: for an *accurate* taste in poetry, and in all the other arts, as Sir Joshua Reynolds has observed, is an *acquired* talent, which can only be produced by thought and a long continued intercourse with the best models of composition. This is mentioned, not with so ridiculous a purpose as to prevent the most inexperienced Reader from judging for himself (I have already said that I wish him to judge for himself); but merely to temper the rashness of decision, and to suggest, that, if Poetry be a subject on which much time has not been bestowed, the judgement may be erroneous; and that in many cases it necessarily will be so.

I know that nothing would have so effectually contributed to further the end which I have in view, as to have shown of what kind the pleasure is, and how that pleasure is produced, which is confessedly produced by metrical composition essentially different from that which I have here endeavoured to recommend: for the Reader will say that he has been pleased by such composition; and what can I do more for him? The power of any art is limited;

and he will suspect, that, if I propose to furnish him with new friends, it is only upon condition of his abandoning his old friends. Besides, as I have said, the Reader is himself conscious of the pleasure which he has received from such composition, composition to which he has peculiarly attached the endearing name of Poetry; and all men feel an habitual gratitude, and something of an honourable bigotry for the objects which have long continued to please them: we not only wish to be pleased, but to be pleased in that particular way in which we have been accustomed to be pleased. There is a host of arguments in these feelings; and I should be the less able to combat them successfully, as I am willing to allow, that, in order entirely to enjoy the Poetry which I am recommending, it would be necessary to give up much of what is ordinarily enjoyed. But, would my limits have permitted me to point out how this pleasure is produced, I might have removed many obstacles, and assisted my Reader in perceiving that the powers of language are not so limited as he may suppose; and that it is possible that poetry may give other enjoyments, of a purer, more lasting, and more exquisite nature. This part of my subject I have not altogether neglected; but it has been less my present aim to prove, that the interest excited by some other kinds of poetry is less vivid, and less worthy of the nobler powers of the mind, than to offer reasons for presuming, that, if the object which I have proposed to myself were adequately attained, a species of poetry would be produced, which is genuine poetry; in its nature well adapted to interest mankind permanently, and likewise important in the multiplicity and quality of its moral relations.

From what has been said, and from a perusal of the Poems, the Reader will be able clearly to perceive the object which I have proposed to myself: he will determine how far I have attained this object; and, what is a much more important question, whether it be worth attaining; and upon the decision of these two questions will rest my claim to the approbation of the public.

Appendix to the Preface (*1802*)

As perhaps I have no right to expect from a Reader of an introduction to a volume of Poems that attentive perusal without which it is impossible, imperfectly as I have been compelled to express my meaning, that what I have said in the Preface should throughout be fully understood, I am the more anxious to give an exact notion of the sense in which I use the phrase *poetic diction*; and for this purpose I will here add a few words concerning the origin of the phraseology which I have condemned under that name. – The earliest Poets of all nations generally wrote from passion excited by real events; they wrote naturally, and as men: feeling powerfully as they did, their language was daring, and figurative. In succeeding times, Poets, and men ambitious of the fame of Poets, perceiving the influence of such language, and desirous of producing the same effect, without having the same animating passion, set themselves to a mechanical adoption of those figures of speech, and made use of them, sometimes with propriety, but much more frequently applied them to feelings and ideas with which they had no natural connexion whatsoever. A language was thus insensibly produced, differing materially from the real language of men in *any situation*. The Reader or Hearer of this distorted language found himself in a perturbed and unusual state of mind: when affected by the genuine language of passion he had been in a perturbed and unusual state of mind also: in both cases he was willing that his common judgement and understanding should be laid asleep, and he had no instinctive and infallible perception of the true to make him reject the false; the one served as a passport for the other. The agitation and confusion of mind were in both cases delightful, and no wonder if he confounded the one with the other, and believed them both to be produced by the same, or similar causes. Besides, the Poet spake to him in the character of a man to be looked up to, a man of genius and authority. Thus, and from a variety of other causes, this distorted language was received with admiration; and Poets, it is probable, who had before contented themselves for the most part with misapplying only expressions which at first had been dictated by real passion, carried the abuse still further, and introduced phrases composed apparently in the spirit of the original figurative language of passion, yet altogether of their own invention, and distinguished by various degrees of wanton deviation from good sense and nature.

It is indeed true that the language of the earliest Poets was felt to differ materially from ordinary language, because it was the language of extraordinary occasions; but it was really spoken by men, language which the Poet himself had uttered when he had been affected by the events which he described, or which he had heard uttered by those around him. To this language it is probable that metre of some sort or other was early superadded. This separated the genuine language of Poetry still further from common life, so that whoever read or heard the poems of these earliest Poets felt himself moved in a way in which he had not been accustomed to be moved in real life, and by causes manifestly different from those which acted upon him in real life. This was the great temptation to all the corruptions which have followed: under the protection of this feeling succeeding Poets constructed a phraseology which had one thing, it is true, in common with the genuine language of poetry, namely, that it was not heard in ordinary conversation; that it was unusual. But the first Poets, as I have said, spake a language which, though unusual, was still the language of men. This circumstance, however, was disregarded by their successors; they found that they could please by easier means: they became proud of a language which they themselves had invented, and which was uttered only by themselves; and, with the spirit of a fraternity, they arrogated it to themselves as their own. In process of time metre became a symbol or promise of this unusual language, and whoever took upon him to write in metre, according as he possessed more or less of true poetic genius, introduced less or more of this adulterated phraseology into his compositions, and the true and the false became so inseparably interwoven that the taste of men was gradually perverted; and this language was received as a natural language; and at length, by the influence of books upon men, did to a certain degree really become so. Abuses of this kind were imported from one nation to another, and with the progress of refinement this diction became daily more and more corrupt, thrusting out of sight the plain humanities of nature by a motley masquerade of tricks, quaintnesses, hieroglyphics, and enigmas.

It would be highly interesting to point out the causes of the pleasure given by this extravagant and absurd language; but this is not the place; it depends upon a great variety of causes, but upon none perhaps more than its influence in impressing a notion of the peculiarity and exaltation of the Poet's character, and in flattering the Reader's self-love by bringing him nearer to a sympathy with that character; an effect which is accomplished by unsettling ordinary habits of thinking, and thus assisting the Reader to approach to that perturbed and dizzy state of mind in which if he does not find himself, he imagines that he is *balked* of a peculiar enjoyment which poetry can, and ought to bestow.

The sonnet which I have quoted from Gray, in the Preface, except the lines printed in Italics, consists of little else but this diction, though not of the worst kind; and indeed, if I may be permitted to say so, it is far too common in the best writers, both ancient and modern. Perhaps I can in no way, by positive example, more easily give my Reader a notion of what I mean by the phrase *poetic diction* than by referring him to a comparison between the metrical paraphrases which we have of passages in the Old and New Testament, and those passages as they exist in our common Translation. See Pope's 'Messiah' throughout, Prior's 'Did sweeter sounds adorn my flowing tongue,' &c. &c. 'Though I speak with the tongues of men and of angels,' &c. &c. See 1st Corinthians, chapter xiiith. By way of immediate example, take the following of Dr Johnson:

> 'Turn on the prudent Ant thy heedless eyes,
> Observe her labours, Sluggard, and be wise;
> No stern command, no monitory voice,
> Prescribes her duties, or directs her choice;
> Yet timely provident she hastes away
> To snatch the blessings of a plenteous day;
> When fruitful Summer loads the teeming plain,
> She crops the harvest and she stores the grain.
> How long shall sloth usurp thy useless hours,
> Unnerve thy vigour, and enchain thy powers?
> While artful shades thy downy couch enclose,

And soft solicitation courts repose,
Amidst the drowsy charms of dull delight,
Year chases year with unremitted flight,
Till want now following, fraudulent and slow,
Shall spring to seize thee, like an ambushed foe.'

From this hubbub of words pass to the original. 'Go to the Ant, thou Sluggard, consider her ways, and be wise: which having no guide, overseer, or ruler, provideth her meat in the summer, and gathereth her food in the harvest. How long wilt thou sleep, O Sluggard? when wilt thou arise out of thy sleep? Yet a little sleep, a little slumber, a little folding of the hands to sleep. So shall thy poverty come as one that travaileth, and thy want as an armed man.' *Proverbs*, chap. 6th.

One more quotation and I have done. It is from Cowper's verses supposed to be written by Alexander Selkirk:

'Religion! what treasure untold
Resides in that heavenly word!
More precious than silver and gold,
Or all that this earth can afford.
But the sound of the church-going bell
These valleys and rocks never heard,
Ne'er sighed at the sound of a knell,
Or smiled when a sabbath appeared.

Ye winds, that have made me your sport,
Convey to this desolate shore
Some cordial endearing report
Of a land I must visit no more.
My Friends, do they now and then send
A wish or a thought after me?
O tell me I yet have a friend,
Though a friend I am never to see.'

I have quoted this passage as an instance of three different styles of composition. The first four lines are poorly expressed; some Critics would call the language prosaic; the fact is, it would be bad prose, so bad, that it is scarcely worse in metre. The epithet 'church-going' applied to a bell, and that by so chaste a writer as Cowper, is an instance of the strange abuses which Poets have introduced into their language till they and their Readers take them as matters of course, if they do not single them out expressly as objects of admiration. The two lines 'Ne'er sighed at the sound,' &c. are, in my opinion, an instance of the language of passion wrested from its proper use, and, from the mere circumstance of the composition being in metre, applied upon an occasion that does not justify such violent expressions; and I should condemn the passage, though perhaps few Readers will agree with me, as vicious poetic diction. The last stanza is throughout admirably expressed: it would be equally good whether in prose or verse, except that the Reader has an exquisite pleasure in seeing such natural language so naturally connected with metre. The beauty of this stanza tempts me here to add a sentiment which ought to be the pervading spirit of a system, detached parts of which have been imperfectly explained in the Preface, – namely, that in proportion as ideas and feelings are valuable, whether the composition be in prose or in verse, they require and exact one and the same language.

[Wordsworth's notes have been incorporated into the text in square brackets.]

The observations prefixed to that portion of these Volumes, which was published many years ago, under the title of 'Lyrical Ballads,' have so little of a special application to the greater part, perhaps, of this collection, as subsequently enlarged and diversified, that they could not with any propriety stand as an Introduction to it. Not deeming it, however, expedient to suppress that exposition, slight and imperfect as it is, of the feelings which had determined the choice of the subjects, and the principles which had regulated the composition of those Pieces, I have transferred it to the end of the second Volume, to be attended to, or not, at the pleasure of the Reader.

In the Preface to that part of 'The Recluse,' lately published under the title of 'The Excursion,' I have alluded to a meditated arrangement of my minor Poems, which should assist the attentive Reader in perceiving their connexion with each other, and also their subordination to that Work. I shall here say a few words explanatory of this arrangement, as carried into effect in the present Volumes.

The powers requisite for the production of poetry are, first, those of observation and description, i.e. the ability to observe with accuracy things as they are in themselves, and with fidelity to describe them, unmodified by any passion or feeling existing in the mind of the Describer: whether the things depicted be actually present to the senses, or have a place only in the memory. This power, though indispensable to a Poet, is one which he employs only in submission to necessity, and never for a continuance of time; as its exercise supposes all the higher qualities of the mind to be passive, and in a state of subjection to external objects, much in the same way as the Translator or Engraver ought to be to his Original. 2dly, Sensibility, – which, the more exquisite it is, the wider will be the range of a Poet's perceptions; and the more will he be incited to observe objects, both as they exist in themselves and as re-acted upon by his own mind. (The distinction between poetic and human sensibility has been marked in the character of the Poet delineated in the original preface, before-mentioned.) 3rdly, Reflection, – which makes the Poet acquainted with the value of actions, images, thoughts, and feelings; and assists the sensibility in perceiving their connexion with each other. 4thly, Imagination and Fancy, – to modify, to create, and to associate. 5thly, Invention, – by which characters are composed out of materials supplied by observation; whether of the Poet's own heart and mind, or of external life and nature; and such incidents and situations produced as are most impressive to the imagination, and most fitted to do justice to the characters, sentiments, and passions, which the Poet undertakes to illustrate. And, lastly, Judgement, – to decide how and where, and in what degree, each of these faculties ought to be exerted; so that the less shall not be sacrificed to the greater; nor the greater, slighting the less, arrogate, to its own injury, more than its due. By judgement, also, is determined what are the laws and appropriate graces of every species of composition.

The materials of Poetry, by these powers collected and produced, are cast, by means of various moulds, into divers forms. The moulds may be enumerated, and the forms specified, in the following order. 1st, the Narrative, – including the Epopoeia, the Historic Poem, the Tale, the Romance, the Mock-heroic, and, if the spirit of Homer will tolerate such neighbourhood, that dear production of our days, the metrical Novel. Of this Class, the distinguishing mark, is, that the Narrator, however liberally his speaking agents be introduced, is himself the source from which everything primarily flows. Epic Poets, in order that their mode of composition may accord with the elevation of their subject, represent themselves as *singing* from the inspiration of the Muse, Arma virum que *cano*; but this is a fiction, in modern times, of slight value: The Iliad or the Paradise Lost would gain little in our estimation by being chaunted. The other poets who belong to this class are commonly content to *tell* their tale; – so that of the whole it may be affirmed that they neither require nor reject the accompaniment of music.

2ndly, The Dramatic, – consisting of Tragedy, Historic Drama, Comedy, and Masque; in which the poet does not appear at all in his own person, and where the whole action is carried on by speech and dialogue of the agents; music being admitted only incidentally and rarely. The Opera may be placed here, in as much as it proceeds by dialogue; though depending, to the degree that it does, upon music, it has a strong claim to be ranked with the Lyrical. The characteristic and impassioned Epistle, of which Ovid and Pope have given examples, considered as a species of monodrama, may, without impropriety, be placed in this class.

3rdly, The Lyrical, – containing the Hymn, the Ode, the Elegy, the Song, and the Ballad; in all which, for the production of their *full* effect, an accompaniment of music is indispensable.

4thly, The Idyllium, – descriptive chiefly either of the processes and appearances of external nature, as the 'Seasons' of Thomson; or of characters, manners, and sentiments, as are Shenstone's School-mistress, The Cotter's Saturday Night of Burns, The Twa Dogs of the same Author; or of these in conjunction with the appearances of Nature, as most of the pieces of Theocritus, the Allegro and Penseroso of Milton, Beattie's Minstrel, Goldsmith's 'Deserted Village.' The Epitaph, the Inscription, the Sonnet, most of the epistles of poets writing in their own persons, and all loco-descriptive poetry, belong to this class.

5thly, Didactic, – the principal object of which is direct instruction; as the Poem of Lucretius, the Georgics of Virgil, 'The Fleece' of Dyer, Mason's 'English Garden,' &c.

And, lastly, philosophical satire, like that of Horace and Juvenal; personal and occasional Satire rarely comprehending sufficient of the general in the individual to be dignified with the name of Poetry.

Out of the three last classes has been constructed a composite species, of which Young's Night Thoughts and Cowper's Task are excellent examples.

It is deducible from the above, that poems, apparently miscellaneous, may with propriety be arranged either with reference to the powers of mind *predominant* in the production of them; or to the mould in which they are cast; or, lastly, to the subjects to which they relate. From each of these considerations, the following Poems have been divided into classes; which, that the work may more obviously correspond with the course of human life, for the

sake of exhibiting in it the three requisites of a legitimate whole, a
beginning, a middle, and an end, have been also arranged, as far
as it was possible, according to an order of time, commencing
with Childhood, and terminating with Old Age, Death, and
Immortality. My guiding wish was, that the small pieces of which
these volumes consist, thus discriminated, might be regarded
under a two-fold view; as composing an entire work within
themselves, and as adjuncts to the philosophical Poem, 'The
Recluse.' This arrangement has long presented itself habitually to
my own mind. Nevertheless, I should have preferred to scatter
the contents of these volumes at random, if I had been persuaded
that, by the plan adopted, anything material would be taken from
the natural effect of the pieces, individually, on the mind of the
unreflecting Reader. I trust there is a sufficient variety in each
class to prevent this; while, for him who reads with reflection, the
arrangement will serve as a commentary unostentatiously directing
his attention to my purposes, both particular and general. But, as
I wish to guard against the possibility of misleading by this
classification, it is proper first to remind the Reader, that certain
poems are placed according to the powers of mind, in the
Author's conception, predominant in the production of them;
predominant, which implies the exertion of other faculties in less
degree. Where there is more imagination than fancy in a poem it
is placed under the head of imagination, and vice versa. Both the
above Classes might without impropriety have been enlarged
from that consisting of 'Poems founded on the Affections'; as
might this latter from those, and from the class 'Proceeding from
Sentiment and Reflection.' The most striking characteristics of
each piece, mutual illustration, variety, and proportion, have
governed me throughout.

It may be proper in this place to state, that the Extracts in the
2nd Class entitled 'Juvenile Pieces,' are in many places altered
from the printed copy, chiefly by omission and compression. The
slight alterations of another kind were for the most part made not
long after the publication of the Poems from which the Extracts
are taken. These Extracts seem to have a title to be placed here as
they were the productions of youth, and represent implicitly some
of the features of a youthful mind, at a time when images of
nature supplied to it the place of thought, sentiment, and almost

of action; or, as it will be found expressed, of a state of mind when

> the sounding cataract
> Haunted me like a passion: the tall rock,
> The mountain, and the deep and gloomy wood,
> Their colours and their forms were then to me
> An appetite, a feeling and a love,
> That had no need of a remoter charm,
> By thought supplied, or any interest
> Unborrowed from the eye –

I will own that I was much at a loss what to select of these descriptions; and perhaps it would have been better either to have reprinted the whole, or suppressed what I have given.

None of the other Classes, except those of Fancy and Imagination, require any particular notice. But a remark of general application may be made. All Poets, except the dramatic, have been in the practice of feigning that their works were composed to the music of the harp or lyre: with what degree of affectation this has been done in modern times, I leave to the judicious to determine. For my own part, I have not been disposed to violate probability so far, or to make such a large demand upon the Reader's charity. Some of these pieces are essentially lyrical; and, therefore, cannot have their due force without a supposed musical accompaniment; but, in much the greatest part, as a substitute for the classic lyre or romantic harp, I require nothing more than an animated or impassioned recitation, adapted to the subject. Poems, however humble in their kind, if they be good in that kind, cannot read themselves: the law of long syllable and short must not be so inflexible – the letter of metre must not be so impassive to the spirit of versification – as to deprive the Reader of a voluntary power to modulate, in subordination to the sense, the music of the poem; – in the same manner as his mind is left at liberty, and even summoned, to act upon its thoughts and images. But, though the accompaniment of a musical instrument be frequently dispensed with, the true Poet does not therefore abandon his privilege distinct from that of the mere Proseman;

> He murmurs near the running brooks
> A music sweeter than their own.

I come now to the consideration of the words Fancy and Imagination, as employed in the classification of the following Poems. 'A man,' says an intelligent Author, has 'imagination,' in proportion as he can distinctly copy in idea the impressions of sense: it is the faculty which *images* within the mind the phenomena of sensation. A man has fancy in proportion as he can call up, connect, or associate, at pleasure, those internal images (Φαυταζειν is to cause to appear) so as to complete ideal representations of absent objects. Imagination is the power of depicting, and fancy of evoking and combining. The imagination is formed by patient observation; the fancy by a voluntary activity in shifting the scenery of the mind. The more accurate the imagination, the more safely may a painter, or a poet, undertake a delineation, or a description, without the presence of the objects to be characterized. The more versatile the fancy, the more original and striking will be the decorations produced. – *British Synonyms discriminated, by W. Taylor.*

Is not this as if a man should undertake to supply an account of a building, and be so intent upon what he had discovered of the foundation as to conclude his task without once looking up at the superstructure? Here, as in other instances throughout the volume, the judicious Author's mind is enthralled by Etymology; he takes up the original word as his guide, his conductor, his escort, and too often does not perceive how soon he becomes its prisoner, without liberty to tread in any path but that to which it confines him. It is not easy to find out how imagination, thus explained, differs from distinct remembrance of images; or fancy from quick and vivid recollection of them: each is nothing more than a mode of memory. If the two words bear the above meaning, and no other, what term is left to designate that Faculty of which the Poet is 'all compact'; he whose eye glances from earth to heaven, whose spiritual attributes body-forth what his pen is prompt in turning to shape; or what is left to characterize fancy, as insinuating herself into the heart of objects with creative activity? – Imagination, in the sense of the word as giving title to a Class of the following Poems, has no reference to images that are merely a faithful copy, existing in the mind, of absent external objects; but is a word of higher import, denoting operations of the mind upon those objects, and processes of creation or of composition, governed by certain fixed laws. I proceed to illustrate my meaning by instances. A parrot *hangs* from the wires of his cage by his beak or by his claws; or a monkey from the bough of a tree by his paws or his tail. Each creature does so literally and actually. In the first Eclogue of Virgil, the Shepherd, thinking of the time when he is to take leave of his Farm, thus addresses his Goats;

> Non ego vos posthac viridi projectus in antro
> Dumosa *pendere* procul de rupe [videbo],

> – half way down
> *Hangs* one who gathers samphire,

is the well-known expression of Shakespeare, delineating an ordinary image upon the Cliffs of Dover. In these two instances is a slight exertion of the faculty which I denominate imagination, in the use of one word: neither the goats nor the samphire-gatherer do literally hang, as does the parrot or the monkey; but, presenting to the senses something of such an appearance, the mind in its activity, for its own gratification, contemplates them as hanging.

> As when far off at Sea a Fleet descried
> *Hangs* in the clouds, by equinoctial winds
> Close sailing from Bengala or the Isles
> Of Ternate or Tydore, whence Merchants bring
> Their spicy drugs; they on the trading flood
> Through the wide Ethiopian to the Cape
> Ply, stemming nightly toward the Pole: so seemed
> Far off the flying Fiend.

Here is the full strength of the imagination involved in the word, *hangs*, and exerted upon the whole image: First, the Fleet, an aggregate of many Ships, is represented as one mighty Person, whose track, we know and feel, is upon the waters; but, taking advantage of its appearance to the senses, the Poet dares to represent it as *hanging in the clouds*, both for the gratification of the mind in contemplating the image itself, and in reference to the motion and appearance of the sublime object to which it is compared.

From images of sight we will pass to those of sound:

> Over his own sweet voice the Stock-dove *broods*;

of the same bird,

> His voice was *buried* among trees,
> Yet to be come at by the breeze;
>
> O, Cuckoo! shall I call thee *Bird*,
> Or but a wandering *Voice*?

The Stock-dove is said to *coo*, a sound well imitating the note of the bird; but, by the intervention of the metaphor *broods*, the affections are called in by the imagination to assist in marking the manner in which the Bird reiterates and prolongs her soft note, as if herself delighting to listen to it, and participating of a still and quiet satisfaction, like that which may be supposed inseparable from the continuous process of incubation. 'His voice was buried among trees,' a metaphor expressing the love of *seclusion* by which this Bird is marked; and characterizing its note as not partaking of the shrill and the piercing, and therefore more easily deadened by the intervening shade; yet a note so peculiar, and withal so pleasing, that the breeze, gifted with that love of the sound which the Poet feels, penetrates the shade in which it is entombed, and conveys it to the ear of the listener.

> Shall I call thee Bird
> Or but a wandering Voice?

This concise interrogation characterizes the seeming ubiquity of the voice of the Cuckoo, and dispossesses the creature almost of a corporeal existence; the imagination being tempted to this exertion of her power by a consciousness in the memory that the Cuckoo is almost perpetually heard throughout the season of Spring, but seldom becomes an object of sight.

Thus far of images independent of each other, and immediately endowed by the mind with properties that do not inhere in them, upon an incitement from properties and qualities the existence of which is inherent and obvious. These processes of imagination are carried on either by conferring additional properties upon an object, or abstracting from it some of those which it actually possesses, and thus enabling it to react upon the mind which hath performed the process, like a new existence.

I pass from the Imagination acting upon an individual image to a consideration of the same faculty employed upon images in a conjunction by which they modify each other. The Reader has already had a fine instance before him in the passage quoted from Virgil, where the apparently perilous situation of the Goat, hanging upon the shaggy precipice, is contrasted with that of the Shepherd, contemplating it from the seclusion of the Cavern in which he lies stretched at ease and in security. Take these images separately, and how unaffecting the picture compared with that produced by their being thus connected with, and opposed to, each other!

> As a huge Stone is sometimes seen to lie
> Couched on the bald top of an eminence,
> Wonder to all who do the same espy
> By what means it could thither come, and whence;
> So that it seems a thing endued with sense,
> Like a Sea-beast crawled forth, which on a shelf
> Of rock or sand reposeth, there to sun himself.
>
> Such seemed this Man; not all alive or dead,
> Nor all asleep, in his extreme old age.
>
> *   *   *   *   *
>
> Motionless as a cloud the old Man stood,
> That heareth not the loud winds when they call,
> And moveth altogether if it move at all.

In these images, the conferring, the abstracting, and the modifying powers of the Imagination, immediately and mediately acting, are all brought into conjunction. The Stone is endowed with something of the power of life to approximate it to the Sea-beast; and the Sea-beast stripped of some of its vital qualities to assimilate it to the stone; which intermediate image is thus treated for the purpose of bringing the original image, that of the stone, to a nearer resemblance to the figure and condition of the aged Man; who is divested of so much of the indications of life and motion as to bring him to the point where the two objects unite and coalesce in just comparison. After what has been said, the image of the Cloud need not be commented upon.

Thus far of an endowing or modifying power: but the Imagination also shapes and *creates*; and how? By innumerable processes; and in none does it more delight than in that of consolidating numbers into unity, and dissolving and separating unity into number, – alternations proceeding from, and governed by, a sublime consciousness of the soul in her own mighty and almost divine powers. Recur to the passage already cited from Milton. When the compact Fleet, as one Person, has been introduced 'Sailing from Bengala,' 'They,' i.e. the 'Merchants,' representing the Fleet resolved into a Multitude of Ships, 'ply' their voyage towards the extremities of the earth: 'So' (referring to the word 'As' in the commencement) 'seemed the flying Fiend;' the image of his Person acting to recombine the multitude of Ships into one body, – the point from which the comparison set out. 'So seemed,' and to whom seemed? To the heavenly Muse who dictates the poem, to the eye of the Poet's mind, and to that of the Reader, present at one moment in the wide Ethiopian, and the next in the solitudes, then first broken in upon, of the infernal regions!

Modo me Thebis, modo ponit Athenis.

Hear again this mighty Poet, – speaking of the Messiah going forth to expel from Heaven the rebellious Angels,

Attended by ten thousand, thousand Saints
He onward came: far off his coming shone, –

the retinue of Saints, and the Person of the Messiah himself, lost almost and merged in the splendour of that indefinite abstraction, 'His coming!'

As I do not mean here to treat this subject further than to throw some light upon the present Volumes, and especially upon one division of them, I shall spare myself and the Reader the trouble of considering the Imagination as it deals with thoughts and sentiments, as it regulates the composition of characters, and determines the course of actions: I will not consider it (more than I have already done by implication) as that power which, in the language of one of my most esteemed Friends, 'draws all things to one, which makes things animate or inanimate, beings with their attributes, subjects with their accessories, take one colour and serve to one effect' [Charles Lamb upon the genius of Hogarth. – W]. The grand store-house of enthusiastic and meditative Imagination, of poetical, as contradistinguished from human and dramatic Imagination, is the prophetic and lyrical parts of the holy Scriptures, and the works of Milton, to which I cannot forbear to add those of Spenser. I select these writers in preference to those of ancient Greece and Rome because the anthropomorphitism of the Pagan religion subjected the minds of the greatest poets in those countries too much to the bondage of definite form; from which the Hebrews were preserved by their abhorrence of idolatry. This abhorrence was almost as strong in our great epic Poet, both from circumstances of his life, and from the constitution of his mind. However imbued the surface might be with classical literature, he was a Hebrew in soul; and all things tended in him towards the sublime. Spenser, of a gentler nature, maintained his freedom by aid of his allegorical spirit, at one time inciting him to create persons out of abstractions; and at another, by a superior effort of genius, to give the universality and permanence of abstractions to his human beings, by means of attributes and emblems that belong to the highest moral truths and the purest sensations, – of which his character of Una is a glorious example. Of the human and dramatic Imagination the works of Shakespeare are an inexhaustible source.

> I tax not you, ye Elements, with unkindness,
> I never gave you Kingdoms, called you Daughters.

And if, bearing in mind the many Poets distinguished by this prime quality, whose names I omit to mention; yet justified by a recollection of the insults which the Ignorant, the Incapable, and the Presumptuous have heaped upon these and my other writings, I may be permitted to anticipate the judgement of posterity upon myself; I shall declare (censurable, I grant, if the notoriety of the fact above stated does not justify me) that I have given, in these unfavourable times, evidence of exertions of this faculty upon its worthiest objects, the external universe, the moral and religious sentiments of Man, his natural affections, and his acquired passions; which have the same ennobling tendency as the productions of men, in this kind, worthy to be holden in undying remembrance.

I dismiss this subject with observing – that, in the series of Poems placed under the head of Imagination, I have begun with one of the earliest processes of Nature in the development of this faculty. Guided by one of my own primary consciousnesses, I have represented a commutation and transfer of internal feelings, co-operating with external accidents to plant, for immortality, images of sound and sight, in the celestial soil of the Imagination. The Boy, there introduced, is listening, with something of a feverish and restless anxiety, for the recurrence of the riotous sounds which he had previously excited; and, at the moment when the intenseness of his mind is beginning to remit, he is surprised into a perception of the solemn and tranquillizing images which the Poem describes. – The Poems next in succession exhibit the faculty exerting itself upon various objects of the external universe; then follow others, where it is employed upon feelings, characters, and actions; and the Class is concluded with imaginative pictures of moral, political, and religious sentiments.

To the mode in which Fancy has already been characterized as the Power of evoking and combining, or, as my friend Mr Coleridge has styled it, 'the aggregative and associative Power,' my objection is only that the definition is too general. To aggregate and to associate, to evoke and to combine, belong as well to the Imagination as to the Fancy; but either the materials evoked and combined are different; or they are brought together under a different law, and for a different purpose. Fancy does not require that the materials which she makes use of should be susceptible of change in their constitution, from her touch; and, where they admit of modification, it is enough for her purpose if it be slight, limited, and evanescent. Directly the reverse of these, are the desires and demands of the Imagination. She recoils from everything but the plastic, the pliant, and the indefinite. She leaves it to Fancy to describe Queen Mab as coming,

> In shape no bigger than an agate stone
> On the fore-finger of an Alderman.

Having to speak of stature, she does not tell you that her gigantic Angel was as tall as Pompey's pillar; much less that he was twelve cubits, or twelve hundred cubits high; or that his dimensions equalled those of Teneriffe or Atlas; – because these, and if they were a million times as high, it would be the same, are bounded: The expression is, 'His stature reached the sky!' the illimitable firmament! – When the Imagination frames a comparison, if it does not strike on the first presentation, a sense of the truth of the likeness, from the moment that it is perceived, grows – and continues to grow – upon the mind; the resemblance depending less upon outline of form and feature than upon expression and effect, less upon casual and outstanding, than upon inherent and internal, properties: – moreover, the images invariably modify each other. – The law under which the processes of Fancy are carried on is as capricious as the accidents of things, and the effects are surprising, playful, ludicrous, amusing, tender, or pathetic, as the objects happen to be appositely produced or fortunately combined. Fancy depends upon the rapidity and profusion with which she scatters her thoughts and images, trusting that their number, and the felicity with which they are linked together, will make amends for the want of individual value: or she prides herself upon the curious subtlety and the successful elaboration with which she can detect their lurking affinities. If she can win you over to her purpose, and impart to you her feelings, she cares not how unstable or transitory may be her influence, knowing that it will not be out of her power to resume it upon an apt occasion. But the Imagination is conscious of an indestructible dominion; – the Soul may fall away from it, not being able to sustain its grandeur, but, if once felt and acknowledged, by no act of any other faculty of the mind can it be relaxed, impaired, or diminished. – Fancy is given to quicken and to beguile the temporal part of our Nature, Imagination to incite and to support the eternal. – Yet is it not the less true that Fancy, as she is an active, is also, under her own laws and in her own spirit, a creative faculty. In what manner Fancy ambitiously aims at a rivalship with the Imagination, and Imagination stoops to work with the materials of Fancy, might be illustrated from the compositions of all eloquent writers, whether in prose or verse; and chiefly from those of our own Country. Scarcely a page of the impassioned parts of Bishop Taylor's Works can be opened that shall not afford examples. – Referring the Reader to those inestimable Volumes, I will content myself with placing a conceit (ascribed to Lord Chesterfield) in contrast with a passage from the Paradise Lost;

> The dews of the evening most carefully shun,
> They are the tears of the sky for the loss of the Sun.

After the transgression of Adam, Milton, with other appearances of sympathizing Nature, thus marks the immediate consequence,

> Sky lowered, and muttering thunder, some sad drops
> Wept at completion of the mortal sin.

The associating link is the same in each instance; – dew or rain, not distinguishable from the liquid substance of tears, are employed as indications of sorrow. A flash of surprise is the effect in the former case, a flash of surprise and nothing more; for the nature of things does not sustain the combination. In the latter, the effects of the act, of which there is this immediate consequence and visible sign, are so momentous that the mind acknowledges the justice and reasonableness of the sympathy in Nature so manifested; and the sky weeps drops of water as if with human eyes, as 'Earth had, before, trembled from her entrails, and Nature given a second groan.'

Awe-stricken as I am by contemplating the operations of the mind of this truly divine Poet, I scarcely dare venture to add that 'An Address to an Infant,' which the Reader will find under the Class of Fancy in the present Volumes, exhibits something of this communion and interchange of instruments and functions between the two powers; and is, accordingly, placed last in the class, as a preparation for that of Imagination which follows.

Finally, I will refer to Cotton's 'Ode upon Winter,' an admirable composition though stained with some peculiarities of the age in which he lived, for a general illustration of the characteristics of Fancy. The middle part of this ode contains a most lively description of the entrance of Winter, with his retinue, as 'A palsied King,' and yet a military Monarch, – advancing for conquest with his Army; the several bodies of which, and their arms and equipments, are described with a rapidity of detail, and a profusion of *fanciful* comparisons, which indicate on the part of the Poet extreme activity of intellect, and a correspondent hurry of delightful feeling. He retires from the Foe into his fortress, where

> a magazine
> Of sovereign juice is cellared in.
> Liquor that will the siege maintain
> Should Phoebus ne'er return again.

Though myself a water-drinker, I cannot resist the pleasure of transcribing what follows, as an instance still more happy of Fancy employed in the treatment of feeling than, in its preceding passages, the Poem supplies of her management of forms.

> 'Tis that, that gives the Poet rage,
> And thaws the gelly'd blood of Age;
> Matures the Young, restores the Old,
> And makes the fainting Coward bold.
>
> It lays the careful head to rest,
> Calms palpitations in the breast,
> Renders our lives' misfortune sweet;
>
> *   *   *   *   *
>
> Then let the chill Sirocco blow,
> And gird us round with hills of snow,
> Or else go whistle to the shore,
> And make the hollow mountains roar.
>
> Whilst we together jovial sit
> Careless, and crowned with mirth and wit;
> Where, though bleak winds confine us home,
> Our fancies round the world shall roam.
>
> We'll think of all the Friends we know,
> And drink to all worth drinking to;
> When having drunk all thine and mine,
> We rather shall want healths than wine.
>
> But where Friends fail us, we'll supply
> Our friendships with our charity;
> Men that remote in sorrows live,
> Shall by our lusty Brimmers thrive.
>
> We'll drink the Wanting into Wealth,
> And those that languish into health,
> The Afflicted into joy; the Opprest
> Into security and rest.
>
> The Worthy in disgrace shall find
> Favour return again more kind,
> And in restraint who stifled lie,
> Shall taste the air of liberty.

The Brave shall triumph in success,
The Lovers shall have Mistresses,
Poor unregarded Virtue, praise,
And the neglected Poet, Bays.

Thus shall our healths do others good,
Whilst we ourselves do all we would;
For freed from envy and from care,
What would we be but what we are?

It remains that I should express my regret at the necessity of separating my compositions from some beautiful Poems of Mr Coleridge, with which they have been long associated in publication. The feelings, with which that joint publication was made, have been gratified; its end is answered, and the time is come when considerations of general propriety dictate the separation. Three short pieces (now first published) are the work of a Female Friend; and the Reader, to whom they may be acceptable, is indebted to me for his pleasure; if anyone regard them with dislike, or be disposed to condemn them, let the censure fall upon him, who, trusting in his own sense of their merit and their fitness for the place which they occupy, *extorted* them from the Authoress.

When I sate down to write this preface it was my intention to have made it more comprehensive; but as all that I deem necessary is expressed, I will here detain the reader no longer: – what I have further to remark shall be inserted, by way of interlude, at the close of this Volume.

Essay, Supplementary to the Preface (*1815*)

By this time, I trust that the judicious Reader, who has now first become acquainted with these poems, is persuaded that a very senseless outcry has been raised against them and their Author. – Casually, and very rarely only, do I see any periodical publication, except a daily newspaper; but I am not wholly unacquainted with the spirit in which my most active and persevering Adversaries have maintained their hostility; nor with the impudent falsehoods and base artifices to which they have had recourse. These, as implying a consciousness on their parts that attacks honestly and fairly conducted would be unavailing, could not but have been regarded by me with triumph; had they been accompanied with such display of talents and information as might give weight to the opinions of the Writers, whether favourable or unfavourable. But the ignorance of those who have chosen to stand forth as my enemies, as far as I am acquainted with their enmity, has unfortunately been still more gross than their disingenuousness, and their incompetence more flagrant than their malice. The effect in the eyes of the discerning is indeed ludicrous: yet, contemptible as such men are, in return for the forced compliment paid me by their long-continued notice (which, as I have appeared so rarely before the public, no one can say has been solicited) I entreat them to spare themselves. The lash, which they are aiming at my productions, does, in fact, only fall on phantoms of their own brain; which, I grant, I am innocently instrumental in raising. – By what fatality the orb of my genius (for genius none of them seem to deny me) acts upon these men like the moon upon a certain description of patients, it would be irksome to inquire; nor would it consist with the respect which I owe myself to take further notice of opponents whom I internally despise.

With the young, of both sexes, Poetry is, like love, a passion; but, for much the greater part of those who have been proud of its power over their minds, a necessity soon arises of breaking the pleasing bondage; or it relaxes of itself; – the thoughts being occupied in domestic cares, or the time engrossed by business. Poetry then becomes only an occasional recreation; while to those whose existence passes away in a course of fashionable pleasure it is a species of luxurious amusement. – In middle and declining age, a scattered number of serious persons resort to poetry, as to religion, for a protection against the pressure of trivial employments, and as a consolation for the afflictions of life. And lastly, there are many, who, having been enamoured of this art, in their youth, have found leisure, after youth was spent, to cultivate general literature; in which poetry has continued to be comprehended *as a study*.

Into the above Classes the Readers of poetry may be divided; Critics abound in them all; but from the last only can opinions be collected of absolute value, and worthy to be depended upon, as prophetic of the destiny of a new work. The young, who in nothing can escape delusion, are especially subject to it in their intercourse with poetry. The cause, not so obvious as the fact is unquestionable, is the same as that from which erroneous judgements in this art, in the minds of men of all ages, chiefly proceed; but upon Youth it operates with peculiar force. The appropriate business of poetry, (which, nevertheless, if genuine is as permanent as pure science) her appropriate employment, her privilege and her *duty*, is to treat of things not as they *are*, but as they *appear*; not as they exist in themselves, but as they *seem* to exist to the *senses* and to the *passions*. What a world of delusion does this acknowledged principle prepare for the inexperienced! what temptations to go astray are here held forth for those whose thoughts have been little disciplined by the understanding, and whose feelings revolt from the sway of reason! – When a juvenile Reader is in the height of his rapture with some vicious passage, should experience throw in doubts, or common-sense suggest suspicions, a lurking consciousness that the realities of the Muse are but shows, and that her liveliest excitements are raised by transient shocks of conflicting feeling and successive assemblages of contradictory thoughts – is ever at hand to justify extravagance, and to sanction absurdity. But, it may be asked, as these illusions are unavoidable, and no doubt eminently useful to the mind as a process, what good can be gained by making observations the tendency of which is to diminish the confidence of youth in its feelings, and thus to abridge its innocent and even profitable pleasures? The reproach implied in the question could not be warded off, if Youth were incapable of being delighted with what is truly excellent; or if these errors always terminated of themselves in due season. But, with the majority, though their force be abated, they continue through life. Moreover, the fire of youth is too vivacious an element to be extinguished or damped by a philosophical remark; and, while there is no danger that what has been said will be injurious or painful to the ardent and the confident, it may prove beneficial to those who, being enthusiastic, are, at the same time, modest and ingenuous. The intimation may unite with their own misgivings to regulate their sensibility, and to bring in, sooner than it would otherwise have arrived, a more discreet and sound judgement.

If it should excite wonder that men of ability, in later life, whose understandings have been rendered acute by practice in affairs, should be so easily and so far imposed upon when they happen to take up a new work in verse, this appears to be the cause; — that, having discontinued their attention to poetry, whatever progress may have been made in other departments of knowledge, they have not, as to this art, advanced in true discernment beyond the age of youth. If then a new poem falls in their way, whose attractions are of that kind which would have enraptured them during the heat of youth, the judgement not being improved to a degree that they shall be disgusted, they are dazzled; and prize and cherish the faults for having had power to make the present time vanish before them, and to throw the mind back, as by enchantment, into the happiest season of life. As they read, powers seem to be revived, passions are regenerated, and pleasures restored. The Book was probably taken up after an escape from the burden of business, and with a wish to forget the world, and all its vexations and anxieties. Having obtained this wish, and so much more, it is natural that they should make report as they have felt.

If Men of mature age, through want of practice, be thus easily beguiled into admiration of absurdities, extravagances, and misplaced ornaments, thinking it proper that their understandings should enjoy a holiday, while they are unbending their minds with verse, it may be expected that such Readers will resemble their former selves also in strength of prejudice, and an inaptitude to be moved by the unostentatious beauties of a pure style. In the higher poetry, an enlightened Critic chiefly looks for a reflexion of the wisdom of the heart and the grandeur of the imagination. Wherever these appear, simplicity accompanies them; Magnificence herself, when legitimate, depending upon a simplicity of her own, to regulate her ornaments. But it is a well known property of human nature that our estimates are ever governed by comparisons, of which we are conscious with various degrees of distinctness. Is it not, then, inevitable (confining these observations to the effects of style merely) that an eye, accustomed to the glaring hues of diction by which such Readers are caught and excited, will for the most part be rather repelled than attracted by an original Work the colouring of which is disposed according to a pure and refined scheme of harmony? It is in the fine arts as in the affairs of life, no man can *serve* (i.e. obey with zeal and fidelity) two Masters.

As Poetry is most just to its own divine origin when it administers the comforts and breathes the spirit of religion, they who have learned to perceive this truth, and who betake themselves to reading verse for sacred purposes, must be preserved from numerous illusions to which the two Classes of Readers, whom we have been considering, are liable. But, as the mind grows serious from the weight of life, the range of its passions is contracted accordingly; and its sympathies become so exclusive that many species of high excellence wholly escape, or but languidly excite, its notice. Besides, Men who read from religious or moral inclinations, even when the subject is of that kind which they approve, are beset with misconceptions and mistakes peculiar to themselves. Attaching so much importance to the truths which interest them, they are prone to overrate the Authors by whom these truths are expressed and enforced. They come prepared to impart so much passion to the Poet's language, that they remain unconscious how little, in fact, they receive from it. And, on the other hand, religious faith is to him who holds it so momentous a thing, and error appears to be attended with such tremendous consequences, that, if opinions touching upon religion occur which the Reader condemns, he not only cannot sympathize with them however animated the expression, but there is, for the most part, an end put to all satisfaction and enjoyment. Love, if it before existed, is converted into dislike; and the heart of the Reader is set against the Author and his book. – To these excesses, they, who from their professions ought to be the most guarded against them, are perhaps the most liable; I mean those sects whose religion, being from the calculating understanding, is cold and formal. For when Christianity, the religion of humility, is founded upon the proudest quality of our nature, what can be expected but contradictions? Accordingly, believers of this cast are at one time contemptuous; at another, being troubled as they are and must be with inward misgivings, they are jealous and suspicious; – and at all seasons, they are under temptation to supply, by the heat with which they defend their tenets, the animation which is wanting to the constitution of the religion itself.

Faith was given to man that his affections, detached from the treasures of time, might be inclined to settle upon those of eternity: – the elevation of his nature, which this habit produces on earth, being to him a presumptive evidence of a future state of existence; and giving him a title to partake of its holiness. The religious man values what he sees chiefly as an 'imperfect shadowing forth' of what he is incapable of seeing. The concerns of religion refer to indefinite objects, and are too weighty for the mind to support them without relieving itself by resting a great part of the burden upon words and symbols. The commerce between Man and his Maker cannot be carried on but by a process where much is represented in little, and the infinite Being accommodates himself to a finite capacity. In all this may be perceived the affinities between religion and poetry; – between religion – making up the deficiencies of reason by faith, and poetry – passionate for the instruction of reason; between religion – whose element is infinitude, and whose ultimate trust is the supreme of things, submitting herself to circumscription and reconciled to substitutions; and poetry – ethereal and transcendent, yet incapable to sustain her existence without sensuous incarnation. In this community of nature may be perceived also the lurking incitements of kindred error; – so that we shall find that no poetry has been more subject to distortion, than that species the argument and scope of which is religious; and no lovers of the art have gone further astray than the pious and the devout.

Whither then shall we turn for that union of qualifications which must necessarily exist before the decisions of a critic can be of absolute value? For a mind at once poetical and philosophical; for a critic whose affections are as free and kindly as the spirit of society, and whose understanding is severe as that of dispassionate government? Where are we to look for that initiatory composure of mind which no selfishness can disturb? For a natural sensibility that has been tutored into correctness without losing anything of its quickness; and for active faculties capable of answering the demands which an Author of original imagination shall make upon them, – associated with a judgement that cannot be duped into admiration by aught that is unworthy of it? – Among those and those only, who, never having suffered their youthful love of poetry to remit much of its force, have applied, to the consideration of the laws of this art, the best power of their understandings. At the same time it must be observed – that, as this Class comprehends the only judgements which are trustworthy, so does it include the most erroneous and perverse. For to be mistaught is worse than to be untaught; and no perverseness equals that which is supported by system, no errors are so difficult to root out as those which the understanding has pledged its credit to uphold. In this Class are contained Censors, who, if they be pleased with what is good, are pleased with it only by imperfect glimpses, and upon false principles; who, should they generalize rightly to a certain point, are sure to suffer for it in the end; – who, if they stumble upon a sound rule, are fettered by misapplying it, or by straining it too far; being incapable of perceiving when it ought to yield to one of higher order. In it are found Critics too petulant to be passive to a genuine Poet, and too feeble to grapple with him; Men, who take upon them to report of the course which *he* holds whom they are utterly unable to accompany, – confounded if he turn quick upon the wing, dismayed if he soar steadily into 'the region;' – Men of palsied imaginations and indurated hearts; in whose minds all healthy action is languid, – who, therefore, feed as the many direct them, or with the many, are greedy after vicious provocatives; – Judges, whose censure is auspicious, and whose praise ominous! In this Class meet together the two extremes of best and worst.

The observations presented in the foregoing series, are of too ungracious a nature to have been made without reluctance; and were it only on this account I would invite the Reader to try them by the test of comprehensive experience. If the number of judges who can be confidently relied upon be in reality so small, it ought to follow that partial notice only, or neglect, perhaps long continued, or attention wholly inadequate to their merits – must have been the fate of most works in the higher departments of poetry; and that, on the other hand, numerous productions have blazed into popularity, and have passed away, leaving scarcely a trace behind them: – it will be, further, found that when Authors have at length raised themselves into general admiration and maintained their ground, errors and prejudices have prevailed concerning their genius and their works, which the few who are conscious of those errors and prejudices would deplore; if they were not recompensed by perceiving that there are select Spirits for whom it is ordained that their fame shall be in the world an existence like that of Virtue, which owes its being to the struggles it makes, and its vigour to the enemies whom it provokes; – a vivacious quality ever doomed to meet with opposition, and still triumphing over it; and, from the nature of its dominion, incapable of being brought to the sad conclusion of Alexander, when he wept that there were no more worlds for him to conquer.

Let us take a hasty retrospect of the poetical literature of this Country for the greater part of the last two Centuries, and see if the facts correspond with these inferences.

Who is there that can now endure to read the 'Creation' of Dubartas? Yet all Europe once resounded with his praise; he was caressed by Kings; and, when his Poem was translated into our language, the Faery Queen faded before it. The name of Spenser, whose genius is of a higher order than even that of Ariosto, is at this day scarcely known beyond the limits of the British Isles. And, if the value of his works is to be estimated from the attention now paid to them by his Countrymen, compared with that which they bestow on those of other writers, it must be pronounced small indeed.

> The laurel, meed of mighty Conquerors
> And Poets *sage* –

are his own words; but his wisdom has, in this particular, been his worst enemy; while, its opposite, whether in the shape of folly or madness, has been their best friend. But he was a great power; and bears a high name: the laurel has been awarded to him.

A Dramatic Author, if he write for the Stage, must adapt himself to the taste of the Audience, or they will not endure him; accordingly the mighty genius of Shakespeare was listened to. The People were delighted; but I am not sufficiently versed in Stage antiquities to determine whether they did not flock as eagerly to the representation of many pieces of contemporary Authors, wholly undeserving to appear upon the same boards. Had there been a formal contest for superiority among dramatic Writers, that Shakespeare, like his predecessors Sophocles and Euripides, would have often been subject to the mortification of seeing the prize adjudged to sorry competitors, becomes too probable when we reflect that the Admirers of Settle and Shadwell were, in a later age, as numerous, and reckoned as respectable in point of talent as those of Dryden. At all events, that Shakespeare stooped to accommodate himself to the People, is sufficiently apparent; and one of the most striking proofs of his almost omnipotent genius, is, that he could turn to such glorious purpose those materials which the prepossessions of the age compelled him to make use of. Yet even this marvellous skill appears not to have been enough to prevent his rivals from having some advantage over him in public estimation; else how can we account for passages and scenes that exist in his works, unless upon a supposition that some of the grossest of them, a fact which in my own mind I have no doubt of, were foisted in by the Players, for the gratification of the many?

But that his Works, whatever might be their reception upon the stage, made little impression upon the ruling Intellects of the time, may be inferred from the fact that Lord Bacon, in his multifarious writings, nowhere either quotes or alludes to him. – [The learned Hakewill (a 3d edition of whose book bears date 1635) writing to refute the error 'touching Nature's perpetual and universal decay,' cites triumphantly the names of Ariosto, Tasso, Bartas, and Spenser, as instances that poetic genius had not degenerated; but he makes no mention of Shakespeare. – W.] His dramatic excellence enabled him to resume possession of the stage after the Restoration; but Dryden tells us that in his time two of Beaumont's and Fletcher's Plays were acted for one of Shakespeare's. And so faint and limited was the perception of the poetic beauties of his dramas in the time of Pope, that, in his Edition of the Plays, with a view of rendering to the general Reader a necessary service, he printed between inverted commas those passages which he thought most worthy of notice.

At this day, the French Critics have abated nothing of their aversion to this darling of our Nation: 'the English with their Bouffon de Shakespeare' is as familiar an expression among them as in the time of Voltaire. Baron Grimm is the only French writer who seems to have perceived his infinite superiority to the first names of the French Theatre; an advantage which the Parisian Critic owed to his German blood and German education. The most enlightened Italians, though well acquainted with our language, are wholly incompetent to measure the proportions of Shakespeare. The Germans only, of foreign nations, are approaching towards a knowledge and feeling of what he is. In some respects they have acquired a superiority over the fellow-countrymen of the Poet; for among us it is a current, I might say, an established opinion that Shakespeare is justly praised when he is pronounced to be 'a wild irregular genius, in whom great faults are compensated by great beauties.' How long may it be before this misconception passes away, and it becomes universally acknowledged that the judgement of Shakespeare in the selection of his materials, and in the manner in which he has made them, heterogeneous as they often are, constitute a unity of their own, and contribute all to one great end, is not less admirable than his imagination, his invention, and his intuitive knowledge of human Nature!

There is extant a small Volume of miscellaneous Poems in which Shakespeare expresses his own feelings in his own Person. It is not difficult to conceive that the Editor, George Stevens, should have been insensible to the beauties of one portion of that Volume, the Sonnets; though there is not a part of the writings of this Poet where is found in an equal compass a greater number of exquisite feelings felicitously expressed. But, from regard to the Critic's own credit, he would not have ventured to talk of an act of parliament not being strong enough to compel the perusal of these, or any production of Shakespeare [This flippant insensibility was publicly reprehended by Mr Coleridge in a course of Lectures upon Poetry given by him at the Royal Institution. For the various merits of thought and language in Shakespeare's Sonnets see Numbers 27, 29, 30, 32, 33, 54, 64, 66, 68, 73, 76, 86, 91, 92, 93, 97, 98, 105, 107, 108, 109, 111, 113, 114, 116, 117, 129, and many others. – W.], if he had not known that the people of England were ignorant of the treasures contained in those little pieces; and if he had not, moreover, shared the too common propensity of human nature to exult over a supposed fall into the mire of a genius whom he had been compelled to regard with admiration, as an inmate of the celestial regions, – 'there sitting where he durst not soar.'

Nine years before the death of Shakespeare, Milton was born;

and early in life he published several small poems, which, though on their first appearance they were praised by a few of the judicious, were afterwards neglected to that degree that Pope, in his youth, could pilfer from them without danger of detection. – Whether these poems are at this day justly appreciated I will not undertake to decide: nor would it imply a severe reflection upon the mass of Readers to suppose the contrary; seeing that a Man of the acknowledged genius of Voss, the German Poet, could suffer their spirit to evaporate; and could change their character, as is done in the translation made by him of the most popular of those pieces. At all events it is certain that these Poems of Milton are now much read, and loudly praised; yet were they little heard of till more than 150 years after their publication; and of the Sonnets, Dr Johnson, as appears from Boswell's Life of him, was in the habit of thinking and speaking as contemptuously as Stevens wrote upon those of Shakespeare.

About the time when the Pindaric Odes of Cowley and his imitators, and the productions of that class of curious thinkers whom Dr Johnson has strangely styled Metaphysical Poets, were beginning to lose something of that extravagant admiration which they had excited, the Paradise Lost made its appearance. 'Fit audience find though few,' was the petition addressed by the Poet to his inspiring Muse. I have said elsewhere that he gained more than he asked; this I believe to be true; but Dr Johnson has fallen into a gross mistake when he attempts to prove, by the sale of the work, that Milton's Countrymen were '*just* to it' upon its first appearance. Thirteen hundred Copies were sold in two years; an uncommon example, he asserts, of the prevalence of genius in opposition to so much recent enmity as Milton's public conduct had excited. But be it remembered that, if Milton's political and religious opinions, and the manner in which he announced them, had raised him many enemies, they had procured him numerous friends; who, as all personal danger was passed away at the time of publication, would be eager to procure the master-work of a Man whom they revered, and whom they would be proud of praising. The demand did not immediately increase; 'for,' says Dr Johnson, 'many more Readers' (he means Persons in the habit of reading poetry) 'than were supplied at first the Nation did not afford.' How careless must a writer be who can make this

assertion in the face of so many existing title pages to belie it!
Turning to my own shelves, I find the folio of Cowley, 7th
Edition, 1681. A book near it is Flatman's Poems, 4th Edition,
1686; Waller, 5th Edition, same date. The Poems of Norris of
Bemerton not long after went, I believe, through nine Editions.
What further demand there might be for these works I do not
know, but I well remember, that 25 Years ago, the Bookseller's
stalls in London swarmed with the folios of Cowley. This is not
mentioned in disparagement of that able writer and amiable Man;
but merely to show – that, if Milton's work was not more read, it
was not because readers did not exist at the time. Only 3000
copies of the Paradise Lost sold in 11 Years; and the Nation, says
Dr Johnson, had been satisfied from 1623 to 1644 [1664?], that is
41 Years, with only two Editions of the Works of Shakespeare;
which probably did not together make 1000 copies; facts adduced
by the critic to prove the 'paucity of Readers.' – There were
Readers in multitudes; but their money went for other purposes,
as their admiration was fixed elsewhere. We are authorized, then,
to affirm that the reception of the Paradise Lost, and the slow
progress of its fame, are proofs as striking as can be desired that
the positions which I am attempting to establish are not erroneous.
– [Hughes is express upon this subject; in his dedication of
Spenser's Works to Lord Somers he writes thus. 'It was your
Lordship's encouraging a beautiful Edition of Paradise Lost that
first brought that incomparable Poem to be generally known and
esteemed.' – W.] How amusing to shape to one's self such a
critique as a Wit of Charles's days, or a Lord of the Miscellanies,
or trading Journalist, of King William's time, would have brought
forth, if he had set his faculties industriously to work upon this
Poem, everywhere impregnated with *original* excellence!

So strange indeed are the obliquities of admiration, that they
whose opinions are much influenced by authority will often be
tempted to think that there are no fixed principles in human
nature for this art to rest upon. [This opinion seems actually to
have been entertained by Adam Smith, the worst critic, David
Hume not excepted, that Scotland, a soil to which this sort of
weed seems natural, has produced. – W.] I have been honoured
by being permitted to peruse in MS. a tract composed between
the period of the Revolution and the close of that Century. It is

the Work of an English Peer of high accomplishments, its object to form the character and direct the studies of his Son. Perhaps nowhere does a more beautiful treatise of the kind exist. The good sense and wisdom of the thoughts, the delicacy of the feelings, and the charm of the style, are, throughout, equally conspicuous. Yet the Author, selecting among the Poets of his own Country those whom he deems most worthy of his son's perusal, particularizes only Lord Rochester, Sir John Denham, and Cowley. Writing about the same time, Shaftsbury, an Author at present unjustly depreciated, describes the English Muses as only yet lisping in their Cradles.

The arts by which Pope, soon afterwards, contrived to procure to himself a more general and a higher reputation than perhaps any English Poet ever attained during his life-time, are known to the judicious. And as well known is it to them, that the undue exertion of these arts, is the cause why Pope has for some time held a rank in literature, to which, if he had not been seduced by an over-love of immediate popularity, and had confided more in his native genius, he never could have descended. He bewitched the nation by his melody, and dazzled it by his polished style, and was himself blinded by his own success. Having wandered from humanity in his Eclogues with boyish inexperience, the praise, which these compositions obtained, tempted him into a belief that nature was not to be trusted, at least in pastoral Poetry. To prove this by example, he put his friend Gay upon writing those Eclogues which the Author intended to be burlesque. The Instigator of the work, and his Admirers, could perceive in them nothing but what was ridiculous. Nevertheless, though these Poems contain some odious and even detestable passages, the effect, as Dr Johnson well observes, 'of reality and truth became conspicuous even when the intention was to show them grovelling and degrading.' These Pastorals, ludicrous to those who prided themselves upon their refinement, in spite of those disgusting passages 'became popular, and were read with delight as just representations of rural manners and occupations.'

Something less than 60 years after the publication of the Paradise Lost appeared Thomson's Winter; which was speedily followed by his other Seasons. It is a work of inspiration; much of it is written from himself, and nobly from himself. How was it received? 'It was no sooner read,' says one of his contemporary Biographers, 'than universally admired: those only excepted who had not been used to feel, or to look for anything in poetry, beyond a *point* of satirical or epigrammatic wit, a smart *antithesis* richly trimmed with rhyme, or the softness of an *elegiac* complaint. To such his manly classical spirit could not readily commend itself; till, after a more attentive perusal, they had got the better of their prejudices, and either acquired or affected a truer taste. A few others stood aloof, merely because they had long before fixed the articles of their poetical creed, and resigned themselves to an absolute despair of ever seeing anything new and original. These were somewhat mortified to find their notions disturbed by the appearance of a poet, who seemed to owe nothing but to nature and his own genius. But, in a short time, the applause became unanimous; everyone wondering how so many pictures, and pictures so familiar, should have moved them but faintly to what they felt in his descriptions. His digressions too, the overflowings of a tender benevolent heart, charmed the reader no less; leaving him in doubt, whether he should more admire the Poet or love the Man.'

This case appears to bear strongly against us: – but we must distinguish between wonder and legitimate admiration. The subject of the work is the changes produced in the appearances of nature by the revolution of the year: and, by undertaking to write in verse, Thomson pledged himself to treat his subject as became a Poet. Now it is remarkable that, excepting a passage or two in the Windsor Forest of Pope, and some delightful pictures in the Poems of Lady Winchilsea, the Poetry of the period intervening between the publication of the Paradise Lost and the Seasons does not contain a single new image of external nature; and scarcely presents a familiar one from which it can be inferred that the eye of the Poet had been steadily fixed upon his object, much less that his feelings had urged him to work upon it in the spirit of genuine imagination. To what a low state knowledge of the most obvious and important phenomena had sunk, is evident from the style in which Dryden has executed a description of Night in one of his Tragedies, and Pope his translation of the celebrated moon-light scene in the Iliad. A blind man, in the habit of attending accurately to descriptions casually dropped from the lips of those around him, might easily depict these appearances with more truth. Dryden's lines are vague, bombastic, and senseless;

> [CORTES *alone, in a night-gown.*
> All things are hushed as Nature's self lay dead:
> The mountains seem to nod their drowsy head:
> The little Birds in dreams their songs repeat,
> And sleeping Flowers beneath the Night-dew sweat:
> Even Lust and Envy sleep; yet Love denies
> Rest to my soul, and slumber to my eyes.
> *Dryden's Indian Emperor* – W.]

those of Pope, though he had Homer to guide him, are throughout false and contradictory. The verses of Dryden, once highly celebrated, are forgotten; those of Pope still retain their hold upon public estimation, – nay, there is not a passage of descriptive poetry, which at this day finds so many and such ardent admirers. Strange to think of an Enthusiast, as may have been the case with thousands, reciting those verses under the cope of a moon-light sky, without having his raptures in the least disturbed by a suspicion of their absurdity. – If these two distinguished Writers could habitually think that the visible universe was of so little consequence to a Poet, that it was scarcely necessary for him to cast his eyes upon it, we may be assured that those passages of the elder Poets which faithfully and poetically describe the phenomena of nature, were not at that time holden in much estimation, and that there was little accurate attention paid to these appearances.

Wonder is the natural product of Ignorance; and as the soil was *in such good condition* at the time of the publication of the Seasons, the crop was doubtless abundant. Neither individuals nor nations become corrupt all at once, nor are they enlightened in a moment. Thomson was an inspired Poet, but he could not work miracles; in cases where the art of seeing had in some degree been learned, the teacher would further the proficiency of his pupils, but he could do little *more*, though so far does vanity assist men in acts of self-deception that many would often fancy they recognized a likeness when they knew nothing of the original. Having shown that much of what his Biographer deemed genuine admiration must in fact have been blind wonderment, – how is the rest to be accounted for? – Thomson was fortunate in the very title of his Poem, which seemed to bring it home to the prepared sympathies of everyone: in the next place, notwithstanding his high powers, he writes a vicious style; and his false ornaments are exactly of that kind which would be most likely to strike the undiscerning. He likewise abounds with sentimental common-places, that from the manner in which they were brought forward bore an imposing air of novelty. In any well-used Copy of the Seasons the Book generally opens of itself with the rhapsody on love, or with one of the stories (perhaps Damon and Musidora); these also are prominent in our Collections of Extracts; and are the parts of his Works which, after all, were probably most efficient in first recommending the Author to general notice. Pope, repaying praises which he had received, and wishing to extol him to the highest, only styles him 'an elegant and philosophical Poet;' nor are we able to collect any unquestionable proofs that the true characteristics of Thomson's genius as an imaginative Poet were perceived, till the elder Warton, almost 40 Years after the publication of the Seasons, pointed them out by a note in his Essay on the life and writings of Pope. In the Castle of Indolence (of which Gray speaks so coldly) these characteristics were almost as conspicuously displayed, and in verse more harmonious and diction more pure. Yet that fine Poem was neglected on its appearance, and is at this day the delight only of a Few!

When Thomson died, Collins breathed his regrets into an Elegiac Poem, in which he pronounces a poetical curse upon *him* who should regard with insensibility the place where the Poet's remains were deposited. The Poems of the mourner himself have now passed through innumerable Editions, and are universally known; but if, when Collins died, the same kind of imprecation had been pronounced by a surviving admirer, small is the number whom it would not have comprehended. The notice which his poems attained during his life-time was so small, and of course the sale so insignificant, that not long before his death he deemed it right to repay to the Bookseller the sum which he had advanced for them, and threw the Edition into the fire.

Next in importance to the Seasons of Thomson, though at considerable distance from that work in order of time, come the Reliques of Ancient English Poetry; collected, new-modelled, and in many instances (if such a contradiction in terms may be used) composed, by the editor, Dr Percy. This Work did not steal silently into the world, as is evident from the number of legendary tales, which appeared not long after its publication; and which were modelled, as the Authors persuaded themselves, after the old Ballad. The Compilation was however ill-suited to the then existing taste of City society; and Dr Johnson, 'mid the little senate to which he gave laws, was not sparing in his exertions to make it an object of contempt. The Critic triumphed, the legendary imitators were deservedly disregarded, and, as undeservedly, their ill-imitated models sank, in this Country, into temporary neglect; while Bürger, and other able Writers of Germany, were translating, or imitating, these Reliques, and composing, with the aid of inspiration thence derived, Poems, which are the delight of the German nation. Dr Percy was so abashed by the ridicule flung upon his labours from the ignorance and insensibility of the Persons with whom he lived, that, though while he was writing under a mask he had not wanted resolution to follow his genius into the regions of true simplicity and genuine pathos (as is evinced by the exquisite ballad of Sir Cauline and by many other pieces), yet, when he appeared in his own person and character as a poetical writer, he adopted, as in the tale of the Hermit of Warkworth, a diction scarcely in any one of its features distinguishable from the vague, the glossy, and unfeeling language of his day. I mention this remarkable fact with regret, esteeming the genius of Dr Percy in this kind of writing superior to that of any other man by whom, in modern times, it has been cultivated. That even Bürger (to whom Klopstock gave, in my hearing, a commendation which he denied to Goethe and Schiller, pronouncing him to be a genuine Poet, and one of the few among the Germans whose works would last) had not the fine sensibility of Percy, might be shown from many passages, in which he has deserted his original only to go astray. For example,

> Now daye was gone, and night was come,
> And all were fast asleepe,
> All, save the Ladye Emmeline,
> Who sate in her bowre to weepe:

> And soone she heard her true Love's voice
> Low whispering at the walle,
> Awake, awake, my deare Ladye,
> 'Tis I thy true-love call.

Which is thus tricked out and dilated,

> Als nun die Nacht Gebirg' und Thal
> Vermummt in Rabenschatten,
> Und Hochburgs Lampen überall
> Schon ausgeflimmert hatten,
> Und alles tief entschlafen war;
> Doch nur das Fräulein immerdar,
> Voll Fieberangst, noch wachte,
> Und seinen Ritter dachte:
> Da horch! Ein süsser Liebeston
> Kam leis' empor geflogen.
> 'Ho, Trudchen, ho! Da bin ich schon!
> Frisch auf! Dich angezogen!'

But from humble ballads we must ascend to heroics.

All hail Macpherson! hail to thee, Sire of Ossian! The Phantom was begotten by the snug embrace of an impudent Highlander upon a cloud of tradition – it travelled southward, where it was greeted with acclamation, and the thin Consistence took its course through Europe, upon the breath of popular applause. The Editor of the 'Reliques' had indirectly preferred a claim to the praise of invention by not concealing that his supplementary labours were considerable: how selfish his conduct contrasted with that of the disinterested Gael, who, like Lear, gives his kingdom away, and is content to become a pensioner upon his own issue for a beggarly pittance! – Open this far-famed Book! – I have done so at random, and the beginning of the 'Epic Poem Temora,' in 8 Books, presents itself. 'The blue waves of Ullin roll in light. The green hills are covered with day. Trees shake their dusky heads in the breeze. Grey torrents pour their noisy streams. Two green hills with aged oaks surround a narrow plain. The blue course of a stream is there. On its banks stood Cairbar of Atha. His spear supports the king; the red eyes of his fear are sad. Cormac rises on his soul with all his ghastly wounds.' Precious memorandums from the pocket-book of the blind Ossian!

If it be unbecoming, as I acknowledge that for the most part it is, to speak disrespectfully of Works that have enjoyed for a length of time a widely spread reputation, without at the same time producing irrefragable proofs of their unworthiness, let me be forgiven upon this occasion. – Having had the good fortune to be born and reared in a mountainous Country, from my very childhood I have felt the falsehood that pervades the volumes imposed upon the World under the name of Ossian. From what I saw with my own eyes, I knew that the imagery was spurious. In nature everything is distinct, yet nothing defined into absolute independent singleness. In Macpherson's work it is exactly the reverse; everything (that is not stolen) is in this manner defined, insulated, dislocated, deadened, – yet nothing distinct. It will always be so when words are substituted for things. To say that the characters never could exist, that the manners are impossible, and that a dream has more substance than the whole state of society, as there depicted, is doing nothing more than pronouncing a censure which Macpherson defied; when, with the steeps of Morven before his eyes, he could talk so familiarly of his Carborne heroes; – Of Morven, which, if one may judge from its appearance at the distance of a few miles, contains scarcely an acre of ground sufficiently accommodating for a sledge to be trailed along its surface. – Mr Malcolm Laing has ably shown that the diction of this pretended translation is a motley assembly from all quarters; but he is so fond of making out parallel passages as to call poor Macpherson to account for his very '*ands*' and his '*buts*!' and he has weakened his argument by conducting it as if he thought that every striking resemblance was a *conscious* plagiarism. It is enough that the coincidences are too remarkable for its being probable or possible that they could arise in different minds without communication between them. Now as the Translators of the Bible, Shakespeare, Milton, and Pope, could not be indebted to Macpherson, it follows that he must have owed his fine feathers to them; unless we are prepared gravely to assert, with Madame de Staël, that many of the characteristic beauties of our most celebrated English Poets, are derived from the ancient Fingallian; in which case the modern translator would have been but giving back to Ossian his own. – It is consistent that Lucien Buonaparte, who could censure Milton for having surrounded Satan in the infernal regions with courtly and regal splendour, should pronounce the modern Ossian to be the glory of Scotland; – a Country that has produced a Dunbar, a Buchanan, a Thomson, and a Burns! These opinions are of ill omen for the Epic ambition of him who has given them to the world.

Yet, much as these pretended treasures of antiquity have been admired, they have been wholly uninfluential upon the literature of the Country. No succeeding Writer appears to have caught from them a ray of inspiration; no Author in the least distinguished, has ventured formally to imitate them – except the Boy, Chatterton, on their first appearance. He had perceived, from the successful trials which he himself had made in literary forgery, how few critics were able to distinguish between a real ancient medal and a counterfeit of modern manufacture; and he set himself to the work of filling a Magazine with *Saxon poems*, – counterparts of those of Ossian, as like his as one of his misty stars is to another. This incapability to amalgamate with the literature of the Island, is, in my estimation, a decisive proof that the book is essentially unnatural; nor should I require any other to demonstrate it to be a forgery, audacious as worthless. – Contrast, in this respect, the effect of Macpherson's publication with the Reliques of Percy, so unassuming, so modest in their pretensions! – I have already stated how much Germany is indebted to this latter work; and for our own Country, its Poetry has been absolutely redeemed by it. I do not think that there is an able Writer in verse of the present day who would not be proud to acknowledge his obligations to the Reliques; I know that it is so with my friends; and, for myself, I am happy in this occasion to make a public avowal of my own.

Dr Johnson, more fortunate in his contempt of the labours of Macpherson than those of his modest friend, was solicited not long after to furnish Prefaces biographical and critical for some of the most eminent English Poets. The Booksellers took upon themselves to make the collection; they referred probably to the most popular miscellanies, and, unquestionably, to their Books of accounts; and decided upon the claim of Authors to be admitted into a body of the most Eminent, from the familiarity of their names with the readers of that day, and by the profits, which, from the sale of his works, each had brought and was bringing to the Trade. The Editor was allowed a limited exercise of discretion, and the Authors whom he recommended are scarcely to be mentioned without a smile. We open the volume of Prefatory Lives, and to our astonishment the *first* name we find is that of Cowley! – What is become of the Morning-star of English Poetry? Where is the bright Elizabethan Constellation? Or, if Names are more acceptable than images, where is the ever-to-be-honoured Chaucer? where is Spenser? where Sydney? and lastly where he, whose rights as a Poet, contradistinguished from those which he is universally allowed to possess as a Dramatist, we have vindicated, where Shakespeare? – These, and a multitude of others not unworthy to be placed near them, their contemporaries and successors, we have *not*. But in their stead, we have (could better be expected when precedence was to be settled by an abstract of reputation at any given period made as in the case before us?) Roscommon, and Stepney, and Phillips, and Walsh, and Smith, and Duke, and King, and Spratt – Halifax, Granville, Sheffield, Congreve, Broome, and other reputed Magnates; Writers in metre utterly worthless and useless, except for occasions like the present, when their productions are referred to as evidence what a small quantity of brain is necessary to procure a considerable stock of admiration, provided the aspirant will accommodate himself to the likings and fashions of his day.

As I do not mean to bring down this retrospect to our own times, it may with propriety be closed at the era of this distinguished event. From the literature of other ages and countries, proofs equally cogent might have been adduced that the opinions announced in the former part of this Essay are founded upon truth. It was not an agreeable office, not a prudent undertaking, to declare them, but their importance seemed to render it a duty. It may still be asked, where lies the particular relation of what has been said to these Volumes? – The question will be easily answered by the discerning Reader who is old enough to remember the taste that was prevalent when some of these Poems were first published, 17 years ago; who has also observed to what degree the Poetry of this Island has since that period been coloured by them; and who is further aware of the unremitting hostility with which, upon some principle or other, they have each and all been opposed. A sketch of my own notion of the constitution of Fame, has been given; and, as far as concerns myself, I have cause to be satisfied. The love, the admiration, the indifference, the slight, the aversion, and even the contempt, with which these Poems have been received, knowing, as I do, the source within my own mind, from which they have proceeded, and the labour and pains, which, when labour and pains appeared needful, have been bestowed upon them, – must all, if I think consistently, be received as pledges and tokens, bearing the same general impression though widely different in value; – they are all proofs that for the present time I have not laboured in vain; and afford assurances, more or less authentic, that the products of my industry will endure.

If there be one conclusion more forcibly pressed upon us than another by the review which has been given of the fortunes and fate of Poetical Works, it is this, – that every Author, as far as he is great and at the same time *original*, has had the task of *creating* the taste by which he is to be enjoyed: so has it been, so will it continue to be. This remark was long since made to me by the philosophical Friend for the separation of whose Poems from my own I have previously expressed my regret. The predecessors of an original Genius of a high order will have smoothed the way for all that he has in common with them; – and much he will have in common; but, for what is peculiarly his own, he will be called upon to clear and often to shape his own road: – he will be in the condition of Hannibal among the Alps.

And where lies the real difficulty of creating that taste by which a truly original Poet is to be relished? Is it in breaking the bonds of custom, in overcoming the prejudices of false refinement, and displacing the aversions of inexperience? Or, if he labour for an object which here and elsewhere I have proposed to myself, does it consist in divesting the Reader of the pride that induces him to dwell upon those points wherein Men differ from each other, to the exclusion of those in which all Men are alike, or the same; and in making him ashamed of the vanity that renders him insensible of the appropriate excellence which civil arrangements, less unjust than might appear, and Nature illimitable in her bounty, have conferred on Men who stand below him in the scale of society? Finally, does it lie in establishing that dominion over the spirits of Readers by which they are to be humbled and humanized, in order that they may be purified and exalted?

If these ends are to be attained by the mere communication of *knowledge*, it does *not* lie here. – TASTE, I would remind the Reader, like IMAGINATION, is a word which has been forced to extend its services far beyond the point to which philosophy would have confined them. It is a metaphor, taken from a *passive* sense of the human body, and transferred to things which are in their essence *not* passive, – to intellectual *acts* and *operations*. The word, imagination, has been overstrained, from impulses honourable to mankind, to meet the demands of the faculty which is perhaps the noblest of our nature. In the instance of taste, the process has been reversed; and from the prevalence of dispositions at once injurious and discreditable, – being no other than that selfishness which is the child of apathy, – which, as Nations decline in productive and creative power, makes them value themselves upon a presumed refinement of judging. Poverty of language is the primary cause of the use which we make of the word, imagination; but the word, Taste, has been stretched to the sense which it bears in modern Europe by habits of self-conceit, inducing that inversion in the order of things whereby a passive faculty is made paramount among the faculties conversant with the fine arts. Proportion and congruity, the requisite knowledge being supposed, are subjects upon which taste may be trusted; it is competent to this office; – for in its intercourse with these the mind is *passive*, and is affected painfully or pleasurably as by an instinct. But the profound and the exquisite in feeling, the lofty and universal in thought and imagination; or in ordinary language the pathetic and the sublime; – are neither of them, accurately speaking, objects of a faculty which could ever without a sinking in the spirit of Nations have been designated by the metaphor – *Taste*. And why? Because without the exertion of a co-operating *power* in the mind of the Reader, there can be no adequate sympathy with either of these emotions: without this auxiliar impulse elevated or profound passion cannot exist.

Passion, it must be observed, is derived from a word which signifies, *suffering*; but the connexion which suffering has with effort, with exertion, and *action*, is immediate and inseparable. How strikingly is this property of human nature exhibited by the fact, that, in popular language, to be in a passion, is to be angry! – But,

> Anger in hasty *words* or *blows*
> Itself discharges on its foes.

To be moved, then, by a passion, is to be excited, often to external, and always to internal, effort; whether for the continuance and strengthening of the passion, or for its suppression, accordingly as the course which it takes may be painful or pleasurable. If the latter, the soul must contribute to its support, or it never becomes vivid, – and soon languishes, and dies. And this brings us to the point. If every great Poet with whose writings men are familiar, in the highest exercise of his genius, before he can be thoroughly enjoyed, has to call forth and to communicate *power*, this service, in a still greater degree, falls upon an original Writer, at his first appearance in the world. – Of genius the only proof is, the act of doing well what is worthy to be done, and what was never done before: Of genius, in the fine arts, the only infallible sign is the widening the sphere of human sensibility, for the delight, honour, and benefit of human nature. Genius is the introduction of a new element into the intellectual universe: or, if that be not allowed, it is the application of powers to objects on which they had not before been exercised, or the employment of them in such a manner as to produce effects hitherto unknown. What is all this but an advance, or a conquest, made by the soul of the Poet? Is it to be supposed that the Reader can make progress of this kind, like an Indian Prince or General – stretched on his Palanquin, and borne by his Slaves? No, he is invigorated and inspirited by his Leader, in order that he may exert himself, for he cannot proceed in quiescence, he cannot be carried like a dead weight. Therefore to create taste is to call forth and bestow power, of which knowledge is the effect; and *there* lies the true difficulty.

As the pathetic participates of an *animal* sensation, it might seem – that, if the springs of this emotion were genuine, all men, possessed of competent knowledge of the facts and circumstances, would be instantaneously affected. And, doubtless, in the works of every true Poet will be found passages of that species of excellence, which is proved by effects immediate and universal. But there are emotions of the pathetic that are simple and direct, and others – that are complex and revolutionary; some – to which

the heart yields with gentleness, others, – against which it strug-
gles with pride: these varieties are infinite as the combinations of
circumstance and the constitutions of character. Remember, also,
that the medium through which, in poetry, the heart is to be
affected – is language; a thing subject to endless fluctuations and
arbitrary associations. The genius of the Poet melts these down
for his purpose; but they retain their shape and quality to him
who is not capable of exerting, within his own mind, a correspond-
ing energy. There is also a meditative, as well as a human, pathos;
an enthusiastic, as well as an ordinary, sorrow; a sadness that has
its seat in the depths of reason, to which the mind cannot sink
gently of itself – but to which it must descend by treading the
steps of thought. And for the sublime, – if we consider what are
the cares that occupy the passing day, and how remote is the
practice and the course of life from the sources of sublimity, in
the soul of Man, can it be wondered that there is little existing
preparation for a Poet charged with a new mission to extend its
kingdom, and to augment and spread its enjoyments?

Away, then, with the senseless iteration of the word, *popular*,
applied to new works in Poetry, as if there were no test of
excellence in this first of the fine arts but that all Men should run
after its productions, as if urged by an appetite, or constrained by
a spell! – The qualities of writing best fitted for eager reception
are either such as startle the world into attention by their audacity
and extravagance; or they are chiefly of a superficial kind, lying
upon the surfaces of manners; or arising out of a selection and
arrangement of incidents, by which the mind is kept upon the
stretch of curiosity, and the fancy amused without the trouble of
thought. But in everything which is to send the soul into herself,
to be admonished of her weakness or to be made conscious of her
power; – wherever life and nature are described as operated upon
by the creative or abstracting virtue of the imagination; wherever
the instinctive wisdom of antiquity and her heroic passions unit-
ing, in the heart of the Poet, with the meditative wisdom of later
ages, have produced that accord of sublimated humanity, which is
at once a history of the remote past and a prophetic annunciation
of the remotest future, *there*, the Poet must reconcile himself for a
season to few and scattered hearers. – Grand thoughts (and
Shakespeare must often have sighed over this truth) as they are

most naturally and most fitly conceived in solitude, so can they
not be brought forth in the midst of plaudits without some
violation of their sanctity. Go to a silent exhibition of the produc-
tions of the Sister Art, and be convinced that the qualities which
dazzle at first sight, and kindle the admiration of the multitude,
are essentially different from those by which permanent influence
is secured. Let us not shrink from following up these principles as
far as they will carry us, and conclude with observing – that there
never has been a period, and perhaps never will be, in which
vicious poetry, of some kind or other, has not excited more
zealous admiration, and been far more generally read, than good;
but this advantage attends the good, that the *individual*, as well as
the species, survives from age to age: whereas, of the depraved,
though the species be immortal the individual quickly *perishes*;
the object of present admiration vanishes, being supplanted by
some other as easily produced; which, though no better, brings
with it at least the irritation of novelty, – with adaptation, more
or less skilful, to the changing humours of the majority of those
who are most at leisure to regard poetical works when they first
solicit their attention.

Is it the result of the whole that, in the opinion of the Writer,
the judgement of the People is not to be respected? The thought
is most injurious; and could the charge be brought against him,
he would repel it with indignation. The People have already been
justified, and their eulogium pronounced by implication, when it
was said, above – that, of *good* Poetry, the *individual*, as well as
the species, *survives*. And how does it survive but through the
People? what preserves it but their intellect and their wisdom?

> – Past and future, are the wings
> On whose support, harmoniously conjoined,
> Moves the great Spirit of human knowledge –
> *MS*

The voice that issues from this Spirit, is that Vox populi which
the Deity inspires. Foolish must he be who can mistake for this a
local acclamation, or a transitory outcry – transitory though it be
for years, local though from a Nation. Still more lamentable is his
error, who can believe that there is anything of divine infallibility
in the clamour of that small though loud portion of the commu-

nity, ever governed by factitious influence, which, under the name of the PUBLIC, passes itself, upon the unthinking, for the PEOPLE. Towards the Public, the Writer hopes that he feels as much deference as it is entitled to: but to the People, philosophically characterized, and to the embodied spirit of their knowledge, so far as it exists and moves, at the present, faithfully supported by its two wings, the past and the future, his devout respect, his reverence, is due. He offers it willingly and readily; and, this done, takes leave of his Readers, by assuring them – that, if he were not persuaded that the Contents of these Volumes, and the Work to which they are subsidiary, evinced something of the 'Vision and the Faculty divine;' and that, both in words and things, they will operate in their degree, to extend the domain of sensibility for the delight, the honour, and the benefit of human nature, notwithstanding the many happy hours which he has employed in their composition, and the manifold comforts and enjoyments they have procured to him, he would not, if a wish could do it, save them from immediate destruction; – from becoming at this moment, to the world, as a thing that had never been.

Notes

Lines Written as a School Exercise

This, Wordsworth's earliest extant poem (composed aetat.15), was written on the occasion of the second centenary of Hawkshead School, celebrated in June 1785. It was first published in the posthumous *Memoirs* (1851), in which Wordsworth claimed that the verses were admired 'more than they deserved, for they were but a tame imitation of Pope's versification, and a little in his style' (see especially lines 85–6). The poem contains a number of eighteenth-century mannerisms: circumlocution (lines 1–4 ask, 'Has the school really existed two hundred years?'), abundant personification, Latinate and artificial diction, and constant classical allusions. 'Academus' Grove' (line 13), scene of Plato's school, was an expression used in William Beattie's *The Minstrel* (1771–4), II, liii. As is true of most poets, Wordsworth began writing steeped in the poetry of his own time. The version printed here follows DCMS 1.

'Science' (line 3) means 'learning'; 'Hebe' (line 20) was the handmaiden of the gods, associated with youthfulness; 'Edward's' (line 56) refers to Edward III, whose reign fell during the Hundred Years War; 'Sandys' (line 65) – pronounced as a monosyllable – was the archbishop who founded the school.

Beauty and Moonlight

This ode in tetrameter couplets (composed perhaps 1786) was apparently Wordsworth's first attempt at love poetry. The 'Mary' of line 4 is perhaps Mary Hutchinson, his future wife. This is one of Wordsworth's early poems that was borrowed (in altered form) by Coleridge to be published for profit in the *Morning Post* in 1798 (see J. W. Smyser, 'Coleridge's Use of Wordsworth's Juvenilia', *Publications of the Modern Language Society of America*, 65, 1950, pp. 419–26). The poem was first published in its present form in 1940.

Extract from the Conclusion of a Poem

This 'extract', revised from a passage near the end of 'The Vale of Esthwaite', was the earliest poem included in Wordsworth's collected poems and was composed probably 1787–8, with some work as early as 1786. From 1815 it was included among 'Poems Written in Youth'.

Its composition is described, and the poem itself paraphrased, in *The Prelude* (1850), VIII, 458–75; and in the *I. F. note*, Wordsworth also comments: 'Hawkshead. The beautiful image with which this poem concludes, suggested itself to me while I was resting in a boat along with my companions under the shade of a magnificent row of Sycamores, which then extended their branches from the shore of the promontory upon which stands the ancient, and at that time the more picturesque, Hall of Coniston ...' This row of sycamores is also described by Wordsworth, in an unpublished tour guide, as having 'once bordered the bay & promontory and in such a manner stretched their boughs over the margin of the lake that a boat might have moved under their shade as along a cloister' (Owen and Smyser, *Prose Works*, 1974, II, p. 309).

Written in Very Early Youth

This sonnet was probably composed during Wordsworth's years at Cambridge – late 1788 to the end of 1791 – but possibly up to early 1802, and was first published in the *Morning Post*, 13 February 1802. It was collected by Wordsworth among 'Miscellaneous Sonnets' from 1807 to 1843 and among 'Poems Written in Youth' in the final, 1850 edition.

'When slow from pensive twilight's latest gleams'

Another of the Cambridge sonnets (composed perhaps between approximately late 1788 and the end of 1791, possibly later), this poem was first published in 1977 in *William Wordsworth: The Poems* (Penguin English Poets).

'Sweet was the walk along the narrow lane'

This sonnet was composed late in Wordsworth's Cambridge career or while in France (that is, probably between June 1789 and April 1792, probably shortly before the latter date) and was first published in 1889. In the manuscript letter in which the only copy of the poem is contained, 'idle' in line 9 reads 'idol'.

Lines Written While Sailing

In its earliest version (joined to 'Remembrance of Collins ...') this poem was composed possibly between about late 1788 and the end of 1791 and, in its final version, between 29 March 1797 and 30 May 1798. It was first published (in its earliest version) in *Lyrical Ballads* (1798). Until 1843 it was collected under 'Poems Proceeding from Sentiment and Reflection', whereupon it was shifted to 'Poems Written in Youth'.

In the *I. F. note*, Wordsworth observed: 'The title is scarcely correct. It was during a solitary walk on the banks of Cam that I was first struck with this appearance, and applied it to my own feelings in the manner here expressed, changing the scene to the Thames, near Windsor. This, and the three stanzas of ... *Remembrance of Collins*, formed one piece: but upon the recommendation of Coleridge, the three last stanzas were separated from the other', in *Lyrical Ballads* (1800).

Critics of the poem have observed that it is not part of the experimentation of *Lyrical Ballads* but rather reflects its composition during the Cambridge years in both tone and the influence of William Bowles, the sonneteer (the first drafts were actually sonnets).

Remembrance of Collins

Originally part of the previous poem, this was separated in *Lyrical Ballads* (1800); it also shares the history of 'Lines Written . . .' in its categorization.

Richmond was the home of James Thomson and the scene of the funeral in William Collins's 'Ode on the Death of Thomson'. Wordsworth is imitating Collins's ode to lament Collins's own death; he is the 'Poet' in line 13, just as the 'later ditty' (14) refers to his ode. Collins's ode is quoted in line 18 – 'and oft suspend the dashing oar' – with 'him' italicized to point up the analogous situation.

The Female Vagrant

In part composed in 1791, but probably written between late July and September 1793, the first version was almost certainly completed by 23 May 1794 (some further work was done probably in 1795). The version printed here was first published in *Lyrical Ballads* (1798). It was collected from 1815 among 'Juvenile Pieces'. The 1798 text was taken from that part of a manuscript poem, *The Adventures on Salisbury Plain*, which tells the story of a female vagrant in her own words. After considerable revision it was again incorporated into a longer poem, *Guilt and Sorrow*, first published in 1842 and collected from 1845 among 'Poems Written in Youth'.

In the 'Advertisement, Prefixed to the First Edition' of *Guilt and Sorrow*, Wordsworth commented:

> Not less than one-third of the following poem, though it has from time to time been altered in the expression, was published so far back as the year 1798, under the title of 'The Female Vagrant'. The extract is of such length that an apology seems to be required for reprinting it here: but it was necessary to restore it to its original position, or the rest would have been unintelligible. The whole was written before the close of the year 1794, and I will detail, rather as matter of literary biography than for any other reason, the circumstances under which it was produced.
>
> During the latter part of the summer of 1793, having passed a month in the Isle of Wight, in view of the fleet which was then preparing for sea off Portsmouth at the commencement of the war, I left the place with melancholy forebodings. The American war was still fresh in memory. The struggle which was beginning, and which many thought would be brought to a speedy close by the irresistible arms of Great Britain being added to those of the allies, I was assured in my own mind would be of long continuance, and productive of distress and misery beyond all possible calculation. This conviction was pressed upon me by having been a witness, during a long residence in revolutionary France, of the spirit which prevailed in that country. After leaving the Isle of Wight, I spent two days in wandering on foot over Salisbury Plain, which, though cultivation was then widely spread through parts of it, had upon the whole a still more impressive appearance than it now retains.
>
> The monuments and traces of antiquity, scattered in abundance over that region, led me unavoidably to compare what we know or guess of those remote times with certain aspects of modern society, and with calamities, principally those consequent upon war, to which, more than

> other classes of men, the poor are subject. In those reflections, joined with particular facts that had come to my knowledge, the following stanzas originated.
>
> In conclusion, to obviate some distraction in the minds of those who are well acquainted with Salisbury Plain, it may be proper to say that, of the features described as belonging to it, one or two are taken from other desolate parts of England.

In a letter to Francis Wrangham (20 November 1795) Wordsworth remarked about the purpose of the poem: 'Its object is partly to expose the vices of the penal law and the calamities of war as they affect individuals.'

As usual with Wordsworth's verse, much of the poem was drawn from life. In the *I. F. note*, he remarks about the female vagrant: 'All that relates to her sufferings as a sailor's wife in America, and her condition of mind during her voyage home, were faithfully taken from the report made to me of her own case by a friend who had been subjected to the same trials and affected in the same way.'

In Chapter IV of *Biographia Literaria*, Coleridge commented on the first complete version of the poem *Salisbury Plain*:

> I was in my twenty-fourth year, when I had the happiness of knowing Mr Wordsworth personally, and while memory lasts, I shall hardly forget the sudden effect produced on my mind, by his recitation of a manuscript poem, which still remains unpublished, but of which the stanza, and tone of style, were the same as those of the 'Female Vagrant', as originally printed in the first volume of the 'Lyrical Ballads'. There was here no mark of strained thought, or forced diction, no crowd or turbulence of imagery, and, as the poet hath himself well described in his lines 'on re-visiting the Wye', manly reflection, and human associations had given both variety, and an additional interest to natural objects, which in the passion and appetite of the first love they had seemed to him neither to need or permit . . .
>
> It was not however the freedom from false taste, whether as to common defects, or to those more properly his own, which made so unusual an impression on my feelings immediately, and subsequently on my judgement. It was the union of deep feeling with profound thought; the fine balance of truth in observing, with the imaginative faculty in modifying the objects observed; and above all the original gift of spreading the tone, the *atmosphere*, and with it the depth and height of the ideal world around forms, incidents, and situations, of which, for the common view, custom had bedimmed all the lustre, had dried up the sparkle and the dew drops.

For a study of the poem, see Enid Welsford, *Salisbury Plain* (Blackwell, 1966). For a full edition of the various versions, see *The Salisbury Plain Poems*, ed. Stephen Gill, 1975.

Some of the words in the poem have changed meaning since the poem was written: 'strain' (line 95) means 'to clasp tightly' and 'amazed' (line 212) means 'bewildered'.

The Convict

This was the only poem to be published solely in the first edition of *Lyrical Ballads* (1798); it had appeared earlier in the *Morning Post* on 14 December 1797 (signed 'Mortimer', the original name of the hero of *The Borderers*). It was composed in 1796, perhaps early but more probably between 21 March and early October. It was not collected by Wordsworth.

Criticism has concerned itself with the poem as a possible collaboration with Coleridge and as typical of the magazine verse of the time.

Animal Tranquillity and Decay

The title in *Lyrical Ballads* (1798), where it was first published, was 'Old Man Travelling: Animal Tranquillity and Decay, a Sketch'. It was composed probably between the second half of 1796 and early June 1797. According to Wordsworth in 1843, the 'verses were an overflowing from *The Old Cumberland Beggar*'. In all collected editions, the poem was included among 'Poems Referring to the Period of Old Age'. Six lines were dropped from the end in 1815:

> I asked him whither he was bound, and what
> The object of his journey: he replied
> That he was going many miles to take
> A last leave of his son, a mariner,
> Who from a sea-fight had been brought to Falmouth,
> And there was dying in a hospital.

Critics have noted that the poem (with the ending dropped) focuses on an interesting if peculiar state of being, and thus they prefer the shortened version, although at least one critic has argued for a unity between the two parts. In the Preface to *Lyrical Ballads* (1802), Wordsworth claimed that the purpose of the poem was 'to attempt to sketch characters under the influence of the less impassioned feelings . . .'

Lines Left upon a Seat in a Yew-tree

Written probably at Racedown just before the move to Alfoxden (perhaps after 8 February but by July 1797), this blank-verse poem was first published in *Lyrical Ballads* (1798). Until 1845, it was included among 'Poems of Sentiment and Reflection', and in the final edition (1849-50), among 'Poems Written in Youth'.

In the *I. F. note*, Wordsworth identified the location of the tree as once growing on a spot that was on his 'favourite walk, in the evenings during the latter part of [his] school-time' at Hawkshead, and he also identified the recluse as 'a gentleman of the neighborhood', now known to be Reverend Mr W. Braethwaite of Satter-how.

Criticism has attended largely to the philosophical content of the poem, but more especially the autobiographical basis of the recluse - how much the philosophy reflects Wordsworth's rejection of William Godwin, and how much the poem shows the influence, perhaps even collaboration, of Coleridge.

To My Sister

Probably composed 1-9 March 1798 (most probably 6, 8 or 9 March), this poem was first published in *Lyrical Ballads* (1798) and was classified among 'Poems of Sentiment and Reflection' from 1815.

The original title was 'Lines Written at a Small Distance from My House, and Sent, by My Little Boy to the Person to Whom They Are Addressed'. In the *I. F.*

note, Wordsworth elaborated: 'Composed in front of Alfoxden House. My little boy-messenger on this occasion was the son of Basil Montagu. The larch mentioned in the first stanza was standing when I revisited the place in May, 1841, more than forty years after.' Critics observe that the poem marked a new, more personal and lyrical step in Wordsworth's poetry.

Goody Blake and Harry Gill

This poem, which perhaps was as close as Wordsworth got to ballad imitation, was written probably between 7 March and about 16 May 1798 and was first published in *Lyrical Ballads* (1798). Until 1845, when the poem was moved in collected editions to 'Miscellaneous Poems', it was included among 'Poems of the Imagination', even though, as Wordsworth observed, it refers rather 'to the imagination than [is] produced by it'.

In the Advertisement to the 1798 volume, Wordsworth claimed the poem was 'founded on a well-authenticated fact which happened in Warwickshire', as recorded in Erasmus Darwin's *Zoönomia* (1794–6). In the Preface to *Lyrical Ballads* (1802), Wordsworth called the poem 'one of the rudest of this collection' and added: 'I wished to draw attention to the truth that the power of the human imagination is sufficient to produce such changes even in our physical nature as might almost appear miraculous.'

The critical discussions of the poem approach it as part of the central experiment of *Lyrical Ballads* (one of the 'curse poems') and examine the artistic techniques, especially the 'portrayal' of the narrator.

'*Canty*' (line 39) means 'cheerful' in north-country dialect.

The Complaint of a Forsaken Indian Woman

This poem was written probably between early March and about 16 May 1798 and was first published in *Lyrical Ballads* (1798). It appeared in all collected editions under 'Poems Founded on the Affections'.

As Wordsworth himself said in the *I. F. note*, he had been reading Samuel Hearne's *A Journey from Prince of Wales's Fort in Hudson Bay to the Northern Ocean* (London, 1795), from which he got the information and even some of the wording for the note prefixed to the poem. He also said the poem was written *for* the *Lyrical Ballads*. In the Preface he said his purpose was 'to follow the fluxes and refluxes of the mind when agitated by the great and simple affections of our nature . . . by accompanying the last struggles of a human being, at the approach of death, cleaving in solitude to life and society . . .' It is usually grouped by critics with 'Her Eyes are Wild', especially for the similar absence of a narrator (after the first stanza of the latter poem) and the use of the first person.

Her Eyes are Wild

Known as 'The Mad Mother' from 1798 to 1805, this poem was composed probably between early March and about 16 May 1798 and was first published in *Lyrical Ballads* (1798). Initially included among 'Poems Founded on the Affections', it was transferred from 1827 to 1832 to 'Poems of the Imagination' but was returned to its original classification thereafter.

In the Preface to *Lyrical Ballads* (1802), Wordsworth said that his plan in writing the poem was 'to follow the fluxes and refluxes of the mind when agitated by the great and simple affections of our nature ... by tracing the maternal passion through many of its more subtle windings ...' This plan does not suggest the various sources Wordsworth followed, especially 'Lady Ann Bothwell's Lament', a traditional ballad included in Percy's *Reliques* (1765). The 'Lament' is a monologue with a similar theme and stanza form, as well as verbal echoes: compare line 5 of the ballad ('Balow, my boy, thy mother's joy') to lines 41–2.

Wordsworth, as usual, went beyond his sources. In line 10, the narrator remarks that the mother spoke in English; in a letter to John Kenyon (late autumn 1836), Wordsworth explained: 'Though she came from far, English was her native tongue – which shows her either to be of these Islands, or a North American. On the latter supposition, while the distance removes her from us, the fact of her speaking our language brings us at once into close sympathy with her.'

Coleridge (*Biographia Literaria*, Chapter XXII) chose lines 39–40 to comment on Wordsworth's imaginative technique:

> They were so expressive of that deranged state, in which from the increased sensibility the sufferer's attention is abruptly drawn off by every trifle, and in the same instant plucked back again by the one despotic thought, and bringing home with it, by the blending, *fusing* power of Imagination and Passion, the alien object to which it had been so abruptly diverted, no longer an alien but an ally and an inmate.

The Idiot Boy

This poem, part of the central experiment of *Lyrical Ballads* (1798), was composed probably between early March and about 16 May 1798. It was collected among 'Poems Founded on the Affections'.

Wordsworth comments on the composition in the *I. F. note*:

> The last stanza – 'The Cocks did crow to-whoo, to-whoo, and the sun did shine so cold' – was the foundation of the whole. The words were reported to me by my dear friend, Thomas Poole; but I have since heard the same repeated of other Idiots. Let me add that this long poem was composed in the groves of Alfoxden, almost extempore; not a word, I believe, being corrected, though one stanza was omitted. I mention this in gratitude to those happy moments, for, in truth, I never wrote anything with so much glee.

Wordsworth always had a high opinion of this poem: In *The Prelude* (1805), he uses it to justify his poetic career (XIV, lines 406–8). In the Preface to *Lyrical Ballads* (1802), he claimed the purpose of the poem was 'to follow the fluxes and refluxes of the mind when agitated by the great and simple affections of our nature ... by tracing the maternal passion through many of its more subtle windings ...' In a long defence of the poem in a letter to John Wilson (June 1802), Wordsworth also claimed he was attempting to change negative attitudes toward idiots.

Critics have dealt with these educational aspects of 'The Idiot Boy' through the conventional eighteenth-century plot of the lost child. But far and away the most attention has been paid to literary influences, including the traditional ballad devices Wordsworth imitates (for example, rhetorical questions, noun–pronoun combinations [the man he] and fill-ins). The largest single literary influence was Gottfried August Bürger's *Lenore* (1773), especially its tempo (with many interjections) and the abrupt opening and closure, but there were others: Robert Burns's *Tam O'Shanter*, with its combination of tenderness and humour, as well as its celebration of life, and William Cowper's *The Diverting History of John Gilpin* (1782), xxiv, which provides a verbal echo (compare lines 115–16 to 'His horse . . ./ What thing upon his back had got / Did wonder more and more'). Novels, especially Cervantes's *Don Quixote*, offered heroes similar to Betty, comic but not contemptible.

The Last of the Flock

Another of the central experiments of *Lyrical Ballads* (1798), this poem was composed probably between early March and about 16 May 1798. It was classified from 1815 among 'Poems Founded on the Affections'.

In the *I. F. note*, Wordsworth claimed that the poem was 'produced at the same time and for the same purpose' as the 'Complaint of a Forsaken Indian Woman' and that the incident actually 'occurred in the village of Holford, close by Alfoxden'. In justifying the use of the word *alone* (line 4), Wordsworth expanded on the background of the poem (letter to John Kenyon, late autumn 1836):

> Funerals, alas! we have all attended, and most of us must have seen then weeping in the public roads . . . I was a witness to a sight of this kind the other day in the streets of Kendal . . . But for my own part, notwithstanding what has here been said in verse, I never in my whole life saw a man weep *alone* in the roads; but a friend of mine did see this poor man weeping *alone*, with the Lamb, the last of his flock, in his arms.

We are Seven

Written probably between early March and about 16 May 1798, this is another of the more experimental poems in *Lyrical Ballads* (1798). It was classified from 1815 among the 'Poems Referring to the Period of Childhood'.

In the *I. F. note*, the composition is described:

> Written at Alfoxden in the spring of 1798, under circumstances somewhat remarkable. The little girl who is the heroine I met within the area of Goodrich Castle in the year 1793 . . . I composed it while walking in the grove at Alfoxden. My friends will not deem it too trifling to relate that while walking to and fro I composed the last stanza first having begun with the last line. When it was all but finished, I came in and recited to Mr. Coleridge and my Sister, and said 'A prefatory stanza must be added, and I should sit down to our little tea-meal with greater pleasure if my task were finished.' I mentioned in substance what I wished to be expressed, and Coleridge immediately threw off the stanza thus:

> 'A little child, dear brother Jem,'

> – I objected to the rhyme, 'dear brother Jem,' as being ludicrous, but we all enjoyed the joke of hitching-in our friend, James Tobin's name, who was familiarly called Jem.

In 1815 the opening line was shortened to its present form. On revisiting Goodrich Castle in 1841, Wordsworth could not find traces of the girl, as he 'did not even know her name'.

In the Preface to *Lyrical Ballads* (1802), Wordsworth described the poem as dealing with: 'the perplexity and obscurity which in childhood attend our notion of death, or rather our utter inability to admit that notion'. As a child, Wordsworth himself experienced such perplexity, as we are informed in the *I. F. note* to 'Ode: Intimations':

> Nothing was more difficult for me in childhood than to admit the notion of death as a state applicable to my own being. I have said, elsewhere [the first stanza of *We are Seven* is quoted]. But it was not so much from [feelings] of animal vivacity that my difficulty came as from a sense of the indomitableness of the spirit within me.

Criticism of the poem deals mainly with the opposition of the narrator and the child, variously seen as reason vs. intuition, physical vs. spiritual and culture vs. Nature. In this regard, the poem is often discussed along with 'Anecdote for Fathers', which it so clearly resembles.

Simon Lee

Like the other experimental poems of *Lyrical Ballads* (1798), this poem was written probably between early March and about 16 May 1798. It was heavily revised over the years, especially the first seven stanzas, and was classified among 'Poems of Sentiment and Reflection' from 1815.

In the *I. F. note*, Wordsworth identified Simon:

> This old man had been huntsman to the Squires of Alfoxden, which, at the time we occupied it, belonged to a minor. The old man's cottage stood upon the common, a little way from the entrance to Alfoxden Park . . . The fact was as mentioned in the poem; and I have, after an interval of 45 years, the image of the old man as fresh before my eyes as if I had seen him yesterday. The expression when the hounds are out, 'I dearly love their voices' was word for word from his own lips.

Wordsworth has clearly fictionalized the background, for Cardigan (line 1) is a county in central Wales. According to a recent critic, he also may have got 'Ivor Hall' from a poem by Evan Evans, a Welsh poet of the late eighteenth century. 'But, oh the heavy change!' (line 25) is taken from Milton's *Lycidas* (line 37.) In the Preface to *Lyrical Ballads* (1802), Wordsworth claimed the purpose of the poem is 'to follow the fluxes and refluxes of the mind when agitated by the great and simple affections of our nature . . . by placing my reader in the way of receiving from ordinary moral sensations another and more salutary impression than we are accustomed to receive from them'.

The criticism of the poem has emphasized the role of the narrator and the deft handling of tone, used, along with other devices, to involve readers in order to re-educate them.

The Thorn

This controversial poem was probably composed between 19 March and about 16

May 1798 and was first published in *Lyrical Ballads* (1798). It was collected from 1815 among 'Poems of the Imagination' and was frequently revised.

In the *I. F. note*, Wordsworth discussed the genesis of the poem:

> Alfoxden. 1798. Arose out of my observing, on the ridge of Quantock Hill, on a stormy day, a thorn which I had often passed in calm and bright weather without noticing it. I said to myself, 'Cannot I by some invention do as much to make this Thorn permanently an impressive object as the storm has made it to my eyes at this moment?' I began the poem accordingly, and composed it with great rapidity.

The entry in Dorothy Wordsworth's *Journal* for 19 March 1798 reads: 'William and Basil and I walked to the hill-tops, a very cold, bleak day. We were met on our return by a severe hailstorm. William wrote some lines describing a stunted thorn'; and for 20 April 1798: 'Came home the Crookham way, by the thorn, and the "little muddy pond"'.

In the Advertisement to *Lyrical Ballads* (1798), Wordsworth wrote: 'The poem of The Thorn, as the reader will soon discover, is not supposed to be spoken in the author's own person: the character of the loquacious narrator will sufficiently show itself in the course of the story.' On the persona of this narrator, Wordsworth expanded in a note to later editions of *Lyrical Ballads*:

> This Poem ought to have been preceded by an introductory Poem, which I have been prevented from writing by never having felt myself in a mood when it was probable that I should write it well. The character which I have here introduced speaking is sufficiently common. The Reader will perhaps have a general notion of it, if he has ever known a man, a Captain of a small trading vessel, for example, who being past the middle age of life, had retired upon an annuity or small independent income to some village or country town of which he was not a native, or in which he had not been accustomed to live. Such men, having little to do, become credulous and talkative from indolence; and from the same cause, and other predisposing causes by which it is probable that such men may have been affected, they are prone to superstition. On which account it appeared to me proper to select a character like this to exhibit some of the general laws by which superstition acts upon the mind. Superstitious men are almost always men of slow faculties and deep feelings; their minds are not loose, but adhesive; they have a reasonable share of imagination, by which word I mean the faculty which produces impressive effects out of simple elements; but they are utterly destitute of fancy, the power by which pleasure and surprise are excited by sudden varieties of situation and an accumulated imagery.
>
> It was my wish in this poem to show the manner in which such men cleave to the same ideas; and to follow the turns of passion, always different, yet not palpably different, by which their conversation is swayed. I had two objects to attain; first, to represent a picture which should not be unimpressive, yet consistent with the character that should describe it; secondly, while I adhered to the style in which such persons describe, to take care that words, which in their minds are impregnated with passion, should likewise convey passion to Readers who are not accustomed to sympathize with men feeling in that manner or using such language. It seemed to me

that this might be done by calling in the assistance of Lyrical and rapid Metre. It was necessary that the Poem, to be natural, should in reality move slowly; yet I hoped that, by the aid of the metre, to those who should at all enter into the spirit of the Poem, it would appear to move quickly. The Reader will have the kindness to excuse this note, as I am sensible that an introductory Poem is necessary to give this Poem its full effect.

Several literary sources for 'The Thorn' have been pointed out. One is William Taylor of Norwich's translation of Gottfried August Bürger's ballad, called by Taylor 'The Lass of Fair Wone', published in the *Monthly Magazine* in 1796, which has similar incidents and even the detail of the pond. The influence here is even clearer in the earlier version of lines 32–3 (revised in 1820): 'I've measured it from side to side: / 'Tis three feet long and two feet wide.' Compare Bürger's ballad (lines 179–80): her skull 'seems to eye the barren grave / Three spans in length, below'. The other sources are variants of an anonymous ballad which likewise contain similar incidents, as well as the detail of the thorn bush – Wordsworth had copied one of these ballads in a commonplace book.

Martha Ray (line 105) was the name of the mother of Basil Montagu, Wordsworth's companion on the walk on 19 March (see extract from Dorothy Wordsworth's *Journal*, above). She was the well-known mistress of the Earl of Sandwich and had been shot in public by a rejected suitor in 1779. Wordsworth must have known she was Montagu's mother.

Beginning with his own contemporaries, the reputation of this, probably the most experimental poem in *Lyrical Ballads*, has been stormy; it has in fact been found a failure a good deal more often than a success. More recent studies have tended to divide over acceptance of Wordsworth's own explanations (given above) of his intentions in writing the poem. For Wordsworth insists on his use of a persona, and the resulting poem has been called a dramatic monologue a number of times, although this view has also been rejected. In addition, several critics have discovered a moral purpose in the poem: an indirect attack by the poet on gossip and stock responses.

Lines Written in Early Spring

One of the more experimental poems in *Lyrical Ballads* (1798), this was composed between probably early April (possibly early March) and about 16 May 1798 and was collected later among 'Poems Proceeding from Sentiment and Reflection'.

In the *I. F. note*, Wordsworth described the scene of composition:

> Actually composed while I was sitting by the side of the brook that runs down from the Comb, in which stands the village of Alford, through the grounds of Alfoxden. It was a chosen resort of mine. The brook fell down a sloping rock so as to make a waterfall considerable for that country, and across the pool below had fallen a tree, an ash, if I rightly remember, from which rose perpendicularly boughs in search of the light interrupted by the deep shade above. The boughs bore leaves of green that for want of sunshine had faded into almost lily-white; and from the underside of this natural sylvan bridge depended long and beautiful tresses of ivy which waved gently in the breeze that might poetically speaking be called the breath of the waterfall. This motion varied of course in proportion to the power of the water in the brook.

Critics deal with the open didacticism of the poem that works through the use of a poet-persona not far from a representation of Wordsworth himself. The qualified animism (lines 11–20) has also received considerable attention.

Anecdote for Fathers

Another of the more experimental poems of *Lyrical Ballads* (1798), this was composed between probably early April (possibly early March) and about 16 May 1798. It was collected among 'Poems Referring to the Period of Childhood' and underwent considerable revision over the years.

Wordsworth identified people and places in the *I. F. note*:

> This was suggested in front of Alfoxden. The boy was a son of my friend, Basil Montagu, who had been two or three years under our care. The name of Kilve is from a village on the Bristol Channel, about a mile from Alfoxden; and the name of Liswyn Farm was taken from a beautiful spot on the Wye.

From 1798 to 1843, the poem carried a subtitle variously worded: 'showing how the art [practice] of Lying may be taught'. In 1845, this was replaced by the present motto, which is a Latin translation by Eusebius (*Preparatio Evangelica*, VI, v) of a Greek line from Porphyro that purports to be the warning from Apollo to any who would try to coerce the oracle: 'Restrain your violence, for I shall lie if you force me.' For the phrase 'cast in beauty's mould' (line 3), see Bishop Percy's version of *The Children in the Wood* (line 20).

Criticism of the poem is usually linked with 'We are Seven', which it resembles in technique, story and the clash between intuition and reason.

Expostulation and Reply

This poem was written probably 23 May 1798 or very shortly after (almost certainly by 12 June) and was first published in *Lyrical Ballads* (1798). From 1815, it was classified among 'Poems of Sentiment and Reflection'.

In the *I. F. note*, Wordsworth said this directly polemical poem was 'a favourite among the Quakers, as I have learnt on many occasions. It was composed in front of the house at Alfoxden in the spring of 1798.'

The poem is most often linked to 'The Tables Turned': the title refers back to 'Expostulation and Reply'; the narrator of 'The Tables Turned' takes up the offensive; and the diction contains phrasings found in the earlier poem ('up! up!' for example). The 'Matthew' (line 15) who opposes 'William's' views was probably William Hazlitt, for in the Advertisement to *Lyrical Ballads* (1798), Wordsworth claimed the setting of the poem 'arose out of conversation with a friend who was somewhat unreasonably attached to modern books of Moral Philosophy'. William Hazlitt argued with Wordsworth about metaphysics at Nether Stowey, where Hazlitt visited Coleridge in 1798 – see Hazlitt's essay 'My First Acquaintance with Poets'.

Critics of the poem have seen it as serious in general intent, even though containing humorous exaggeration.

The Tables Turned

Composition, publication and classification are identical to the previous poem, to which it is clearly related by title and parallel phrasings, although the issues go far beyond the conflict between reading and passive reception found in the previous poem.

The same exaggeration continues here in any case; compare Wordsworth's views provided in a later *I. F. note* (to 'This Lawn, a carpet all alive'):

> Some are of opinion that the habit of analysing, decomposing, and anatomizing is inevitably unfavourable to the perception of beauty. People are led into this mistake by overlooking the fact that such processes being to a certain extent within the reach of a limited intellect, we are apt to ascribe to them that insensibility of which they are in truth the effect and not the cause. Admiration and love, to which all knowledge truly vital must tend, are felt by men of real genius in proportion as their discoveries in natural Philosophy are enlarged; and the beauty in form of a plant or an animal is not made less but more apparent as a whole by more accurate insight into its constituent properties and powers. A *Savant* who is not also a Poet in soul and a religionist in heart is a feeble and unhappy Creature.

Lines Composed a Few Miles above Tintern Abbey

'Tintern Abbey' was probably composed between 11 and 13 July 1798 (possibly begun 10 July, possibly finished 14 July), was first published in *Lyrical Ballads* (1798) and was collected from 1815 among 'Poems of the Imagination'.

Wordsworth describes the circumstances of composition in the *I. F. note*:

> July 1798. No poem of mine was composed under circumstances more pleasant for me to remember than this. I began it upon leaving Tintern, after crossing the Wye, and concluded it just as I was entering Bristol in the evening, after a ramble of 4 or 5 days, with my sister. Not a line of it was altered, and not any part of it written down till I reached Bristol. It was published immediately after . . .

In a note appended to the poem from 1800 to 1805, Wordsworth commented further: 'I have not ventured to call this poem an Ode; but it was written with a hope that in the transitions, and the impassioned music of the versification would be found the principal requisites of that species of composition.'

Verbal and rhythmic echoes from eighteenth-century poetry occur frequently in the poem (see Mary Jacobus, *Tradition and Experiment in Wordsworth's Lyrical Ballads*, 1976, and John Hayden, 'The Road to Tintern Abbey', *The Wordsworth Circle*, 1981).

There are a number of other echoes of a popular guidebook to the region. The phrasing in lines 7-8 and the smoke of line 17 may come from Gilpin's *Observations on the River Wye* (1782): 'Many of the furnaces, on the banks of the river, consume charcoal, which is manufactured on the spot; and the smoke, which is frequently seen issuing from the sides of the hills; and spreading its thin veil over a part of them, beautifully breaks their lines, and unites them with the sky' (p. 12).

Wordsworth wrote notes to two passages in the poem. He commented on line 4:

'The river is not affected by the tides a few miles above Tintern.' He also explained a borrowing in line 106: 'This line has a close resemblance to an admirable line of Young's, the exact expression of which I do not recollect.' The work in question is Young's *Night Thoughts* (1742–4), VI, lines 417, 424: 'Senses . . . half create the wondrous world they see.'

Besides providing information on the semi-industrial nature of the Wye valley, Gilpin discussed at some length the homeless beggars who inhabited the ruins of the abbey, thus perhaps bringing on Wordsworth's 'vagrant dwellers' (line 20). The 'Hermit' (lines 21–2) may result from another comment by Gilpin: 'Every thing around breathes an air so calm, and tranquil; so sequestered from the commerce of life, that it is easy to conceive, a man of warm imagination, in monkish times, might have been allured by such a scene to become an inhabitant of it' (p. 32).

Some echoes come from other sources. The phrasing in line 33 should be compared to Milton's Preface to *The Judgment of Martin Bucer Concerning Divorce*: '. . . Whereby good men in the best portion of their lives'; and the phrase 'evil tongues' (line 128) was used in *Paradise Lost*, VII, line 26. Line 110 is remarkably similar to line 22 of Akenside's 'Pleasures of Imagination' (1744): 'The guide, the guardian of their lovely sports'.

'Genial' (line 113) means both cheerful *and* creative – a play on words pointing up their common root which is often also made by Coleridge.

Everyone who deals with 'Tintern Abbey' agrees that it is a complex poem, and it is this complexity that has produced a wide range of critical response. All commentators acknowledge the greatness of the poem, yet there are a good many adverse criticisms along the way.

Many topographical elegies were written in the eighteenth century, notably by Mark Akenside and William Cowper. Much of the theme is likewise not original – the attempt to understand man's relationship to Nature. Many critics mention the speaker's problem in reconciling his own changing self and the essential permanence of Nature, as well as the other stark contrasts in the poem.

The ensuing mixture of certainty and doubts in the poem (seen in the many qualifications) is both attacked as destabilizing and defended as part of the argument directed towards Wordsworth's true audience, Coleridge and Dorothy, both sceptical for different reasons (see Richard Matlak, *Studies in Romanticism*, 1986).

A number of individual passages have been scrutinized and questioned. Chief among these are lines 93–102, which William Empson (*Seven Types of Ambiguity*, 1930) found to have unclear syntax, thus inciting a variety of defences. Seeing 'into the life of things' (line 49) is another phrase usually taken to signify the mystical or visionary, although at times it has been interpreted along non-spiritual lines.

A final line to be considered – 'the still, sad music of humanity' (line 91) – has been interpreted as either awareness of death or, more usually, general human suffering, and is usually taken to be at the moral centre of the poem. The examples of suffering given in the poem, however, are often seen as insufficiently great evils to warrant such phrasing, while the real examples – the beggars described by Gilpin as inhabiting the ruin – are largely ignored, and may even have been responsible for shifting the scene 'a few miles' (as specified in the title) from the abbey, the centre of popular tours of the valley.

The structure of the poem has also been found wanting, especially in what some see as the anticlimactic address to the companion at the end, also interpreted as a sudden change from what was thought to be a monologue. Defences, when considered necessary, run from what is taken as a natural progression of thoughts and associations in the poem, to Wordsworth's reliance on the form of an impromptu Pindaric ode, to a classical rhetorical structure in five parts (not reflected in the paragraphing), the result of Wordsworth's classical education.

A minor consideration is the question of place, already mentioned, and of time given in the title. There is a possibility that the time given in line 1, 'five years' earlier, did not refer to 1793 but 1791, the date of a possibly earlier tour more in keeping with Wordsworth's joyful mood in the poem. Even the day of composition, 13 July, one scholar has suggested, was perhaps changed from the real date of completion, 14 July, to avoid any political link with the anniversary of Bastille Day.

The Reverie of Poor Susan

Probably composed between 30 March 1797 and 13 August 1800, this poem was first published in Lyrical Ballads (1800) as 'Poor Susan'. The expanded title (given in 1815) is a translation of the title of a poem by Gottfried August Bürger, Das Arme Süsschen's Traum (1781). From 1815 it was included among 'Poems of the Imagination'.

Wordsworth commented in the I. F. note: 'This arose out of my observation of the affecting music of these birds hanging in this way in the London streets during the freshness and stillness of the Spring morning.'

In a letter to Wordsworth (28 April 1815), Charles Lamb wrote:

> Susan stood for the representative of poor Rus in Urbe [country in the city]. There was quite enough to stamp the moral of the thing never to be forgotten. 'Fast volumes of vapour' &c. The last verse of Susan was to be got rid of at all events. It threw a kind of dubiety upon Susan's moral conduct. Susan is a servant maid. I see her trundling her mop and contemplating the whirling phenomenon thro' blurred optics; but to term her a poor outcast seems as much as to say that poor Susan was no better than she should be, which I trust was not what you meant to express.

Perhaps because of such concerns, the original final stanza was dropped earlier (1802):

> Poor Outcast! return – to receive thee once more
> The house of thy Father will open its door,
> And thou once again, in thy plain russet gown,
> May'st hear the thrush sing from a tree of its own.

In a note (1815) to 'The Farmer of Tilsbury Vale', Wordsworth asked the reader to compare its real-life picture to 'the imaginative one of "The Reverie of Poor Susan"' and remarked (in the I. F. note to 'The Farmer') that 'the latter part of the poem, perhaps, requires some apology as being too much of an echo to the "Reverie of Poor Susan"'.

All three streets mentioned in the poem (Wood, Lothbury and Cheapside) are situated in the City of London, the mercantile district.

Recent criticism of the poem has tended to work from Lamb's suggestion that Susan may be a prostitute, except for a convincing article by F. H. Langman (Southern Review, 1978), who argues that it really concerns Susan's loss of the visionary capacity.

A Night-Piece

Probably composed mainly on 25 January 1798 (the first version at least was completed by 5 March 1798), this poem was first published in 1815 and included from then on among 'Poems of the Imagination'.

In the *I. F. note*, Wordsworth provides background to the poem: 'Composed on the road between Nether Stowey and Alfoxden, extempore. I distinctly recollect the very moment when I was struck, as described "He looks up at the clouds, etc."' A description of the same phenomenon occurs in Dorothy Wordsworth's *Journal* (25 January 1798):

> Went to Poole's after tea. The sky spread over with one continuous cloud, whitened by the light of the moon, which, though her dim shape were seen, did not throw forth so strong a light as to chequer the earth with shadows. At once the clouds seemed to cleave asunder, and left her in the centre of a black-blue vault. She sailed along, followed by multitudes of stars, small, and bright, and sharp. Their brightness seemed concentrated (half-moon).

This poem has attracted considerable attention in the last few years, most probably because of the recent view of Wordsworth as a visionary poet. The most illuminating of these critics is Kenneth Johnston, who used the poem as a paradigm of one of two kinds of visionary poem (*New Perspectives on Coleridge and Wordsworth*, ed. G. Hartman, 1972). Johnston is especially good on the function of the stylistic eccentricities of the poem.

The Old Cumberland Beggar

Probably written between 25 January and 5 March 1798 (with much revision before 10 October 1800), this poem was first published in *Lyrical Ballads* (1800) and was collected in all editions among 'Poems Referring to the Period of Old Age'.

In the *I. F. note*, Wordsworth commented:

> Observed, and with great benefits to my own heart, when I was a child: written at Racedown and Alfoxden ... The political economists were about that time beginning their war upon mendicity in all its forms, and by implication, if not directly, on Almsgiving also.

'HOUSE, misnamed of INDUSTRY' (line 179) refers to the workhouse, where work was supposed to be provided (but sometimes wasn't) for able-bodied paupers in return for food and lodgings provided by the parish. (For a description of the changes in the Poor Laws that were taking place at the time, see T. W. Thompson, *Wordsworth's Hawkshead*, 1970, pp. 276–81.)

There are several literary echoes in the poem. 'Hill and dale' (line 49) occurs in *Paradise Lost* VI, line 641, and 'the cottage curs' (line 61) in William Beattie's 'The Minstrel' (1771–4), I, line 39. Other words have obsolete meanings: 'easy' (line 116) means 'comfortable'; 'monitor' (line 123) means 'reminder'; 'chartered' (line 175) means 'privileged, unrestrained'; and 'free of' (line 183) means 'allowed the use or enjoyment of'.

Criticism of the poem has tended to debate whether Wordsworth was indifferent to the plight of the beggar and to social justice in general. Frequent mention is made to other contemporary works concerned with the same social issues.

The most useful criticism is a close analysis of the poem by Cleanth Brooks (*From Sensibility to Romanticism*, ed. F. Hilles and H. Bloom, 1965), who notes the non-modern ideas, the honesty and realism, the subtlety and the rhetoric.

'*A whirl-blast from behind the hill*'

Probably composed on 19 March 1798, this poem was first published in *Lyrical Ballads* (1800) and from 1815 was collected among 'Poems of the Fancy'.

Wordsworth identified both the scene of the poem and place of composition in the *I. F. note*: 'Observed in the holly grove at Alfoxden, where these verses were written . . .' Dorothy also described the occasion (*Journal*, 18 March 1798): 'On our return [from Nether Stowey to Alfoxden] we sheltered under the hollies during a hailshower. The withered leaves danced with the hailstones. William wrote a description of the storm.'

'Robin Good-fellow' (line 20) is another name for Puck.

Four lines were dropped from the end of the poem in 1815:

> Oh! grant me, Heaven, a heart at ease,
> That I may never cease to find,
> Even in appearances like these,
> Enough to nourish and to stir my mind!

[THE LUCY POEMS]

The 'Lucy poems' make up the one group that requires a separate introduction because they have presented so many problems to critics over the years. Some question whether there is in fact a group of poems at all – a proposition put forward by H. S. Davies in 1965 (*Essays in Criticism*). Then, if one accepts that there is a group, there is the issue of *which* poems belong to it. Most critics see five in the group (as given here in the text), but others add 'Lucy Gray', 'Louisa' or even 'The Danish Boy'.

Wordsworth seems to have been almost totally indifferent to the order of the five poems, placing them in two different categories in the first collected edition of 1815. Undeterred, many critics continue to argue for one order or another, for an order is essential when arguing for an integrated whole with some sort of progression or unified pattern. Still others run all the 'Lucy poems' together and discuss them as if they are one poem.

A further 'problem', one that seems unnecessary and non-productive, is autobiographical: who was Lucy and what was Wordsworth's actual relation to her? This issue was popular early on, and one critic narrowed Lucy down to a particular girl in a particular Welsh valley. Critics today tend to see Lucy's identity as irrelevant, although recent psycho-biographical studies have identified Lucy as Dorothy Wordsworth, for one reason or another disposed of by the poet under the poetic cover of Lucy's death.

Such efforts towards identification, of course, are intended to uncover the meaning of the 'Lucy poems', the last and most important problem. These poems, individually and collectively, are sufficiently difficult to interpret that one or more have been used to probe the general question of poetic meaning (see E. D. Hirsch in his early study of literary meaning, *Validity in Interpretation*, 1967, and Brian Caraker in his recent work on hermeneutics, *Wordsworth's 'Slumber' and the*

Problematics of Reading, 1991). The best brief readings of all the Lucy poems are by Geoffrey Durrant (*William Wordsworth*, 1969).

'*A slumber did my spirit seal*'

This 'Lucy poem' was probably composed between 6 October and December 1798 (possibly in January 1799) and was first published in *Lyrical Ballads* (1800). From 1815 it was collected among 'Poems of the Imagination'.

In a letter to Thomas Poole (6 April 1799), Coleridge quotes the poem and remarks: 'Some months ago Wordsworth transmitted to me a most sublime epitaph – whether it had any reality, I cannot say. – Most probably, in some gloomier moment he had fancied the moment in which his sister might die.'

'Motion' and 'force' (line 5) are terms used in Newtonian physics. But the first term may, along with 'rolled' (line 7), also involve a literary echo: compare William Habington's 'Labia Mea': 'Time controls / Our pride, whose motion all things rolls'.

Because of its dramatic economy, this poem is probably considered the most difficult of the 'Lucy poems'. It is easily the most attended to. Analysis of the poem has been used by a number of critics to demonstrate various literary approaches, from Freudian to deconstructivist. It is, nevertheless, usually interpreted as centring upon the awakening of the naïve speaker to a sense of reality (mortality). The ending is sometimes said to be positive, inasmuch as Wordsworth's animism makes rocks, stones and trees vital and sentient.

'*She dwelt among the untrodden ways*'

Probably composed between 6 October and probably 21 or 28 December (possibly by 14 December) 1798, this 'Lucy poem' was first published in *Lyrical Ballads* (1800) and was collected from 1815 among 'Poems Founded on the Affections'.

An additional stanza of a draft was dropped from the beginning of the poem before publication:

> My hope was one, from cities far,
> Nursed on a lonesome heath;
> Her lips were red as roses are,
> Her hair a woodbine wreath.

An additional stanza appeared in the same draft between the second and third stanzas of the present version:

> And she was graceful as the broom
> That flowers by Carron's side;
> But slow distemper checked her bloom,
> And on the Heath she died.

Three rivers in England have the name 'Dove' (line 2), any one of which (or none of which) Wordsworth may have had in mind.

There has been less criticism of this 'Lucy poem' than the others, perhaps because of its apparent simplicity. A very close and complex reading of the poem was, however, rendered by R. Slakey in 1972 (*Studies in English Literature*).

'Strange fits of passion have I known'

This 'Lucy poem' was probably written between 6 October and probably 21 or 28 December (possibly by 14 December) 1798 and was first published in *Lyrical Ballads* (1800). It was included from 1815 among 'Poems Founded on the Affections'. A draft of this poem had included a final stanza:

> I told her this: her laughter light
> Is ringing in my ears:
> And when I think upon that night
> My eyes are dim with tears.

There is a possible literary echo in line 6: compare the ballad 'Dulcina', line 17 (in Percy's *Reliques*) – 'And cheeks, as fresh as rose in June'.

Critical attention has largely been directed at the sudden premonition in the last stanza, variously explained by reference to the theories of Erasmus Darwin (a late eighteenth-century psychologist), Freud and Jung, or to simple association. Since Lucy is not dead in this poem, there is little attempt to identify Lucy or to analyse any sublimation of desires Wordsworth might have had. In fact, one scholar insists that the speaker is clearly a persona.

'Three years she grew in sun and shower'

Probably composed between 23 and 27 February 1799, this 'Lucy poem' was first published in *Lyrical Ballads* (1800) and was collected from 1815 among 'Poems of the Imagination'.

The *I. F. note* is very brief: '1799. Composed in the Hartz Forest'.

'Impulse' (line 8) means 'incitement, impetus'.

Criticism of this poem often refers to the Persephone myth, with Nature as the benevolent protectress or, as argued once, the violent male, Hades.

'I travelled among unknown men'

This, the last of the 'Lucy poems', was probably composed shortly before 29 April 1801. It was first published in 1807 and was collected from 1815 among 'Poems Founded on the Affections'.

Probably because this 'Lucy poem' was written several years after the others, it has attracted very little individual attention and is often separated in some way in discussions of the group. It is even seen by critics as a return to more conventional ideas.

Nutting

This blank-verse poem, originally intended for *The Prelude*, was probably composed between 6 October and probably 21 or 28 December (possibly by 14 December) 1798 and was first published in *Lyrical Ballads* (1800). From 1815 it was collected among 'Poems Founded on the Affections'. A fifty-two-line opening addressed to 'Lucy', which was discarded, survives (Clarendon edition, II, pp. 504–6).

The 'Dame' (line 11) was Ann Tyson, with whom Wordsworth boarded while attending Hawkshead School.

Autobiographical background is given in the *I. F. note*:

> Written in Germany; intended as part of a poem on my own life, but struck out as not being wanted there. Like most of my schoolfellows I was an impassioned nutter. For this pleasure, the vale of Esthwaite, abounding in coppice-wood, furnished a very wide range. These verses arose out of the remembrance of feelings I had often had when a boy, and particularly, in the extensive woods that still stretch from the side of Esthwaite Lake towards Graythwaite, the seat of the ancient family of Sandys.

Criticism of the poem always addresses the sexual imagery latent in the poem, and many critics also consider the effect of the experience of the child on the speaker – whether a moral education or an archetypal initiation. Some are dissatisfied with the ending, finding it inadequate for the experience described or simply too sentimental.

Matthew

Probably composed between 6 October 1798 and 23 February 1799 (almost certainly by late April 1799), this poem was first published in *Lyrical Ballads* (1800) and from 1815 was collected among 'Poems of Sentiment and Reflection'. Entitled in the table of contents (1800–1820) 'Lines Written on a Tablet in a School' and (1827–32) 'If Nature, for a Favourite Child' (with no title in the text), the present title was given in 1837. This poem is usually treated as the first of three published 'Matthew poems'.

In the *I. F. note*, Wordsworth comments on Matthew:

> Such a Tablet as is here spoken of continued to be preserved in Hawkshead School, though the inscriptions were not brought down to our time. This and other poems connected with Matthew would not gain by a literal detail of facts. Like the Wanderer in 'The Excursion', this Schoolmaster was made up of several both of his class and men of other occupations. I do not ask pardon for what there is of untruth in such verses, considered strictly as matters of fact. It is enough if, being true and consistent in spirit, they move and teach in a manner not unworthy of a Poet's calling.

T. W. Thompson has suggested three contemporaries as forming part of Matthew's portrait (see *Wordsworth's Hawkshead*, 1970, pp. 171–90).

In line 25 there is in the mention of a 'secret cup', perhaps an allusion to the Passion of Christ: 'O my Father, if it be possible, let this cup pass from me . . .' (Matthew, 26: 39).

'Matthew' is usually considered along with the next two poems. All three are seen as dealing with the same general themes, even though 'Matthew' is thought to have a more straightforward elegiac form. The group generally receives very favourable treatment. The autobiographical dimension is often emphasized, sometimes even naïvely assumed, yet the poet is usually taken to agree with Matthew rather than with the speaker. Geoffrey Durrant offers the most interesting interpretation of the group of poems (*William Wordsworth*, 1969).

The Two April Mornings

Like the previous and following works this 'Matthew poem' (see the note to 'Matthew') was probably composed between 6 October 1798 and 23 February 1799 (almost certainly by late April 1799), was first published in *Lyrical Ballads* (1800) and from 1815 was collected among 'Poems of Sentiment and Reflection'. It more closely resembles 'The Fountain' than 'Matthew' in form.

Criticism tends to deal with time and memory, with Matthew's rejection of the girl in the churchyard, and with the meaning of the 'bough of wilding' (a wild plant, a crab apple) at the end of the poem. For Geoffrey Durrant (*William Wordsworth*, 1969), the poem shows Matthew teaching the speaker that life does not just involve the present but rather all past experience.

The Fountain

Like the two previous works, this 'Matthew poem' (see note to 'Matthew') was probably composed between 6 October 1798 and 23 February 1799 (almost certainly by late April 1799), was first published in *Lyrical Ballads* (1800) and from 1815 was collected among 'Poems of Sentiment and Reflection'.

The word *approved* (line 54) means 'proved good'.

Points of critical interest have been issues of time and memory complicated by art (the various songs), the question of what age takes away and leaves behind, and the rejection by Matthew of the narrator, paralleling his rejection of the girl in the previous poem. For Geoffrey Durrant (*William Wordsworth*, 1969), the poem supports the ultimate separateness of all humans in what he claims is Matthew's honest acceptance of man's position in time and in the world.

Lucy Gray; or, Solitude

This poem (not one of 'the Lucy poems') was probably written between 6 October 1798 and 23 February 1799. It was first published in *Lyrical Ballads* (1800) and was included from 1815 among 'Poems Referring to the Period of Childhood'.

Wordsworth provides considerable background information in the *I. F. note*:

> Written at Goslar in Germany in 1799. It was founded on a circumstance told me by my Sister, of a little girl who, not far from Halifax in Yorkshire, was bewildered in a snow-storm. Her footsteps were traced by her parents to the middle of the lock of a canal, and no other vestige of her, backward or forward, could be traced. The body however was found in the canal. The way in which the incident was treated and the spiritualizing of the character might furnish hints for contrasting the imaginative influences which I have endeavoured to throw over common life with Crabbe's matter of fact style of treating subjects of the same kind.

Further information is provided by Henry Crabb Robinson's *Diary* (11 September 1816): Wordsworth told him that in writing the poem his 'object was to exhibit poetically entire *solitude* . . .', a point reinforced by the second part of the title. Robinson also recorded Wordsworth as saying that he 'represents the child as observing the day-*moon*, which no town or village girl would ever notice'.

In lines 30–32, Wordsworth echoes what he called in the 1800 Preface 'one of the most justly admired stanzas' of the traditional ballad *The Babes in the Wood*: 'Those pretty babes with hand in hand / Went wandering up and down; / But never more they saw the Man / Approaching from the town.'

A Poet's Epitaph

Probably composed between 6 October 1798 and 23 February 1799, this poem was first published in *Lyrical Ballads* (1800) and was included from 1815 among 'Poems of Sentiment and Reflection'.

The composition of the poem is mentioned by Wordsworth in the *I. F. note* for 'Written in Germany': in Goslar 'I walked daily on the ramparts, or in a sort of public ground or garden ... During these walks I composed the poem that follows, *The* [*sic*] *Poet's Epitaph*.'

There are several possible sources for the poem. Theocritus' *Epigram XIX* reads: 'Here lies the poet Hipponax! If thou art a sinner draw not near this tomb, but if thou art a true man, and the son of righteous sires, sit boldly down here, yea, and sleep if thou wilt' – (trans. Lang). Robert Burns's 'A Bard's Epitaph' (1786) contains repeated questions similar to those in Wordsworth's poem. The detail of 'russet brown' (line 38) probably derives from James Thomson's *Castle of Indolence* (1748), II, xxxiii: 'the bard ... in russet brown bedight'.

The identity of the occupations of those rejected by the speaker is sometimes unclear: the 'Statist' (line 1) is a statesman or politician; the 'Man of purple cheer' (line 9) a clergyman or 'Doctor' (line 11) of Divinity; the 'Philosopher' (line 18) a natural scientist.

Recent critics have emphasized the comic, even satiric, qualities of the poem.

The Brothers

Composition of this poem began certainly by 24 December 1799 (probably shortly before) and finished probably in early 1800. It was first published in *Lyrical Ballads* (1800) and was collected from 1815 among 'Poems Founded on the Affections'.

Wordsworth commented twice on the poem. In a note to the poem (1802–32), he wrote: 'This poem was intended to be the concluding poem of a series of pastorals, the scene of which was laid among the mountains of Cumberland and Westmoreland. I mention this to apologise for the abruptness with which the poem begins.' In the *I. F. note* he added: '1800. This poem was composed in a grove at the north-eastern end of Grasmere Lake ... The poem arose out of the fact, mentioned to me at Ennerdale, that a shepherd had fallen asleep upon the top of the rock called The Pillar, and perished as here described, his staff being left midway on the rock.' Coleridge, during a tour with Wordsworth in the Lake District, recorded the same incident in his diary (12 November 1799), with the additional detail of the mouldering of the staff.

Coleridge referred to the poem in the *Biographia Literaria* (Chapter XVIII) as 'that model of English pastoral, which I have never yet read with unclouded eye'. Wordsworth also mentioned the poem in the Preface of 1802 (see Appendix I, p. 435).

Wordsworth wrote several notes to specific lines. On lines 59–65 he commented: 'This description of the Calenture [a tropical fever] is sketched from an imperfect recollection of an admirable one in prose, by Mr. Gilbert, author of the *Hurricane* [1796].' In editions 1815–36, he annotated lines 141–5: 'This actually took place upon Kidstow Pike at the head of Haweswater'. And in a note to lines 310–11 he identified Great Gable, a mountain, the Liza and Ehen rivers, and Egremont, a town – all in Cumberland. Wordsworth, moreover, might well have annotated line

13, concerning the absence of epitaphs and monuments, with the following passage from *Essays on Epitaphs* (1800):

> There is not anything more worthy of remark in the manners of the inhabitants of these mountains, than the tranquillity, I might say indifference, with which they think and talk upon the subject of death. Some of the country churchyards, as here described, do not contain a single tombstone, and most of them have a very small number.

'Homely' (line 16) means 'kindly, simple', and 'piety' (line 267) means 'faithfulness to family responsibilities'.

To M. H.

Composed between 20 and 28 December 1799 (probably on or shortly before 28 December), this poem was first published in *Lyrical Ballads* (1800) and was collected from 1815 among 'Poems on the Naming of Places'.

In the *I. F. note*, Wordsworth identified people and places in the poem: 'To Mary Hutchinson, two years before our marriage. The pool alluded to is in Rydal Upper Park.'

Hart-Leap Well

This poem was probably composed early 1800 (certainly by about early June) and was first published in *Lyrical Ballads* (1800). It was included from 1815 among 'Poems of the Imagination'.

In the *I. F. note*, Wordsworth described the occasion and composition of the poem:

> Town-End. 1800. *Grasmere*. The first eight stanzas were composed extempore one winter evening in the cottage; when, after having tired myself with labouring at an awkward passage in 'The Brothers', I started with a sudden impulse to this to get rid of the other, and finished it in a day or two. My sister and I had past the place a few weeks before in our wild winter journey from Sockburn on the banks of the Tees to Grasmere. A peasant whom we met near the spot told us the story so far as concerned the name of the well, and the hart, and pointed out the stones. Both the stones and the well are objects that may easily be missed; the tradition by this time may be extinct in the neighbourhood: the man who related it to us was very old.

Wensley Moor (line 1) is situated in Yorkshire between the rivers Swale (line 75) and Ure (line 76).

There are some possible literary influences. Both the central incident of the curse on the cruel hunter and the moral of the poem are similar to Gottfried August Bürger's *Der Wilde Jäger* (1778). The phrase 'moving accident' (line 97) occurs in *Othello*, I, iii, line 135.

'It was an April morning: fresh and clear'

This poem was probably composed in 1800 (perhaps between April and 13 October; certainly by 15 October 1800) and was first published in *Lyrical Ballads*

(1800). It was included from 1815 among 'Poems on the Naming of Places'.

Wordsworth located the scene of the poem in the *I. F. note*: 'Grasmere, 1800. This poem was suggested on the banks of the brook that runs through Easedale, which is, in some parts of its course, as wild and beautiful as brook can be. I have composed thousands of verses by the side of it.'

Emma (line 39) is always identified as Dorothy Wordsworth. 'Various' (line 10) means 'undergoing change'.

To Joanna

Probably composed about (but at least by) 23 August 1800, this poem was first published in *Lyrical Ballads* (1800) and was collected from 1815 among 'Poems on the Naming of Places'.

In the *I. F. note*, Wordsworth comments on the echoes:

> Grasmere, 1800. The effect of her laugh is an extravagance; though the effect of the reverberation of voices in some parts of the mountains is very striking. There is, in the Excursion, an allusion to the bleat of a lamb thus re-echoed, and described without any exaggeration, as I heard it, on the side of Stickle Tarn, from the precipice that stretches on to Langdale Pikes.

In a notebook, Wordsworth wrote:

> The poem supposes that at the Rock something had taken place in my mind either then, or afterwards in thinking upon what then took place which, if related, will cause the Vicar to smile. For something like this you are prepared by the phrase 'Now, by those dear immunities', etc. [lines 32-5]. I begin to relate the story, meaning in a certain degree to divert or partly play upon the Vicar. I begin – my mind partly forgets its purpose, being softened by the images of beauty in the description of the rock, and the delicious morning, and when I come to the 2 lines 'The Rock, like something' etc. [lines 54-5], I am caught in the trap of my own imagination. I entirely lose sight of my first purpose. I take fire in the lines 'That ancient Woman' [lines 56-61]. I go in that strain of fancy 'old Skiddaw' [line 62] and terminate the description in tumult 'And Kirkstone' etc. [line 65], describing what for a moment I believed either actually took place at the time, or when I have been reflecting on what did take place I have had a temporary belief, in some fit of imagination, did really or might have taken place. When the description is closed, or perhaps partly before I waken from the dream and see that the Vicar thinks I have been extravagating, as I intended he should, I then tell the story as it happened really; and as the recollection of it exists permanently and regularly in my mind, mingling allusions suffused with humour, partly to the trance in which I have been, and partly to the trick I have been playing on the Vicar. The poem then concludes in a strain of deep tenderness.

For identification of places, see Wordsworth's note at the end of the poem. 'The old steeple-tower' (line 20) is St Oswald's, Grasmere, and 'that tall rock' (line 42) is part of Helm-crag (line 56), according to Knight. Coleridge in *Biographia Literaria* (Chapter XX) notes the influence of Drayton's *Polyolbion* (Song XXX, lines 155-64) on the image of echoes (lines 54-65).

Recent criticism of the poem treats it as subtle, although only on a close reading. The most convincing interpretation is F. H. Langman's article (*Southern Review*, 1978), which shows the clear oppositions Wordsworth sets up in the poem, especially Man vs. Nature and Christianity vs. paganism (and how they are reconciled through the speaker's dealings with Joanna and the Vicar), as well as the humour and self-mockery of the poem.

'When, to the attractions of the busy world'

The first version of this poem was composed on 29–30 August 1800, with additions written possibly until about late 1805, and the final 1815 version was probably composed between 9 September and late October 1814. It was first published in 1815 and was included among 'Poems on the Naming of Places'.

Wordsworth identified the scene further in the *I. F. note*: '... The grove still exists, but the plantation has been walled in, and is not so accessible as when my brother John wore the path in the manner here described. The grove was a favourite haunt with us all while we lived at Town-End.' 'Esthwaite's pleasant shore' (line 67) refers to the town of Hawkshead, where Wordsworth's brother John had attended grammar school.

Michael

This highly esteemed poem was probably composed between about early October (certainly by 11 October) and perhaps 9 December (certainly by 19 December) 1800. It was first published in *Lyrical Ballads* (1800) and was collected from 1815 among 'Poems Founded on the Affections'.

Wordsworth provided background information in the *I. F. note*:

> Town-End, 1801. Written about the same time as *The Brothers*. The sheepfold, on which so much of the poem turns, remains, or rather the ruins of it. The character and circumstances of Luke were taken from a family to whom had belonged, many years before, the house we lived in at Town-End, along with some fields and woodlands on the eastern shore of Grasmere. The name of the Evening Star was not in fact given to this house but to another on the same side of the valley more to the north.

According to Christopher Wordsworth's *Memoirs* (1851, II, p. 305), Wordsworth told Mr Justice Coleridge: '"Michael" was founded on the son of an old couple having become dissolute and run away from his parents; and on an old shepherd having been seven years in building up a sheepfold in a solitary valley ...' In a letter to Thomas Poole (9 April 1801), Wordsworth wrote of 'Michael':

> I have attempted to give a picture of a man, of strong mind and lively sensibility, agitated by two of the most powerful affections of the human heart; the parental affection, and the love of property, *landed* property, including the feelings of inheritance, home, and personal and family independence ... I had a still further wish that this poem should please you, because in writing it I had your character often before my eyes, and sometimes thought I was delineating such a man as you yourself would have been under the same circumstances.

Wordsworth wrote to Charles James Fox (14 January 1801) that in 'Michael' (and in 'The Brothers') he was describing the 'domestic affections' of north-country small landowners, whose 'little tract of land serves as a kind of permanent rallying-point for their domestic feelings . . .'

In the Clarendon edition (II, pp. 479-84) are given a number of MS passages probably intended for 'Michael'.

In a series of notes, Wordsworth identified elements in the poem. In a reference to line 169, he explained, 'Clipping is a word used in the north of England for shearing.' In another note (1802-5) concerning Richard Bateman (line 258), he commented: 'The story alluded to here is well known in the country. The chapel is called Ings Chapel and is on the road leading from Kendal to Ambleside.' And in a note (1802-5) to line 324, he explained: '. . . A sheepfold in these mountains is an unroofed building of stone walls, with different divisions. It is generally placed by the side of a brook . . .' Such a brook runs through the 'ghyll' found in the poem, 'a steep narrow valley, with a stream running through it' (note to 'The Idle Shepherd Boys').

'Green-head Ghyll' (line 2) is located in the north-east of Grasmere Vale, and 'forest-side' (line 40) was at the eastern side of Grasmere (Lake). The 'kites' in line 11 refer to the birds of prey, 'the South' in line 50 is the south wind, and 'parish-boy' in line 259 is a poor boy supported by the parish.

There has been a good deal of critical comment on the poem, the subtitle, 'A Pastoral', stimulating perhaps the most discussion. 'Michael' tends to be set against the background of the entire pastoral tradition − there are a number of authentic pastoral conventions in the poem, such as the contrast between the rural and the urban − and the question often raised concerns its place within that tradition. Some put the poem in a middle ground between the hard (the crude reality) and the soft (Arcadian) pastoral, but others consider it beyond the tradition altogether, for containing one of the most human portraits in eighteenth-century pastoral and for professing the effect of landscape on humans.

Judith Page provides a useful brief discussion of 'Michael' as a pastoral (*Studies in English Literature*, 1989).

The so-called 'Ballad-Michael', a manuscript fragment with similar elements in burlesque form first presented by Stephen M. Parrish (*Bicentenary Wordsworth Studies*, ed. J. Wordsworth, 1970), being also a pastoral, has caused a tempest in an ink-well. Was it an earlier version, a simple divertissement or the prologue to another poem? Judith Page makes a good case for it being the beginning of a poem in the pastoral burlesque tradition, dropped by Wordsworth probably when he realized the serious nature of his subject.

Most, in any event, see the subtitle 'A Pastoral' as Wordsworth delivering a deliberate challenge by treating pastoral more seriously than was customary. A contemporary of Wordsworth objected to the use of blank verse, considered an elevated verse form, but there are other elements of a higher style noted by critics: a kind of indirection provided by circumlocution and muted personifications. Karl Kroeber has also argued that a number of factors, such as the auditory appeal over the visual, were calculated to keep readers from obtaining a simple perspective on subjects and events (*Articulate Images*, ed. R. Wendorf, 1983).

The stylistic influence of the King James Old Testament has also been noted, especially in the scene of the covenant. The general influence of the Old Testament is usually argued, made obvious as it is by that covenant and the patriarchal stature of Michael. The story of Abraham and Isaac has often been singled out because Luke's birth, like Isaac's, was a gift of God, because of the 'sacrifice' of Luke by Michael, and even because of the suggestion of a sacrificial altar in the piled rocks of the unfinished sheepfold.

Some critics have also turned to social and political issues, taken in historical context. Most of them mention that Wordsworth wrote to the politician Charles James Fox (14 January 1801) referring to such concerns in connection with the poem, although they then seem to assume as a corollary that 'Michael' was written originally as a polemic rather than merely used in the letter as an illustration. Several critics go further and see Michael's shepherding as a metaphor for Wordsworth's poetic creativity, based on the poet-speaker's desire to pass on the tale, just as Michael wishes to pass on the land.

Such analogies lead often to surprisingly negative readings of the poem, called by one scholar the 'dark' view. Most of the critical bombardment falls on Michael, who is said to be wrong in his treatment of Luke to begin with (he should have sold part of the land instead of sending Luke away) and whose word is our only evidence that Luke was guilty of falling on evil ways. He is, moreover, not sociable enough, choosing solitude, as he does, over his family. A more level-headed reading is provided by David Ellis (*English*, 1987), who deals with Wordsworth's realistic handling of psychology and of shepherds.

To a Young Lady

Composed perhaps between 23 and 27 January 1802 (certainly by 9 February), this poem was first published 12 February 1802 in the *Morning Post*. In collected editions it appeared from 1815 to 1832 among 'Poems of Sentiment and Reflection' and thereafter among 'Poems of the Imagination'.

In the *I. F. note*, Wordsworth connected the poem to 'Louisa': 'Composed at the same time and on the same view as "I met Louisa in the shade". Indeed, they were designed to make one piece.' The 'young lady' of the title has been variously identified as his sister-in-law, Joanna Hutchinson, and his sister, Dorothy, who said she had been rebuked in 1794 by her aunt for 'rambling about the country on foot' (letter to Mrs C. Crackenthorpe, 21 April 1794).

The Sailor's Mother

Composed on 11 and 12 March 1802, this poem was first published in 1807 and was collected from 1815 among 'Poems Founded on the Affections'.

In the *I. F. note*, Wordsworth provided background to the poem: 'Town-End, 1800. I met this woman near the Wishing-Gate, on the high-road that then led from Grasmere to Ambleside. Her appearance was exactly as here described, and such was her account, nearly to the letter.' Coleridge observed (*Biographia Literaria*, Chapter XVIII) that the last three stanzas 'furnish the only fair instance that I have been able to discover in all Mr. Wordsworth's writings, of an *actual* adoption, or true imitation, of the *real* and *very* language of *low and rustic life*, freed from provincialisms'.

In the context, Coleridge is attacking the incompatibility of this style with the more elevated one of the opening. However, several critics have recently defended Wordsworth on this point.

Alice Fell; or, Poverty

Composed on 12 and 13 March 1802, this poem was first published in 1807. When contained in collected editions from 1815, it was included among 'Poems Referring to the Period of Childhood', but it was dropped from editions from 1820 to 1832 inclusive.

In the *I. F. note*, Wordsworth discussed the source and history of the poem:

> Written to gratify Mr. Graham of Glasgow, brother of the Author of the Sabbath. He was a zealous coadjutor of Mr. Clarkson, and a man of ardent humanity. The incident had happened to himself, and he urged me to put it into verse for humanity's sake. The humbleness, meanness if you like, of the subject, together with the homely mode of treating it, brought upon me a world of ridicule by the small critics, so that in policy I excluded it from many editions of my poems, till it was restored at the request of my son-in-law, Edward Quillinan.

Dorothy Wordsworth recorded the story in her *Journal* (16 February 1802):

> Mr. Graham said he wished Wm had been with him the other day – he was riding in a post-chaise and he heard a strange cry that he could not understand, the sound continued, and he called to the chaise driver to stop. It was a little girl that was crying as if her heart would burst. She had got up behind the chaise, and her cloak had been caught by the wheel, and was jammed in, and it hung there. She was crying after it. Poor thing. Mr. Graham took her into the chaise, and her cloak was released from the wheel, but the child's misery did not cease, for her cloak was torn to rags; it had been a miserable cloak before, but she had no other, and it was the greatest sorrow that could befall her. Her name was Alice Fell. She had no parents, and belonged to the next town. At the next town Mr. G. left money with some respectable people in the town, to buy her a new cloak.

Beggars

Composed on 13 and 14 March 1802, this poem was first published in 1807 and from 1815 was collected among 'Poems of the Imagination'.

In the *I. F. note*, Wordsworth mentions the source of the poem: 'Town-end, 1802. Met, and described to me by my Sister, near the quarry at the head of Rydal lake, a place still a chosen resort of vagrants travelling with their families.' Wordsworth told Henry Crabb Robinson (Edith J. Morley, *Henry Crabb Robinson on Books and their Writers*, 1938, I, pp. 10–11) that he wrote the poem 'to exhibit the power of physical beauty and health and vigour in childhood even in a state of moral depravity'.

Wordsworth found the incident described in Dorothy Wordsworth's *Journal* (10 June 1800):

> On Tuesday May 27th [1800] a very tall woman, tall much beyond the measure of tall women, called at the door. She had on a very long brown cloak, and a very white cap without Bonnet – her face was excessively brown, but it had plainly once been fair. She led a little bare-footed child about two years old by the hand, and said her husband, who was a tinker, was gone before with the other children. I gave her a piece of Bread. Afterwards on my road to Ambleside, beside the Bridge at Rydal, I saw her

husband sitting by the roadside, his two asses feeding beside him, and the young children at play upon the grass. The man did not beg. I passed on and about a quarter of a mile further I saw two boys before me, one about 10, the other about 8 years old, at play chasing a butterfly. They were wild figures, not very ragged, but without shoes and stockings. The hat of the elder was wreathed round with yellow flowers; the younger, whose hat was only a rimless crown, had stuck it round with laurel leaves. They continued at play till I drew very near, and then they addressed me with the Beggars' cant and the whining voice of sorrow. I said 'I served your mother this morning' (the Boys were so like the woman who had called at the door that I could not be mistaken). 'O!' says the elder, 'you could not serve my mother, for she's dead, and my father's on at the next town – he's a potter.' I persisted in my assertion, and that I would give them nothing. Says the elder, 'Come, let's away,' and away they flew like lightning.

Wordsworth had difficulty avoiding Dorothy's exact wording (compare her *Journal*, 13 March 1802, and lines 21–6). This poem underwent considerable revision; the sixth stanza was added in 1827. In the same year Wordsworth published 'Sequel to "Beggars"'. For the 'weed of glorious feature' (line 18), see Spenser's *Muiopotmos* (line 218).

To a Butterfly ('Stay near me')

Composed in the orchard at Dove Cottage, Grasmere (*I. F. note*), on 14 March 1802, this poem was first published in 1807 among 'Moods of My Own Mind'. It was collected from 1815 among 'Poems Referring to the Period of Childhood'.

Emmeline is probably a pseudonym for Dorothy Wordsworth. In the *I. F. note*, Wordsworth comments: '. . . My sister and I were parted immediately after the death of our Mother who died in 1778, both being very young.' Dorothy's *Journal* (14 March 1802) adds corroboration:

The thought first came upon him as we were talking about the pleasure we both always feel at the sight of a Butterfly. I told him I used to chase them a little, but that I was afraid of brushing the dust off their wings, and did not catch them – He told me how they used to kill all the white ones when he went to school because they were Frenchmen.

To the Cuckoo ('O blithe New-Comer!')

This poem was perhaps composed largely on 23–26 March 1802 (with further composition possible about 14 May and about 3 June) and was first published in 1807 among 'Moods of My Own Mind'. It was collected from 1815 among 'Poems of the Imagination'.

In the Preface of 1815, Wordsworth commented on the questions posed in the first stanza:

This concise interrogation characterizes the seeming ubiquity of the voice of the cuckoo, and dispossesses the creature almost of a corporeal existence; the imagination being tempted to this exertion of her power by a consciousness in the memory that the cuckoo is almost perpetually heard throughout the season of spring, but seldom becomes an object of sight.

In his *Guide to the Lakes* (third edition, 1822, p. 106), Wordsworth further observed: 'There is also an imaginative influence in the voice of the cuckoo, when that voice has taken possession of a deep mountain valley . . .' Similarities have been noted between this poem and Michael Bruce's 'Ode: To the Cuckoo' (1770).

'*My heart leaps up*'

This poem was probably composed on 26 March 1802 and was first published in 1807 among 'Moods of My Own Mind'. It was collected from 1815 among 'Poems Referring to the Period of Childhood'. In 1815 the entire poem was placed first in that category, and the last three lines also became an epigraph to 'Ode: Intimations . . .', begun the next day.

In *The Friend* (10 August 1809), Coleridge commented in a note on 'those who are not good and wise enough to contemplate the Past in the Present and so to produce by a virtuous and thoughtful sensibility that continuity in their self-consciousness, which Nature has made the law of their animal Life':

> Ingratitude, sensuality, and hardness of heart all flow from this source. Men are ungrateful to others only when they have ceased to look back on their former selves with joy and tenderness. They exist in fragments. Annihilated as to the Past, they are dead to the Future, or seek for the proofs of it everywhere, only not (where alone they can be found) in themselves. A contemporary poet has exprest and illustrated this sentiment with equal fineness of thought and tenderness of feeling. ['My heart leaps up . . .' is then quoted.]

To H. C., Six Years Old

This poem about Hartley Coleridge, eldest son of Samuel Taylor Coleridge, was composed probably between 27 March and about 17 June 1802 (at least before 14 October 1803) and was first published in 1807. From 1815 it was included among 'Poems Referring to the Period of Childhood'.

In a note (1807) to lines 6–9, Wordsworth referred to Jonathan Carver's *Travels Through the Interior Parts of North America* (1778), p. 133: 'The water at this time was as pure and transparent as air; and my canoe seemed as if it hung suspended in that element.' There is a possible literary echo in line 27: compare Andrew Marvell's 'On a Drop of Dew' (lines 1–2) – 'See how the Orient Dew / Shed from the bosom of the Morn . . .'

Ode: Intimations of Immortality

Often seen as Wordsworth's most important poem, the 'Immortality Ode' was probably written between 27 March 1802 (stanzas I–IV) and probably early 1804 (by 6 March). It was first published in 1807 at the end of the second volume, and from 1815 was placed at the end and was not included among any classification. In 1807 the poem was entitled simply 'Ode' and the epigraph was '*Paulo majora canamus*' ('Let us sing a little higher'), taken from Virgil's *Fourth Eclogue*. From 1815 the poem carried the present title and epigraph.

Wordsworth commented at length in the *I. F. note*:

This was composed during my residence at Town-End, Grasmere; two years at least passed between the writing of the four first stanzas and the remaining part. To the attentive and competent reader the whole sufficiently explains itself; but there may be no harm in adverting here to particular feelings or *experiences* of my own mind on which the structure of the poem partly rests. Nothing was more difficult for me in childhood than to admit the notion of death as a state applicable to my own being. I have said elsewhere –

'A simple child,
That lightly draws its breath,
And feels its life in every limb,
What should it know of death!'

But it was not so much from [feelings] of animal vivacity that *my* difficulty came as from a sense of the indomitableness of the spirit within me. I used to brood over the stories of Enoch and Elijah, and almost to persuade myself that, whatever might become of others, I should be translated, in something of the same way, to heaven. With a feeling congenial to this, I was often unable to think of external things as having external existence, and I communed with all that I saw as something not apart from, but inherent in, my own immaterial nature. Many times while going to school have I grasped at a wall or tree to recall myself from this abyss of idealism to the reality. At that time I was afraid of such processes. In later periods of life I have deplored, as we have all reason to do, a subjugation of an opposite character, and have rejoiced over the remembrances, as is expressed in the lines –

'Obstinate questionings
Of sense and outward things,
Fallings from us, vanishings;' etc.

To that dream-like vividness and splendour which invest objects of sight in childhood, everyone, I believe, if he would look back, could bear testimony, and I need not dwell upon it here: but having in the Poem regarded it as presumptive evidence of a prior state of existence, I think it right to protest against a conclusion, which has given pain to some good and pious persons, that I mean to inculcate such a belief. It is far too shadowy a notion to be recommended to faith, as more than an element in our instincts of immortality. But let us bear in mind that, though the idea is not advanced in revelation, there is nothing there to contradict it, and the fall of Man presents an analogy in its favor. Accordingly, a pre-existent state has entered into the popular creeds of many nations; and, among all persons acquainted with classic literature, is known as an ingredient in Platonic philosophy. Archimedes said that he could move the world if he had a point whereon to rest his machine. Who has not felt the same aspiration as regards the world of his own mind? Having to wield some of its elements when I was impelled to write this Poem on the 'Immortality of the Soul', I took hold of the notion of pre-existence as having sufficient foundation in humanity for authorizing me to make for my purpose the best use of it I could as a Poet.

In Christopher Wordsworth, *Memoirs* (1851, II, p. 476), Wordsworth observed further:

> In my Ode on the *Initimations of Immortality in Childhood*, I do not profess to give a literal representation of the state of the affections and of the moral being in childhood. I record my own feelings at that time – my absolute spirituality, my 'all-soulness,' if I may so speak. At that time I could not believe that I should lie down quietly in the grave, and that my body would moulder into dust.

In the same *Memoirs* (II, p. 480), R. P. Graves is quoted as reporting:

> I remember Mr. Wordsworth saying that, at a particular stage of his mental progress, he used to be frequently so rapt into an unreal transcendental world of ideas that the external world seemed no longer to exist in relation to him, and he had to reconvince himself of its existence by *clasping a tree*, or something that happened to be near him.

In a letter to Mrs Clarkson (January 1815), Wordsworth further observed of the ode:

> This poem rests entirely upon two recollections of childhood, one that of a splendour in the objects of sense which is passed away, and the other an indisposition to bend to the law of death, as applying to our particular case. A Reader who has not a vivid recollection of these feelings having existed in his mind cannot understand that poem.

After 1815 Wordsworth deleted the following passage (after line 121), to which Coleridge objected in the *Biographia Literaria* (Chapter XXII):

> To whom the grave
> Is but a lonely bed without the sense or sight
> Of day or the warm light,
> A place of thought where we in waiting lie.

Coleridge disliked the 'frightful notion of lying *awake* in the grave', but a passage in Dorothy Wordsworth's *Journal* (29 April 1802) evinces a quite different attitude: 'We then went to John's Grove, sate a while at first. Afterwards William lay, and I lay, in the trench under the fence . . . He thought that it would be as sweet thus to lie so in the grave, to hear the *peaceful* sounds of the earth, and just to know that our dear friends were near.'

'. . . thy Immortality / Broods like the Day' (lines 119–20) should be compared to Wordsworth's *Essay upon Epitaphs I* (fifth paragraph): 'If we look back upon the days of childhood, we shall find that the time is not in remembrance when, with respect to our own individual Being, the mind was without this assurance [of immortality].'

This passage has many literary echoes. Milton's *Paradise Lost* possibly supplied 'celestial light' (line 4) from Book III, lines 51–2 – 'So much the rather thou celestial Light / Shine inward . . .' – and 'abolish or destroy' (line 161) from Book II, lines 92–3 – 'More destroyed than thus / We should be quite abolisht and expire.' *Hamlet* is perhaps echoed in line 148 – 'And then it started like a guilty thing / Upon a fearful summons' (I, ii, lines 148–9) – and 'in my heart of hearts' (line 190) also occurs in *Hamlet* (III, ii, line 78). 'Shades of the prison-house begin to close' (line 67) is perhaps indebted to Virgil's *Aeneid* (VI, line 734):

'*clausae tenebris et carcene caeco*' – closed in the shades of the dark prison. '. . . humorous stage' (line 104) is also found in Samuel Daniel's dedicatory sonnet (line 1) to Fulke Greville in *Musophilus*. Corinthians I, 9: 24–5 may be behind line 200 – 'Know ye not that they which run in a race, run all, but one receiveth the prize?' And Gray's 'Ode on the Pleasure Arising from Vicissitude' (1754), line 49 ('The meanest floweret of the vale') may have supplied the phrase 'the meanest flower' in line 203.

Wordsworth's own poetry and prose seem to be echoed as well. For lines 1–2, compare 'The Voice from the Side of Etna' (possibly by Wordsworth), lines 9–16:

> There was a time when earth, and sea, and skies,
> The bright green vale and forest's dark recess,
> When all things lay before my eyes
> In steady loveliness.
> But now I feel on earth's uneasy scene
> Such motions as will never cease!
> I only ask for peace –
> Then wherefore must I know that such a time has been?

Lines 36–40 should also be compared to 'The Idle Shepherd-Boys' (lines 27–30), lines 74–5 to 'The Barberry Tree' (lines 63–4), lines 127–8 to *The Prelude*, XIV (lines 157 9) and lines 155–6 to 'Address to Silence' (probably by Wordsworth) (line 50) and 'On the Power of Sound' (lines 217–18).

The meaning of some words has become obsolete: 'cons' (line 103) means 'memorizes', 'humorous' (line 104) means 'fanciful' and 'Persons' (line 105) means 'dramatis personae'.

More has been written about 'The Ode' than about any other poem by Wordsworth save *The Prelude*. It is usually seen as the greatest of his shorter works, even when it is not considered entirely successful. Over the last fifty years or so, Lionel Trilling's 1941 essay (reprinted in *The Liberal Imagination*, 1950) on this poem as an essentially positive one has engendered supporters and adversaries in about equal numbers, Helen Vendler's attack (1978) being the best known of the latter (reprinted in *The Music of What Happens*, 1988).

This division very nearly mirrors another split: between those who see the poem as strictly naturalistic (like Trilling) and those who find it to be transcendental, even Christian. But while there may well be a Christian thrust to the poem, one scholar has pointed out that there is no commitment to that faith. Perhaps the best article on the religious aspects is by Anya Taylor (*Studies in English Literature*, 1986), who claims that the real argument for immortality is not pre-existence but the traditional 'argument from discontent', that the 'obstinate questionings' and 'blank misgivings' offer the real proof for an afterlife.

On the formalist side, critics often discuss the genre–pastoral elegy moving towards prophetic ode. The structure of the poem is usually divided into three parts, strophes I–IV, V–VIII and IX–XI, almost always with a strong difference noted between the first four strophes, written in 1802, and the remainder, written in 1804. The central images, often called symbols, are usually said to be light and the child, and image patterns discovered by critics range from the myth of the Fall to May-day celebrations.

The theme of the work is most often seen as not immortality but the growth of the mind or soul, sometimes with the related problem of the continuity of individual identity added. This theme is said to be conveyed by a number of what are referred to as contradictions (for example, the glory is lost but not lost) but which more correctly, according to E. D. Hirsch (*Wordsworth and Schelling*, 1960), should be called paradoxes, natural to this kind of argument.

The issue of the pre-existence of the soul is widely addressed, especially early on. Some claim that Wordsworth certainly believed in pre-existence, despite his insistence that he was simply using it as part of the machinery of the poem. Another problem is the hyperbolic description of the child in strophes VII–VIII, first attacked by Coleridge as '*mental* bombast' in the *Biographia Literaria* (Chapter XXII) and best defended by Vendler (see above), who saw the description as a satire of the human socialization process. The identity of the 'timely utterance' (line 23) has likewise been conjectured by many critics; the candidates are 'My heart leaps up . . .', 'Resolution and Independence', strophes I–II of the poem itself, and the sounds the speaker hears around him. A final important obscurity is the meaning of line 28 – 'The Winds come to me from the fields of sleep . . .' – which is never adequately explained.

The larger literary influences have not been slighted. They include Milton's *Lycidas* and *Paradise Lost* IX, Virgil's *Fourth Eclogue* and Spenser's *Prothalamion*, which provided thirty-one out of forty-two rhymes. E. D. Hirsch (see above), however, goes beyond the literary to argue for the connection of the 'immortality ode' to a specific scene.

The Sparrow's Nest

This poem was probably composed about March–April (certainly by 7 May) 1802 and was first published in 1807 among a group entitled 'Moods of My Own Mind'. From 1815 to 1843 it was collected among the category 'Poems Founded on the Affections', and thereafter among 'Poems Referring to the Period of Childhood'.

The poem may have had a basis in the poet's life; for 'Emmeline' (line 9) read 'Dorothy' in the manuscript sent to the printer, and Wordsworth observed in the *I. F. note*:

> The Orchard, Grasmere Town-End, 1801. At the end of the garden at my Father's house at Cockermouth was a high terrace . . . The terrace wall, a low one, was covered with closely clipt privet and roses, which gave an almost impervious shelter to birds that built their nests there. The latter of these stanzas alludes to one of the nests.

Lines 15–17 contain an echo of lines 42–3 of Charles Churchill's 'Independence' (1764): 'The blessing she [Nature] bestow'd – she gave them eyes, / And they could see; she gave them ears – they heard . . .'

Written in March

Composed on 16 April 1802, this poem was first published in 1807 among a group entitled 'Moods of My Own Mind'. From 1815 it was collected among 'Poems of the Imagination'.

Brother's Water is a small lake near the foot of Kirkstone Pass. In her *Journal* (16 April 1802) Dorothy Wordsworth described the composition of the poem:

When we came to the foot of Brother's Water I left William sitting on the bridge ... When I returned I found William writing a poem descriptive of the sights and sounds we saw and heard. There was the gentle flowing of the stream, the glittering, lively lake, green fields without a living creature to be seen on them; behind us, a flat pasture with forty-two cattle feeding ... The people were at work ploughing, harrowing, and sowing; lasses spreading dung, a dog's barking now and then; cocks crowing, birds twittering; the snow in patches at the top of the highest hills ... William finished his poem before we got to the foot of Kirkstone.

In the *I. F. note*, Wordsworth observed that the poem was composed 'extempore' and that it 'was a favourite with Joanna Baillie' (1762-1851), a Scottish poet and playwright. One recent commentator has remarked that the scene given in lines 8-10 conveys a psychological phenomenon, that in these circumstances a herd of cattle does somehow appear to be one cow.

The Green Linnet

This poem was perhaps composed between 16 April and 8 July 1802, and was first published in 1807. It was collected from 1815 among 'Poems of the Fancy'.
In the *I. F. note*, Wordsworth observed: 'Composed in the Orchard, Town-End, where the bird was often seen as here described.'

To the Daisy ('Bright Flower')

This poem was perhaps composed at least partly between 16 April and 8 July 1802, but was possibly not completed until between 6 March 1804 and about March 1805. First published in 1807, it was collected from 1815 to 1832 among 'Poems of the Fancy' and thereafter among 'Poems of Sentiment and Reflection'.
This was one of three poems Wordsworth addressed to the daisy. In the *I. F. note*, he claimed all three 'were composed at Town-End, Grasmere, during the earlier part of my residence there'. In a note (1807), he also observed they 'were written in the year 1802; which is mentioned, because in some of the ideas, though not in the manner in which those ideas are connected, and likewise even in some of the expressions, there is a resemblance to passages in a Poem (lately published) of Mr. Montgomery entitled A Field Flower ...' In yet another note (1807), he claimed this and another of the poems 'were overflowings of the mind in composing' 'To the Daisy' ('In Youth').
In the *I. F. note*, Wordsworth defended line 23:

I have been censured for the last line but one – 'Thy function apostolical' – as being little less than profane. How could it be thought so? The word is adopted with reference to its derivation, implying something sent on a mission; and assuredly this little flower, especially when the subject of verse, may be regarded, in its humble degree, as administering both to moral and to spiritual purposes.

To a Butterfly ('I've watched')

Composed 20 April 1802, this poem was first published in 1807 among a group entitled 'Moods of My Own Mind' and was collected from 1815 among 'Poems Founded on the Affections'.

To the Small Celandine ('Pansies')

This poem was probably composed between 30 April and 1 May 1802. It was first published in 1807 and was collected from 1815 among 'Poems of the Fancy'.

In a note to the title Wordsworth identified the celandine simply as a 'Common Pilewort', but in the *I. F. note* observed, 'It is remarkable that this flower, coming out so early in the Spring as it does, and so bright and beautiful, and in such profusion, should not have been noticed earlier in English verse.'

To the Same Flower [*The Small Celandine*]

This poem was probably composed on 1 May 1802. It was first published in 1807 and from 1815 was collected among 'Poems of the Fancy'.

In a note to the previous poem, Wordsworth commented on the phenomenon described in the fifth stanza: 'What adds much to the interest that attaches to [the celandine] is its habit of shutting itself up and opening out according to the degree of light and temperature of the air.'

The phrase 'beneath our shoon' (shoes), set off in quotation marks in line 50, contains an echo of lines 634–5 of Milton's *Comus*: 'And the dull swain / Treads on it daily with his clouted shoon.' 'Thrid' (line 51) means 'make way through'.

Resolution and Independence

The first version of this poem (often called 'The Leech-gatherer' by the Wordsworth family) was composed on 3–7 May 1802, with revisions on 9 May and heavy revisions perhaps between 14 June and 4 July 1802. It was first published in 1807 and was collected from 1815 among 'Poems of the Imagination'.

In the *I. F. note*, Wordsworth provides information on two elements in the poem:

> This old man I met a few hundred yards from my cottage at Town-End, Grasmere; and the account of him is taken from his own mouth. I was in the state of feeling described in the beginning of the poem, while crossing over Barton Fell from Mr. Clarkson's, at the foot of Ullswater, towards Askam. The image of the hare I then observed on the ridge of the Fell.

Henry Crabb Robinson reported a conversation with Wordsworth (in his *Diary* for 11 September 1816): 'The Leech Gatherer he did actually meet near Grasmere, except that he gave to his poetic character powers of mind which his original did not possess.'

Dorothy Wordsworth's *Journal* (3 October 1800) provides more information on the leech-gatherer:

> When William and I returned from accompanying Jones, we met an old man almost double. He had on a coat, thrown over his shoulders above his waistcoat and coat. Under this he carried a bundle, and had an apron on and a nightcap. His face was interesting. He had dark eyes and a long nose. John, who afterwards met him at Wytheburn, took him for a Jew. He was of Scotch parents, but had been born in the army. He had had a wife, and 'a good woman, and it pleased God to bless us with ten children'. All these were dead but one, of whom he had not heard for many years, a sailor. His trade was to gather leeches, but now leeches are scarce, and he had not strength for it. He lived by begging, and was making his way to Carlisle,

where he should buy a few godly books to sell. He said leeches were very scarce, partly owing to the dry season, but many years they have been scarce. He supposed it owing to their being much sought after, that they did not breed fast, and were of slow growth. Leeches were formerly 2s. 6d. [per] 100; now they are 30s.

The leech-gatherer catches leeches by allowing them to attach themselves to his feet (lines 122-3). Leeches were used in medicine at the time.

Wordsworth offers an interpretation of the poem in a letter to Sara Hutchinson (14 June 1802) – some of the quotations given are from an early draft (see the Clarendon edition, II, p. 536):

> I describe myself as having been exalted to the highest pitch of delight by the joyousness and beauty of Nature and then as depressed, even in the midst of those beautiful objects, to the lowest dejection and despair. A young Poet in the midst of the happiness of Nature is described as overwhelmed by the thought of the miserable reverses which have befallen the happiest of all men, viz Poets – I think of this till I am so deeply impressed by it, that I consider the manner in which I was rescued from my dejection and despair almost as an interposition of Providence. 'Now whether it was by peculiar grace, A leading from above.' A person reading this Poem with feelings like mine will have been awed and controlled, expecting almost something spiritual or supernatural – What is brought forward? 'A lonely place, a Pond' 'by which an old man *was*, far from all house or home' – not stood, not sat, but '*was*' – the figure presented in the most naked simplicity possible. This feeling of spirituality or supernaturalness is again referred to as being strong in my mind in this passage – '*How came he here* thought I or what can he be doing?' I then describe him, whether ill or well is not for me to judge with perfect confidence, but this I can *confidently* affirm, that, though I believe God has given me a strong imagination, I cannot conceive a figure more impressive than that of an old Man like this, the survivor of a Wife and ten children, travelling alone among the mountains and all lonely places, carrying with him his own fortitude, and the necessities which an unjust state of society has entailed upon him. You say and Mary (that is you can say no more than that) the Poem is *very well* after the introduction of the old man; this is not true, if it is not more than very well it is very bad, there is no intermediate state. You speak of his speech as tedious: everything is tedious when one does not read with the feelings of the Author – '*The Thorn*' is tedious to hundreds; and so is the *Idiot Boy* to hundreds. It is in the character of the old man to tell his story in a manner which an *impatient* reader must necessarily feel as tedious. But Good God! Such a figure, in such a place, a pious self-respecting, miserably infirm, and [   ] Old Man telling such a tale!
>
> My dear Sara, it is not a matter of indifference whether you are pleased with this figure and his employment; it may be comparatively so, whether you are pleased or not with *this Poem*; but it is of the utmost importance that you should have had pleasure from contemplating the fortitude, independence, persevering spirit, and the general moral dignity of this old man's character.

The following stanza, which originally came after line 56, was deleted in 1820, probably because it was criticized by Coleridge for demonstrating 'inconstancy of style' (*Biographia Literaria*, Chapter XXII):

> My course I stopped as soon as I espied
> The Old Man in that naked wilderness:
> Close by a Pond, upon the further side,
> He stood alone: a minute's space I guess
> I watched him, he continuing motionless:
> To the Pool's further margin then I drew;
> He being all the while before me full in view.

There were two comments by Wordsworth about the poem in his 1815 Preface. The first refers to line 5:

> The Stock-dove is said to *coo*, a sound well imitating the note of the bird; but, by intervention of the metaphor *broods*, the affections are called in by the imagination to assist in marking the manner in which the bird reiterates and prolongs her soft note, as if herself delighting to listen to it, and participating of a still and quiet satisfaction, like that which may be supposed inseparable from the continuous process of incubation.

Lines 57–65 and 75–7 were also quoted, with the observation: 'In these images, the conferring, the abstracting, and the modifying powers of the Imagination, immediately and mediately acting, are all brought into conjunction.' Wordsworth continues by describing how each image prepares for the next.

There were a number of literary influences on the poem, especially Spenser on the diction. There are two echoes from Wordsworth's own modernization of Chaucerian and pseudo-Chaucerian poems. For lines 48–9, compare *The Cuckoo and the Nightingale* – thought at the time to have been by Chaucer – (lines 171–2): 'For thereof come all contraries to gladness: / The sickness comes, and overwhelming sadness . . .' For lines 20–21, compare *Troilus and Cresida* (lines 104–5): 'All which he of himself conceited wholly / Out of his weakness and his melancholy.' 'Peculiar grace' (line 50) echoes James Thomson's *Castle of Indolence* (1748), II, lxxv. Thomas Chatterton's 'Excellent Ballad of Charitie' uses the same stanza form as 'Resolution and Independence' and has a similar focus on an old man.

Two items in the text require illumination. The poet in lines 45–6 is Robert Burns and the word 'genial' (line 39) is a play on words, signifying both 'cheerful' and 'creative', also used at times by Coleridge.

Probably among Wordsworth's five most important poems, 'Resolution and Independence' has been connected by critics with other poems. Chief among these is Coleridge's 'Dejection: An Ode', for Wordsworth's poem is said to be an answer to Coleridge's and to contain advice about curing his dejection; there are even contrasts, such as the storm at the opening of both poems, one coming, the other past. 'Stanzas Written in My Pocket-Copy' is said to have also been directed towards Coleridge, perhaps to reassure him of Wordsworth's continued affection after its more blunt predecessor. Another connection has been made to 'A Narrow Girdle', which was written a week after the meeting with the leech-gatherer and concerns another old man, this one, unlike the speaker of 'Resolution and Independence', abandoned by nature. There are, moreover, many references to 'The Leech-gatherer' (the manuscript first version), especially the revision made in the second version by dropping the direct speech of the leech-gatherer and the effect that has on the published poem.

Autobiographical considerations are also found in the many discussions of the cause of the poet's depression in the poem, most often said to be Wordsworth's poor financial situation at the time of his impending marriage. Some critics, however, claim that the depression was caused by the pressures of life itself, the fate of all humans. One asserted – what seems obvious – that the poet in the poem is not Wordsworth at all, but simply a persona, 'a young poet', as Wordsworth himself puts it in the letter to Sara Hutchinson quoted above.

As with the 'Immortality Ode', the interpretations of the poem fall fairly evenly between what could be called the spiritual and the naturalistic readings. About half see the poet in the poem as turning to religion for help, even seeking Christian 'grace' after having been disappointed by Nature. The two episodes of the speaker fading out from the scene at hand (lines 107–12 and 127–31) are seen as having a visionary quality. The naturalistic readings, on the other hand, are usually psychological – Jungian or Freudian – and take the 'events' in the poem to mirror events happening in Wordsworth's psyche. More lately, critics have seen an economic or social point to the poem.

The leech-gatherer is frequently placed at the very centre of the poem. He is sometimes distinguished from Wordsworth's other 'solitaries', yet he is nevertheless seen as an image of suffering humanity, his envisioned 'wandering' (line 131) identifying him with the Wandering Jew. He is also discussed as a figure of the poet himself, partly because of the simile of 'reading in a book' (line 81), with the absence of leeches signifying Wordsworth's recent lack of inspiration.

Two problem passages are also discussed. The odd, rather stilted address of the poet to the leech-gatherer, and the inattention and subsequent repetition of the questioning, are seen as either comic or a dramatically effective deflation. But the moral pronounced in the final couplet received more criticism; it is obvious or false or poorly expressed. One critic commented on the consequent ironic lack of independence in the speaker, relying on the example of the leech-gatherer rather than on himself. Another claimed the real moral of the poem is the speaker's recognition of his limitations and his humanity.

Travelling

This poem was perhaps composed about (but by) 4 May 1802 and was revised slightly before 6 March 1804. It was first published in 1947.

Dorothy Wordsworth refers to this poem in her *Journal* (4 May 1802): 'I repeated verses to William while he was in bed; he was soothed and I left him. "This is the spot" over and over again.'

Stanzas Written in my Pocket-Copy

This poem was probably composed on 9–11 May 1802 and was first published in 1815 among 'Poems Founded on the Affections'.

Wordsworth commented on the two portraits in the *I. F. note*: 'Composed in the Orchard, Grasmere, Town-End. Coleridge was living with us much at the time; his son Hartley has said, that his father's character and habits are here preserved in a livelier way than anything that has been written about him.' The last four stanzas refer to Coleridge, the first four to Wordsworth himself. Words-worth's portrait of himself owes a good deal to Beattie's characterization of Edwin, the hero of *The Minstrel* (1771–4). The poem should be read with James

Thomson's *Castle of Indolence* (1748) fresh in mind, for Wordsworth's poem imitates Thomson's style and mood.

The phrase 'like a naked Indian' (line 27) echoes *The Prelude*, I, line 300. 'Deftly' (line 58) means 'softly' in north-country dialect.

Milton Teichman (*Publications of the Modern Language Society of America*, 1971) has argued convincingly that this poem is a reply to 'Coleridge's Dejection: An Ode', like 'Resolution and Independence', and perhaps in its more light-hearted tone a palliative to that other, more didactic poem.

1801 ('I grieved for Buonoparté')

One of the first of the political sonnets of 1802–3, this poem was probably written on 21 May 1802. It was first published on 16 September 1803 in the *Morning Post*, and from 1815 it was contained among 'Poems Dedicated to National Independence and Liberty'.

The occasion of the sonnet was Dorothy's reading aloud Milton's sonnets. Scholars have noted the syllogistic structure of the sonnet, a pattern noted in Wordsworth's sonnets to liberty; the recurrent theme of 'magnanimous meekness' as essential to individual and national character; and the significance of the date in the title as the reference point for the political stance taken, in this case before Napoleon's consulship and the Treaty of Amiens.

'Methought I saw the footsteps of a throne'

One of a group of sonnets that celebrates victory over death, this poem was probably composed between 21 May and about late 1802, possibly late July or 25 December 1802. It was first published in 1807 and from 1815 was contained among 'Miscellaneous Sonnets'.

The opening probably intentionally echoes Milton's sonnet, 'Methought I Saw My Late Espoused Saint', and Wordsworth recorded in the *I. F. note*: 'The latter part . . . was a great favourite with my Sister [-in-law] Sara Hutchinson.'

'England! the time is come'

This political sonnet was composed between 21 May and about late 1802, possibly by 25 December, and was first published in 1807. In 1815 it appeared among 'Poems Dedicated to National Independence and Liberty'.

'It is not to be thought of that the Flood'

First published in the *Morning Post* of 16 April 1803, this political sonnet was written probably between 21 May and about late 1802, possibly by 25 December. It was included from 1815 among 'Poems Dedicated to National Independence and Liberty'.

The quotation in line 4 is from Samuel Daniel's *Civil Wars* (1595), II, line 7. In 1827, the more conservative Wordsworth replaced the original lines 5–6: 'Road by which all might come and go that would, / And bear out freights of worth to foreign Lands.'

'When I have borne in memory what has tamed'

One of the poems included from 1815 in the category 'Poems Dedicated to National Independence and Liberty', this sonnet was composed probably between 21 May and about late 1802 (possibly by 25 December) and was first published (with the title 'England') on 17 September 1803 in the *Morning Post*.

' "Beloved Vale!" I said, "When I shall con" '

This humorous sonnet about returning to the Vale of Esthwaite was composed probably between 21 May and about late 1802 (possibly by 25 December) and was first published in 1807. It was collected among 'Miscellaneous Sonnets' from 1815.

Personal Talk

This poem, composed of four sonnets, was written probably between 21 May 1802 and 6 March 1804 and was first published in 1807. Originally included among 'Poems of Sentiment and Reflection', it was moved to the category 'Miscellaneous Sonnets' in 1820, but was returned to its original category in 1845.

The poem begins as a relatively slight work directed against gossip and small talk. Indeed, Isabella Fenwick, Wordsworth's note-taker, objected to 'maidens withering on the stalk' (line 6) as 'vulgar, and worthy only of having been composed by a country Squire' (*I. F. note*). In its final six lines, however, the poem contains the inscription chosen for the pedestal of Wordsworth's statue in Westminster Abbey.

The poem contains several literary echoes. The line quoted above echoes Milton's *Comus* (lines 743-4) and Shakespeare's *A Midsummer Night's Dream* (I, i, lines 76-8), just as 'by distance made more sweet' (line 26) draws on Collins's 'Ode, The Passions' (1747, line 60). The literary allusions in lines 41-2 are to Desdemona in *Othello* and to Una in Spenser's *Faerie Queene*, I.

'The world is too much with us; late and soon'

One of the most popular of Wordsworth's poems, this sonnet was probably written between 21 May 1802 and 6 March 1804 and was first published in 1807. It was included from 1815 among 'Miscellaneous Sonnets'.

Probably because of its popularity, this relatively straightforward poem has received a surprising number of adverse (and unconvincing) criticisms for alleged inconsistencies and suspect sentiments. The identification of sources has been more fruitful. In the passage at the end referring to the two brother gods (sons of Poseidon and Amphitrite) there are echoes of Milton (*Paradise Lost*, III, lines 603-4: 'And call up unbound / In various shapes old *Proteus* from the Sea') and from Spenser (*Colin Clouts Come Home Againe*: 'pleasant lea', line 283, and '*Triton* blowing loud his wreathèd horn', line 245). Other phrasings have been traced to Henry Headleys's 'An Invocation to Melancholy' (1785) – 'Oh, God, I'd rather be a looby Peasant . . .', followed by a reference to Proteus five lines later – and to Dryden's *The Indian Emperor*, III, ii, line 4 – a reference to 'sleeping flowers'.

To the Memory of Raisley Calvert

This sonnet was composed probably between 21 May 1802 and 6 March 1804 and was first published in 1807. It was included from 1815 among 'Miscellaneous Sonnets'.

In the *I. F. note*, Wordsworth identifies the person addressed: 'This young man, Raisley Calvert, to whom I was so much indebted [for a legacy], died at Penrith 1795.' In lines 11–12 there is an echo of line 87 of Milton's *Lycidas*: 'That strain I heard was of a higher mood.'

'Where lies the Land to which yon Ship must go'

Written probably between 21 May 1802 and 6 March 1804, this sonnet was first published in 1807 and was included among 'Miscellaneous Sonnets' from 1815.

In Henry Crabb Robinson's *Diary* (3 June 1812), Wordsworth is quoted as saying the poem 'expressed the delight he had felt on thinking of the first feelings of men before navigation had so completely made the world known, and while a ship exploring unknown regions was an object of high interest and sympathy'.

'With Ships the sea was sprinkled far and nigh'

This sonnet was composed probably between 21 May 1802 and 6 March 1804 and was first published in 1807. It was contained among 'Miscellaneous Sonnets' from 1815.

Wordsworth explained the psychology of the poem in a letter to Lady Beaumont (21 May 1807):

> There is scarcely one of my Poems which does not aim to direct the attention to some moral sentiment, or to some general principle, or law of thought, or of our intellectual constitution. For instance, in the present case, who is there that has not felt that the mind can have no rest among a multitude of objects, of which it either cannot make one whole or from which it cannot single out one individual, whereupon may be concentrated the attention divided among or distracted by a multitude? After a certain time we must either select one image or object, which must put out of view the rest wholly, or must subordinate them to itself while it stands forth as a Head ...

In a note, Wordsworth identified the source of the wording in lines 5–8, Skelton's 'Bowge of Court', lines 36–8: 'Methought I saw a ship, goodly of sail, / Come sailing forth into that haven broad, / Her tackling rich and of high apparel.'

On the Extinction of the Venetian Republic

The date of composition of this sonnet is uncertain; it was perhaps written, like so many of Wordsworth's political sonnets, as early as 21 May 1802, but it was possibly written between late December 1806 and early February 1807. It was first published in 1807 and in all collected editions appeared among 'Poems Dedicated to National Independence and Liberty'.

At the height of her greatness in the fifteenth century, Venice was a considerable commercial power as a centre of trade with the East. The maritime basis of her power was celebrated in an annual ceremony during which the Doge of Venice wedded his city with the Adriatic (line 8). She was also a bulwark against Turkish invasion of Europe (line 2). The 'final day' of Venice (line 12) has two possible meanings. In 1797 Napoleon brought an end to the Republic of Venice, but Alan Hill (*Review of English Studies*, 1979) has argued for a later date of composition because of the absence of any adverse reference to Napoleon and because of Wordsworth's use of the 'extinction' to bemoan the fate of all institutions. Hill suggests the date 19 January 1806, when Venice was 'incorporated into the new kingdom of Italy', a move towards unification that Wordsworth strongly supported.

A Farewell

This light-hearted poem was composed for the most part probably about late May (by 29 May) 1802, with revision between 30 May and 14 June 1802, and was first published in 1815 in the category 'Poems Founded on the Affections'.

The 'little Nook' (line 1) was Dove Cottage. In the *I. F. note*, Wordsworth said the poem was 'composed just before [his] sister and [he] went to fetch Mary [Hutchinson] from Gallowhill, near Scarborough'. In a letter (14 June 1802) to Mary, his fiancée, Wordsworth refers to the poem as 'Spenserian', thus allowing it to accommodate slightly more extravagant imagery. The 'one song' referred to in line 56 is 'The Sparrow's Nest'.

Composed Upon Westminster Bridge

Among the best known of Wordsworth's poems, this sonnet was composed perhaps on 31 July 1802 and was probably completed on 3 September 1802. It was first published in 1807 and in collected editions always appeared among 'Miscellaneous Sonnets'.

Wordsworth claimed in the *I. F. note* that the poem was 'composed on the roof of a coach on [his] way to France Sept. 1802'. The scene is also described by Dorothy Wordsworth in her *Journal* (31 July 1802):

> We left London on Saturday morning at half past five or six, the 31st of July (I have forgot which). We mounted the Dover Coach at Charing Cross. It was a beautiful morning. The City, St. Paul's, with the River and a multitude of little Boats, made a most beautiful sight as we crossed Westminster Bridge. The houses were not overhung by their cloud of smoke and they were spread out endlessly, yet the sun shone so brightly with such a pure light, that there was even something like the purity of one of nature's own grand spectacles.

There is a fairly obvious paradox at the centre of the poem – that an urban scene, witnessed under the right circumstances, is as fair as, and more calm than, any scene in nature – and this paradox was used by Cleanth Brooks (*The Well Wrought Urn*, 1947) to support his theory that paradox is an important poetical device.

It is the poem's imagery that has attracted the most attention. Its balance of the urban and nature has been praised, but, overall, opinions of the imagery have been unfavourable. Most critics see it as worn out, and at best static. Wordsworth himself defended the image in lines 4–5 from the charge of confusion in a letter to

John Kenyon (late autumn 1836): 'The contradiction is in the *words* only – bare, as not being covered with smoke or vapour; – clothed, as being attired in the beams of morning.' Critics have also pointed out the confusion in the image of the last line where the 'heart . . . lying still' makes the city a corpse.

Calais, August, 1802

This sonnet was written probably between 1 and 29 August 1802 and was first published on 13 January 1803 in the *Morning Post*. It was placed from 1815 among 'Poems Dedicated to National Independence and Liberty'.

Napoleon was made First Consul for life on 2 August 1802. In October 1802, Sir Francis Romilly wrote in his *Diary*: 'I had been disgusted at the eagerness with which the English crowded to do homage at the new court of a usurper and a tyrant . . .' The questions asked in lines 1–2 are a paraphrase of Matthew, 11: 7.

Composed by the Sea-Side, near Calais

Probably written between 1 and 29 August 1802, this sonnet was first published in 1807 and was placed among 'Poems Dedicated to National Independence and Liberty' from 1815.

The same scene is described by Dorothy Wordsworth in her *Journal* (August 1802): 'We had delightful walks after the heat of the day was passed away – seeing far off in the West the Coast of England like a cloud crested with Dover Castle, which was but like the summit of the cloud. The Evening star and the glory of the sky.'

'It is a beauteous evening, calm and free'

This sonnet was composed 'on the beach near Calais' (*I. F. note*) probably between 1 and 29 August 1802 and was first published in 1807. From 1815 it was collected among 'Miscellaneous Sonnets'.

The child addressed in line 9 was Caroline, who was Wordsworth's daughter by Annette Vallon and was ten years old at the time. Dorothy Wordsworth in her *Journal* (August 1802) comments: 'The weather was very hot. We walked by the seashore almost every evening with Annette and Caroline, or William and I alone . . . It was also beautiful, on the calm hot night . . . Caroline was delighted.' For the reference to 'Abraham's bosom' (line 12), see Luke, 16: 22.

To Toussaint L'Ouverture

This sonnet was written possibly between 1 and 29 August 1802 and was first published in the *Morning Post* on 2 February 1803. It was collected from 1815 among 'Poems Dedicated to National Independence and Liberty'.

François Dominique Toussaint L'Ouverture was the son of a Negro slave; as governor of Haiti, he resisted Napoleon's re-establishment of slavery and was imprisoned in 1802. Wordsworth borrowed the phrase 'unconquerable mind' (line 14) from Gray's *The Progress of Poesy* (1754), line 65.

September, 1802. Near Dover

One of the poems included in 'Poems Dedicated to National Independence and Liberty' from 1815, this sonnet was probably composed on 30 August 1802 (or shortly after) and was first published in 1807.

In Dorothy Wordsworth's *Journal* (30 August 1802) the scene was described: 'We ... sate upon the Dover Cliffs, and looked upon France with many a melancholy and tender thought. We could see the shores almost as plain as if it were but an English Lake.'

London, 1802

Included from 1815 among 'Poems Dedicated to National Independence and Liberty', this sonnet was probably composed in September (by 22 September) 1802 and was first published in 1807.

The structure of the sonnet has received most critical attention. Cleanth Brooks and Austen Warren considered the poem poorly organized (*Approach to Literature*, 1938), but more lately the structure has been seen as tripartite as a deliberate reflection of Milton, with Wordsworth consciously ignoring the two-part structure of the Italian sonnet.

Written in London, September, 1802

This sonnet was probably written in September (by 22 September) 1802 and was first published in 1807. It was included among 'Poems Dedicated to National Independence and Liberty' from 1815.

Wordsworth provided background information in the *I. F. note*:

> This was written immediately after my return from France to London, when I could not but be struck, as here described, with the vanity and parade of our own country, especially in great towns and cities, as contrasted with the quiet, and I may say the desolation, that the revolution had produced in France. This must be borne in mind, or else the reader may think that in this and the succeeding sonnets I have exaggerated the mischief engendered and fostered among us by undisturbed wealth.

In one manuscript, 'O Friend' (line 1) reads 'Coleridge'. In line 9, there is an echo of Milton's 'Sonnet to Fairfax' (lines 13-14): 'In vain doth Valour bleed / While Avarice and Rapine share the land.'

'Nuns fret not at their convent's narrow room'

This sonnet, one of several written about the sonnet form, was composed perhaps around late 1802 and was first published in 1807. From 1815 it was contained among 'Miscellaneous Sonnets', where it served as the prefatory sonnet until 1827.

The phrase 'narrow room' (line 1) also occurs in a letter Wordsworth wrote to an unknown correspondent in November 1802, at about the same time that he composed the poem: '[The music of Milton's sonnets] has an energetic and varied flow of sound crowding into narrow room more of the combined effect of rhyme and blank verse than can be done by any other kind of verse I know of.'

'Furness-fells' (line 6) are the hills west of Lake Windermere.

To the Men of Kent. October, 1803

Composed probably between 25 September and 14 October 1803, this sonnet was first published in 1807 and was included from 1815 among 'Poems Dedicated to National Independence and Liberty'.

In lines 9–11 Wordsworth draws upon the legend that the men of Kent (those born east of the Medway) went out to meet William the Conqueror with 'green boughs' and as a consequence obtained confirmation of their ancient privileges and charters from the invading Normans.

Sonnet in the Pass of Killicranky

This sonnet was composed perhaps between 14 and 31 October 1803 and was first published in 1807. It appeared in the collected poems from 1815 to 1820 among 'Sonnets Dedicated to Liberty' and from 1827 among 'Memorials of a Tour in Scotland, 1803'.

In her *Recollections of a Tour Made in Scotland*, Dorothy Wordsworth described the same sentiment as that found in the poem (8 September 1803):

> Before breakfast we walked to the Pass of Killiecrankie . . . When we were travelling in Scotland an invasion [by Napoleon] was hourly looked for, and one could not but think with some regret of the times when from the now depopulated Highlands forty or fifty thousand men might have been poured down for the defence of the country, under such leaders as the Marquis of Montrose or [Viscount Dundee].

In a note of 1807, Wordsworth referred to 'an anecdote related in Mr. Scott's *Border Minstrelsy*' as background to line 11:

> [Viscount Dundee] is still remembered in the Highlands as the most successful leader of their clans. An old soldier told the editor that on the field of battle at Sheriffmuir an old veteran urged the Earl of Mar to order the Highlanders to charge before the regular army of Argyle had formed their line. Mar repeatedly answered that it was not yet time, till the old chieftain turned from him in disdain and despair, and stamping with rage exclaimed aloud 'O for one hour of Dundee!'

October, 1803 ['These times']

This sonnet was composed probably between 14 October 1803 and early January 1804 (possibly by 31 October 1803) and was first published in 1807. In all collected editions it appeared among 'Poems Dedicated to National Independence and Liberty'. There are two other sonnets with this title.

Yarrow Unvisited

This poem was probably composed between 14 October 1803 and 6 March 1804 (possibly by 21 November, especially early or mid-November, 1803) and was first published in 1807. It was included from 1815 to 1820 among 'Poems of the Imagination' and thereafter among 'Memorials of a Tour in Scotland, 1803'. It is the first of a series of three poems: see also 'Yarrow Visited' and 'Yarrow Revisited'.

In her *Recollections of a Tour Made in Scotland*, Dorothy Wordsworth recorded (18 September 1803): 'At Clovenford, being so near to the Yarrow [river], we could not but think of the possibility of going thither, but came to the conclusion of reserving the pleasure for some future time, in consequence of which, after our return, William wrote the poem . . .' In the *I. F. note* to 'Yarrow Revisited', Wordsworth claimed that in 1803 they 'declined going in search of this celebrated stream, not altogether . . . for the reasons assigned in the poem on the occasion'.

The Yarrow was celebrated in Scottish ballads such as 'The Braes of Yarrow' (1724) by William Hamilton of Bangour, mentioned in Wordsworth's prefatory note and echoed (line 51) in line 35 of Wordsworth's poem, as he noted. Another Yarrow ballad was 'Dowie Dens of Yarrow', which provided the rhyme for lines 38 and 40.

Perhaps the most important ballad influencing the poem, though, was 'Leader Haughs', written by the Border poet Nicol Burne (*fl.* 1581). As Wordsworth wrote in a letter to Sir Walter Scott (16 January 1805), describing the poem: 'A few stanzas, which I hope, for the subject at least, will give you some pleasure. I wrote them, not without a view of pleasing you, soon after our return from Scotland . . . They are in the same sort of metre as the *Leader Haughs* . . .' In the letter, Wordsworth also asked Scott to supply a substitute for 'Burn-mill' (line 42), a name found in 'Leader Haughs' but not actually located in the Yarrow valley; Scott suggested 'Broad Meadow', but the change was never made. Line 64, moreover, echoes line 88 of 'Leader Haughs'.

Some of the vocabulary in Wordsworth's poem is Scottish: '*Marrow*' (line 6) is a 'companion'; 'lintwhites' (line 20) are 'linnets'; and 'Strath' (line 37) is a 'wide valley'.

The Pedlar and the Ruined Cottage (MS M)

The history of the composition of the poem is complicated. Begun in 1797 as a short tale about Margaret, in 1798 the poem was expanded to include a history of the pedlar (the Wanderer) who tells the tale. The following year the two parts were separated, only to be recombined in 1803–4 (MS E), and then copied and revised in March 1804 for Coleridge to carry with him to Malta (MS M). The combined parts, further revised, were first published in 1814 as Book I of *The Excursion*.

In the *I. F. note*, Wordsworth provides background concerning the Pedlar:

> Had I been born in a class which would have deprived me of what is called a liberal education, it is not unlikely that, being strong in body, I should have taken to a way of life such as that in which my Pedlar passed the greater part of his days. At all events, I am here called upon freely to acknowledge that the character I have represented in his person is chiefly an idea of what I fancied my own character might have become in his circumstances. Nevertheless, much of what he says and does had an external existence that fell under my own youthful and subsequent observation. An individual named [James] Patrick, by birth and education a Scotchman, followed this humble occupation for many years, and afterward settled in the Town of Kendal. He married a kinswoman of my wife's, and her sister Sarah was brought up from early childhood under this good man's eye. My own imaginations I was happy to find clothed in reality, and fresh ones suggested, by what she reported of this man's tenderness of

heart, his strong and pure imagination, and his solid attainments in
literature, chiefly religious whether in prose or verse. At Hawkshead also,
while I was a schoolboy, there occasionally resided a Packman (the name
then generally given to [persons of] this calling) with whom I had frequent
conversations upon what had befallen him, and what he had observed,
during his wandering life; and, as was natural, we took much to each other;
and, upon the subject of *Pedlarism* in general, as *then* followed, and its
favourableness to an intimate knowledge of human concerns, not merely
among the humbler classes of society, I need say nothing here in addition
to what is to be found in *The Excursion*, and a note attached to it.

The note referred to was attached to line 350 ('much did he see of men'). The
former profession of the Wanderer was to bring the greatest amount of criticism
and scorn upon *The Excursion*. Apparently in anticipation of this, Wordsworth
added this note, defending his choice of this 'class of men, from whom my own
personal knowledge emboldened me to draw this portrait'. As further evidence,
Wordsworth quotes two long paragraphs from Robert Heron's *Journey in Scotland*
(1793, I, p. 91), the most pertinent passage of which is as follows (italics added by
Wordsworth):

Their dealings form [Scottish pedlars] to great quickness of wit, and
acuteness of judgement . . . As, in their peregrinations, they have opportu-
nity of contemplating the manners of various men and various cities, they
become eminently skilled in the knowledge of the world. *As they wander,
each alone, through thinly inhabited districts, they form habits of reflection,
and of sublime contemplation.*

In reference to lines 498–504 concerning Margaret, Wordsworth also com-
mented in the *I. F. note*:

[These lines] faithfully delineate, as far as they go, the character possessed
in common by many women whom it has been my happiness to know in
humble life; and . . . several of the most touching things which she is
represented as saying and doing are taken from actual observation of the
distresses and trials under which different persons were suffering, some of
them strangers to me, and others daily under my notice.

About Robert, her husband, Wordsworth added:

I was born too late to have a distinct remembrance of the origin of the
American war, but the state in which I represent Robert's mind to be I
had frequent opportunities of observing at the commencement of our
rupture with France in '93, opportunities of which I availed myself in the
story of the Female Vagrant, as told in the poem on Guilt and Sorrow.

There are a number of literary echoes in the poem. Line 195 echoes 'Il
Penseroso', lines 109–10: 'Or call up him that left half told / The story of
Cambuscan bold'; line 285 echoes Milton's *Paradise Lost*, VII, lines 374–5: 'the
Pleiades before him danced / Shedding sweet influence'; lines 378–9 echo *The
Tempest*, I, ii, line 506: 'O, I have suffered / With those that I saw suffer'; 'And
their place knew them not' (line 532) echoes Psalms, 103: 16: 'And the place
thereof shall know it no more' (see also *Paradise Lost*, VII, line 144); '"trotting
brooks,"' (line 686) echoes Burns's 'To William Simpson' (1785), line 87: 'Adown

some trottin' burn's [brook's] meander'; and line 691 echoes *A Midsummer Night's Dream*, I, i, line 211.

Some phrasing is similar to that found in other works by Wordsworth himself. Lines 352-6 echo a passage in the Preface to *Lyrical Ballads* (1800): 'Low and rustic life was generally chosen, because, in that situation, the essential passions of the heart . . . speak a plainer . . . language; because in that situation our elementary feelings coexist in a state of greater simplicity . . .' Lines 378-9 also occur in an unpublished memoir of Wordsworth by Barron Field, where Wordsworth is quoted as remarking of Coleridge: 'He could not afford to suffer with those whom he saw suffer.' The phrase 'deepest noon' (line 577) echoes *The Waggoner* (line 6). The description of the visitation of the sheep (lines 724-30), moreover, may owe something to Dorothy Wordsworth's *Alfoxden Journal* (4 February 1798): 'The moss rubbed from the pailings by the sheep, that leave locks of wool, and the red marks with which they are spotted, upon the wood'.

Biographical connections between Wordsworth and the Pedlar are commonly made. 'The market village' (line 42), for example, is taken to refer to Hawkshead, where Wordsworth attended grammar school. Much that is said about the youth of the Wanderer (lines 134-424) does have parallels in Wordsworth's autobiographical *The Prelude*; and one passage was transferred from the MS to that poem.

In the phrase 'Last human tenant' (line 894), the deletion of an MS passage about 'non-human' tenants has robbed the poem' of its significance.

Some of the meanings of words in the poem have changed or become obsolete. 'Access' (line 230) means 'state, fit (of mind)'; 'nervous' (line 415) means 'vigorous'; 'trivial' (line 595) means 'commonplace'; 'trick' (line 808) means 'expression, habit'; and 'reckless' (line 883) means 'with no regard for oneself'.

Criticism has been concerned with the manner in which the setting of the poem (especially the garden) represents the psychological and spiritual events, with the dramatic role of the Wanderer in communicating the story, and with the credibility and acceptability of his words of 'natural wisdom'. But lately a most prominent critical question has concerned the separation of the two parts of the poem and the establishment of *The Ruined Cottage* (MS D, 1799), the tale of Margaret, as the standard text. This was first published as an appendix to Volume V of the Clarendon edition (1949) and received its most important critical support as the best text in Jonathan Wordsworth's *The Music of Humanity* (1969).

Since then, however, a good number of critics have questioned the separation of the history of the pedlar, for the absence of the part providing his history is said to deprive the poem as a whole of its psychological complexity and of much of the dramatic interplay between the narrator and the Wanderer, especially in his role as educator. Several scholars further argue that the most damaging result of omitting the background of the Wanderer is that his persuasive power is lessened and that the 'natural wisdom' he instils into the narrator is made a good deal less credible in the remaining context and is largely unacceptable as a result. We are thus left, they claim, with only a very moving story of suffering and some puzzlement over the Wanderer's cheerful, calm reaction to it.

The best version of the complete poem is clearly a determination of some importance. Many scholars choose the first published version, Book I of *The Excursion*, even though the diction had become more elevated and less forceful than in *The Ruined Cottage* of MS D. But an intermediate manuscript version, MS M, seems to me to offer arguably the best of the complete versions; it lacks the stylistic weaknesses of Book I and contains three passages omitted elsewhere:

the charming description of the little girl – without the sentimental passage on singing and weeping – (MS M, lines 64–89; omitted Book I); the passage about the silent poets (MS M, lines 98–120; missing MS E); and the account of the effect of nature on the Wanderer and the description of the tumult of his heart (MS M, lines 300–320; missing MS E). MS M, which I consulted directly, was first published (in very rough form) in *The Ruined Cottage* and *The Pedlar*, ed. James Butler, 1979). It is given here in its final form – that is, as revised in the manuscript – and is now printed in a readable copy for the first time. The first fifty lines, missing from MS M, are taken from MS E and some missing punctuation has been supplied from MS E.

The best short criticism of the poem is by Cleanth Brooks (*From Sensibility to Romanticism*, ed. F. Hilles and H. Bloom, 1965).

'She was a Phantom of delight'

Probably written between 14 October 1803 and 6 March 1804 (perhaps early 1804), this poem was first published in 1807 and was collected from 1815 among 'Poems of the Imagination'.

The subject of the poem was identified in Christopher Wordsworth's *Memoirs*, 1851, (II, p. 306), where William Wordsworth is quoted as saying the poem was written 'on "his dear wife"'. A remark on the composition was contained in the *I. F. note*: '1804 Town-End. The germ of this poem was four lines composed as part of the verses on the Highland Girl ['To a Highland Girl']. Though beginning in this way, it was written from my heart, as is sufficiently obvious.'

The term 'machine' (line 22) is one 'applied to the human and animal frame as a combination of several parts' (*Oxford English Dictionary*). Compare William Bartram's *Travels Through North and South Carolina* (1791), which Wordsworth knew well: 'At the return of the morning, by the powerful influence of light, the pulse of nature becomes more active, and the universal vibration of life insensibly and irresistibly moves the wondrous machine' (p. 179).

The Small Celandine

Composed possibly in 1803 or early 1804 (by 6 March), this poem was first published in 1807, when it appeared among 'Moods of My Own Mind'. In all collected editions it appeared among 'Poems Referring to the Period of Old Age'.

In the *I. F. note* to 'To the Small Celandine' ('Pansies') Wordsworth commented on the phenomenon described in the first stanza: 'What adds much to the interest that attaches [to the flower] is its habit of shutting itself up and opening out according to the degree of light and temperature of the air.'

Ode to Duty

Basically, this ode was probably composed in early 1804 (by 6 March), with the first stanza probably added between late March 1804 and early December 1806, and was first published in 1807. In all collected editions it appeared among 'Poems of Sentiment and Reflection'. The Latin epigraph, added in 1837, is taken from Seneca's description of a man of perfect virtue in his *Moral Epistles*, CXX, line 10 (with a change to the first person) and reads in English: 'Not only consciously good but so habituated by training that I not only can act rightly but cannot act otherwise.' This poem underwent considerable revision.

The sixth stanza (lines 41-8), deleted by Wordsworth after 1807, is here reinstated (in brackets) in line with the policy of later editors. It makes the transition in thought clearer, but was perhaps excised by Wordsworth because it tends to qualify his submission in a manner that could be mistaken for latent wilfulness.

In the *I. F. note*, Wordsworth talked of literary sources: 'This ode, written 1805, is on the model of Gray's Ode to Adversity which is copied from Horace's Ode to Fortune . . .' Critics have noted a return by Wordsworth in the poem to eighteenth-century modes, especially generalizations and personifications. There is even a borrowing of a phrase in line 63 ('confidence of reason') from Dr Johnson's *Life of Addison*. But far and away the most borrowings are Miltonic. The phrasing in line 1 is indebted to Milton's *Paradise Lost*, IX, lines 652-3 – 'God so commanded, and left that Command / Sole Daughter of his voice' – and the phrase 'lowly wise' (line 61) is borrowed from Book VIII, line 173. The phrasing of line 46, moreover, is adapted from Milton's Dedication to *The Doctrine and Discipline of Divorce*: 'empty and over-dignified precepts'.

The ode has attracted considerable attention. Some critics have seen it as marking a moral turning-point in Wordsworth's life; others have questioned whether there was such a change at all. This issue depends to a large extent on what Wordsworth meant by 'Duty'. One critic interprets duty as simple household duties, but most see the concept as more serious, in keeping with the tone. The ode is sometimes seen as a response to Coleridge, who was himself considering the issue of moral responsibility at the time and seemed to favour certain Kantian ethical views.

Wordsworth himself, in the *I. F. note*, apparently takes 'Duty' to mean the self-discipline necessary to avoid procrastination in composition:

> Many and many a time have I been twitted by my wife and sister for having forgotten this dedication of myself to the stern lawgiver. Transgressor indeed I have been from hour to hour, from day to day; I would fain hope, however, not more flagrantly nor in a worse way than most of my tuneful brethren. But these last words are in a wrong strain. We should be rigorous to ourselves, and forbearing if not indulgent to others, and if we make comparison at all it ought to be with those who have morally excelled us.

In a letter to *The Friend* (4 January 1810), referring to lines 55-6 of the ode Wordsworth wrote in the more serious vein in which the *I. F. note* ended:

> When, in his character of philosophical Poet, having thought of Morality as implying in its essence voluntary obedience, and producing the effect of order, [the speaker] transfers in the transport of imagination, the law of moral to physical natures, and, having contemplated, through the medium of that order, all modes of existence as subservient to one spirit, concludes his address to the power of Duty in the following words: [last stanza quoted].

'I wandered lonely as a cloud'

This poem, undoubtedly Wordsworth's best known, was probably written between late March 1804 and early April 1807 (possibly by the end of 1804). It was first published in 1807, placed among 'Moods of My Own Mind', and was collected from 1815 among 'Poems of the Imagination', in 1815 with the following note: 'The subject of these Stanzas is rather an elementary feeling and simple impression (approaching to the nature of an ocular spectrum) upon the imaginative faculty, than an *exertion* of it . . .' The second stanza was added in 1815, and several other revisions were made. Lines 21-2 were written by Wordsworth's wife and he considered them the 'two best lines in it' (*I. F. note*). Coleridge, however, thought them an example of '*mental* bombast' (*Biographia Literaria*, Chapter XXII).

In the *I. F. note*, Wordsworth commented on the scene: 'Town End, 1804 . . . The daffodils grew and still grow on the margin of Ullswater and probably may be seen to this day as beautiful in the month of March, nodding their golden heads beside the dancing and foaming waves.'

Dorothy Wordsworth also described the scene in her *Journal* (15 April 1802):

> We saw a few daffodils close to the water-side. We fancied that the lake had floated the seeds ashore, and that the little colony had so sprung up. But as we went along there were more and yet more; and at last, under the boughs of the trees, we saw that there was a long belt of them along the shore, about the breadth of a country turnpike road. I never saw daffodils so beautiful. They grew among the mossy stones about and about them; some rested their heads upon these stones as on a pillow for weariness; and the rest tossed and reeled and danced, and seemed as if they verily laughed with the wind that blew upon them over the lake; they looked so gay, ever glancing, ever changing. This wind blew directly over the lake to them. There was here and there a little knot, and a few stragglers a few yards higher up; but they were so few as not to disturb the simplicity, and unity, and life of that one busy highway.

Criticism of the poem stresses the deceptive simplicity that hides a deeper, visionary meaning. Several scholars mention the presence of an archetypal dance image used in each stanza that points towards cosmic unity and order, which the speaker re-embraces at the end of the poem.

Yew-Trees

The early part of this poem (lines 1-13) was possibly composed on 24 September 1804 (or shortly after) and the poem was completed by late October 1814. It was first published in 1815 among 'Poems of the Imagination'.

In the *I. F. note*, Wordsworth provided some background information:

> Grasmere, 1803. These yew-trees are still standing, but the spread of that at Lorton is much diminished by mutilation. I will here mention that a little way up the hill, on the road leading from Rosthwaite to Stonethwaite, lay the trunk of a yew-tree . . . Calculating upon what I have observed of the slow growth of this tree in rocky situations, and of its durability, I have often thought that the one I am describing must have been as old as the Christian era . . . In no part of England, or of Europe, have I ever seen a yew-tree at all approaching this in magnitude, as it must have stood . . .

The historical references in lines 4-8 are to English battles against Scotland and France. 'Umfraville' and 'Percy' (line 5) are probably Robert de Umfraville (1277-1325) and Sir Henry Percy (1364-1403), both of whom fought against the Scots. 'Azincour, Crecy, Poictiers' (lines 7-8) – Agincourt, Crécy and Poitiers –

were three battles England fought against France in the Hundred Years War (1337–1453). There is also a literary allusion in 'ghostly Shapes' (line 25); see the *Aeneid*, VI, lines 273–84 for a similar congregation of allegorical figures: 'And in the midst an ancient elm spreads its shadowing arms' (line 282–3).

Both Wordsworth (Henry Crabb Robinson's *Diary*, 9 May 1815) and Coleridge (*Biographia Literaria*, Chapter XXII) considered 'Yew-Trees' among Wordsworth's most imaginative poems. Later critical attention has been sparse. Most refers back to an article by Michael Riffaterre (*New Literary History*, 1973) which questions the referentiality of all literary meaning. Subsequent criticism has been more concerned with theory than with the text, although some attention has been given to the identity of the speaker. An exception to this pattern is an article by Gene Ruoff (*Modern Language Quarterly*, 1973), who is convincing in finding two opposed perceptions (the yew in Lorton and the yews of Borrowdale), giving two distinct perspectives, profane and sacred respectively (following an approach originated by Mircea Eliade).

Elegiac Stanzas Suggested by a Picture of Peele Castle

Probably written between about 20 May and 27 June 1806, this elegy on Wordsworth's brother, John, was first published in 1807 and was collected from 1815 among 'Epitaphs and Elegiac Pieces'.

In the *I. F. note*, Wordsworth observed: 'Sir George Beaumont painted two pictures on this subject, one of which he gave to Mrs. Wordsworth . . .' Lines 1–2, moreover, refer to Wordsworth's stay at Rampside in the summer of 1794, within full view of Peele (or Piel) Castle, situated near Barrow-in-Furness in Cumbria.

'A power is gone, which nothing can restore' (line 35) echoes a letter to James Losh (16 March 1805) in which Wordsworth refers to his brother's death: 'I feel that there is something cut out of my life which cannot be restored'. The 'deep distress' (line 36) also refers to the death. John was lost at sea 6 February 1805.

'Deplore' (line 42) means 'mourn' and 'the Kind' (line 54) means 'humankind'.

In editions 1820–27, lines 14–16 read 'add a gleam, / Of lustre, known to neither sea nor land / But borrowed from the youthful Poet's dream'. On the insistence of a friend, Wordsworth restored the original wording in 1832.

Criticism of the poem centres on the question of what has been lost, what the 'power' (line 35) refers to. Related questions are how much of a crisis the poem demonstrates and whether the hope offered at the end is real.

Stepping Westward

Probably composed on 3 June 1805, this poem was first published in 1807. It was placed among 'Poems of the Imagination' from 1815 to 1820, and thereafter among 'Memorials of a Tour in Scotland, 1803'.

Dorothy Wordsworth also described the event in her *Recollections* (11 September 1803):

> The sun had been set for some time, when, being within a quarter of a mile of the ferryman's hut, our path having led us close to the shore of the calm lake we met two neatly dressed women, without hats, who had probably been taking their Sunday evening's walk. One of them said to us in a friendly, soft tone of voice, 'What! you are stepping westward?' I cannot

describe how affecting this simple expression was in that remote place, with the Western sky in front, *yet* glowing with the departed sun. William wrote this poem long after in remembrance of his feelings and mine.

The Solitary Reaper

This poem, one of Wordsworth's best known, was probably composed on 5 November 1805 and was first published in 1807. In 1815 and 1820 it was collected among 'Poems of the Imagination', but was moved thereafter to 'Memorials of a Tour in Scotland, 1803'.

In a note (1807) Wordsworth described the composition of the poem: 'This poem was suggested by a beautiful sentence in a MS. Tour in Scotland written by a friend, the last line being taken from it *verbatim*.' The passage, from Thomas Wilkinson's *Tours to the British Mountains* (finally published 1824), is as follows (p. 12): 'Passed a female who was reaping alone: she sung in Erse as she bended over her sickle; the sweetest human voice I ever heard: her strains were tenderly melancholy, and felt delicious, long after they were heard no more.'

Dorothy Wordsworth (*Recollections*, 13 September 1803) provided more information: 'It was harvest time, and the fields were quietly – might I be allowed to say pensively? – enlivened by small companies of reapers. It is not uncommon in the more lonely parts of the Highlands to see a single person so employed.'

There are possible sources for the patterns of imagery, especially the song of a bird or singer heard coming from a vale, in several eighteenth-century poems (see A. A. Mendelow, *Studies in Western Literature*, ed. D. Fineman, 1962).

Criticism of the poem has been uniformly positive. The poem is seen to centre upon the speaker as it records a moment of vision. Even though it is not based on an experience Wordsworth had, he is often identified as the speaker; several biographical readings even depend upon such an identification. The form of the poem is sometimes described as simple, but more often as *appearing* deceptively simple. Geoffrey Finch (*Ariel*, 1975) points out the many paradoxes hidden in the poem, and many critics analyse the deft use of rhetorical questions to draw the reader into the poem. Others concentrate on the movement within the regular stanzaic structure: the introduction to the scene (stanza 1), speculation that moves away from it (stanzas 2–3) and a return (stanza 4). The sudden change to the past tense in the last stanza has received a good deal of favourable attention.

Character of the Happy Warrior

This clearly didactic poem was probably composed between about 6 December 1805 and early January 1806, and was first published in 1807. It was contained in collected editions among 'Poems of Sentiment and Reflection'.

Wordsworth identified the model for the poem in a note (1807): 'The above verses were written soon after tidings had been received of the Death of Lord Nelson [*d.* 21 October 1805], which event directed the author's thoughts to the subject . . .' In the *I. F. note*, he expanded on this information:

The course of the great war with the French naturally fixed one's attention upon the military character, and, to the honour of our country, there were many illustrious instances of the qualities that constitute its highest excellence. Lord Nelson carried most of the virtues that the trials he was exposed to in his department of the service necessarily call forth and sustain ... Many elements of the character here portrayed were found in my brother John, who perished by shipwreck as mentioned elsewhere. His messmates used to call him the Philosopher, from which it must be inferred that the qualities and dispositions I allude to had not escaped their notice.

When told by Harriet Martineau that Dr Channing admired the poem, Wordsworth replied (Harriet Martineau, *Autobiography*, 1877, II, p. 237): 'Ay, that was not on account of the *poetic conditions* being best fulfilled in that poem: but because it is [solemnly] a chain of extremely valooable thoughts.'

In both style and content Wordsworth was apparently influenced by Samuel Daniel's 'Funeral Poem Upon the Earl of Devonshire' (see the notes to the Clarendon edition, IV, p. 420). Wordsworth identified in a note (1807) a borrowing in lines 75-6: '"For Knightes ever should be persevering / To seek honour without feintise or slouth / Fro well to better in all manner thing." CHAUCER. – The Floure and the Leafe' (now known not to be Chaucer's).

The Waggoner

Basically composed between 1 and 14 January 1806 (but possibly some parts were composed as early as 1802), this mock-heroic poem was first published in 1819. It was collected among 'Poems of the Fancy' in 1820, then between 'Poems Founded on the Affections' and 'Poems of the Fancy' from 1827 to 1836, and finally it was placed last among 'Poems of the Fancy' from 1845. For the various versions of the poem, see *Benjamin the Waggoner by William Wordsworth*, ed. Paul F. Betz, 1981.

In the *I. F. note*, Wordsworth commented: 'Written at Town-End, Grasmere. The characters and story from fact'. In another note (1836) he observed:

> Several years after the event that forms the subject of the poem, in company with my friend, the late Mr. Coleridge, I happened to fall in with the person to whom the name of Benjamin is given. Upon our expressing regret that we had not, for a long time, seen upon the road either him or his wagon, he said: – 'They could not do without me; and as to the man who was put in my place, no good could come out of him; he was a man of no *ideas*.'
>
> The fact of my discarded hero's getting the horses out of a great difficulty with a word, as related in the poem, was told me by an eye-witness.

According to Christopher Wordsworth, *Memoirs* (1851, II, p. 310), Justice Coleridge recorded in his *Memoranda* (10 October 1836) that Wordsworth

> read much of *The Waggoner* to me. It seems a very favourite poem of his, and he read me splendid descriptions from it. He said his object in it had not been understood. It was a play of the fancy on a domestic incident and lowly character: he wished by the opening descriptive lines to put his reader into the state of mind in which he wished it to be read. If he failed in doing that, he wished him to lay it down. He pointed out, with the same view, the glowing lines on the state of exaltation in which Ben and his companion are under the influence of liquor. Then he read the sickening

languor of the morning walk, contrasted with the glorious uprising of Nature, and the songs of the birds. Here he has added about six most exquisite lines [IV, 71-82].

Charles Lamb, to whom the poem was dedicated in 1819, wrote to Wordsworth (7 June 1819): '. . . Benjamin is no common favorite – there is a spirit of beautiful tolerance in it – it is as good as it was in 1806 – and will be as good in 1829 if our dim eyes shall be awake to peruse it.' The epigraph, added in 1845, is from Thomson's *Seasons: Summer*, lines 977-9.

'The DOVE and OLIVE-BOUGH' (I, line 53) refers to Dove Cottage, in which Wordsworth lived at Town-End, Grasmere; it was once an inn. According to tradition, Dunmail (I, line 210), the last king of Cumberland, is buried under a cairn on the top of Dunmail Raise, the boundary between Cumberland and Westmorland. Caesar's crossing of the Rubicon river in 49 BC (II, line 81) on his return to Rome to fight Pompey signified an irreversible step. Lord Nelson defeated the French at the Battle of the Nile (II, line 115) in 1798. For the tale of Sir Lancelot and Clifford (IV, lines 47-8), see Wordsworth's 'Song at the Feast of Brougham Castle . . .', lines 95-101.

Some words have obsolete or obscure meanings. 'Crazy' (II, line 6) means 'damaged'; 'vibrate' (II, line 42) means 'vacillate'; 'foundrous' (III, line 92) means 'likely to cause to stick fast or break down'; 'carl' (III, line 101) means 'fellow'; 'pricked' (IV, line 123) means 'rode' (archaic, with a Spenserian flavour – see *The Faerie Queene*, I, i, line 1); 'heartless' (IV, line 259) means 'dejected'.

There are several literary echoes in the poem. Compare I, line 26 with Gray's *Elegy* (line 8): 'And drowsy tinklings lull the distant folds'; II, lines 128-34 with Sterne's *Tristram Shandy* (IX, xxviii): 'And this, said he, is the town *Namur* – and this the citadel – and there lay the French – and here lay his honour and myself'; IV, line 12 with *Hamlet*, I, v, line 58: 'Methinks I scent the morning air'; and IV, line 198 with Milton's *Paradise Lost*, I, line 13: 'Invoke thy aid to my adventurous Song.'

Wordsworth himself wrote a series of notes to the poem over the years:

I, 3 *The buzzing dor-hawk* 'When the poem was first written the note of the bird was thus described: "The Night-hawk is singing his frog-like tune, / Twirling his watchman's rattle about –" but from unwillingness to startle the reader at the outset by so bold a mode of expression, the passage was altered as it now stands.' (1836-7)

I, 90 *painted by the Host* 'This rude piece of self-taught art (such is the progress of refinement) has been supplanted by a professional production.'

I, 168 *Helm-crag* 'A mountain of Grasmere, the broken summit of which presents two figures, full as distinctly shaped as that of the famous Cobbler near Arroquhar in Scotland.' (Sidrophel is the name of the astrologer [line 171] in Butler's *Hudibras* II, iii.)

II, 30 MERRY-NIGHT 'A term well known in the North of England, and applied to rural Festivals where young persons meet in the evening for the purpose of dancing.'

II, 97 *The fiddle's squeak* 'At the close of each strathspey, or jig, a particular note from the fiddle summons the Rustic to the agreeable duty of saluting his partner.'

III, 28 'After [this line] followed in the MS. an incident which has been kept back. Part of the suppressed verses shall here be given as a gratification of private feeling, which the well-disposed reader will find no difficulty in excusing. They are now printed for the first time:
Can any mortal clog come to her?
It can: . . .

* * * * *

But Benjamin, in his vexation,
Possesses inward consolation;
He knows his ground, and hopes to find
A spot with all things to his mind,
An upright mural block of stone,
Moist with pure water trickling down.
A slender spring; but kind to man
It is, a true Samaritan;
Close to the highway, pouring out
Its offering from a chink or spout;
Whence all, howe'er athirst, or dropping
With toil, may drink, and without stooping.
Cries Benjamin "Where is it, where?
Voice hath it none, but must be near,"
– A star, declining towards the west,
Upon the watery surface threw
Its image tremulously imprest,
That just marked out the object and withdrew,
Right welcome service! . . .

* * * * *

ROCK OF NAMES!

Light is the strain, but not unjust
To Thee and Thy memorial-trust
That once seemed only to express
Love that was love in idleness;
Tokens, as year hath followed year
How changed, alas, in character!
For they were graven on thy smooth breast
By hands of those my soul loved best;
Meek women, men as true and brave
As ever went to a hopeful grave:

> Their hands and mine, when side by side
> With kindred zeal and mutual pride,
> We worked until the Initials took
> Shapes that defied a scornful look. –
> Love as for us a genial feeling
> Survives, or one in need of healing,
> The power, dear Rock, around thee cast,
> Thy monumental power, shall last
> For me and mine! O thought of pain,
> That would impair it or profane!
> Take all in kindness then, as said
> With a staid heart but playful head;
> And fail not Thou, loved Rock! to keep
> Thy charge when we are laid asleep.'

                                                                        (1836)

IV, 21 *Ghimmer-crag*   'The crag of the ewe lamb'. [Identified in Knight's edition (1896, III, line 116) as the rock now known as Fisher Crag.]

Star-Gazers

This poem was probably written between 4 April and 14 November 1806 and was first published in 1807. It appeared from 1815 among 'Poems of the Imagination'.

   In the *I. F. note*, Wordsworth commented: 'Observed by me in Leicester Square as here described, 1806'.

'Yes, it was the mountain Echo'

Written on 15 June 1806 or shortly thereafter, this poem was first published in 1807 and was collected from 1815 among 'Poems of the Imagination'.

   In the *I. F. note*, Wordsworth describes the occasion and composition of the poem: 'Town-end ... The echo came from Nab-Scar, when I was walking on the opposite side of Rydal Mere ... On my return from my walk I recited these verses to Mary ...' In his *Guide to the Lakes* (third edition, 1822, p. 106), Wordsworth comments on the 'imaginative influence in the voice of the cuckoo, when that voice has taken possession of a deep mountain valley, very different from anything which can be excited by the same sound in a flat country'.

The Recluse. Home at Grasmere

Not published in Wordsworth's lifetime, this poem was in part composed perhaps early 1800 but most of it probably between about late June and early September 1806. (Jonathan Wordsworth makes a strong, but not altogether convincing, case that the poem was composed as a whole in 1800 with mostly minor revisions in 1806 – at the periods listed above for both years – *Review of English Studies*, 1980.) It was first published in 1888.

   The text given here follows the last version of the poem (MS D) as closely as is consonant with clarity; punctuation was also left intact, which is not true of the Cornell edition, edited by Beth Darlington (1977). Lines 754–860 were printed by Wordsworth as 'The Prospectus to *The Excursion*' in 1814, but are included here as an integral part of *Home at Grasmere*.

As the full title indicates, *Home at Grasmere* was intended to be the first book of the first part of *The Recluse*, the only entire part of which to reach completion being *The Excursion* – see the note to that poem.

There are a good many Miltonic echoes in the poem. 'Indefatigable flight' (line 216) possibly summons up *Paradise Lost*, II, lines 407–8: ' . . . Spread his aerie flight / Upborn with indefatigable wings'; 'Numerous verse' (line 766) is from V, line 150; the quotation marked in line 776 from VII, lines 30–31; 'empyreal thrones' (line 787) from II, line 430; and 'Shedding benignant influence' (line 843) from VII, 374–5 ('the *Pleiades* before him danced / Shedding sweet influence'). 'Chaos' (line 788) in *Paradise Lost* is an unformed region existing before the creation of the universe and 'Erebus' (line 789) is the classical underworld.

There are also echoes from Shakespeare. In a note to lines 836–8, Wordsworth points out one: '"Not my own fears, nor the prophetic soul / Of the wide world dreaming on things to come." Shakespeare's *Sonnets* [107].' 'Wanton boys' (line 559) is borrowed from *King Lear*, IV, i, line 38.

Two words have obscure meanings: 'devious' (line 6) means 'rambling' and '*bield*' (line 334) means 'shelter'.

Home at Grasmere attracted little attention (and most of it unfavourable) until the 1970s, when three very useful articles appeared, each addressing a different but important feature of the poem. Muriel Mellown (*The Wordsworth Circle*, 1974) argues that the narrative and reflective merge in the use of three themes; Karl Kroeber (*Publications of the Modern Language Association of America*, 1974) also stresses the coherence of the poem but emphasizes Wordsworth's unconventional, even paradoxical views on matters such as property; and Kenneth Johnston (*Studies in Romanticism*, 1975) emphasizes the structure of the poem, with the swans at the centre, as well as unusual elements of argument, imagery and syntax. Otherwise, most critics deal with the vale as a unified microcosm, with the poet's public function and with the 'Prospectus' as a fitting end to the poem.

Lines, Composed at Grasmere

Probably composed about early September 1806 (before 14 September), this poem was first published in 1807 and appeared in all collected editions among 'Epitaphs and Elegiac Pieces'.

Wordsworth had a high opinion of Charles James Fox (d. 13 September 1806); see his letter to Fox of 14 January 1801, which accompanied a presentation copy of *Lyrical Ballads*. Wordsworth annotated line 10: 'Importuna e grave salma. – Michael Angelo'. This is the first line of Sonnet CIII of Michelangelo, translated later by Wordsworth in its entirety (see *Memorials of a Tour in Italy*, XXII).

Thought of a Briton on the Subjugation of Switzerland

Probably composed between 30 October 1806 and late February 1807, this sonnet was first published in 1807 and was collected from 1815 among 'Poems Dedicated to National Independence and Liberty'.

The voice of the sea represents England, as suggested by the 'Briton' in the title.

The French subjugated Switzerland in 1802. According to the *I. F. note*: 'This was composed while pacing to and fro between the Hall of Coleorton, then rebuilding, and the principal Farm-house of the Estate, in which we lived for nine or ten months.'

The sonnet has been highly esteemed. Wordsworth himself (in a letter to Richard Sharp, 27 September 1808) considered it 'as being the best I had written' of the sonnets. In *The Friend* (21 December 1809) Coleridge declared it 'one of the noblest Sonnets in our language, and the happiest comment on the line of Milton – "the *mountain* Nymph, sweet Liberty . . ."' And modern critics have praised the balance and unity found in the poem.

November, 1806

This sonnet was composed probably between 30 October 1806 and late February 1807 (perhaps by early December, especially 7 December 1806) and was first published in 1807. It was included from 1815 among 'Poems Dedicated to National Independence and Liberty'.

The event that occasioned the poem was the defeat (at the Battle of Jena, 14 October 1806) of Prussia, the last continental power considered strong enough to resist Napoleon. In a note to lines 13–14, Wordsworth announced: 'These two lines are from Lord Brookes' *Life of Sir Philip Sidney.*' The passage, found near the beginning of Chapter VIII, reads: 'The stirring spirits sent abroad as fuel, to keep the flame far off: and the effeminate made judges of danger which they fear and honour which they understand not.'

Song at the Feast of Brougham Castle

Composed at Coleorton (*I. F. note*) probably between 30 October 1806 and early April 1807, this poem was first published in 1807 and was collected from 1815 among 'Poems of the Imagination'.

The opponents in the Wars of the Roses, which ran for thirty years (line 7) from 1455, were the house of Lancaster (the red rose) and the house of York (the white rose). The marriage (line 13) in 1486 of Elizabeth Neville (York) and Henry VII (Lancaster) brought the two houses together.

In a note (1807) Wordsworth conveyed the pertinent portion of the history of the Wars of the Roses:

> Henry Lord Clifford . . . the subject of this poem, was the son of John, Lord Clifford, who was slain at Towton Field [and who] after the Battle of Wakefield slew, in the pursuit, the young Earl of Rutland, son of the Duke of York . . . 'in part of revenge, for the Earl's Father had slain his' . . . But independent of this act, at best a cruel and savage one, the family of Clifford had done enough to draw upon them the vehement hatred of the House of York: so that after the Battle of Towton, there was no hope for them but in flight and concealment. Henry, the subject of the poem, was deprived of his estate and honours during the space of twenty-four years; all which time he lived as a shepherd in Yorkshire, or in Cumberland, where the estate of his father-in-law [step-father] (Sir Lancelot Threlkeld) lay. He was restored to his estate and honours in the first year of Henry the Seventh.

Wordsworth further described the historical background in a note to lines 142–3: 'The martial character of the Cliffords is well known to the readers of English History; but it may not be improper here to say ... that, besides several others, who perished in the same manner, the four immediate progenitors of the person in whose hearing this is supposed to be spoken, all died in the Field.' All the castles mentioned in lines 36–49 were part of the Clifford estate.

In another note to the poem (1807), Wordsworth explained the reference to 'the undying fish' (line 122): 'It is imagined by the people of the Country that there are two immortal Fish, Inhabitants of this Tarn, which lies in the mountains not far from Threlkeld. – Blencathara, mentioned before, is the old and proper name of the mountain vulgarly called Saddle-back.'

Wordsworth also points out in a note (1807) a borrowing in line 27 from Sir John Beaumont's *The Battle of Bosworth Field* (1629), line 100: 'The earth assists thee with the cry of blood.' There is also an echo in lines 9–10 from Butler's *Hudibras*, II, i, lines 567–8: 'That shall infuse Eternal Spring, / And everlasting flourishing'.

Gypsies

Probably written about (but not before) 26 February 1807, this poem was first published in 1807 among the group 'Moods of My Own Mind' and was collected from 1815 among 'Poems of the Imagination'.

In the *I. F. note*, Wordsworth provides very little background to the poem: 'Composed at Coleorton, 1807. I had observed them, as here described, near Castle Donnington, on my way to and from Derby.' Lines 25–8 were added in 1820. In a letter to Barron Field (24 October 1828), Wordsworth promised to drop 'the concluding apology', but failed to do so.

Coleridge began, and epitomizes, the criticism of this controversial poem by attacking it (*Biographia Literaria*, Chapter XXII) for '*mental* bombast', or 'thoughts and images too great for the subject'. Coleridge assumes the speaker is Wordsworth and that he is a 'tourist', who has 'gone out for a day's tour of pleasure', and comments:

> The poet, without seeming to reflect that the poor tawny wanderers might probably have been tramping for weeks together through road and lane, over moor and mountain, and consequently must have been right glad to rest themselves, their children and cattle, for one whole day; and overlooking the obvious truth, that such repose might be quite as necessary for *them*, as a walk of the same continuance was pleasing or healthful for the more fortunate poet; expresses his indignation in a series of lines, the diction and imagery of which would have been rather above, than below the mark, had they been applied to the immense empire of China improgressive for thirty centuries ...

Later critics have similarly dealt with the speaker's alleged condescension, agreeing with Coleridge's view. Others have defended Wordsworth by dissociating the speaker's view from the poet's. One critic, however, has argued against them all that Wordsworth was taking a serious moral position against the gypsies' sloth, not to be confused with 'wise passiveness'.

[*St Paul's*]

Probably composed between 6 April and early autumn 1808, this poem was not published until 1947.

In a letter to Sir George Beaumont (8 April 1808), Wordsworth described the scene of the poem:

> I left Coleridge at seven o'clock on Sunday morning, and walked towards the City in a very thoughtful and melancholy state of mind. I had passed through Temple Bar and by St. Dunstan's, noticing nothing, and entirely occupied with my own thoughts, when, looking up, I saw before me the avenue of Fleet Street, silent, empty, and pure white, with a sprinkling of new-fallen snow, not a cart or carriage to obstruct the view, no noise, only a few soundless and dusky foot-passengers here and there. You remember the elegant curve of Ludgate Hill in which this avenue would terminate, and beyond, towering above it, was the huge and majestic form of St. Paul's, solemnised by a thin veil of falling snow. I cannot say how much I was affected at this unthought-of sight in such a place, and what a blessing I felt there is in habits of exalted Imagination. My sorrow was controlled, and my uneasiness of mind – not quieted and relieved altogether – seemed at once to receive the gift of an anchor of security.

Epitaph

This little-known epitaph for Thomas Wordsworth was perhaps composed between the date of his death, 1 December 1812, and 20 January 1817 (probably during the later of these years) and was first published in 1837. It was included from 1837 among 'Epitaphs and Elegiac Pieces'.

In a letter to Edward Quillinan (19 September 1822), Mary Wordsworth wrote about the poet and this poem: 'It took him years to produce those 6 simple lines upon the stone at the head of the earthly remains of our own dear boy . . . yet he could not give it up.'

Characteristics of a Child Three Years Old

This poem was composed possibly in 1811 but probably between 3 January 1813 and about late May 1814. It was first published in 1815 among 'Poems Referring to the Period of Childhood'.

In the *I. F. note*, Wordsworth claimed the poem was written at Allan Bank, his house in Grasmere, in 1811, and he identified the subject of the poem: 'Picture of my Daughter Catharine, who died the year after'. The phrasing in lines 12–13 echoes Milton's *Paradise Lost*, IX, line 249: 'For solitude sometimes is best society.'

'Surprised by joy – impatient as the Wind'

This poem was probably written between sometime in 1813 and about the middle of October 1814. It was first published in 1815 among 'Miscellaneous Sonnets'.

In the *I. F. note*, Wordsworth commented: 'This was in fact suggested by my daughter Catharine, long after her death [4 June 1812, at the age of three].'

The Excursion

The whole of *The Excursion* was composed between 1797 and 1814 and was first published in 1814.

In the Preface to the 1814 edition, Wordsworth describes (in the second paragraph) the genesis of his 'philosophical poem', *The Recluse*, an account which is not quite accurate (see the Clarendon edition, V, p. 363). In any case, of the plan as set forth by Wordsworth, very little materialized, at least in the manner described. *The Prelude* ('That Work, addressed to a dear Friend') was finished, and published posthumously, in 1850; the first part of *The Recluse* is represented by only one book, *Home at Grasmere*, first published in 1888; *The Excursion*, the second part, was thus the only section of *The Recluse* to be completed and the only one to be published in Wordsworth's lifetime. In de Selincourt's witty phrase (Clarendon edition, V, p. 368), all that came of Wordsworth's original plan 'apart from one Book, was a Prelude to the main theme and an Excursion from it'.

The Excursion has never been a popular poem, from the time of the contemporary reviewer Francis Jeffrey's 'This will never do' to the most recent criticisms. With the exception of the story of Margaret in Book I (in this edition contained in *The Pedlar and the Ruined Cottage*) the best part of the poem is often said to be the tales contained in the poem, especially those told in Book VI by the Pastor to help in the conversion of the Solitary, a man given over to disillusion and depression. Two of these tales are especially well done: [The Tale of the Whig and the Jacobite] and [The Story of Ellen]. The passage from Book IV, entitled here [Greek Nature Myths], has also had many admirers, including John Keats, who is said to have specifically admired lines 858-64. The brief passage from Book VIII, [The Pastor's Children], contains perhaps the most charming picture of children Wordsworth ever wrote.

from BOOK IV
[*Greek Nature Myths*]

The 'beardless youth' (line 859) is Apollo and the 'beaming Goddess' (line 865) is Diana, goddess of the hunt and of the moon.

from BOOK VI
[*The Whig and the Jacobite*]

In the *I. F. note*, Wordsworth provides background information for the pair:

> From this point the conversation leads to the mention of two Individuals who, by their several fortunes, were, at different times, driven to take refuge at the small and obscure town of Hawkshead on the skirt of these mountains. Their stories I had from the dear old Dame with whom, as a schoolboy and afterwards, I lodged for nearly the space of ten years. The elder, the Jacobite, was named Drummond, and was of a high family in Scotland; the Hanoverian Whig bore the name of Vandepat, and might perhaps be a descendant of some Dutchman who had come over in the train of King William. At all events his zeal was such that he ruined himself by a contest for the representation of London or Westminster, undertaken to support his party, and retired to this corner of the world, selected, as it had been by Drummond, for that obscurity which, since visiting the Lakes became fashionable, it has no longer retained.

'The Stuart' (line 417) was Prince Charles, defeated at Culloden in 1745. There is perhaps a literary echo in 'lenient hand of time' (line 423): compare Bowles's 'Influence of Time on Grief' (1789), l: 'O Time, who know'st a lenient hand to lay'.

from BOOK VI
[*The Story of Ellen*]

In the *I. F. note*, Wordsworth tells the background to the story:

> The story that follows was told to Mrs. Wordsworth and my Sister by the sister of this unhappy young woman; every particular was exactly as I have related. The party was not known to me, though she lived at Hawkshead, but it was after I left school. The Clergyman, who administered comfort to her in her distress, I knew well. Her Sister who told the story was the wife of a leading yeoman in the Vale of Grasmere, and they were an affectionate pair and greatly respected by everyone who knew them.

There are several literary echoes in this long passage. Compare line 905 with *Hamlet*, III, i, line 72 – 'The pangs of despised love, the law's delay' – and line 1005 with Milton's *Paradise Regained*, IV, line 639 – 'Home to his Mother's house private returned'.

'Nicest' (line 841) means 'most intricately made', and for the background to the reference to Moses smiting the rock in lines 919–20, see Numbers, 20: 11.

from BOOK VIII
[*The Pastor's Children*]

The 'He' of the first line quoted is the Solitary, whose entire family, including a young boy and girl, had succumbed to disease.

The most complete study of the poem is *The Excursion: A Study* (1950) by J. S. Lyon.

Yarrow Visited

This poem is the second in the Yarrow 'series' (see also 'Yarrow Unvisited' and 'Yarrow Revisited'). Composition began certainly by 1 September but the poem was probably composed between 2 and 16 September 1814, and it was first published in 1815. In 1815 and 1820 it was included among 'Poems of the Imagination', and thereafter among 'Memorials of a Tour in Scotland, 1814'.

In the *I. F. note*, Wordsworth observed:

> As mentioned in my verses on the death of the Ettrick Shepherd ('Extempore Effusion'), my first visit to Yarrow was in his company. We had lodged the night before at Traquhair, where Hogg had joined us . . . I seldom read or think of this poem without regretting that my dear Sister was not of the party as she would have had so much delight in recalling the time when, travelling together in Scotland, we declined going in search of this celebrated stream . . .

The relation of this poem to 'Yarrow Unvisited' is mentioned in two letters. The first is by Wordsworth, writing to R. P. Gillies (23 November 1814): 'Second parts, if much inferior to the first, are always disgusting, and as I had succeeded in *Yarrow Unvisited*, I was anxious that there should be no falling off; but that was unavoidable, perhaps, from the subject, as imagination almost always transcends reality.' In a letter to Wordsworth (28 April 1815), Charles Lamb praised the sixth stanza ('no lovelier stanza can be found in the wide world of poetry') but commented that 'the poem on the whole seems condemned to leave behind it a melancholy of imperfect satisfaction, as if you had wronged the feeling with which in what preceded it you had resolved never to visit it, and as if the Muse had determined in the most delicate manner to make you, and *scarce make you*, feel it. Else, it is far superior to the other . . .'

Literary allusions abound in the poem. The opening four lines refer to 'Yarrow Unvisited' (lines 49–56) and lines 25–6 contain a reference to the ballad 'The Dowie Dens of Yarrow', in which a knight is slain and compared to a cropped rose. 'Newark's Towers' (line 55) were the setting of Scott's *The Lay of the Last Minstrel* (1805). The 'bower of bliss' (line 61) alludes to Spenser's *The Faerie Queene*, II, xii, line 42.

Laodamia

Composed for the most part (130-line version) about mid-October (certainly by 27 October) 1814, this poem was first published in 1815. In 1815 and 1820 it was included among 'Poems Founded on the Affections', and thereafter among 'Poems of the Imagination'.

In the *I. F. note*, Wordsworth observed:

> Rydal Mount, 1814. Written at the same time as *Dion* and *Artegal and Elidure*. The incident of the trees growing and withering put the subject into my thoughts, and I wrote with the hope of giving it a loftier tone than, so far as I know, has been given to it by any of the Ancients who have treated of it. It cost me more trouble than almost anything of equal length I have ever written.

This poem is the fruit of Wordsworth's renewed reading of classical authors, which he undertook to help prepare his son for university. The main source for the poem is Book VI of the *Aeneid*, but use was also made of Ovid's *Heroides* XIII, Catullus's lyrics and Euripides' *Iphigenia in Aulis*.

In a note (1815), Wordsworth commented on line 112: 'For this feature in the character of Protesilaus, see the *Iphigenia in Aulis* of Euripides.'

For the plans of Protesilaus (line 132) see the *Iliad*, II, line 700. And Wordsworth added a note to line 174:

> For the account of these long-lived trees, see Pliny's 'Natural History', ib. xvi. cap. 44; and for the features in the character of Protesilaus, see the 'Iphigenia in Aulis' of Euripides. Virgil places the Shade of Laodamia in a mournful region, among unhappy Lovers,
> ————— His Laodamia
> It Comes. —————

The 'Parcae' (line 65) are the Fates and 'Erebus' (line 71) is the region through which the Shades pass on the way to Hades. In lines 79–82, we are reminded that Hercules successfully wrestled with Death for the return of Alcestis alive to her husband, Admetus. In the next two lines (83–4), Protesilaus is told that when Jason returned from his voyage on the *Argo*, Medea rejuvenated his ageing father, Aeson, by spells.

Much of the diction is appropriately Latinate, and often has meanings that have become obsolete: 'required' (line 4) means 'requested': 'expects' (line 12) means 'awaits'; 'self-devoted' (line 48) means 'self-doomed'; 'redundant' (line 59) means 'plentiful'; 'conscious' (line 65) means 'aware'; 'pensive' (line 96) means 'serious, reflective'; and 'fondly' (line 167) means 'foolishly'.

The ending for the poem proved difficult for Wordsworth. In 1815 and 1820, lines 158-63 read:

> Ah, judge her gently who so deeply loved!
> Her, who, in reason's spite, yet without crime,
> Was in a trance of passion thus removed;
> Delivered from the galling yoke of time
> And these frail elements – to gather flowers
> Of blissful quiet mid unfading bowers.

In 1827, Laodamia is said to be 'not without crime' and 'was doomed to wander in a grosser clime'. The reason for this revision is contained in Wordsworth's letter to his nephew, John Wordsworth (October 1831): 'As first written the heroine was dismissed to happiness in Elysium. To what purpose then the mission of Protesilaus? He exhorts her to moderate her passion; the exhortation is fruitless, and no punishment follows.' In 1832, the punishment is changed to 'to wear out her appointed time', which also consorts well enough with the *Aeneid*.

Criticism of the poem has been generally favourable; 'Laodamia' is often considered one of the last successful poems Wordsworth wrote (Matthew Arnold, however, while admiring the poem, considered it 'not wholly free from something artificial'). The source of its success is often seen to be the tension caused by the conflict between passion and reason (or duty), a conflict identified by one scholar as posing a special problem for Wordsworth in his own life.

Composed upon an Evening of Extraordinary Splendour and Beauty

'Felt and in a great measure composed [probably summer 1817] upon the little mount in front of our abode at Rydal' (*I. F. note*), this poem was first published in 1820 and was placed among 'Poems of the Imagination' until 1837, at which time it was transferred to 'Evening Voluntaries'.

Wordsworth added a note to line 49: 'In these lines I am under obligation to the exquisite picture of "Jacob's Dream," by Mr. Alstone, now in America.' Washington Allston (1779-1843), an American painter, was a friend of Wordsworth.

'Sole listener, Duddon! to the breeze that played'

Sonnet V in *The River Duddon* sonnet series, this poem was composed between 1806 and 1820 (probably in December 1818) and was first published in 1820.

The probable locale dealt with in this sonnet (on the course of the small river in the Lake District) is discussed in Knight's edition (1896), Volume VI.

'Return, Content! for fondly I pursued'

Sonnet XXVI of *The River Duddon* sonnet series, this poem is a revised version of 'Dear Native Brooks', a manuscript poem composed possibly 1803-4. 'Return, Content!' was first published in 1820, as part of the series.

After-thought

This thirty-fourth and concluding sonnet of *The River Duddon* series was composed between 1806 and 1820 (possibly in December 1818) and first published in 1820.

There are several conscious literary echoes in the poem that Wordsworth himself pointed out in a note. He gives Milton's *Paradise Lost*, VIII, line 282 – 'And feel that I am happier than I know' – as the source of line 14. In referring to line 7, he commented, 'The allusion to the Greek poet will be obvious to the Classical reader.' Compare his 'In Part from Moschus's Lament for Bion' (line 5), 'But we, the great, the mighty and the wise' (a translation of line 102 of Moschus's 'Lament').

Critics usually agree that this sonnet is both one of Wordsworth's best and one of the best of his later poems. Lee Johnson (*Wordsworth and the Sonnet*, 1973) provides the most extended analysis, noting the complexity of the four sections, the four parallel lists, and the reversal of the octave and sestet.

Mutability

One of the *Ecclesiastical Sketches* (III, xxxiv), this poem was composed in 1821 and first published in 1822 as part of that sonnet series (in 1837 renamed *Ecclesiastical Sonnets*).

In the last line is a borrowing from Milton's *Education*: 'Unimaginable touches' of music. Wordsworth had used the phrase before, as well as some of the images, in 'Fragment of a "Gothic" Tale' (lines 67–71): 'The unimaginable touch of time / Or shouldering rend had split with ruin deep / Those towers that stately stood ... / And plumed their heads with trees ...' These lines in turn may have been suggested by John Dyer's 'The Ruins of Rome' (1740), lines 38–42.

Inside of King's College Chapel, Cambridge

One of the *Ecclesiastical Sketches* (III, xliii), this poem was composed probably in November or December 1820 and first published in 1822 as part of that sonnet series (in 1837 renamed *Ecclesiastical Sonnets*).

The 'royal Saint' (line 1) was Henry VI.

To a Skylark ('Ethereal Minstrel')

Probably composed in 1825, this poem was first published in 1827 among 'Poems of the Imagination'.

The *I. F. note* reads: 'Rydal Mount 1825. (Where there are no skylarks, but the poet is everywhere [pencil addition].)'

The original second stanza to this poem was transferred in 1845 to 'A Morning Exercise' (lines 43–8) and reads:

> To the last point of vision, and beyond,
> Mount, daring warbler! – that love-prompted strain
> ('Twixt thee and thine a never-failing bond)
> Thrills not the less the bosom of the plain:
> Yet mightst thou seem, proud privilege! to sing
> All independent of the leafy spring.

In the *I. F. note* to the later poem, Wordsworth asked that the last five stanzas be read with 'To a Skylark'.

'*Scorn not the Sonnet; Critic, you have frowned*'

One of Wordsworth's several sonnets on the sonnet form itself (see also 'Nuns fret not . . .'), this poem was probably composed in 1827 (before May) and was first published in 1827 among 'Miscellaneous Sonnets'.

In the *I. F. note*, Wordsworth commented: 'Composed, almost extempore, in a short walk on the western side of Rydal Lake.'

Yarrow Revisited

This poem, the last in a 'series' (see also 'Yarrow Unvisited' and 'Yarrow Visited'), was probably written in autumn 1831, and was first published in 1835 as part of a collection, *Yarrow Revisited, and Other Poems*.

Wordsworth observed in the *I. F. note*:

> In the autumn of 1831, my daughter and I set off from Rydal to visit Sir Walter Scott before his departure for Italy . . . On Tuesday morning Sir Walter Scott accompanied us and most of the party to Newark Castle on the Yarrow. When we alighted from the carriages he walked pretty stoutly, and had great pleasure in revisiting those his favourite haunts. Of that excursion the verses 'Yarrow revisited' are a memorial. Notwithstanding the romance that pervades Sir W.'s works and attaches to many of his habits, there is too much pressure of fact for these verses to harmonise as much as I could wish with the two preceding Poems.

There are a number of literary allusions and echoes in the poem. The 'Great Minstrel of the Border' (line 8) is Sir Walter Scott, 'Winsome Marrow' (line 2) is taken from William Hamilton's *The Braes of Yarrow* (1724), line 2 (also quoted in 'Yarrow Unvisited', line 6), and 'the silent portal arch' (line 99) is perhaps an echo of 'The embattled portal arch' (line 32) in Scott's *The Lay of the Last Minstrel* (1805).

On the Departure of Sir Walter Scott

This poem, which H. C. Robinson considered 'the most perfect sonnet in the language' (letter to James Masquerier, 19 October 1833), was probably composed in September 1831 and was first published in 1833 in the *Literary Souvenir*. It was included by Wordsworth in *Yarrow Revisited, and Other Poems* (1835), and was included under that title in the collected editions that followed.

In the *I. F. note*, Wordsworth observed:

> On our return [from Newark Castle] in the afternoon we had to cross the Tweed directly opposite Abbotsford. The wheels of our carriage grated upon the pebbles in the bed of the stream, that there flows somewhat rapidly; a rich but sad light of rather a purple than a golden hue was spread over the Eildon hills at that moment; and, thinking it probable that it might be the last time Sir Walter would cross the stream, I was not a

little moved, and expressed some of my feelings in the sonnet beginning –
'A trouble, not of clouds, or weeping rain'.

'Parthenope' (line 14) is Naples, Scott's destination.

'Calm is the fragrant air, and loth to lose'

This poem was probably composed in 1832 and was first published in 1835. From
1835 it was contained among 'Evening Voluntaries'.

'Most sweet it is with unuplifted eyes'

This sonnet was probably composed in summer 1833, and was first published in
1835 as part of 'Poems Composed or Suggested During a Tour, 1833'.

Extempore Effusion upon the Death of James Hogg

Probably written between 21 November and early December (by 4 December)
1835, this elegy was first published 5 December 1835 in the *Newcastle Journal* and
from 1836–7 was included among 'Epitaphs and Elegiac Pieces'.

In the *I. F. note*, Wordsworth commented, 'These verses were written extempore, immediately after reading a notice of the Ettrick Shepherd's [Hogg's]
death in the Newcastle paper . . .' In a note, Wordsworth listed those mourned:

> Walter Scott ... died 21st Sept., 1832.
> S. T. Coleridge. „   25th July, 1834.
> Charles Lamb.. „   27th Dec., 1834.
> Geo. Crabbe... „   3rd Feb., 1832.
> Felicia Hemans.. „   16th May, 1835.

Some of the deceased, Wordsworth refers to obliquely. 'The Ettrick Shepherd'
(line 4) and 'the Shepherd-poet' (line 12) refer to James Hogg, the author of *The
Queen's Wake* and *Private Memoirs and Confessions of a Justified Sinner*, who died
21 November 1835. The 'Border-minstrel' (line 8) was Sir Walter Scott, who was
buried in Dryburgh Abbey (line 10). The 'holy Spirit' (line 37) was Felicia
Hemans, a minor poet befriended by Wordsworth.

There are a number of literary allusions and echoes in the poem. 'When first
. . . When last' (lines 1, 5) refer to his own 'Yarrow Visited' and 'Yarrow
Revisited' respectively and echo a construction ('When first . . . When now', (lines
2, 4) used by John Logan (1747–88) in his *The Braes of Yarrow*. 'The rolling year'
(line 13), moreover, comes from Logan's 'Ode to the Cuckoo' (line 8). 'Clouds
that rake the mountain-summits' (line 21) was given a note, possibly by
Wordsworth, in Henry Reed's *Poetical Works of William Wordsworth* (1837): 'This
expression is borrowed from a sonnet by Mr. G. Bell, the author of a small volume
of poems lately printed at Penrith. Speaking of Skiddaw, he says "Yon dark cloud
'rakes,' and shrouds its noble brow." '

The Prelude [Final, Fourteen-Book Version; MS E]

The Prelude, Wordsworth's longest poem, was begun in 1798 and published posthumously in 1850. The earliest two-book version of 1799 is sometimes published, but although it is more unified in argument, it contains only a small fraction of the later versions. The two versions most often encountered are the 1805 version in thirteen books and the 1850 version in fourteen books published posthumously; but problems with that first published edition (see below) have caused the two versions to be redesignated the thirteen-book and the fourteen-book *Prelude* respectively to accommodate re-editing of the last version from late manuscripts. The difference in number of books derives from the division of one book into two; otherwise, one long passage (the story of Vaudracour and Julia) is missing from the later version, but there were also a number of added passages.

These two versions are often published together with facing texts that allow for examination of the revisions made over the years. A good deal of discussion has taken place over which of the two is preferable; the earlier is said to be more vital in its style and imagery, the later to have fewer rough and confusing passages but also to be more pedestrian, since the poet is further from the events described in this semi-autobiographical poem about his early life. A third view is that the preference between the two versions involves a trade-off.

The text of the final version is difficult to determine, despite both the half-century Wordsworth had the poem to hand and his customary concern over the accuracy of the final texts of his poems, for the first, posthumous edition (1850) contains unauthorized revisions made by three editors, who were themselves working with two late manuscripts with many questionable readings between them. The two manuscripts are MS D, written and revised mostly in the hand of Mary Wordsworth, and the later MS E, written in the hands of Dora Wordsworth and Elizabeth Cookson and revised in the hands of Mary and William Wordsworth.

W. J. B. Owen, the editor of the Cornell edition of *The Fourteen-Book Prelude* (1985), used MS D as the basic copy text since, he argued, it is 'the latest manuscript to which the poet is known to have given prolonged and close attention' (p. 11). This procedure is followed even though the correctness of the readings 'cannot be rigorously proved' (p. 12) and 'whether or not they make or seem to make good sense' (p. 14). Owen goes on to argue the existence of misreadings in MS E (pp. 11–15), somewhat unconvincingly, and then uses the high incidence of the alleged misreadings to prove his case. He does, however, follow many of the substantive revisions found in MS E.

MS E, nevertheless, was the version mainly used to produce the 1850 edition, which in wording generally follows it. According to Ernest de Selincourt, MS E 'was obviously intended to be the final fair copy' (Clarendon edition, p. xxiv), and the manuscript contains a note near the end: 'reviewed July 1839'. Moreover, Christopher Wordsworth, one of the editors of the 1850 edition, claimed that the poem 'was left ready for the Press by the author' (p. xxiv). In the absence of convincing arguments to the contrary, the final text produced and reviewed by Wordsworth should hold a special place among the versions of the poem.

Without a clearly authoritative text to follow, every editor of the final version of *The Prelude* must, in an especially crucial way, resort to frequent scholarly and critical judgements, as well as choose a basic text or editorial policy. I have stuck to MS E in its final revised form ('final E'), since Wordsworth had read it and made revisions to it. Only where a mistranscription has obviously been made (as in I, line 353: 'like hurtless lightning', *not* 'like hurtless light') have I reverted to a MS D reading. To be 'obviously' a mistranscription requires, I believe, more than that a word was replaced (between the manuscripts) by a similar word – especially when the original word is clearly written in MS D (making a mistake less likely) and when the MS E reading makes perfectly good, or better, sense. In the case of punctuation, only when the sense of the passage is totally changed from all previous manuscripts do I revert to MS D; otherwise, whenever possible I have removed unnecessary punctuation, following MS E. Capitals were frequently removed by the 1850 editors and since they were most likely following contemporary usage and since the text is otherwise overburdened with mostly meaningless capitalization, I have followed those editors in most instances, as did the editors of the Norton edition (*The Prelude, 1799, 1805, 1850,* 1970).

Of the four or five full-length studies of *The Prelude,* the most useful are R. D. Havens, *The Mind of a Poet* (1941) and Herbert Lindenberger, *On Wordsworth's Prelude* (1963). Several chapters and articles also provide useful ways of approaching the poem: Donald Davie's 'Syntax in the Blank Verse of Wordsworth's *Prelude*' (*Articulate Energy,* 1955), Max Wildi's 'Wordsworth and the Simplon Pass' (*English Studies,* 1959, 1962) and Jonathan Bishop's 'Wordsworth and the "Spots of Time"' (*English Literary History,* 1959).

BOOK FIRST
Introduction, Childhood & School-time

The autobiographical nature of the poem is soon apparent in the references to landmarks in Wordsworth's life. The 'Vale' in line 72 is Grasmere Vale; the 'Vale' in line 304 is Esthwaite (Hawkshead); 'the shattered monument / Of feudal sway' (lines 284–5) is Cockermouth Castle, situated in Wordsworth's birthplace. The 'Friend' addressed in line 46 and throughout the poem is Samuel Taylor Coleridge. The previous forty-five lines of the poem are the 'glad preamble', mentioned later in the poem (V, line 4).

Some items in Book I need illumination. The Aeolian harp of line 96 is an eighteenth-century device, much like a wind-chime but using instead the passage of wind over strings to make a pleasant sound – a conceit often used, as here, as a metaphor for the poet. The 'Orphean lyre' (line 233), on the other hand, is intended to convey the idea of a philosophic poem. The 'false steward' (line 268) is an allusion to the parable in Matthew, 25: 14–30. The game being played in line 511 is called 'noughts and crosses' in Britain and 'tick-tack-toe' in the United States.

Mention is also made of certain relatively little-known historical characters in the long passage in which the poet considered choosing a military theme for his epic. Mithridates (131–63 BC) in line 187 was King of Pontus, mentioned, along with Odin, in Gibbon's *Decline and Fall of the Roman Empire* (1776), Chapter 10. Sertorius (c. 112–72 BC) in line 191 was a Roman general and ally of Mithridates; his followers are supposed to have fled to the Canary Islands ('the Fortunate Isles', line 192). The 'Frenchman' (line 206) was identified by Wordsworth in a note (1850): 'Dominique de Gourges, a French gentleman who went in 1568 to Florida to avenge the massacre of the French by the Spaniards there'. Gustavus I (1496–1560) in line 212 freed Sweden from the Danes in 1523. William Wallace (c. 1272–1305) in line 214 was the Scottish hero executed by the English.

Of the books in *The Prelude* Book I has had the most literary echoes identified.

Echoes of Milton's *Paradise Lost* occur in lines 14 (XII, line 646: 'The world was all before them'), 62 (VIII, lines 286–7: 'On a green shady bank profuse of flow'rs / Pensive I sat me down'), 102–3 (VII, line 375: 'Shedding sweet influence'), 140–41 (I, line 21: 'Dove-like sat'st brooding'), 233 (III, line 17: 'Orphean lyre'), 460 (VII, line 22: 'Within the visible diurnal sphere'), 511 (VIII, line 83: 'With centric and eccentric scribbled o'er') and 544–5 (IX, line 27: 'Not sedulous by nature'). In the passage (IX, lines 25–41) of *Paradise Lost* from which the last citation was taken, Milton rejects a 'Romantic Tale' considered later by Wordsworth (line 169). There are borrowings as well from Milton's *L'Allegro* (line 137: 'immortal verse') in line 232, from *Samson Agonistes* (line 675: 'wand'ring loose about') in line 121, and elsewhere from eighteenth-century Miltonists: in line 85 (James Beattie's *The Minstrel*, II, xxiii: 'with startling sounds'), line 326 (William Shenstone's *Elegy*, XXV, 18: 'cultured vales') and line 370 (William Cowper's *The Task*, IV, line 57: 'craggy ridge'). Two Shakespearean borrowings have been identified: in line 537 (*As You Like It*, II, vii, line 177: 'Thy tooth is not so keen') and in line 551 (*Measure for Measure*, I, iv, line 59: 'The wanton strings and motions of the sense'). Spenser provided one phrase in line 185 (*The Faerie Queene*, I, proem, i: 'faithful loves'); Pope provided two others in line 246 (*Imitations of Horace*, Epistle I, i, line 40: 'That lock up all the Functions of my soul') and in line 522 (*Rape of the Lock*, III, line 54: 'plebeian card'); and Erasmus Darwin supplied another in lines 433–4 (*Economy of Vegetation*, 1791, III, line 570: 'Hang o'er the gliding steel, and hiss along the ice').

Many more words than in later books require caution because of their obscure or obsolete meanings. In line 37, 'redundant' means 'superfluous'; in line 112, 'self-congratulation' means 'rejoicing'; in line 230, 'cherishes' means 'cheers'; in line 253, 'vacant' means 'carefree'; in line 275, 'holms' means 'islands'; in line 326, 'cultured' means 'cultivated'; in line 379, 'instinct' means 'endowed'; in lines 408 and 581, 'vulgar' means 'common'; in line 450, 'reflex' means 'reflection'; in line 460, 'diurnal' means 'daily'; in line 461, 'train' means 'succession'; in line 471, 'characters' means 'marks'; in line 475, 'work' means 'seethe'; in line 543, 'Bothnic' means 'northern Baltic'; in line 544, 'sedulous' means 'diligent'; in line 553, 'intellectual' means 'spiritual'; in line 555, 'first-born' means 'innate'; in line 564 'organic' means 'physical'; and in line 593, 'collateral' means 'indirect'.

BOOK SECOND
School-time continued

In a note (1850) to line 333, Wordsworth identified the 'Friend' as 'The late Rev. John Fleming, of Rayrigg, Windermere'.

Fewer literary borrowings have been discovered in Book II and those come from more varied sources. Milton's *Paradise Lost* supplied only three phrasings that have been identified: in line 228 (V, line 564: 'Sad task and hard'), in line 364 (VIII, line 470: 'Under his forming hands'), and specifically quoted by Wordsworth in line 295 (IX, line 249: 'For solitude sometimes is best society'). Shakespeare also supplies two phrasings: in line 18, (*The Tempest*, IV, i, line 163: 'To still my beating mind') and in line 419 (Sonnet 116: 'If this be error'). The remainder are from other sources: in line 40 (William Cowper's *The Task*, IV, line 478: 'The fiddle screams'), in line 144 (the traditional ballad 'Sir Patrick Spens', line 2: 'the blood-red wine'), in lines 342–3 (James Thomson's *Seasons: Summer*, line 942: 'Sad on the jutting eminence he sits'), in line 427 (Matthew, 5: 8: 'Blessed are the pure in heart'), and in lines 451–2 (Coleridge's 'Frost at

Midnight', lines 51–2: 'reared / In the great city'). In line 28 Wordsworth quotes his own 'Tintern Abbey', line 43: 'corporeal frame'.

A number of words used in Book II have obsolete, changed, or allusive meanings: in line 30, 'self-presence' means 'sense of reality'; in line 53, 'grateful' means 'pleasing'; in line 78, 'Sabine' means 'frugal' (probably alluding to the temperate life of Horace, the Roman poet, who lived on a Sabine farm); in line 134, 'breathed' means 'let the horses recover their breath'; in line 214, 'succedaneum' means 'substitute'; in line 282, 'influxes' means 'influences'; in line 309, 'ghostly' means 'spiritual'; in line 315, 'intellectual' means 'spiritual'; in line 362, 'plastic' means 'shaping'; in line 377, 'still' means 'always'; in line 413, 'the Uncreated' means 'God'; and in line 450, 'principle' means 'source'.

from BOOK THIRD
Residence at Cambridge

In the passages from Book III, there are a few items requiring explanation. In line 278, Trompington is Trumpington, near Cambridge, and is the scene of Chaucer's *Reeve's Tale*. The 'blind Poet' in line 286 is Milton. Such 'a floating island' as described in lines 336–9 appeared at times on Derwentwater (see *The Prose Works*, II, p. 184).

In the selections are also a number of literary echoes. Milton supplied wording in line 57 (*Il Penseroso*, line 161: 'pealing organ') and in line 288 (*Paradise Lost*, VII, line 27: 'In darkness, and with dangers compassed round'). Spenser is echoed in line 293, taken from *The Shepheards Calender*, line 1: 'A Shepheards boye (no better doe him call)'. There are, moreover, two borrowings from the Bible: in lines 69–70 (Daniel, 5: 27: 'Thou art weighed in the balances, and art found wanting') and in line 82 (Psalms, 42: 11: 'Why art thou cast down, O my soul?').

Some words in the passages have obsolete, changed or allusive meanings: in line 44 'housekeeping' means 'hospitality'; in line 119, 'incumbencies' means 'spiritual broodings'; in line 190, 'Breathings' means 'pauses'; in line 193, 'heartless' means 'discouraged'; in line 310, 'Cassandra' means 'doom-laden'; and in line 372, 'magisterial' means 'masterful'.

from BOOK FOURTH
Summer Vacation

Some material in Book IV requires explanation. Wordsworth in a note (1850) identified the 'sweet Valley' (line 19) as Hawkshead (actually Esthwaite Vale) and the 'old Dame' (line 28) was Ann Tyson, with whom Wordsworth boarded at Colthouse, near Hawkshead, while attending grammar school. There are also two classical allusions: in Greek mythology, 'Charon' (line 14) was the ferryman who took the dead over the River Styx in Hades, and the 'fair Seven' (line 245) were the Pleiades, the Seven Sisters who were placed by Zeus among the stars. For the matter of unveiling in the presence of God (lines 150–52), see Exodus, 34: 34.

There are a number of literary echoes in the passages. Milton's *Paradise Lost* provided two phrasings: in line 328 (V, line 285: 'sky-tinctured grain') and in line 331 (VIII, line 528: 'and the melody of birds'), and in line 282 his *L'Allegro* (line 127): 'Pomp, and feast, and revelry'. 'Strenuous idleness' (line 378) echoes 'strenua . . . inertia' of Horace's *Epistle I*, xi, line 28, as well as Edward Young's *Night Thoughts*, I, line 150. The phrase is also used in Wordsworth's own 'This Lawn, a Carpet All Alive' (line 6), just as his 'The Dog – An Idyllium' (lines 20–23) provided phrasing for lines 113–16 and his 'A Guide through the District of the Lakes' ('an instantaneous map-like burst' – *Prose Works*, II, line 264n) provided a phrase for line 10.

A few words have changed meaning. In line 123, 'passenger' means 'pedestrian'; in line 281, 'gawds' means 'gaieties'; in line 288, 'feeding' means 'supplying the mind'; in line 297, 'heartless' means 'discouraging'; and in line 383, 'lapse' means 'flow'.

from BOOK FIFTH
Books

The only item that might need identification in the selected passages is 'the famous history' (line 60), which is *Don Quixote*. For the possible sources of the dream presented in lines 70–141, see J. W. Smyser, *Publications of the Modern Language Association of America* (1956). Descartes, it is claimed, probably supplied the dream with the two 'books', while Wordsworth himself added the stone and shell, as well as the Arab, 'semi-Quixote'.

There are two borrowings identified in the selections. Milton's *Paradise Lost* supplied phrasing for line 200 (V, line 150: 'in prose or numerous verse') and *Henry IV, Part II* provided a phrase for line 409 (IV, iv, line 54: 'Most subject is the fattest soil to weeds'). Some word meanings, changed over the years, need explanation. In line 153, 'enow' means 'enough'; in line 179, 'slender' means 'graceful'; and in line 200, 'native' means 'natural' and 'numerous' means 'metrical'.

In his *Recollections* (1839), Thomas De Quincey remarked of the word 'far' (line 383): 'This expression, "far," by which space and its infinites are attributed to the human heart, and to its capacities of re-echoing the sublimities of nature, has always struck me as with a flash of sublime revelation' (p. 161).

from BOOK SIXTH
Cambridge, and the Alps

A number of items found in the selections require explanation. 'Granta' (line 6) stands for Cambridge and the castle in line 205 is Brougham Castle, near Penrith in the Lake District, which was mistakenly thought to have been visited by Sir Philip Sidney (line 208), who wrote *Arcadia* for his sister (lines 210–11). At line 203, Wordsworth puns on the name of his sister, Dorothy, which means 'gift of God', and the 'maid' in line 224 is Mary Hutchinson, his future wife. Line 247 contains a playful reference to Coleridge's ship (to Malta), the *Speedwell*. The 'confusion' (line 239) of imagining Coleridge to be also present is no doubt psychological, caused by his closeness to the group at the time the passage was written. The 'youthful friend' in line 323 was Robert Jones. The 'federal day' in line 346 was Bastille Day, 14 July, 1790. The 'willow wreath' (line 552) would be appropriate for rejected lovers. The 'narrow chasm' (line 621) was the extraordinarily rugged Gorge of Gondo, which has been described by Max Wildi (*English Studies*, 1959, 1962).

There are a number of literary borrowings. Milton's *Paradise Lost* provided two phrasings: in lines 197–8 (V, lines 310–11: 'seems another morn / Risen on midnoon') and in line 640 (V, line 165: 'Him first, him last, him midst, and without end'). Shakespeare afforded two other wordings: in line 340 (Sonnet 16: 'Now stand you on the top of happy hours') and in line 647 (*Macbeth*, II, ii, line 33: 'innocent sleep'). Another borrowing, in line 193, is from John Dyer's *The Fleece* (1757) I, line 658: 'spiry rocks'. The remainder are from Wordsworth's own 'Descriptive

Sketches' (1793): lines 361-3 echo line 48 of that poem; and lines 530-32 echo line 682; line 629 echoes line 130; and lines 632-3 echo lines 249-50.

In line 10, 'coves' means 'caves' or 'caverns', and in line 251, 'Etesian' means 'north-west'.

from BOOK SEVENTH
Residence in London

A number of items in the selected passages need explanation. The story of 'those' (line 369) unharmed by the fiery furnace is biblical: see Daniel, 3: 23-7. The 'one' (line 494) who rose to speak was William Pitt the Younger, and for the reference to Henry V that follows (line 498), see *Henry V*, IV, iii, lines 51-5. The apology that follows (lines 512-43) to Edmund Burke, the great Tory politician, was added to *The Prelude* in 1832. There are three classical allusions: Aurora (line 502) was the goddess of dawn, drawn in the chariot ('car') of the sun; Aeolus was the god of the winds, which he chained in his cave (line 533); and Athena, goddess of wisdom, sprang from 'Jove's brain' (line 538). St Bartholomew's Fair (lines 676-8) was held in Smithfield, London, on 23-5 August each year. The one borrowing in the selections concerns the fair: line 714 echoes *Paradise Lost*, II, line 625: 'Perverse, all monstruous, all prodigious things'.

In line 347, 'had been' means 'would have been'; in line 374, 'preferred' means 'presented'; in line 695 'roundabouts' means 'merry-go-rounds'; and in line 715, 'Promethean' means 'creative'.

from BOOK EIGHTH
Retrospect, Love of Nature leading to Love of Man

Several items in the selected passages need identification. Helvellyn (line 1) is a mountain (3,118 ft) overlooking Grasmere Fair. Chartreuse (line 275) refers to the monastery of La Grande Chartreuse, in the French Alps near Grenoble, home of the Carthusian monks. 'Corin' and 'Phyllis' (lines 285, 287) were names conventionally used by poets to portray shepherds.

The selections contain a good number of literary borrowings. In line 680 Wordsworth sets off in quotation marks a phrase from Milton's *L'Allegro* (line 118) and there is an echo in line 273 from *Paradise Lost*, III, 58: 'Above all height'. James Thomson's *Seasons* supplies two other echoes: in lines 229-30, *Winter* (line 16): 'Looked out the joyous Spring – looked out and smiled', and in lines 264-6, *Autumn* (lines 726-9): 'Objects appear, and, wildered, o'er the waste / The shepherd stalks gigantic; / . . . in deeper circles still . . . / sits the general fog . . .' In a note (1850), Wordsworth identified a passage (lines 48-52) set off by quotation marks as 'from a descriptive Poem – "Malvern Hills" – by one of Mr. Wordsworth's oldest friends, Mr. Joseph Cottle'. The echo in line 356 is from John, 2: 4: 'Mine hour is not yet come.'

A number of words have obsolete or altered meanings. In line 21, 'byre' means 'cow-shed'; in line 22, 'chaffering' means 'bargaining'; in line 33, 'raree-show' means 'peep-show'; in line 55, 'want' means 'lack'; in line 246, 'portending' means 'extending'; in line 256, 'native man' means 'human nature'; and in line 288, 'for the purposes of kind' means 'by nature'.

from BOOK NINTH
Residence in France

A few items in the passages need clarification. The 'town' (line 40) on the Loire is

Orleans and the 'one' exception (line 132) to the mostly Royalist officers was Michel Beaupuy, who was 'a patriot' (line 123) – that is, a Republican.

The sole literary borrowing identified is 'hubbub wild' (line 58), taken from Milton's *Paradise Lost*, II, line 951.

There are several words that need explanation because of altered or obsolete meanings: in line 21, 'argument' means 'theme'; in line 296, 'sensibly' means 'sense-appealingly'; in line 318, 'Complacently' means 'enjoyably'; and in line 515, 'heartless' means 'dejected'.

from BOOK TENTH
France continued

Several items in the passages require clarification. Translated into English, the 'last words' (line 383) of Mme Roland were, 'O Liberty, what crimes they commit in your name'. One of the perpetrators of those crimes was the tyrant Robespierre, whose death (line 573) was reported to Wordsworth in summer 1794. There are two references to classical myths concerning Hercules: lines 391–3 allude to his killing of the snakes in his cradle as an infant, and lines 583–6 to one of his labours, the cleaning of the stables of King Augeas by diverting two rivers.

There are a number of literary borrowings. Shakespeare supplies the wording in three passages: in line 74 (*Hamlet*, I, ii, line 147: 'A little month'), in line 78 (*As You Like it*, I, i, lines 11–13: 'His horses ... are taught their manage'), and quoted in line 87 (*Macbeth*, II, ii, line 32: 'Methought I heard a voice cry, "Sleep no more!"'). Milton's *Samson Agonistes*, line 695, 'unjust tribunals', is echoed in line 412. Lines 293–4 borrow from Coleridge's *Rime of the Ancient Mariner* (line 607): 'While each to his great Father bends'. And Sidney's *Apology* provides an echo for line 357 ('old men from the chimney corner').

Words with changed or obsolete meanings occur here and there: in line 67, 'hotel' means 'town-house'; in line 77, 'admonishments' means 'reminders'; in line 230, 'haply' means 'perhaps'; and in line 388, 'flattered' means 'encouraged'.

from BOOK ELEVENTH
France concluded

In line 140, Wordsworth refers to 'subterranean fields'. The only such Utopia seems to be that found in Ludvig Holberg's *Nicolai Klimii Iter Subterraneum* (1741).

A number of literary echoes appear in the selections. In line 163, Milton's Sonnet XII supplies key words: 'Licence they mean when they cry liberty.' Samuel Daniel's *Civil Wars*, VI, 36 ('Weary the soul with contrarieties') provides phrasing for line 304, just as Peter II, 2: 22 ('The dog is turned to his own vomit again') supplies lines 362–3. In lines 243–4, Wordsworth echoes his own *The Borderers*, lines 1495–6: 'From the clear light of circumstances, flashed / Upon an independent Intellect'.

Two words have undergone a change in meaning: in line 242, 'magisterially' means 'masterfully' and in line 297, 'titles' means 'entitlements'.

from BOOK TWELFTH
Imagination and Taste, how impaired and restored

There are two references in the selected passage to Mary Hutchinson, Wordsworth's future wife: 'a maid' (line 151) and 'the loved one' (line 262).

There are also several literary echoes. Milton's *Paradise Lost*, VII, lines 364–5

('Hither, as to their fountain, other stars / Repairing') supplies phrasing for lines 325–6. Then there are borrowings from Wordsworth's own works: in lines 7–8, from 'The Idiot Boy' (lines 435–6): 'And with the owls began my song, / And with the owls must end'; and in line 143, from 'To the Daisy' ['In Youth'] (lines 1–2): 'In youth from rock to rock I went, / From hill to hill in discontent.'

Several words have obsolete meanings. In line 38, 'complacency' means 'contentedness'; in line 121, 'insensible' means 'insensitive'; in line 193, 'degradation' means 'decline'; and in line 235, 'bottom' means 'valley floor'.

from BOOK THIRTEENTH
Subject concluded

In line 333, 'the giant wicker' was the gigantic figure of a man made of wicker in which men were imprisoned and then burned alive (the movie *The Wicker Man*, 1973, ends with such a sacrifice).

There are few literary echoes in the passages from Book XIII. Milton is the source of one in line 229 (*Paradise Lost*, I, line 372: 'full of pomp and gold'). In lines 315–47, Wordsworth borrows a good deal of phrasing from his own unpublished *Salisbury Plain* (lines 177–96) and *Adventures on Salisbury Plain* (lines 36, 158–9).

Words with changed meanings are 'vulgar' (line 188), which means 'common', and 'unadulterated' (line 239), which means 'uncorrupted'.

from BOOK FOURTEENTH
Conclusion

A few items need clarification. The 'youthful friend' (line 3) was Robert Jones, with whom Wordsworth was touring Wales ('Cambria') in 1791. The idea of the sea of mist and the chasm providing an audial phenomenon (lines 35–62) was not unique, or even rare. Such a scene occurs in at least three other travel narratives of the time, as well as in two other of Wordsworth's poems (*Descriptive Sketches* and *The Excursion*). The 'One' (line 267), the 'phantom' (line 268), was Mary Hutchinson, Wordsworth's future wife and the subject of his 'She Was a Phantom of Delight'.

There are a good number of literary borrowings here, especially from Milton. In line 43, there is phrasing from *Paradise Lost* (VII, line 286: 'and their broad bare backs upheave'), as also in lines 71–2 (I, line 21: 'sat'st brooding on the vast abyss'), in line 120 (V, line 488: 'discursive, or intuitive'), in line 160 (II, line 622: 'a universe of death'), and in lines 245–6 (IX, lines 490–91: 'though terror be in love, / And beauty'). Milton's *Samson Agonistes* (lines 1382–3) also provides wording for lines 104–5 ('Some rousing motions in me which dispose / To something extraordinary my thoughts'). Shakespeare supplies phrasing for lines 229–30 (*Much Ado About Nothing*, I, i, line 303: 'soft and delicate desires'), as does also Wordsworth's own 'The Sparrow's Nest' (line 18): 'And humble cares, and delicate fears'. The New Testament, Philippians, 4: 7, provides the wording for lines 126–7: 'The peace of God, which passeth all understanding'.

Words with altered or obsolete meanings also occur in the passages: in line 4, 'couching-time' means 'bed-time'; in line 12, 'glaring' means 'dreary'; in line 22, 'lurcher' means 'mongrel'; in line 209, 'Dividually' means 'separately'; in line 227, 'want' means 'lack'; and in line 254, 'twinkle' means 'flutter'.

Index of Titles

Index of First Lines

READ MORE IN PENGUIN

In every corner of the world, on every subject under the sun, Penguin represents quality and variety – the very best in publishing today.

For complete information about books available from Penguin – including Puffins, Penguin Classics and Arkana – and how to order them, write to us at the appropriate address below. Please note that for copyright reasons the selection of books varies from country to country.

In the United Kingdom: Please write to *Dept. EP, Penguin Books Ltd, Bath Road, Harmondsworth, West Drayton, Middlesex UB7 0DA*

In the United States: Please write to *Consumer Sales, Penguin Putnam Inc., P.O. Box 12289 Dept. B, Newark, New Jersey 07101-5289.* VISA and MasterCard holders call 1-800-788-6262 to order Penguin titles

In Canada: Please write to *Penguin Books Canada Ltd, 10 Alcorn Avenue, Suite 300, Toronto, Ontario M4V 3B2*

In Australia: Please write to *Penguin Books Australia Ltd, P.O. Box 257, Ringwood, Victoria 3134*

In New Zealand: Please write to *Penguin Books (NZ) Ltd, Private Bag 102902, North Shore Mail Centre, Auckland 10*

In India: Please write to *Penguin Books India Pvt Ltd, 11 Community Centre, Panchsheel Park, New Delhi 110017*

In the Netherlands: Please write to *Penguin Books Netherlands bv, Postbus 3507, NL-1001 AH Amsterdam*

In Germany: Please write to *Penguin Books Deutschland GmbH, Metzlerstrasse 26, 60594 Frankfurt am Main*

In Spain: Please write to *Penguin Books S. A., Bravo Murillo 19, 1° B, 28015 Madrid*

In Italy: Please write to *Penguin Italia s.r.l., Via Benedetto Croce 2, 20094 Corsico, Milano*

In France: Please write to *Penguin France, Le Carré Wilson, 62 rue Benjamin Baillaud, 31500 Toulouse*

In Japan: Please write to *Penguin Books Japan Ltd, Kaneko Building, 2-3-25 Koraku, Bunkyo-Ku, Tokyo 112*

In South Africa: Please write to *Penguin Books South Africa (Pty) Ltd, Private Bag X14, Parkview, 2122 Johannesburg*

READ MORE IN PENGUIN

A CHOICE OF CLASSICS

Leopoldo Alas	**La Regenta**
Leon B. Alberti	**On Painting**
Ludovico Ariosto	**Orlando Furioso** (in two volumes)
Giovanni Boccaccio	**The Decameron**
Baldassar Castiglione	**The Book of the Courtier**
Benvenuto Cellini	**Autobiography**
Miguel de Cervantes	**Don Quixote**
	Exemplary Stories
Dante	**The Divine Comedy** (in three volumes)
	La Vita Nuova
Machado de Assis	**Dom Casmurro**
Bernal Díaz	**The Conquest of New Spain**
Niccolò Machiavelli	**The Discourses**
	The Prince
Alessandro Manzoni	**The Betrothed**
Emilia Pardo Bazán	**The House of Ulloa**
Benito Pérez Galdós	**Fortunata and Jacinta**
Eça de Quierós	**The Maias**
Sor Juana Inés de la Cruz	**Poems, Protest and a Dream**
Giorgio Vasari	**Lives of the Artists** (in two volumes)

and

Five Italian Renaissance Comedies
  (Machiavelli/**The Mandragola**; Ariosto/**Lena**; Aretino/**The
  Stablemaster**; Gl'Intronati/**The Deceived**; Guarini/**The Faithful
  Shepherd**)
The Poem of the Cid
Two Spanish Picaresque Novels
  (Anon/**Lazarillo de Tormes**; de Quevedo/**The Swindler**)

READ MORE IN PENGUIN

A CHOICE OF CLASSICS

Adomnan of Iona	**Life of St Columba**
St Anselm	**The Prayers and Meditations**
Thomas Aquinas	**Selected Writings**
St Augustine	**Confessions**
	The City of God
Bede	**Ecclesiastical History of the English People**
Geoffrey Chaucer	**The Canterbury Tales**
	Love Visions
	Troilus and Criseyde
Marie de France	**The Lais of Marie de France**
Jean Froissart	**The Chronicles**
Geoffrey of Monmouth	**The History of the Kings of Britain**
Gerald of Wales	**History and Topography of Ireland**
	The Journey through Wales and The Description of Wales
Gregory of Tours	**The History of the Franks**
Robert Henryson	**The Testament of Cresseid and Other Poems**
Robert Henryson/ William Dunbar	**Selected Poems**
Walter Hilton	**The Ladder of Perfection**
St Ignatius	**Personal Writings**
Julian of Norwich	**Revelations of Divine Love**
Thomas à Kempis	**The Imitation of Christ**
William Langland	**Piers the Ploughman**
Sir Thomas Malory	**Le Morte d'Arthur** (in two volumes)
Sir John Mandeville	**The Travels of Sir John Mandeville**
Marguerite de Navarre	**The Heptameron**
Christine de Pisan	**The Treasure of the City of Ladies**
Chrétien de Troyes	**Arthurian Romances**
Marco Polo	**The Travels**
Richard Rolle	**The Fire of Love**
François Villon	**Selected Poems**
Jacobus de Voragine	**The Golden Legend**

READ MORE IN PENGUIN

A CHOICE OF CLASSICS

ANTHOLOGIES AND ANONYMOUS WORKS

The Age of Bede
Alfred the Great
Beowulf
A Celtic Miscellany
The Cloud of Unknowing and Other Works
The Death of King Arthur
The Earliest English Poems
Early Christian Lives
Early Irish Myths and Sagas
Egil's Saga
English Mystery Plays
The Exeter Book of Riddles
Eyrbyggja Saga
Hrafnkel's Saga and Other Stories
The Letters of Abelard and Heloise
Medieval English Lyrics
Medieval English Verse
Njal's Saga
The Orkneyinga Saga
Roman Poets of the Early Empire
The Saga of King Hrolf Kraki
Seven Viking Romances
Sir Gawain and the Green Knight

READ MORE IN PENGUIN

A CHOICE OF CLASSICS

Francis Bacon	**The Essays**
Aphra Behn	**Love-Letters between a Nobleman and His Sister**
	Oroonoko, The Rover and Other Works
George Berkeley	**Principles of Human Knowledge/Three Dialogues between Hylas and Philonous**
James Boswell	**The Life of Samuel Johnson**
Sir Thomas Browne	**The Major Works**
John Bunyan	**Grace Abounding to The Chief of Sinners**
	The Pilgrim's Progress
Edmund Burke	**A Philosophical Enquiry into the Origin of our Ideas of the Sublime and Beautiful**
	Reflections on the Revolution in France
Frances Burney	**Evelina**
Margaret Cavendish	**The Blazing World and Other Writings**
William Cobbett	**Rural Rides**
William Congreve	**Comedies**
Cowley/Waller/Oldham	**Selected Poems**
Thomas de Quincey	**Confessions of an English Opium Eater**
	Recollections of the Lakes
Daniel Defoe	**A Journal of the Plague Year**
	Moll Flanders
	Robinson Crusoe
	Roxana
	A Tour Through the Whole Island of Great Britain
	The True-Born Englishman
John Donne	**Complete English Poems**
	Selected Prose
Henry Fielding	**Amelia**
	Jonathan Wild
	Joseph Andrews
	The Journal of a Voyage to Lisbon
	Tom Jones
George Fox	**The Journal**
John Gay	**The Beggar's Opera**

READ MORE IN PENGUIN

A CHOICE OF CLASSICS

Oliver Goldsmith	**The Vicar of Wakefield**
Gray/Churchill/Cowper	**Selected Poems**
William Hazlitt	**Selected Writings**
George Herbert	**The Complete English Poems**
Thomas Hobbes	**Leviathan**
Samuel Johnson	**Gabriel's Ladder**
	History of Rasselas, Prince of Abissinia
	Selected Writings
Samuel Johnson/	**A Journey to the Western Islands of**
James Boswell	**Scotland and The Journal of a Tour of**
	the Hebrides
Matthew Lewis	**The Monk**
John Locke	**An Essay Concerning Human**
	Understanding
Andrew Marvell	**Complete Poems**
Thomas Middleton	**Five Plays**
John Milton	**Complete Poems**
	Paradise Lost
Samuel Richardson	**Clarissa**
	Pamela
Earl of Rochester	**Complete Works**
Richard Brinsley	
Sheridan	**The School for Scandal and Other Plays**
Sir Philip Sidney	**Arcadia**
Christopher Smart	**Selected Poems**
Adam Smith	**The Wealth of Nations (Books I–III)**
Tobias Smollett	**Humphrey Clinker**
	Roderick Random
Edmund Spenser	**The Faerie Queene**
Laurence Sterne	**The Life and Opinions of Tristram Shandy**
	A Sentimental Journey Through France
	and Italy
Jonathan Swift	**Complete Poems**
	Gulliver's Travels
Thomas Traherne	**Selected Poems and Prose**
Henry Vaughan	**Complete Poems**

READ MORE IN PENGUIN

A CHOICE OF CLASSICS

Matthew Arnold	**Selected Prose**
Jane Austen	**Emma**
	Lady Susan/The Watsons/Sanditon
	Mansfield Park
	Northanger Abbey
	Persuasion
	Pride and Prejudice
	Sense and Sensibility
William Barnes	**Selected Poems**
Mary Braddon	**Lady Audley's Secret**
Anne Brontë	**Agnes Grey**
	The Tenant of Wildfell Hall
Charlotte Brontë	**Jane Eyre**
	Juvenilia: 1829–35
	The Professor
	Shirley
	Villette
Emily Brontë	**Complete Poems**
	Wuthering Heights
Samuel Butler	**Erewhon**
	The Way of All Flesh
Lord Byron	**Don Juan**
	Selected Poems
Lewis Carroll	**Alice's Adventures in Wonderland**
	The Hunting of the Snark
Thomas Carlyle	**Selected Writings**
Arthur Hugh Clough	**Selected Poems**
Wilkie Collins	**Armadale**
	The Law and the Lady
	The Moonstone
	No Name
	The Woman in White
Charles Darwin	**The Origin of Species**
	Voyage of the Beagle
Benjamin Disraeli	**Coningsby**
	Sybil

READ MORE IN PENGUIN

A CHOICE OF CLASSICS

Charles Dickens	**American Notes for General Circulation**
	Barnaby Rudge
	Bleak House
	The Christmas Books (in two volumes)
	David Copperfield
	Dombey and Son
	Great Expectations
	Hard Times
	Little Dorrit
	Martin Chuzzlewit
	The Mystery of Edwin Drood
	Nicholas Nickleby
	The Old Curiosity Shop
	Oliver Twist
	Our Mutual Friend
	The Pickwick Papers
	Pictures from Italy
	Selected Journalism 1850–1870
	Selected Short Fiction
	Sketches by Boz
	A Tale of Two Cities
George Eliot	**Adam Bede**
	Daniel Deronda
	Felix Holt
	Middlemarch
	The Mill on the Floss
	Romola
	Scenes of Clerical Life
	Silas Marner
Fanny Fern	**Ruth Hall**
Elizabeth Gaskell	**Cranford/Cousin Phillis**
	The Life of Charlotte Brontë
	Mary Barton
	North and South
	Ruth
	Sylvia's Lovers
	Wives and Daughters

READ MORE IN PENGUIN

A CHOICE OF CLASSICS

Edward Gibbon	**The Decline and Fall of the Roman Empire** (in three volumes)
	Memoirs of My Life
George Gissing	**New Grub Street**
	The Odd Women
William Godwin	**Caleb Williams**
	Concerning Political Justice
Thomas Hardy	**Desperate Remedies**
	The Distracted Preacher and Other Tales
	Far from the Madding Crowd
	Jude the Obscure
	The Hand of Ethelberta
	A Laodicean
	The Mayor of Casterbridge
	A Pair of Blue Eyes
	The Return of the Native
	Selected Poems
	Tess of the d'Urbervilles
	The Trumpet-Major
	Two on a Tower
	Under the Greenwood Tree
	The Well-Beloved
	The Woodlanders
George Lyell	**Principles of Geology**
Lord Macaulay	**The History of England**
Henry Mayhew	**London Labour and the London Poor**
George Meredith	**The Egoist**
	The Ordeal of Richard Feverel
John Stuart Mill	**The Autobiography**
	On Liberty
	Principles of Political Economy
William Morris	**News from Nowhere and Other Writings**
John Henry Newman	**Apologia Pro Vita Sua**
Margaret Oliphant	**Miss Marjoribanks**
Robert Owen	**A New View of Society and Other Writings**
Walter Pater	**Marius the Epicurean**
John Ruskin	**Unto This Last and Other Writings**

READ MORE IN PENGUIN

A CHOICE OF CLASSICS

Walter Scott	**The Antiquary**
	Heart of Mid-Lothian
	Ivanhoe
	Kenilworth
	The Tale of Old Mortality
	Rob Roy
	Waverley
Robert Louis Stevenson	**Kidnapped**
	Dr Jekyll and Mr Hyde and Other Stories
	In the South Seas
	The Master of Ballantrae
	Selected Poems
	Weir of Hermiston
William Makepeace Thackeray	**The History of Henry Esmond**
	The History of Pendennis
	The Newcomes
	Vanity Fair
Anthony Trollope	**Barchester Towers**
	Can You Forgive Her?
	Doctor Thorne
	The Eustace Diamonds
	Framley Parsonage
	He Knew He Was Right
	The Last Chronicle of Barset
	Phineas Finn
	The Prime Minister
	The Small House at Allington
	The Warden
	The Way We Live Now
Oscar Wilde	**Complete Short Fiction**
Mary Wollstonecraft	**A Vindication of the Rights of Woman**
	Mary and **Maria** (includes Mary Shelley's **Matilda**)
Dorothy and William Wordsworth	**Home at Grasmere**